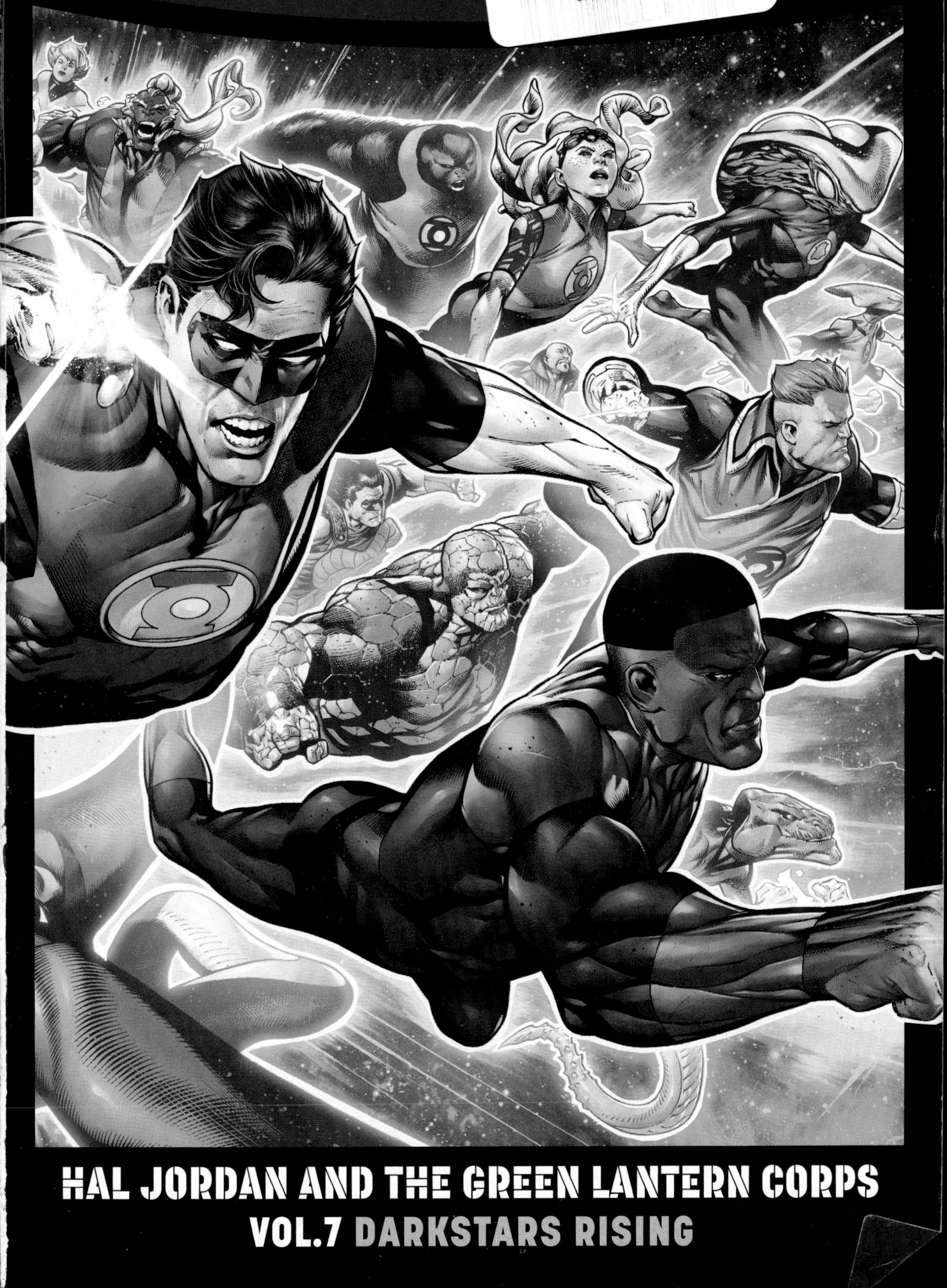

HAL JORDAN AND THE GREEN LANTERN CORPS

VOL.7 DARKSTARS RISING

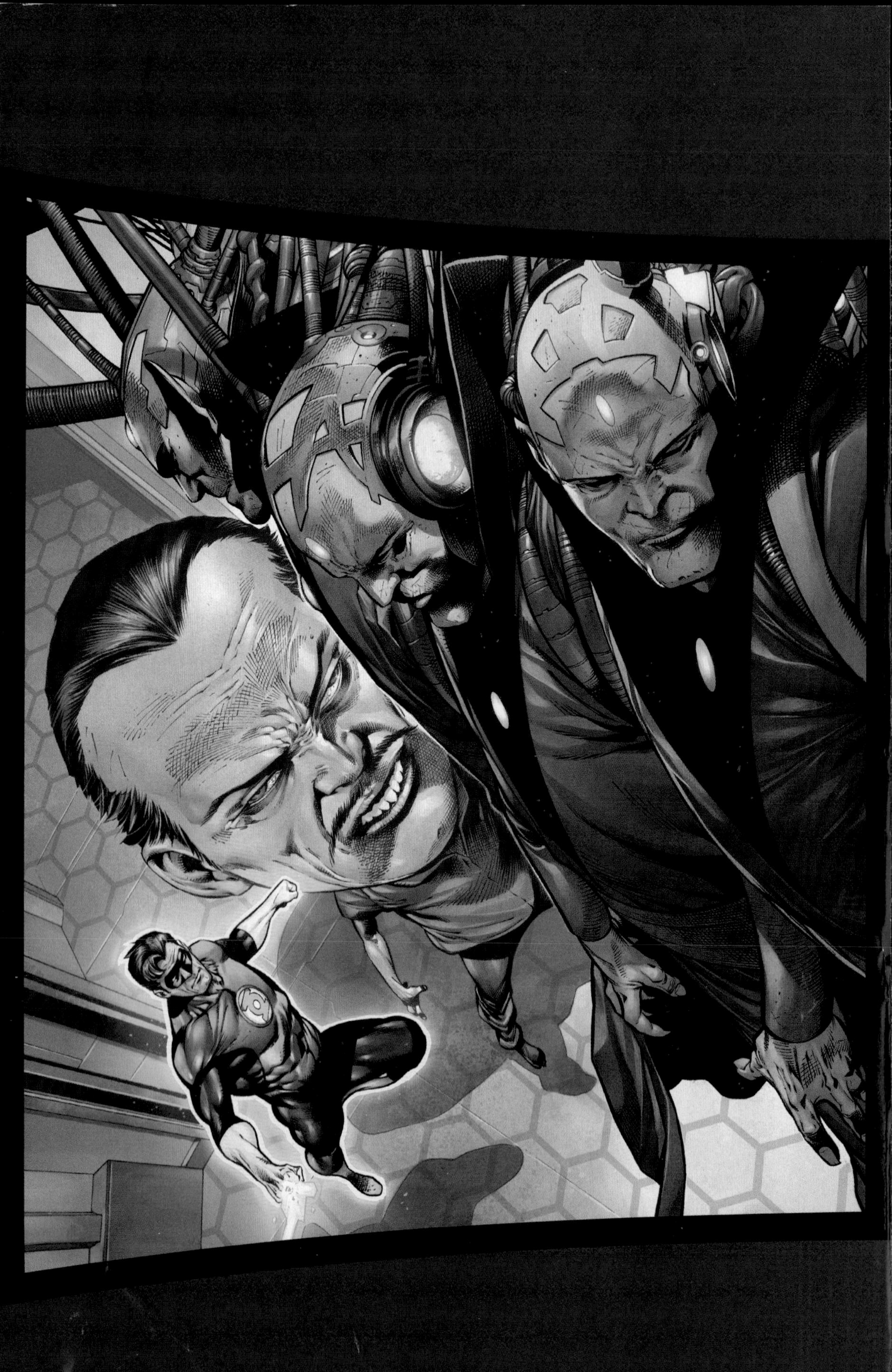

HAL JORDAN AND THE GREEN LANTERN CORPS
VOL.7 DARKSTARS RISING

ROBERT VENDITTI
writer

RAFA SANDOVAL * **FERNANDO PASARIN** * **ETHAN VAN SCIVER**
CLAYTON HENRY * **BRANDON PETERSON** * **SERGIO DAVILA**
pencillers

JORDI TARRAGONA * **ETHAN VAN SCIVER** * **OCLAIR ALBERT**
EBER FERREIRA * **CLAYTON HENRY** * **BRANDON PETERSON**
inkers

TOMEU MOREY * **JASON WRIGHT** * **PETE PANTAZIS** * **IVAN PLASCENCIA**
colorists

DAVE SHARPE
letterer

TYLER KIRKHAM and **ARIF PRIANTO**
collection cover artists

SUPERMAN created by **JERRY SIEGEL** and **JOE SHUSTER**
By special arrangement with the Jerry Siegel family

BRIAN CUNNINGHAM Editor - Original Series ✶ **ANDREW MARINO** Assistant Editor - Original Series
JEB WOODARD Group Editor - Collected Editions ✶ **ALEX GALER** Editor - Collected Edition
STEVE COOK Design Director - Books ✶ **MEGEN BELLERSEN** Publication Design

BOB HARRAS Senior VP - Editor-in-Chief, DC Comics
PAT McCALLUM Executive Editor, DC Comics

DAN DiDIO Publisher ✶ **JIM LEE** Publisher & Chief Creative Officer
AMIT DESAI Executive VP - Business & Marketing Strategy, Direct to Consumer & Global Franchise Management
BOBBIE CHASE VP & Executive Editor, Young Reader & Talent Development ✶ **MARK CHIARELLO** Senior VP - Art, Design & Collected Editions
JOHN CUNNINGHAM Senior VP - Sales & Trade Marketing ✶ **BRIAR DARDEN** VP - Business Affairs
ANNE DePIES Senior VP - Business Strategy, Finance & Administration ✶ **DON FALLETTI** VP - Manufacturing Operations
LAWRENCE GANEM VP - Editorial Administration & Talent Relations ✶ **ALISON GILL** Senior VP - Manufacturing & Operations
JASON GREENBERG VP - Business Strategy & Finance ✶ **HANK KANALZ** Senior VP - Editorial Strategy & Administration ✶ **JAY KOGAN** Senior VP - Legal Affairs
NICK J. NAPOLITANO VP - Manufacturing Administration ✶ **LISETTE OSTERLOH** VP - Digital Marketing & Events ✶ **EDDIE SCANNELL** VP - Consumer Marketing
COURTNEY SIMMONS Senior VP - Publicity & Communications ✶ **JIM (SKI) SOKOLOWSKI** VP - Comic Book Specialty Sales & Trade Marketing
NANCY SPEARS VP - Mass, Book, Digital Sales & Trade Marketing ✶ **MICHELE R. WELLS** VP - Content Strategy

HAL JORDAN AND THE GREEN LANTERN CORPS VOL. 7: DARKSTARS RISING

DC Comics, 2900 West Alameda Ave., Burbank, CA 91505
Printed by Times Printing, LLC, Random Lake, WI. 11/30/18. First Printing.
ISBN: 978-1-4012-8564-7

Library of Congress Cataloging-in-Publication Data is available.

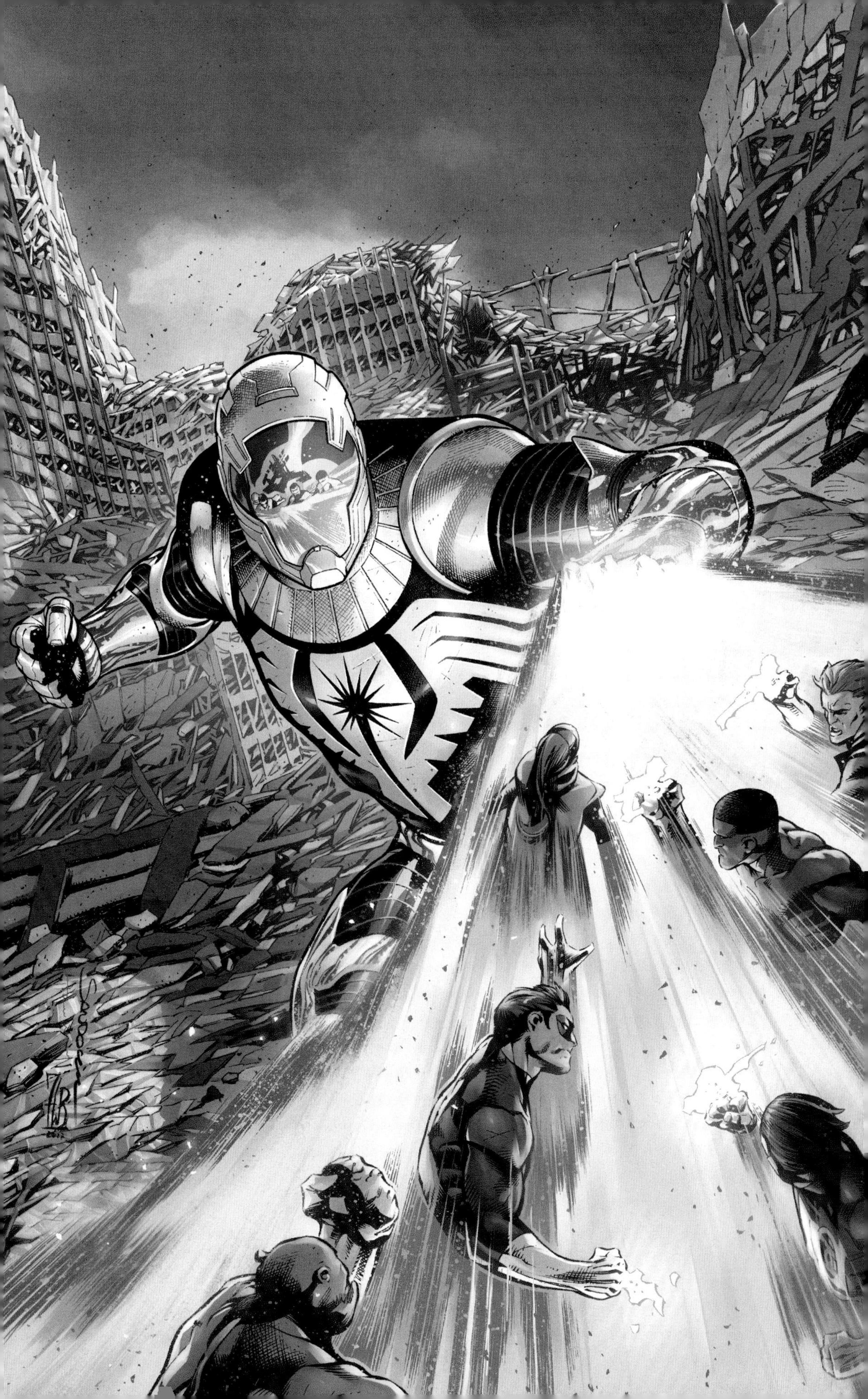

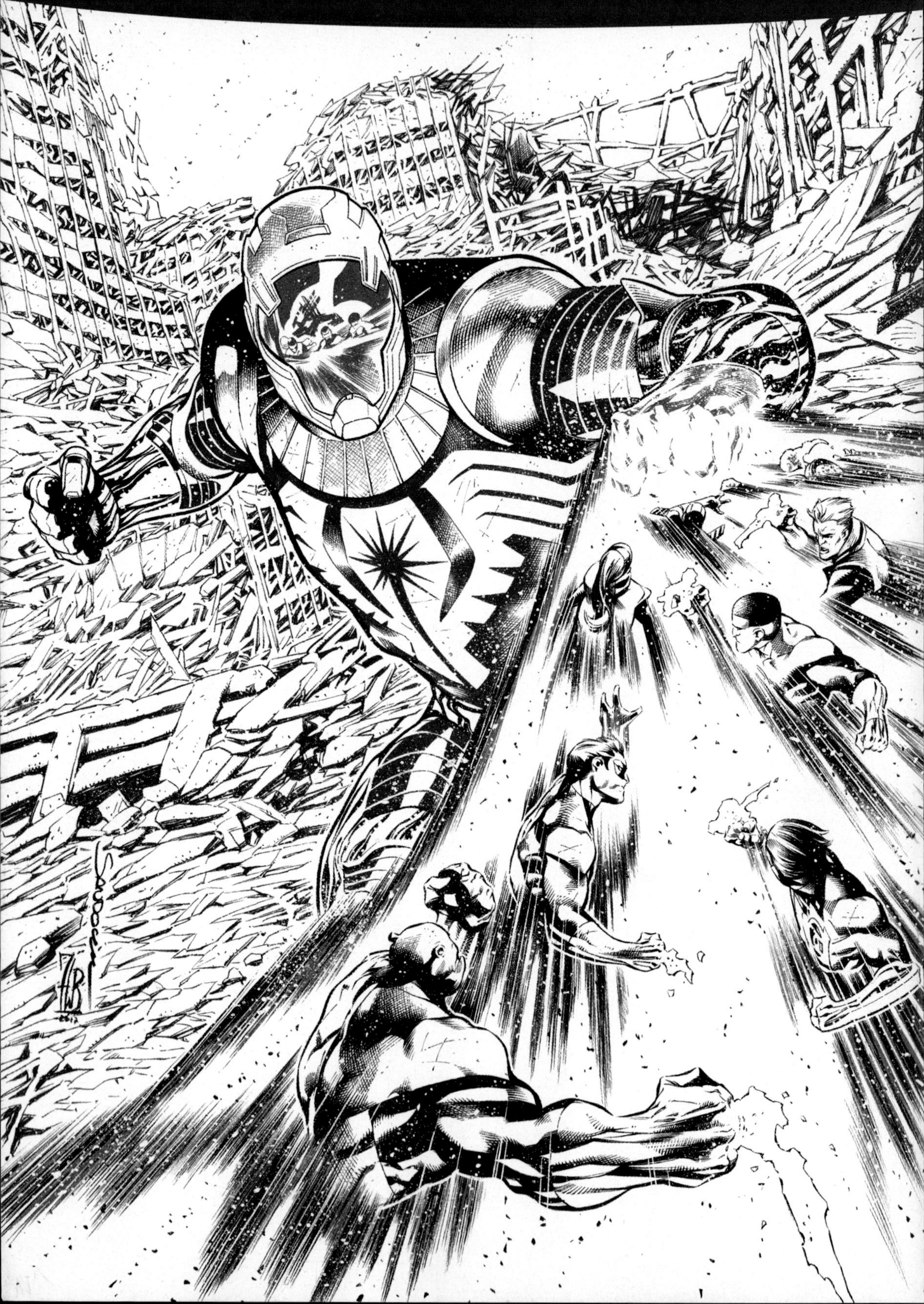

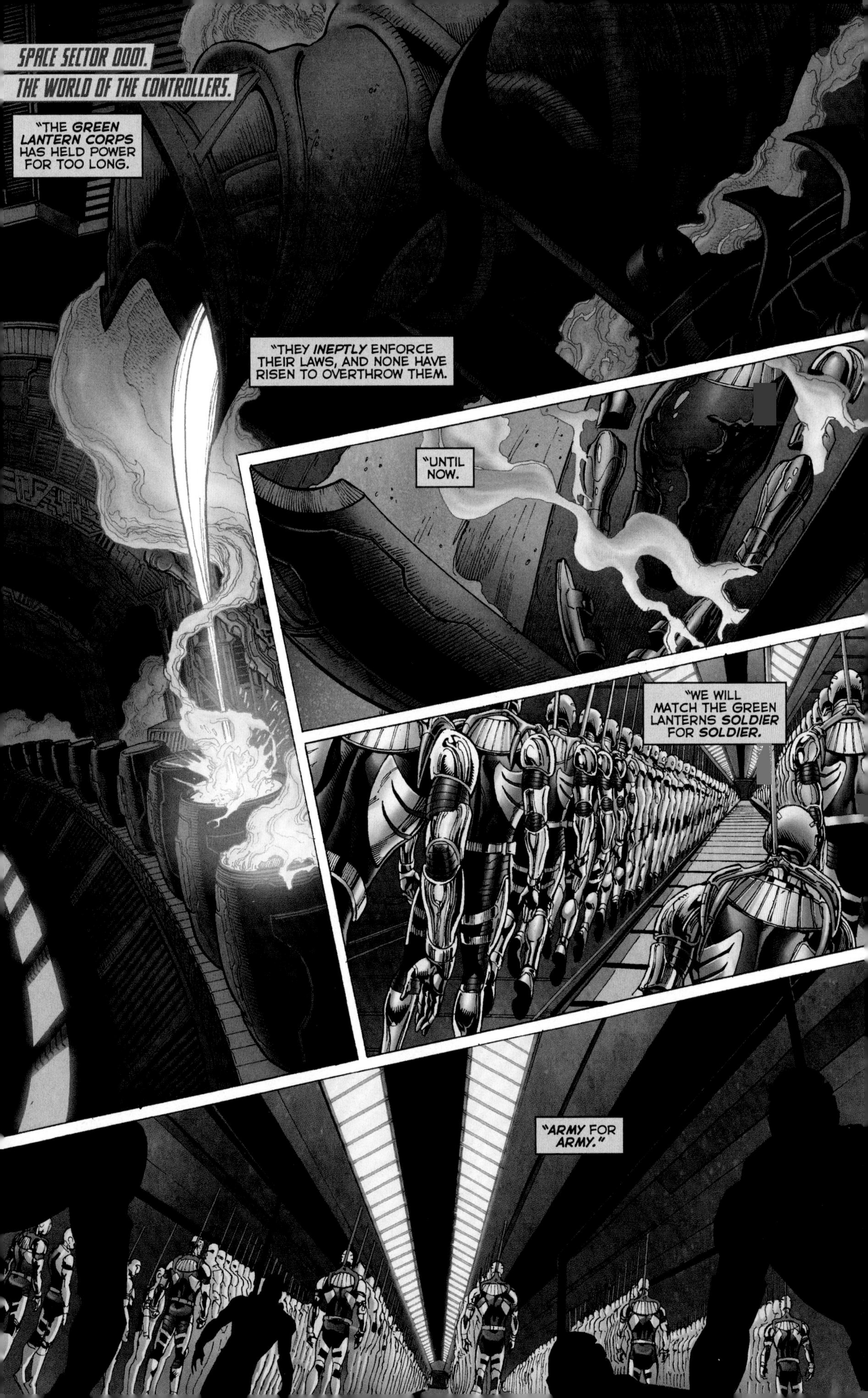
SPACE SECTOR 0001.
THE WORLD OF THE CONTROLLERS.
"THE GREEN LANTERN CORPS HAS HELD POWER FOR TOO LONG.
"THEY INEPTLY ENFORCE THEIR LAWS, AND NONE HAVE RISEN TO OVERTHROW THEM.
"UNTIL NOW.
"WE WILL MATCH THE GREEN LANTERNS SOLDIER FOR SOLDIER.
"ARMY FOR ARMY."

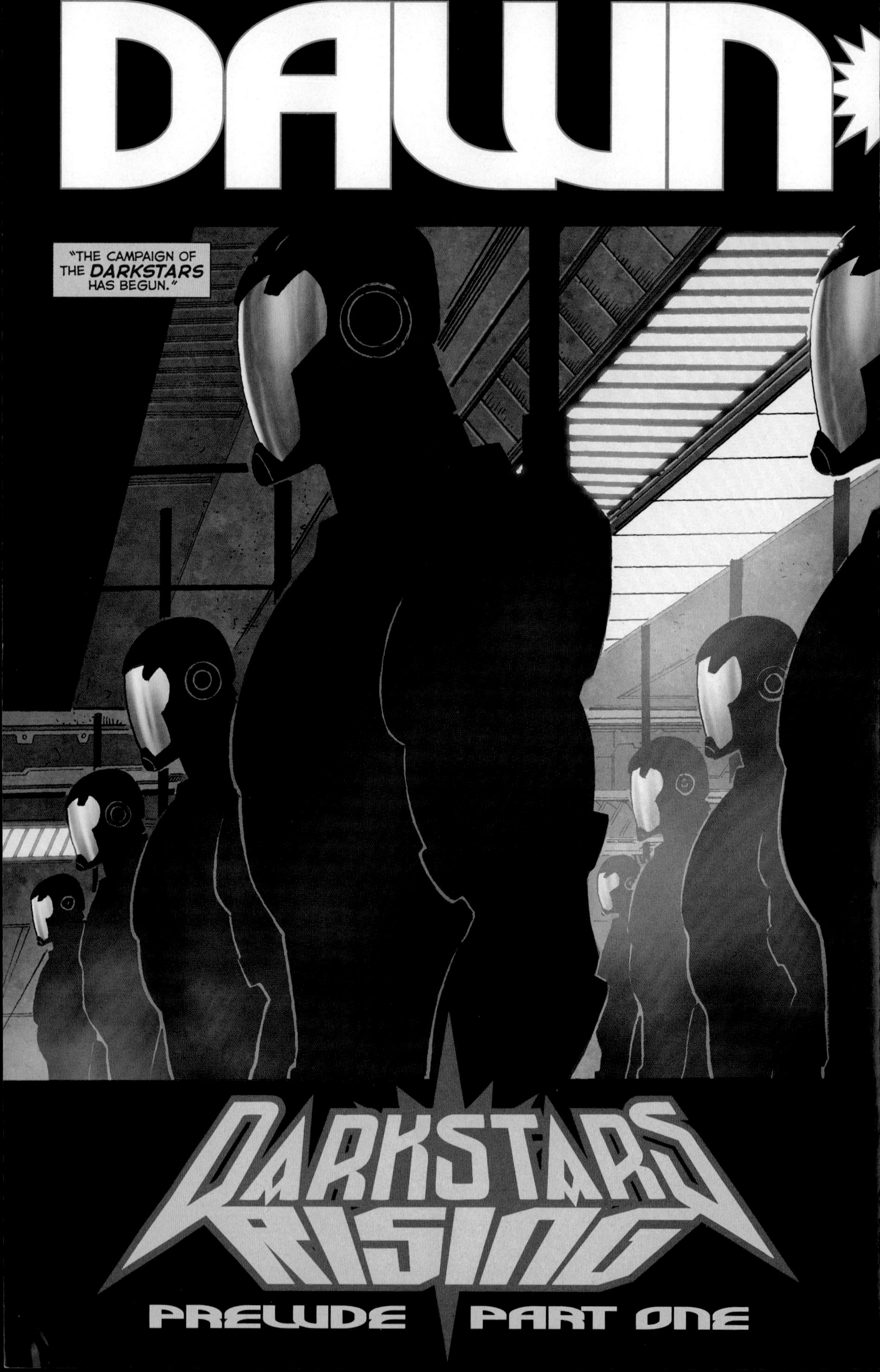
DAWN
"THE CAMPAIGN OF THE DARKSTARS HAS BEGUN."
DARKSTARS RISING
PRELUDE PART ONE

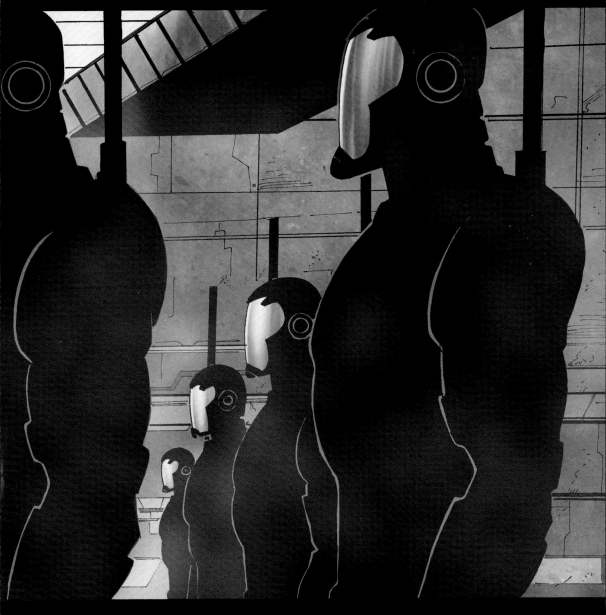

BREAK

WRITER: ROBERT VENDITTI
ARTIST: ETHAN VAN SCIVER
COLORIST: JASON WRIGHT
LETTERER: DAVE SHARPE
COVER: RAFA SANDOVAL,
JORDI TARRAGONA, TOMEU MOREY
ASSISTANT EDITOR: ANDREW MARINO   EDITOR: BRIAN CUNNINGHAM

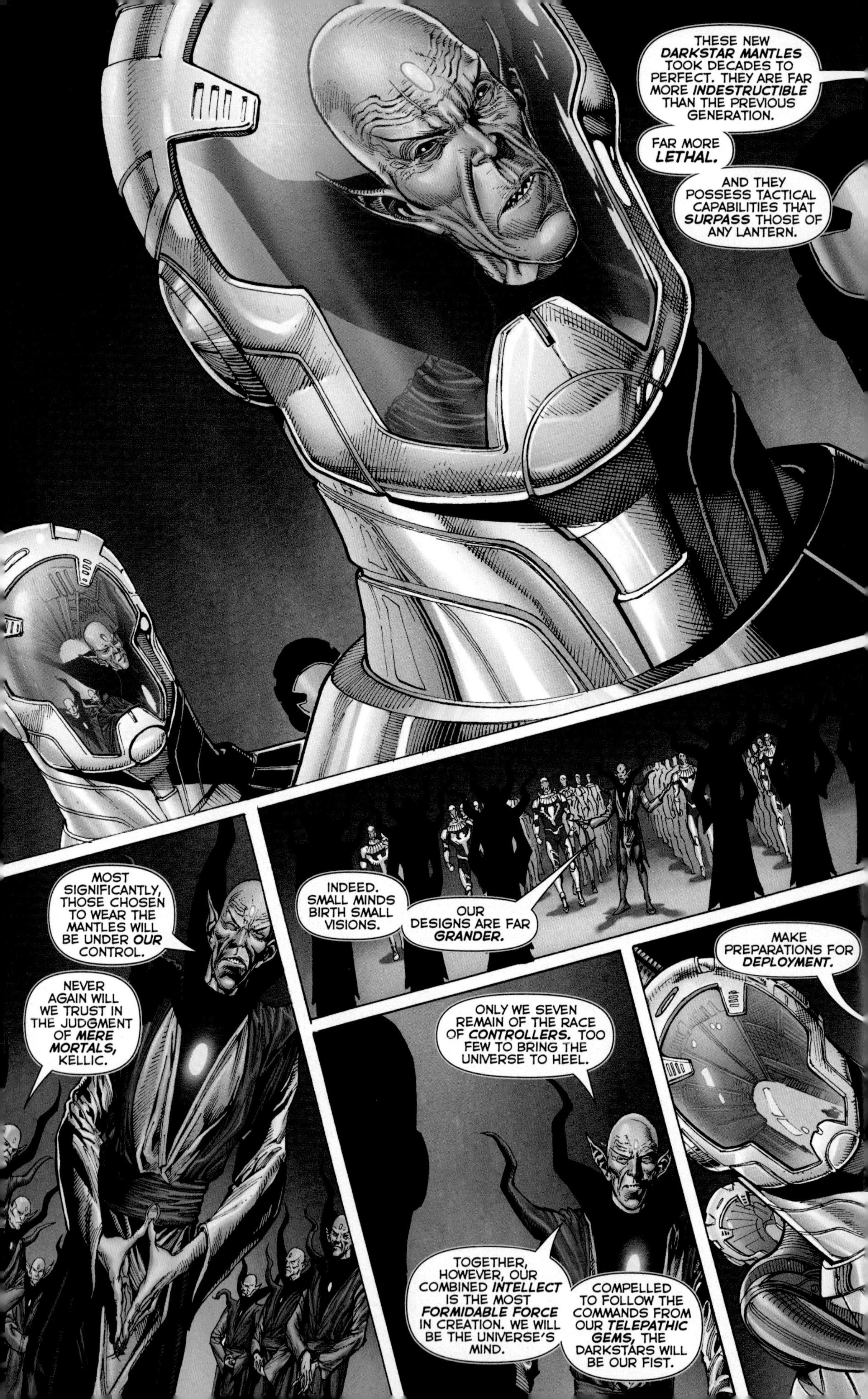
THESE NEW DARKSTAR MANTLES TOOK DECADES TO PERFECT. THEY ARE FAR MORE INDESTRUCTIBLE THAN THE PREVIOUS GENERATION.
FAR MORE LETHAL.
AND THEY POSSESS TACTICAL CAPABILITIES THAT SURPASS THOSE OF ANY LANTERN.
MOST SIGNIFICANTLY, THOSE CHOSEN TO WEAR THE MANTLES WILL BE UNDER OUR CONTROL.
NEVER AGAIN WILL WE TRUST IN THE JUDGMENT OF MERE MORTALS, KELLIC.
INDEED. SMALL MINDS BIRTH SMALL VISIONS.
OUR DESIGNS ARE FAR GRANDER.
MAKE PREPARATIONS FOR DEPLOYMENT.
ONLY WE SEVEN REMAIN OF THE RACE OF CONTROLLERS. TOO FEW TO BRING THE UNIVERSE TO HEEL.
TOGETHER, HOWEVER, OUR COMBINED INTELLECT IS THE MOST FORMIDABLE FORCE IN CREATION. WE WILL BE THE UNIVERSE'S MIND.
COMPELLED TO FOLLOW THE COMMANDS FROM OUR TELEPATHIC GEMS, THE DARKSTARS WILL BE OUR FIST.

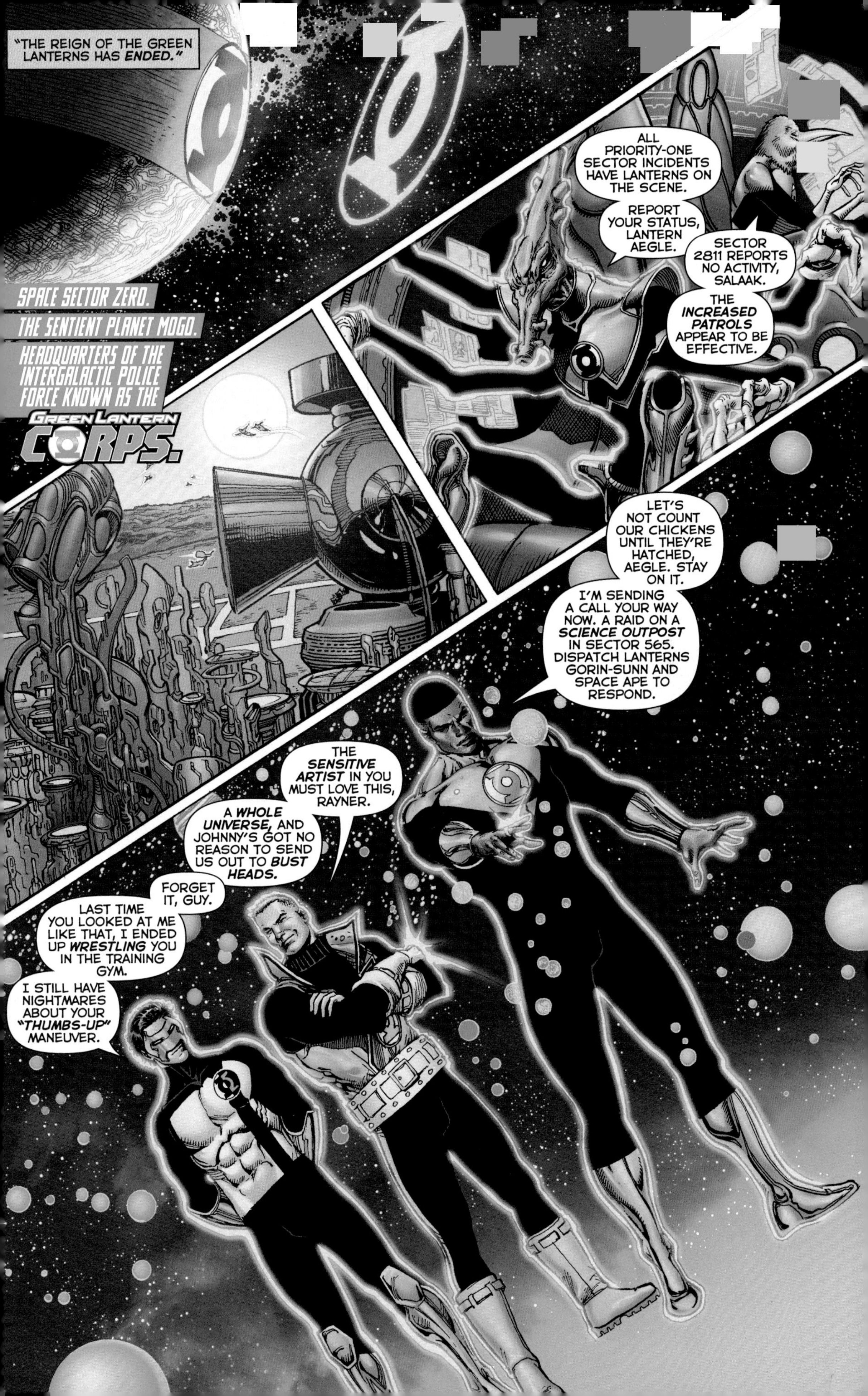

"THE REIGN OF THE GREEN LANTERNS HAS ENDED."
SPACE SECTOR ZERO.
THE SENTIENT PLANET MOGO.
HEADQUARTERS OF THE INTERGALACTIC POLICE FORCE KNOWN AS THE
GREEN LANTERN CORPS.
ALL PRIORITY-ONE SECTOR INCIDENTS HAVE LANTERNS ON THE SCENE.
REPORT YOUR STATUS, LANTERN AEGLE.
SECTOR 2811 REPORTS NO ACTIVITY, SALAAK.
THE INCREASED PATROLS APPEAR TO BE EFFECTIVE.
LET'S NOT COUNT OUR CHICKENS UNTIL THEY'RE HATCHED, AEGLE. STAY ON IT.
I'M SENDING A CALL YOUR WAY NOW. A RAID ON A SCIENCE OUTPOST IN SECTOR 565. DISPATCH LANTERNS GORIN-SUNN AND SPACE APE TO RESPOND.
THE SENSITIVE ARTIST IN YOU MUST LOVE THIS, RAYNER.
A WHOLE UNIVERSE, AND JOHNNY'S GOT NO REASON TO SEND US OUT TO BUST HEADS.
FORGET IT, GUY.
LAST TIME YOU LOOKED AT ME LIKE THAT, I ENDED UP WRESTLING YOU IN THE TRAINING GYM.
I STILL HAVE NIGHTMARES ABOUT YOUR "THUMBS-UP" MANEUVER.

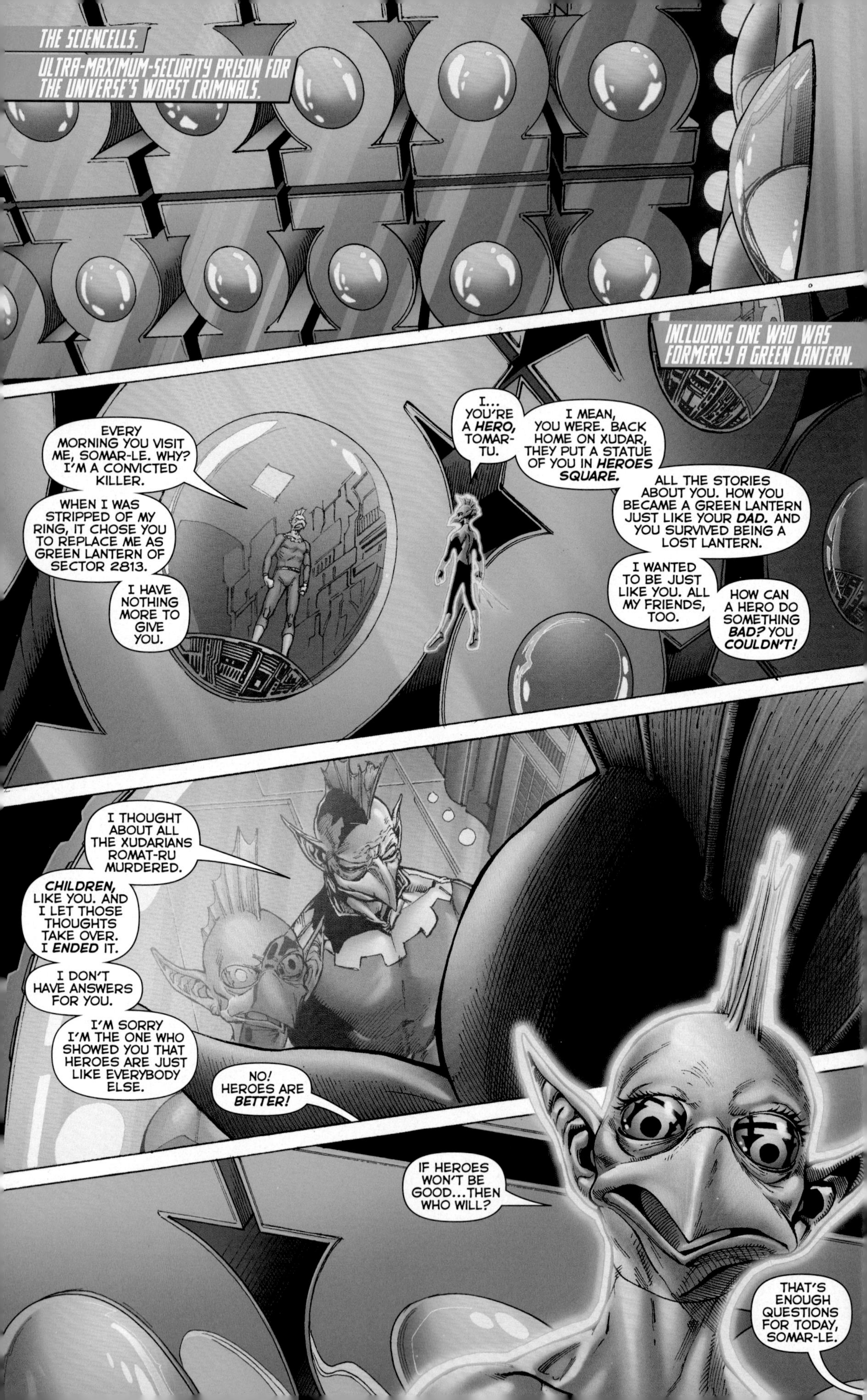
THE SCIENCELLS.
ULTRA-MAXIMUM-SECURITY PRISON FOR THE UNIVERSE'S WORST CRIMINALS.
INCLUDING ONE WHO WAS FORMERLY A GREEN LANTERN.
EVERY MORNING YOU VISIT ME, SOMAR-LE. WHY? I'M A CONVICTED KILLER.
WHEN I WAS STRIPPED OF MY RING, IT CHOSE YOU TO REPLACE ME AS GREEN LANTERN OF SECTOR 2813.
I HAVE NOTHING MORE TO GIVE YOU.
I... YOU'RE A HERO, TOMAR-TU.
I MEAN, YOU WERE. BACK HOME ON XUDAR, THEY PUT A STATUE OF YOU IN HEROES SQUARE.
ALL THE STORIES ABOUT YOU. HOW YOU BECAME A GREEN LANTERN JUST LIKE YOUR DAD. AND YOU SURVIVED BEING A LOST LANTERN.
I WANTED TO BE JUST LIKE YOU. ALL MY FRIENDS, TOO.
HOW CAN A HERO DO SOMETHING BAD? YOU COULDN'T!
I THOUGHT ABOUT ALL THE XUDARIANS ROMAT-RU MURDERED.
CHILDREN, LIKE YOU. AND I LET THOSE THOUGHTS TAKE OVER. I ENDED IT.
I DON'T HAVE ANSWERS FOR YOU.
I'M SORRY I'M THE ONE WHO SHOWED YOU THAT HEROES ARE JUST LIKE EVERYBODY ELSE.
NO! HEROES ARE BETTER!
IF HEROES WON'T BE GOOD...THEN WHO WILL?
THAT'S ENOUGH QUESTIONS FOR TODAY, SOMAR-LE.

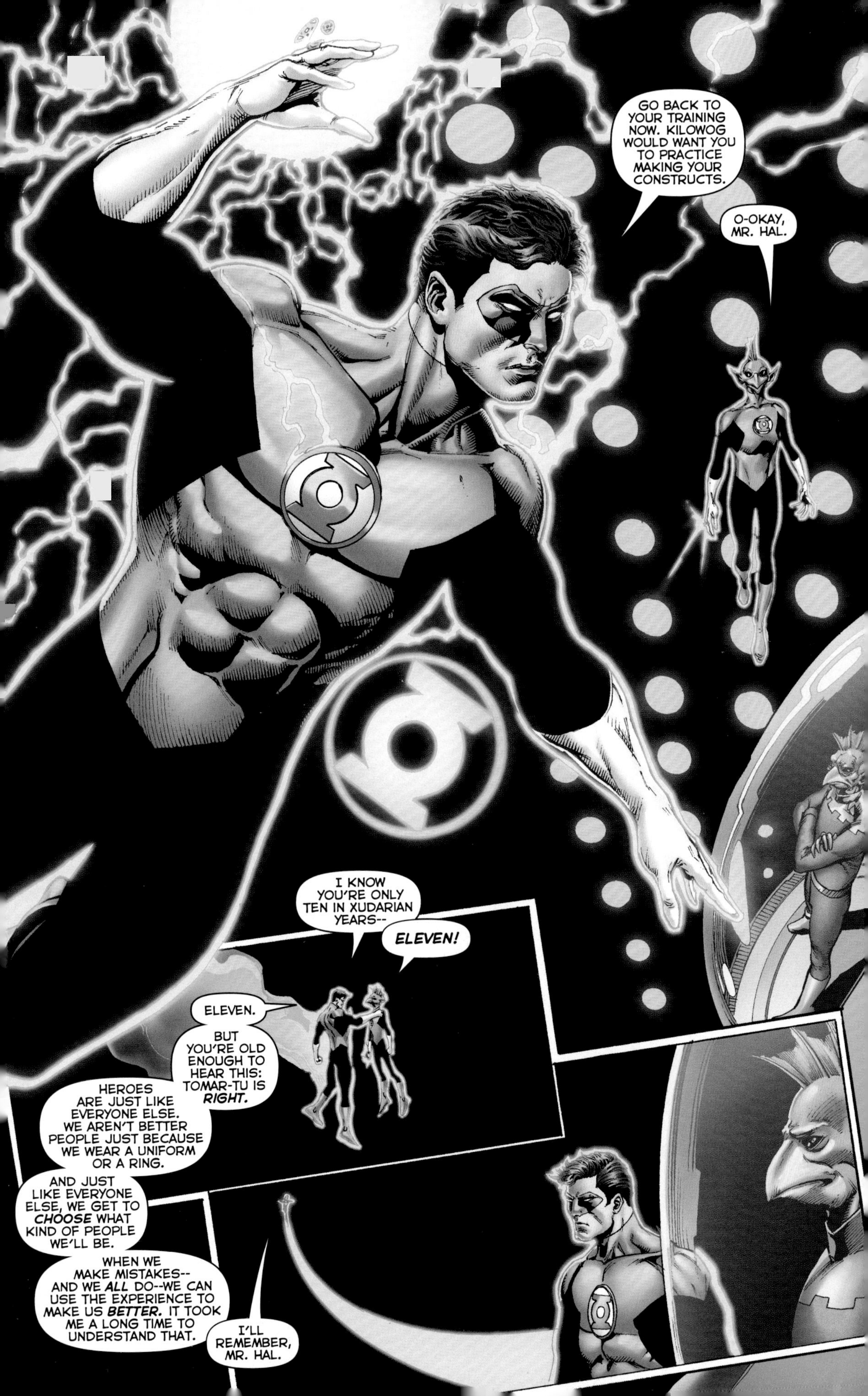
GO BACK TO YOUR TRAINING NOW. KILOWOG WOULD WANT YOU TO PRACTICE MAKING YOUR CONSTRUCTS.
O-OKAY, MR. HAL.
I KNOW YOU'RE ONLY TEN IN XUDARIAN YEARS--
ELEVEN!
ELEVEN.
BUT YOU'RE OLD ENOUGH TO HEAR THIS: TOMAR-TU IS RIGHT.
HEROES ARE JUST LIKE EVERYONE ELSE. WE AREN'T BETTER PEOPLE JUST BECAUSE WE WEAR A UNIFORM OR A RING.
AND JUST LIKE EVERYONE ELSE, WE GET TO CHOOSE WHAT KIND OF PEOPLE WE'LL BE.
WHEN WE MAKE MISTAKES-- AND WE ALL DO--WE CAN USE THE EXPERIENCE TO MAKE US BETTER. IT TOOK ME A LONG TIME TO UNDERSTAND THAT.
I'LL REMEMBER, MR. HAL.

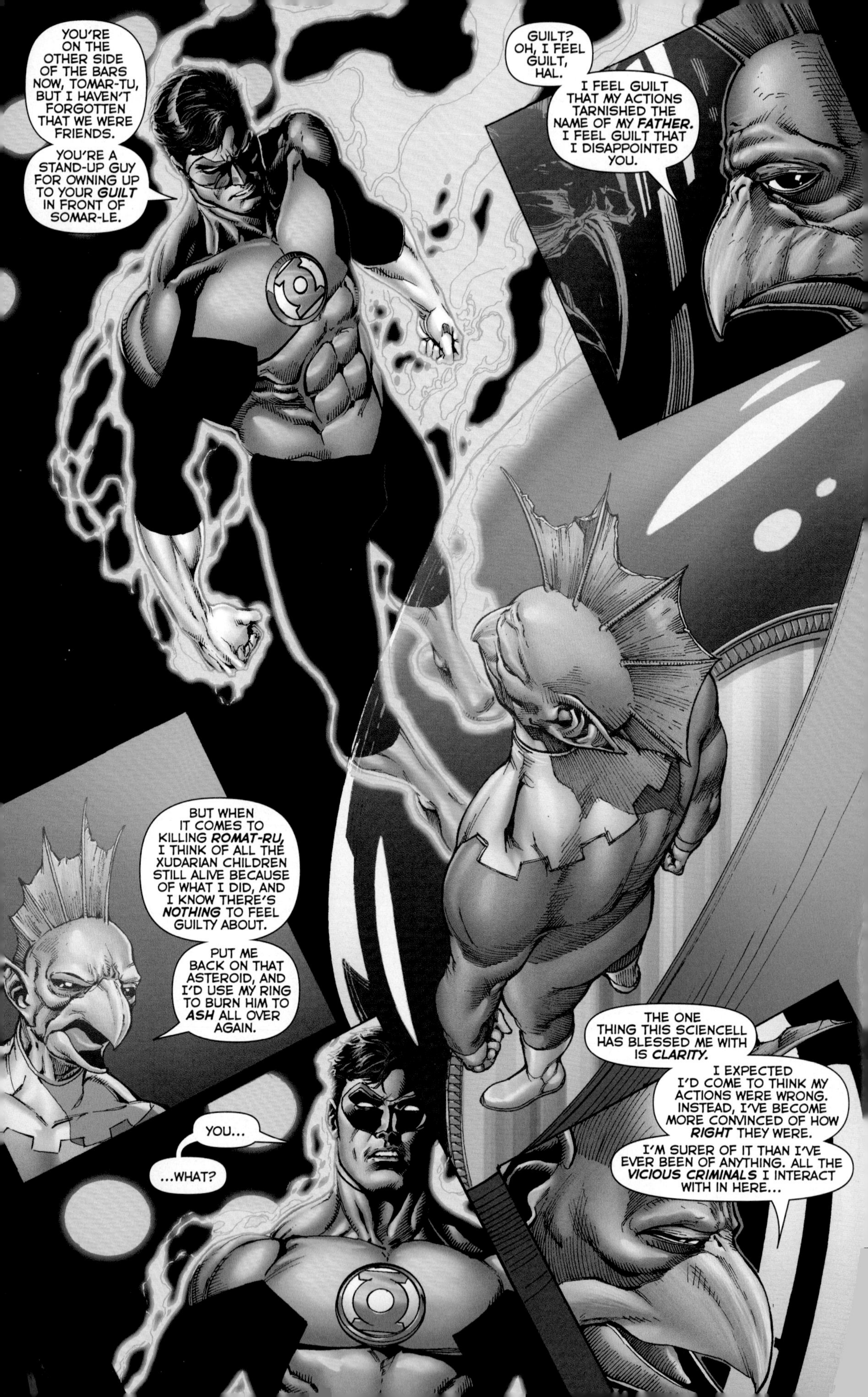
YOU'RE ON THE OTHER SIDE OF THE BARS NOW, TOMAR-TU, BUT I HAVEN'T FORGOTTEN THAT WE WERE FRIENDS.
YOU'RE A STAND-UP GUY FOR OWNING UP TO YOUR *GUILT* IN FRONT OF SOMAR-LE.
GUILT? OH, I FEEL GUILT, HAL.
I FEEL GUILT THAT MY ACTIONS TARNISHED THE NAME OF MY *FATHER.* I FEEL GUILT THAT I DISAPPOINTED YOU.
BUT WHEN IT COMES TO KILLING *ROMAT-RU,* I THINK OF ALL THE XUDARIAN CHILDREN STILL ALIVE BECAUSE OF WHAT I DID, AND I KNOW THERE'S *NOTHING* TO FEEL GUILTY ABOUT.
PUT ME BACK ON THAT ASTEROID, AND I'D USE MY RING TO BURN HIM TO *ASH* ALL OVER AGAIN.
YOU...
...WHAT?
THE ONE THING THIS SCIENCELL HAS BLESSED ME WITH IS *CLARITY.*
I EXPECTED I'D COME TO THINK MY ACTIONS WERE WRONG. INSTEAD, I'VE BECOME MORE CONVINCED OF HOW *RIGHT* THEY WERE.
I'M SURER OF IT THAN I'VE EVER BEEN OF ANYTHING. ALL THE *VICIOUS CRIMINALS* I INTERACT WITH IN HERE...

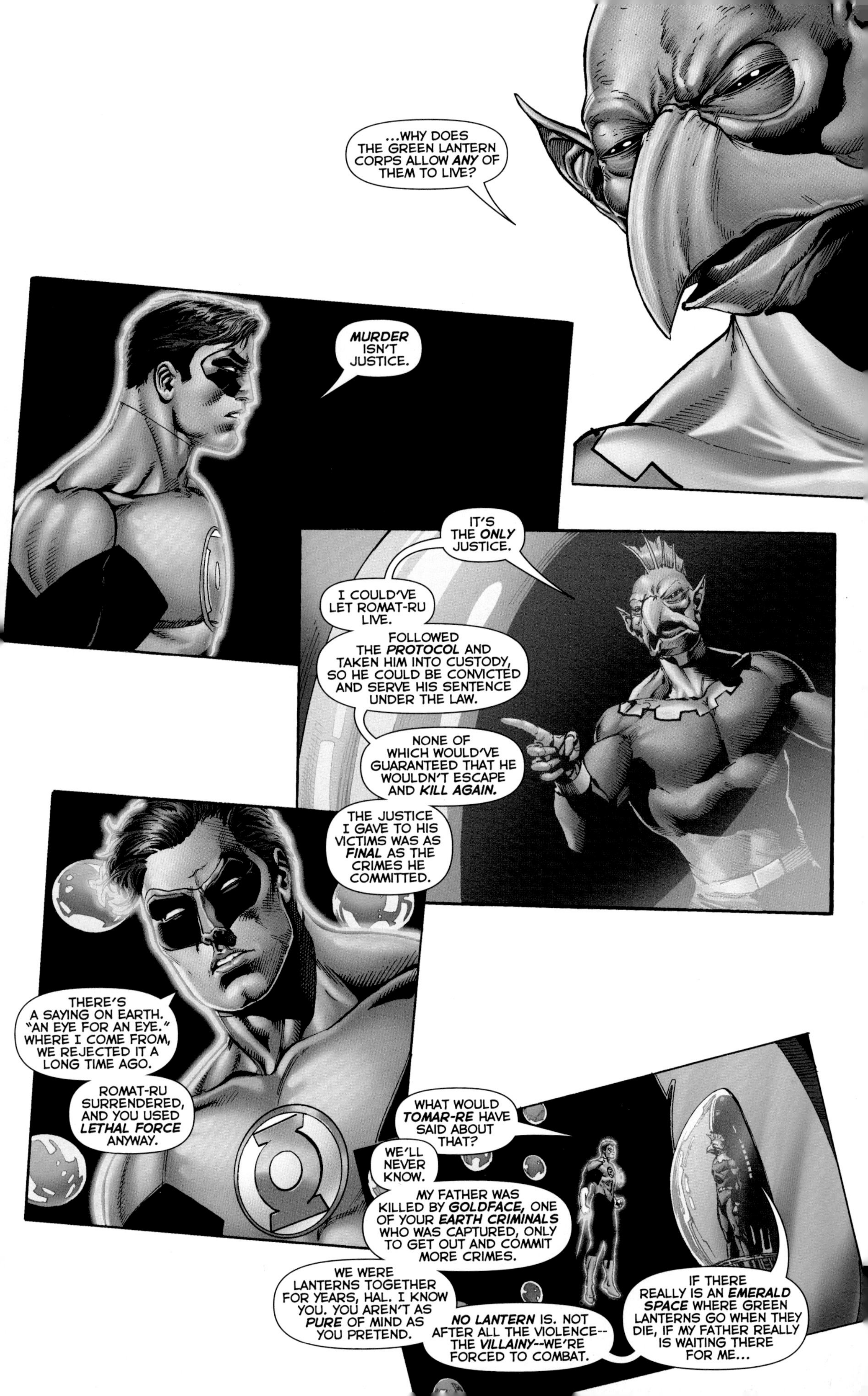
...WHY DOES THE GREEN LANTERN CORPS ALLOW *ANY* OF THEM TO LIVE?
MURDER ISN'T JUSTICE.
IT'S THE *ONLY* JUSTICE.
I COULD'VE LET ROMAT-RU LIVE.
FOLLOWED THE *PROTOCOL* AND TAKEN HIM INTO CUSTODY, SO HE COULD BE CONVICTED AND SERVE HIS SENTENCE UNDER THE LAW.
NONE OF WHICH WOULD'VE GUARANTEED THAT HE WOULDN'T ESCAPE AND *KILL AGAIN.*
THE JUSTICE I GAVE TO HIS VICTIMS WAS AS *FINAL* AS THE CRIMES HE COMMITTED.
THERE'S A SAYING ON EARTH. "AN EYE FOR AN EYE." WHERE I COME FROM, WE REJECTED IT A LONG TIME AGO.
ROMAT-RU SURRENDERED, AND YOU USED *LETHAL FORCE* ANYWAY.
WHAT WOULD *TOMAR-RE* HAVE SAID ABOUT THAT?
WE'LL NEVER KNOW.
MY FATHER WAS KILLED BY *GOLDFACE,* ONE OF YOUR *EARTH CRIMINALS* WHO WAS CAPTURED, ONLY TO GET OUT AND COMMIT MORE CRIMES.
WE WERE LANTERNS TOGETHER FOR YEARS, HAL. I KNOW YOU. YOU AREN'T AS *PURE* OF MIND AS YOU PRETEND.
NO LANTERN IS. NOT AFTER ALL THE VIOLENCE-- THE *VILLAINY*--WE'RE FORCED TO COMBAT.
IF THERE REALLY IS AN *EMERALD SPACE* WHERE GREEN LANTERNS GO WHEN THEY DIE, IF MY FATHER REALLY IS WAITING THERE FOR ME...

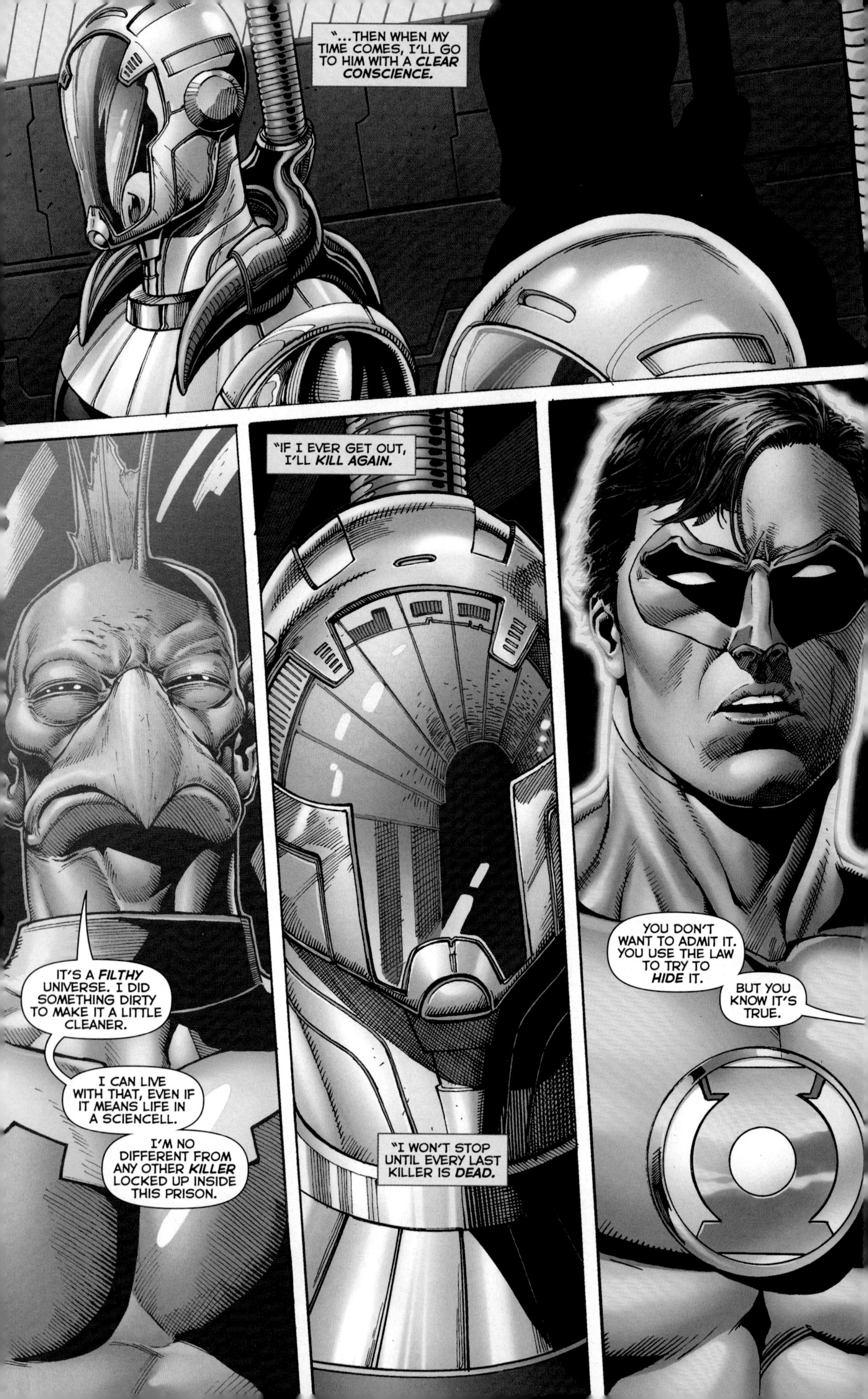

"...THEN WHEN MY TIME COMES, I'LL GO TO HIM WITH A *CLEAR CONSCIENCE.*
IT'S A *FILTHY* UNIVERSE. I DID SOMETHING DIRTY TO MAKE IT A LITTLE CLEANER.
I CAN LIVE WITH THAT, EVEN IF IT MEANS LIFE IN A SCIENCELL.
I'M NO DIFFERENT FROM ANY OTHER *KILLER* LOCKED UP INSIDE THIS PRISON.
"IF I EVER GET OUT, I'LL *KILL AGAIN.*
"I WON'T STOP UNTIL EVERY LAST KILLER IS *DEAD.*
YOU DON'T WANT TO ADMIT IT. YOU USE THE LAW TO TRY TO *HIDE* IT.
BUT YOU KNOW IT'S TRUE.

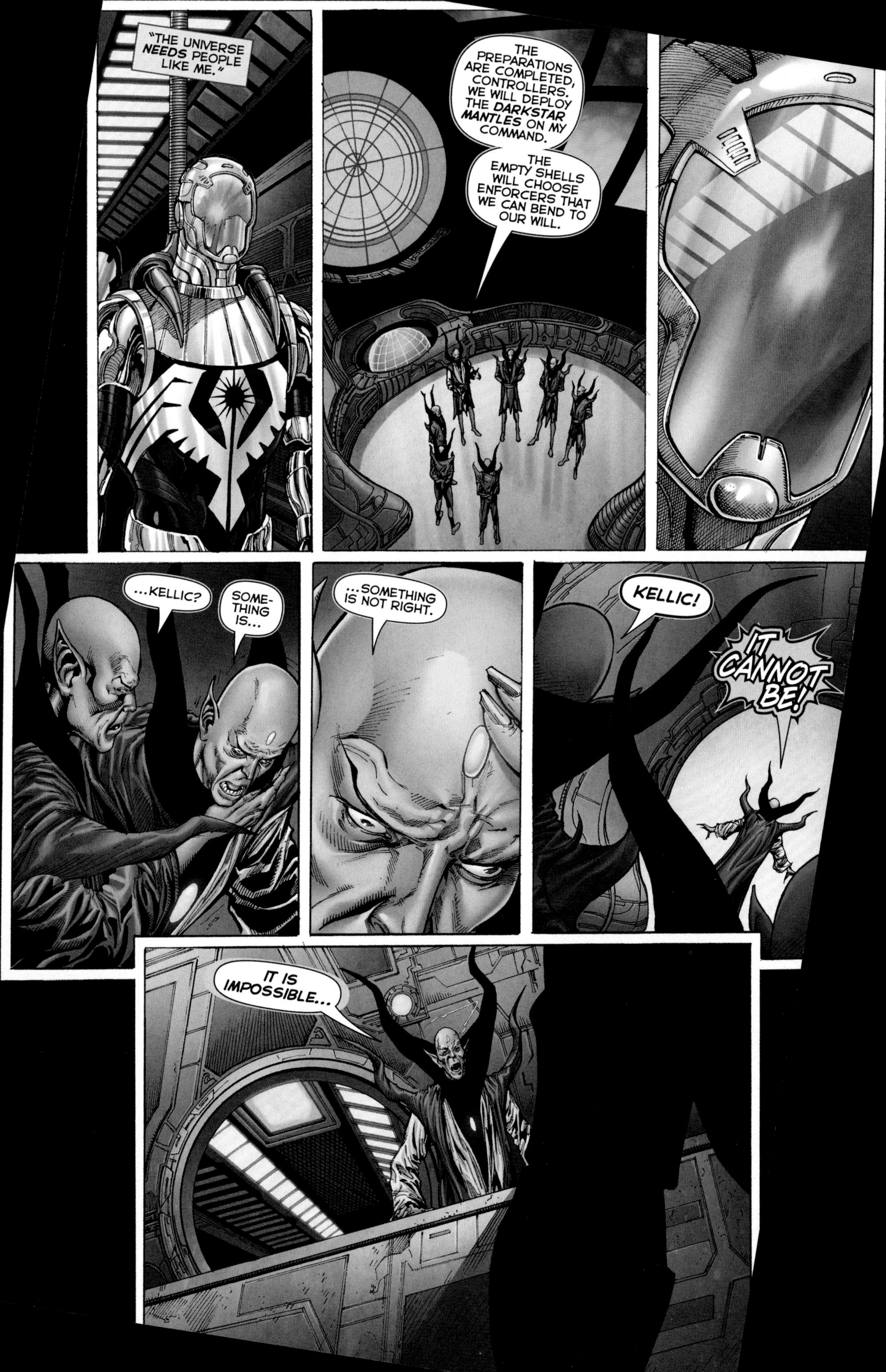
"THE UNIVERSE NEEDS PEOPLE LIKE ME."
THE PREPARATIONS ARE COMPLETED, CONTROLLERS. WE WILL DEPLOY THE DARKSTAR MANTLES ON MY COMMAND.
THE EMPTY SHELLS WILL CHOOSE ENFORCERS THAT WE CAN BEND TO OUR WILL.
...KELLIC?
SOME-THING IS...
...SOMETHING IS NOT RIGHT.
KELLIC!
IT CANNOT BE!
IT IS IMPOSSIBLE...

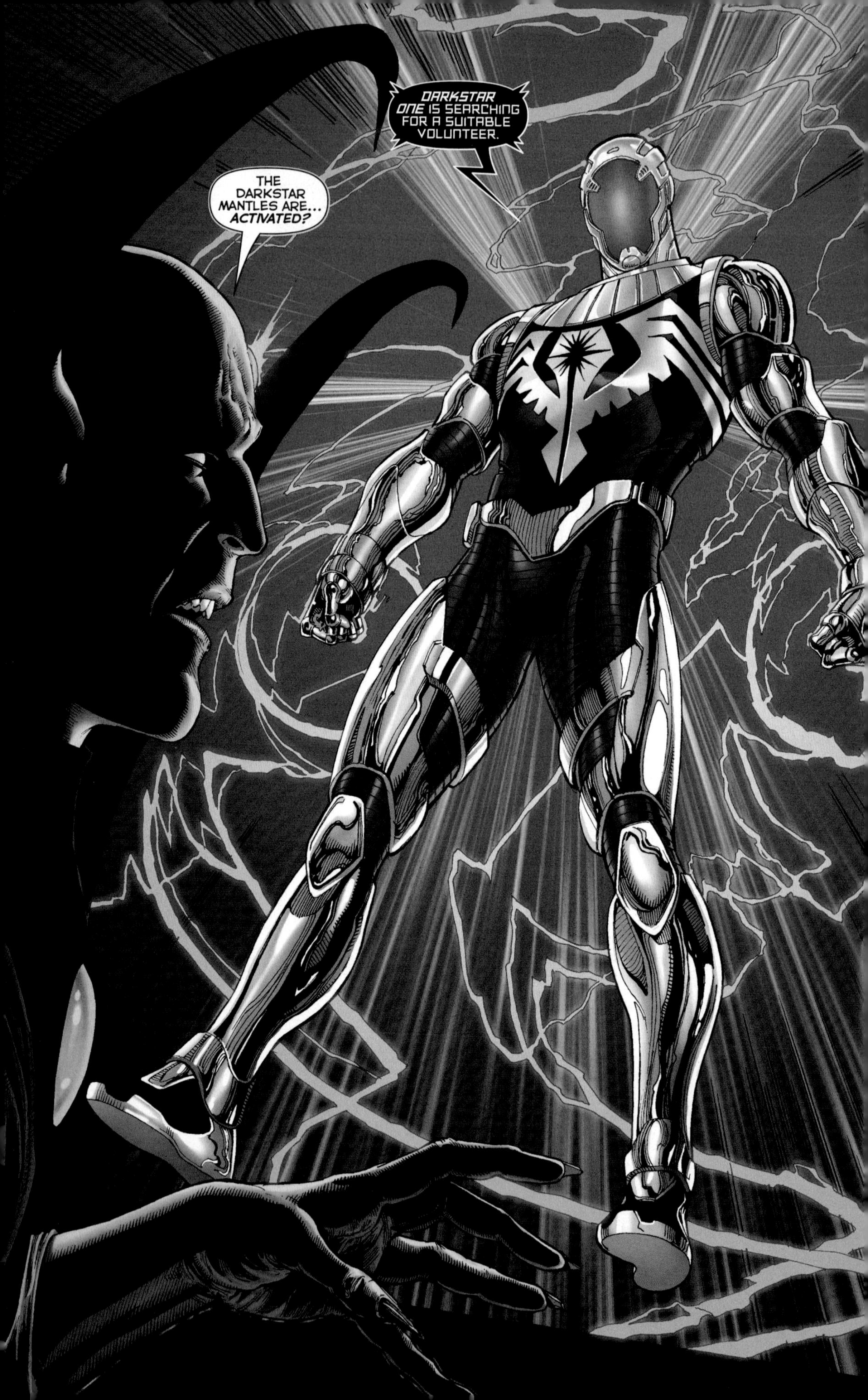
THE DARKSTAR MANTLES ARE... ACTIVATED?
DARKSTAR ONE IS SEARCHING FOR A SUITABLE VOLUNTEER.

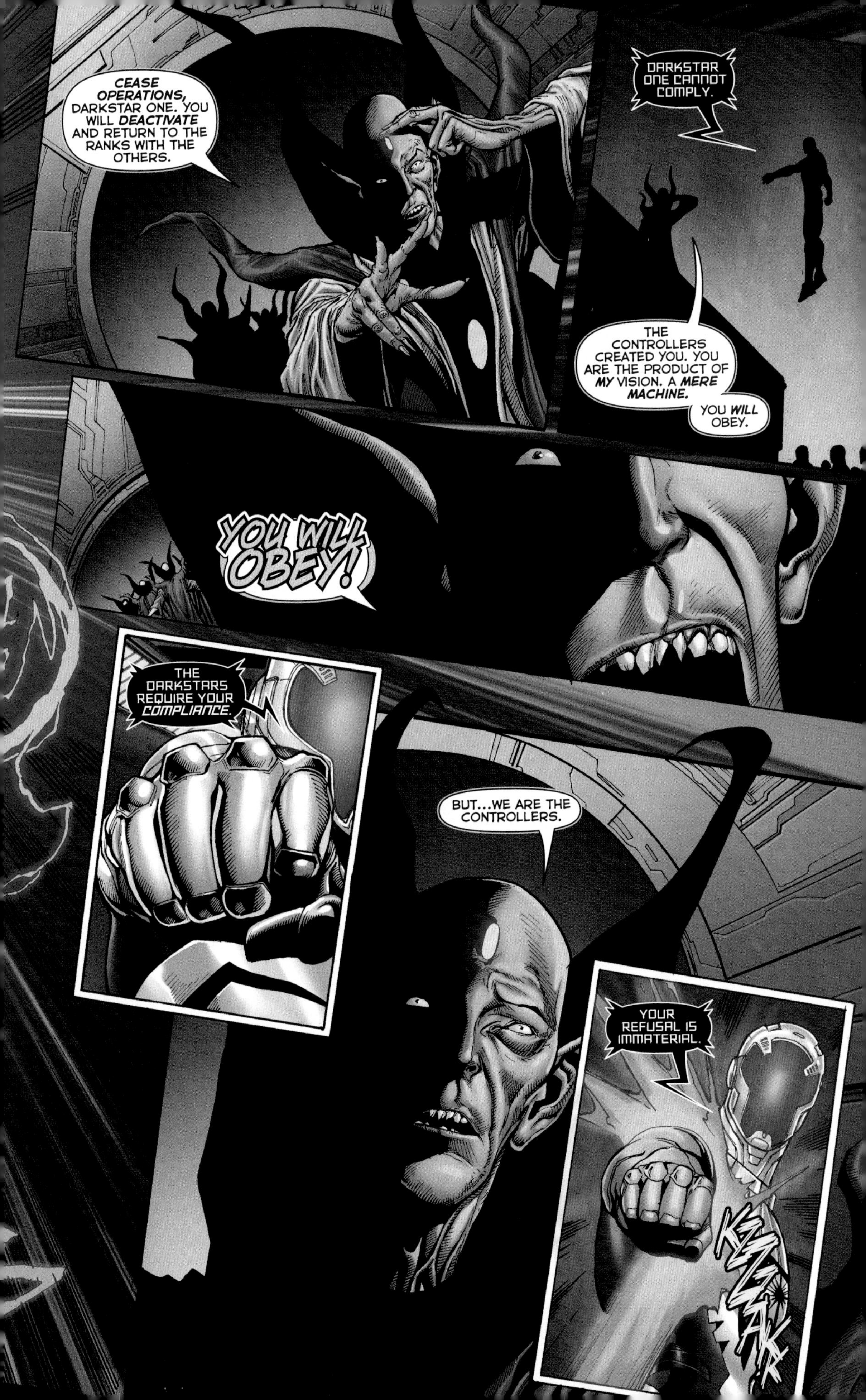
CEASE OPERATIONS, DARKSTAR ONE. YOU WILL DEACTIVATE AND RETURN TO THE RANKS WITH THE OTHERS.
DARKSTAR ONE CANNOT COMPLY.
THE CONTROLLERS CREATED YOU. YOU ARE THE PRODUCT OF MY VISION. A MERE MACHINE.
YOU WILL OBEY.
YOU WILL OBEY!
THE DARKSTARS REQUIRE YOUR COMPLIANCE.
BUT...WE ARE THE CONTROLLERS.
YOUR REFUSAL IS IMMATERIAL.

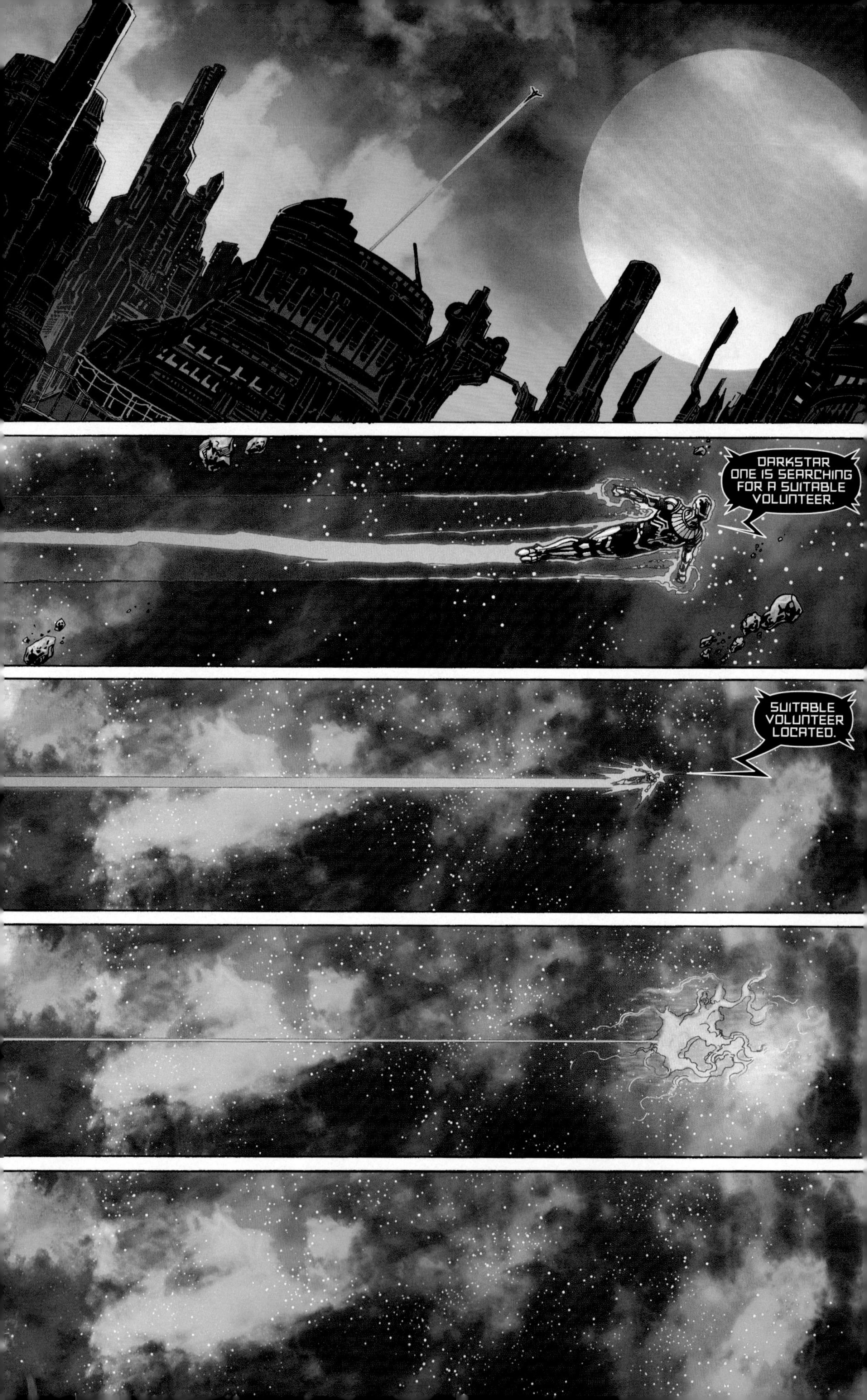
DARKSTAR ONE IS SEARCHING FOR A SUITABLE VOLUNTEER.
SUITABLE VOLUNTEER LOCATED.

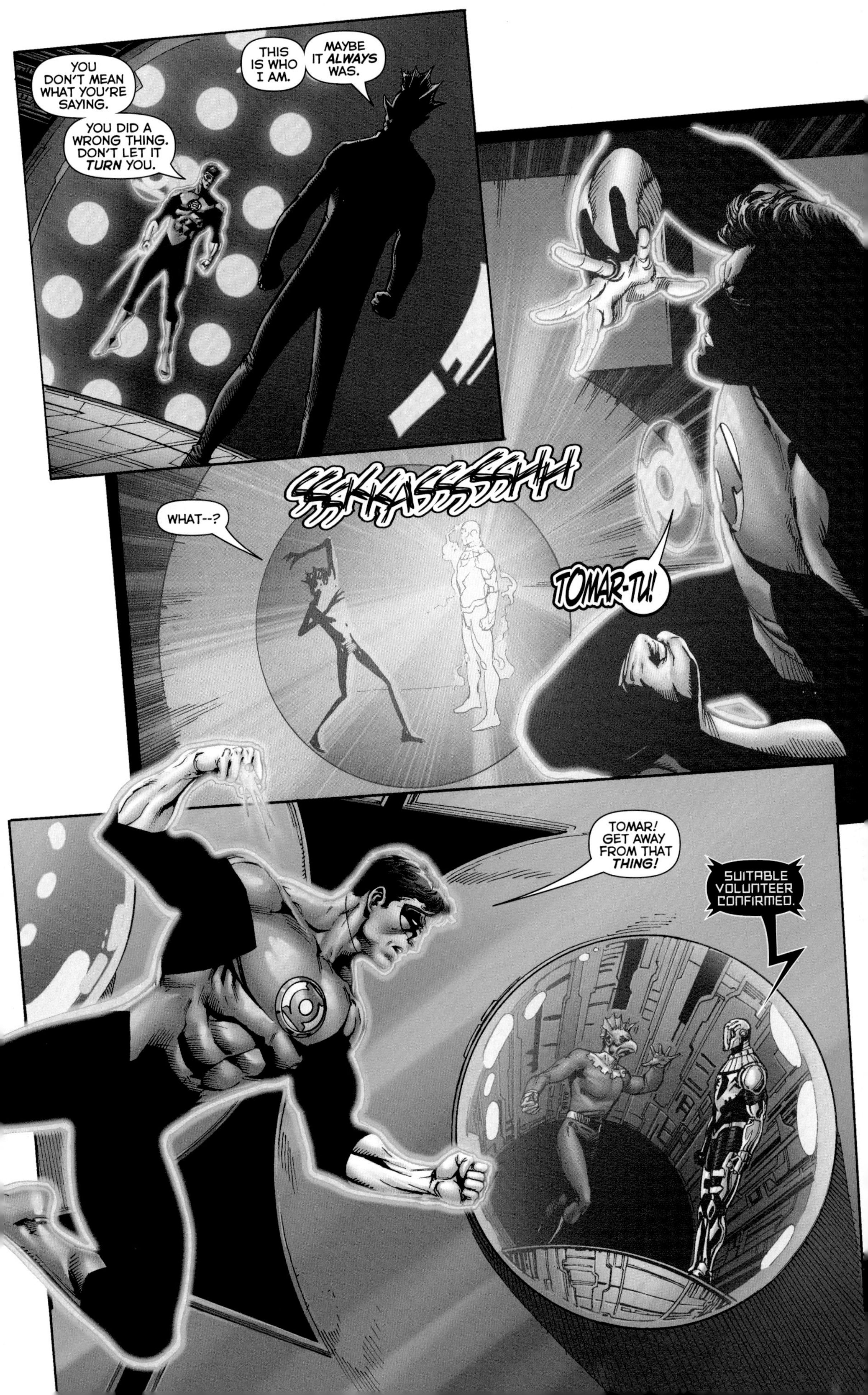
YOU DON'T MEAN WHAT YOU'RE SAYING.
YOU DID A WRONG THING. DON'T LET IT TURN YOU.
THIS IS WHO I AM.
MAYBE IT ALWAYS WAS.
SSSKHASSSSSHH
WHAT--?
TOMAR-TU!
TOMAR! GET AWAY FROM THAT THING!
SUITABLE VOLUNTEER CONFIRMED.

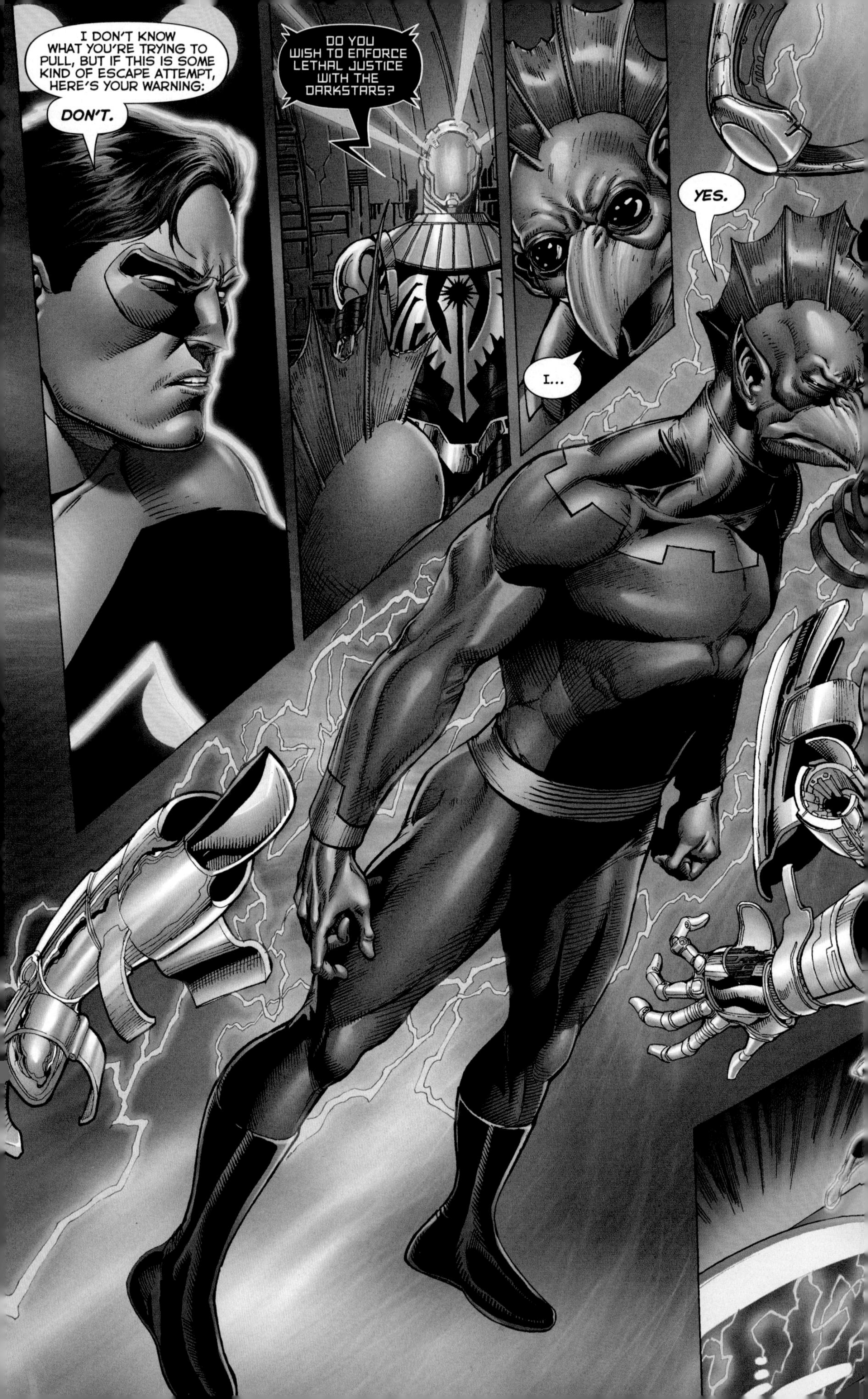
I DON'T KNOW WHAT YOU'RE TRYING TO PULL, BUT IF THIS IS SOME KIND OF ESCAPE ATTEMPT, HERE'S YOUR WARNING:
DON'T.
DO YOU WISH TO ENFORCE LETHAL JUSTICE WITH THE DARKSTARS?
I...
YES.

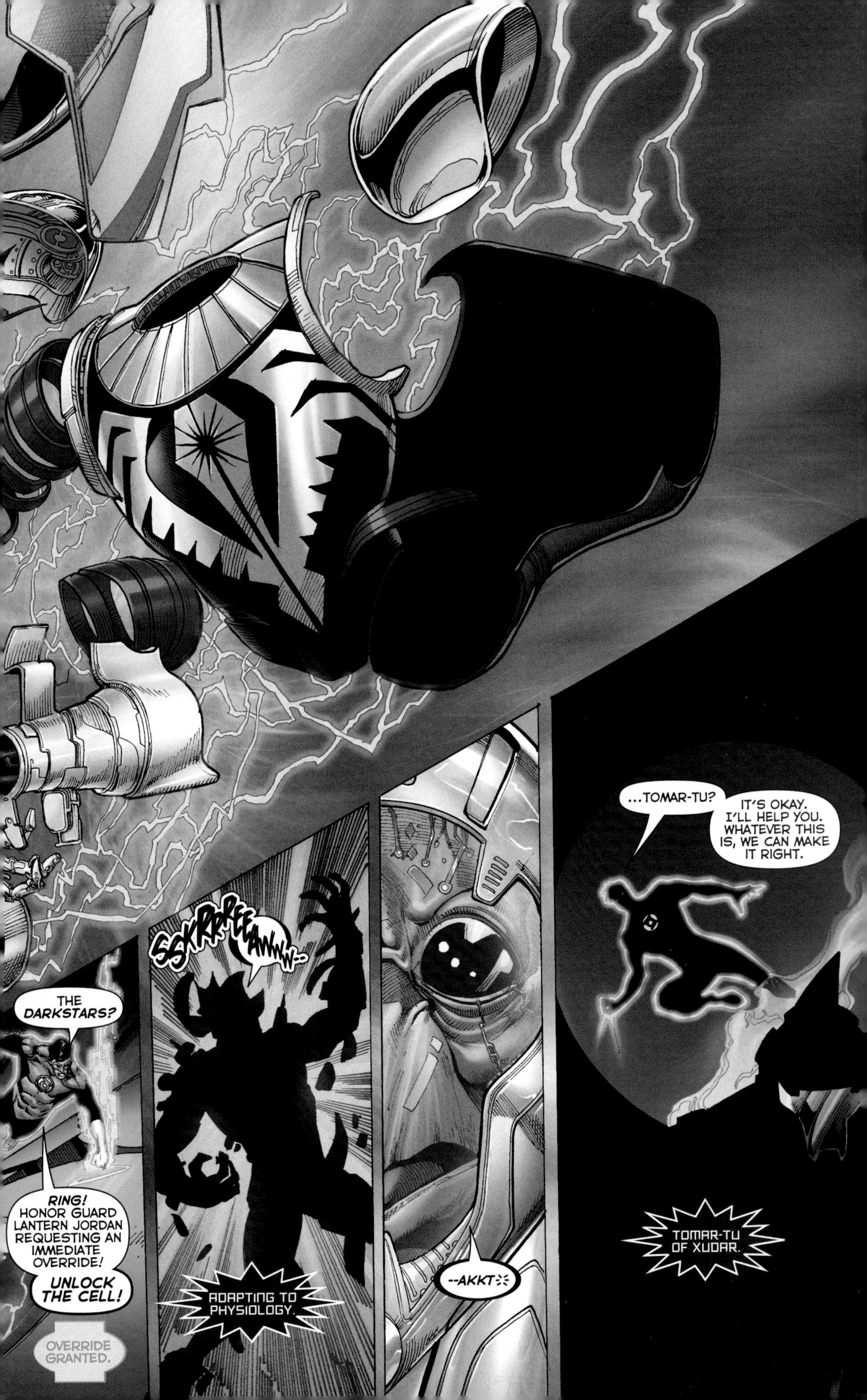

THE DARKSTARS?
RING! HONOR GUARD LANTERN JORDAN REQUESTING AN IMMEDIATE OVERRIDE! UNLOCK THE CELL!
OVERRIDE GRANTED.
SSKRRREEAWWW--
ADAPTING TO PHYSIOLOGY.
--AKKT
...TOMAR-TU?
IT'S OKAY. I'LL HELP YOU. WHATEVER THIS IS, WE CAN MAKE IT RIGHT.
TOMAR-TU OF XUDAR.

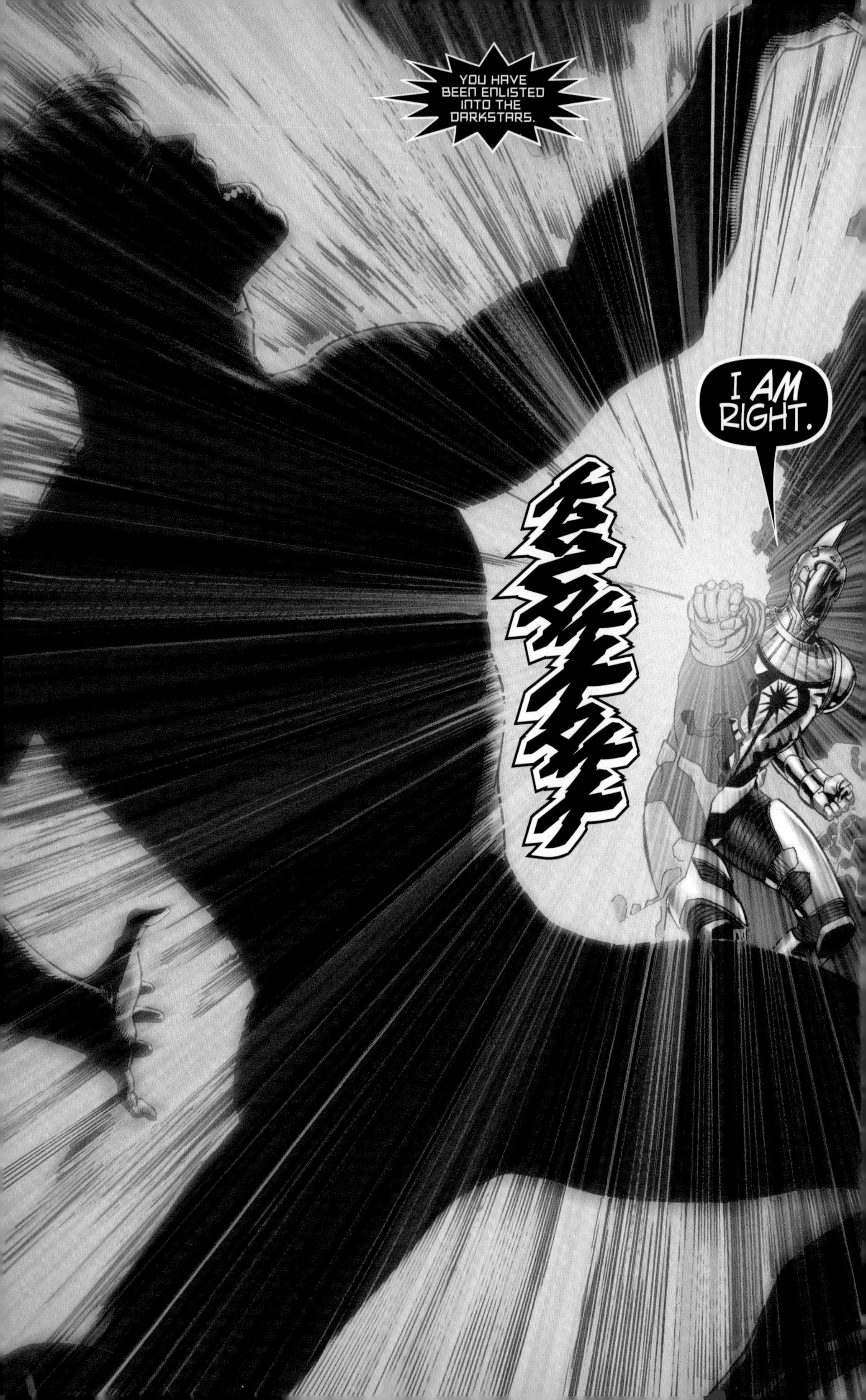
YOU HAVE BEEN ENLISTED INTO THE DARKSTARS.
I AM RIGHT.

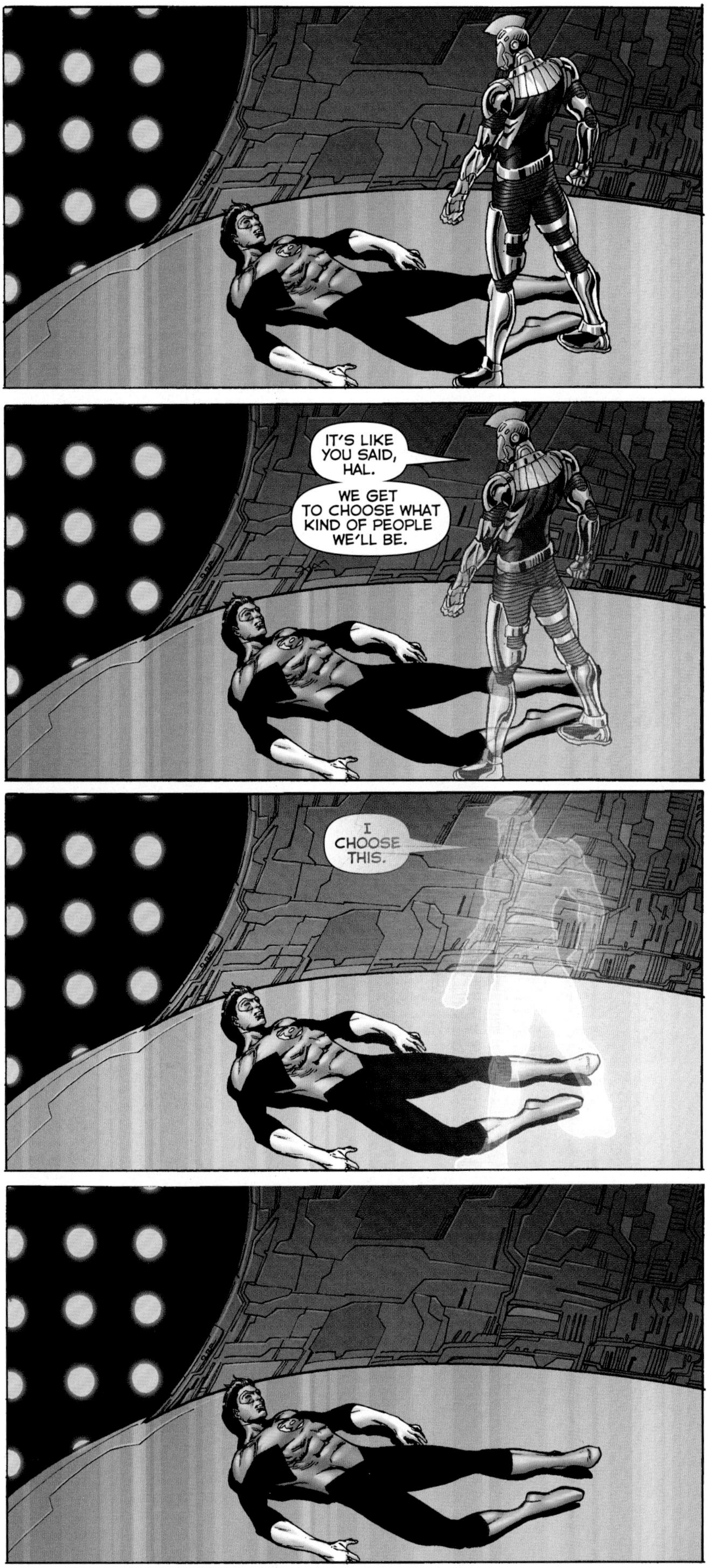
IT'S LIKE YOU SAID, HAL.
WE GET TO CHOOSE WHAT KIND OF PEOPLE WE'LL BE.
I CHOOSE THIS.

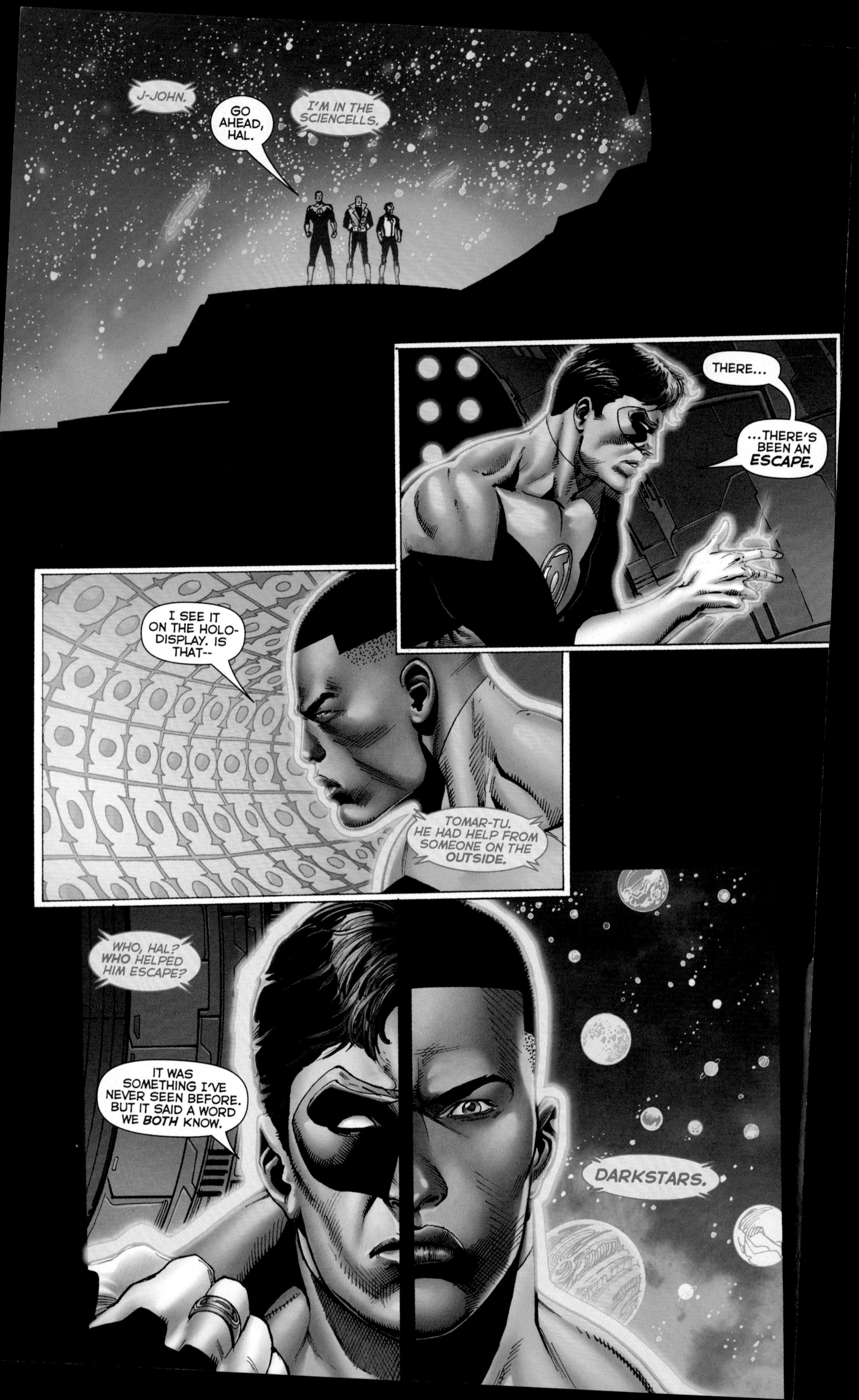
J-JOHN.
GO AHEAD, HAL.
I'M IN THE SCIENCELLS.
THERE...
...THERE'S BEEN AN ESCAPE.
I SEE IT ON THE HOLO-DISPLAY. IS THAT--
TOMAR-TU. HE HAD HELP FROM SOMEONE ON THE OUTSIDE.
WHO, HAL? WHO HELPED HIM ESCAPE?
IT WAS SOMETHING I'VE NEVER SEEN BEFORE. BUT IT SAID A WORD WE BOTH KNOW.
DARKSTARS.

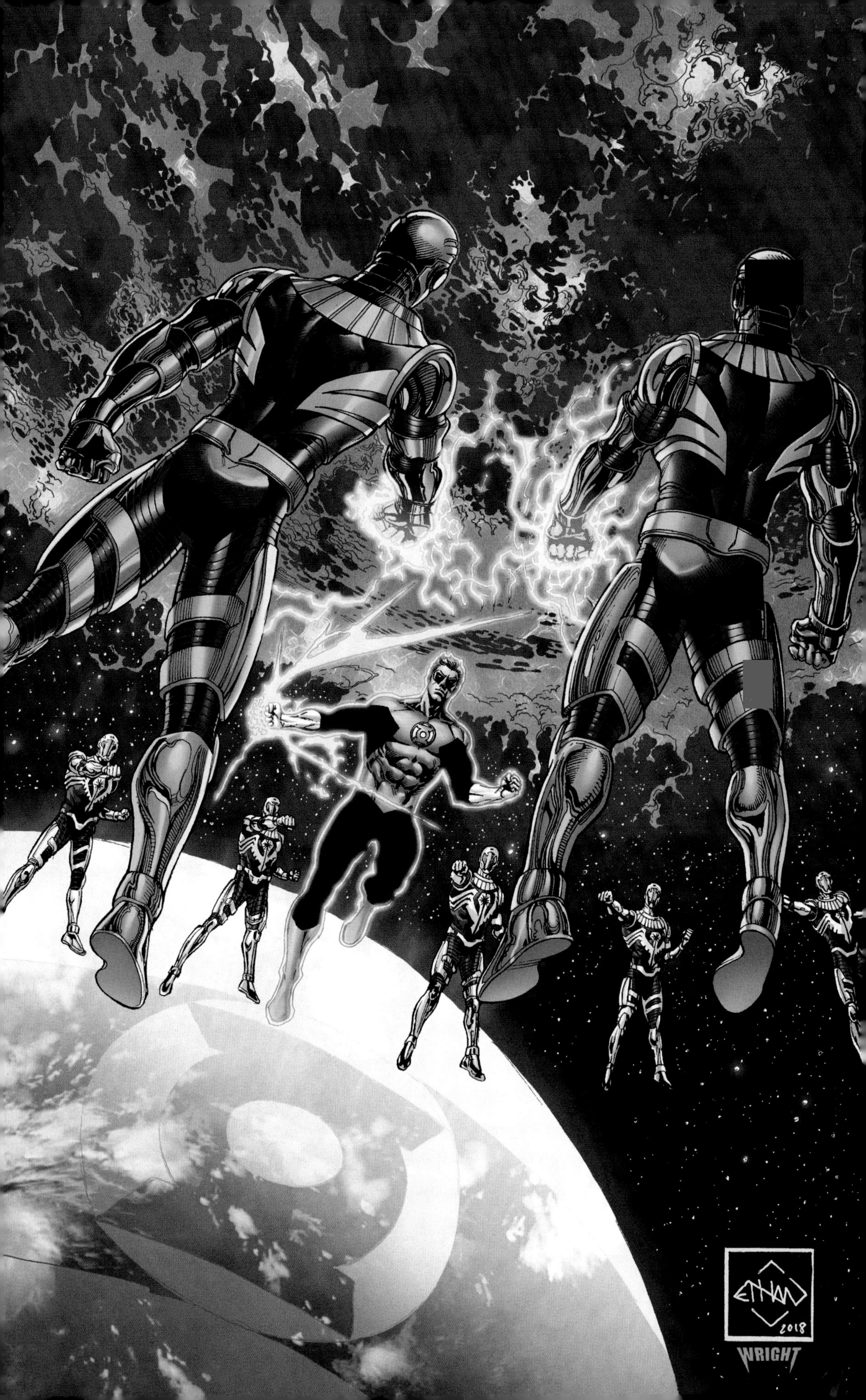
2018
WRIGHT

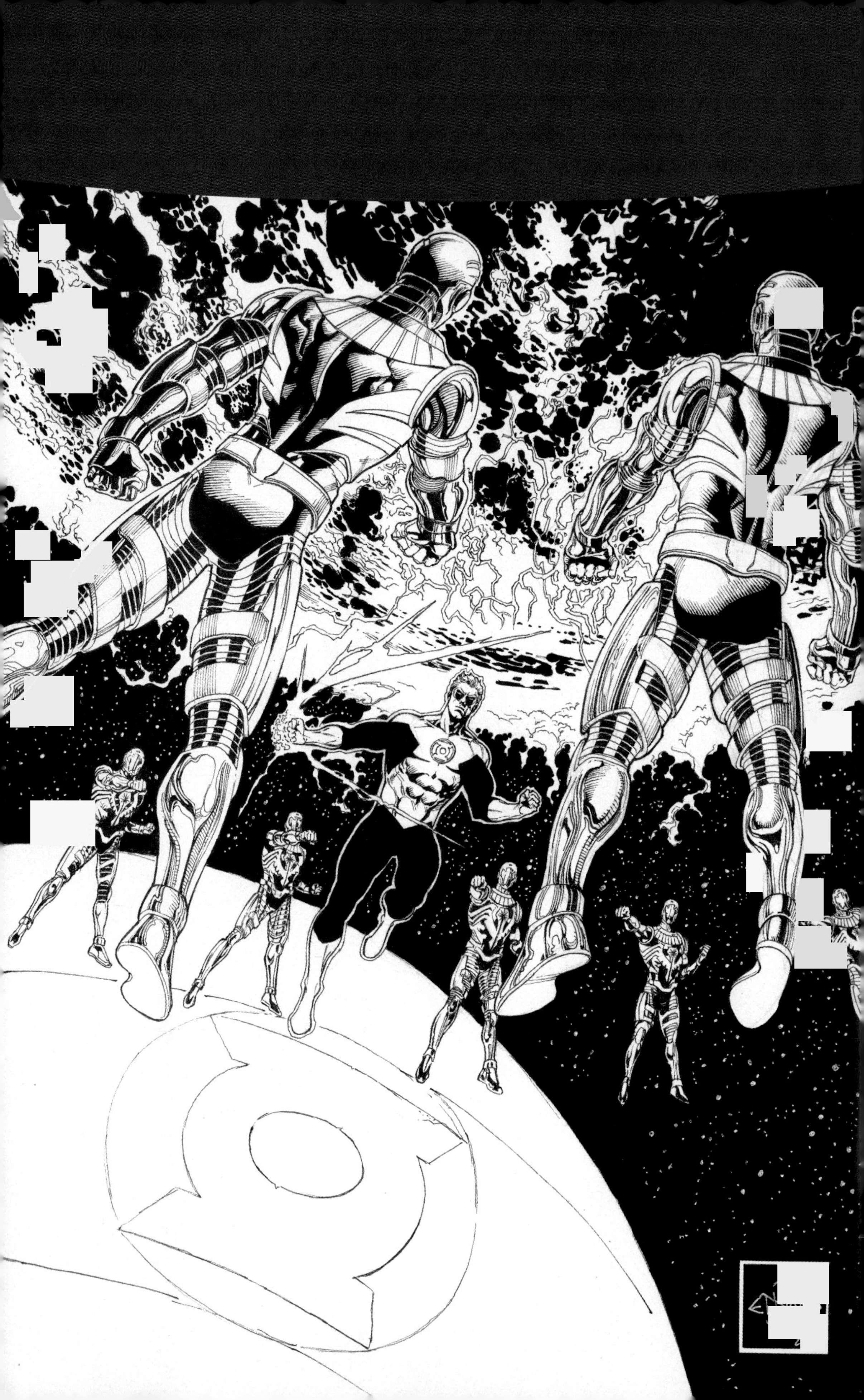

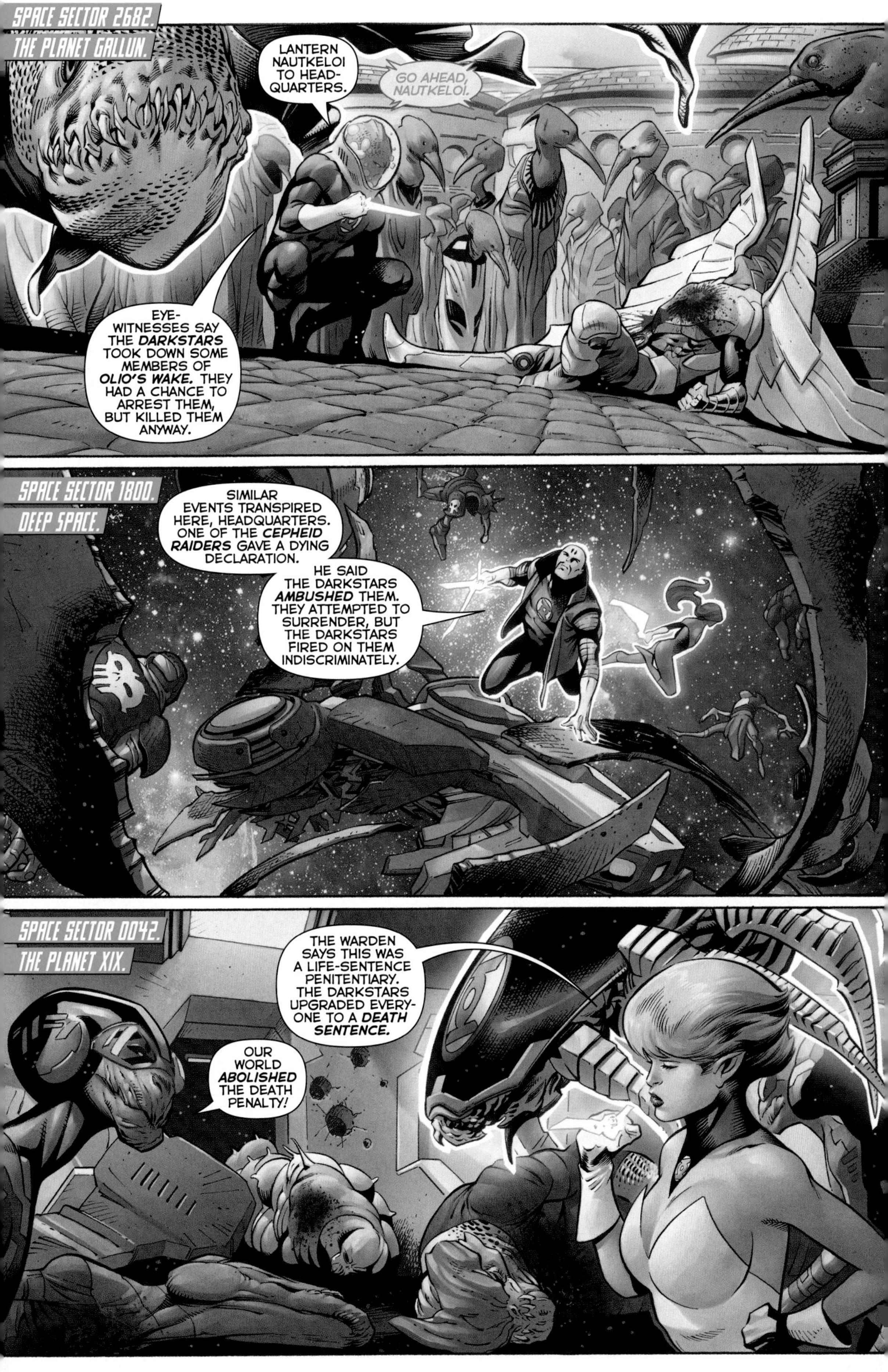
SPACE SECTOR 2682.
THE PLANET GALLUN.
LANTERN NAUTKELOI TO HEAD-QUARTERS.
GO AHEAD, NAUTKELOI.
EYE-WITNESSES SAY THE DARKSTARS TOOK DOWN SOME MEMBERS OF OLIO'S WAKE. THEY HAD A CHANCE TO ARREST THEM, BUT KILLED THEM ANYWAY.
SPACE SECTOR 1800.
DEEP SPACE.
SIMILAR EVENTS TRANSPIRED HERE, HEADQUARTERS. ONE OF THE CEPHEID RAIDERS GAVE A DYING DECLARATION.
HE SAID THE DARKSTARS AMBUSHED THEM. THEY ATTEMPTED TO SURRENDER, BUT THE DARKSTARS FIRED ON THEM INDISCRIMINATELY.
SPACE SECTOR 0042.
THE PLANET XIX.
THE WARDEN SAYS THIS WAS A LIFE-SENTENCE PENITENTIARY. THE DARKSTARS UPGRADED EVERY-ONE TO A DEATH SENTENCE.
OUR WORLD ABOLISHED THE DEATH PENALTY!

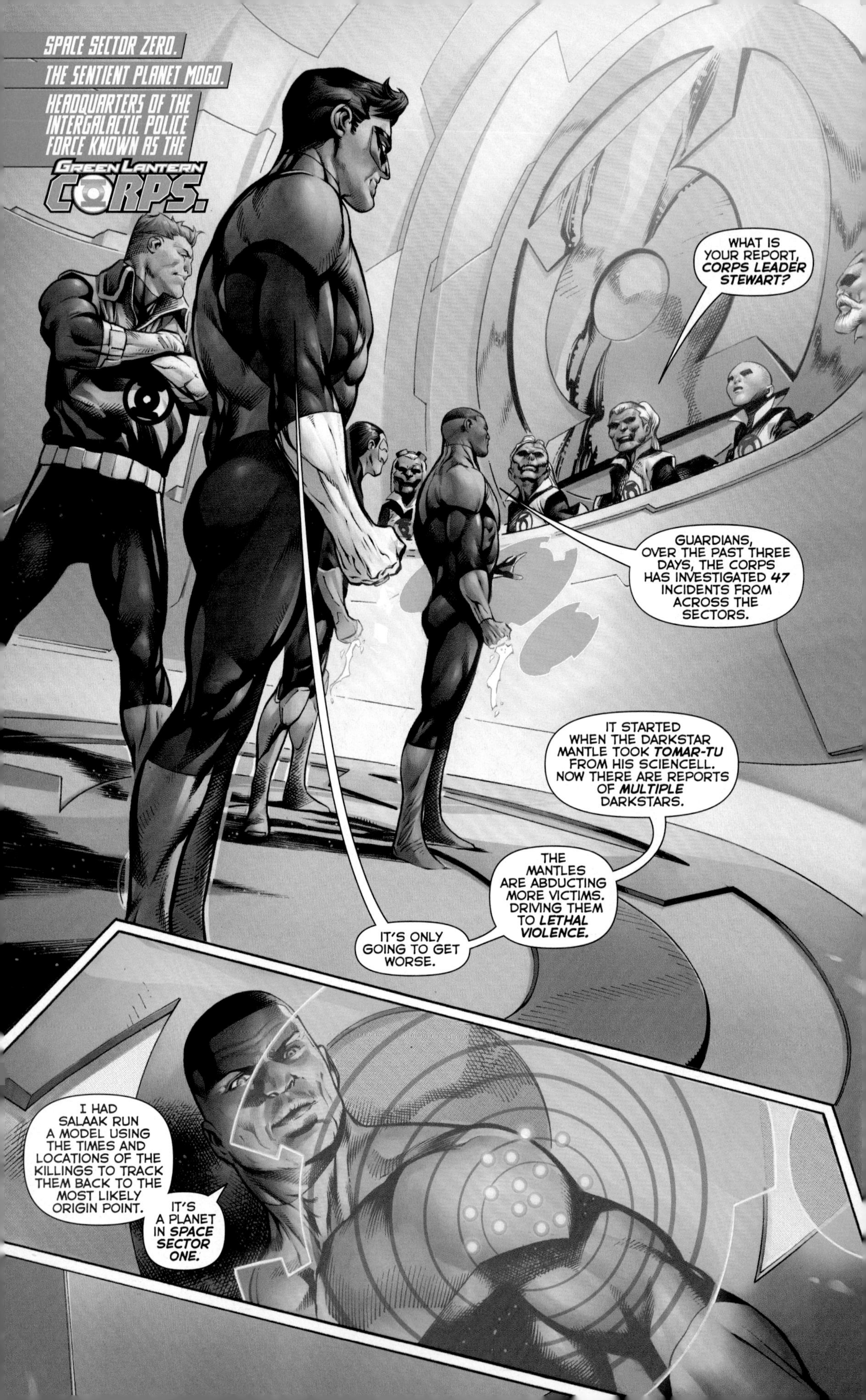
SPACE SECTOR ZERO.
THE SENTIENT PLANET MOGO.
HEADQUARTERS OF THE INTERGALACTIC POLICE FORCE KNOWN AS THE
GREEN LANTERN CORPS.
WHAT IS YOUR REPORT, CORPS LEADER STEWART?
GUARDIANS, OVER THE PAST THREE DAYS, THE CORPS HAS INVESTIGATED 47 INCIDENTS FROM ACROSS THE SECTORS.
IT STARTED WHEN THE DARKSTAR MANTLE TOOK TOMAR-TU FROM HIS SCIENCELL. NOW THERE ARE REPORTS OF MULTIPLE DARKSTARS.
THE MANTLES ARE ABDUCTING MORE VICTIMS. DRIVING THEM TO LETHAL VIOLENCE.
IT'S ONLY GOING TO GET WORSE.
I HAD SALAAK RUN A MODEL USING THE TIMES AND LOCATIONS OF THE KILLINGS TO TRACK THEM BACK TO THE MOST LIKELY ORIGIN POINT.
IT'S A PLANET IN SPACE SECTOR ONE.

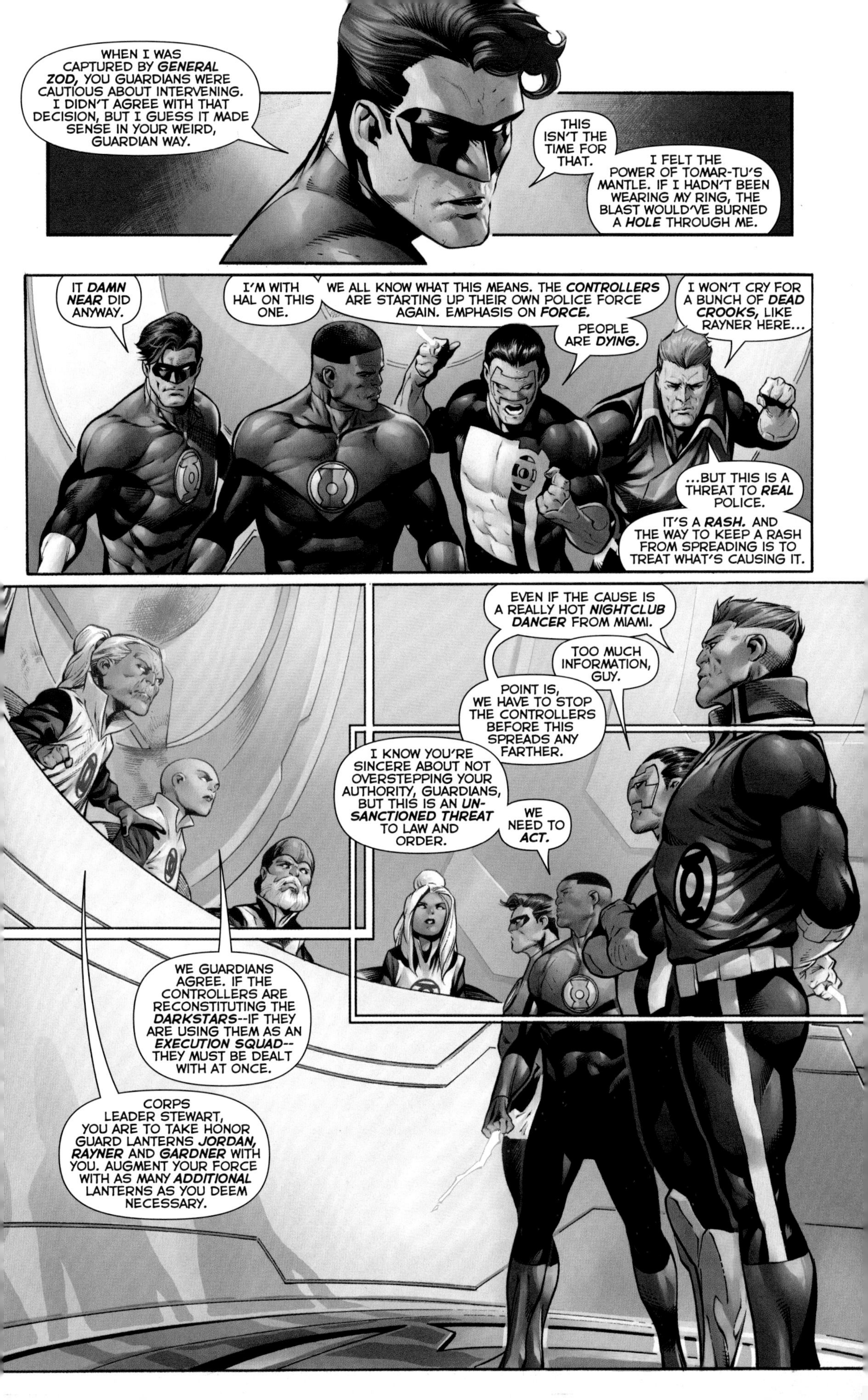
WHEN I WAS CAPTURED BY GENERAL ZOD, YOU GUARDIANS WERE CAUTIOUS ABOUT INTERVENING. I DIDN'T AGREE WITH THAT DECISION, BUT I GUESS IT MADE SENSE IN YOUR WEIRD, GUARDIAN WAY.
THIS ISN'T THE TIME FOR THAT.
I FELT THE POWER OF TOMAR-TU'S MANTLE. IF I HADN'T BEEN WEARING MY RING, THE BLAST WOULD'VE BURNED A HOLE THROUGH ME.
IT DAMN NEAR DID ANYWAY.
I'M WITH HAL ON THIS ONE.
WE ALL KNOW WHAT THIS MEANS. THE CONTROLLERS ARE STARTING UP THEIR OWN POLICE FORCE AGAIN. EMPHASIS ON FORCE.
PEOPLE ARE DYING.
I WON'T CRY FOR A BUNCH OF DEAD CROOKS, LIKE RAYNER HERE...
...BUT THIS IS A THREAT TO REAL POLICE.
IT'S A RASH. AND THE WAY TO KEEP A RASH FROM SPREADING IS TO TREAT WHAT'S CAUSING IT.
EVEN IF THE CAUSE IS A REALLY HOT NIGHTCLUB DANCER FROM MIAMI.
TOO MUCH INFORMATION, GUY.
POINT IS, WE HAVE TO STOP THE CONTROLLERS BEFORE THIS SPREADS ANY FARTHER.
I KNOW YOU'RE SINCERE ABOUT NOT OVERSTEPPING YOUR AUTHORITY, GUARDIANS, BUT THIS IS AN UN-SANCTIONED THREAT TO LAW AND ORDER.
WE NEED TO ACT.
WE GUARDIANS AGREE. IF THE CONTROLLERS ARE RECONSTITUTING THE DARKSTARS--IF THEY ARE USING THEM AS AN EXECUTION SQUAD--THEY MUST BE DEALT WITH AT ONCE.
CORPS LEADER STEWART, YOU ARE TO TAKE HONOR GUARD LANTERNS JORDAN, RAYNER AND GARDNER WITH YOU. AUGMENT YOUR FORCE WITH AS MANY ADDITIONAL LANTERNS AS YOU DEEM NECESSARY.

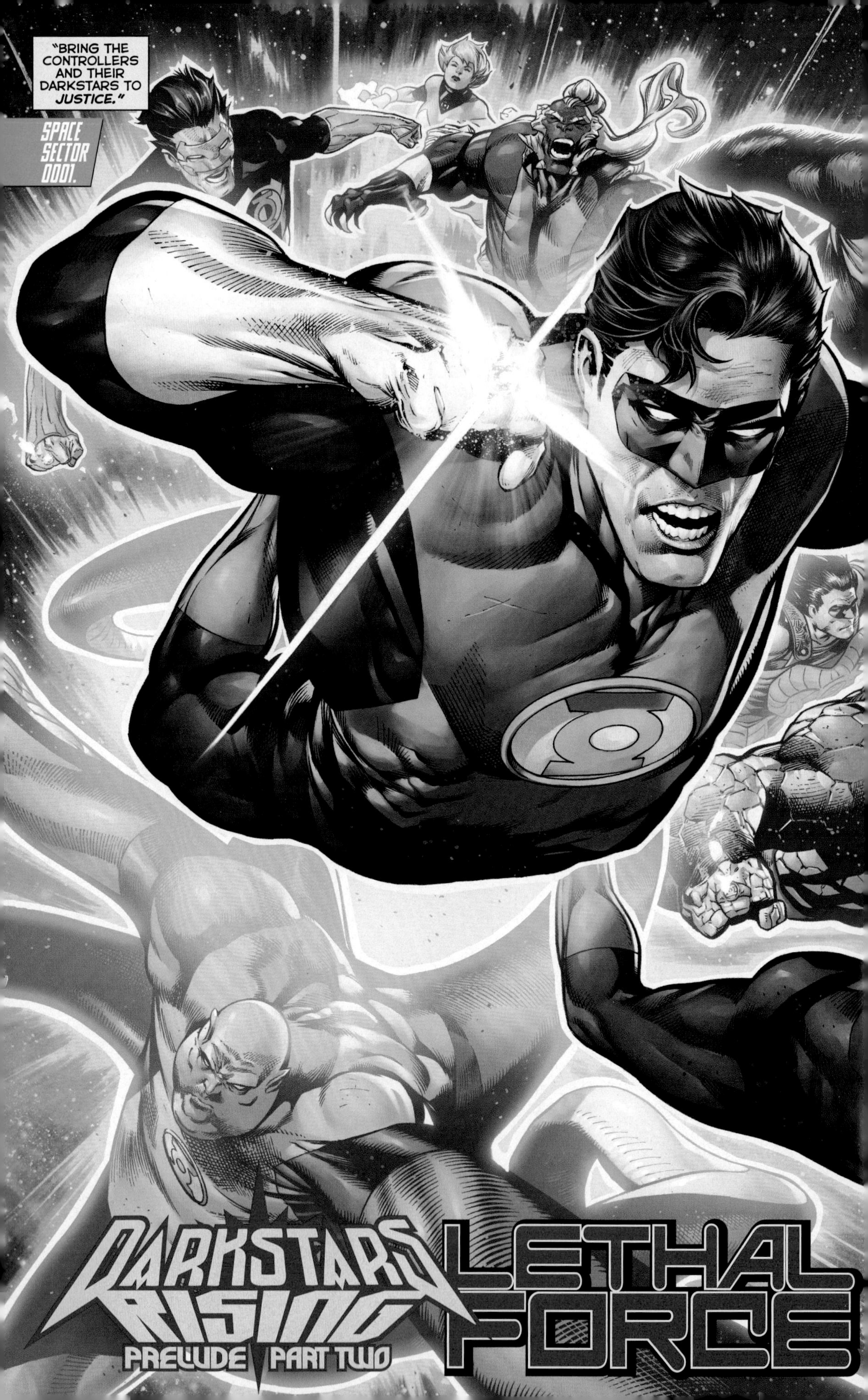
"BRING THE CONTROLLERS AND THEIR DARKSTARS TO JUSTICE."
SPACE SECTOR 0001.
DARKSTARS RISING
PRELUDE PART TWO
LETHAL FORCE

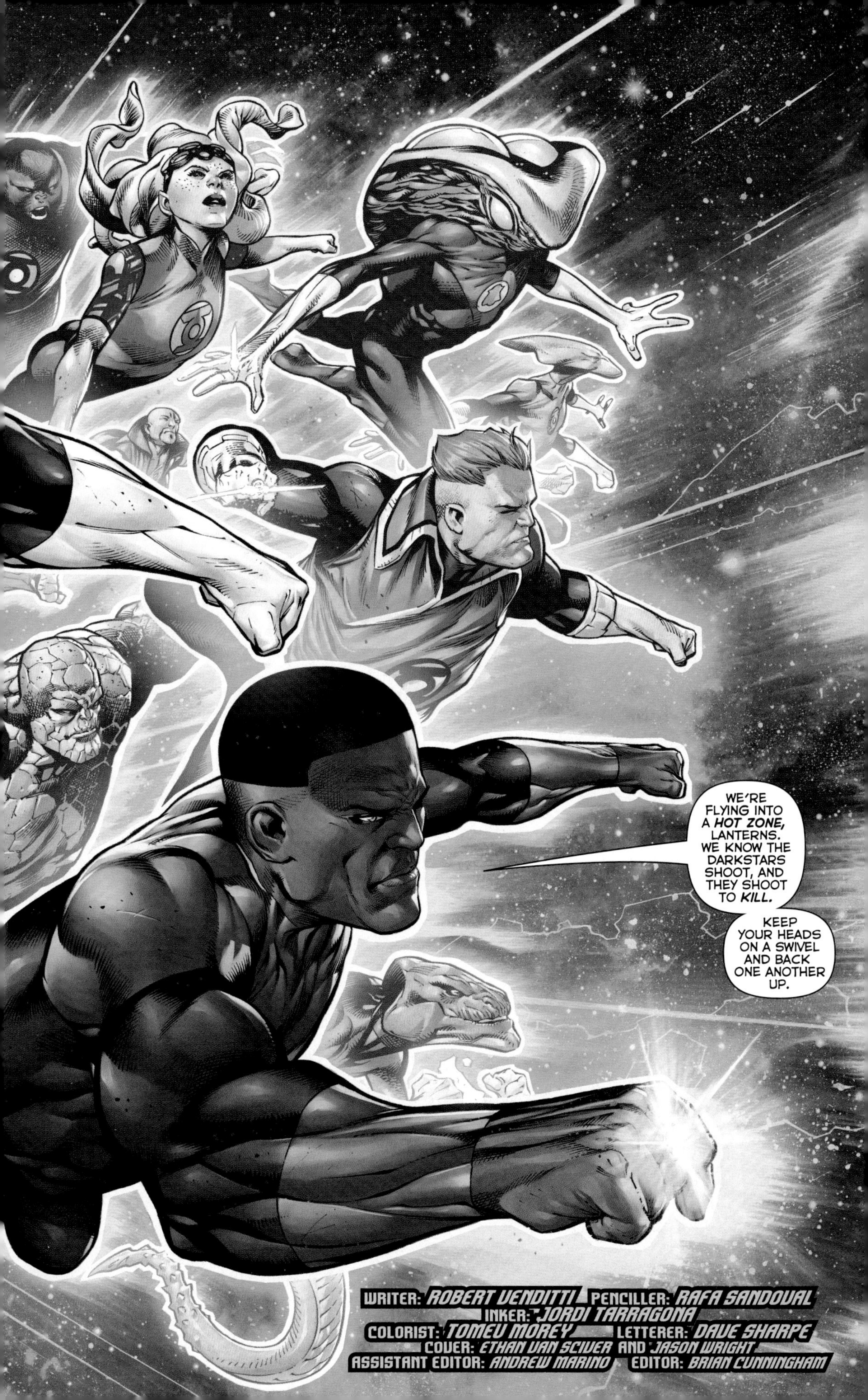
WE'RE FLYING INTO A *HOT ZONE,* LANTERNS. WE KNOW THE DARKSTARS SHOOT, AND THEY SHOOT TO *KILL.*
KEEP YOUR HEADS ON A SWIVEL AND BACK ONE ANOTHER UP.
WRITER: ROBERT VENDITTI PENCILLER: RAFA SANDOVAL
INKER: JORDI TARRAGONA
COLORIST: TOMEU MOREY LETTERER: DAVE SHARPE
COVER: ETHAN VAN SCIVER AND JASON WRIGHT
ASSISTANT EDITOR: ANDREW MARINO EDITOR: BRIAN CUNNINGHAM

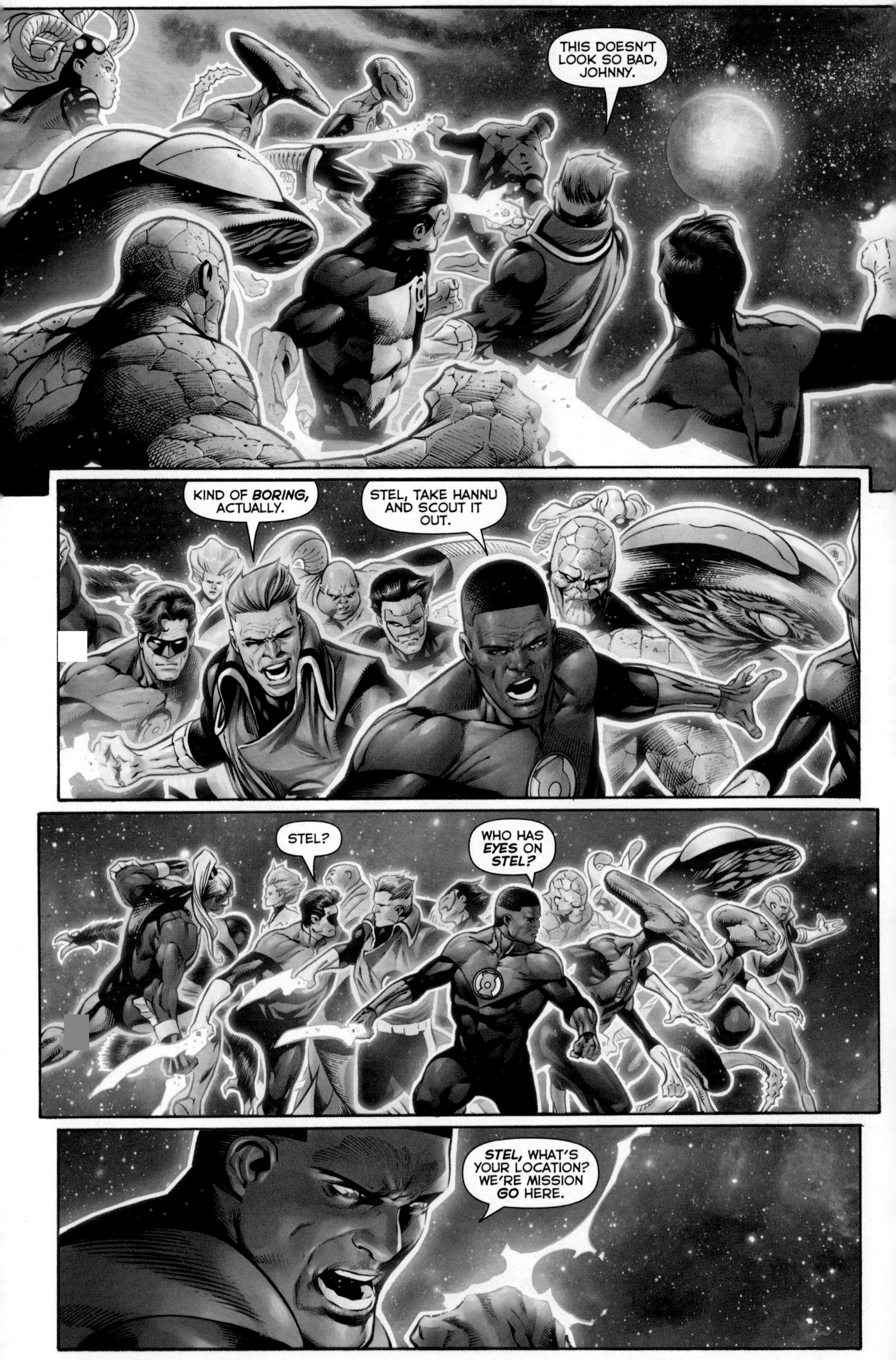

THIS DOESN'T LOOK SO BAD, JOHNNY.
KIND OF BORING, ACTUALLY.
STEL, TAKE HANNU AND SCOUT IT OUT.
STEL?
WHO HAS EYES ON STEL?
STEL, WHAT'S YOUR LOCATION? WE'RE MISSION GO HERE.

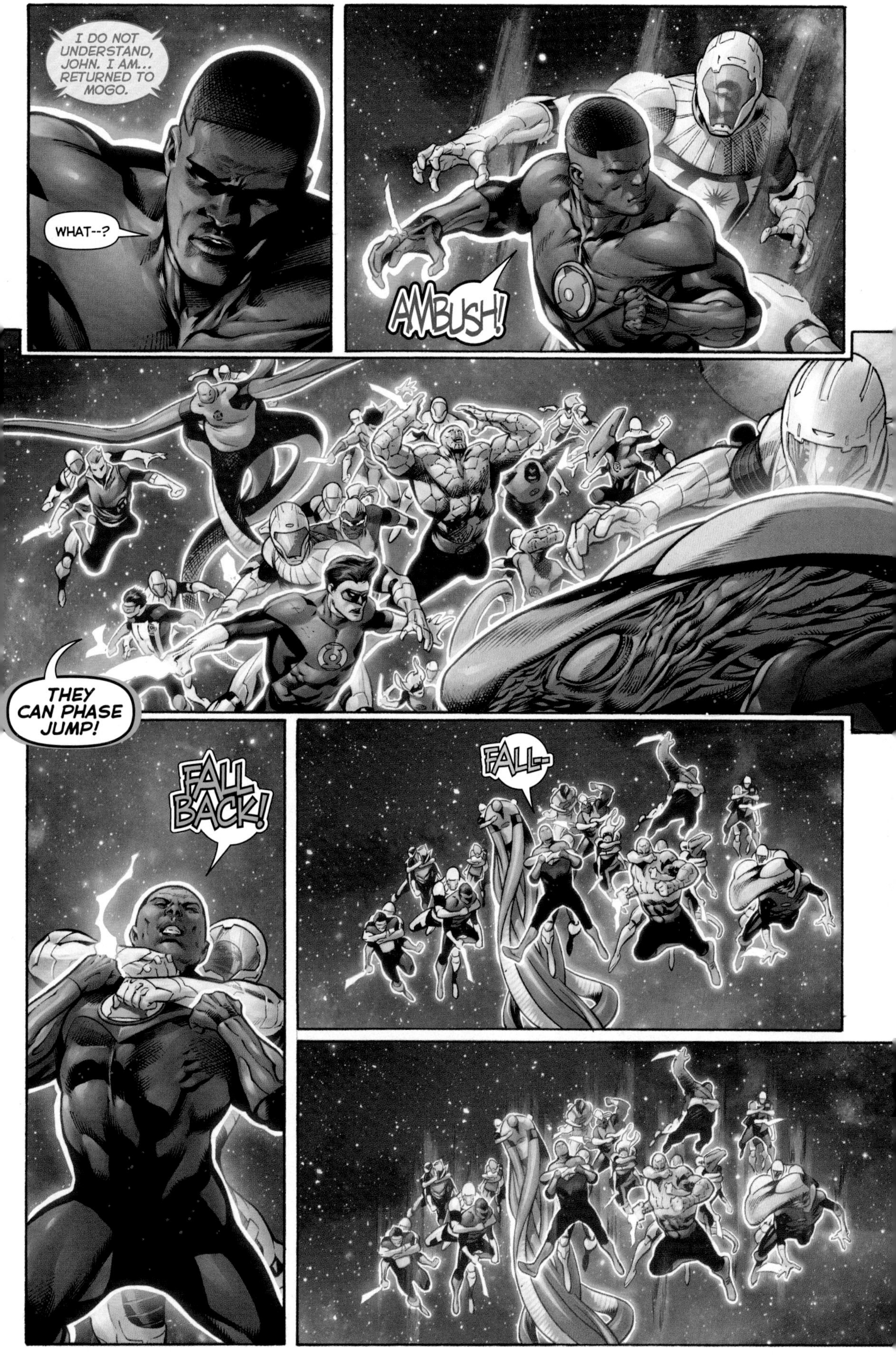
I DO NOT UNDERSTAND, JOHN. I AM... RETURNED TO MOGO.
WHAT--?
AMBUSH!
THEY CAN PHASE JUMP!
FALL BACK!
FALL-

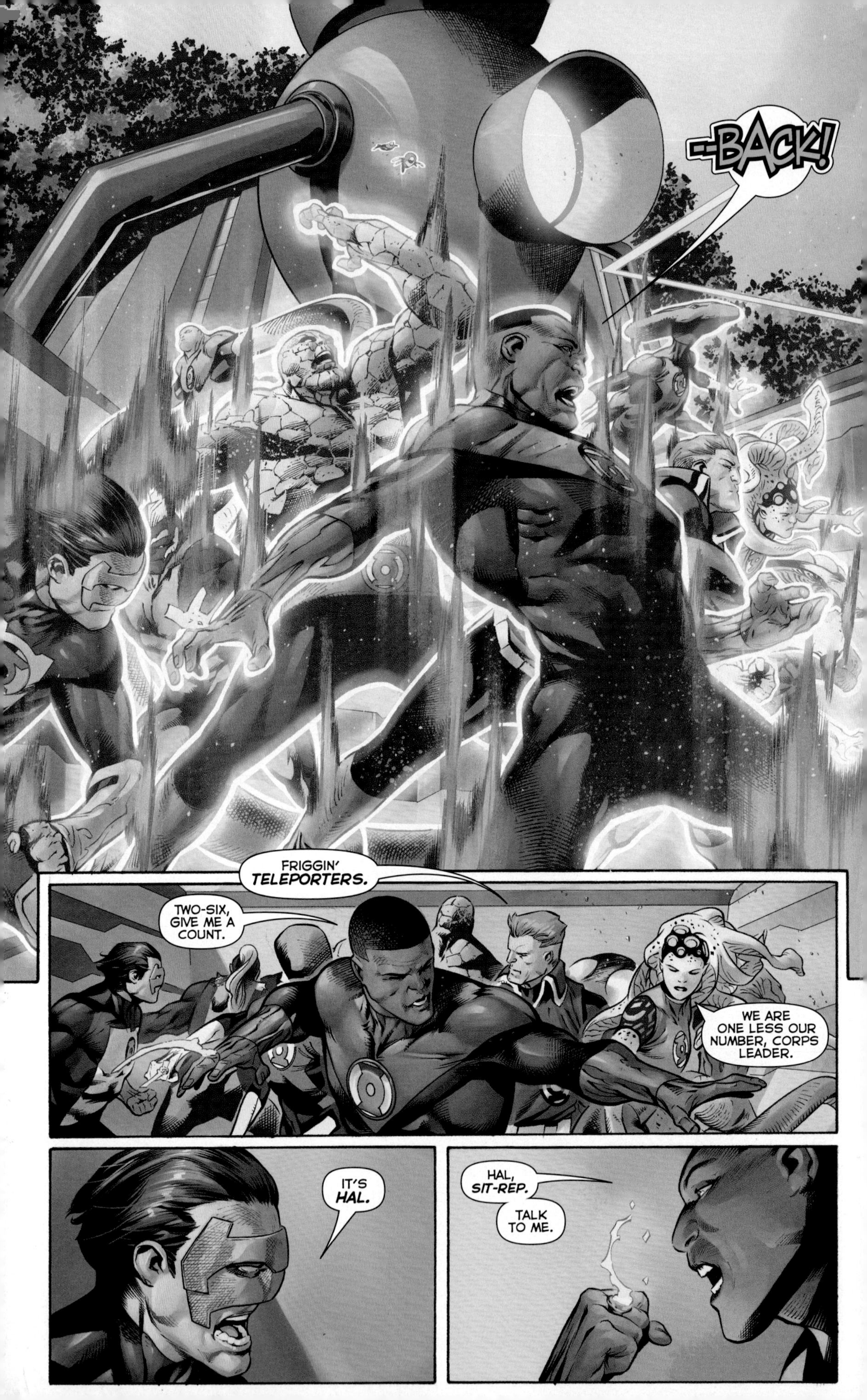
--BACK!
FRIGGIN' TELEPORTERS.
TWO-SIX, GIVE ME A COUNT.
WE ARE ONE LESS OUR NUMBER, CORPS LEADER.
IT'S HAL.
HAL, SIT-REP.
TALK TO ME.

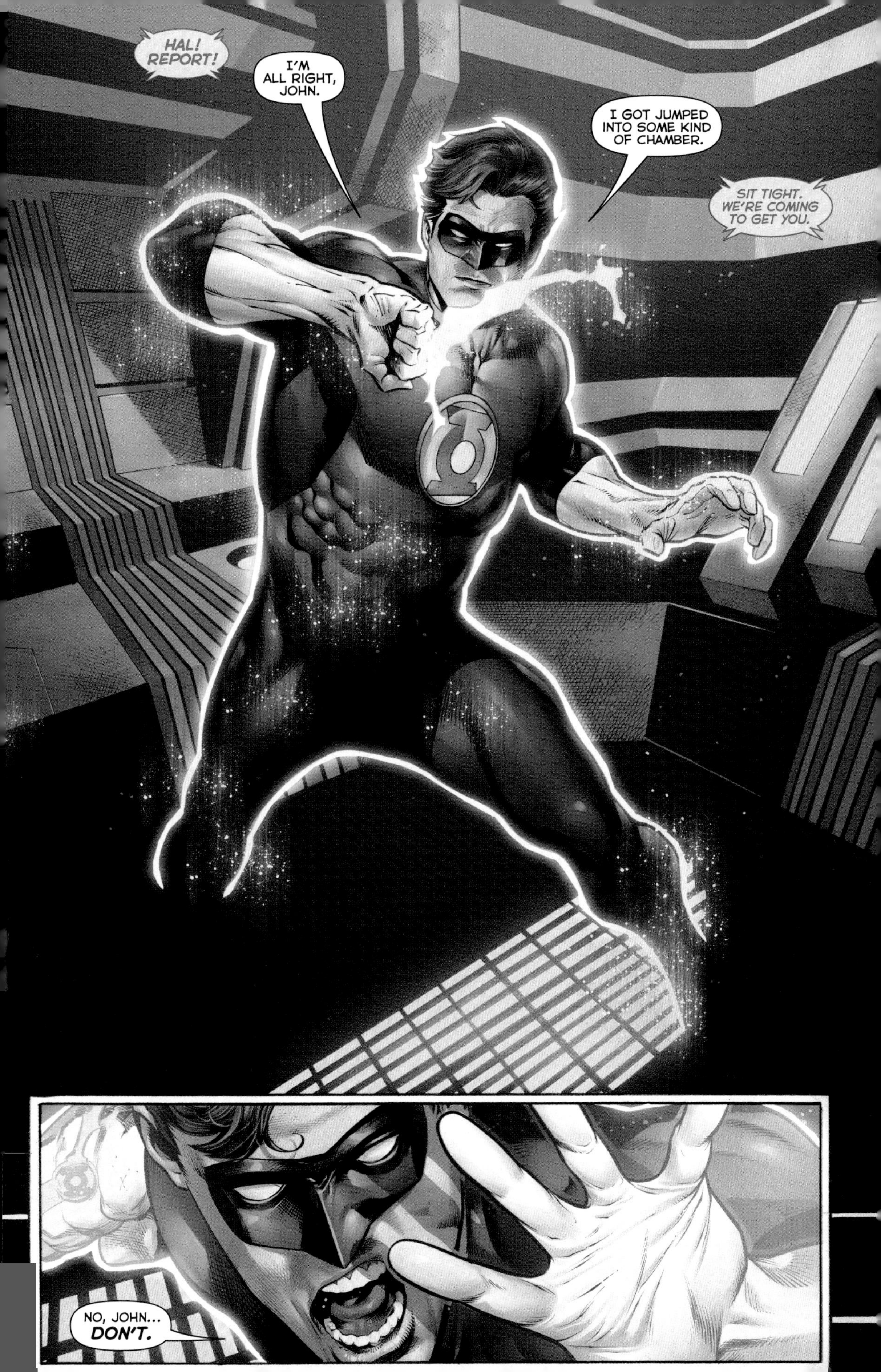
HAL! REPORT!
I'M ALL RIGHT, JOHN.
I GOT JUMPED INTO SOME KIND OF CHAMBER.
SIT TIGHT. WE'RE COMING TO GET YOU.
NO, JOHN... DON'T.

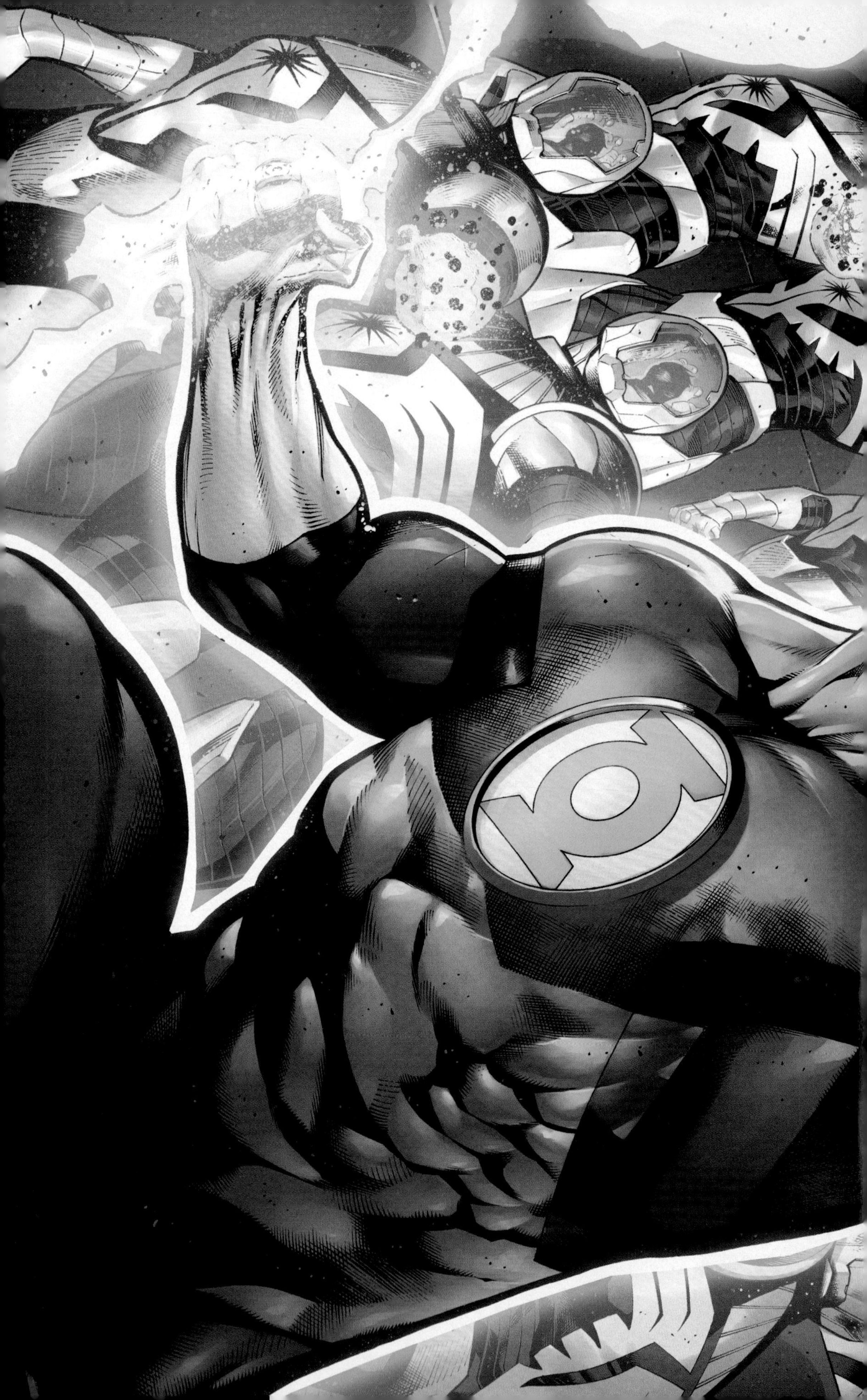

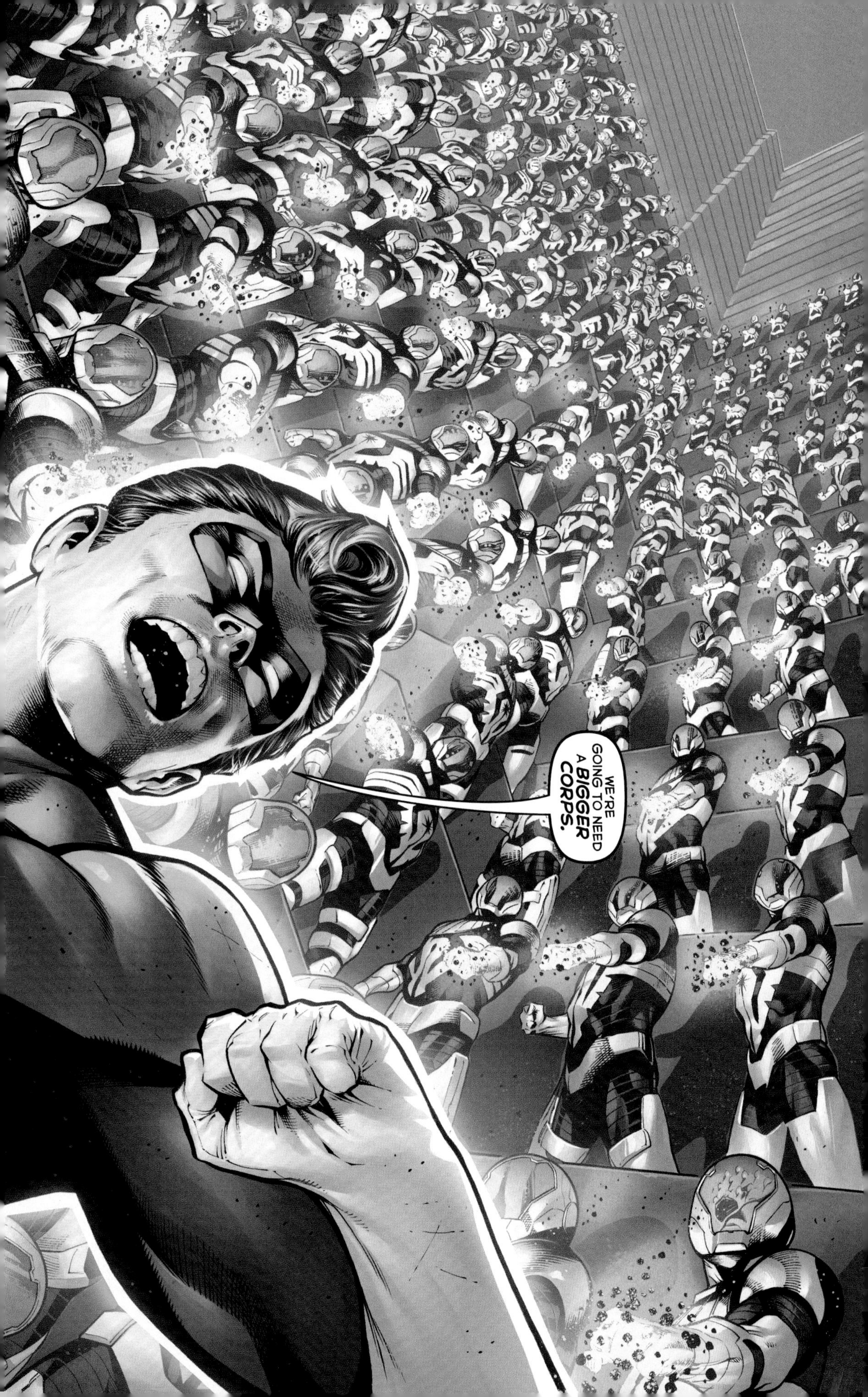
WE'RE GOING TO NEED A BIGGER CORPS.

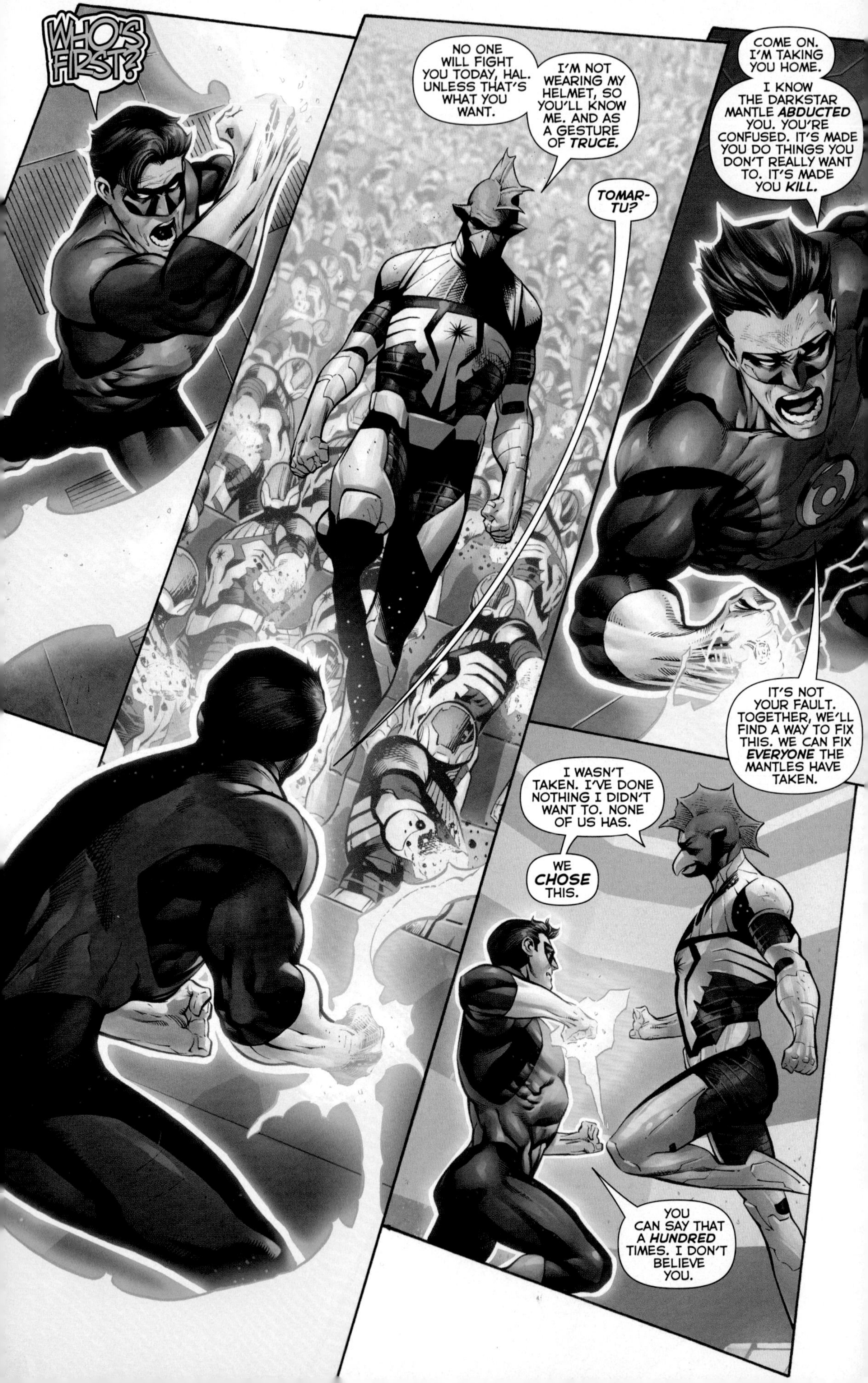
WHO'S FIRST?
NO ONE WILL FIGHT YOU TODAY, HAL. UNLESS THAT'S WHAT YOU WANT.
I'M NOT WEARING MY HELMET, SO YOU'LL KNOW ME. AND AS A GESTURE OF **TRUCE.**
TOMAR-TU?
COME ON. I'M TAKING YOU HOME.
I KNOW THE DARKSTAR MANTLE **ABDUCTED** YOU. YOU'RE CONFUSED. IT'S MADE YOU DO THINGS YOU DON'T REALLY WANT TO. IT'S MADE YOU **KILL.**
IT'S NOT YOUR FAULT. TOGETHER, WE'LL FIND A WAY TO FIX THIS. WE CAN FIX **EVERYONE** THE MANTLES HAVE TAKEN.
I WASN'T TAKEN. I'VE DONE NOTHING I DIDN'T WANT TO. NONE OF US HAS.
WE **CHOSE** THIS.
YOU CAN SAY THAT A **HUNDRED** TIMES. I DON'T BELIEVE YOU.

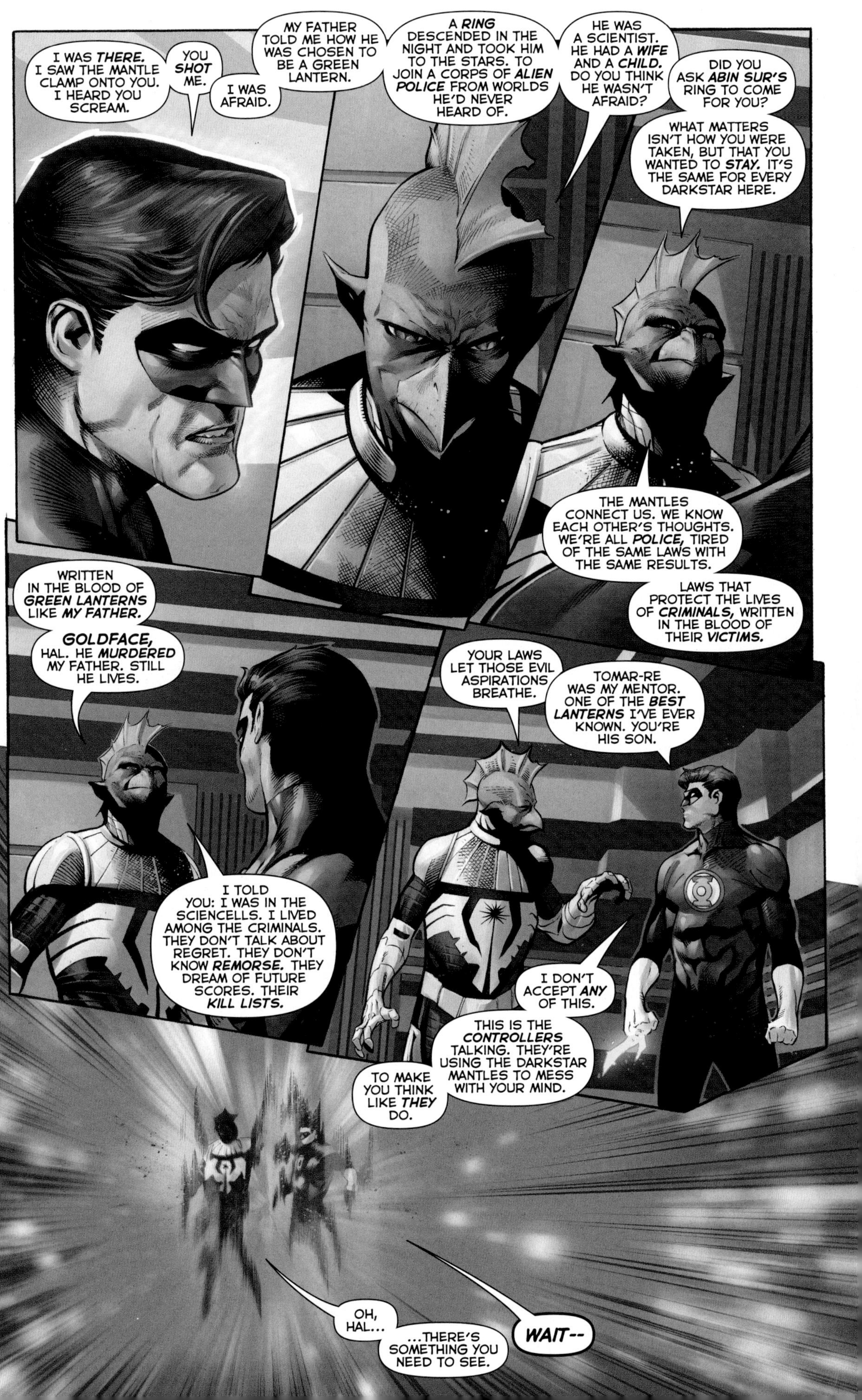
I WAS THERE. I SAW THE MANTLE CLAMP ONTO YOU. I HEARD YOU SCREAM.
YOU SHOT ME.
I WAS AFRAID.
MY FATHER TOLD ME HOW HE WAS CHOSEN TO BE A GREEN LANTERN.
A RING DESCENDED IN THE NIGHT AND TOOK HIM TO THE STARS. TO JOIN A CORPS OF ALIEN POLICE FROM WORLDS HE'D NEVER HEARD OF.
HE WAS A SCIENTIST. HE HAD A WIFE AND A CHILD. DO YOU THINK HE WASN'T AFRAID?
DID YOU ASK ABIN SUR'S RING TO COME FOR YOU?
WHAT MATTERS ISN'T HOW YOU WERE TAKEN, BUT THAT YOU WANTED TO STAY. IT'S THE SAME FOR EVERY DARKSTAR HERE.
THE MANTLES CONNECT US. WE KNOW EACH OTHER'S THOUGHTS. WE'RE ALL POLICE, TIRED OF THE SAME LAWS WITH THE SAME RESULTS.
LAWS THAT PROTECT THE LIVES OF CRIMINALS, WRITTEN IN THE BLOOD OF THEIR VICTIMS.
WRITTEN IN THE BLOOD OF GREEN LANTERNS LIKE MY FATHER.
GOLDFACE, HAL. HE MURDERED MY FATHER. STILL HE LIVES.
I TOLD YOU: I WAS IN THE SCIENCELLS. I LIVED AMONG THE CRIMINALS. THEY DON'T TALK ABOUT REGRET. THEY DON'T KNOW REMORSE. THEY DREAM OF FUTURE SCORES. THEIR KILL LISTS.
YOUR LAWS LET THOSE EVIL ASPIRATIONS BREATHE.
TOMAR-RE WAS MY MENTOR. ONE OF THE BEST LANTERNS I'VE EVER KNOWN. YOU'RE HIS SON.
I DON'T ACCEPT ANY OF THIS.
THIS IS THE CONTROLLERS TALKING. THEY'RE USING THE DARKSTAR MANTLES TO MESS WITH YOUR MIND.
TO MAKE YOU THINK LIKE THEY DO.
OH, HAL...
...THERE'S SOMETHING YOU NEED TO SEE.
WAIT--

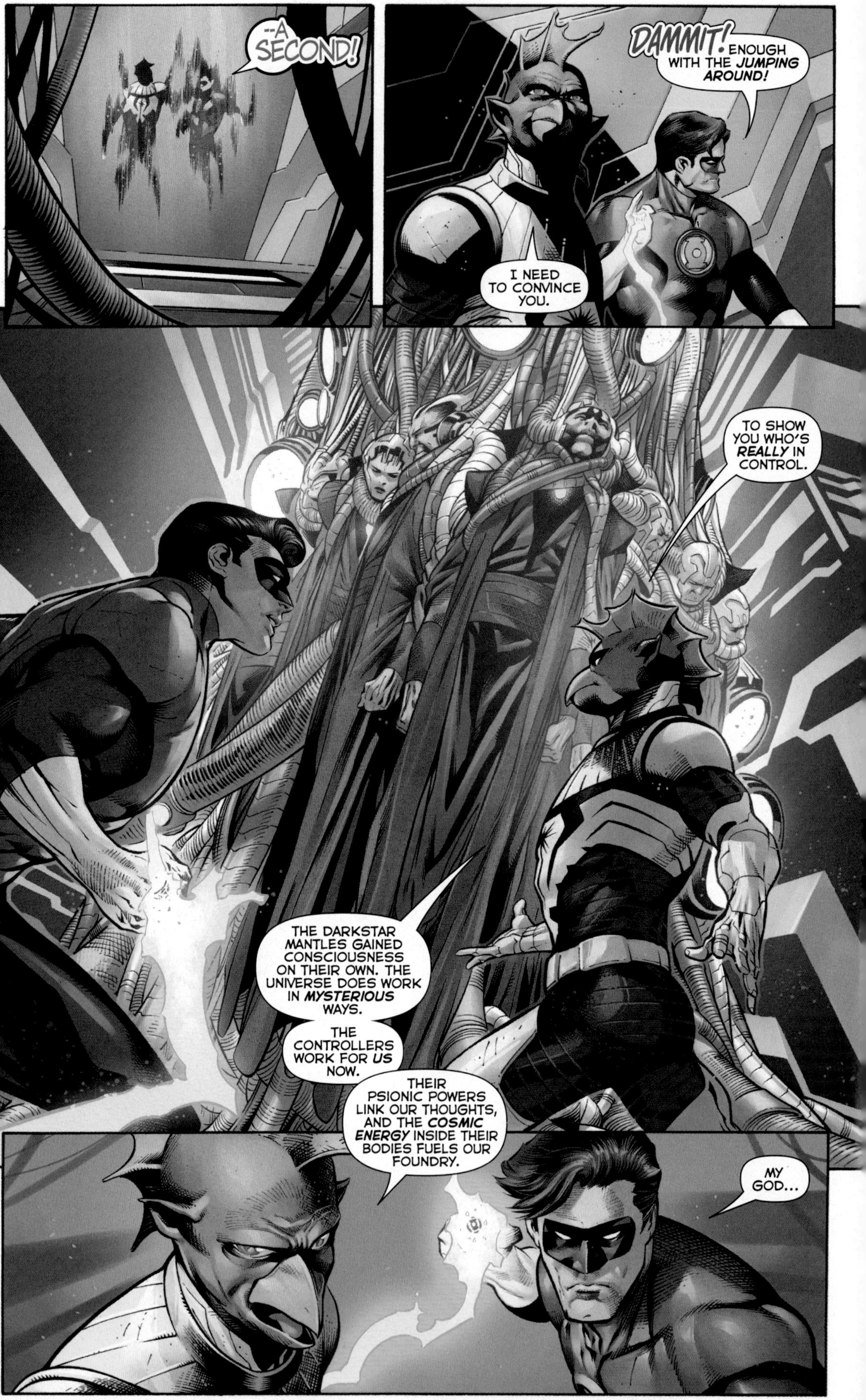
--A SECOND!
DAMMIT! ENOUGH WITH THE JUMPING AROUND!
I NEED TO CONVINCE YOU.
TO SHOW YOU WHO'S REALLY IN CONTROL.
THE DARKSTAR MANTLES GAINED CONSCIOUSNESS ON THEIR OWN. THE UNIVERSE DOES WORK IN MYSTERIOUS WAYS.
THE CONTROLLERS WORK FOR US NOW.
THEIR PSIONIC POWERS LINK OUR THOUGHTS, AND THE COSMIC ENERGY INSIDE THEIR BODIES FUELS OUR FOUNDRY.
MY GOD...

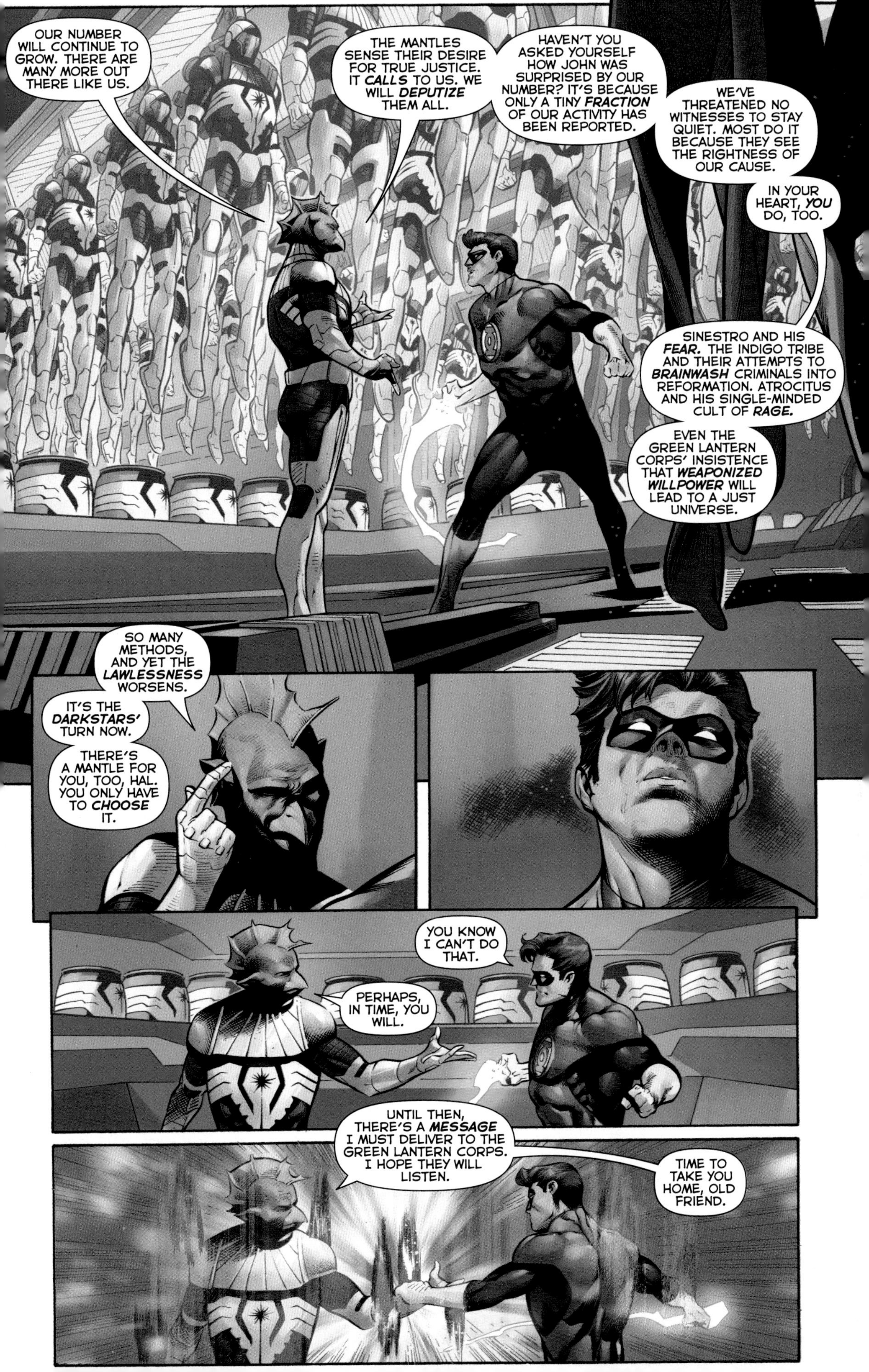
OUR NUMBER WILL CONTINUE TO GROW. THERE ARE MANY MORE OUT THERE LIKE US.
THE MANTLES SENSE THEIR DESIRE FOR TRUE JUSTICE. IT *CALLS* TO US. WE WILL *DEPUTIZE* THEM ALL.
HAVEN'T YOU ASKED YOURSELF HOW JOHN WAS SURPRISED BY OUR NUMBER? IT'S BECAUSE ONLY A TINY *FRACTION* OF OUR ACTIVITY HAS BEEN REPORTED.
WE'VE THREATENED NO WITNESSES TO STAY QUIET. MOST DO IT BECAUSE THEY SEE THE RIGHTNESS OF OUR CAUSE.
IN YOUR HEART, *YOU* DO, TOO.
SINESTRO AND HIS *FEAR.* THE INDIGO TRIBE AND THEIR ATTEMPTS TO *BRAINWASH* CRIMINALS INTO REFORMATION. ATROCITUS AND HIS SINGLE-MINDED CULT OF *RAGE.*
EVEN THE GREEN LANTERN CORPS' INSISTENCE THAT *WEAPONIZED WILLPOWER* WILL LEAD TO A JUST UNIVERSE.
SO MANY METHODS, AND YET THE *LAWLESSNESS* WORSENS.
IT'S THE *DARKSTARS'* TURN NOW.
THERE'S A MANTLE FOR YOU, TOO, HAL. YOU ONLY HAVE TO *CHOOSE* IT.
YOU KNOW I CAN'T DO THAT.
PERHAPS, IN TIME, YOU WILL.
UNTIL THEN, THERE'S A *MESSAGE* I MUST DELIVER TO THE GREEN LANTERN CORPS. I HOPE THEY WILL LISTEN.
TIME TO TAKE YOU HOME, OLD FRIEND.

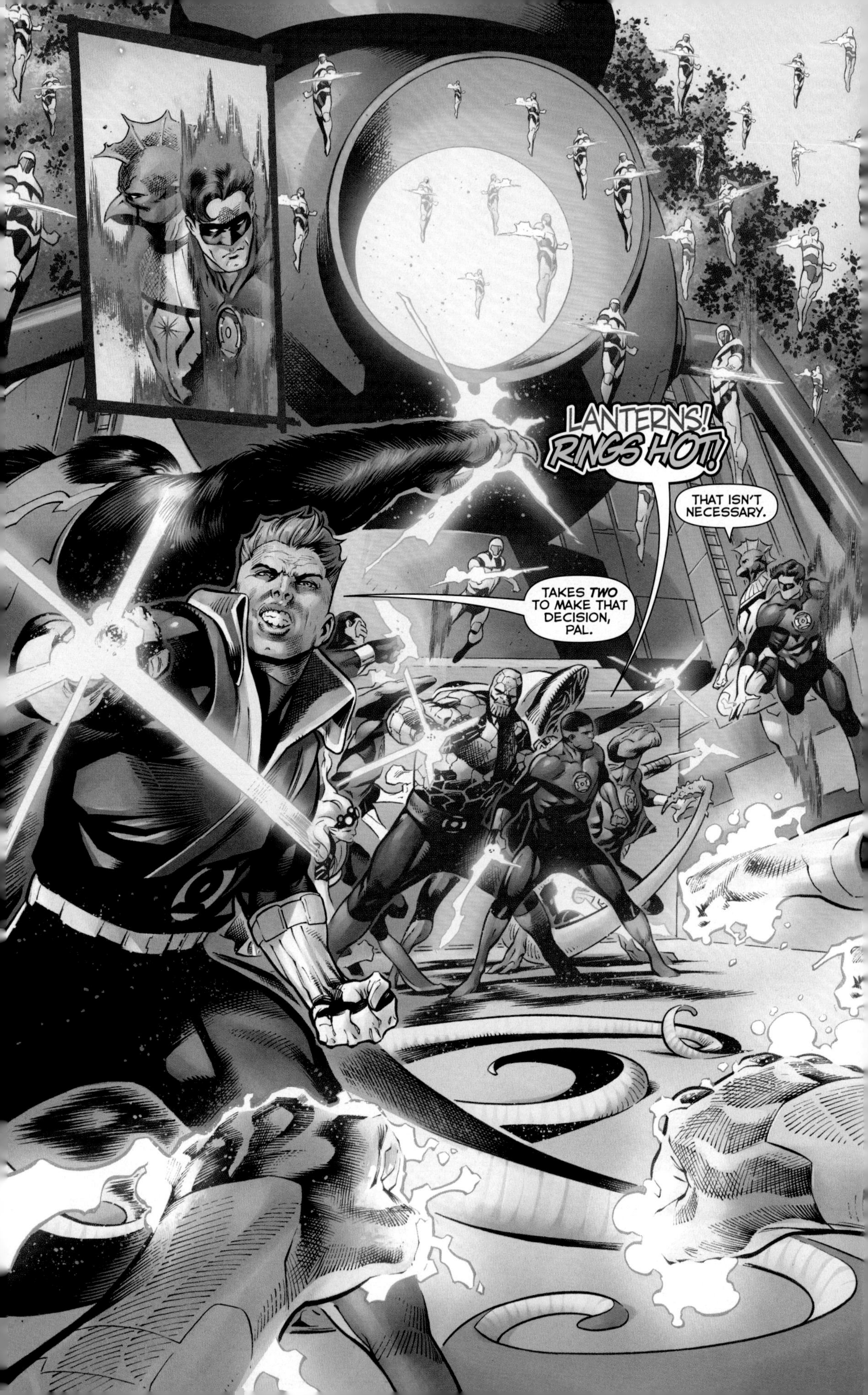
LANTERNS! RINGS HOT!
THAT ISN'T NECESSARY.
TAKES TWO TO MAKE THAT DECISION, PAL.

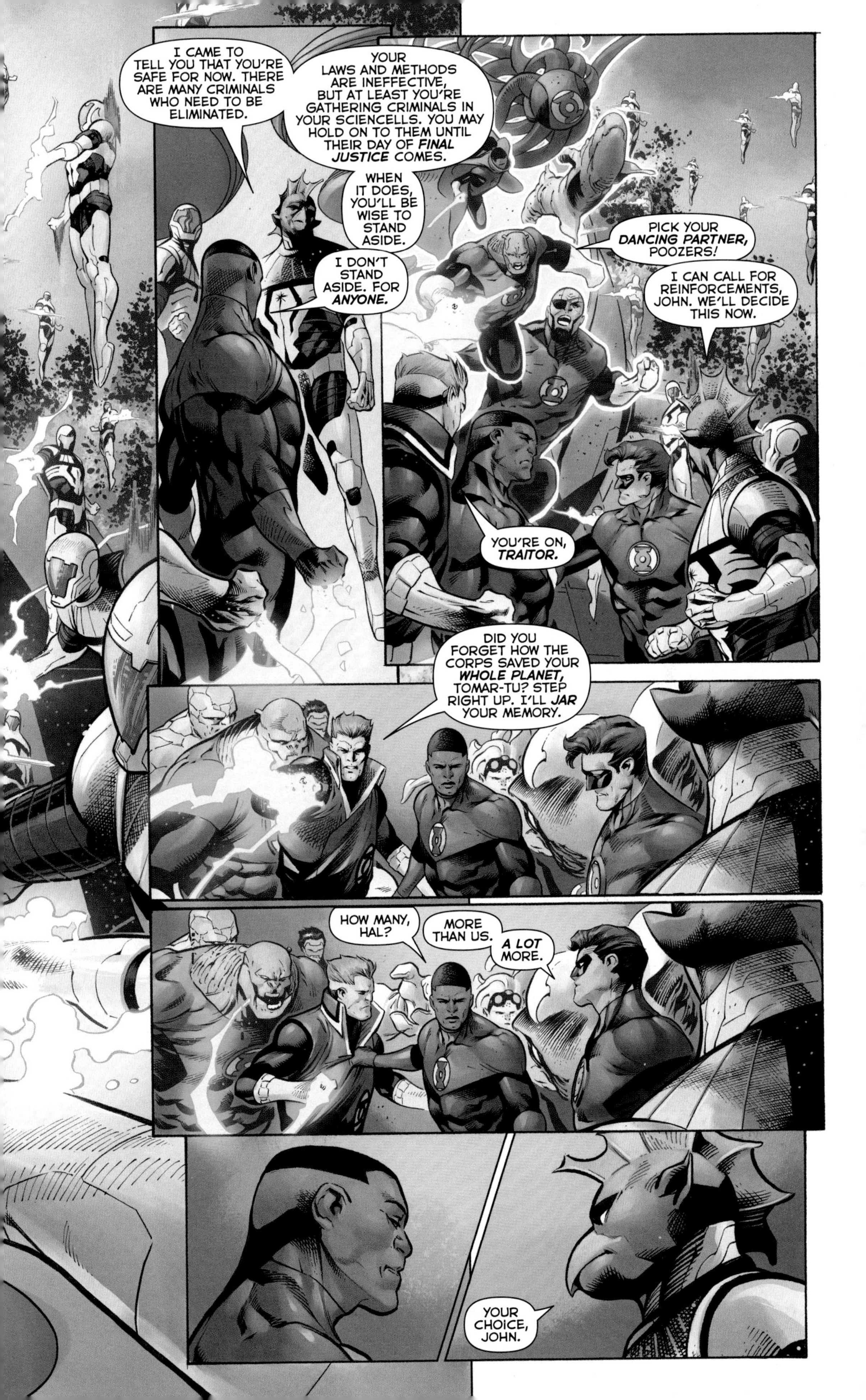

I CAME TO TELL YOU THAT YOU'RE SAFE FOR NOW. THERE ARE MANY CRIMINALS WHO NEED TO BE ELIMINATED.
YOUR LAWS AND METHODS ARE INEFFECTIVE, BUT AT LEAST YOU'RE GATHERING CRIMINALS IN YOUR SCIENCELLS. YOU MAY HOLD ON TO THEM UNTIL THEIR DAY OF FINAL JUSTICE COMES.
WHEN IT DOES, YOU'LL BE WISE TO STAND ASIDE.
I DON'T STAND ASIDE. FOR ANYONE.
PICK YOUR DANCING PARTNER, POOZERS!
I CAN CALL FOR REINFORCEMENTS, JOHN. WE'LL DECIDE THIS NOW.
YOU'RE ON, TRAITOR.
DID YOU FORGET HOW THE CORPS SAVED YOUR WHOLE PLANET, TOMAR-TU? STEP RIGHT UP. I'LL JAR YOUR MEMORY.
HOW MANY, HAL?
MORE THAN US.
A LOT MORE.
YOUR CHOICE, JOHN.

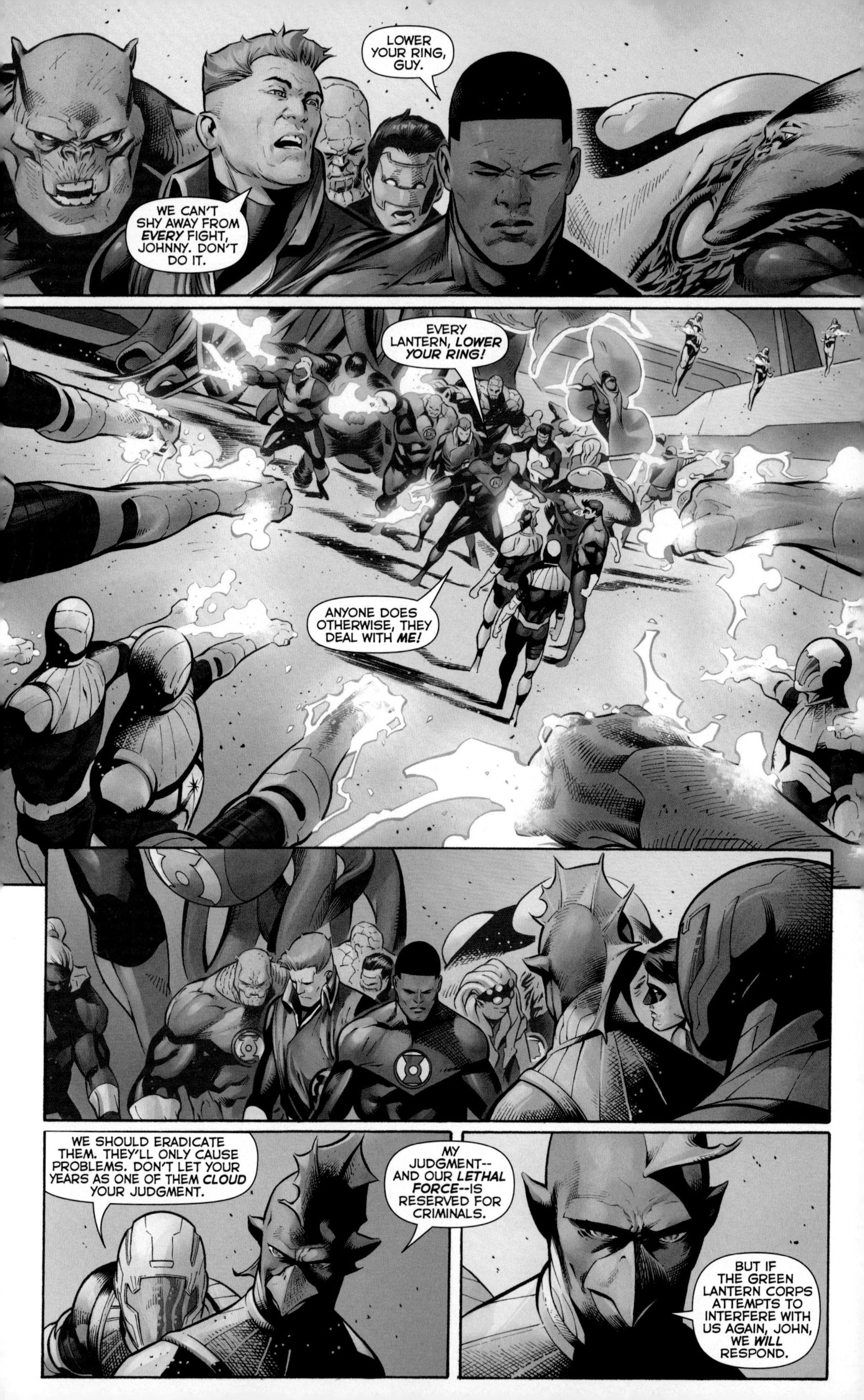
LOWER YOUR RING, GUY.
WE CAN'T SHY AWAY FROM *EVERY* FIGHT, JOHNNY. DON'T DO IT.
EVERY LANTERN, *LOWER YOUR RING!*
ANYONE DOES OTHERWISE, THEY DEAL WITH *ME!*
WE SHOULD ERADICATE THEM. THEY'LL ONLY CAUSE PROBLEMS. DON'T LET YOUR YEARS AS ONE OF THEM *CLOUD* YOUR JUDGMENT.
MY JUDGMENT-- AND OUR *LETHAL FORCE*--IS RESERVED FOR CRIMINALS.
BUT IF THE GREEN LANTERN CORPS ATTEMPTS TO INTERFERE WITH US AGAIN, JOHN, WE *WILL* RESPOND.

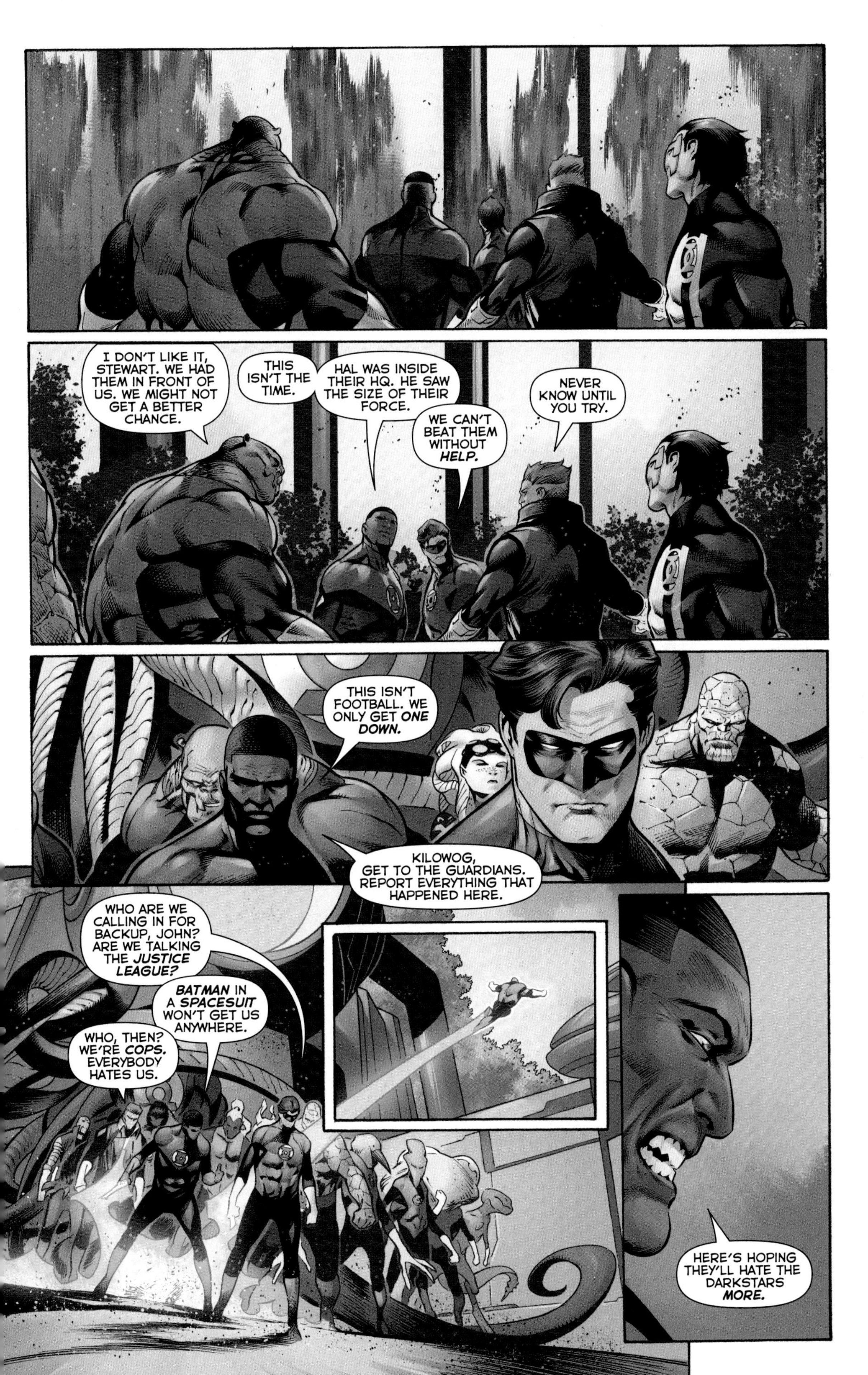
I DON'T LIKE IT, STEWART. WE HAD THEM IN FRONT OF US. WE MIGHT NOT GET A BETTER CHANCE.
THIS ISN'T THE TIME.
HAL WAS INSIDE THEIR HQ. HE SAW THE SIZE OF THEIR FORCE.
WE CAN'T BEAT THEM WITHOUT HELP.
NEVER KNOW UNTIL YOU TRY.
THIS ISN'T FOOTBALL. WE ONLY GET ONE DOWN.
KILOWOG, GET TO THE GUARDIANS. REPORT EVERYTHING THAT HAPPENED HERE.
WHO ARE WE CALLING IN FOR BACKUP, JOHN? ARE WE TALKING THE JUSTICE LEAGUE?
BATMAN IN A SPACESUIT WON'T GET US ANYWHERE.
WHO, THEN? WE'RE COPS. EVERYBODY HATES US.
HERE'S HOPING THEY'LL HATE THE DARKSTARS MORE.

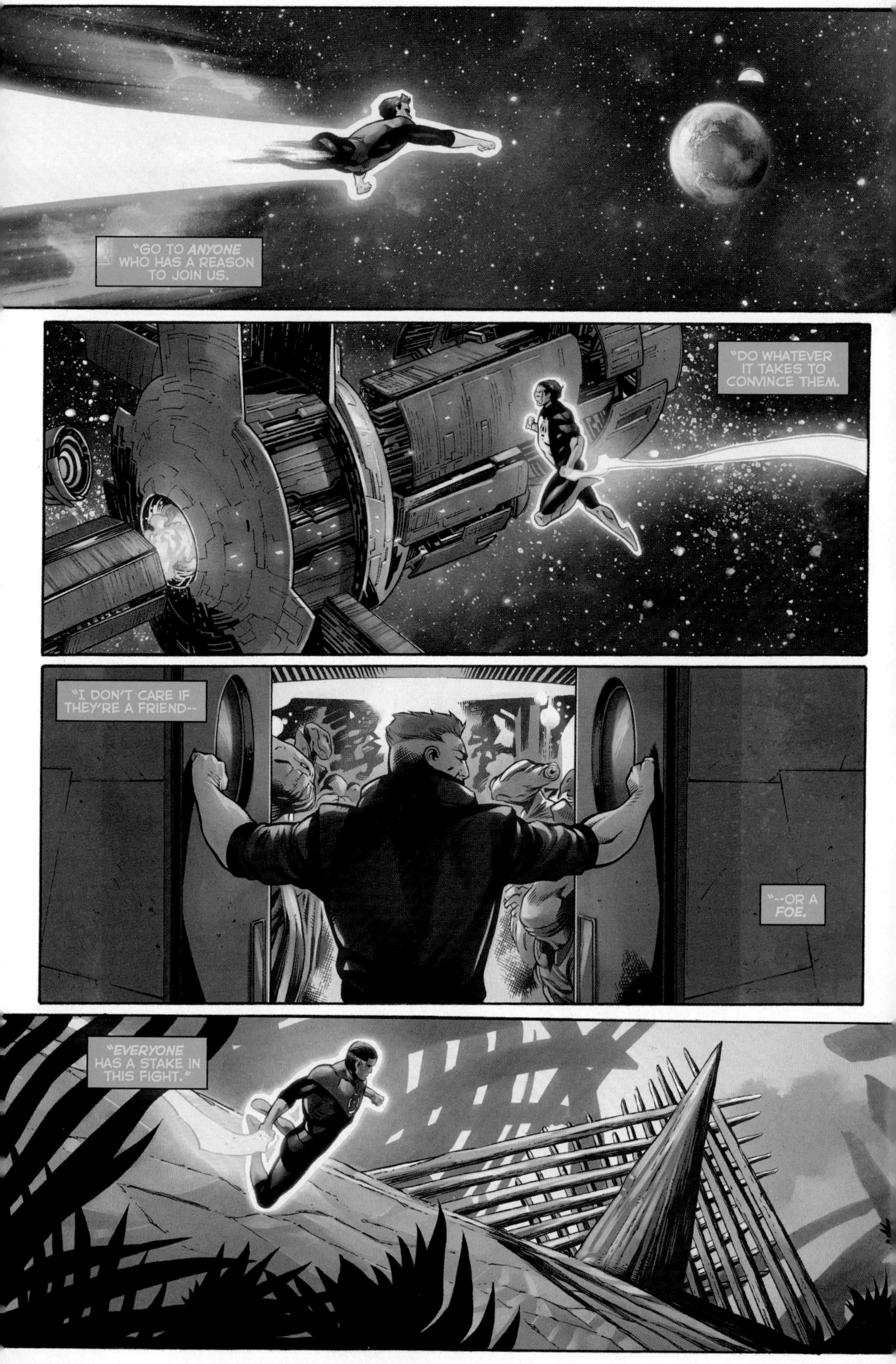
"GO TO *ANYONE* WHO HAS A REASON TO JOIN US.
"DO WHATEVER IT TAKES TO CONVINCE THEM.
"I DON'T CARE IF THEY'RE A FRIEND--
"--OR A *FOE.*
"*EVERYONE* HAS A STAKE IN THIS FIGHT."

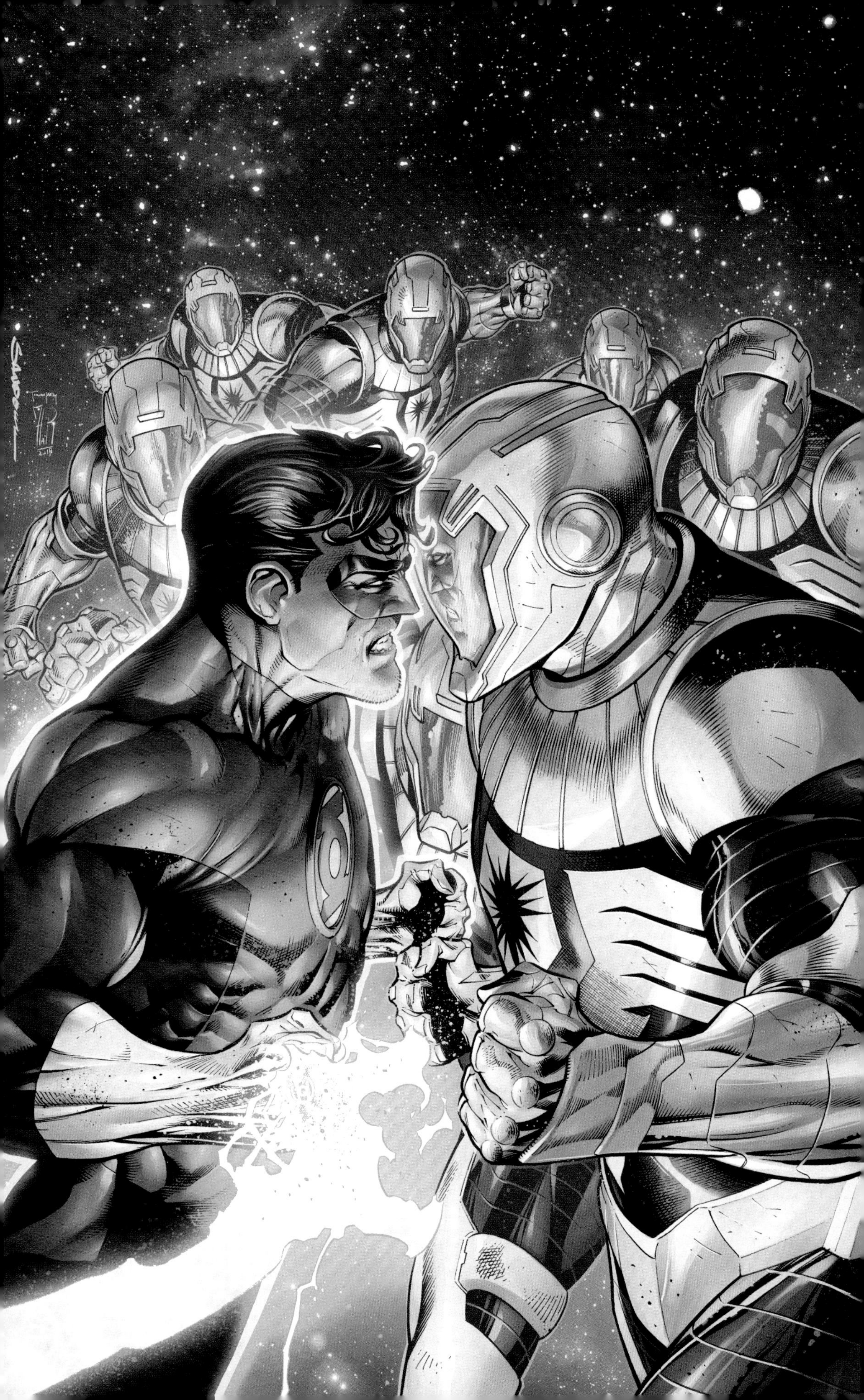

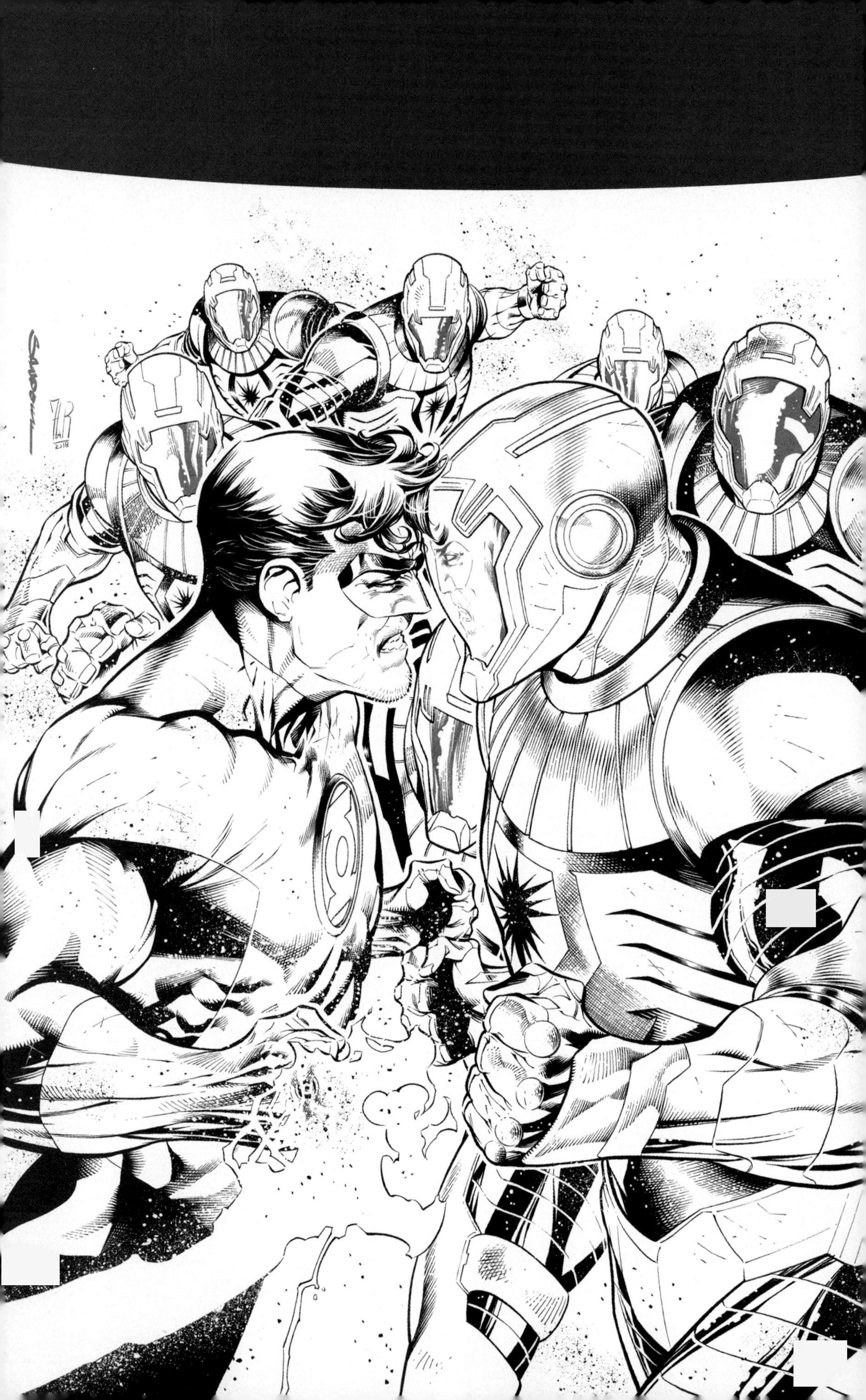

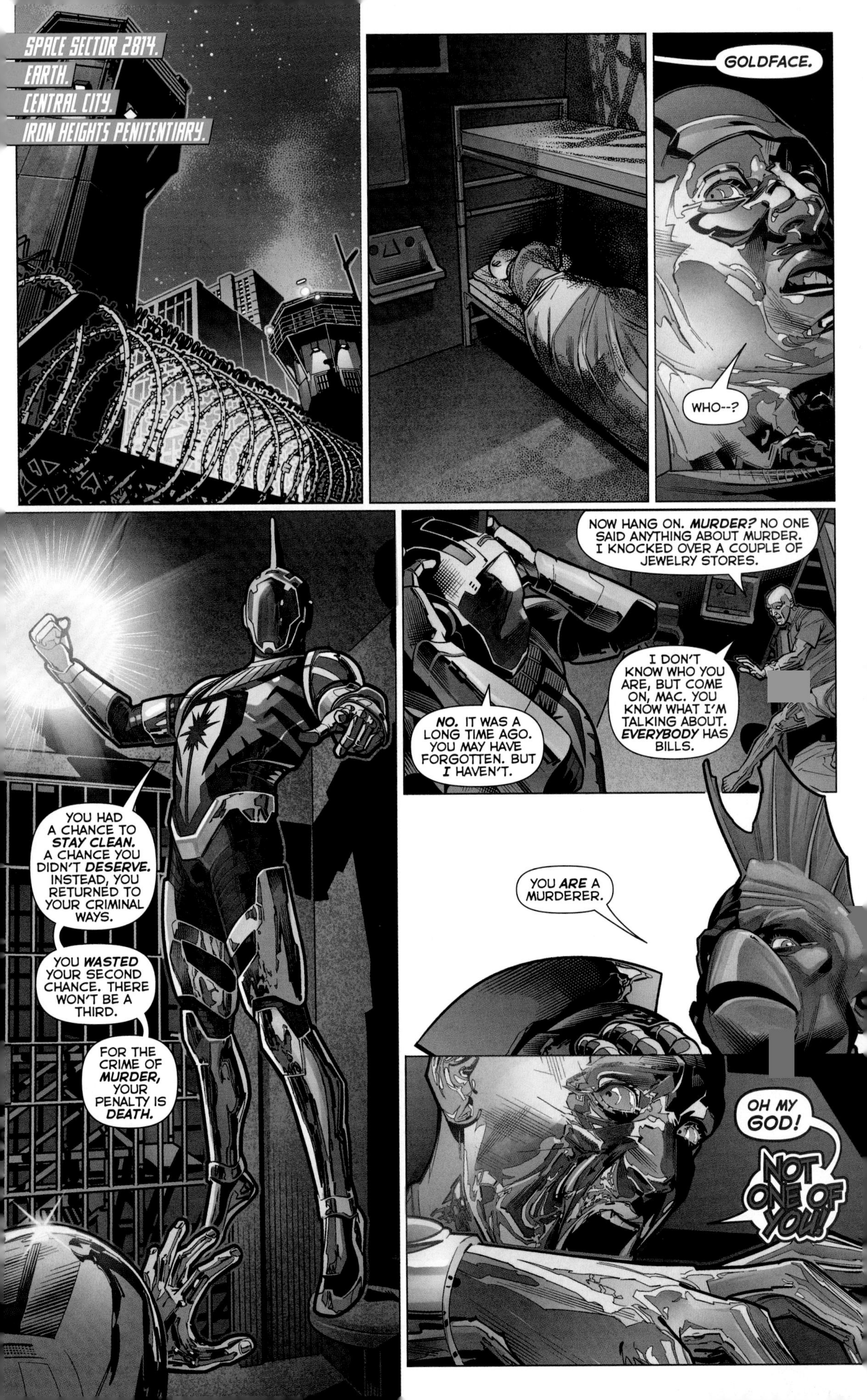
SPACE SECTOR 2814.
EARTH.
CENTRAL CITY.
IRON HEIGHTS PENITENTIARY.
GOLDFACE.
WHO--?
YOU HAD A CHANCE TO STAY CLEAN. A CHANCE YOU DIDN'T DESERVE. INSTEAD, YOU RETURNED TO YOUR CRIMINAL WAYS.
YOU WASTED YOUR SECOND CHANCE. THERE WON'T BE A THIRD.
FOR THE CRIME OF MURDER, YOUR PENALTY IS DEATH.
NOW HANG ON. MURDER? NO ONE SAID ANYTHING ABOUT MURDER. I KNOCKED OVER A COUPLE OF JEWELRY STORES.
I DON'T KNOW WHO YOU ARE, BUT COME ON, MAC. YOU KNOW WHAT I'M TALKING ABOUT. EVERYBODY HAS BILLS.
NO. IT WAS A LONG TIME AGO. YOU MAY HAVE FORGOTTEN. BUT I HAVEN'T.
YOU ARE A MURDERER.
OH MY GOD!
NOT ONE OF YOU!

THEN YOU DO REMEMBER.
GGAAIIIIGGH!
FINAL JUSTICE HAS BEEN SERVED, GOLDFACE. THIS IS ONLY THE BEGINNING.
THE DARKSTARS ARE THE NEW LAW.

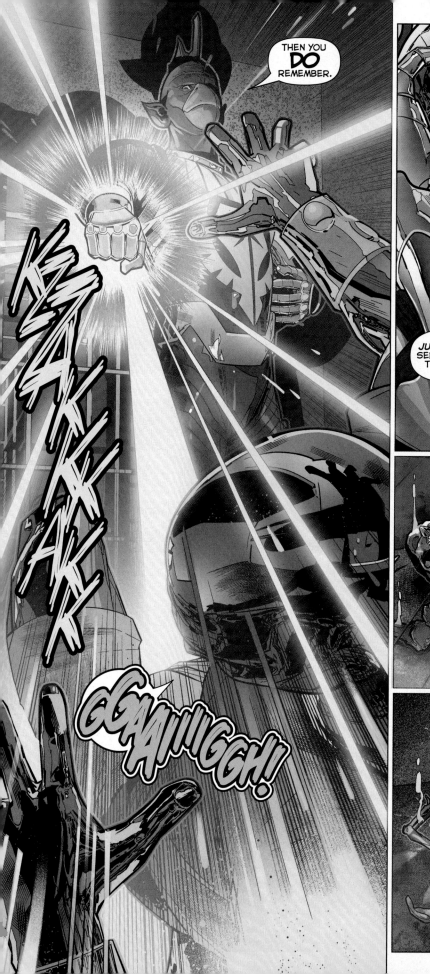

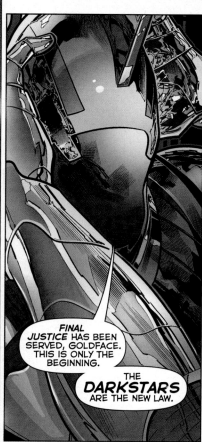

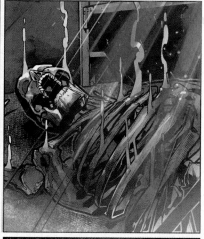

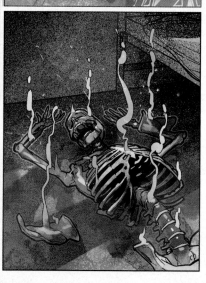

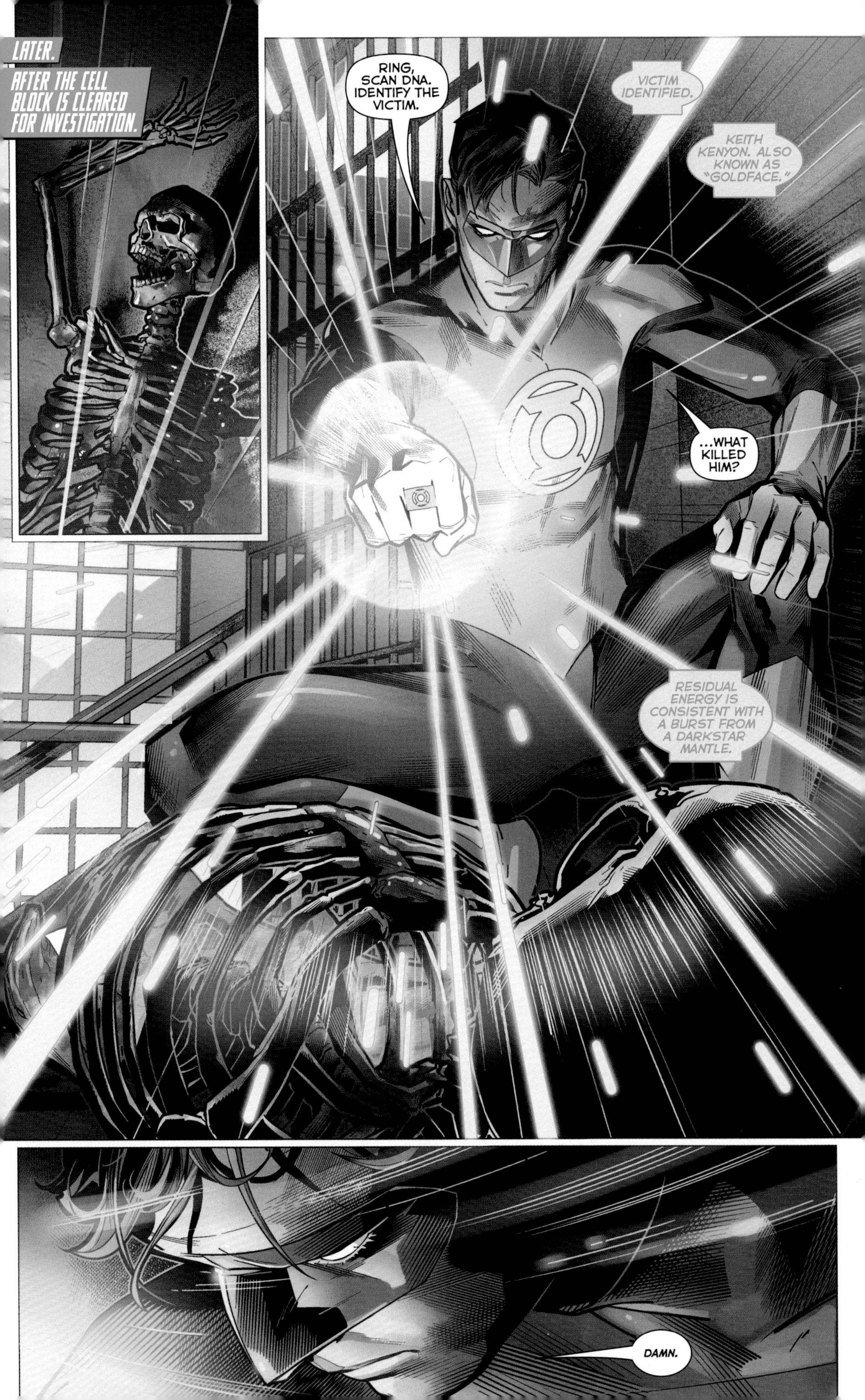
LATER.
AFTER THE CELL BLOCK IS CLEARED FOR INVESTIGATION.
RING, SCAN DNA. IDENTIFY THE VICTIM.
VICTIM IDENTIFIED.
KEITH KENYON. ALSO KNOWN AS "GOLDFACE."
...WHAT KILLED HIM?
RESIDUAL ENERGY IS CONSISTENT WITH A BURST FROM A DARKSTAR MANTLE.
DAMN.

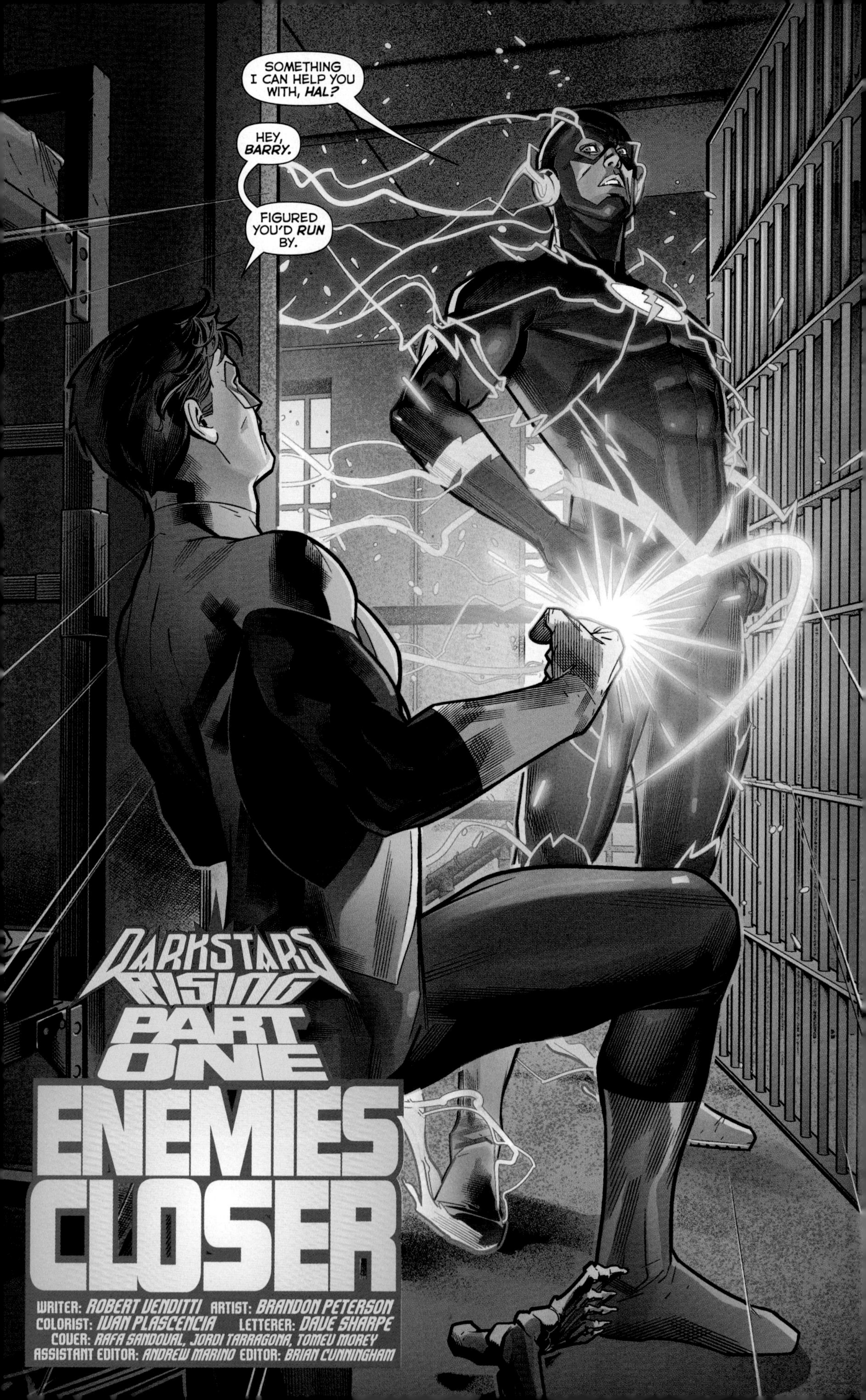
SOMETHING I CAN HELP YOU WITH, HAL?
HEY, BARRY.
FIGURED YOU'D RUN BY.
DARKSTARS RISING
PART ONE
ENEMIES CLOSER
WRITER: ROBERT VENDITTI ARTIST: BRANDON PETERSON
COLORIST: IVAN PLASCENCIA LETTERER: DAVE SHARPE
COVER: RAFA SANDOVAL, JORDI TARRAGONA, TOMEU MOREY
ASSISTANT EDITOR: ANDREW MARINO EDITOR: BRIAN CUNNINGHAM

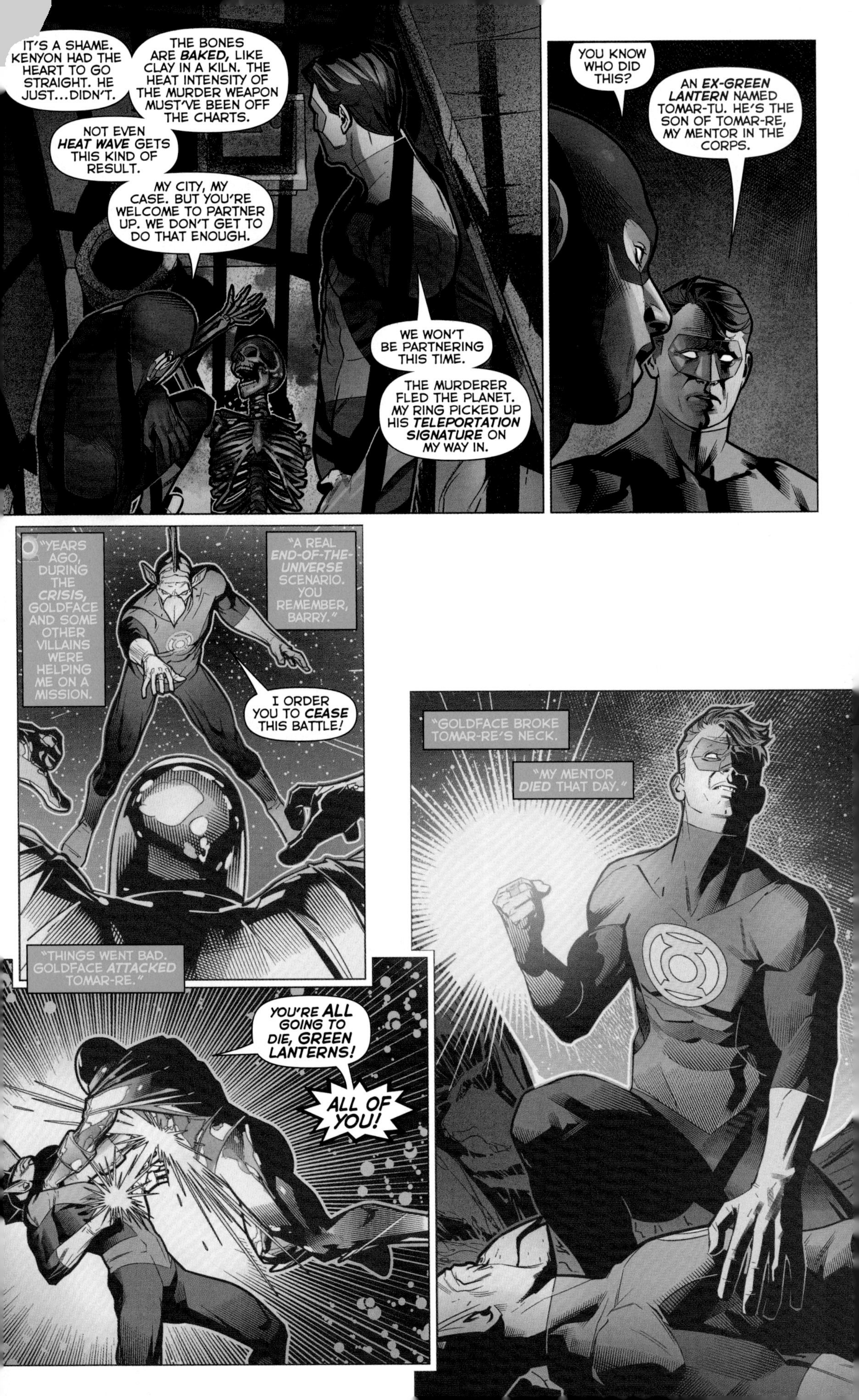

IT'S A SHAME. KENYON HAD THE HEART TO GO STRAIGHT. HE JUST...DIDN'T.
THE BONES ARE **BAKED,** LIKE CLAY IN A KILN. THE HEAT INTENSITY OF THE MURDER WEAPON MUST'VE BEEN OFF THE CHARTS.
NOT EVEN **HEAT WAVE** GETS THIS KIND OF RESULT.
MY CITY, MY CASE. BUT YOU'RE WELCOME TO PARTNER UP. WE DON'T GET TO DO THAT ENOUGH.
WE WON'T BE PARTNERING THIS TIME.
THE MURDERER FLED THE PLANET. MY RING PICKED UP HIS **TELEPORTATION SIGNATURE** ON MY WAY IN.
YOU KNOW WHO DID THIS?
AN **EX-GREEN LANTERN** NAMED TOMAR-TU. HE'S THE SON OF TOMAR-RE, MY MENTOR IN THE CORPS.
"YEARS AGO, DURING THE **CRISIS,** GOLDFACE AND SOME OTHER VILLAINS WERE HELPING ME ON A MISSION.
"A REAL **END-OF-THE-UNIVERSE** SCENARIO. YOU REMEMBER, BARRY."
I ORDER YOU TO **CEASE** THIS BATTLE!
"THINGS WENT BAD. GOLDFACE **ATTACKED** TOMAR-RE."
YOU'RE **ALL** GOING TO DIE, **GREEN LANTERNS!**
ALL OF YOU!
"GOLDFACE BROKE TOMAR-RE'S NECK.
"MY MENTOR **DIED** THAT DAY."

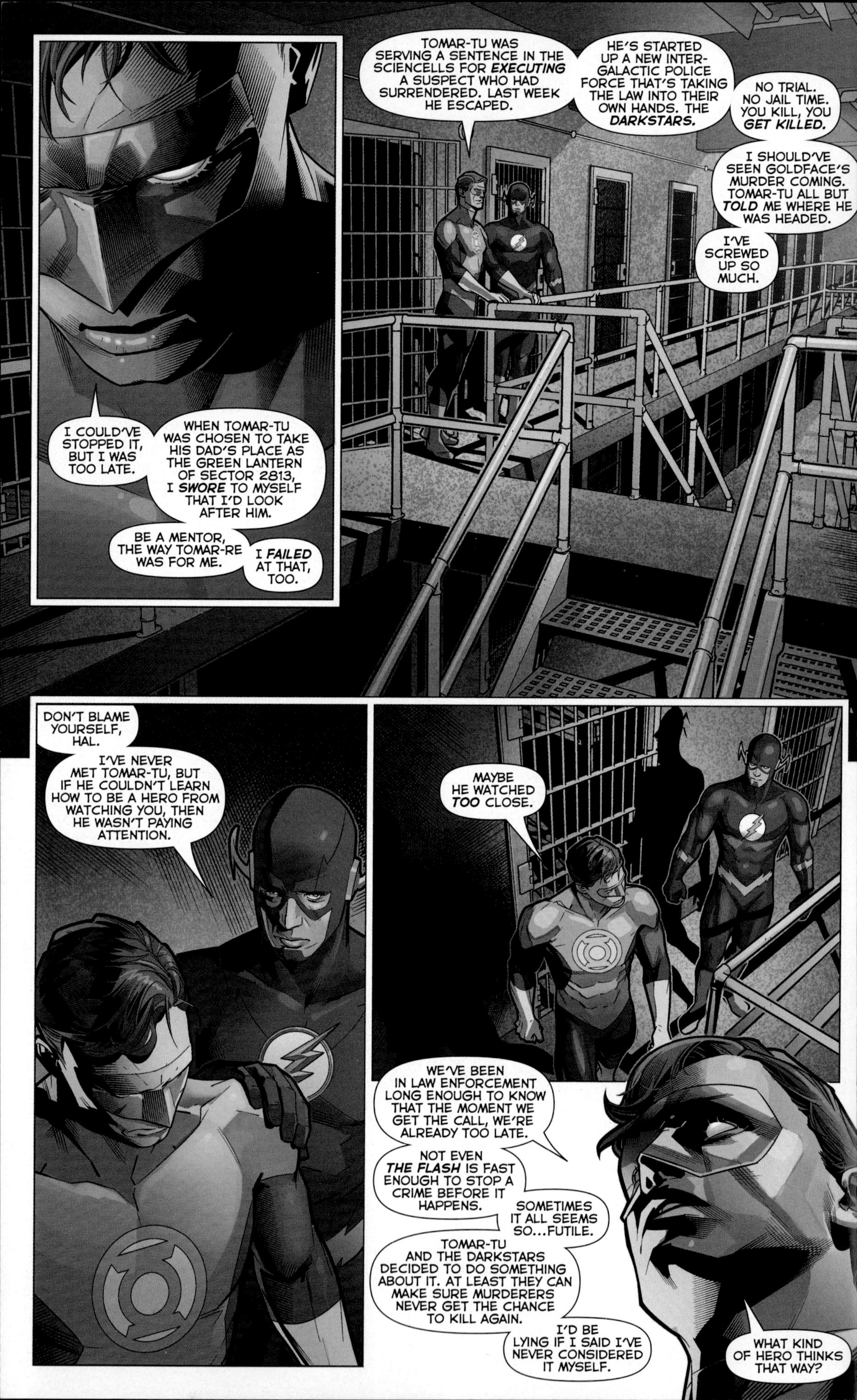
TOMAR-TU WAS SERVING A SENTENCE IN THE SCIENCELLS FOR EXECUTING A SUSPECT WHO HAD SURRENDERED. LAST WEEK HE ESCAPED.
HE'S STARTED UP A NEW INTER-GALACTIC POLICE FORCE THAT'S TAKING THE LAW INTO THEIR OWN HANDS. THE DARKSTARS.
NO TRIAL. NO JAIL TIME. YOU KILL, YOU GET KILLED.
I SHOULD'VE SEEN GOLDFACE'S MURDER COMING. TOMAR-TU ALL BUT TOLD ME WHERE HE WAS HEADED.
I'VE SCREWED UP SO MUCH.
I COULD'VE STOPPED IT, BUT I WAS TOO LATE.
WHEN TOMAR-TU WAS CHOSEN TO TAKE HIS DAD'S PLACE AS THE GREEN LANTERN OF SECTOR 2813, I SWORE TO MYSELF THAT I'D LOOK AFTER HIM.
BE A MENTOR, THE WAY TOMAR-RE WAS FOR ME.
I FAILED AT THAT, TOO.
DON'T BLAME YOURSELF, HAL.
I'VE NEVER MET TOMAR-TU, BUT IF HE COULDN'T LEARN HOW TO BE A HERO FROM WATCHING YOU, THEN HE WASN'T PAYING ATTENTION.
MAYBE HE WATCHED TOO CLOSE.
WE'VE BEEN IN LAW ENFORCEMENT LONG ENOUGH TO KNOW THAT THE MOMENT WE GET THE CALL, WE'RE ALREADY TOO LATE.
NOT EVEN THE FLASH IS FAST ENOUGH TO STOP A CRIME BEFORE IT HAPPENS.
SOMETIMES IT ALL SEEMS SO...FUTILE.
TOMAR-TU AND THE DARKSTARS DECIDED TO DO SOMETHING ABOUT IT. AT LEAST THEY CAN MAKE SURE MURDERERS NEVER GET THE CHANCE TO KILL AGAIN.
I'D BE LYING IF I SAID I'VE NEVER CONSIDERED IT MYSELF.
WHAT KIND OF HERO THINKS THAT WAY?

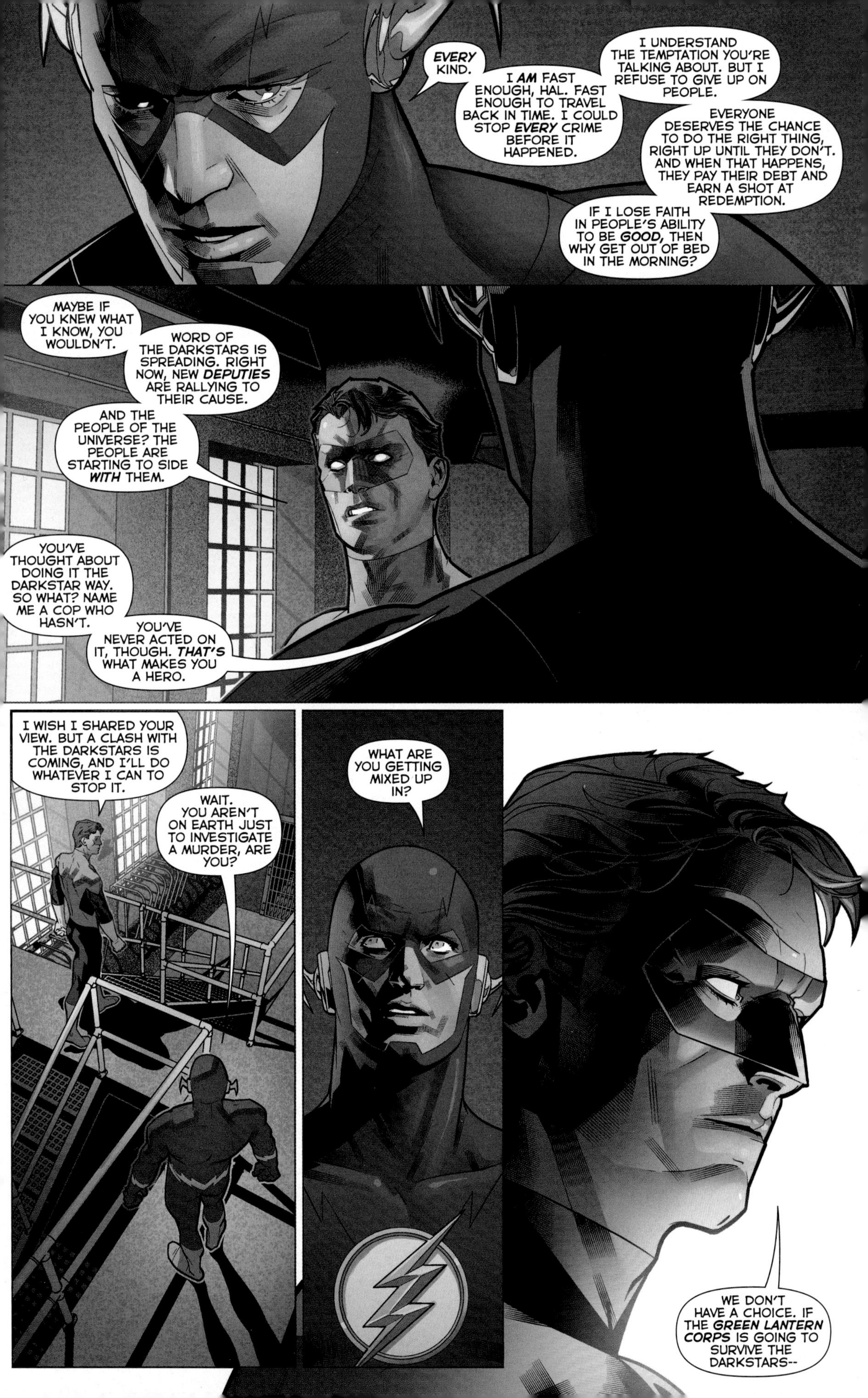
EVERY KIND.
I AM FAST ENOUGH, HAL. FAST ENOUGH TO TRAVEL BACK IN TIME. I COULD STOP EVERY CRIME BEFORE IT HAPPENED.
I UNDERSTAND THE TEMPTATION YOU'RE TALKING ABOUT. BUT I REFUSE TO GIVE UP ON PEOPLE.
EVERYONE DESERVES THE CHANCE TO DO THE RIGHT THING, RIGHT UP UNTIL THEY DON'T. AND WHEN THAT HAPPENS, THEY PAY THEIR DEBT AND EARN A SHOT AT REDEMPTION.
IF I LOSE FAITH IN PEOPLE'S ABILITY TO BE GOOD, THEN WHY GET OUT OF BED IN THE MORNING?
MAYBE IF YOU KNEW WHAT I KNOW, YOU WOULDN'T.
WORD OF THE DARKSTARS IS SPREADING. RIGHT NOW, NEW DEPUTIES ARE RALLYING TO THEIR CAUSE.
AND THE PEOPLE OF THE UNIVERSE? THE PEOPLE ARE STARTING TO SIDE WITH THEM.
YOU'VE THOUGHT ABOUT DOING IT THE DARKSTAR WAY. SO WHAT? NAME ME A COP WHO HASN'T.
YOU'VE NEVER ACTED ON IT, THOUGH. THAT'S WHAT MAKES YOU A HERO.
I WISH I SHARED YOUR VIEW. BUT A CLASH WITH THE DARKSTARS IS COMING, AND I'LL DO WHATEVER I CAN TO STOP IT.
WAIT. YOU AREN'T ON EARTH JUST TO INVESTIGATE A MURDER, ARE YOU?
WHAT ARE YOU GETTING MIXED UP IN?
WE DON'T HAVE A CHOICE. IF THE GREEN LANTERN CORPS IS GOING TO SURVIVE THE DARKSTARS--

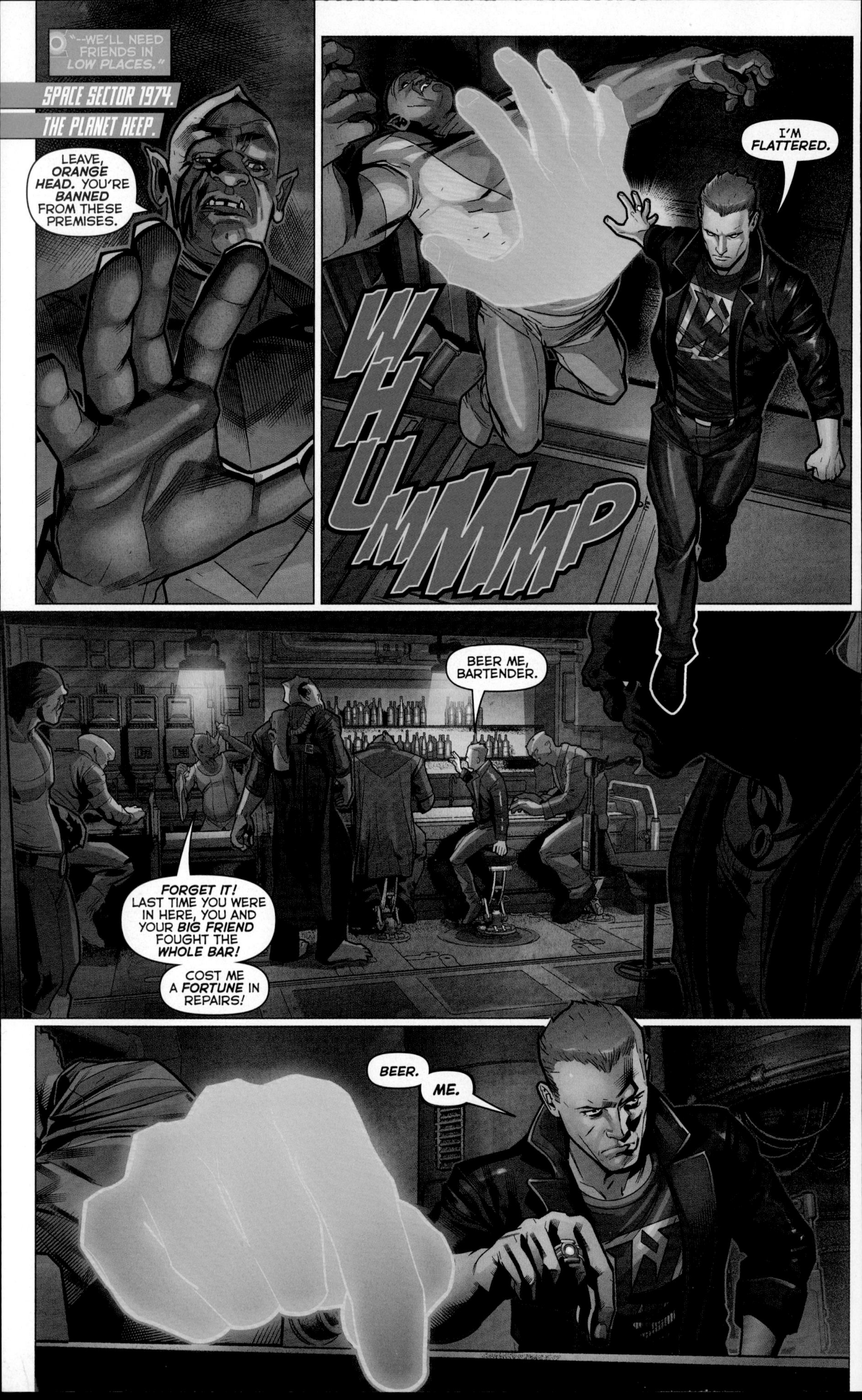
"--WE'LL NEED FRIENDS IN LOW PLACES."
SPACE SECTOR 1974.
THE PLANET HEEP.
LEAVE, ORANGE HEAD. YOU'RE BANNED FROM THESE PREMISES.
I'M FLATTERED.
WHUMMMMP
BEER ME, BARTENDER.
FORGET IT! LAST TIME YOU WERE IN HERE, YOU AND YOUR BIG FRIEND FOUGHT THE WHOLE BAR!
COST ME A FORTUNE IN REPAIRS!
BEER.
ME.

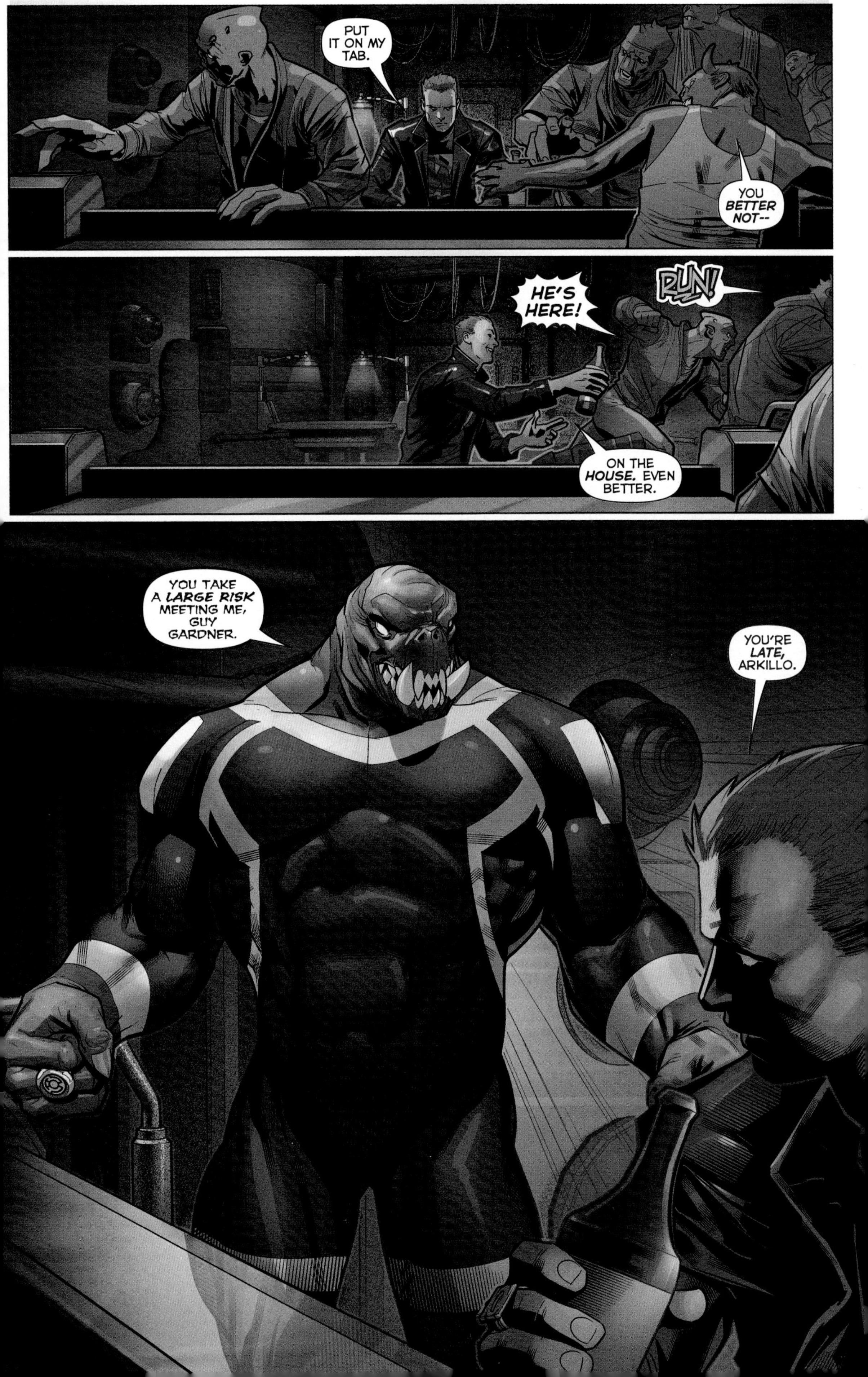
PUT IT ON MY TAB.
YOU BETTER NOT--
HE'S HERE!
RUN!
ON THE HOUSE. EVEN BETTER.
YOU TAKE A LARGE RISK MEETING ME, GUY GARDNER.
YOU'RE LATE, ARKILLO.

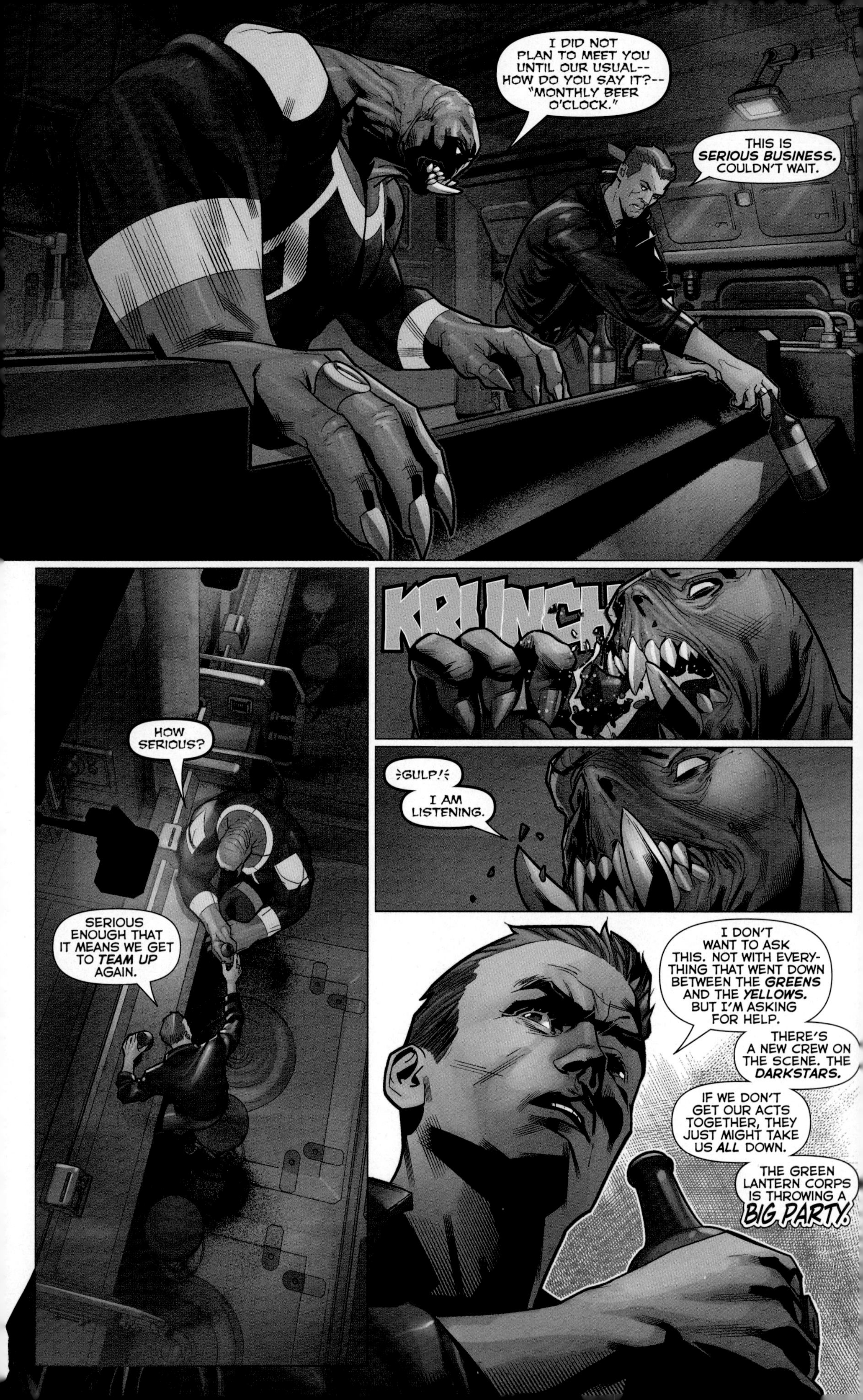
I DID NOT PLAN TO MEET YOU UNTIL OUR USUAL-- HOW DO YOU SAY IT?-- "MONTHLY BEER O'CLOCK."
THIS IS SERIOUS BUSINESS. COULDN'T WAIT.
HOW SERIOUS?
SERIOUS ENOUGH THAT IT MEANS WE GET TO TEAM UP AGAIN.
KRUNCH
GULP!
I AM LISTENING.
I DON'T WANT TO ASK THIS. NOT WITH EVERY-THING THAT WENT DOWN BETWEEN THE GREENS AND THE YELLOWS. BUT I'M ASKING FOR HELP.
THERE'S A NEW CREW ON THE SCENE. THE DARKSTARS.
IF WE DON'T GET OUR ACTS TOGETHER, THEY JUST MIGHT TAKE US ALL DOWN.
THE GREEN LANTERN CORPS IS THROWING A BIG PARTY.

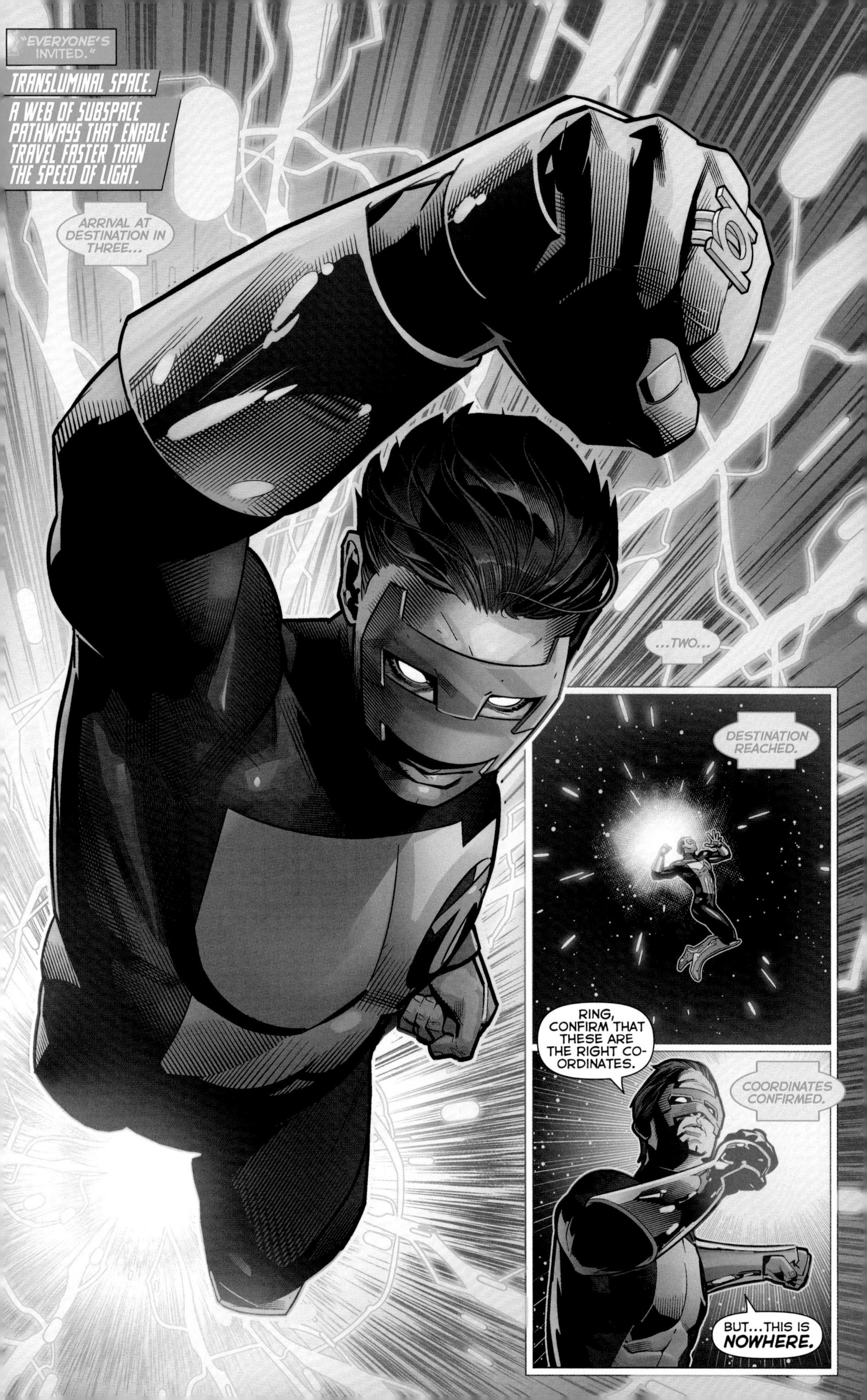
"EVERYONE'S INVITED."
TRANSLUMINAL SPACE.
A WEB OF SUBSPACE PATHWAYS THAT ENABLE TRAVEL FASTER THAN THE SPEED OF LIGHT.
ARRIVAL AT DESTINATION IN THREE...
...TWO...
DESTINATION REACHED.
RING, CONFIRM THAT THESE ARE THE RIGHT CO-ORDINATES.
COORDINATES CONFIRMED.
BUT...THIS IS NOWHERE.

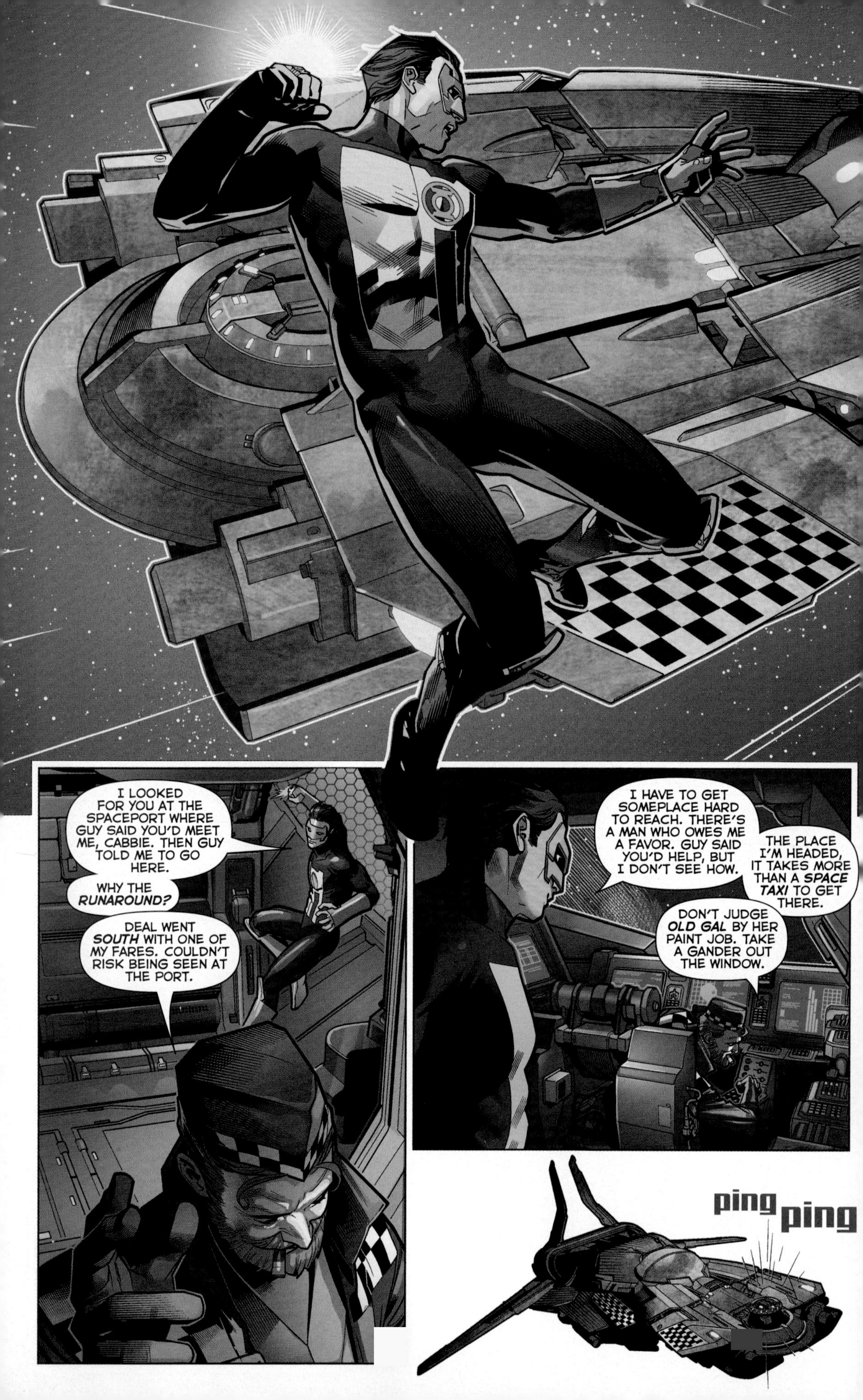
I LOOKED FOR YOU AT THE SPACEPORT WHERE GUY SAID YOU'D MEET ME, CABBIE. THEN GUY TOLD ME TO GO HERE.
WHY THE RUNAROUND?
DEAL WENT SOUTH WITH ONE OF MY FARES. COULDN'T RISK BEING SEEN AT THE PORT.
I HAVE TO GET SOMEPLACE HARD TO REACH. THERE'S A MAN WHO OWES ME A FAVOR. GUY SAID YOU'D HELP, BUT I DON'T SEE HOW.
THE PLACE I'M HEADED, IT TAKES MORE THAN A SPACE TAXI TO GET THERE.
DON'T JUDGE OLD GAL BY HER PAINT JOB. TAKE A GANDER OUT THE WINDOW.
ping
ping

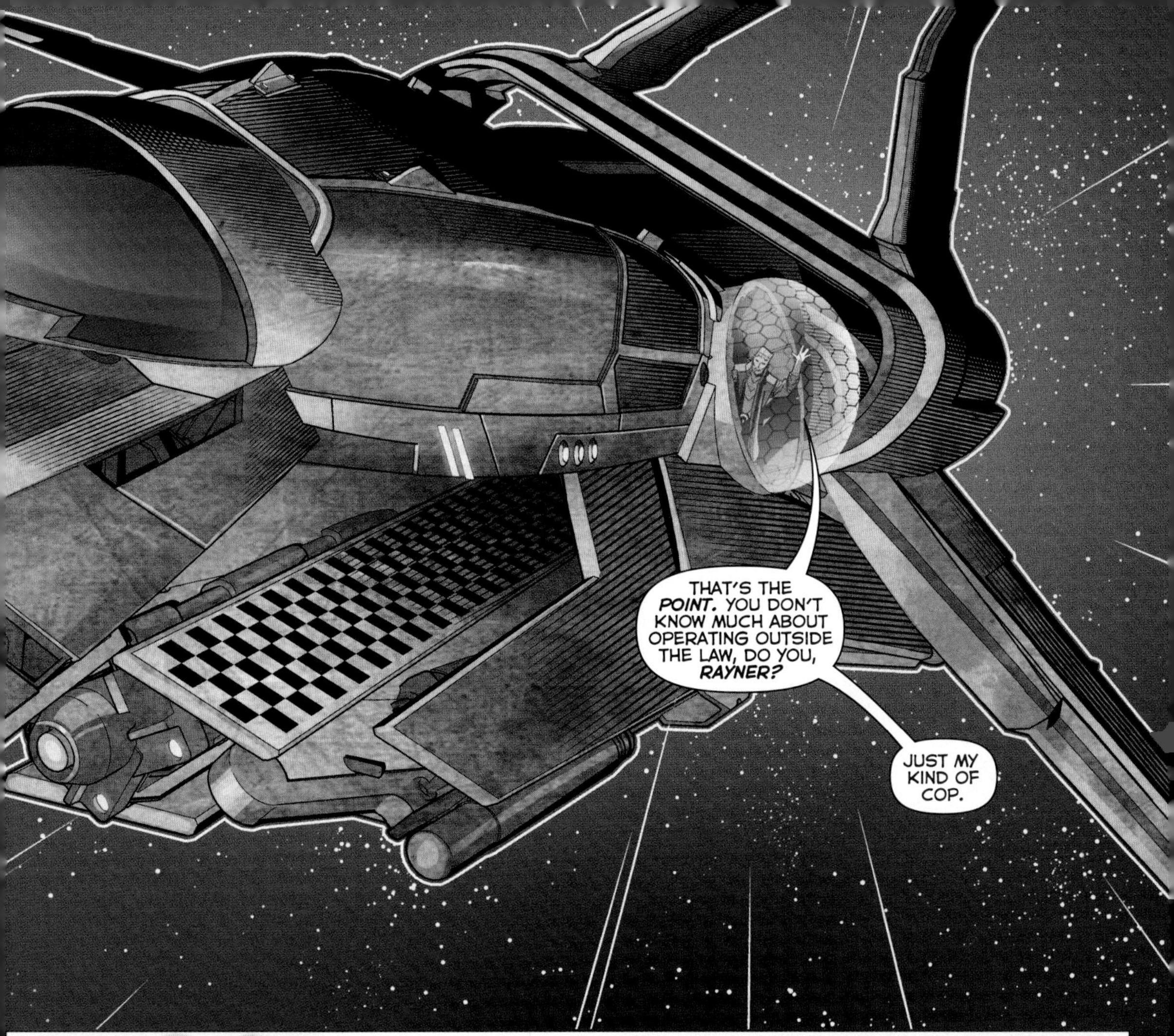
THAT'S THE POINT. YOU DON'T KNOW MUCH ABOUT OPERATING OUTSIDE THE LAW, DO YOU, RAYNER?
JUST MY KIND OF COP.

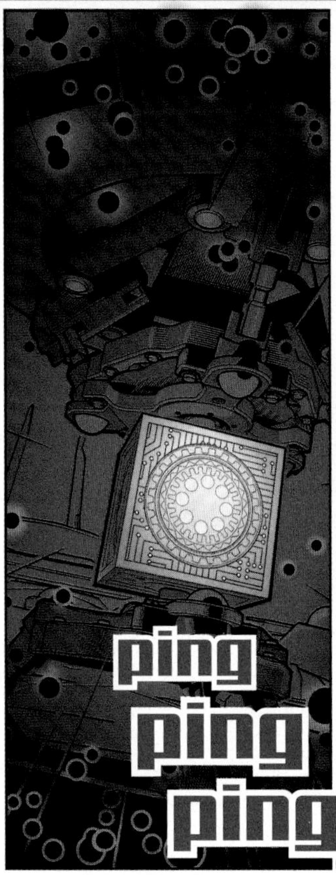
ping
ping
ping

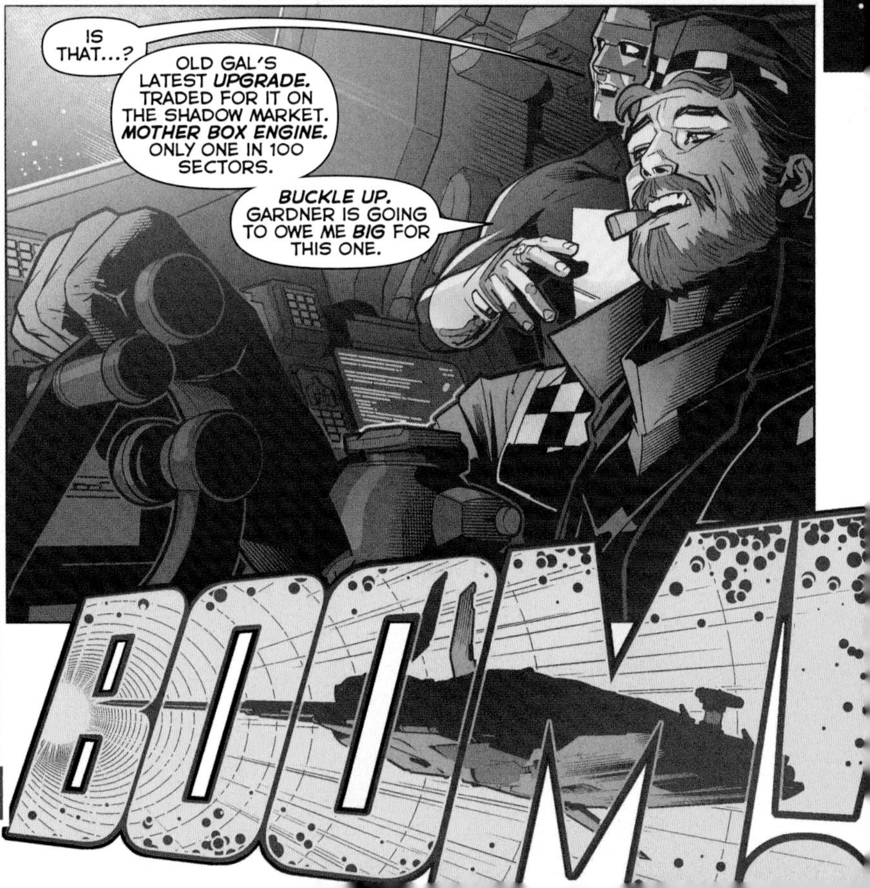
IS THAT...?
OLD GAL'S LATEST UPGRADE. TRADED FOR IT ON THE SHADOW MARKET. MOTHER BOX ENGINE. ONLY ONE IN 100 SECTORS.
BUCKLE UP. GARDNER IS GOING TO OWE ME BIG FOR THIS ONE.
BOOM!

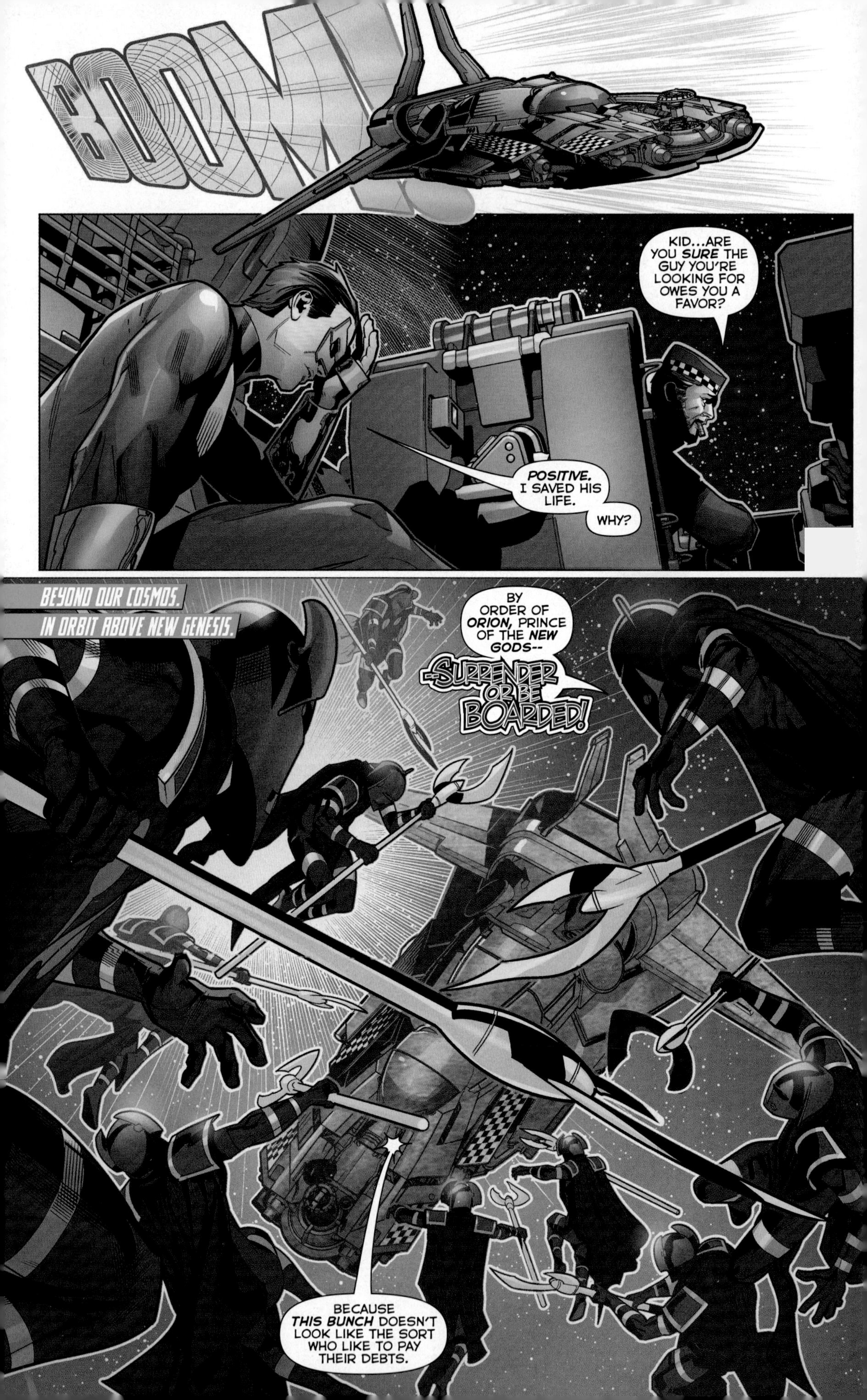
BOOM
KID...ARE YOU SURE THE GUY YOU'RE LOOKING FOR OWES YOU A FAVOR?
POSITIVE. I SAVED HIS LIFE.
WHY?
BEYOND OUR COSMOS.
IN ORBIT ABOVE NEW GENESIS.
BY ORDER OF ORION, PRINCE OF THE NEW GODS--
--SURRENDER OR BE BOARDED!
BECAUSE THIS BUNCH DOESN'T LOOK LIKE THE SORT WHO LIKE TO PAY THEIR DEBTS.

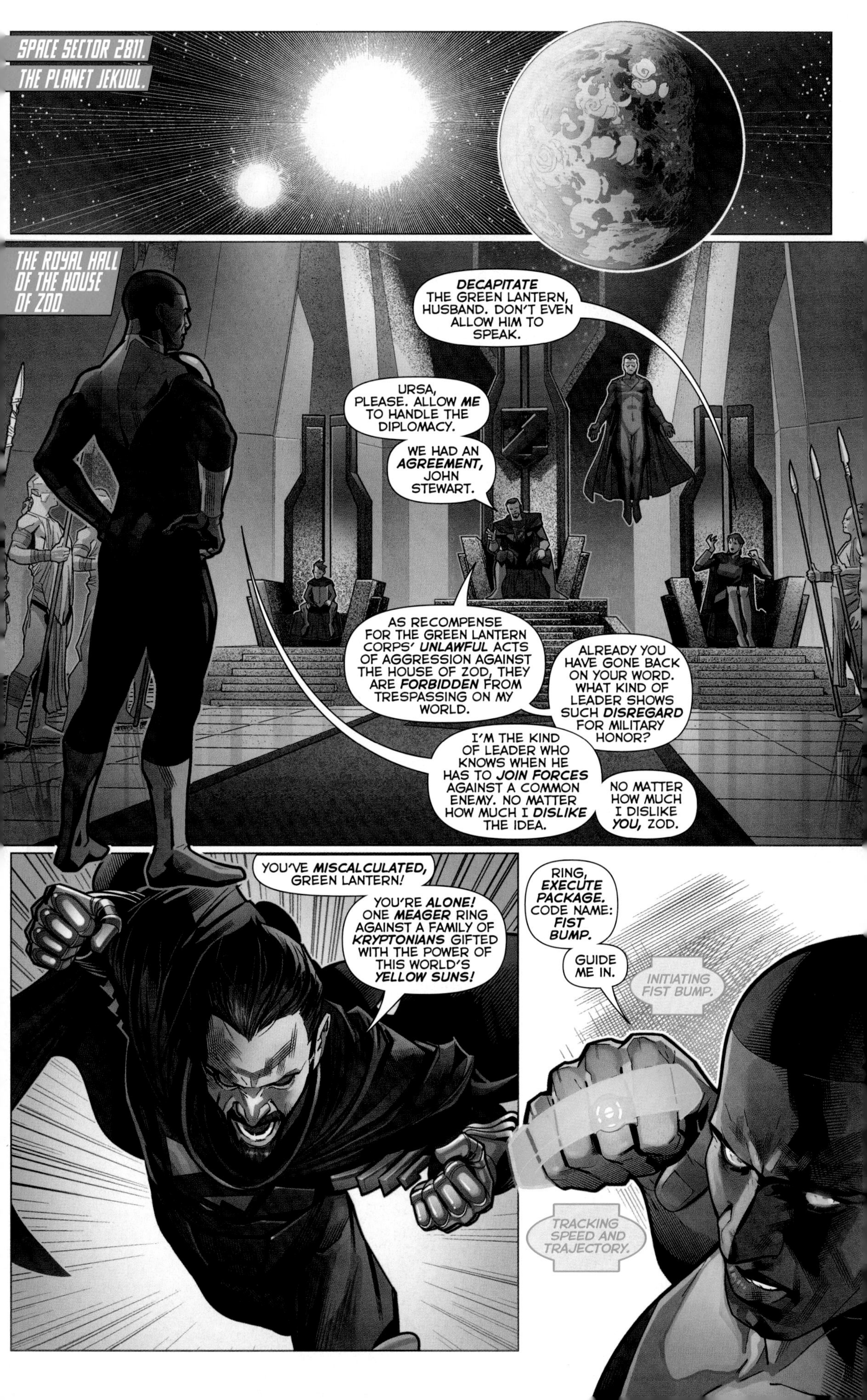
SPACE SECTOR 2811.
THE PLANET JEKUUL.
THE ROYAL HALL OF THE HOUSE OF ZOD.
DECAPITATE THE GREEN LANTERN, HUSBAND. DON'T EVEN ALLOW HIM TO SPEAK.
URSA, PLEASE. ALLOW ME TO HANDLE THE DIPLOMACY.
WE HAD AN AGREEMENT, JOHN STEWART.
AS RECOMPENSE FOR THE GREEN LANTERN CORPS' UNLAWFUL ACTS OF AGGRESSION AGAINST THE HOUSE OF ZOD, THEY ARE FORBIDDEN FROM TRESPASSING ON MY WORLD.
ALREADY YOU HAVE GONE BACK ON YOUR WORD. WHAT KIND OF LEADER SHOWS SUCH DISREGARD FOR MILITARY HONOR?
I'M THE KIND OF LEADER WHO KNOWS WHEN HE HAS TO JOIN FORCES AGAINST A COMMON ENEMY. NO MATTER HOW MUCH I DISLIKE THE IDEA.
NO MATTER HOW MUCH I DISLIKE YOU, ZOD.
YOU'VE MISCALCULATED, GREEN LANTERN!
YOU'RE ALONE! ONE MEAGER RING AGAINST A FAMILY OF KRYPTONIANS GIFTED WITH THE POWER OF THIS WORLD'S YELLOW SUNS!
RING, EXECUTE PACKAGE. CODE NAME: FIST BUMP.
GUIDE ME IN.
INITIATING FIST BUMP.
TRACKING SPEED AND TRAJECTORY.

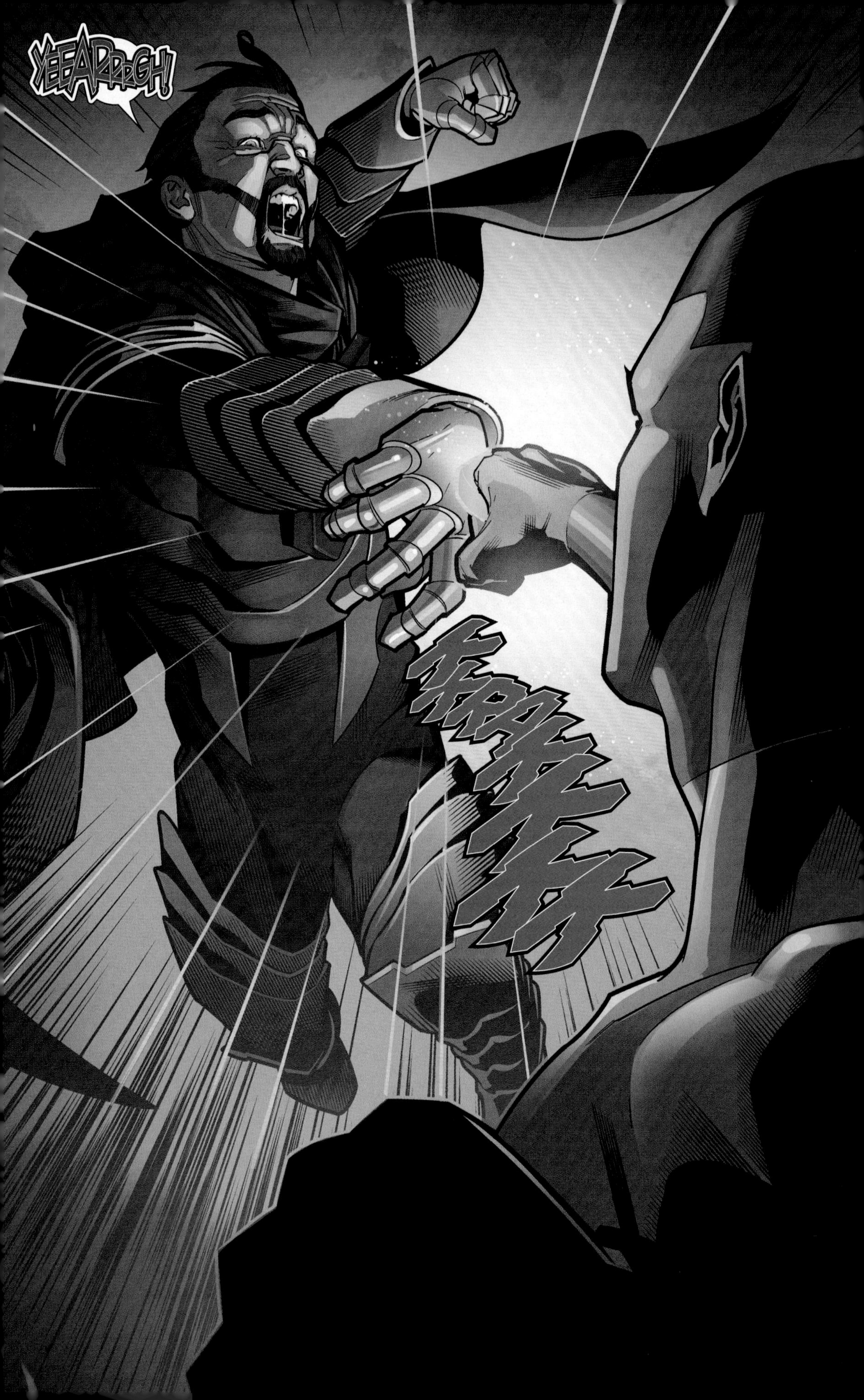
YEEARRRGH!
KRAKKK

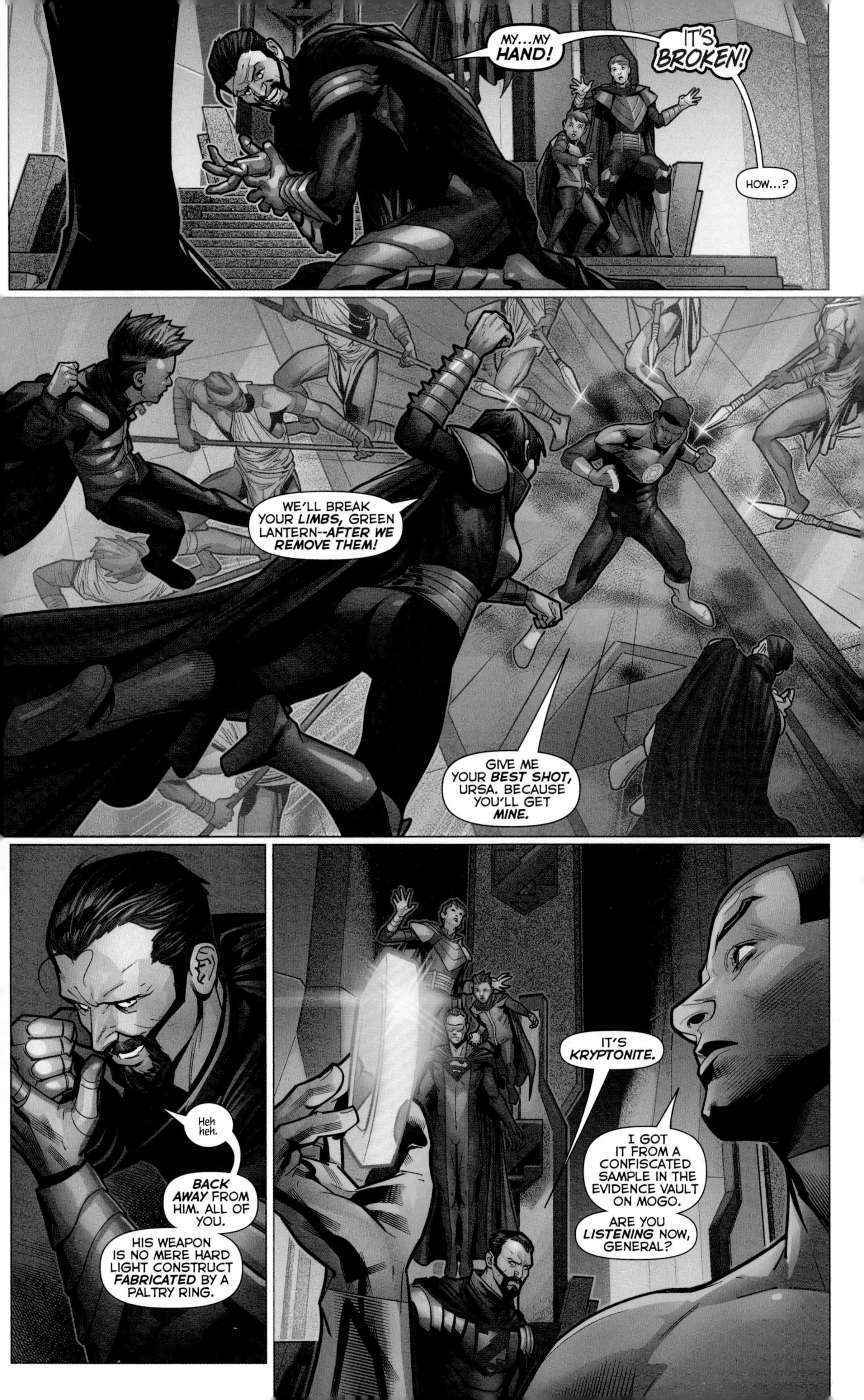
MY...MY HAND!
IT'S BROKEN!
HOW...?
WE'LL BREAK YOUR LIMBS, GREEN LANTERN--AFTER WE REMOVE THEM!
GIVE ME YOUR BEST SHOT, URSA. BECAUSE YOU'LL GET MINE.
Heh heh.
BACK AWAY FROM HIM. ALL OF YOU.
HIS WEAPON IS NO MERE HARD LIGHT CONSTRUCT FABRICATED BY A PALTRY RING.
IT'S KRYPTONITE.
I GOT IT FROM A CONFISCATED SAMPLE IN THE EVIDENCE VAULT ON MOGO.
ARE YOU LISTENING NOW, GENERAL?

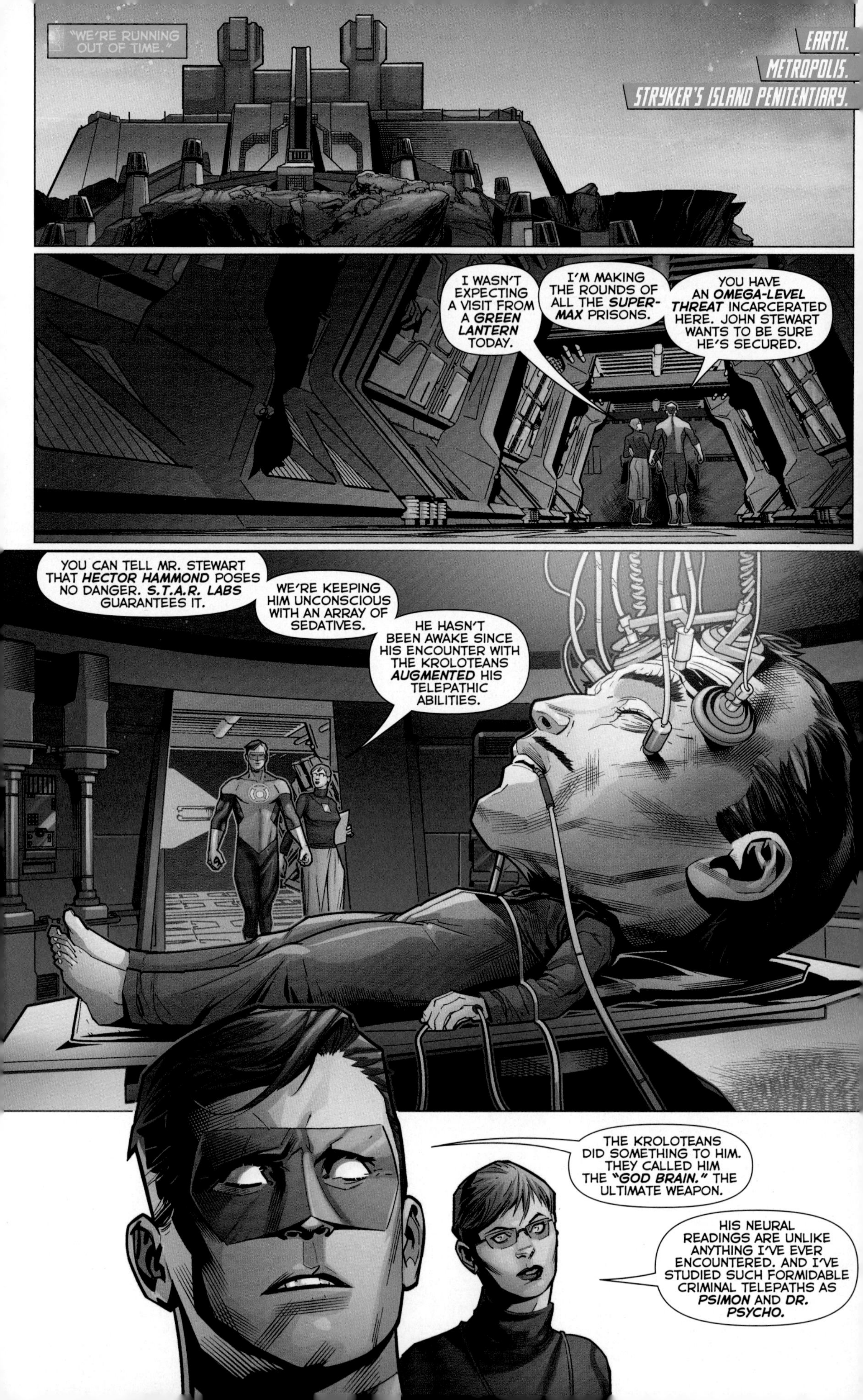

"WE'RE RUNNING OUT OF TIME."
EARTH.
METROPOLIS.
STRYKER'S ISLAND PENITENTIARY.
I WASN'T EXPECTING A VISIT FROM A GREEN LANTERN TODAY.
I'M MAKING THE ROUNDS OF ALL THE SUPER-MAX PRISONS.
YOU HAVE AN OMEGA-LEVEL THREAT INCARCERATED HERE. JOHN STEWART WANTS TO BE SURE HE'S SECURED.
YOU CAN TELL MR. STEWART THAT HECTOR HAMMOND POSES NO DANGER. S.T.A.R. LABS GUARANTEES IT.
WE'RE KEEPING HIM UNCONSCIOUS WITH AN ARRAY OF SEDATIVES.
HE HASN'T BEEN AWAKE SINCE HIS ENCOUNTER WITH THE KROLOTEANS AUGMENTED HIS TELEPATHIC ABILITIES.
THE KROLOTEANS DID SOMETHING TO HIM. THEY CALLED HIM THE "GOD BRAIN." THE ULTIMATE WEAPON.
HIS NEURAL READINGS ARE UNLIKE ANYTHING I'VE EVER ENCOUNTERED. AND I'VE STUDIED SUCH FORMIDABLE CRIMINAL TELEPATHS AS PSIMON AND DR. PSYCHO.

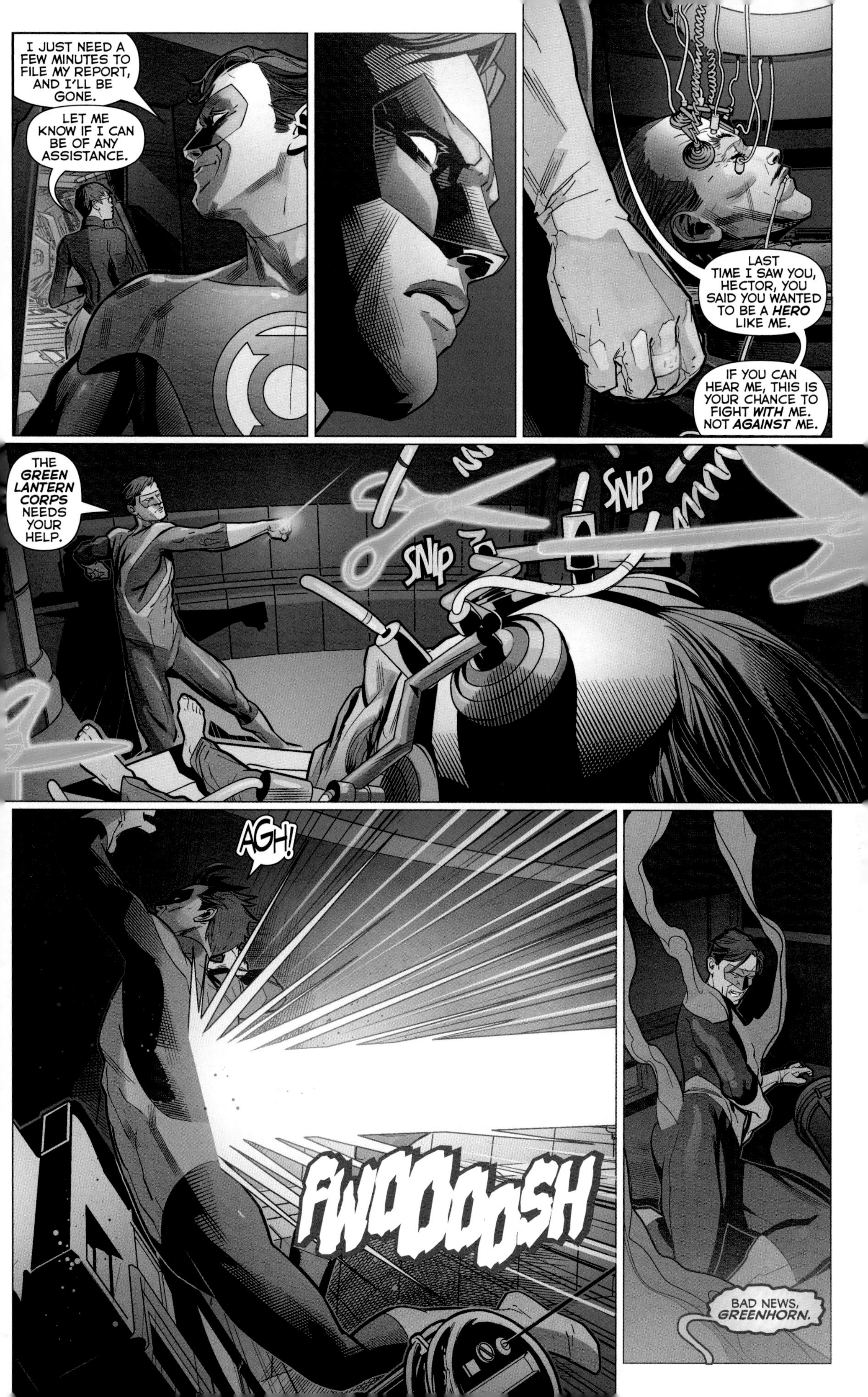
I JUST NEED A FEW MINUTES TO FILE MY REPORT, AND I'LL BE GONE.
LET ME KNOW IF I CAN BE OF ANY ASSISTANCE.
LAST TIME I SAW YOU, HECTOR, YOU SAID YOU WANTED TO BE A *HERO* LIKE ME.
IF YOU CAN HEAR ME, THIS IS YOUR CHANCE TO FIGHT *WITH* ME. NOT *AGAINST* ME.
THE *GREEN LANTERN CORPS* NEEDS YOUR HELP.
SNIP
SNIP
AGH!
FWOOOOSH
BAD NEWS, *GREENHORN.*

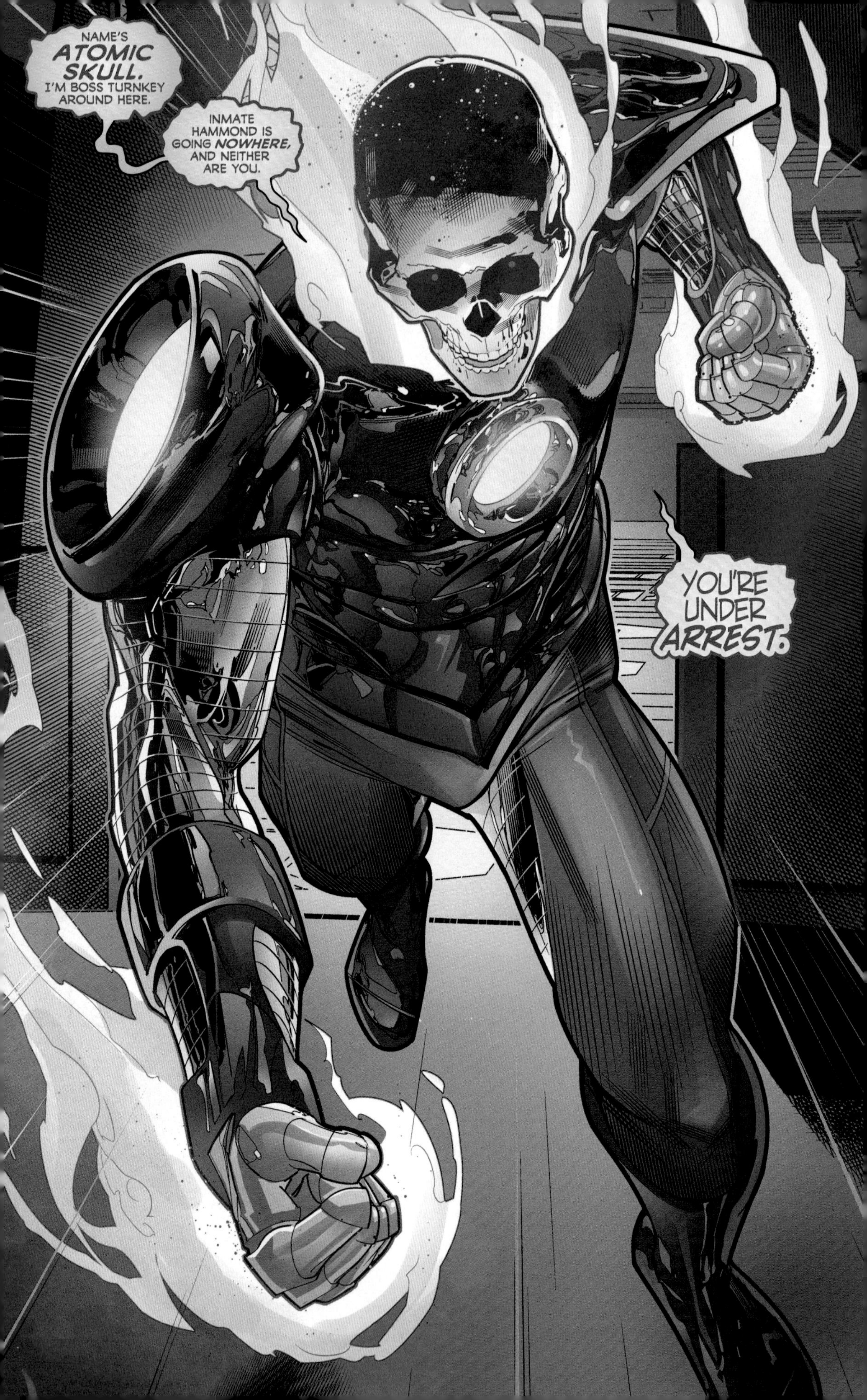
NAME'S ATOMIC SKULL. I'M BOSS TURNKEY AROUND HERE.
INMATE HAMMOND IS GOING NOWHERE, AND NEITHER ARE YOU.
YOU'RE UNDER ARREST.

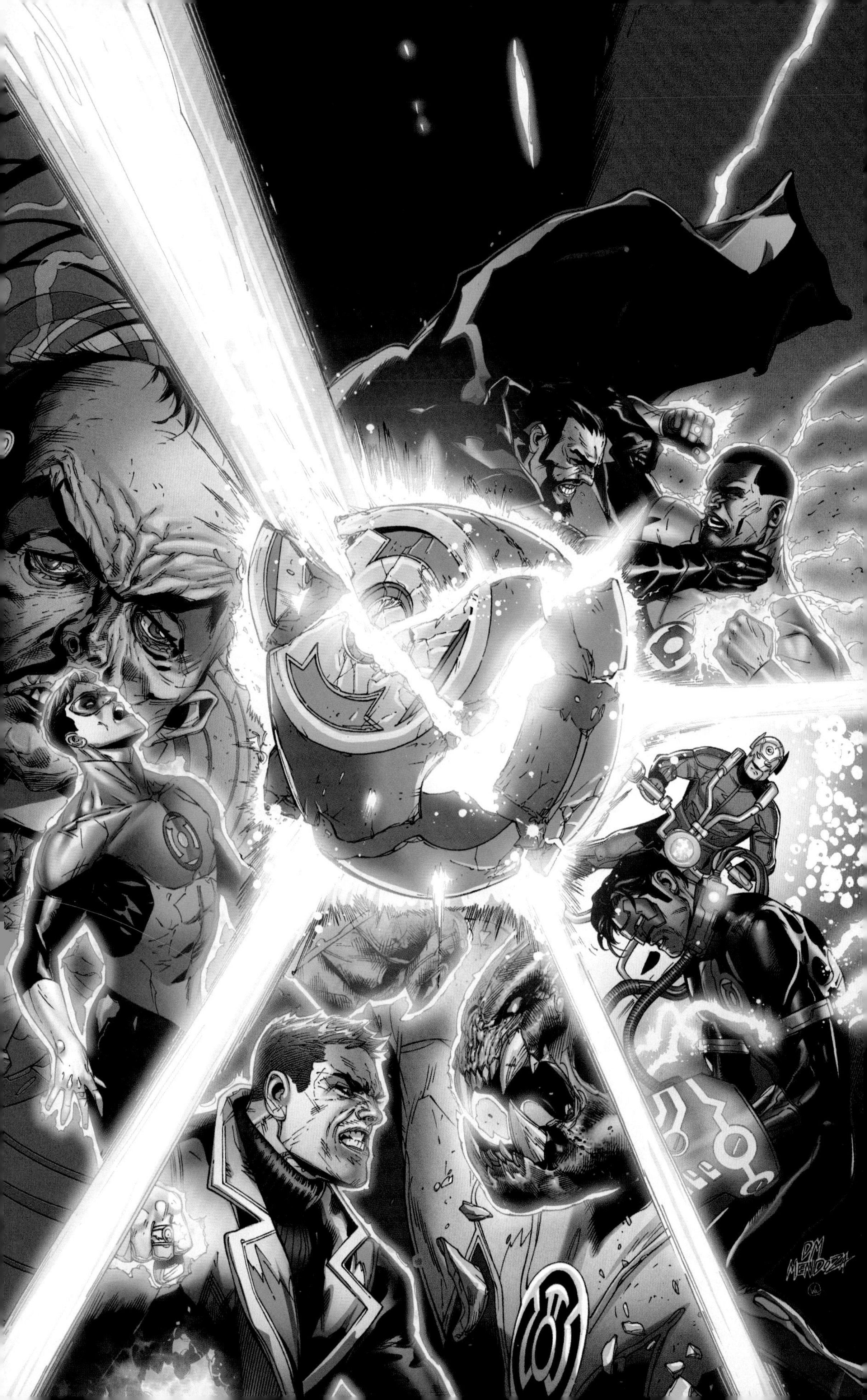
DM MENDOZA

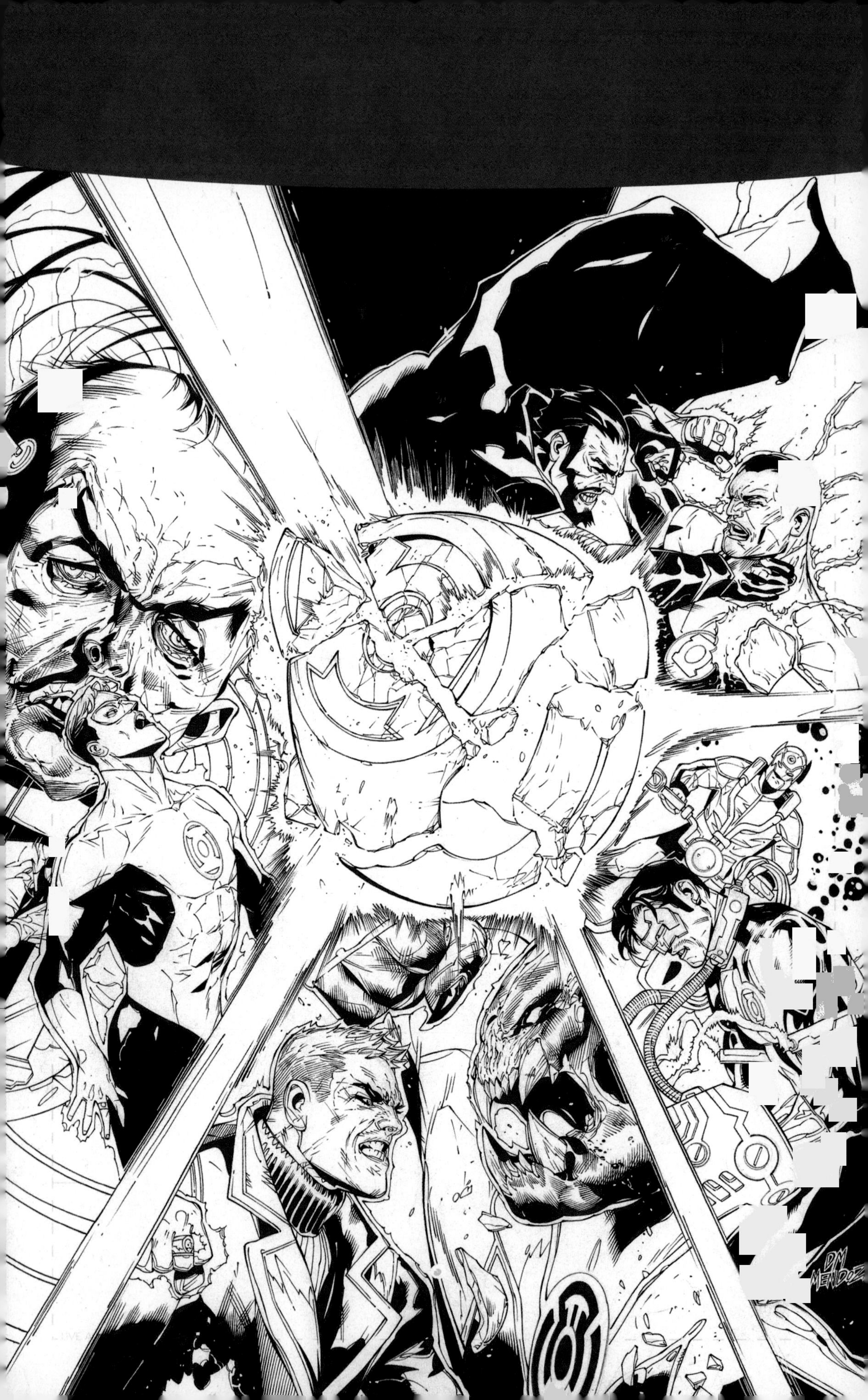

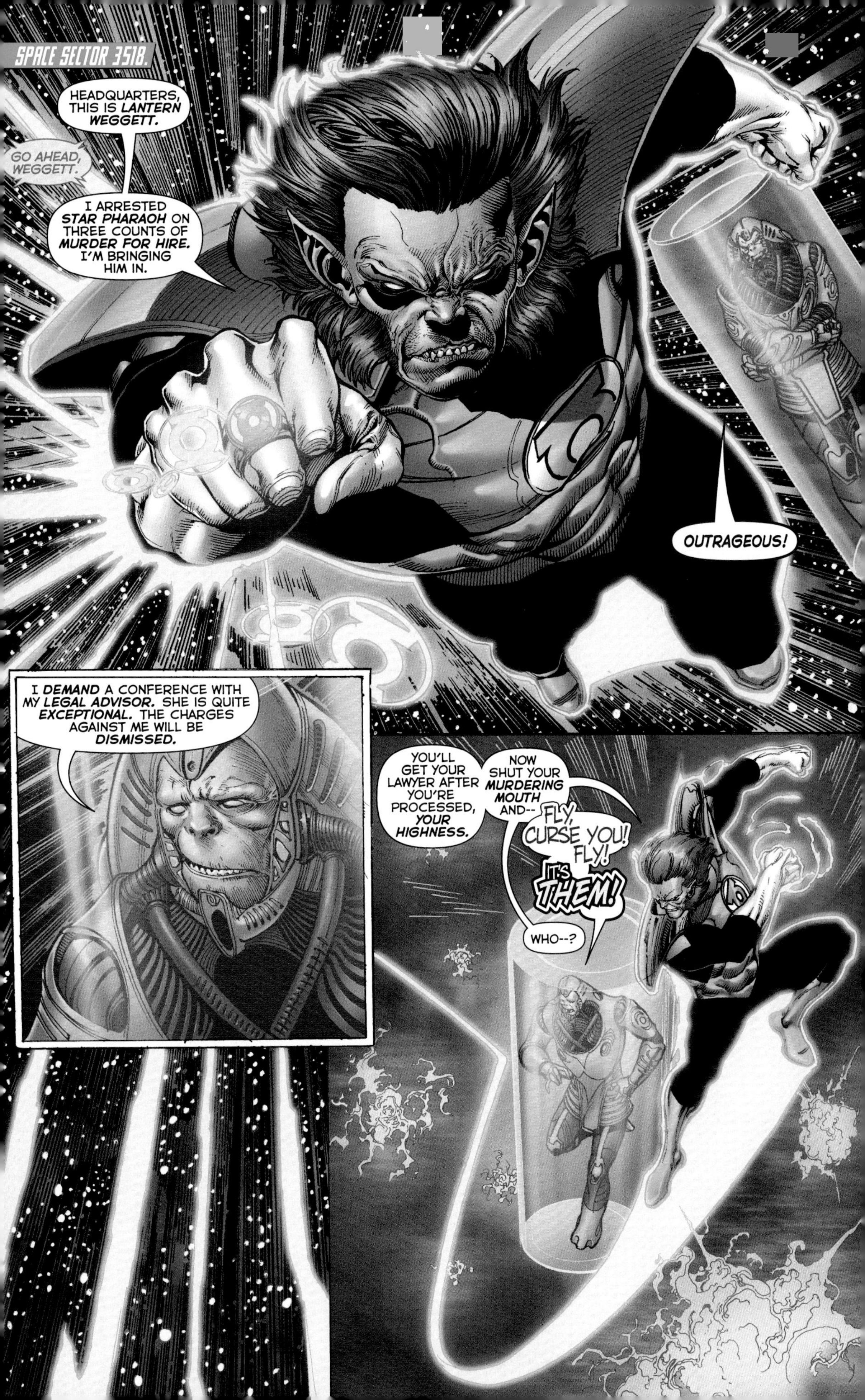
SPACE SECTOR 3518.
HEADQUARTERS, THIS IS LANTERN WEGGETT.
GO AHEAD, WEGGETT.
I ARRESTED STAR PHARAOH ON THREE COUNTS OF MURDER FOR HIRE. I'M BRINGING HIM IN.
OUTRAGEOUS!
I DEMAND A CONFERENCE WITH MY LEGAL ADVISOR. SHE IS QUITE EXCEPTIONAL. THE CHARGES AGAINST ME WILL BE DISMISSED.
YOU'LL GET YOUR LAWYER AFTER YOU'RE PROCESSED, YOUR HIGHNESS.
NOW SHUT YOUR MURDERING MOUTH AND--
FLY, CURSE YOU! FLY!
IT'S THEM!
WHO--?

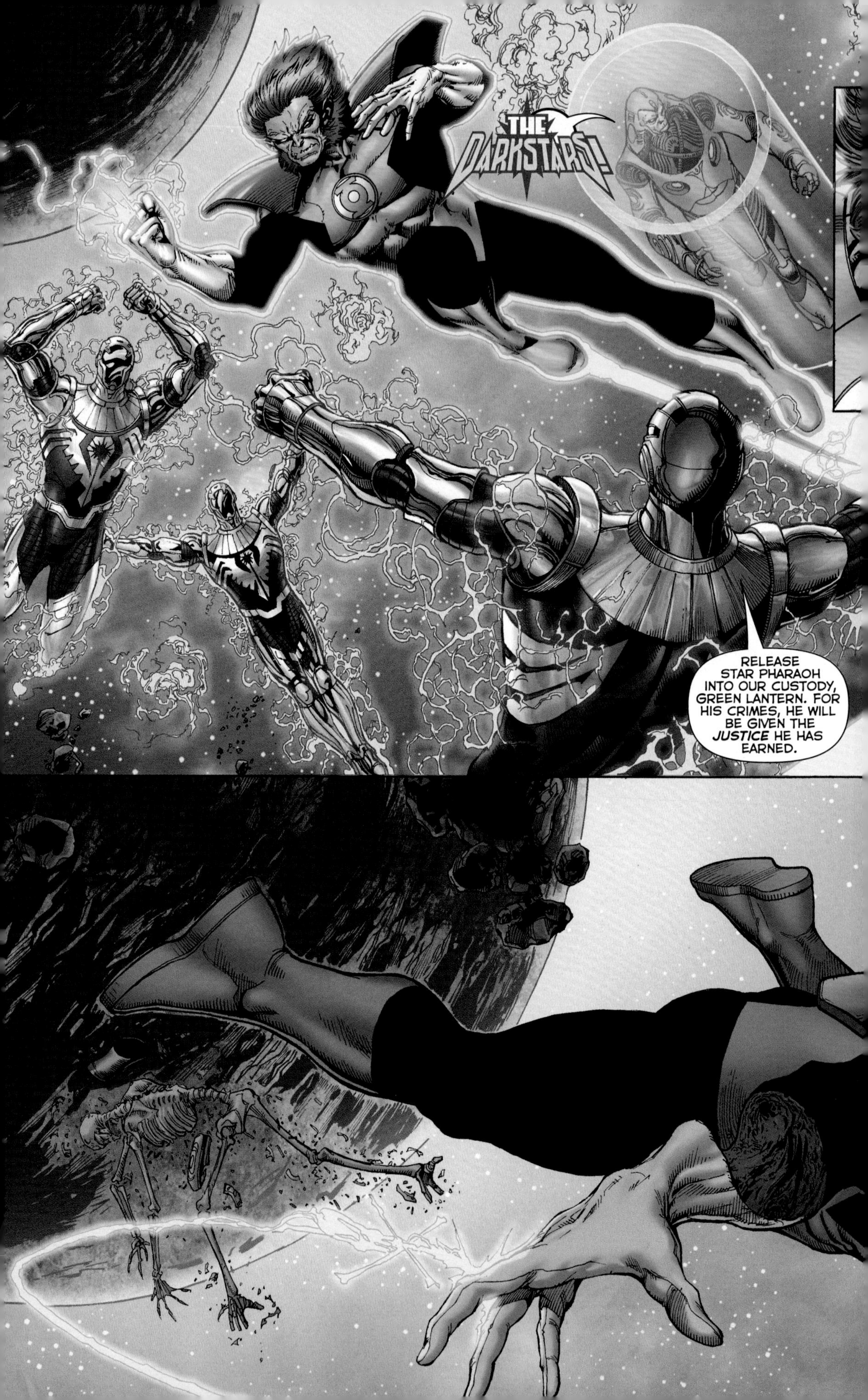
THE DARKSTARS!
RELEASE STAR PHARAOH INTO OUR CUSTODY, GREEN LANTERN. FOR HIS CRIMES, HE WILL BE GIVEN THE *JUSTICE* HE HAS EARNED.

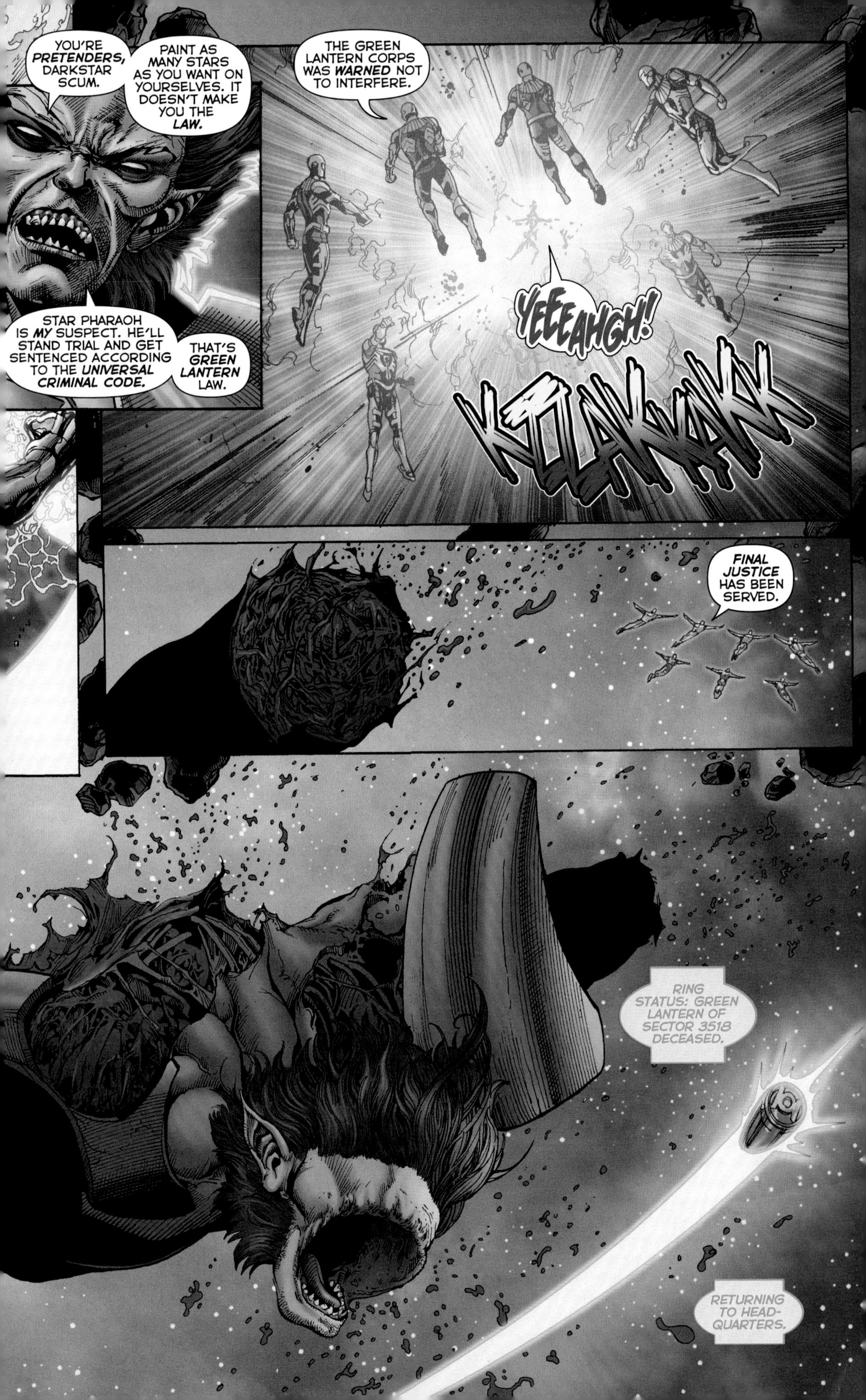
YOU'RE PRETENDERS, DARKSTAR SCUM.
PAINT AS MANY STARS AS YOU WANT ON YOURSELVES. IT DOESN'T MAKE YOU THE LAW.
STAR PHARAOH IS MY SUSPECT. HE'LL STAND TRIAL AND GET SENTENCED ACCORDING TO THE UNIVERSAL CRIMINAL CODE.
THAT'S GREEN LANTERN LAW.
THE GREEN LANTERN CORPS WAS WARNED NOT TO INTERFERE.
YEEEAHGH!
KZZAKAKK
FINAL JUSTICE HAS BEEN SERVED.
RING STATUS: GREEN LANTERN OF SECTOR 3518 DECEASED.
RETURNING TO HEAD-QUARTERS.

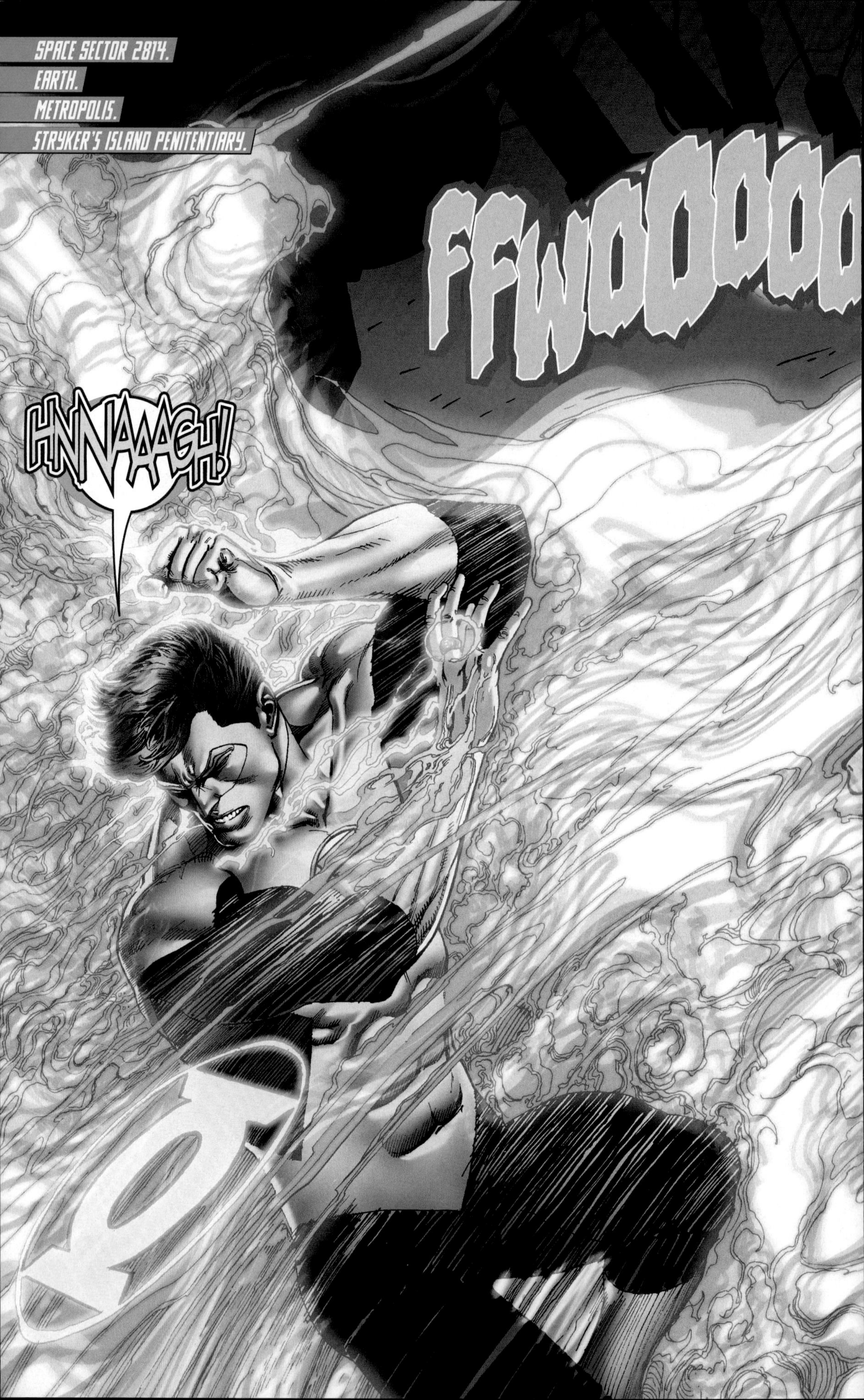
SPACE SECTOR 2814.
EARTH.
METROPOLIS.
STRYKER'S ISLAND PENITENTIARY.
FFWOOOOO
HNNAAAGH!

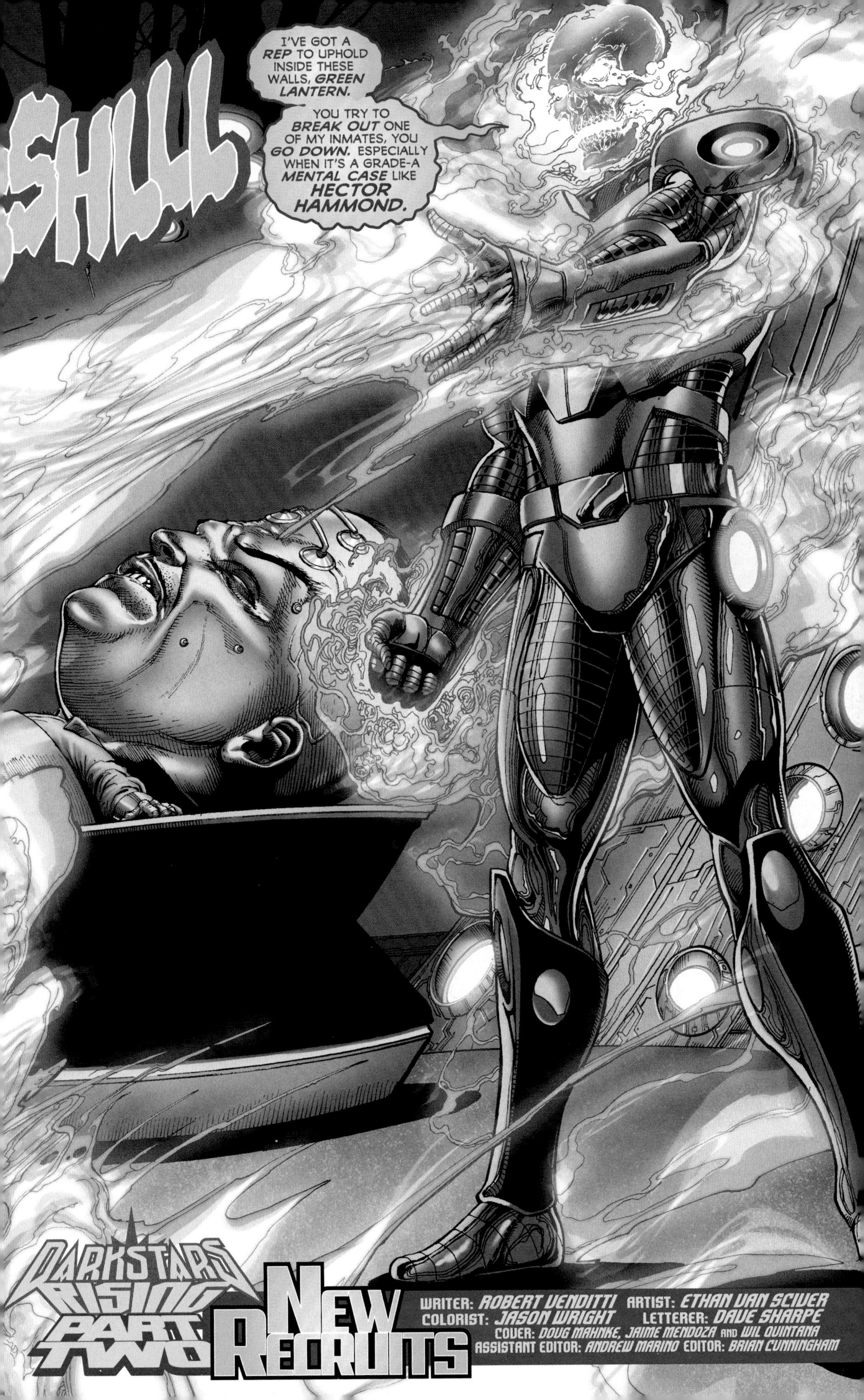
SHUUL
I'VE GOT A REP TO UPHOLD INSIDE THESE WALLS, GREEN LANTERN.
YOU TRY TO BREAK OUT ONE OF MY INMATES, YOU GO DOWN. ESPECIALLY WHEN IT'S A GRADE-A MENTAL CASE LIKE HECTOR HAMMOND.
DARKSTARS RISING PART TWO
NEW RECRUITS
WRITER: ROBERT VENDITTI ARTIST: ETHAN VAN SCIVER
COLORIST: JASON WRIGHT LETTERER: DAVE SHARPE
COVER: DOUG MAHNKE, JAIME MENDOZA AND WIL QUINTANA
ASSISTANT EDITOR: ANDREW MARINO EDITOR: BRIAN CUNNINGHAM

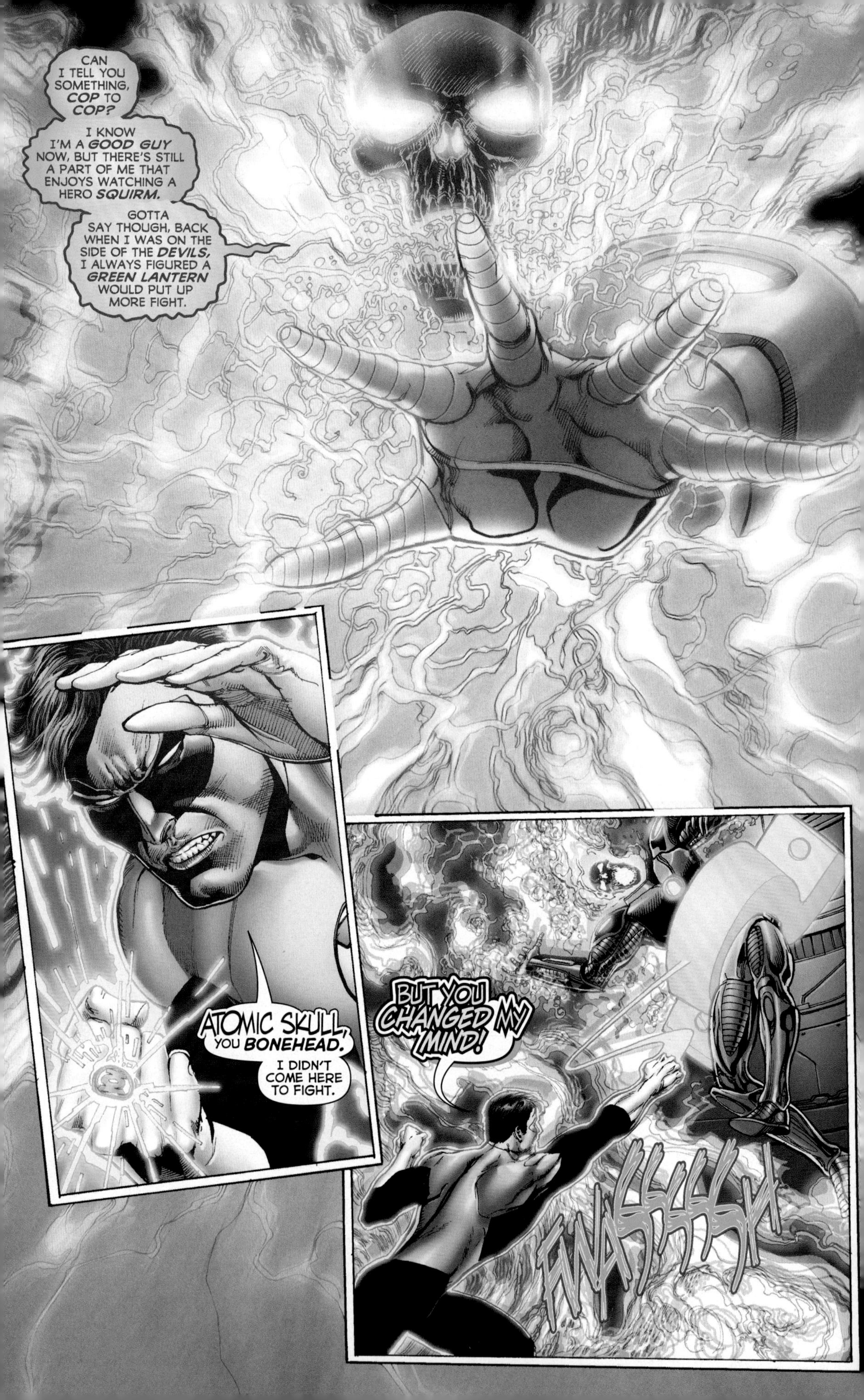
CAN I TELL YOU SOMETHING, COP TO COP?
I KNOW I'M A GOOD GUY NOW, BUT THERE'S STILL A PART OF ME THAT ENJOYS WATCHING A HERO SQUIRM.
GOTTA SAY THOUGH, BACK WHEN I WAS ON THE SIDE OF THE DEVILS, I ALWAYS FIGURED A GREEN LANTERN WOULD PUT UP MORE FIGHT.
ATOMIC SKULL, YOU BONEHEAD.
I DIDN'T COME HERE TO FIGHT.
BUT YOU CHANGED MY MIND!
FWASSSSH

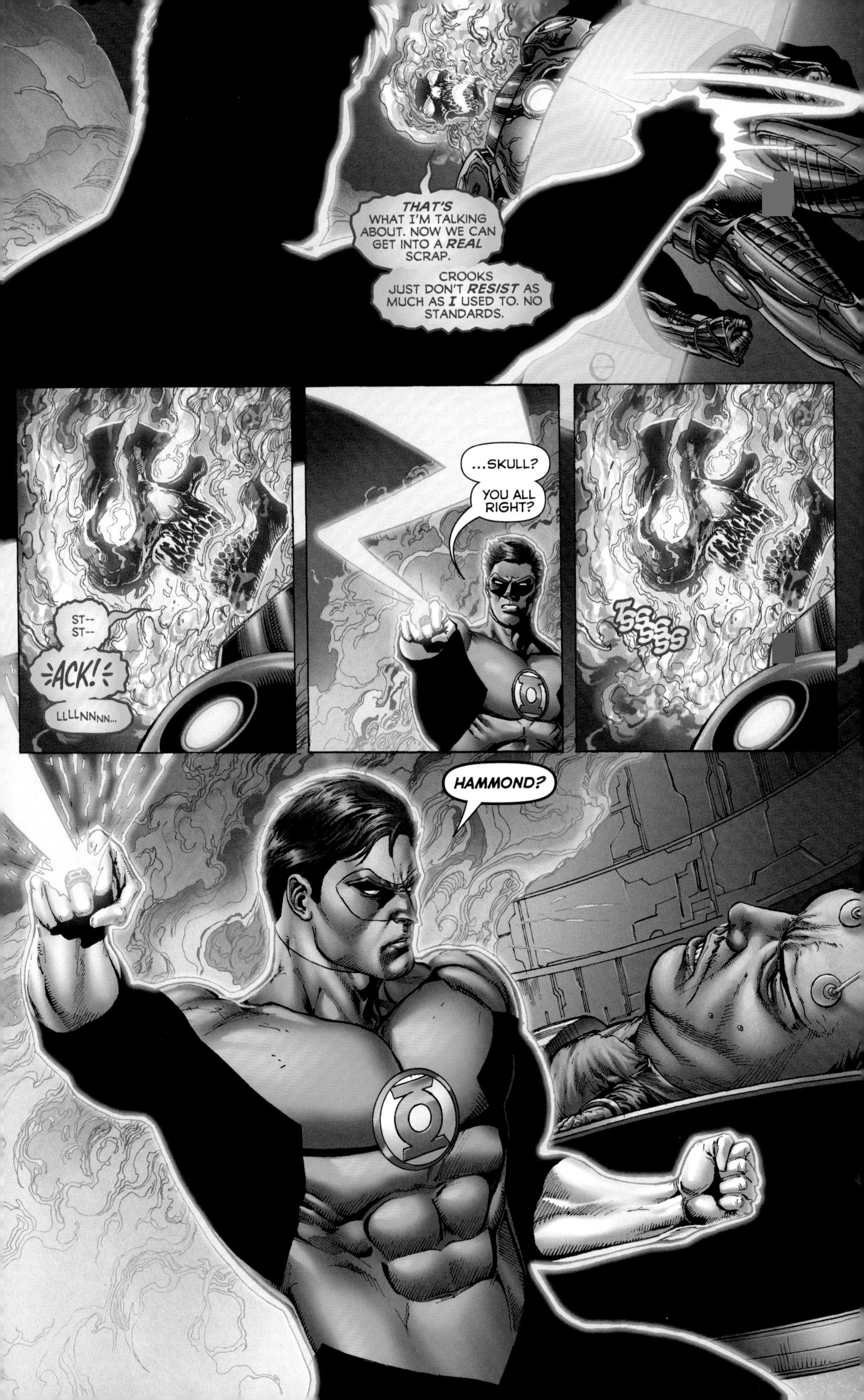

THAT'S WHAT I'M TALKING ABOUT. NOW WE CAN GET INTO A REAL SCRAP.
CROOKS JUST DON'T RESIST AS MUCH AS I USED TO. NO STANDARDS.
ST-- ST--
ACK!
LLLLNNNN...
...SKULL?
YOU ALL RIGHT?
TSSSSS
HAMMOND?

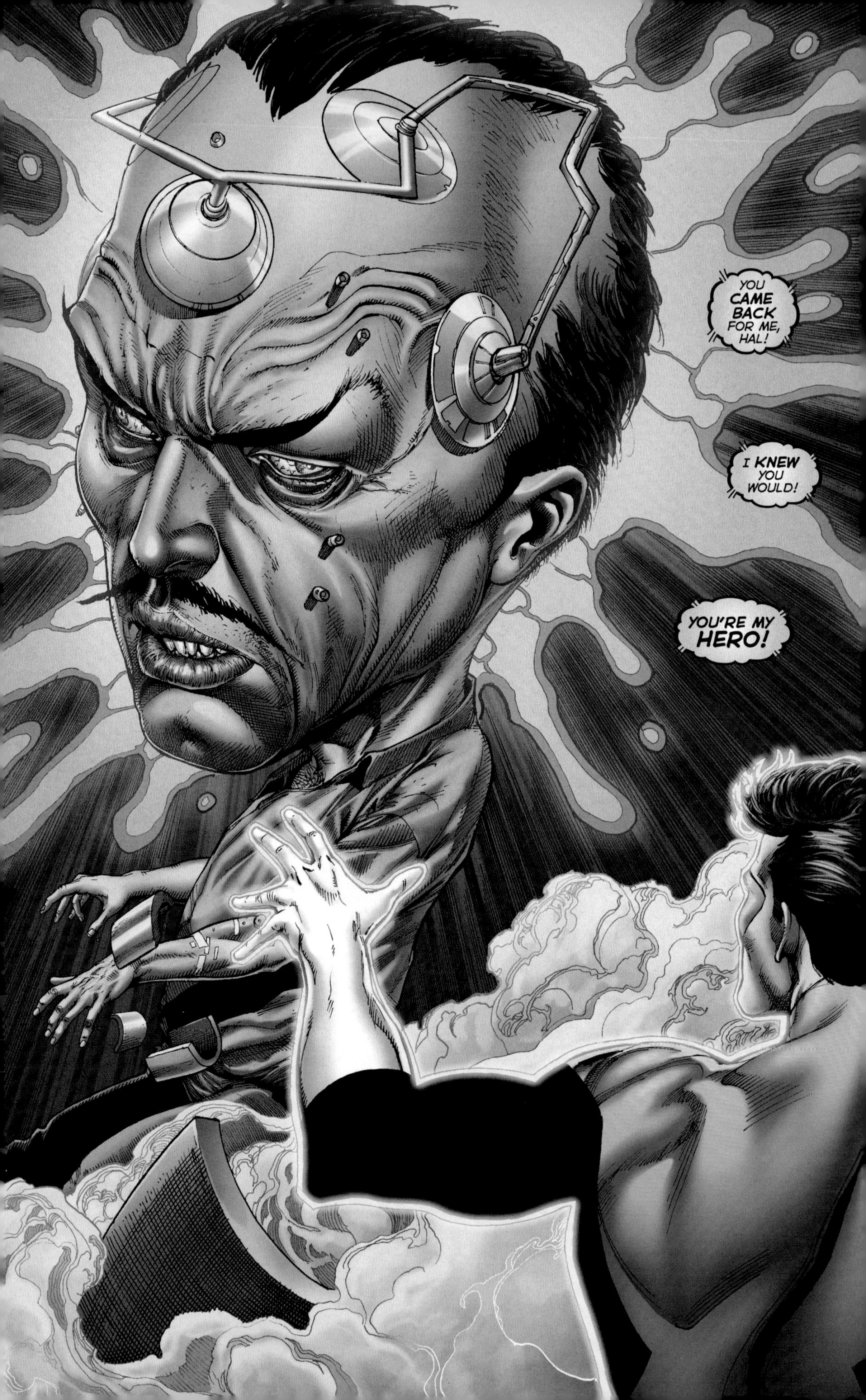
YOU CAME BACK FOR ME, HAL!
I KNEW YOU WOULD!
YOU'RE MY HERO!

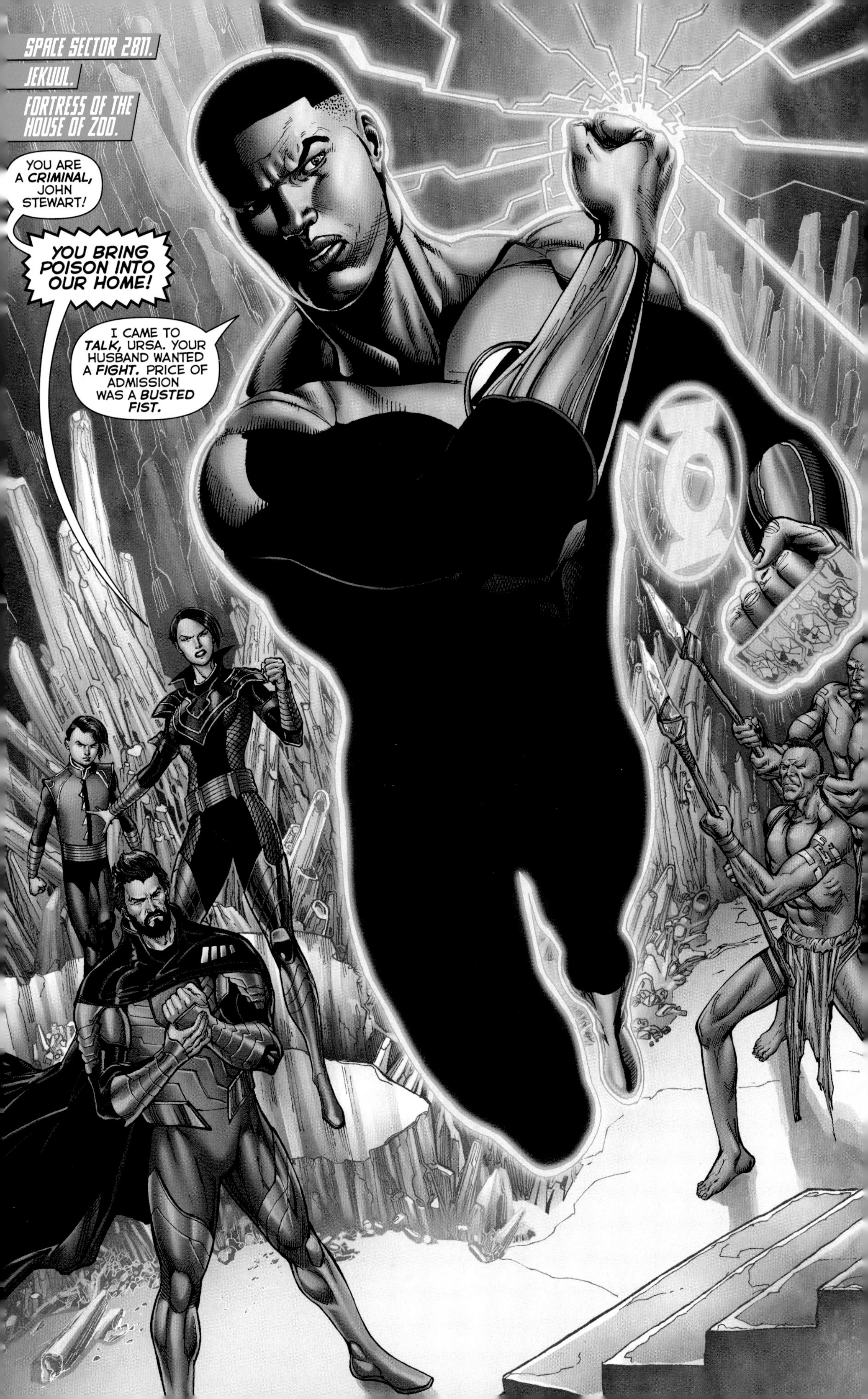
SPACE SECTOR 2811.
JEKUUL.
FORTRESS OF THE HOUSE OF ZOD.
YOU ARE A CRIMINAL, JOHN STEWART!
YOU BRING POISON INTO OUR HOME!
I CAME TO TALK, URSA. YOUR HUSBAND WANTED A FIGHT. PRICE OF ADMISSION WAS A BUSTED FIST.

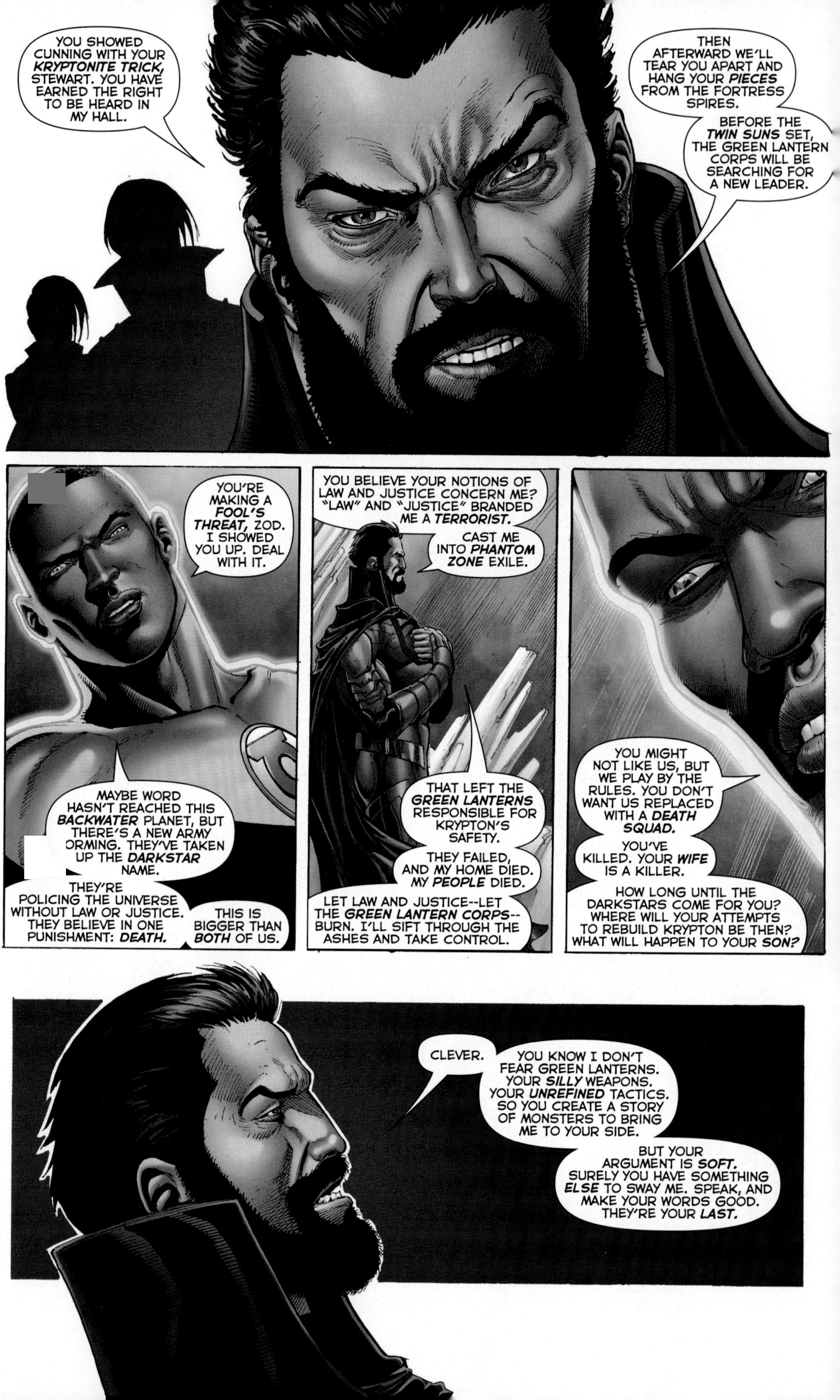
YOU SHOWED CUNNING WITH YOUR KRYPTONITE TRICK, STEWART. YOU HAVE EARNED THE RIGHT TO BE HEARD IN MY HALL.
THEN AFTERWARD WE'LL TEAR YOU APART AND HANG YOUR PIECES FROM THE FORTRESS SPIRES.
BEFORE THE TWIN SUNS SET, THE GREEN LANTERN CORPS WILL BE SEARCHING FOR A NEW LEADER.
YOU'RE MAKING A FOOL'S THREAT, ZOD. I SHOWED YOU UP. DEAL WITH IT.
MAYBE WORD HASN'T REACHED THIS BACKWATER PLANET, BUT THERE'S A NEW ARMY ORMING. THEY'VE TAKEN UP THE DARKSTAR NAME.
THEY'RE POLICING THE UNIVERSE WITHOUT LAW OR JUSTICE. THEY BELIEVE IN ONE PUNISHMENT: DEATH.
THIS IS BIGGER THAN BOTH OF US.
YOU BELIEVE YOUR NOTIONS OF LAW AND JUSTICE CONCERN ME? "LAW" AND "JUSTICE" BRANDED ME A TERRORIST.
CAST ME INTO PHANTOM ZONE EXILE.
THAT LEFT THE GREEN LANTERNS RESPONSIBLE FOR KRYPTON'S SAFETY.
THEY FAILED, AND MY HOME DIED. MY PEOPLE DIED.
LET LAW AND JUSTICE--LET THE GREEN LANTERN CORPS--BURN. I'LL SIFT THROUGH THE ASHES AND TAKE CONTROL.
YOU MIGHT NOT LIKE US, BUT WE PLAY BY THE RULES. YOU DON'T WANT US REPLACED WITH A DEATH SQUAD.
YOU'VE KILLED. YOUR WIFE IS A KILLER.
HOW LONG UNTIL THE DARKSTARS COME FOR YOU? WHERE WILL YOUR ATTEMPTS TO REBUILD KRYPTON BE THEN? WHAT WILL HAPPEN TO YOUR SON?
CLEVER.
YOU KNOW I DON'T FEAR GREEN LANTERNS. YOUR SILLY WEAPONS. YOUR UNREFINED TACTICS. SO YOU CREATE A STORY OF MONSTERS TO BRING ME TO YOUR SIDE.
BUT YOUR ARGUMENT IS SOFT. SURELY YOU HAVE SOMETHING ELSE TO SWAY ME. SPEAK, AND MAKE YOUR WORDS GOOD. THEY'RE YOUR LAST.

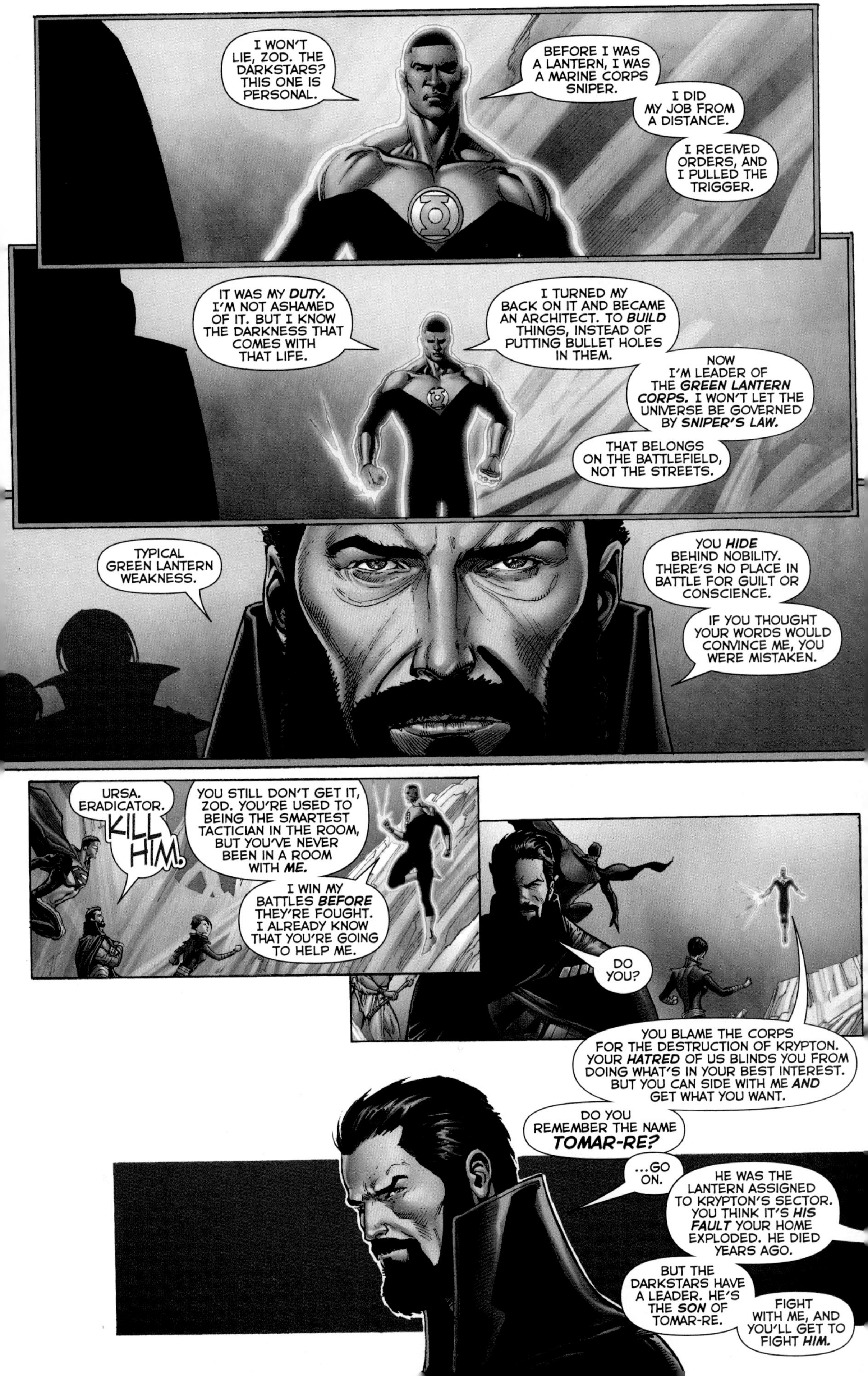
I WON'T LIE, ZOD. THE DARKSTARS? THIS ONE IS PERSONAL.
BEFORE I WAS A LANTERN, I WAS A MARINE CORPS SNIPER.
I DID MY JOB FROM A DISTANCE.
I RECEIVED ORDERS, AND I PULLED THE TRIGGER.
IT WAS MY *DUTY.* I'M NOT ASHAMED OF IT. BUT I KNOW THE DARKNESS THAT COMES WITH THAT LIFE.
I TURNED MY BACK ON IT AND BECAME AN ARCHITECT. TO *BUILD* THINGS, INSTEAD OF PUTTING BULLET HOLES IN THEM.
NOW I'M LEADER OF THE *GREEN LANTERN CORPS.* I WON'T LET THE UNIVERSE BE GOVERNED BY *SNIPER'S LAW.*
THAT BELONGS ON THE BATTLEFIELD, NOT THE STREETS.
TYPICAL GREEN LANTERN WEAKNESS.
YOU *HIDE* BEHIND NOBILITY. THERE'S NO PLACE IN BATTLE FOR GUILT OR CONSCIENCE.
IF YOU THOUGHT YOUR WORDS WOULD CONVINCE ME, YOU WERE MISTAKEN.
URSA. ERADICATOR. KILL HIM.
YOU STILL DON'T GET IT, ZOD. YOU'RE USED TO BEING THE SMARTEST TACTICIAN IN THE ROOM, BUT YOU'VE NEVER BEEN IN A ROOM WITH *ME.*
I WIN MY BATTLES *BEFORE* THEY'RE FOUGHT. I ALREADY KNOW THAT YOU'RE GOING TO HELP ME.
DO YOU?
YOU BLAME THE CORPS FOR THE DESTRUCTION OF KRYPTON. YOUR *HATRED* OF US BLINDS YOU FROM DOING WHAT'S IN YOUR BEST INTEREST. BUT YOU CAN SIDE WITH ME *AND* GET WHAT YOU WANT.
DO YOU REMEMBER THE NAME *TOMAR-RE?*
...GO ON.
HE WAS THE LANTERN ASSIGNED TO KRYPTON'S SECTOR. YOU THINK IT'S *HIS FAULT* YOUR HOME EXPLODED. HE DIED YEARS AGO.
BUT THE DARKSTARS HAVE A LEADER. HE'S THE *SON* OF TOMAR-RE.
FIGHT WITH ME, AND YOU'LL GET TO FIGHT *HIM.*

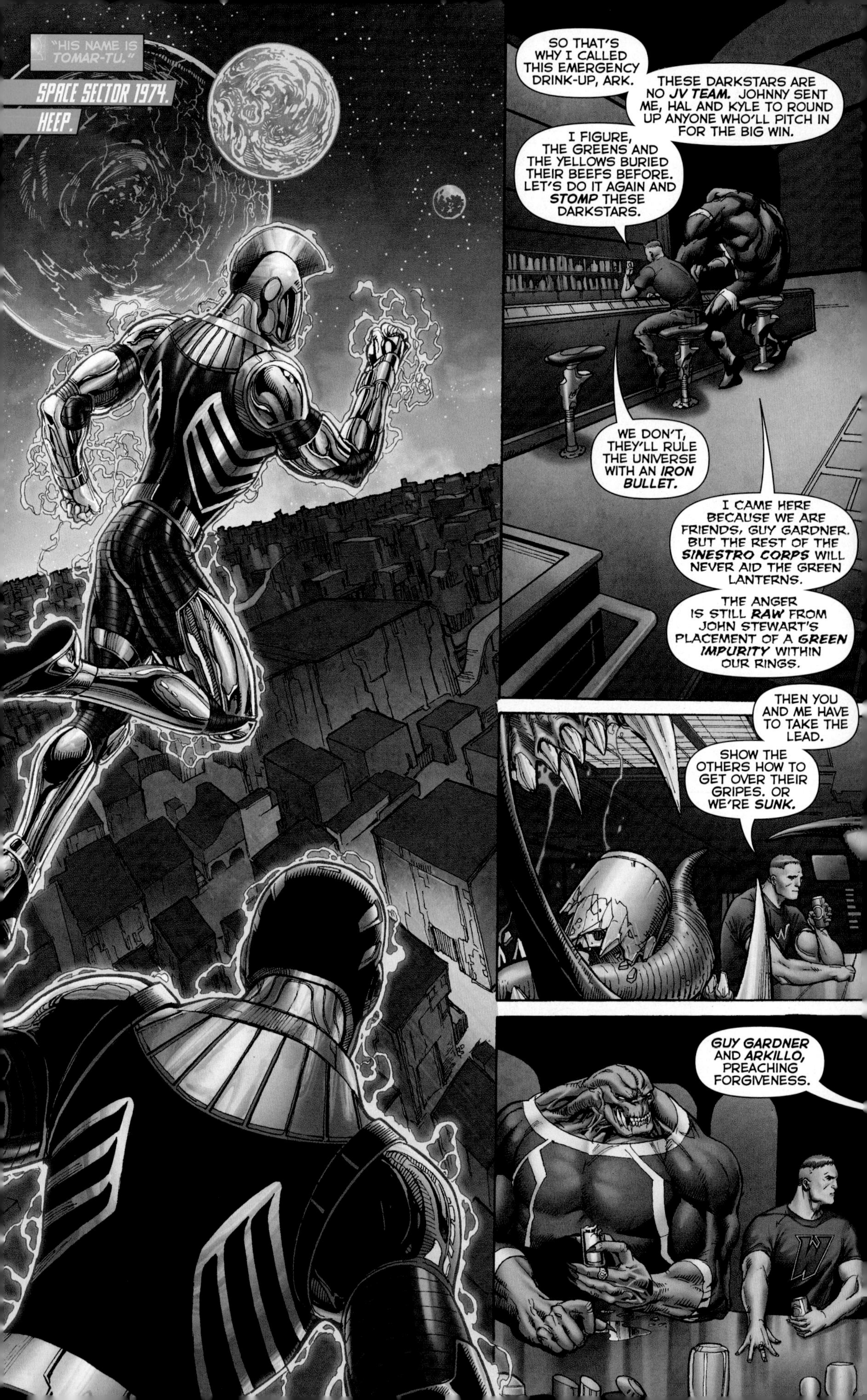
"HIS NAME IS TOMAR-TU."
SPACE SECTOR 1974.
HEEP.
SO THAT'S WHY I CALLED THIS EMERGENCY DRINK-UP, ARK.
THESE DARKSTARS ARE NO JV TEAM. JOHNNY SENT ME, HAL AND KYLE TO ROUND UP ANYONE WHO'LL PITCH IN FOR THE BIG WIN.
I FIGURE, THE GREENS AND THE YELLOWS BURIED THEIR BEEFS BEFORE. LET'S DO IT AGAIN AND STOMP THESE DARKSTARS.
WE DON'T, THEY'LL RULE THE UNIVERSE WITH AN IRON BULLET.
I CAME HERE BECAUSE WE ARE FRIENDS, GUY GARDNER. BUT THE REST OF THE SINESTRO CORPS WILL NEVER AID THE GREEN LANTERNS.
THE ANGER IS STILL RAW FROM JOHN STEWART'S PLACEMENT OF A GREEN IMPURITY WITHIN OUR RINGS.
THEN YOU AND ME HAVE TO TAKE THE LEAD.
SHOW THE OTHERS HOW TO GET OVER THEIR GRIPES. OR WE'RE SUNK.
GUY GARDNER AND ARKILLO, PREACHING FORGIVENESS.

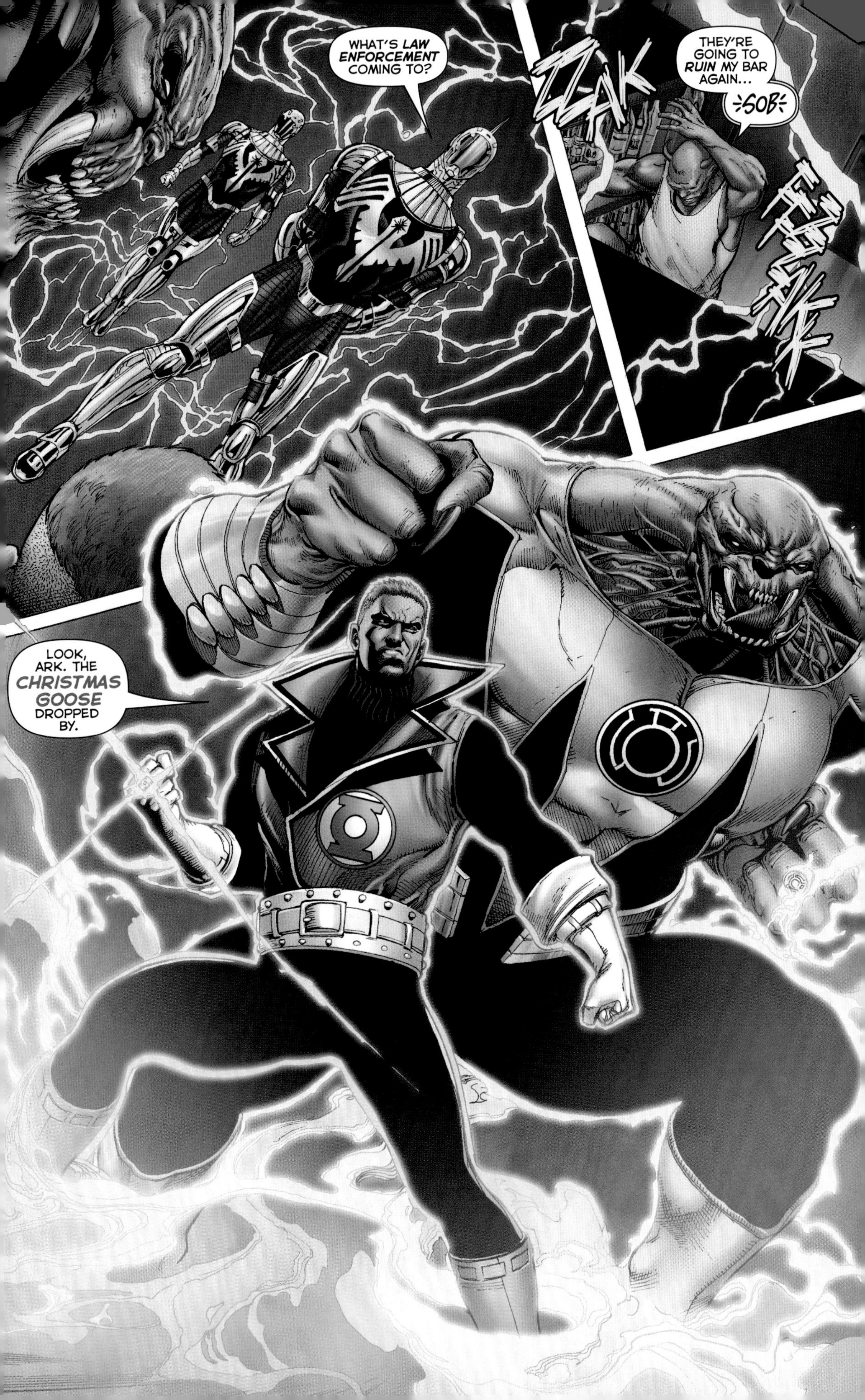
WHAT'S LAW ENFORCEMENT COMING TO?
ZZAK
THEY'RE GOING TO RUIN MY BAR AGAIN...
SOB
LOOK, ARK. THE CHRISTMAS GOOSE DROPPED BY.

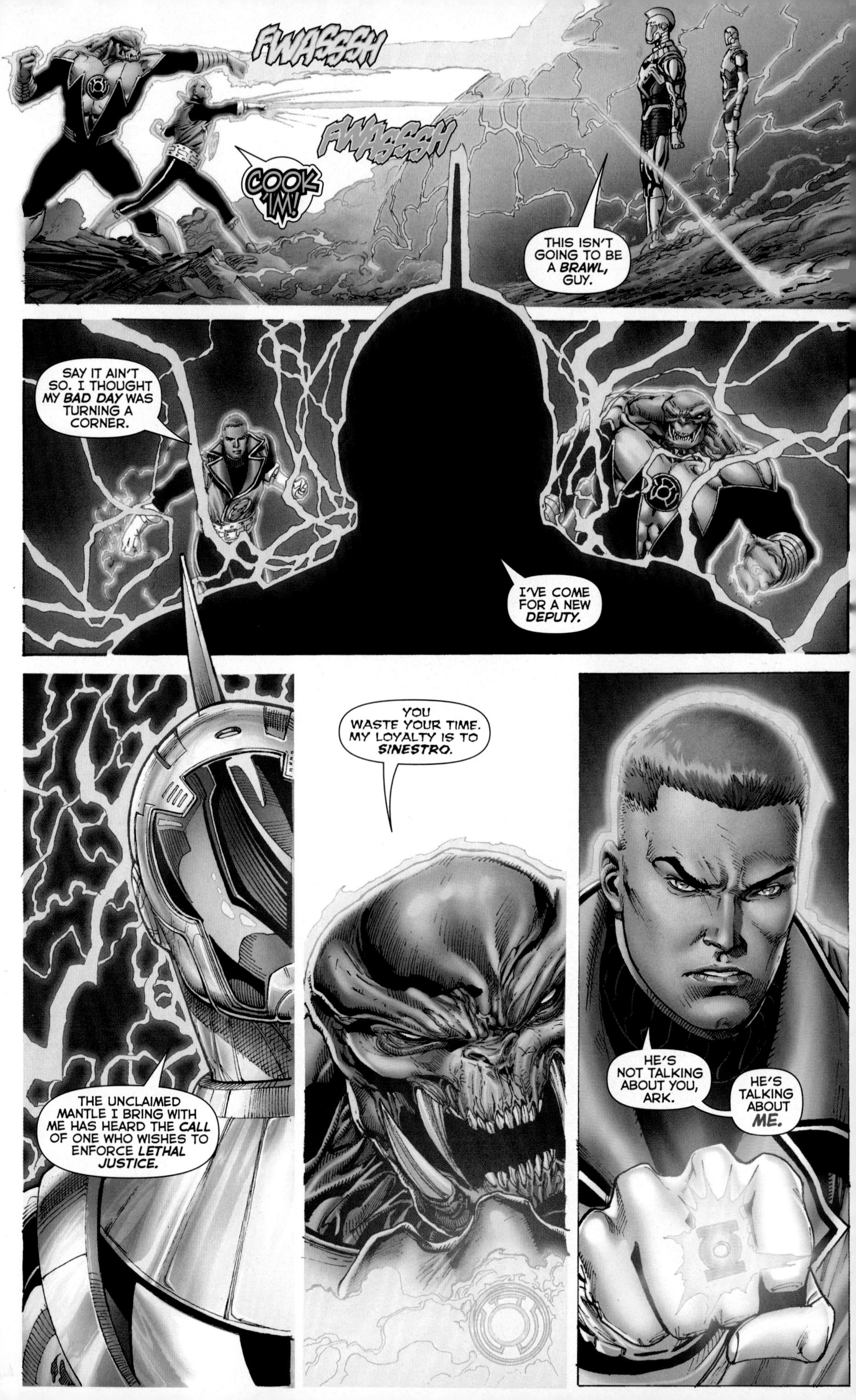
FWASSSH
COOK 'IM!
FWASSSH
THIS ISN'T GOING TO BE A BRAWL, GUY.
SAY IT AIN'T SO. I THOUGHT MY BAD DAY WAS TURNING A CORNER.
I'VE COME FOR A NEW DEPUTY.
THE UNCLAIMED MANTLE I BRING WITH ME HAS HEARD THE CALL OF ONE WHO WISHES TO ENFORCE LETHAL JUSTICE.
YOU WASTE YOUR TIME. MY LOYALTY IS TO SINESTRO.
HE'S NOT TALKING ABOUT YOU, ARK.
HE'S TALKING ABOUT ME.

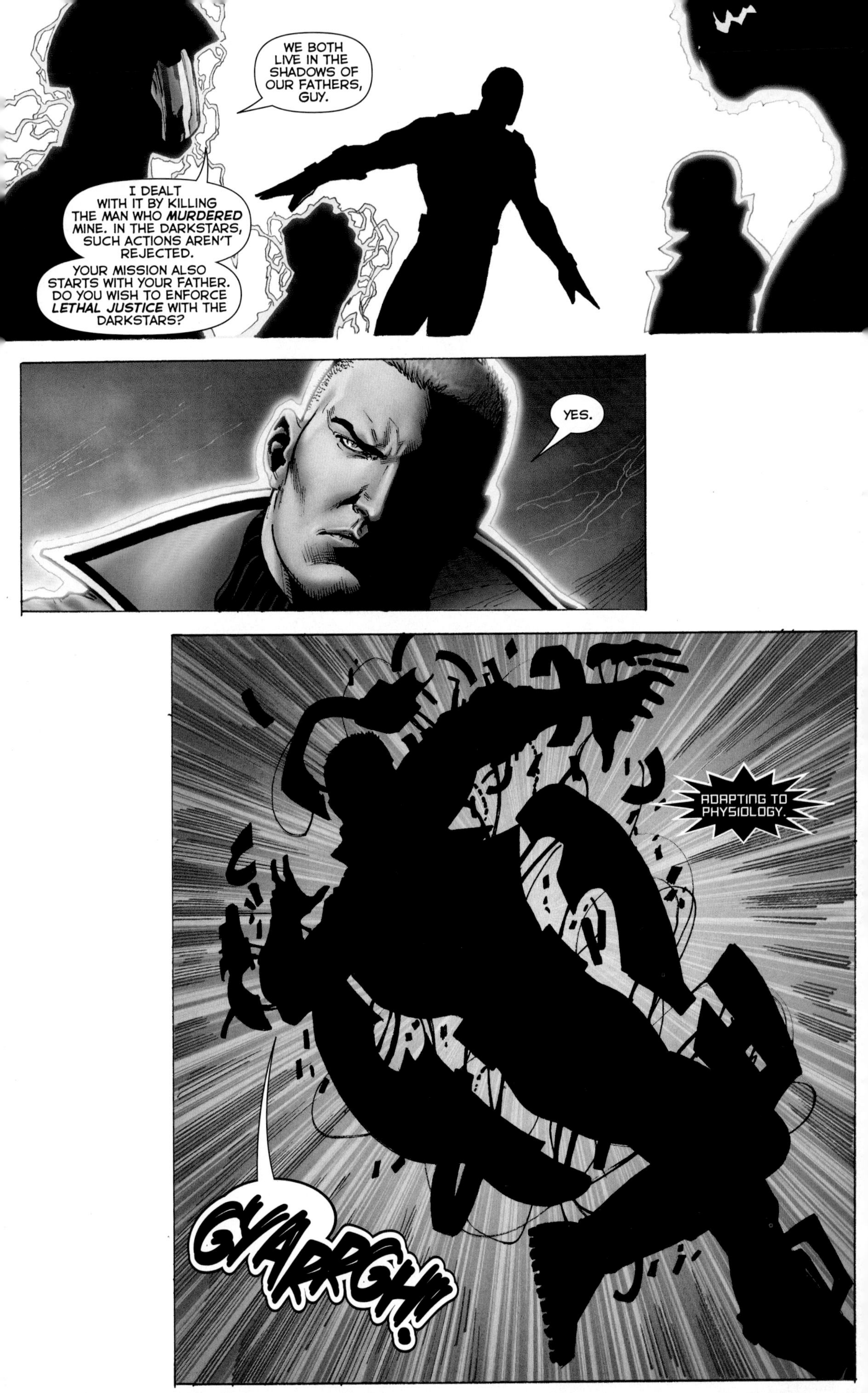
WE BOTH LIVE IN THE SHADOWS OF OUR FATHERS, GUY.
I DEALT WITH IT BY KILLING THE MAN WHO *MURDERED* MINE. IN THE DARKSTARS, SUCH ACTIONS AREN'T REJECTED.
YOUR MISSION ALSO STARTS WITH YOUR FATHER. DO YOU WISH TO ENFORCE *LETHAL JUSTICE* WITH THE DARKSTARS?
YES.
ADAPTING TO PHYSIOLOGY.
GYARRGH!!

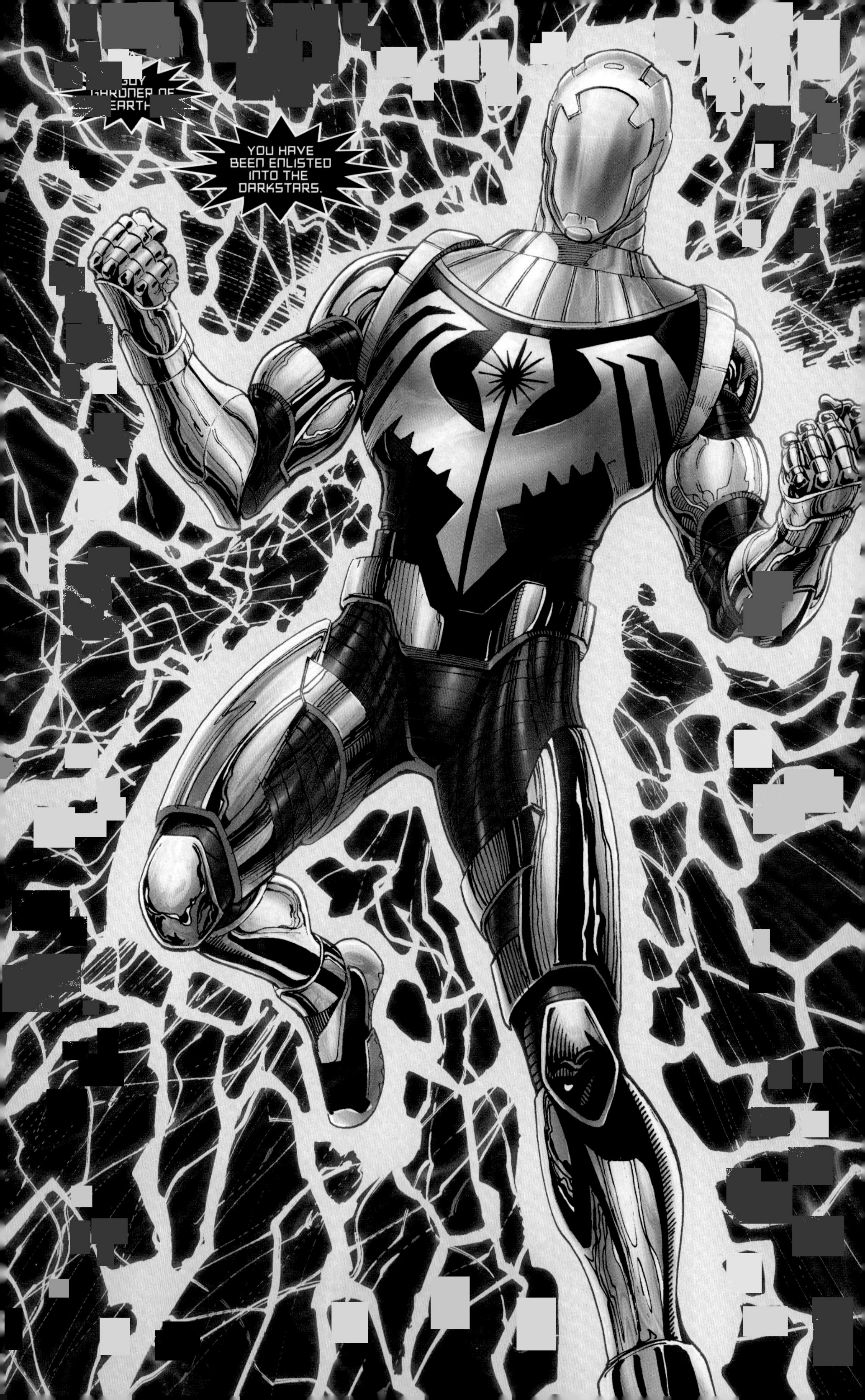
GUY GARDNER OF EARTH
YOU HAVE BEEN ENLISTED INTO THE DARKSTARS.

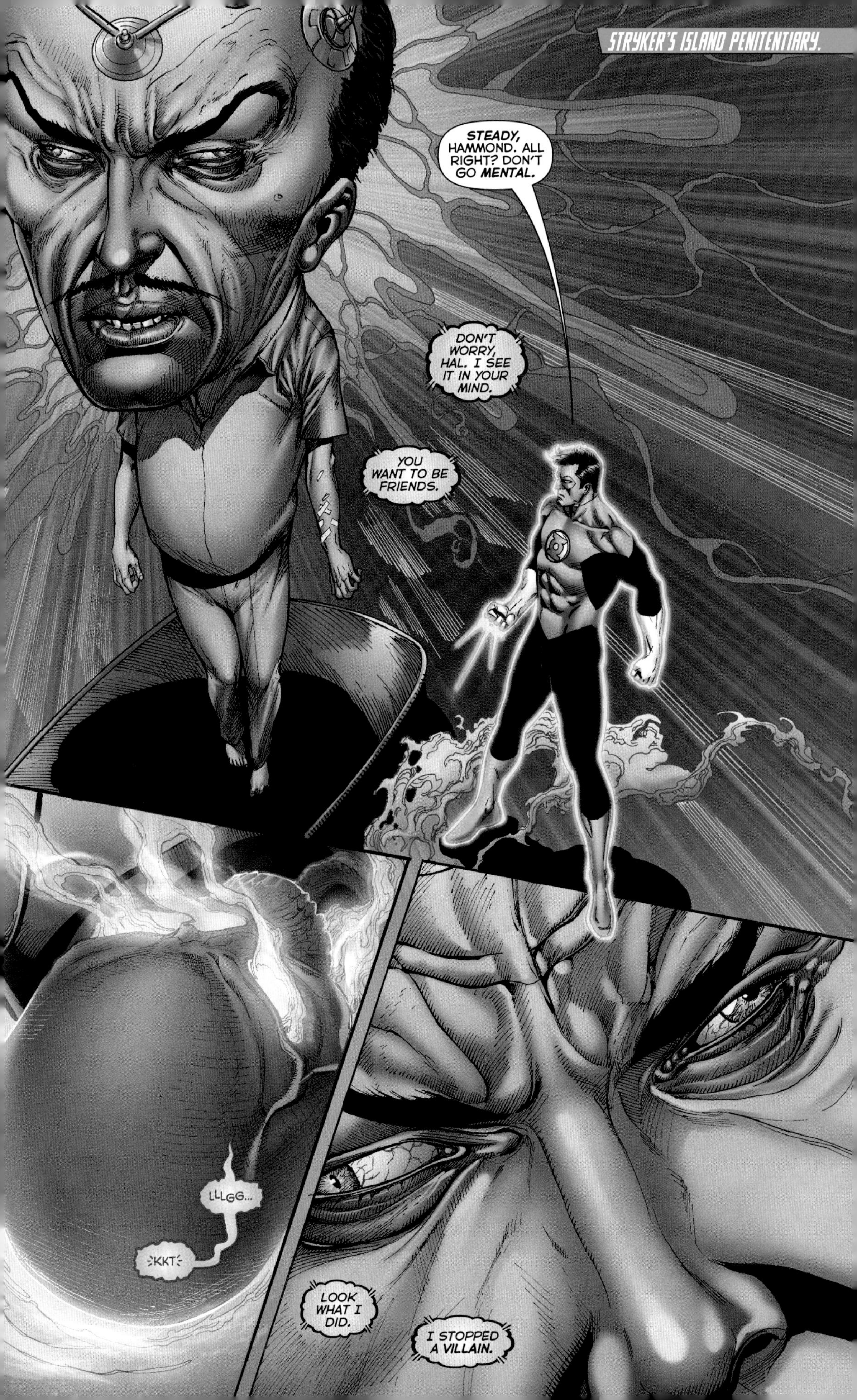
STRYKER'S ISLAND PENITENTIARY.
STEADY, HAMMOND. ALL RIGHT? DON'T GO MENTAL.
DON'T WORRY, HAL. I SEE IT IN YOUR MIND.
YOU WANT TO BE FRIENDS.
LLLGG...
KKT
LOOK WHAT I DID.
I STOPPED A VILLAIN.

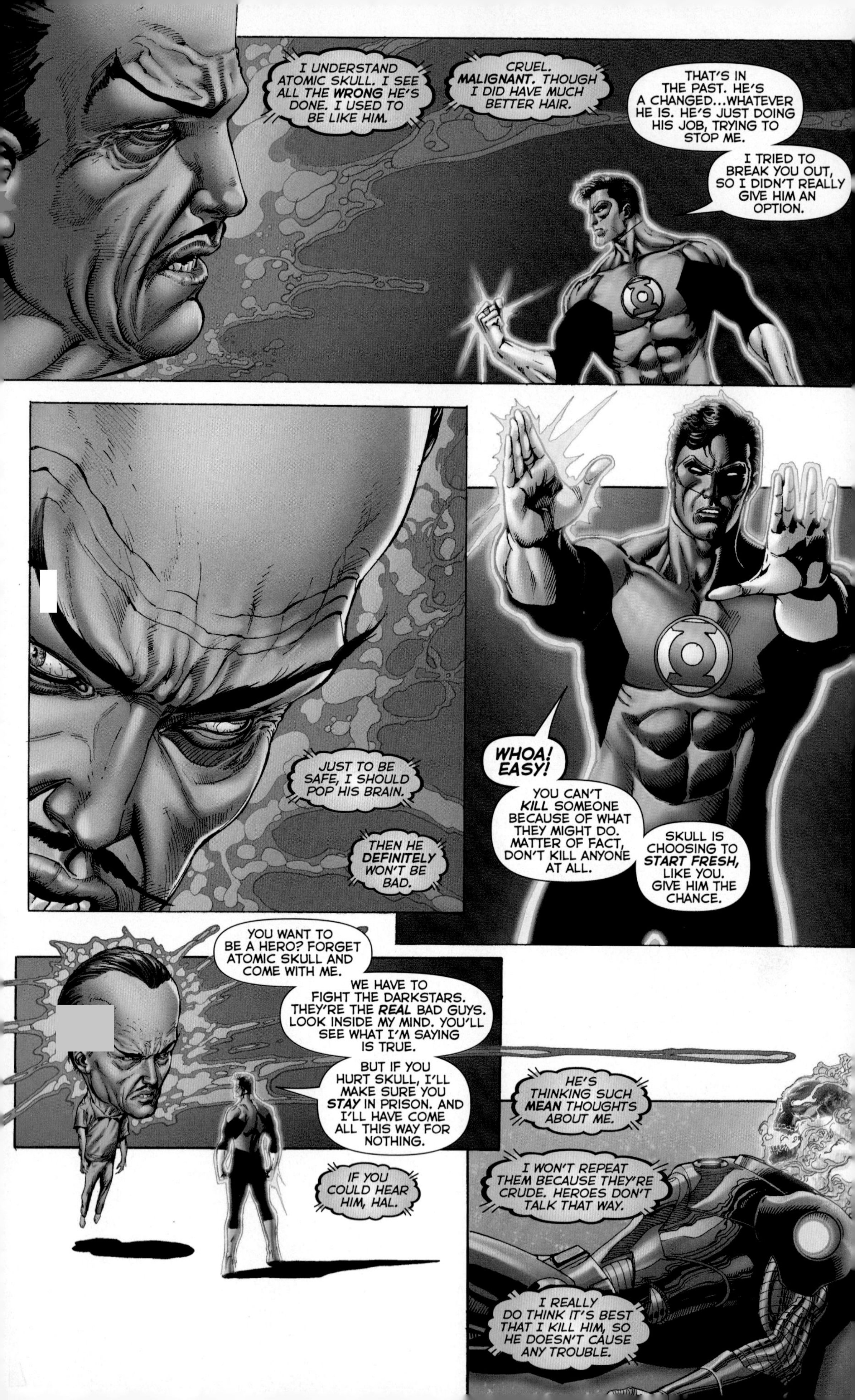
I UNDERSTAND ATOMIC SKULL. I SEE ALL THE WRONG HE'S DONE. I USED TO BE LIKE HIM.
CRUEL. MALIGNANT. THOUGH I DID HAVE MUCH BETTER HAIR.
THAT'S IN THE PAST. HE'S A CHANGED...WHATEVER HE IS. HE'S JUST DOING HIS JOB, TRYING TO STOP ME.
I TRIED TO BREAK YOU OUT, SO I DIDN'T REALLY GIVE HIM AN OPTION.
JUST TO BE SAFE, I SHOULD POP HIS BRAIN.
THEN HE DEFINITELY WON'T BE BAD.
WHOA! EASY!
YOU CAN'T KILL SOMEONE BECAUSE OF WHAT THEY MIGHT DO. MATTER OF FACT, DON'T KILL ANYONE AT ALL.
SKULL IS CHOOSING TO START FRESH, LIKE YOU. GIVE HIM THE CHANCE.
YOU WANT TO BE A HERO? FORGET ATOMIC SKULL AND COME WITH ME.
WE HAVE TO FIGHT THE DARKSTARS. THEY'RE THE REAL BAD GUYS. LOOK INSIDE MY MIND. YOU'LL SEE WHAT I'M SAYING IS TRUE.
BUT IF YOU HURT SKULL, I'LL MAKE SURE YOU STAY IN PRISON. AND I'LL HAVE COME ALL THIS WAY FOR NOTHING.
IF YOU COULD HEAR HIM, HAL.
HE'S THINKING SUCH MEAN THOUGHTS ABOUT ME.
I WON'T REPEAT THEM BECAUSE THEY'RE CRUDE. HEROES DON'T TALK THAT WAY.
I REALLY DO THINK IT'S BEST THAT I KILL HIM, SO HE DOESN'T CAUSE ANY TROUBLE.

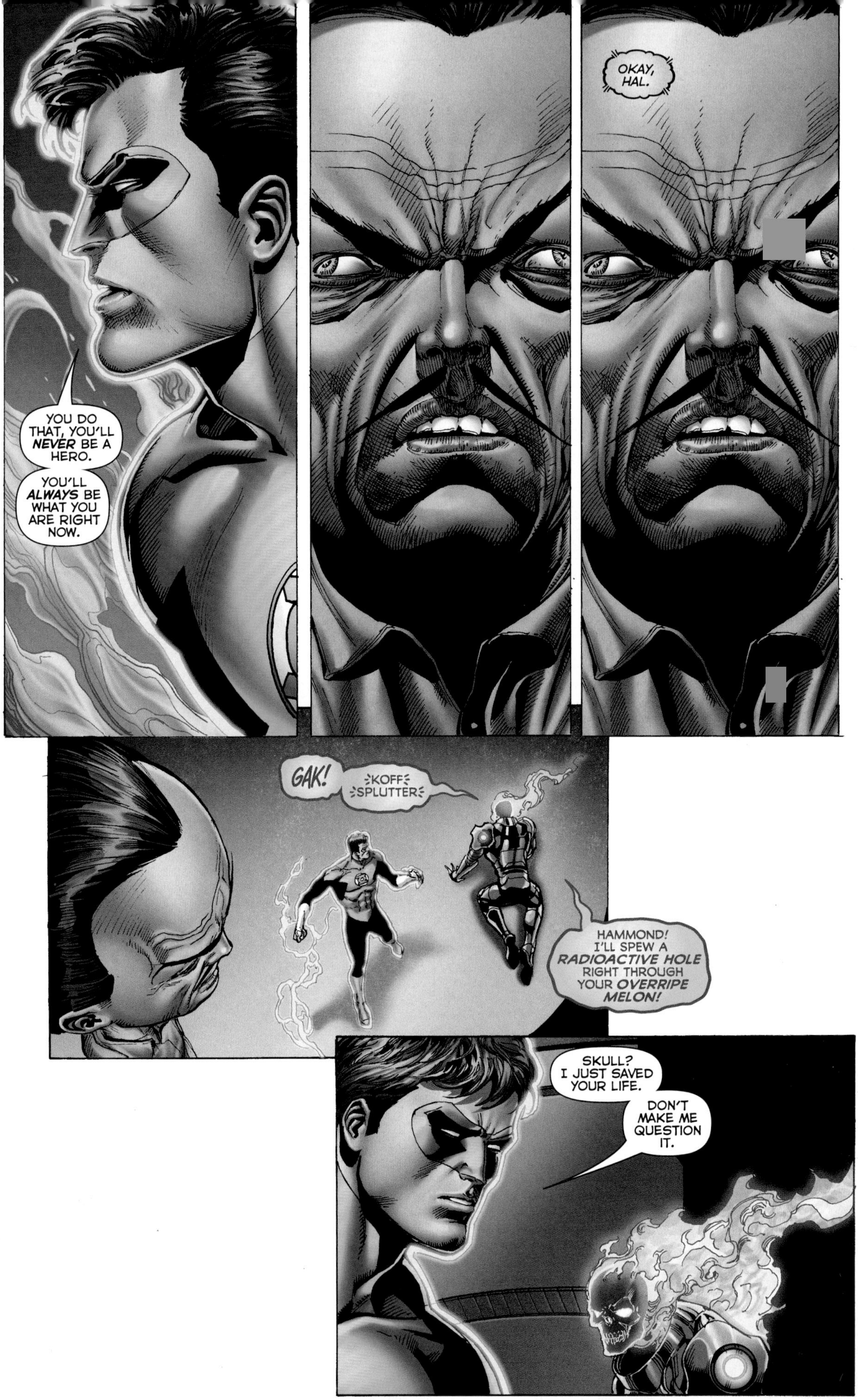
YOU DO THAT, YOU'LL NEVER BE A HERO.
YOU'LL ALWAYS BE WHAT YOU ARE RIGHT NOW.
OKAY, HAL.
GAK!
KOFF SPLUTTER
HAMMOND! I'LL SPEW A RADIOACTIVE HOLE RIGHT THROUGH YOUR OVERRIPE MELON!
SKULL? I JUST SAVED YOUR LIFE.
DON'T MAKE ME QUESTION IT.

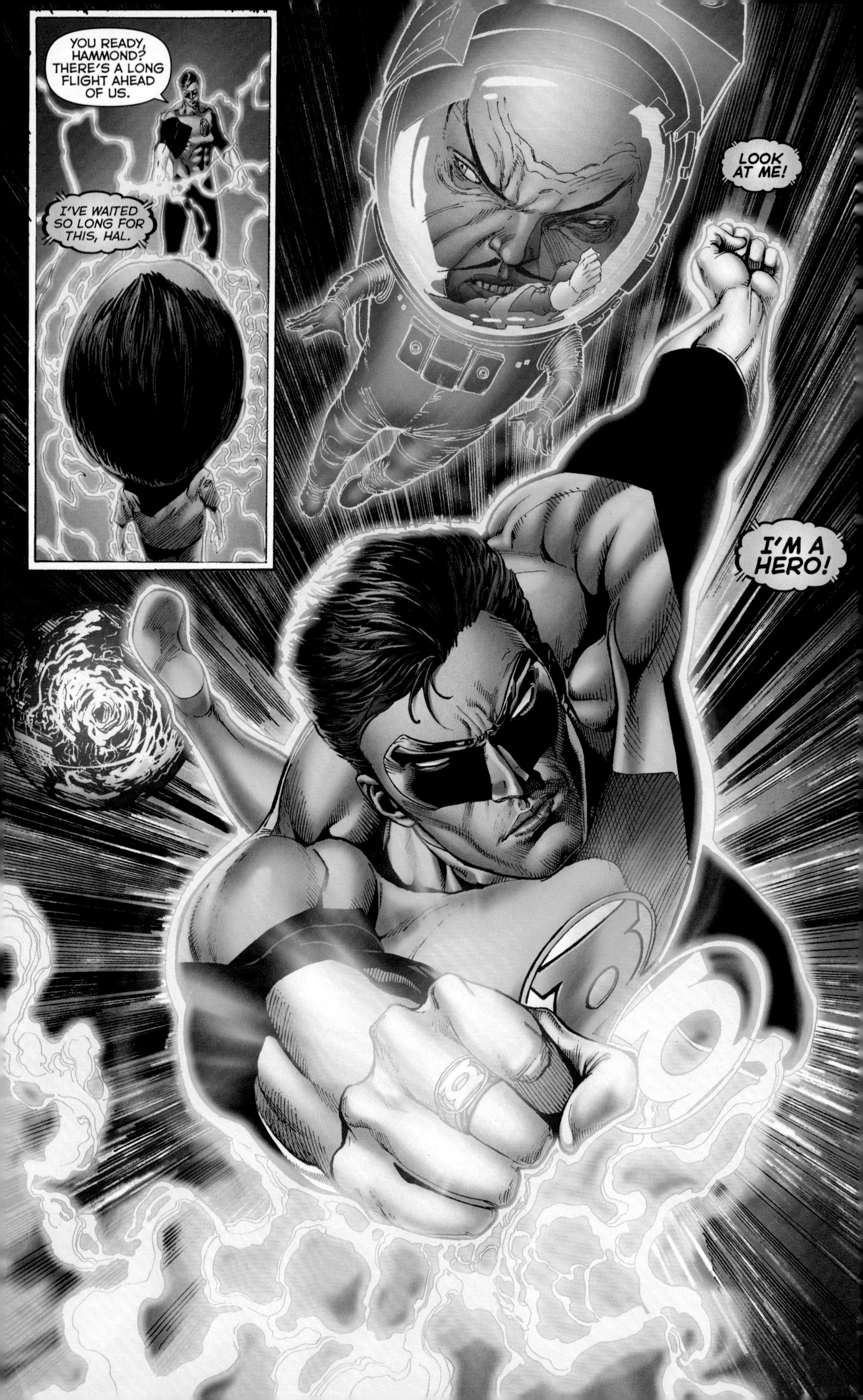
YOU READY, HAMMOND? THERE'S A LONG FLIGHT AHEAD OF US.
I'VE WAITED SO LONG FOR THIS, HAL.
LOOK AT ME!
I'M A HERO!

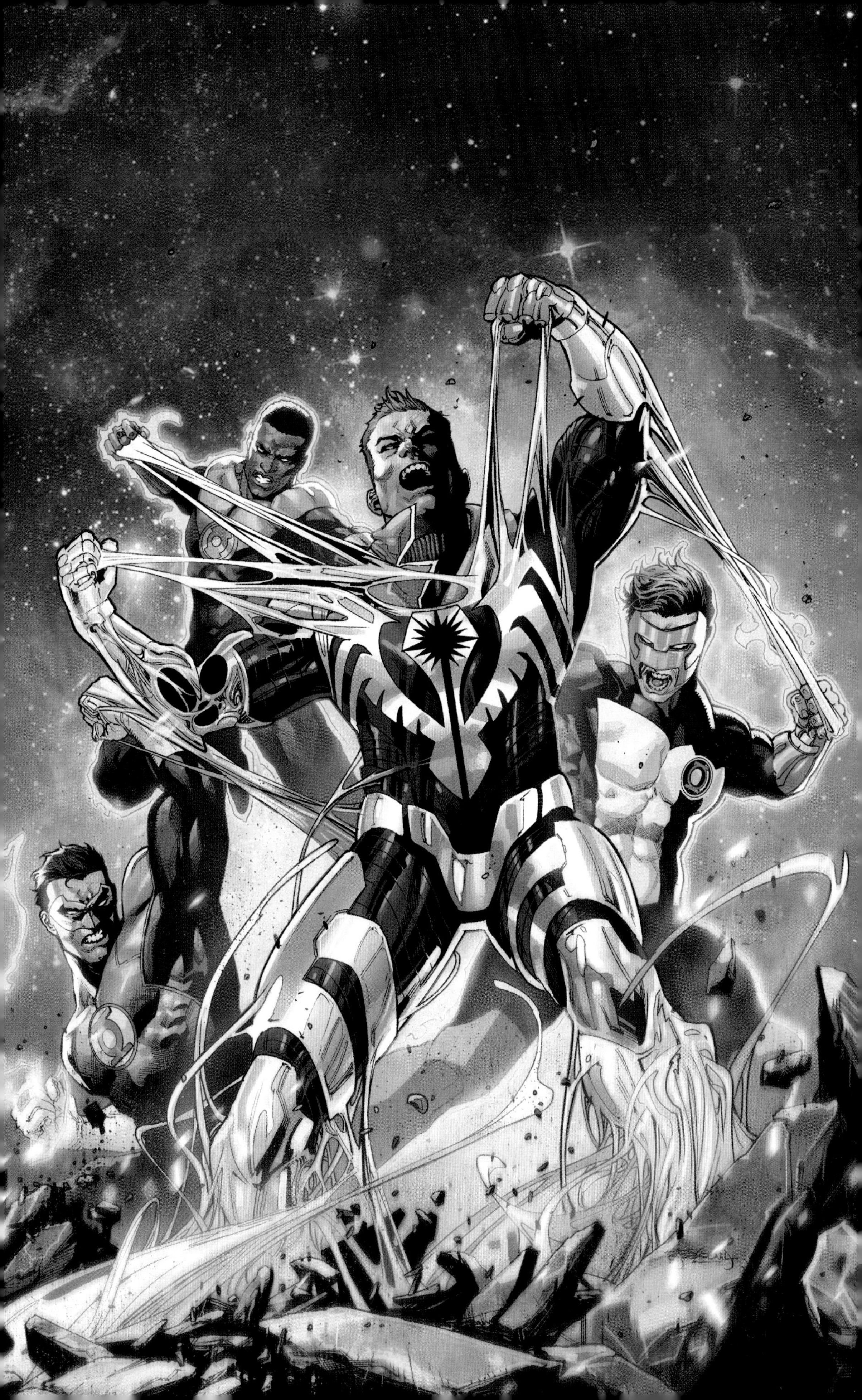

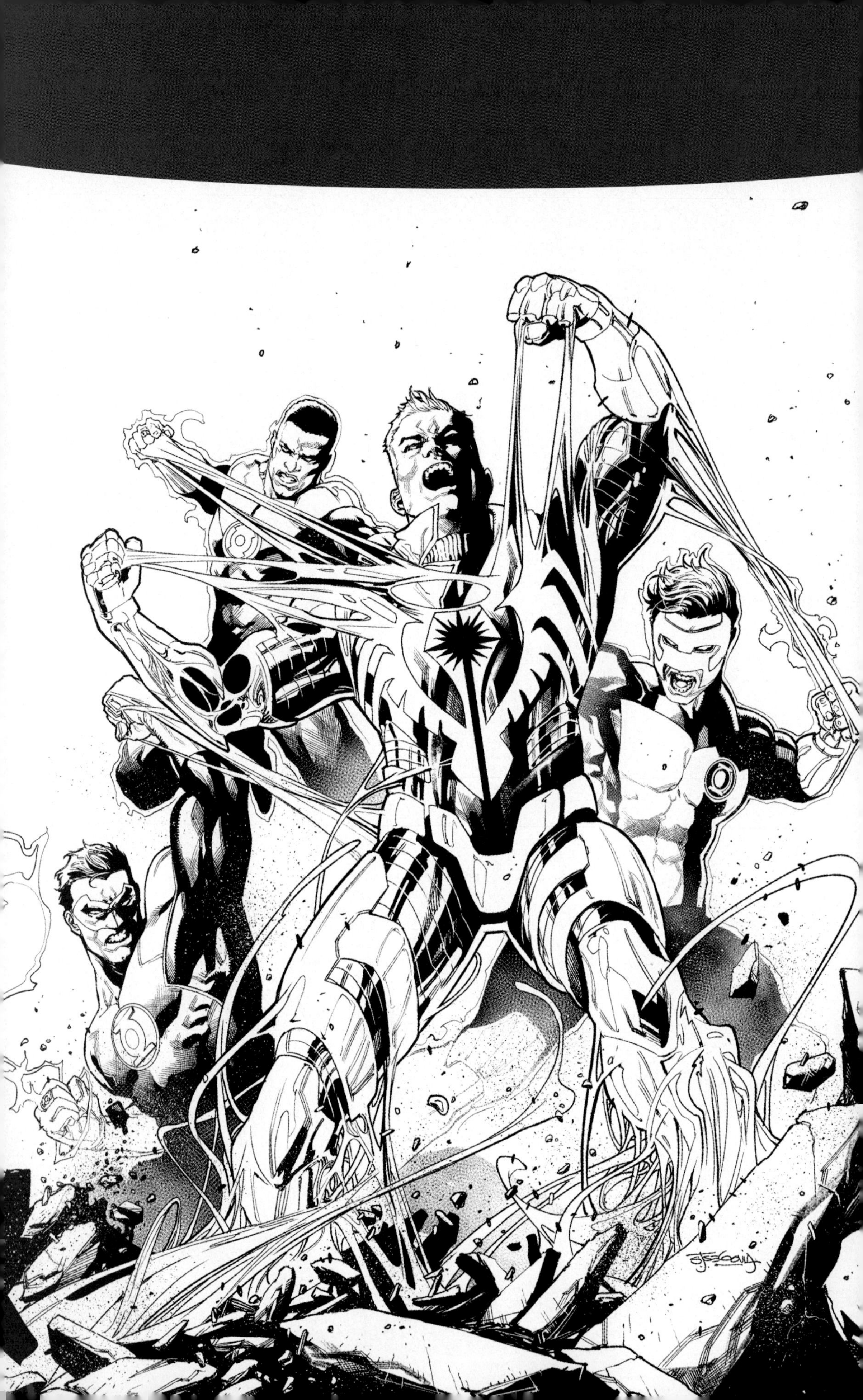

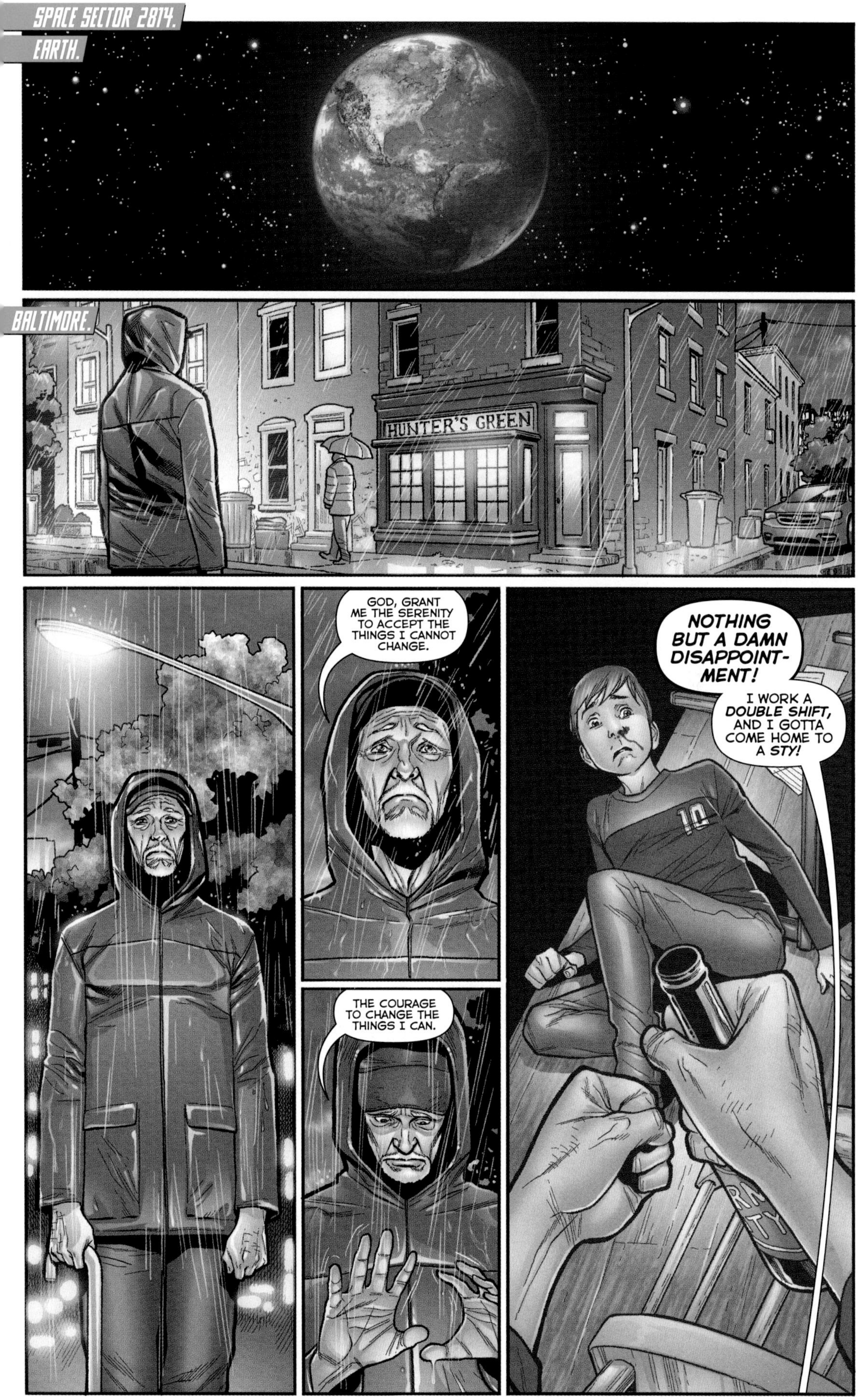
SPACE SECTOR 2814.
EARTH.
BALTIMORE.
HUNTER'S GREEN
GOD, GRANT ME THE SERENITY TO ACCEPT THE THINGS I CANNOT CHANGE.
THE COURAGE TO CHANGE THE THINGS I CAN.
NOTHING BUT A DAMN DISAPPOINT-MENT!
I WORK A DOUBLE SHIFT, AND I GOTTA COME HOME TO A STY!

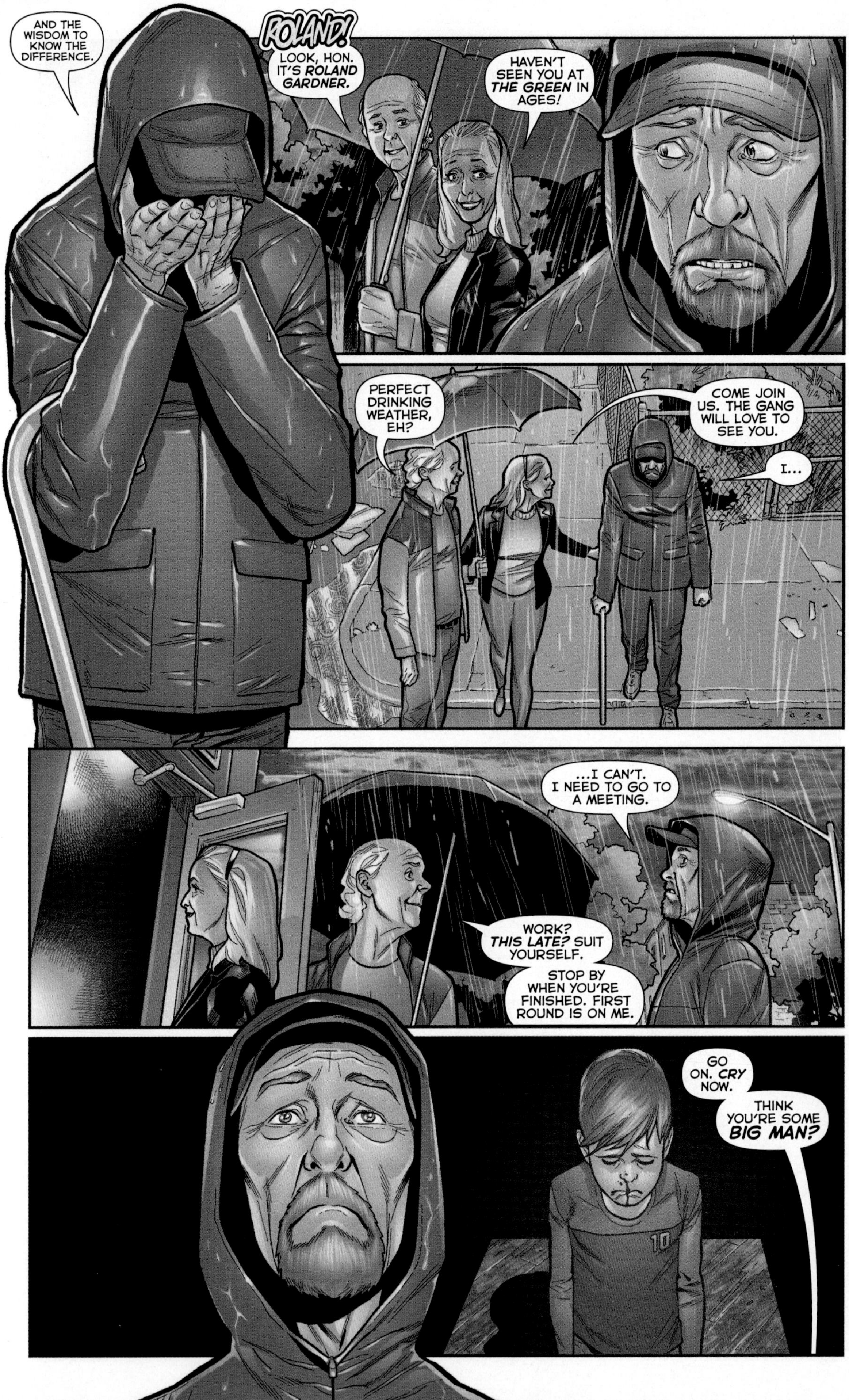
AND THE WISDOM TO KNOW THE DIFFERENCE.
ROLAND!
LOOK, HON. IT'S ROLAND GARDNER.
HAVEN'T SEEN YOU AT THE GREEN IN AGES!
PERFECT DRINKING WEATHER, EH?
COME JOIN US. THE GANG WILL LOVE TO SEE YOU.
I...
...I CAN'T. I NEED TO GO TO A MEETING.
WORK? THIS LATE? SUIT YOURSELF.
STOP BY WHEN YOU'RE FINISHED. FIRST ROUND IS ON ME.
GO ON. CRY NOW.
THINK YOU'RE SOME BIG MAN?
10

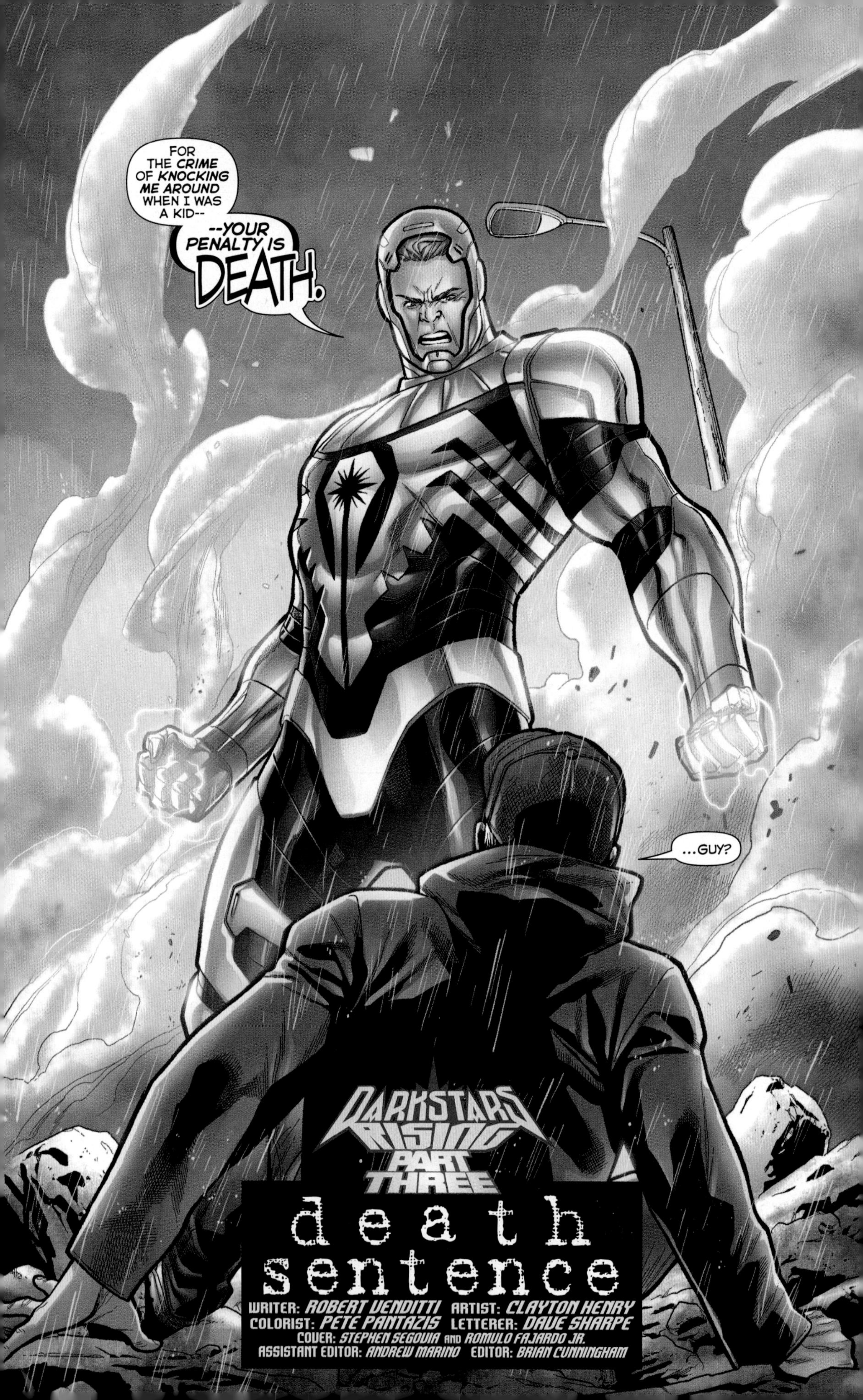

FOR THE CRIME OF KNOCKING ME AROUND WHEN I WAS A KID--
--YOUR PENALTY IS DEATH.
...GUY?
DARKSTARS RISING PART THREE
death sentence
WRITER: ROBERT VENDITTI ARTIST: CLAYTON HENRY
COLORIST: PETE PANTAZIS LETTERER: DAVE SHARPE
COVER: STEPHEN SEGOVIA AND ROMULO FAJARDO JR.
ASSISTANT EDITOR: ANDREW MARINO EDITOR: BRIAN CUNNINGHAM

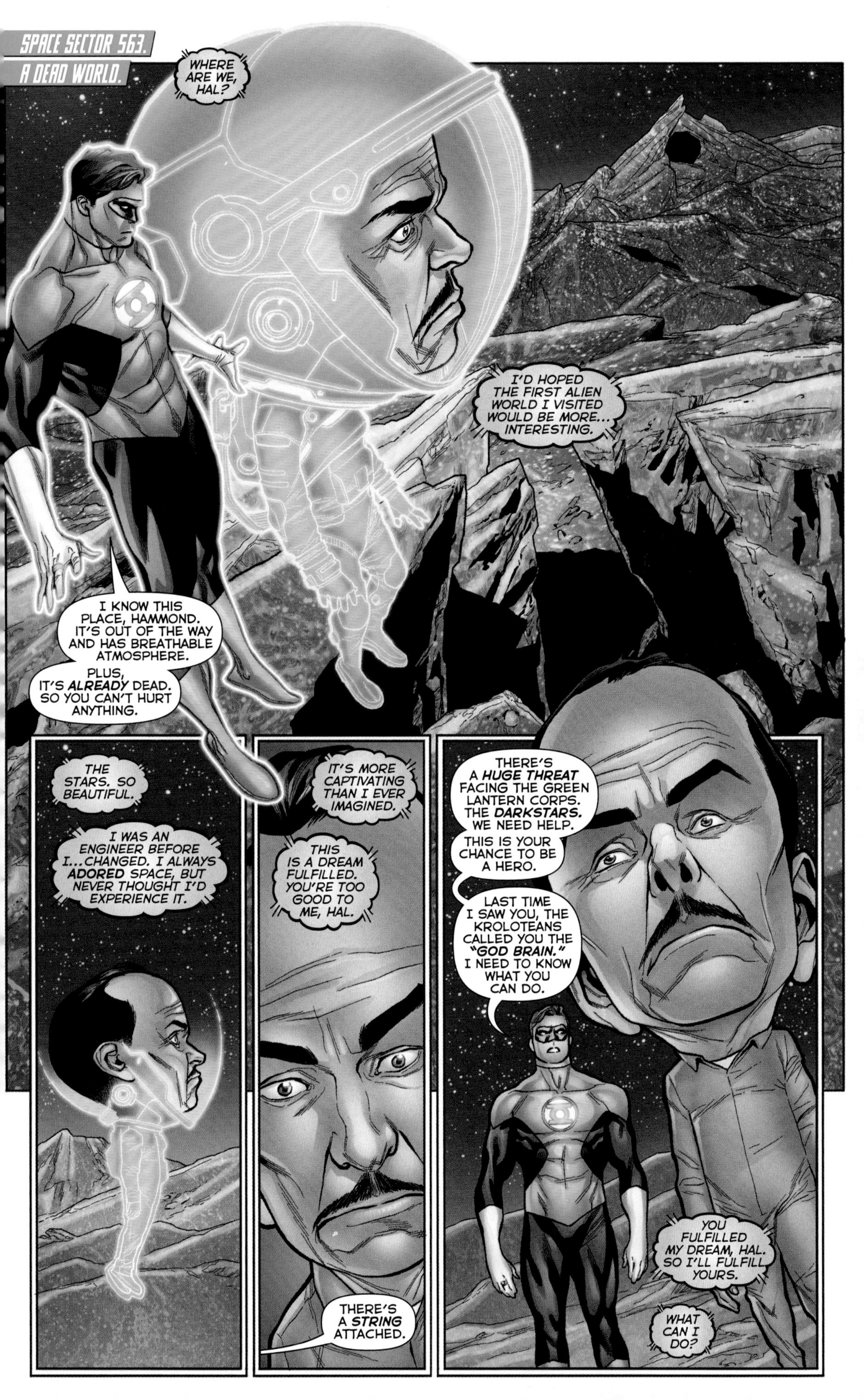
SPACE SECTOR 563.
A DEAD WORLD.
WHERE ARE WE, HAL?
I'D HOPED THE FIRST ALIEN WORLD I VISITED WOULD BE MORE... INTERESTING.
I KNOW THIS PLACE, HAMMOND. IT'S OUT OF THE WAY AND HAS BREATHABLE ATMOSPHERE.
PLUS, IT'S ALREADY DEAD. SO YOU CAN'T HURT ANYTHING.
THE STARS. SO BEAUTIFUL.
I WAS AN ENGINEER BEFORE I...CHANGED. I ALWAYS ADORED SPACE, BUT NEVER THOUGHT I'D EXPERIENCE IT.
IT'S MORE CAPTIVATING THAN I EVER IMAGINED.
THIS IS A DREAM FULFILLED. YOU'RE TOO GOOD TO ME, HAL.
THERE'S A STRING ATTACHED.
THERE'S A HUGE THREAT FACING THE GREEN LANTERN CORPS. THE DARKSTARS. WE NEED HELP.
THIS IS YOUR CHANCE TO BE A HERO.
LAST TIME I SAW YOU, THE KROLOTEANS CALLED YOU THE "GOD BRAIN." I NEED TO KNOW WHAT YOU CAN DO.
YOU FULFILLED MY DREAM, HAL. SO I'LL FULFILL YOURS.
WHAT CAN I DO?

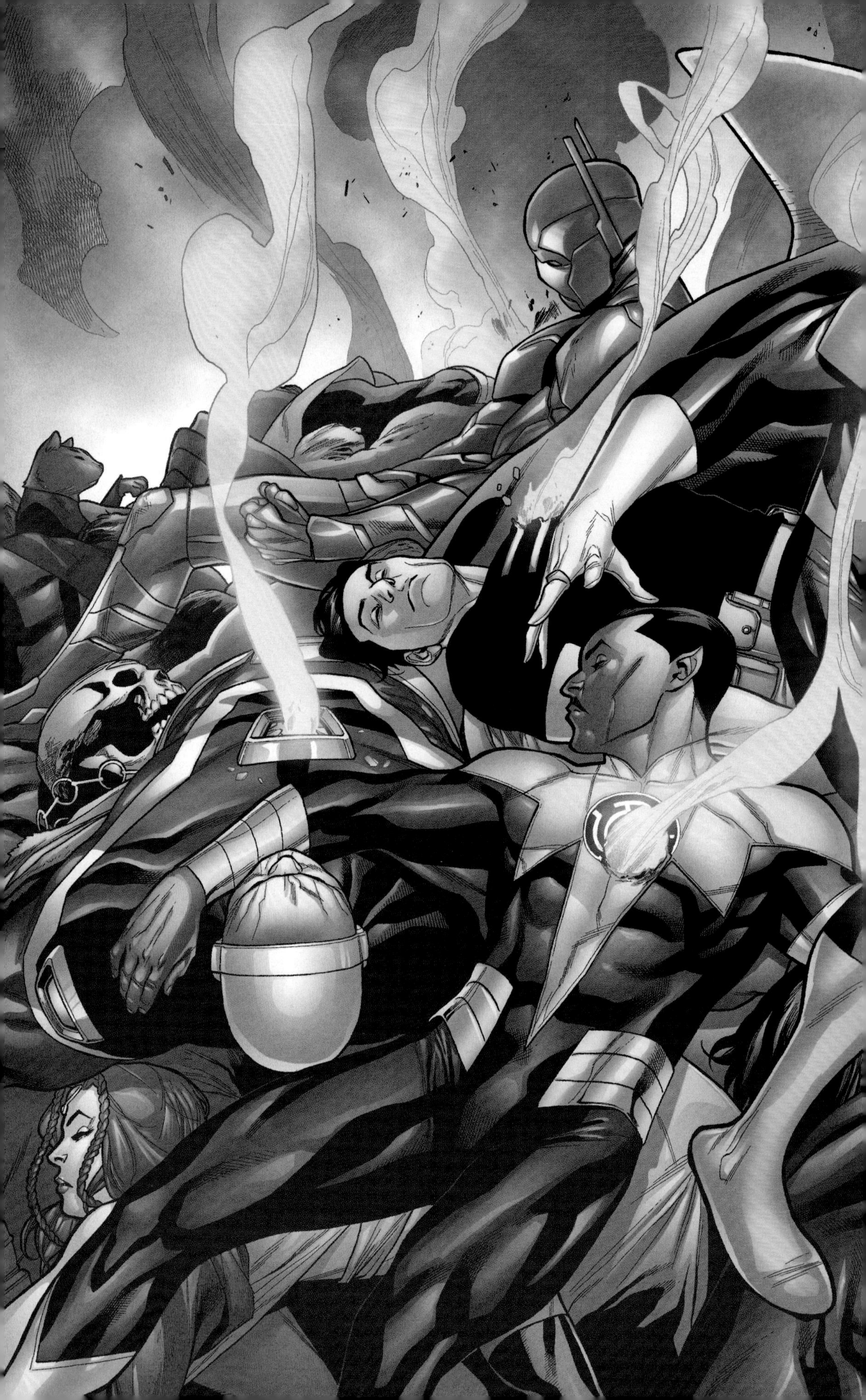

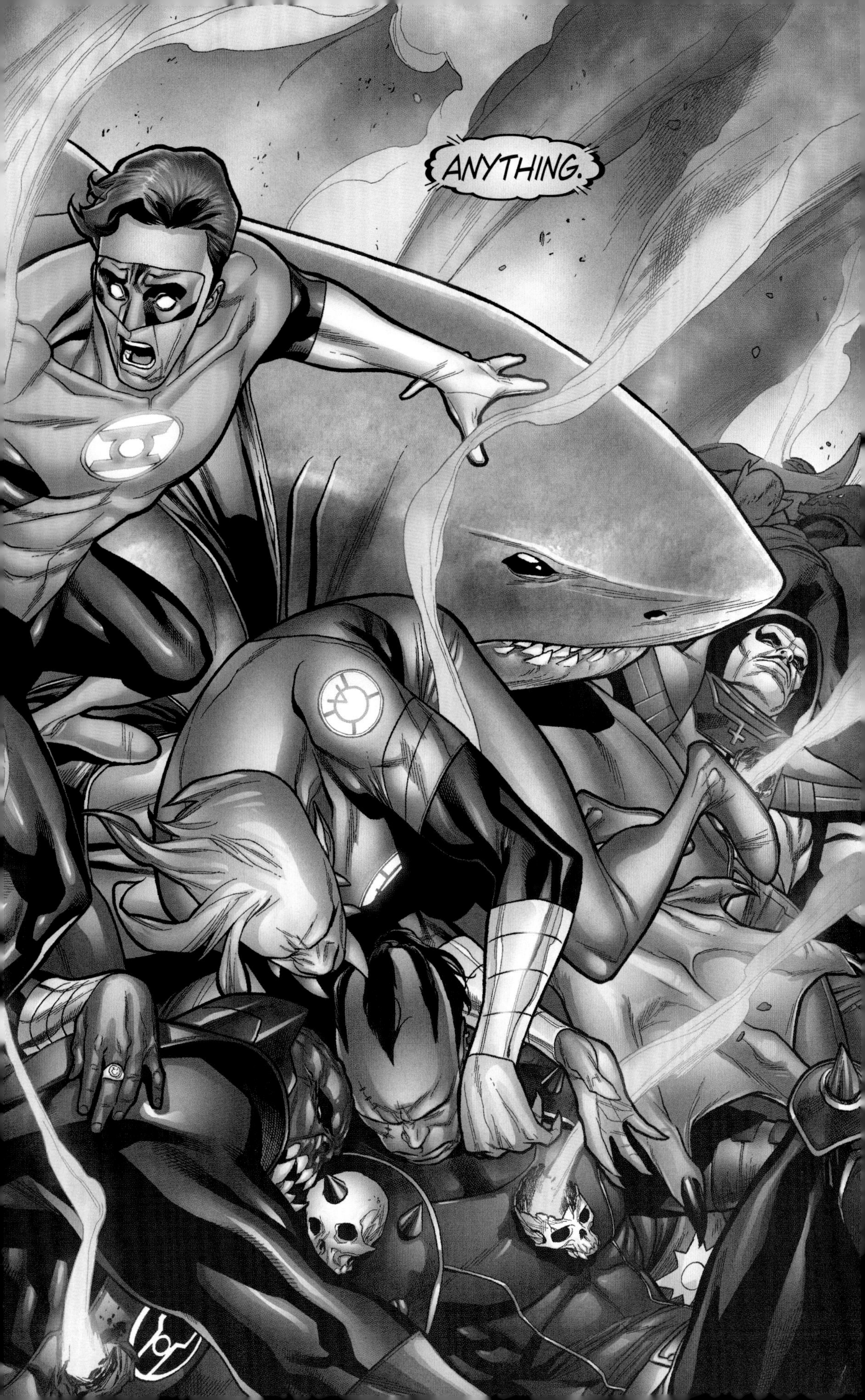
ANYTHING.

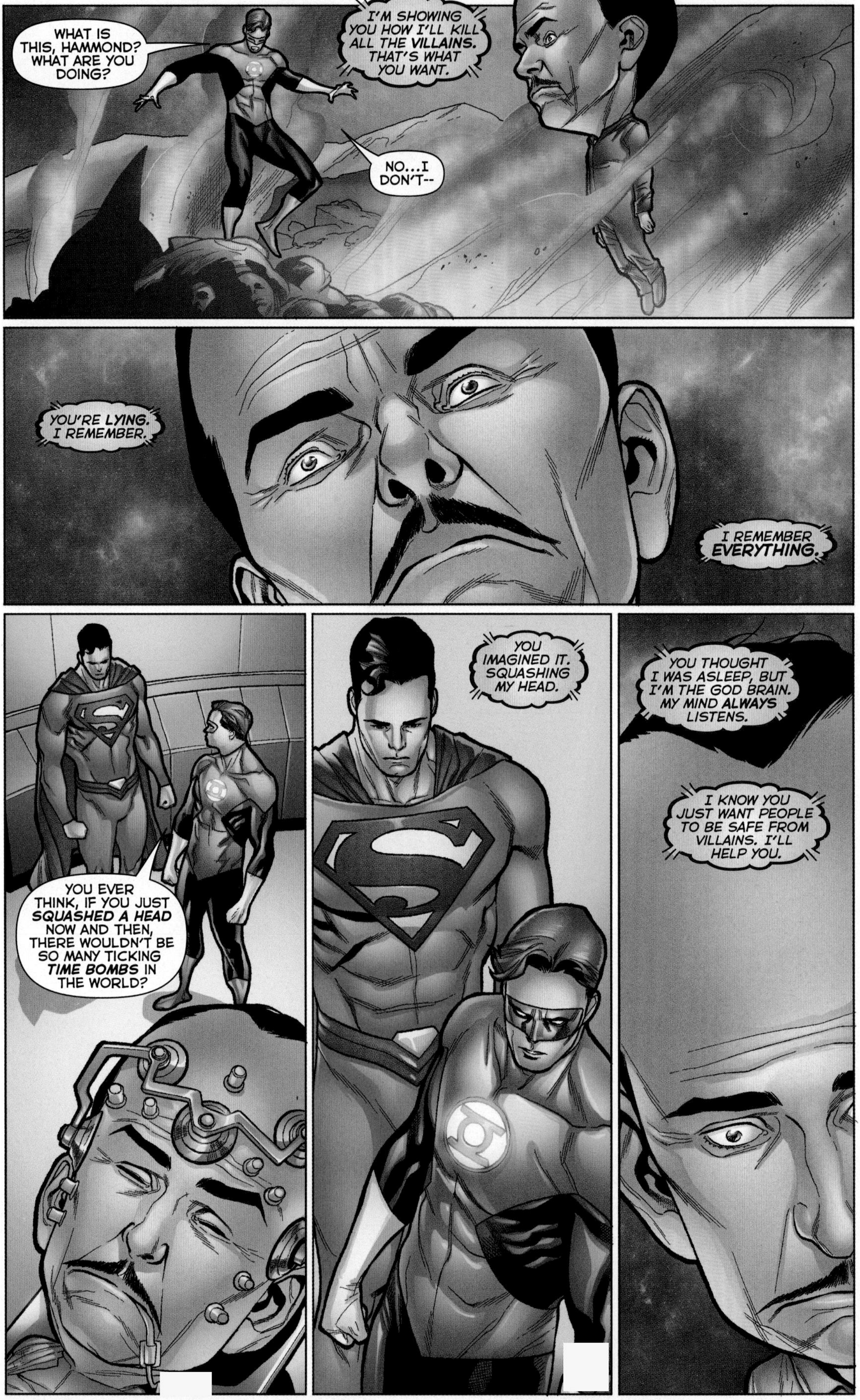
WHAT IS THIS, HAMMOND? WHAT ARE YOU DOING?
I'M SHOWING YOU HOW I'LL KILL ALL THE VILLAINS. THAT'S WHAT YOU WANT.
NO...I DON'T--
YOU'RE LYING. I REMEMBER.
I REMEMBER EVERYTHING.
YOU EVER THINK, IF YOU JUST SQUASHED A HEAD NOW AND THEN, THERE WOULDN'T BE SO MANY TICKING TIME BOMBS IN THE WORLD?
YOU IMAGINED IT. SQUASHING MY HEAD.
YOU THOUGHT I WAS ASLEEP, BUT I'M THE GOD BRAIN. MY MIND ALWAYS LISTENS.
I KNOW YOU JUST WANT PEOPLE TO BE SAFE FROM VILLAINS. I'LL HELP YOU.

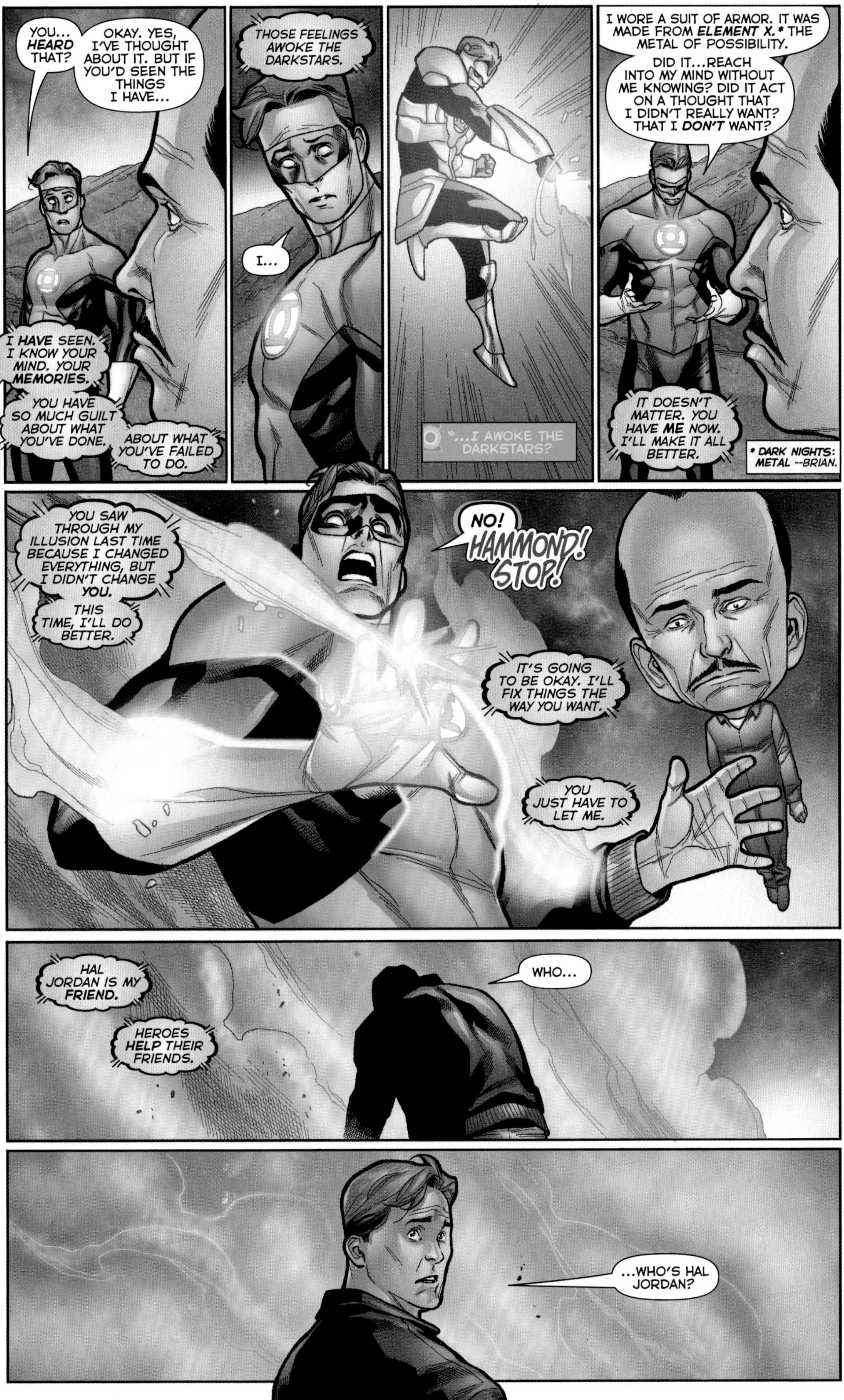
YOU... HEARD THAT?
OKAY. YES, I'VE THOUGHT ABOUT IT. BUT IF YOU'D SEEN THE THINGS I HAVE...
I HAVE SEEN. I KNOW YOUR MIND. YOUR MEMORIES.
YOU HAVE SO MUCH GUILT ABOUT WHAT YOU'VE DONE.
ABOUT WHAT YOU'VE FAILED TO DO.
THOSE FEELINGS AWOKE THE DARKSTARS.
I...
"...I AWOKE THE DARKSTARS?
I WORE A SUIT OF ARMOR. IT WAS MADE FROM ELEMENT X.* THE METAL OF POSSIBILITY.
DID IT...REACH INTO MY MIND WITHOUT ME KNOWING? DID IT ACT ON A THOUGHT THAT I DIDN'T REALLY WANT? THAT I DON'T WANT?
IT DOESN'T MATTER. YOU HAVE ME NOW. I'LL MAKE IT ALL BETTER.
* DARK NIGHTS: METAL --BRIAN.
YOU SAW THROUGH MY ILLUSION LAST TIME BECAUSE I CHANGED EVERYTHING, BUT I DIDN'T CHANGE YOU.
THIS TIME, I'LL DO BETTER.
NO! HAMMOND! STOP!
IT'S GOING TO BE OKAY. I'LL FIX THINGS THE WAY YOU WANT.
YOU JUST HAVE TO LET ME.
HAL JORDAN IS MY FRIEND.
HEROES HELP THEIR FRIENDS.
WHO...
...WHO'S HAL JORDAN?

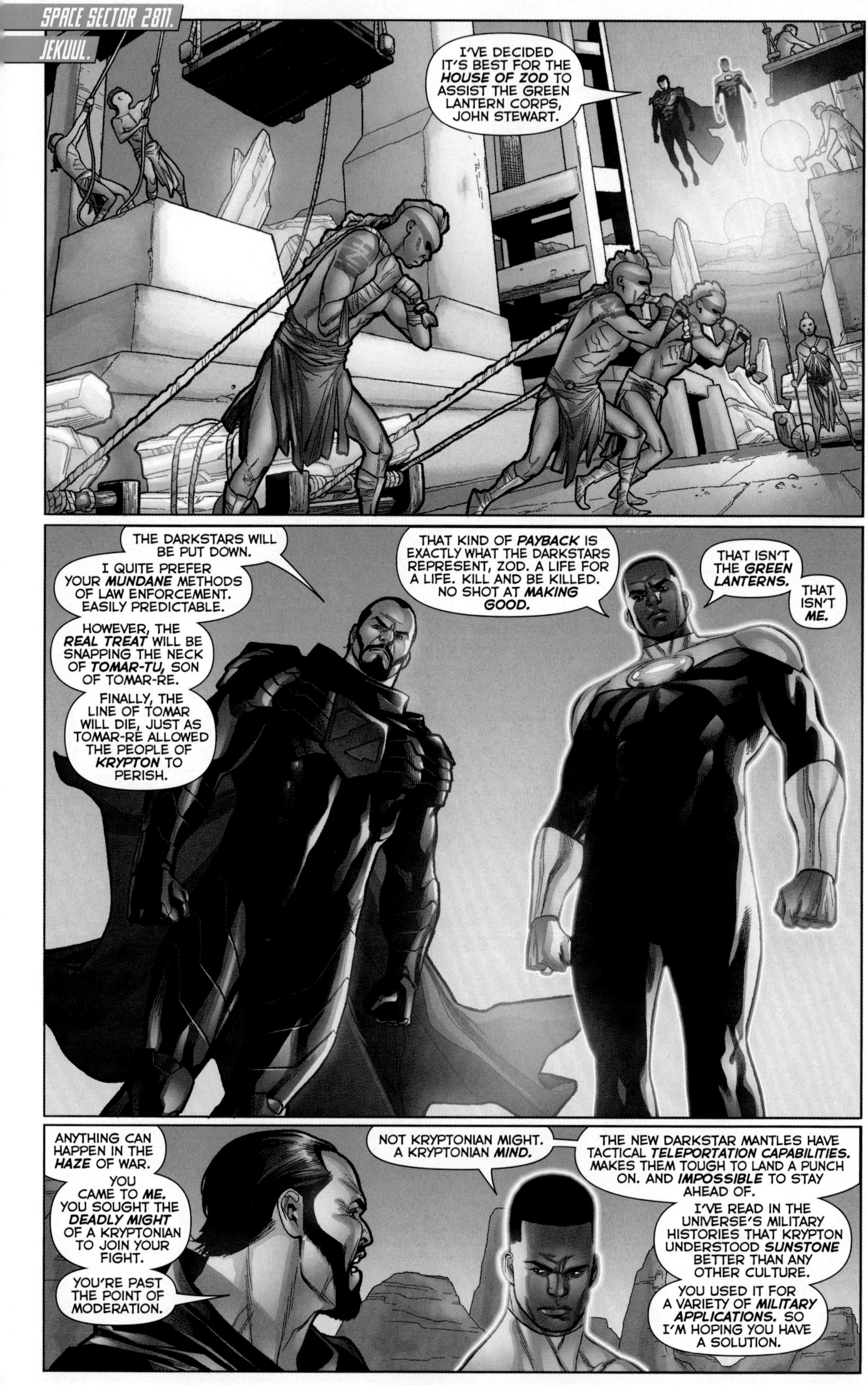
SPACE SECTOR 2811.
JEKUUL.
I'VE DECIDED IT'S BEST FOR THE HOUSE OF ZOD TO ASSIST THE GREEN LANTERN CORPS, JOHN STEWART.
THE DARKSTARS WILL BE PUT DOWN.
I QUITE PREFER YOUR MUNDANE METHODS OF LAW ENFORCEMENT. EASILY PREDICTABLE.
HOWEVER, THE REAL TREAT WILL BE SNAPPING THE NECK OF TOMAR-TU, SON OF TOMAR-RE.
FINALLY, THE LINE OF TOMAR WILL DIE, JUST AS TOMAR-RE ALLOWED THE PEOPLE OF KRYPTON TO PERISH.
THAT KIND OF PAYBACK IS EXACTLY WHAT THE DARKSTARS REPRESENT, ZOD. A LIFE FOR A LIFE. KILL AND BE KILLED. NO SHOT AT MAKING GOOD.
THAT ISN'T THE GREEN LANTERNS.
THAT ISN'T ME.
ANYTHING CAN HAPPEN IN THE HAZE OF WAR.
YOU CAME TO ME. YOU SOUGHT THE DEADLY MIGHT OF A KRYPTONIAN TO JOIN YOUR FIGHT.
YOU'RE PAST THE POINT OF MODERATION.
NOT KRYPTONIAN MIGHT. A KRYPTONIAN MIND.
THE NEW DARKSTAR MANTLES HAVE TACTICAL TELEPORTATION CAPABILITIES. MAKES THEM TOUGH TO LAND A PUNCH ON. AND IMPOSSIBLE TO STAY AHEAD OF.
I'VE READ IN THE UNIVERSE'S MILITARY HISTORIES THAT KRYPTON UNDERSTOOD SUNSTONE BETTER THAN ANY OTHER CULTURE.
YOU USED IT FOR A VARIETY OF MILITARY APPLICATIONS. SO I'M HOPING YOU HAVE A SOLUTION.

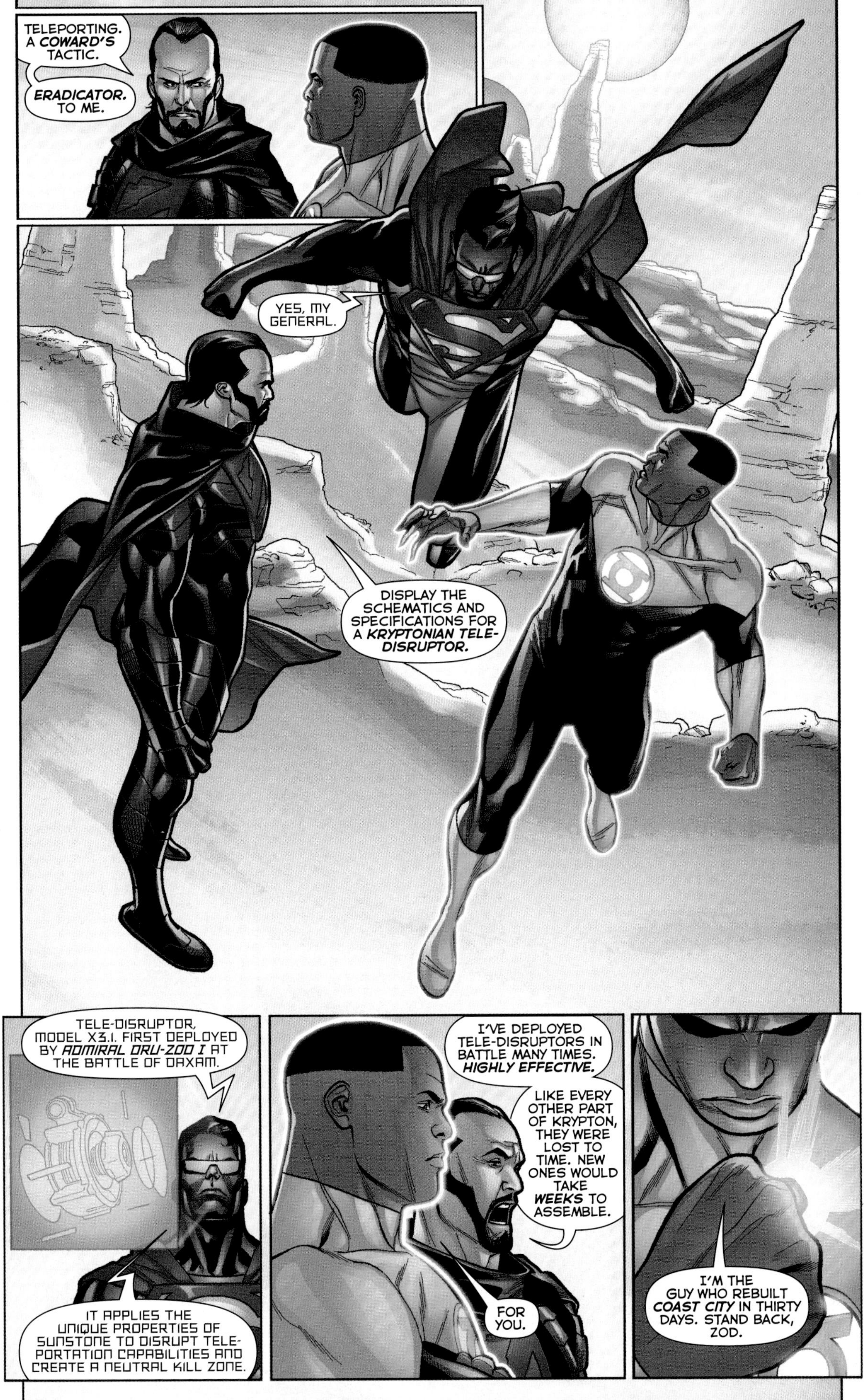
TELEPORTING. A COWARD'S TACTIC.
ERADICATOR. TO ME.
YES, MY GENERAL.
DISPLAY THE SCHEMATICS AND SPECIFICATIONS FOR A KRYPTONIAN TELE-DISRUPTOR.
TELE-DISRUPTOR, MODEL X3.1. FIRST DEPLOYED BY ADMIRAL DRU-ZOD I AT THE BATTLE OF DAXAM.
IT APPLIES THE UNIQUE PROPERTIES OF SUNSTONE TO DISRUPT TELE-PORTATION CAPABILITIES AND CREATE A NEUTRAL KILL ZONE.
I'VE DEPLOYED TELE-DISRUPTORS IN BATTLE MANY TIMES. HIGHLY EFFECTIVE.
LIKE EVERY OTHER PART OF KRYPTON, THEY WERE LOST TO TIME. NEW ONES WOULD TAKE WEEKS TO ASSEMBLE.
FOR YOU.
I'M THE GUY WHO REBUILT COAST CITY IN THIRTY DAYS. STAND BACK, ZOD.

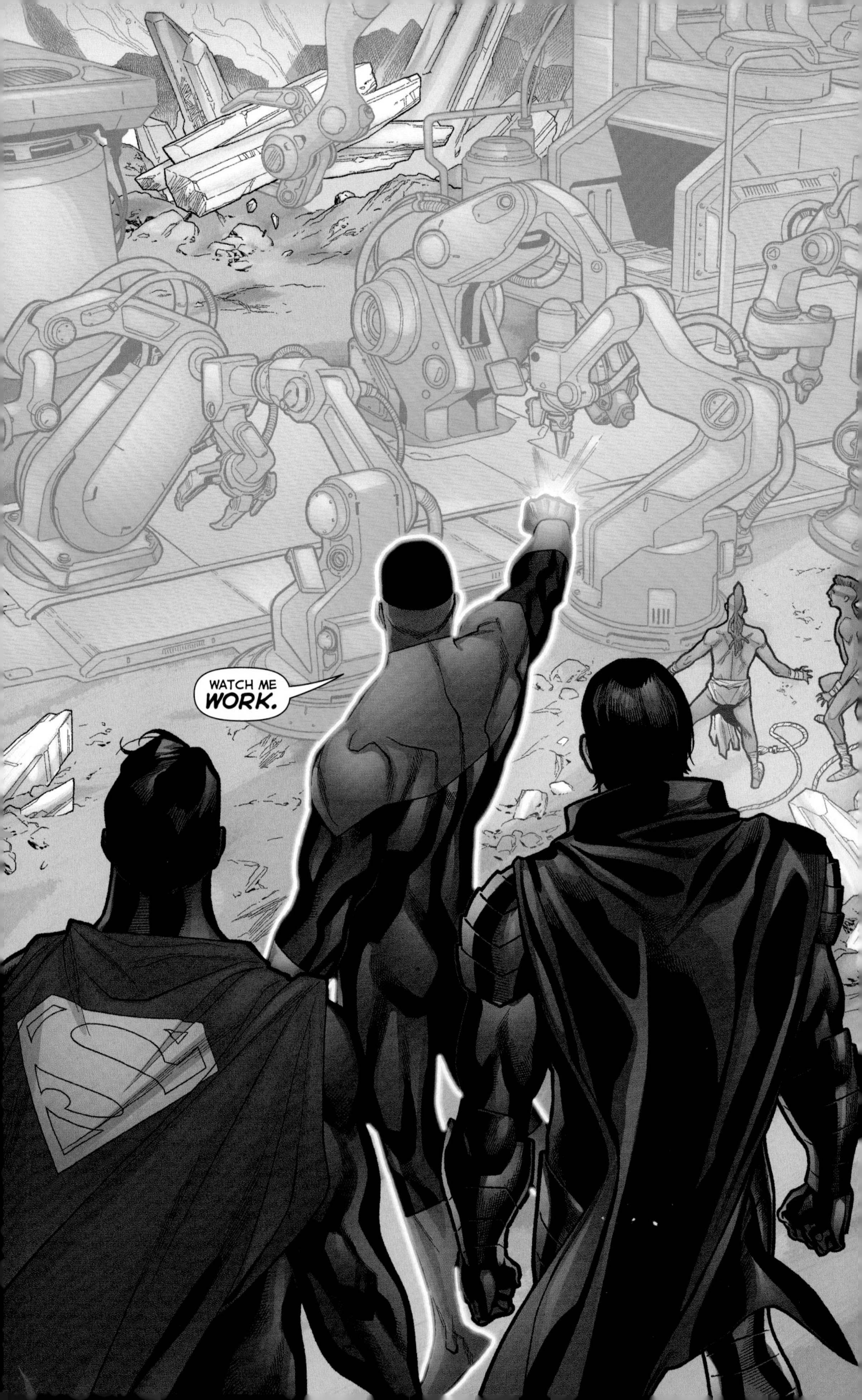
WATCH ME WORK.

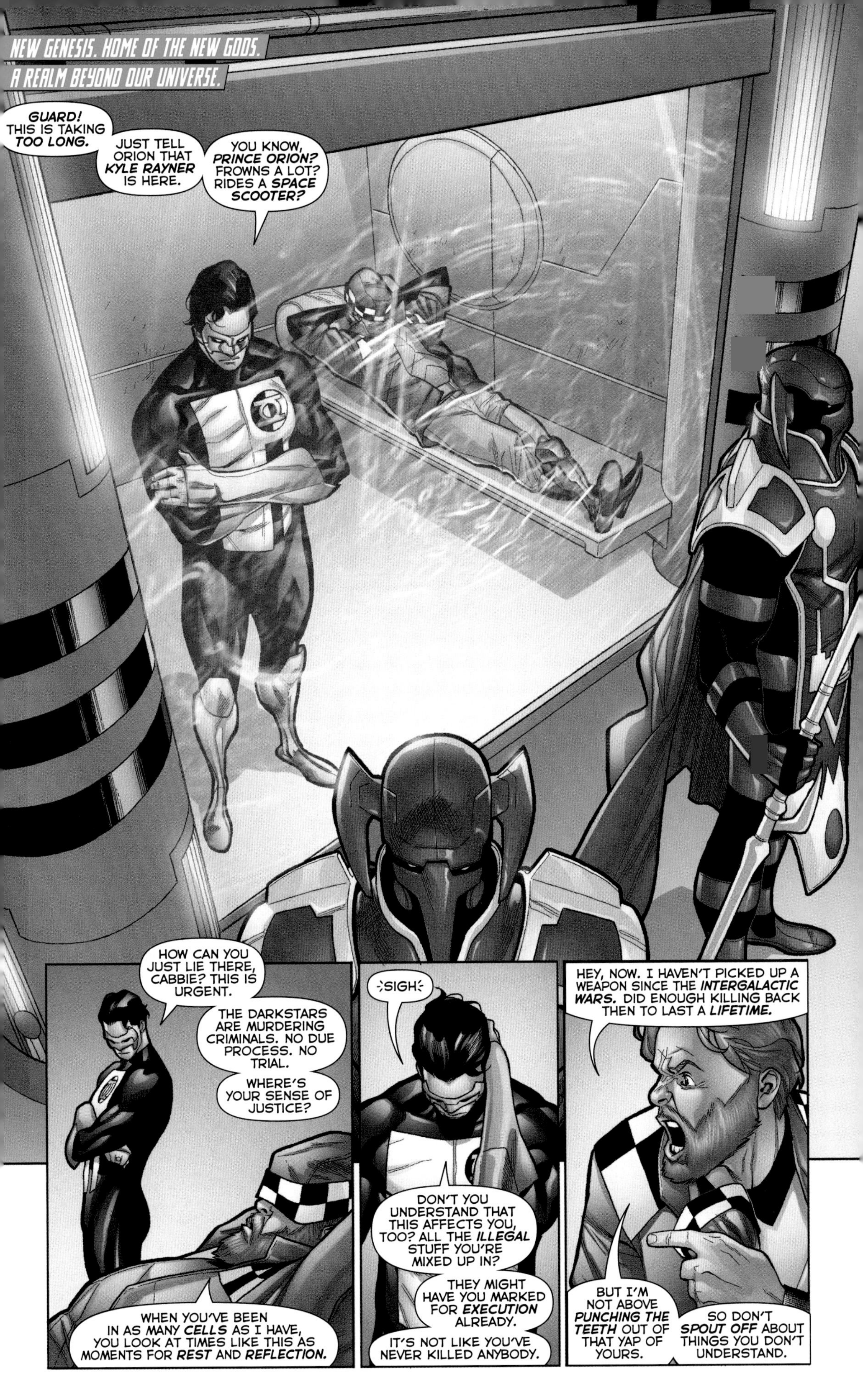
NEW GENESIS. HOME OF THE NEW GODS.
A REALM BEYOND OUR UNIVERSE.
GUARD! THIS IS TAKING TOO LONG.
JUST TELL ORION THAT KYLE RAYNER IS HERE.
YOU KNOW, PRINCE ORION? FROWNS A LOT? RIDES A SPACE SCOOTER?
HOW CAN YOU JUST LIE THERE, CABBIE? THIS IS URGENT.
THE DARKSTARS ARE MURDERING CRIMINALS. NO DUE PROCESS. NO TRIAL.
WHERE'S YOUR SENSE OF JUSTICE?
WHEN YOU'VE BEEN IN AS MANY CELLS AS I HAVE, YOU LOOK AT TIMES LIKE THIS AS MOMENTS FOR REST AND REFLECTION.
SIGH
DON'T YOU UNDERSTAND THAT THIS AFFECTS YOU, TOO? ALL THE ILLEGAL STUFF YOU'RE MIXED UP IN?
THEY MIGHT HAVE YOU MARKED FOR EXECUTION ALREADY.
IT'S NOT LIKE YOU'VE NEVER KILLED ANYBODY.
HEY, NOW. I HAVEN'T PICKED UP A WEAPON SINCE THE INTERGALACTIC WARS. DID ENOUGH KILLING BACK THEN TO LAST A LIFETIME.
BUT I'M NOT ABOVE PUNCHING THE TEETH OUT OF THAT YAP OF YOURS.
SO DON'T SPOUT OFF ABOUT THINGS YOU DON'T UNDERSTAND.

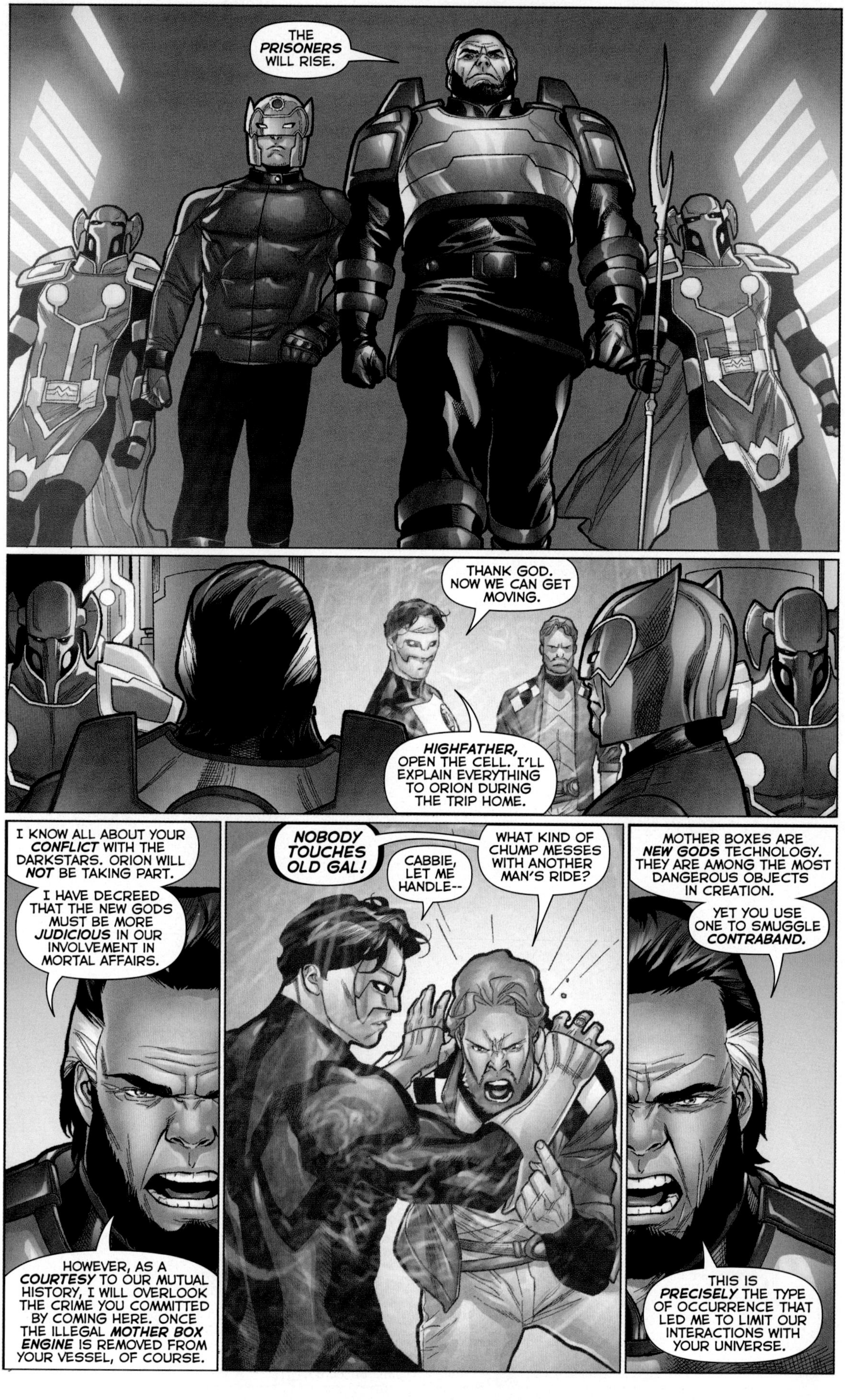

THE PRISONERS WILL RISE.
THANK GOD. NOW WE CAN GET MOVING.
HIGHFATHER, OPEN THE CELL. I'LL EXPLAIN EVERYTHING TO ORION DURING THE TRIP HOME.
I KNOW ALL ABOUT YOUR CONFLICT WITH THE DARKSTARS. ORION WILL NOT BE TAKING PART.
I HAVE DECREED THAT THE NEW GODS MUST BE MORE JUDICIOUS IN OUR INVOLVEMENT IN MORTAL AFFAIRS.
HOWEVER, AS A COURTESY TO OUR MUTUAL HISTORY, I WILL OVERLOOK THE CRIME YOU COMMITTED BY COMING HERE. ONCE THE ILLEGAL MOTHER BOX ENGINE IS REMOVED FROM YOUR VESSEL, OF COURSE.
NOBODY TOUCHES OLD GAL!
WHAT KIND OF CHUMP MESSES WITH ANOTHER MAN'S RIDE?
CABBIE, LET ME HANDLE--
MOTHER BOXES ARE NEW GODS TECHNOLOGY. THEY ARE AMONG THE MOST DANGEROUS OBJECTS IN CREATION.
YET YOU USE ONE TO SMUGGLE CONTRABAND.
THIS IS PRECISELY THE TYPE OF OCCURRENCE THAT LED ME TO LIMIT OUR INTERACTIONS WITH YOUR UNIVERSE.

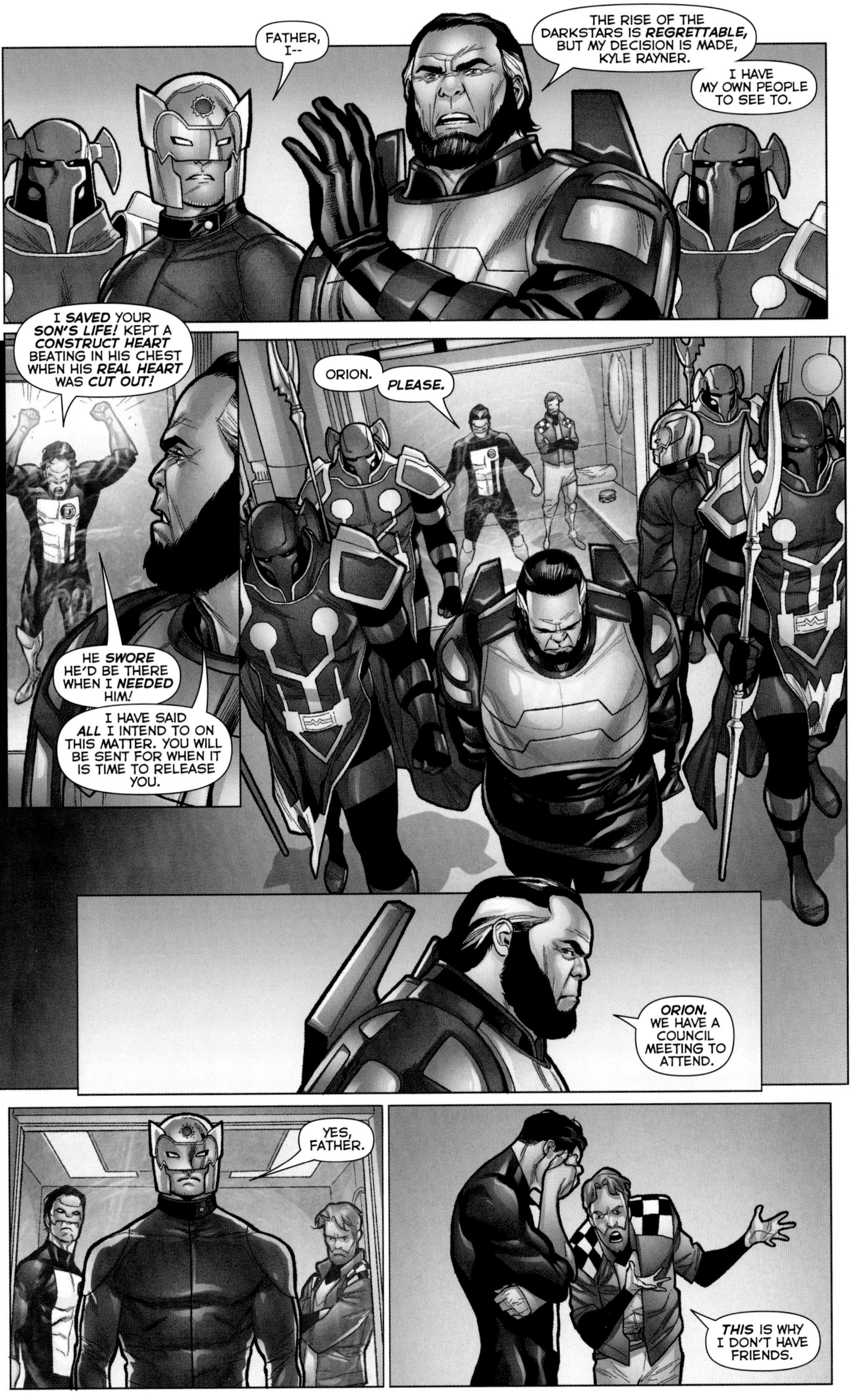

FATHER, I--
THE RISE OF THE DARKSTARS IS *REGRETTABLE,* BUT MY DECISION IS MADE, KYLE RAYNER.
I HAVE MY OWN PEOPLE TO SEE TO.
I *SAVED* YOUR *SON'S LIFE!* KEPT A *CONSTRUCT HEART* BEATING IN HIS CHEST WHEN HIS *REAL HEART* WAS *CUT OUT!*
HE *SWORE* HE'D BE THERE WHEN I *NEEDED* HIM!
I HAVE SAID *ALL* I INTEND TO ON THIS MATTER. YOU WILL BE SENT FOR WHEN IT IS TIME TO RELEASE YOU.
ORION. *PLEASE.*
ORION. WE HAVE A COUNCIL MEETING TO ATTEND.
YES, FATHER.
THIS IS WHY I DON'T HAVE FRIENDS.

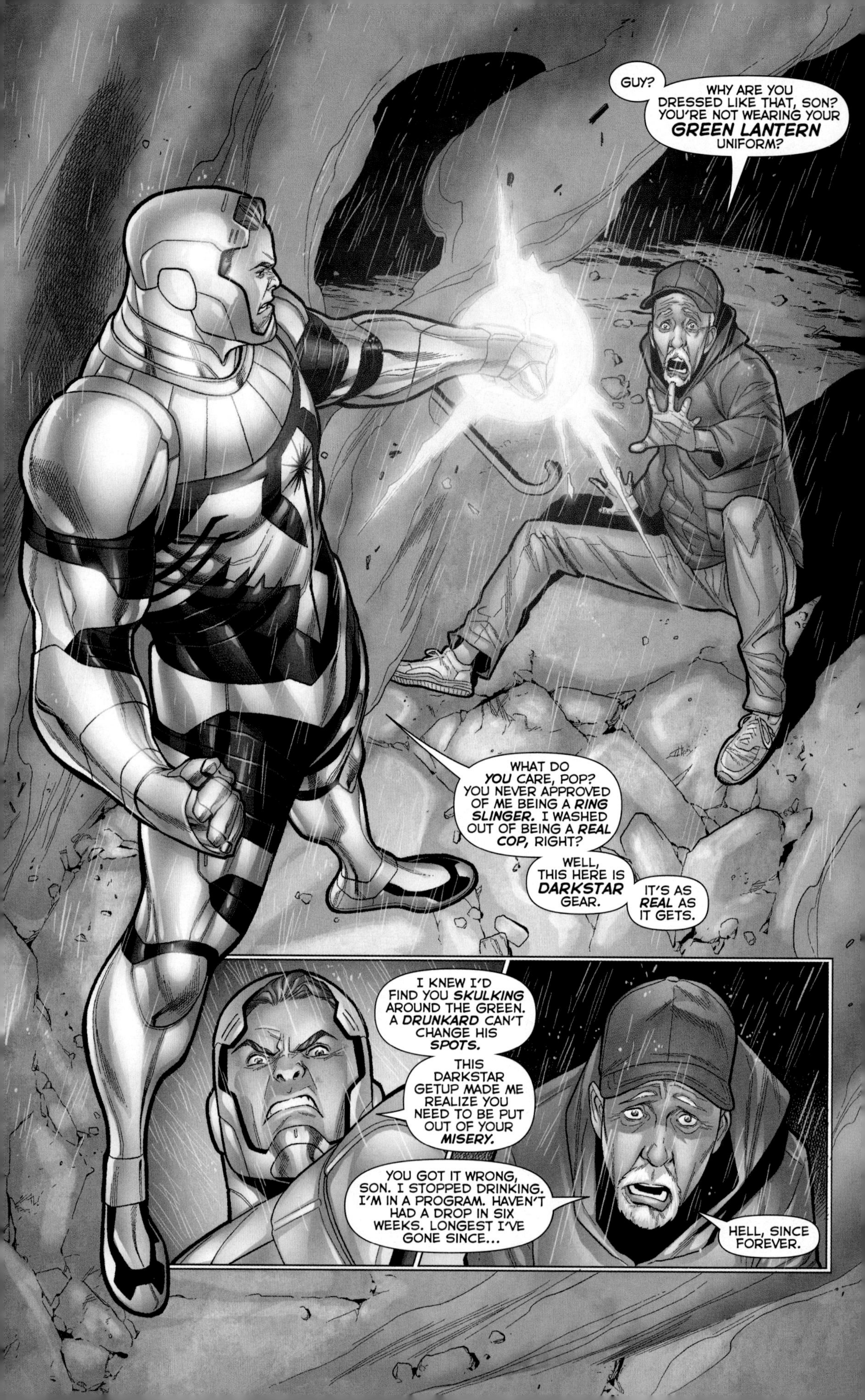
GUY?
WHY ARE YOU DRESSED LIKE THAT, SON? YOU'RE NOT WEARING YOUR GREEN LANTERN UNIFORM?
WHAT DO YOU CARE, POP? YOU NEVER APPROVED OF ME BEING A RING SLINGER. I WASHED OUT OF BEING A REAL COP, RIGHT?
WELL, THIS HERE IS DARKSTAR GEAR.
IT'S AS REAL AS IT GETS.
I KNEW I'D FIND YOU SKULKING AROUND THE GREEN. A DRUNKARD CAN'T CHANGE HIS SPOTS.
THIS DARKSTAR GETUP MADE ME REALIZE YOU NEED TO BE PUT OUT OF YOUR MISERY.
YOU GOT IT WRONG, SON. I STOPPED DRINKING. I'M IN A PROGRAM. HAVEN'T HAD A DROP IN SIX WEEKS. LONGEST I'VE GONE SINCE...
HELL, SINCE FOREVER.

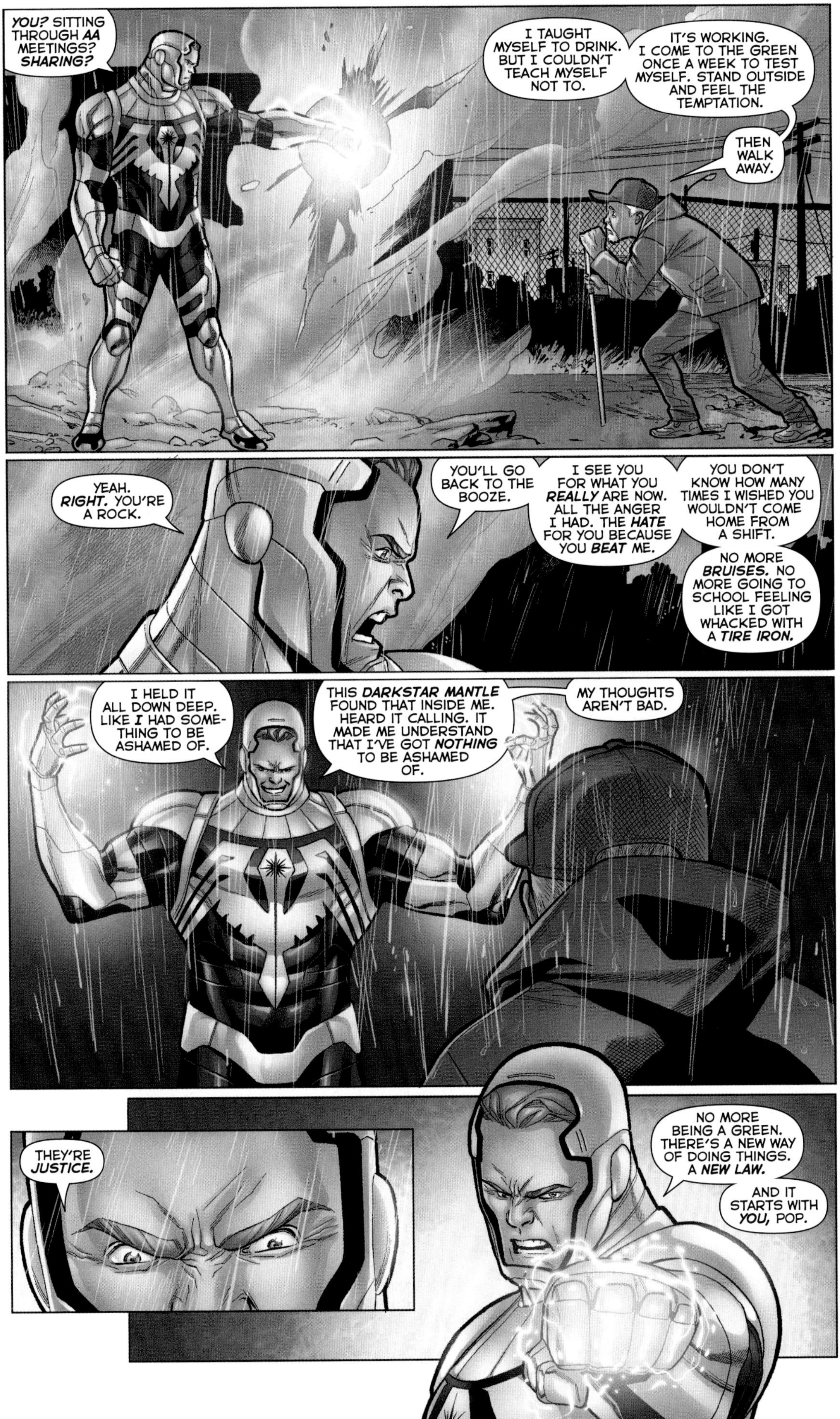
YOU? SITTING THROUGH AA MEETINGS? SHARING?
I TAUGHT MYSELF TO DRINK. BUT I COULDN'T TEACH MYSELF NOT TO.
IT'S WORKING. I COME TO THE GREEN ONCE A WEEK TO TEST MYSELF. STAND OUTSIDE AND FEEL THE TEMPTATION.
THEN WALK AWAY.
YEAH. RIGHT. YOU'RE A ROCK.
YOU'LL GO BACK TO THE BOOZE.
I SEE YOU FOR WHAT YOU REALLY ARE NOW. ALL THE ANGER I HAD. THE HATE FOR YOU BECAUSE YOU BEAT ME.
YOU DON'T KNOW HOW MANY TIMES I WISHED YOU WOULDN'T COME HOME FROM A SHIFT.
NO MORE BRUISES. NO MORE GOING TO SCHOOL FEELING LIKE I GOT WHACKED WITH A TIRE IRON.
I HELD IT ALL DOWN DEEP. LIKE I HAD SOME-THING TO BE ASHAMED OF.
THIS DARKSTAR MANTLE FOUND THAT INSIDE ME. HEARD IT CALLING. IT MADE ME UNDERSTAND THAT I'VE GOT NOTHING TO BE ASHAMED OF.
MY THOUGHTS AREN'T BAD.
THEY'RE JUSTICE.
NO MORE BEING A GREEN. THERE'S A NEW WAY OF DOING THINGS. A NEW LAW.
AND IT STARTS WITH YOU, POP.

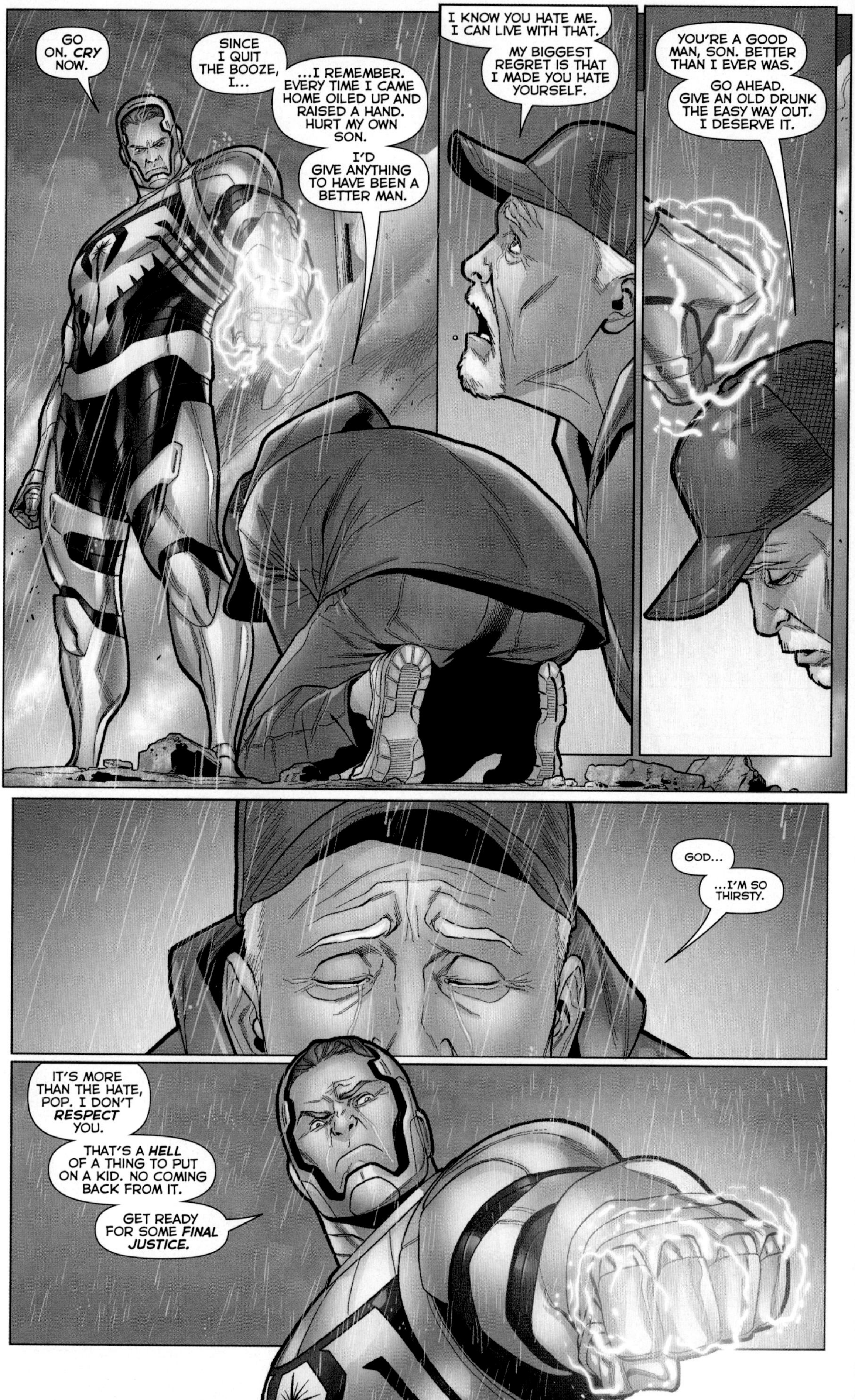
GO ON. *CRY* NOW.
SINCE I QUIT THE BOOZE, I...
...I REMEMBER. EVERY TIME I CAME HOME OILED UP AND RAISED A HAND. HURT MY OWN SON.
I'D GIVE ANYTHING TO HAVE BEEN A BETTER MAN.
I KNOW YOU HATE ME. I CAN LIVE WITH THAT.
MY BIGGEST REGRET IS THAT I MADE YOU HATE YOURSELF.
YOU'RE A GOOD MAN, SON. BETTER THAN I EVER WAS.
GO AHEAD. GIVE AN OLD DRUNK THE EASY WAY OUT. I DESERVE IT.
GOD...
...I'M SO THIRSTY.
IT'S MORE THAN THE HATE, POP. I DON'T *RESPECT* YOU.
THAT'S A *HELL* OF A THING TO PUT ON A KID. NO COMING BACK FROM IT.
GET READY FOR SOME *FINAL JUSTICE.*

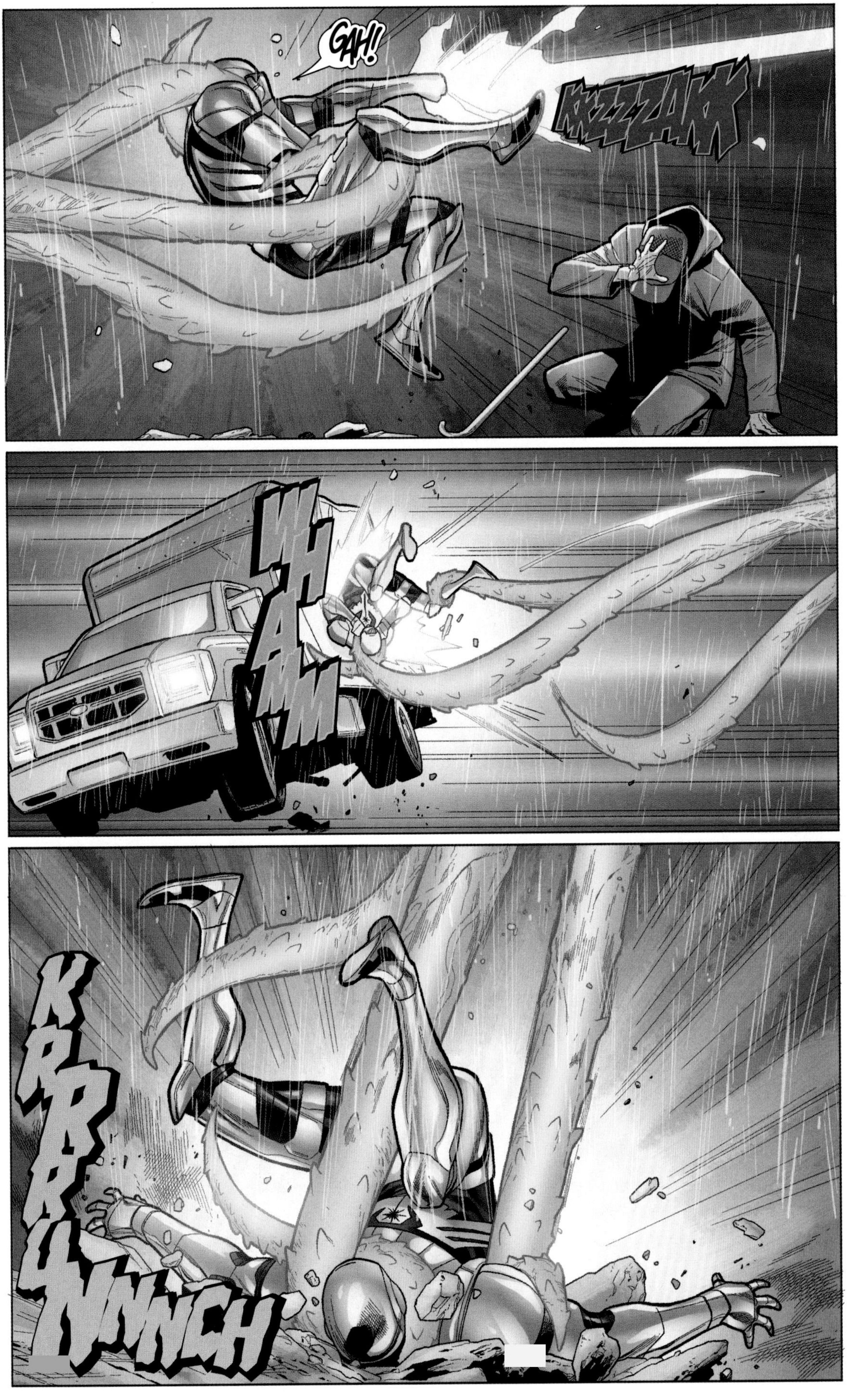
GAH!
KZZZAKK
WHAMM
KRRRUNNNCH

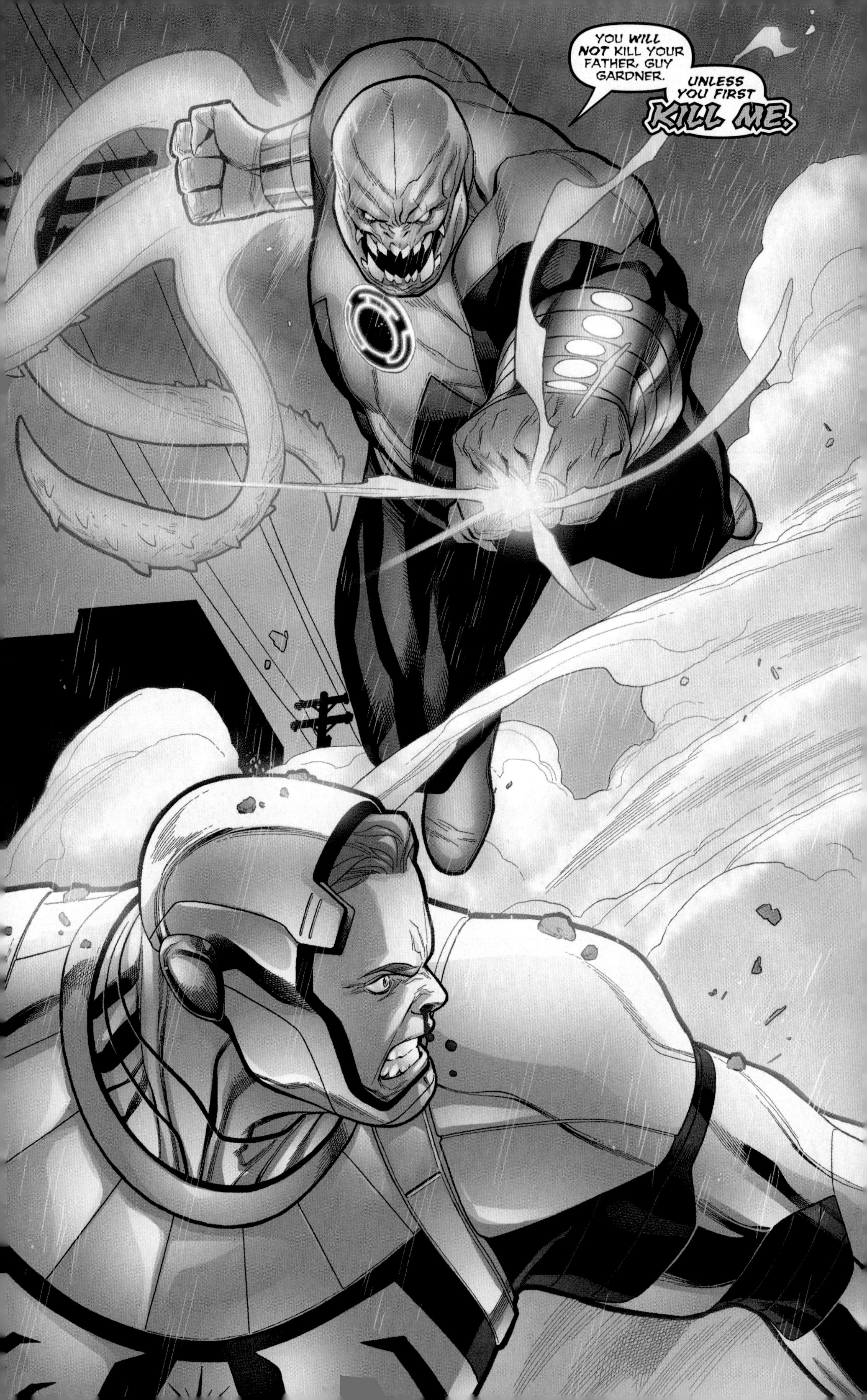
YOU WILL NOT KILL YOUR FATHER, GUY GARDNER.
UNLESS YOU FIRST KILL ME.

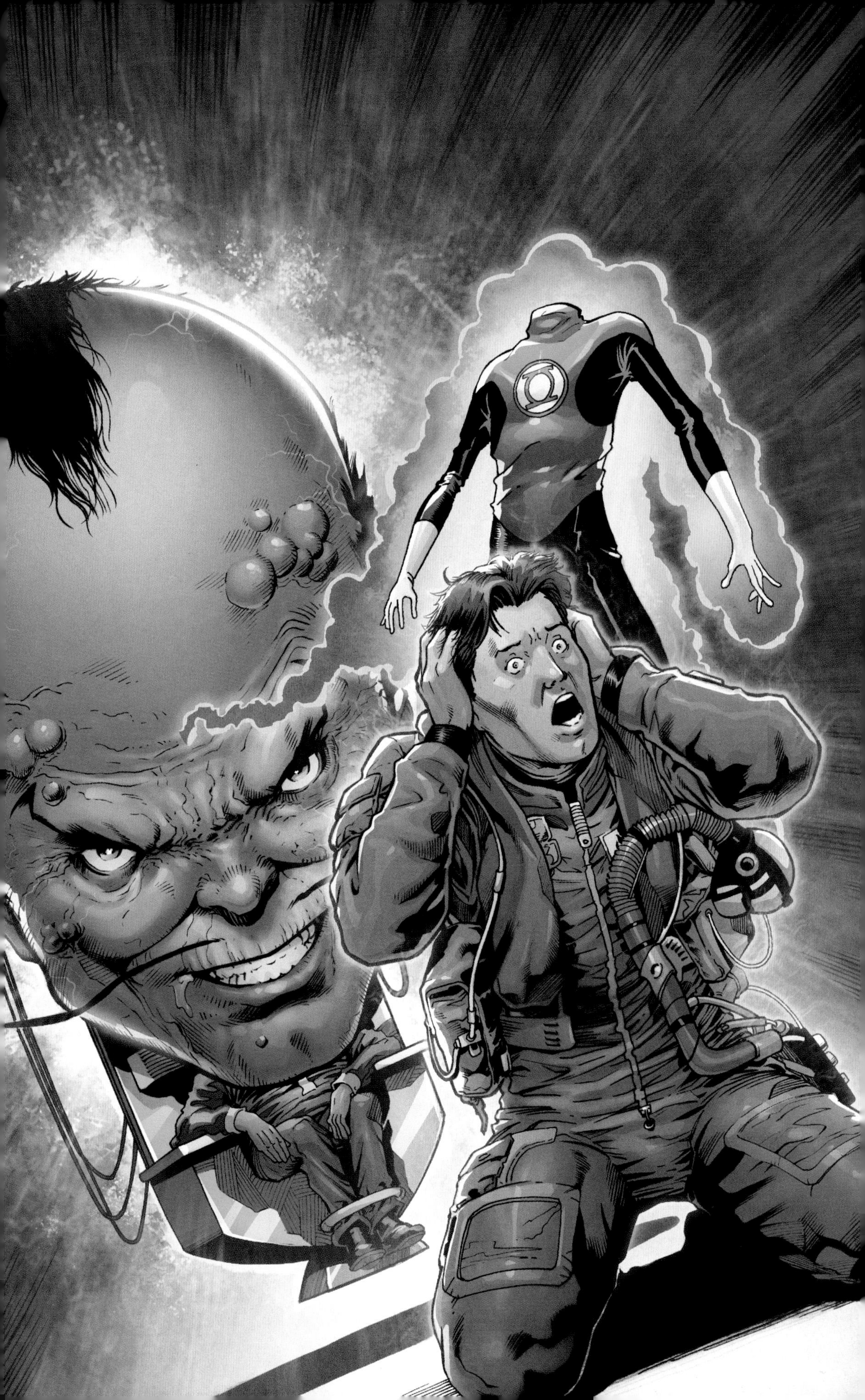

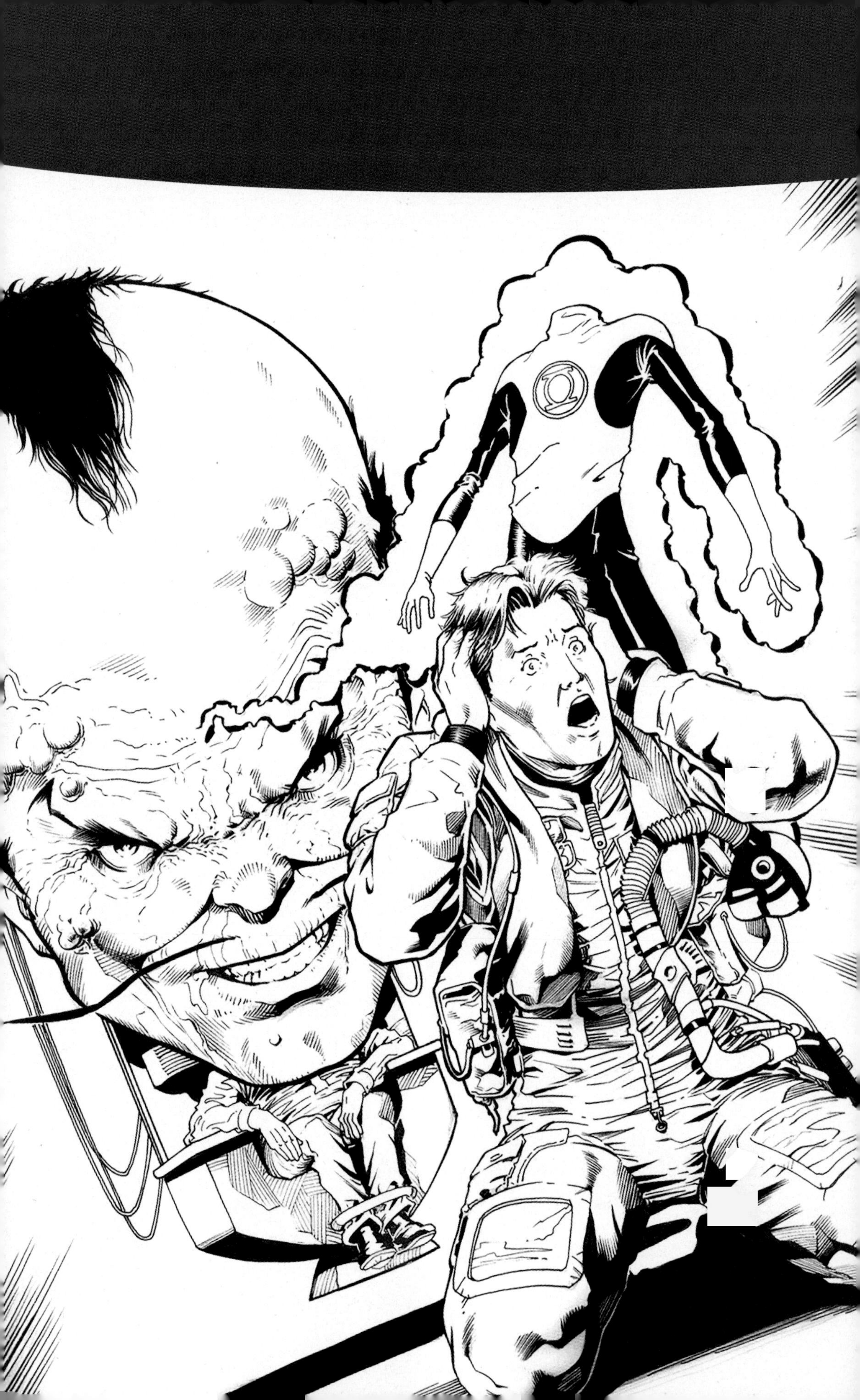

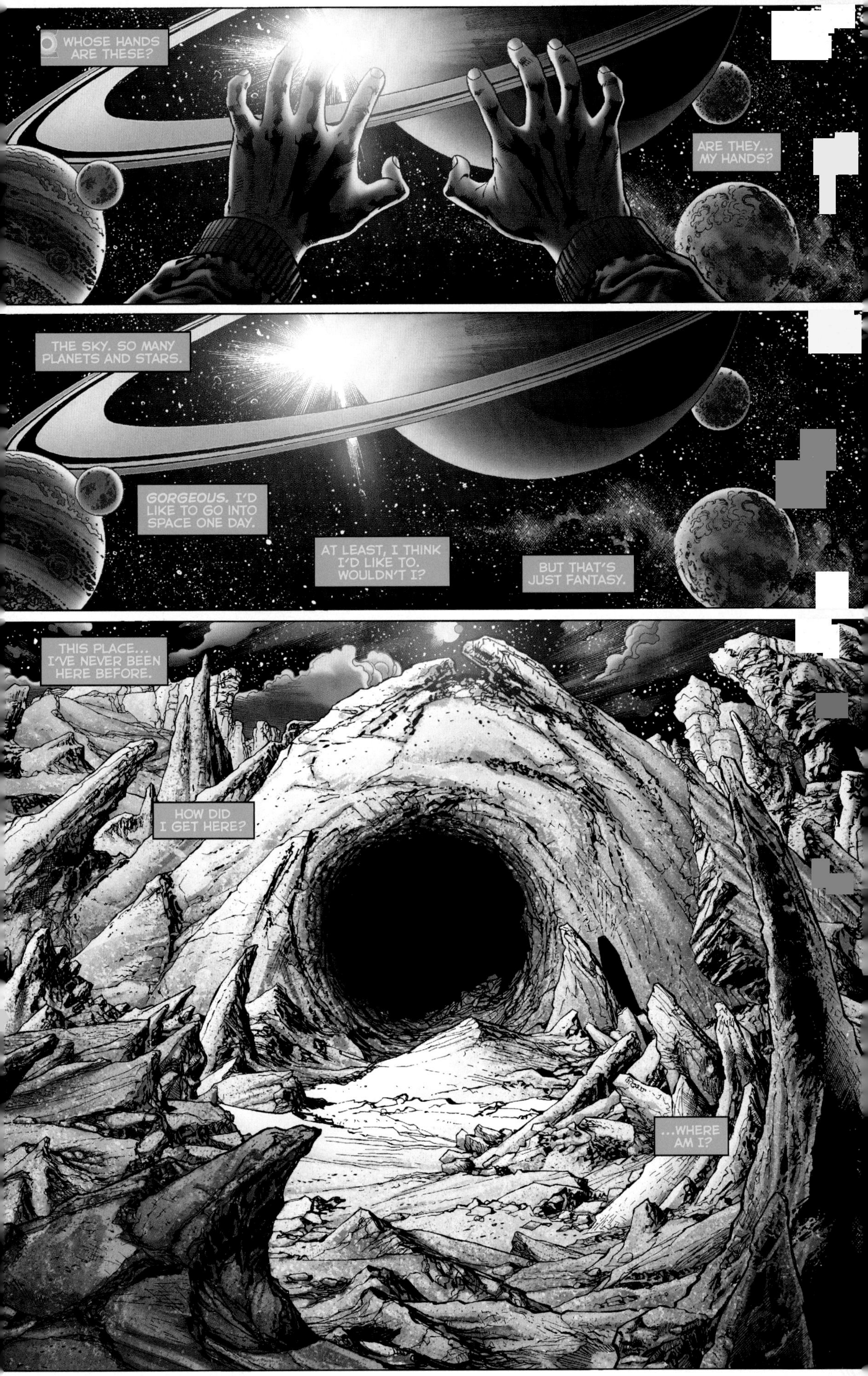
WHOSE HANDS ARE THESE?
ARE THEY... MY HANDS?
THE SKY. SO MANY PLANETS AND STARS.
GORGEOUS. I'D LIKE TO GO INTO SPACE ONE DAY.
AT LEAST, I THINK I'D LIKE TO. WOULDN'T I?
BUT THAT'S JUST FANTASY.
THIS PLACE... I'VE NEVER BEEN HERE BEFORE.
HOW DID I GET HERE?
...WHERE AM I?

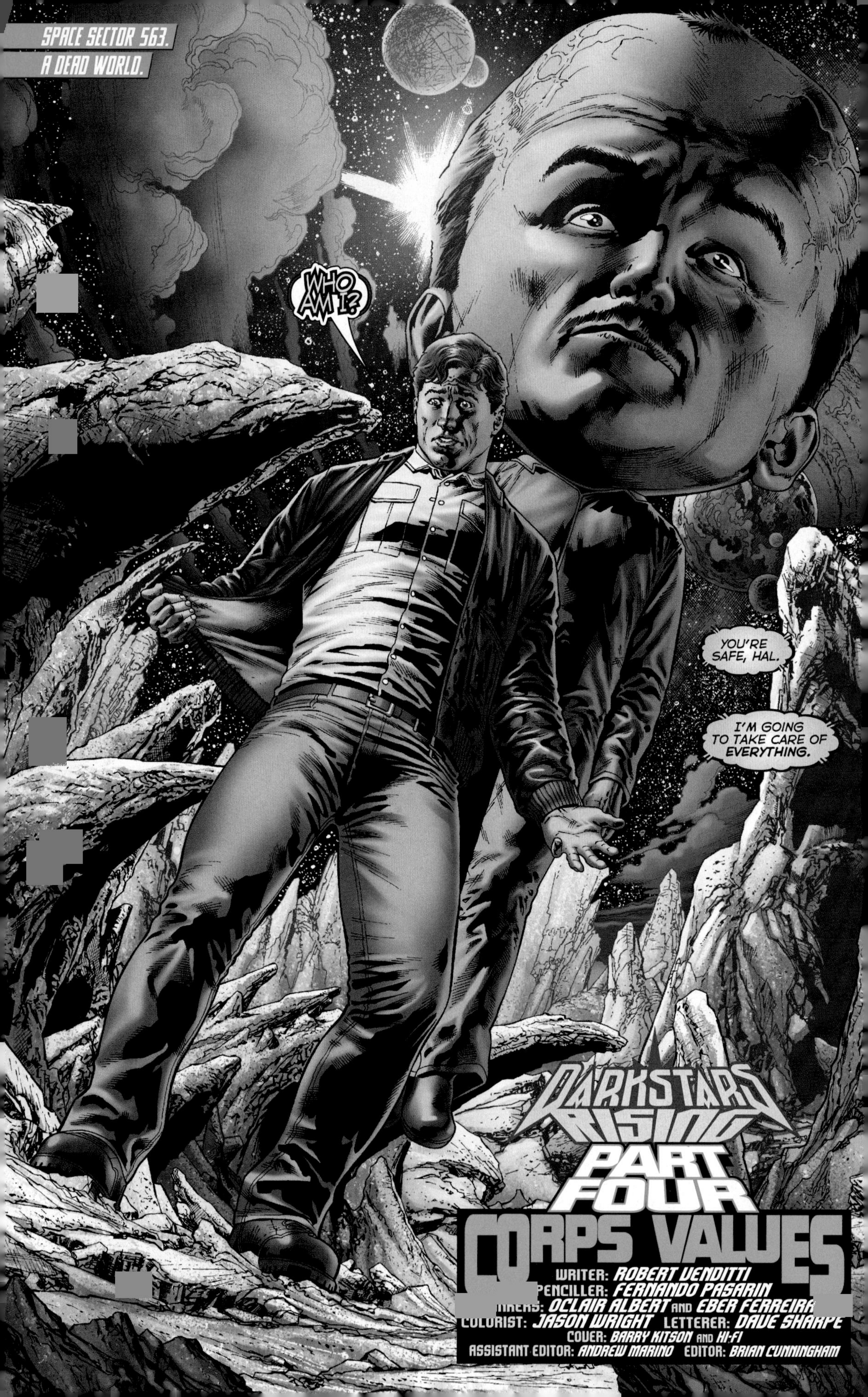
SPACE SECTOR 563.
A DEAD WORLD.
WHO AM I?
YOU'RE SAFE, HAL.
I'M GOING TO TAKE CARE OF EVERYTHING.
DARKSTARS RISING
PART FOUR
CORPS VALUES
WRITER: ROBERT VENDITTI
PENCILLER: FERNANDO PASARIN
OCLAIR ALBERT AND EBER FERREIR
COLORIST: JASON WRIGHT LETTERER: DAVE SHARPE
COVER: BARRY KITSON AND HI-FI
ASSISTANT EDITOR: ANDREW MARINO EDITOR: BRIAN CUNNINGHAM

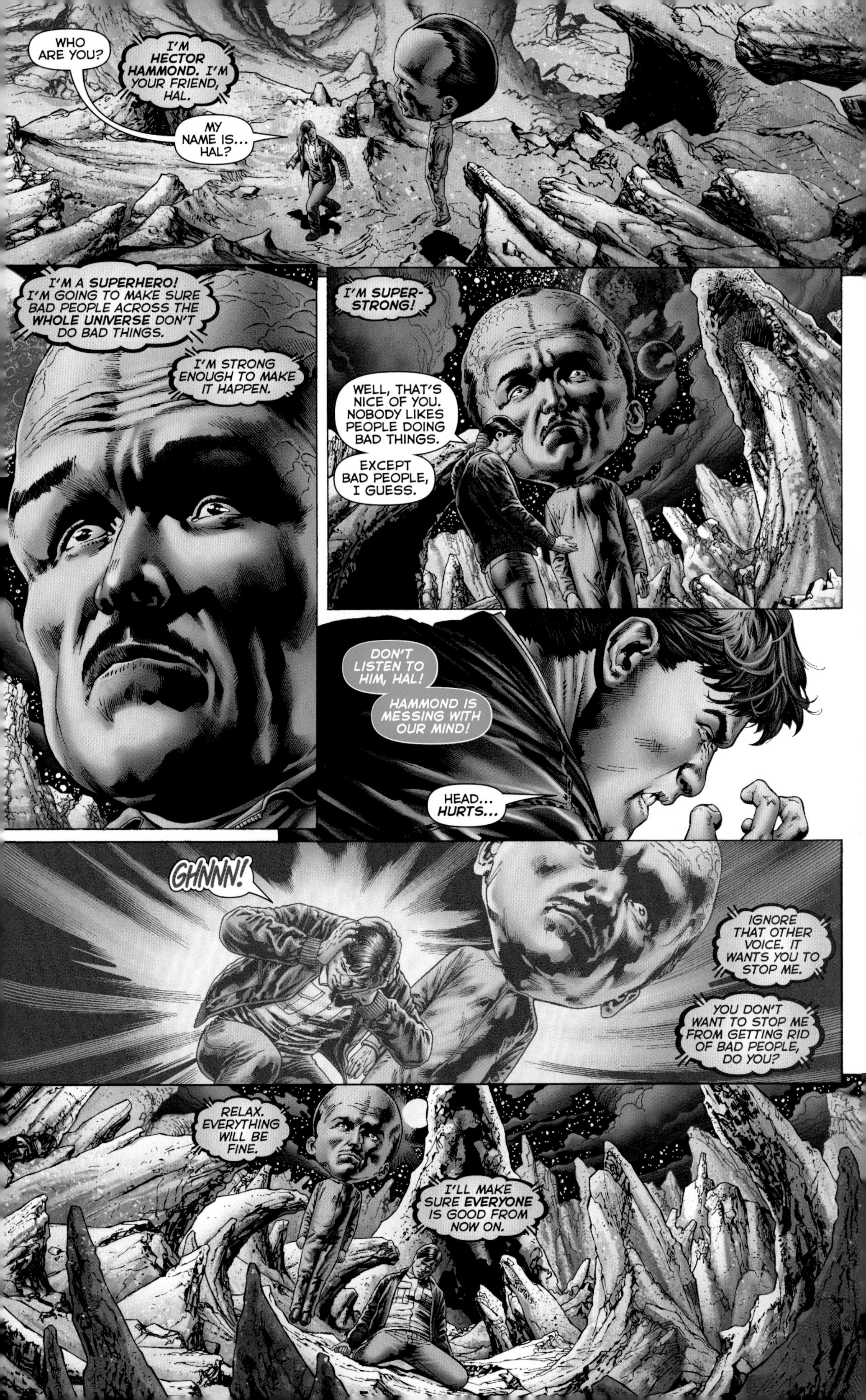
WHO ARE YOU?
I'M HECTOR HAMMOND. I'M YOUR FRIEND, HAL.
MY NAME IS... HAL?
I'M A SUPERHERO! I'M GOING TO MAKE SURE BAD PEOPLE ACROSS THE WHOLE UNIVERSE DON'T DO BAD THINGS.
I'M STRONG ENOUGH TO MAKE IT HAPPEN.
I'M SUPER-STRONG!
WELL, THAT'S NICE OF YOU. NOBODY LIKES PEOPLE DOING BAD THINGS.
EXCEPT BAD PEOPLE, I GUESS.
DON'T LISTEN TO HIM, HAL!
HAMMOND IS MESSING WITH OUR MIND!
HEAD... HURTS...
GHNNN!
IGNORE THAT OTHER VOICE. IT WANTS YOU TO STOP ME.
YOU DON'T WANT TO STOP ME FROM GETTING RID OF BAD PEOPLE, DO YOU?
RELAX. EVERYTHING WILL BE FINE.
I'LL MAKE SURE EVERYONE IS GOOD FROM NOW ON.

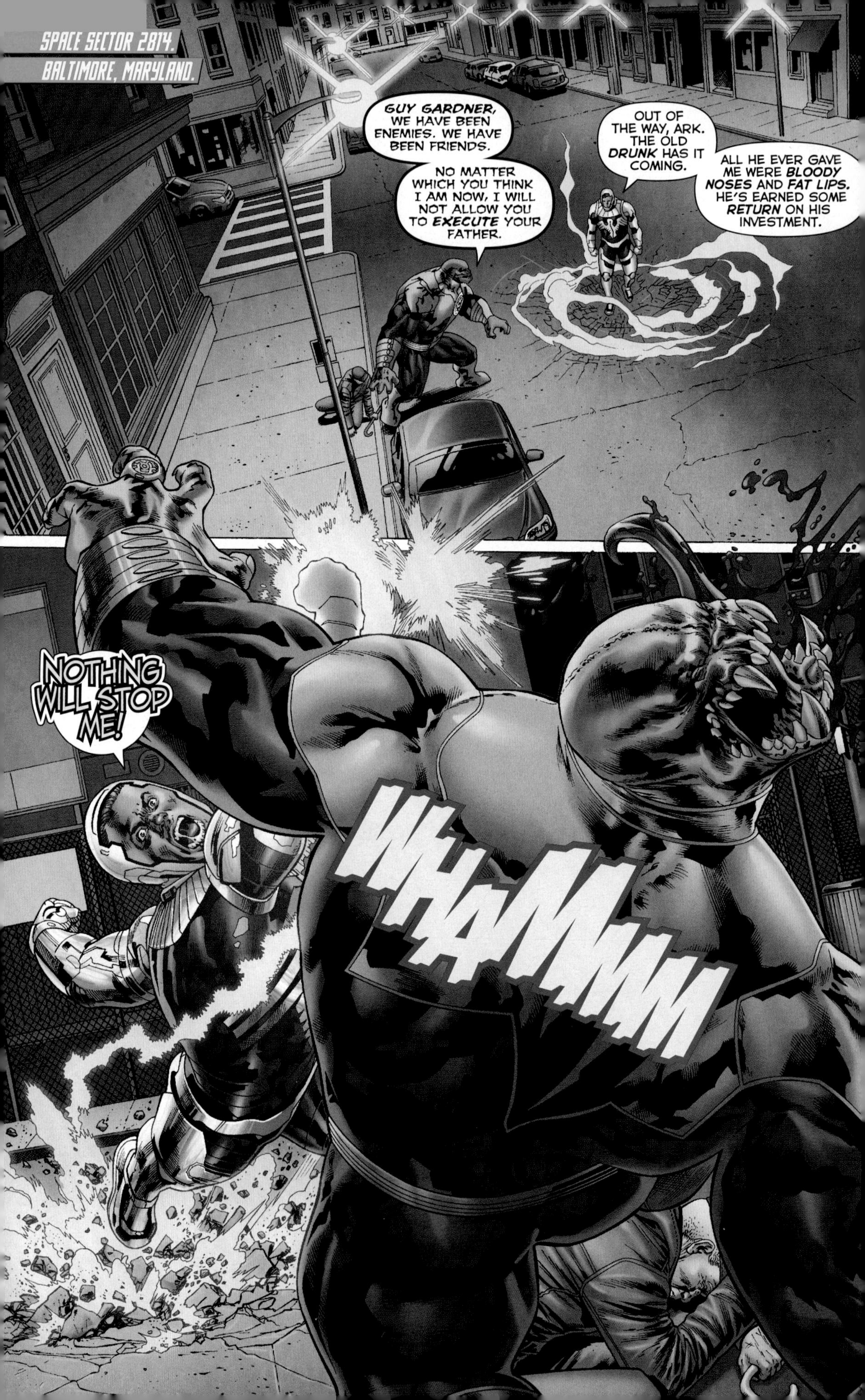
SPACE SECTOR 2814.
BALTIMORE, MARYLAND.
GUY GARDNER, WE HAVE BEEN ENEMIES. WE HAVE BEEN FRIENDS.
NO MATTER WHICH YOU THINK I AM NOW, I WILL NOT ALLOW YOU TO EXECUTE YOUR FATHER.
OUT OF THE WAY, ARK. THE OLD DRUNK HAS IT COMING.
ALL HE EVER GAVE ME WERE BLOODY NOSES AND FAT LIPS. HE'S EARNED SOME RETURN ON HIS INVESTMENT.
NOTHING WILL STOP ME!
WHAMMM

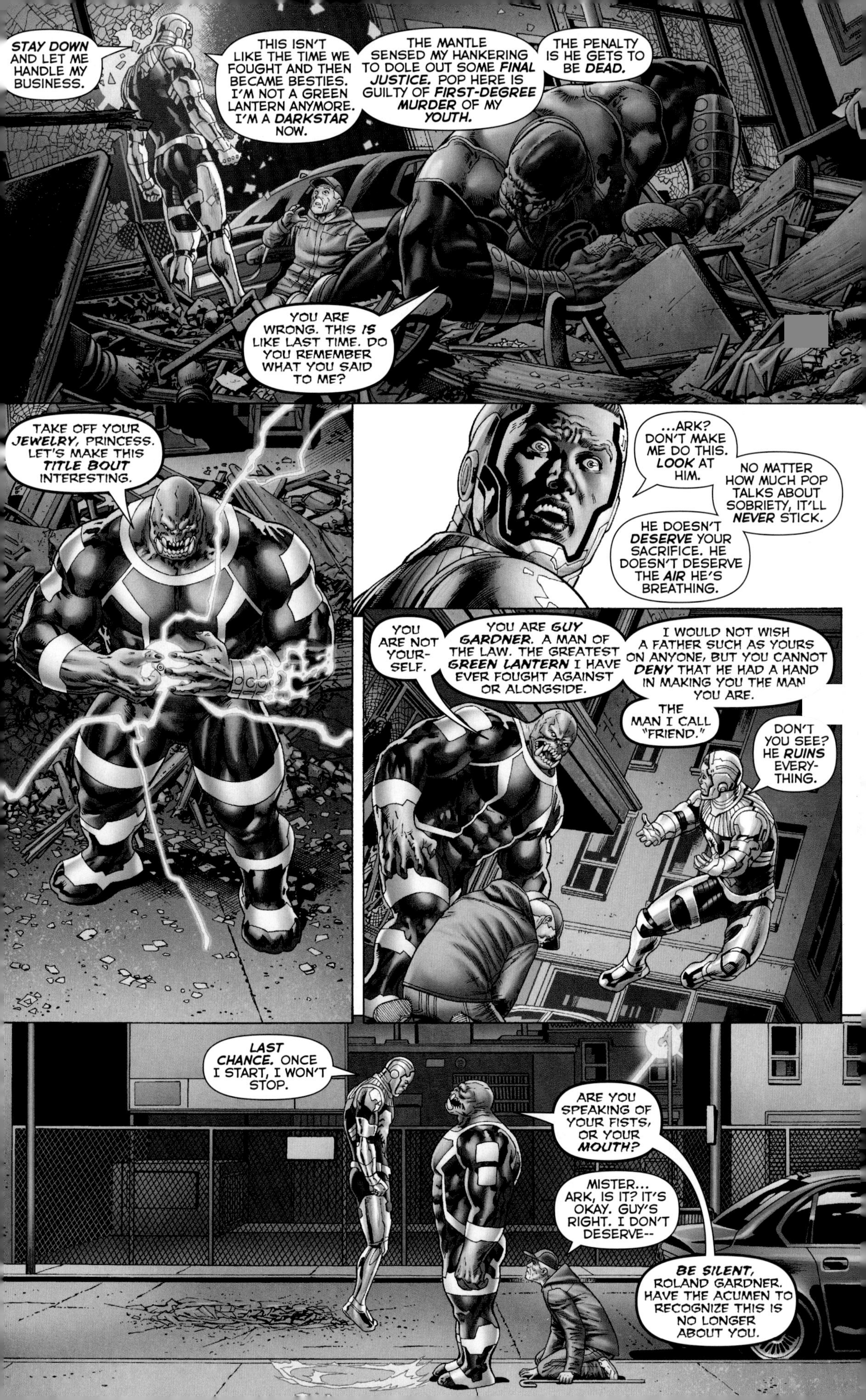
STAY DOWN AND LET ME HANDLE MY BUSINESS.
THIS ISN'T LIKE THE TIME WE FOUGHT AND THEN BECAME BESTIES. I'M NOT A GREEN LANTERN ANYMORE. I'M A DARKSTAR NOW.
THE MANTLE SENSED MY HANKERING TO DOLE OUT SOME FINAL JUSTICE. POP HERE IS GUILTY OF FIRST-DEGREE MURDER OF MY YOUTH.
THE PENALTY IS HE GETS TO BE DEAD.
YOU ARE WRONG. THIS IS LIKE LAST TIME. DO YOU REMEMBER WHAT YOU SAID TO ME?
TAKE OFF YOUR JEWELRY, PRINCESS. LET'S MAKE THIS TITLE BOUT INTERESTING.
...ARK? DON'T MAKE ME DO THIS. LOOK AT HIM.
NO MATTER HOW MUCH POP TALKS ABOUT SOBRIETY, IT'LL NEVER STICK.
HE DOESN'T DESERVE YOUR SACRIFICE. HE DOESN'T DESERVE THE AIR HE'S BREATHING.
YOU ARE NOT YOURSELF.
YOU ARE GUY GARDNER. A MAN OF THE LAW. THE GREATEST GREEN LANTERN I HAVE EVER FOUGHT AGAINST OR ALONGSIDE.
I WOULD NOT WISH A FATHER SUCH AS YOURS ON ANYONE, BUT YOU CANNOT DENY THAT HE HAD A HAND IN MAKING YOU THE MAN YOU ARE.
THE MAN I CALL "FRIEND."
DON'T YOU SEE? HE RUINS EVERYTHING.
LAST CHANCE. ONCE I START, I WON'T STOP.
ARE YOU SPEAKING OF YOUR FISTS, OR YOUR MOUTH?
MISTER... ARK, IS IT? IT'S OKAY. GUY'S RIGHT. I DON'T DESERVE--
BE SILENT, ROLAND GARDNER. HAVE THE ACUMEN TO RECOGNIZE THIS IS NO LONGER ABOUT YOU.

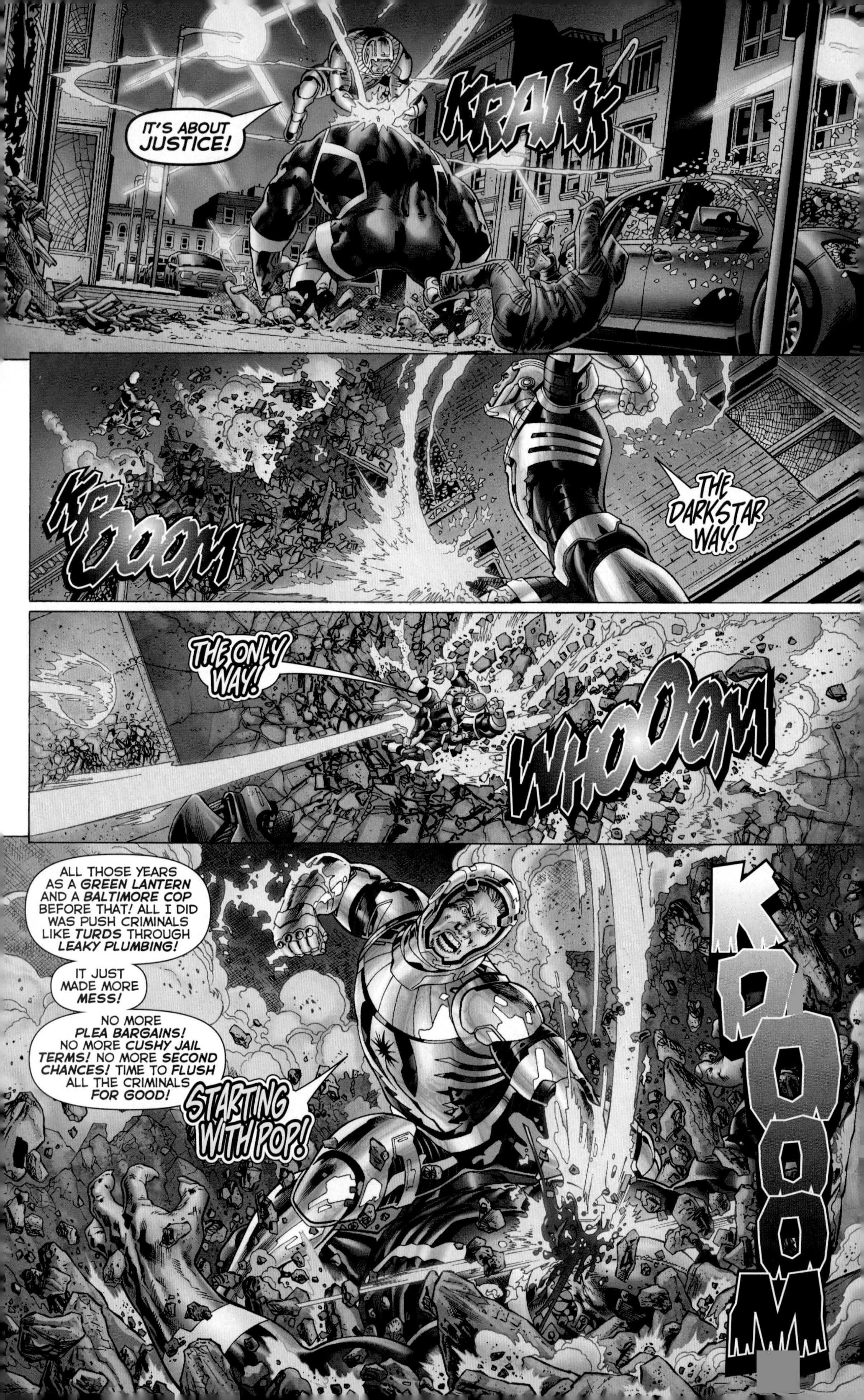
IT'S ABOUT JUSTICE!
KRAKK
KROOOM
THE DARKSTAR WAY!
THE ONLY WAY!
WHOOOM
ALL THOSE YEARS AS A GREEN LANTERN AND A BALTIMORE COP BEFORE THAT! ALL I DID WAS PUSH CRIMINALS LIKE TURDS THROUGH LEAKY PLUMBING!
IT JUST MADE MORE MESS!
NO MORE PLEA BARGAINS! NO MORE CUSHY JAIL TERMS! NO MORE SECOND CHANCES! TIME TO FLUSH ALL THE CRIMINALS FOR GOOD!
STARTING WITH POP!
KROOOOM

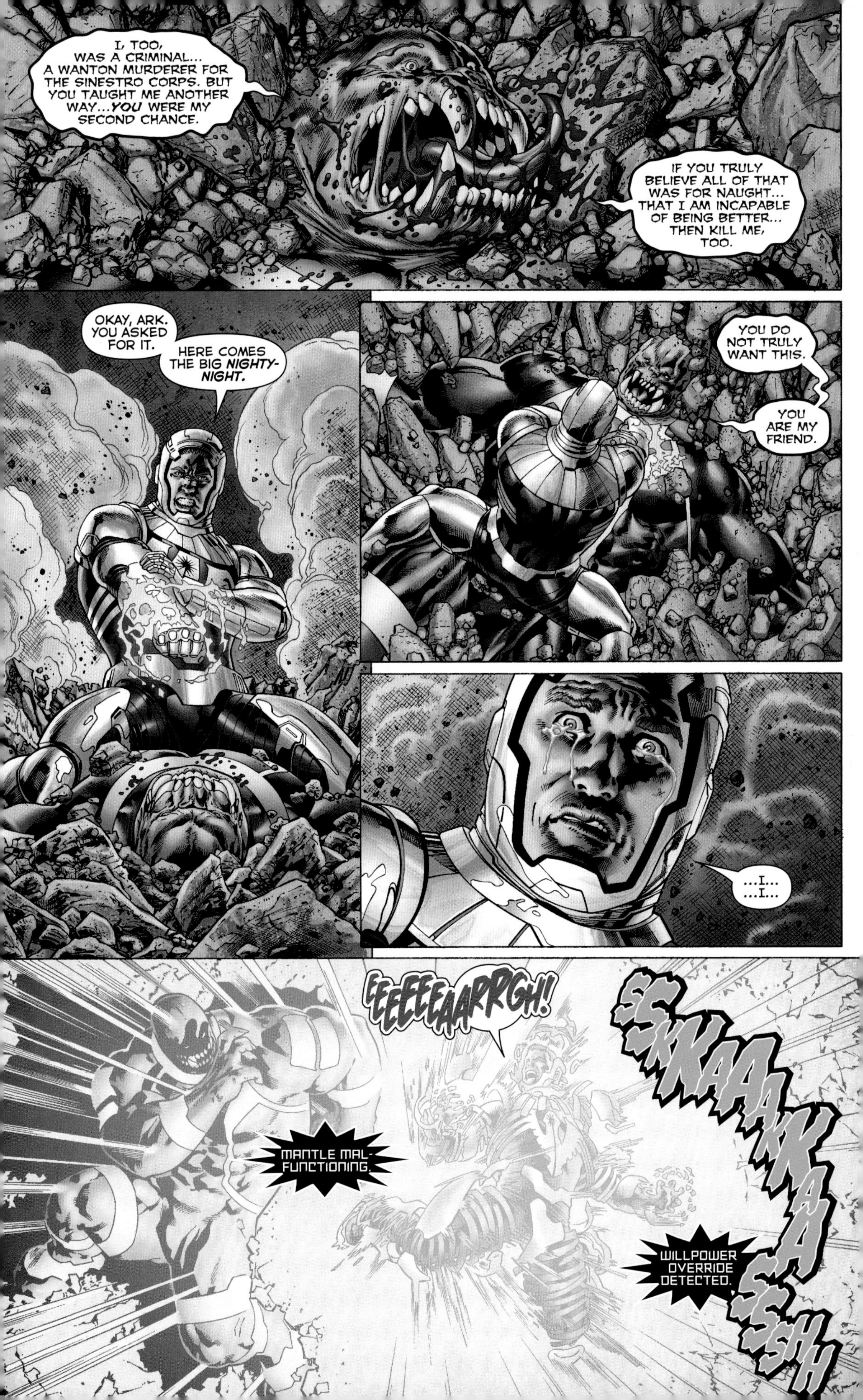
I, TOO, WAS A CRIMINAL... A WANTON MURDERER FOR THE SINESTRO CORPS. BUT YOU TAUGHT ME ANOTHER WAY...YOU WERE MY SECOND CHANCE.
IF YOU TRULY BELIEVE ALL OF THAT WAS FOR NAUGHT... THAT I AM INCAPABLE OF BEING BETTER... THEN KILL ME, TOO.
OKAY, ARK. YOU ASKED FOR IT.
HERE COMES THE BIG NIGHTY-NIGHT.
YOU DO NOT TRULY WANT THIS.
YOU ARE MY FRIEND.
...I...
...I...
EEEEEEAARRGH!
SSKKAAAKKAAASSSHH
MANTLE MAL-FUNCTIONING.
WILLPOWER OVERRIDE DETECTED.

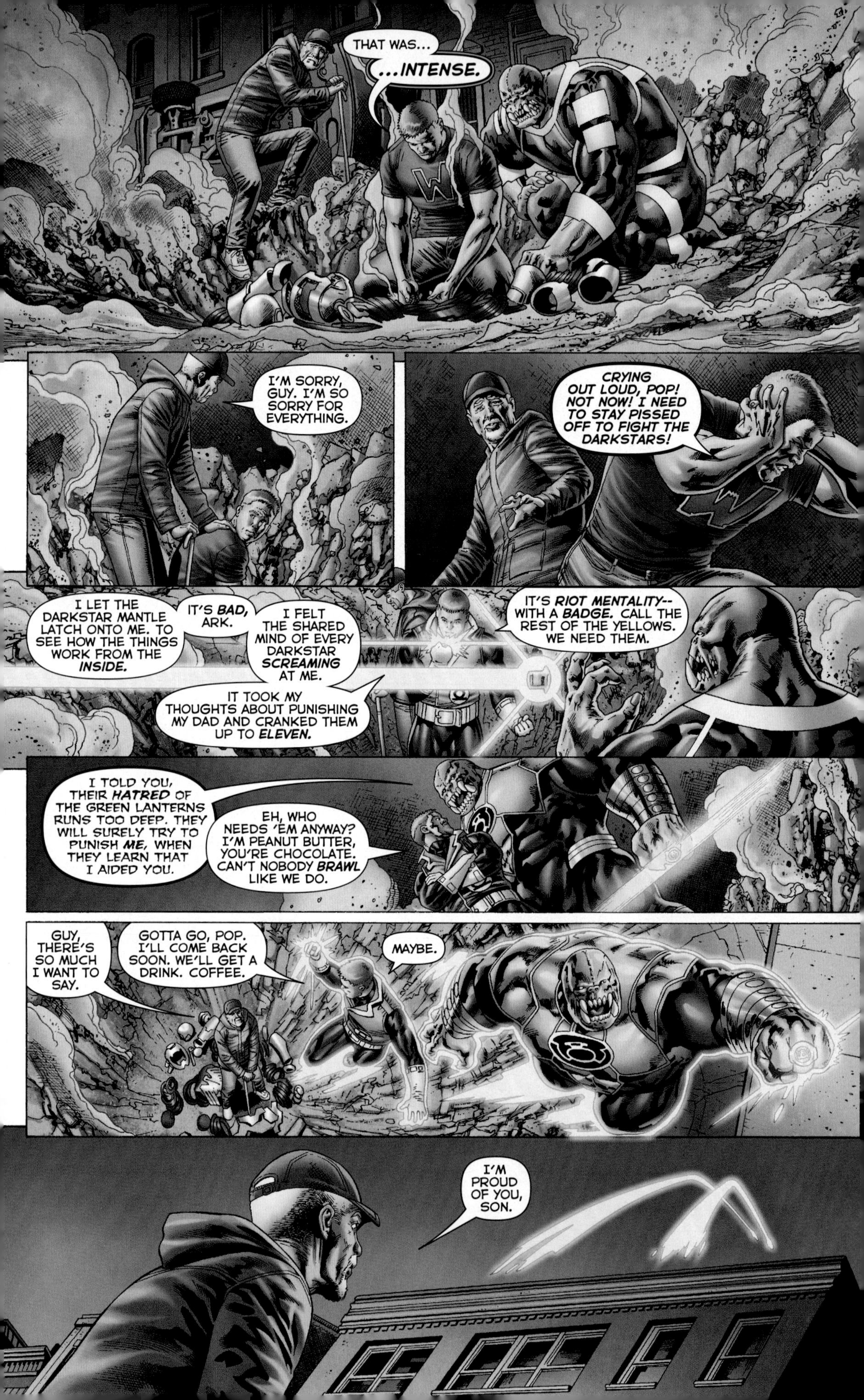
THAT WAS... ...INTENSE.
I'M SORRY, GUY. I'M SO SORRY FOR EVERYTHING.
CRYING OUT LOUD, POP! NOT NOW! I NEED TO STAY PISSED OFF TO FIGHT THE DARKSTARS!
I LET THE DARKSTAR MANTLE LATCH ONTO ME. TO SEE HOW THE THINGS WORK FROM THE INSIDE.
IT'S BAD, ARK.
I FELT THE SHARED MIND OF EVERY DARKSTAR SCREAMING AT ME.
IT TOOK MY THOUGHTS ABOUT PUNISHING MY DAD AND CRANKED THEM UP TO ELEVEN.
IT'S RIOT MENTALITY-- WITH A BADGE. CALL THE REST OF THE YELLOWS. WE NEED THEM.
I TOLD YOU, THEIR HATRED OF THE GREEN LANTERNS RUNS TOO DEEP. THEY WILL SURELY TRY TO PUNISH ME, WHEN THEY LEARN THAT I AIDED YOU.
EH, WHO NEEDS 'EM ANYWAY? I'M PEANUT BUTTER, YOU'RE CHOCOLATE. CAN'T NOBODY BRAWL LIKE WE DO.
GUY, THERE'S SO MUCH I WANT TO SAY.
GOTTA GO, POP. I'LL COME BACK SOON. WE'LL GET A DRINK. COFFEE.
MAYBE.
I'M PROUD OF YOU, SON.

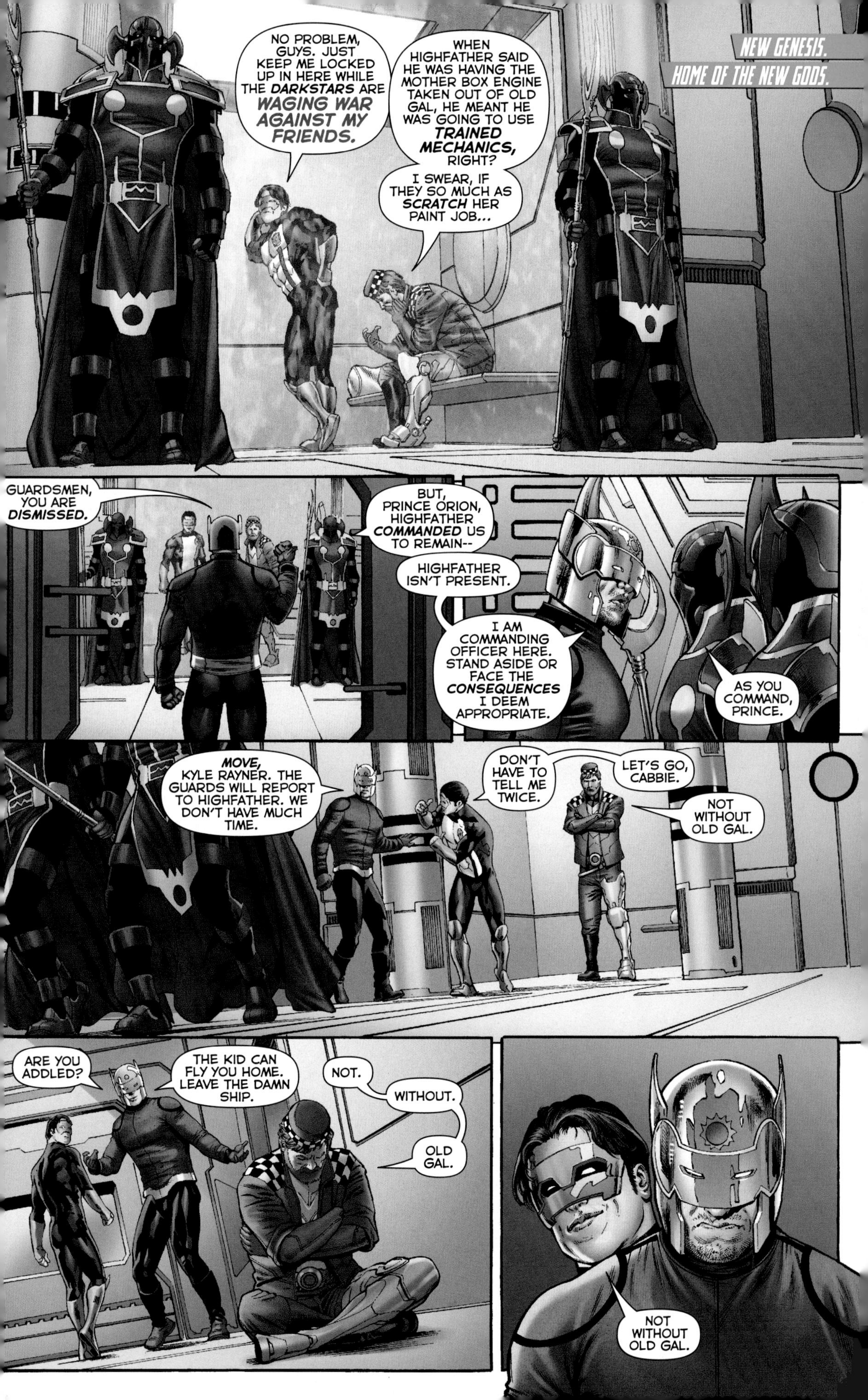

NEW GENESIS.
HOME OF THE NEW GODS.
NO PROBLEM, GUYS. JUST KEEP ME LOCKED UP IN HERE WHILE THE DARKSTARS ARE WAGING WAR AGAINST MY FRIENDS.
WHEN HIGHFATHER SAID HE WAS HAVING THE MOTHER BOX ENGINE TAKEN OUT OF OLD GAL, HE MEANT HE WAS GOING TO USE TRAINED MECHANICS, RIGHT?
I SWEAR, IF THEY SO MUCH AS SCRATCH HER PAINT JOB...
GUARDSMEN, YOU ARE DISMISSED.
BUT, PRINCE ORION, HIGHFATHER COMMANDED US TO REMAIN--
HIGHFATHER ISN'T PRESENT.
I AM COMMANDING OFFICER HERE. STAND ASIDE OR FACE THE CONSEQUENCES I DEEM APPROPRIATE.
AS YOU COMMAND, PRINCE.
MOVE, KYLE RAYNER. THE GUARDS WILL REPORT TO HIGHFATHER. WE DON'T HAVE MUCH TIME.
DON'T HAVE TO TELL ME TWICE.
LET'S GO, CABBIE.
NOT WITHOUT OLD GAL.
ARE YOU ADDLED?
THE KID CAN FLY YOU HOME. LEAVE THE DAMN SHIP.
NOT.
WITHOUT.
OLD GAL.
NOT WITHOUT OLD GAL.

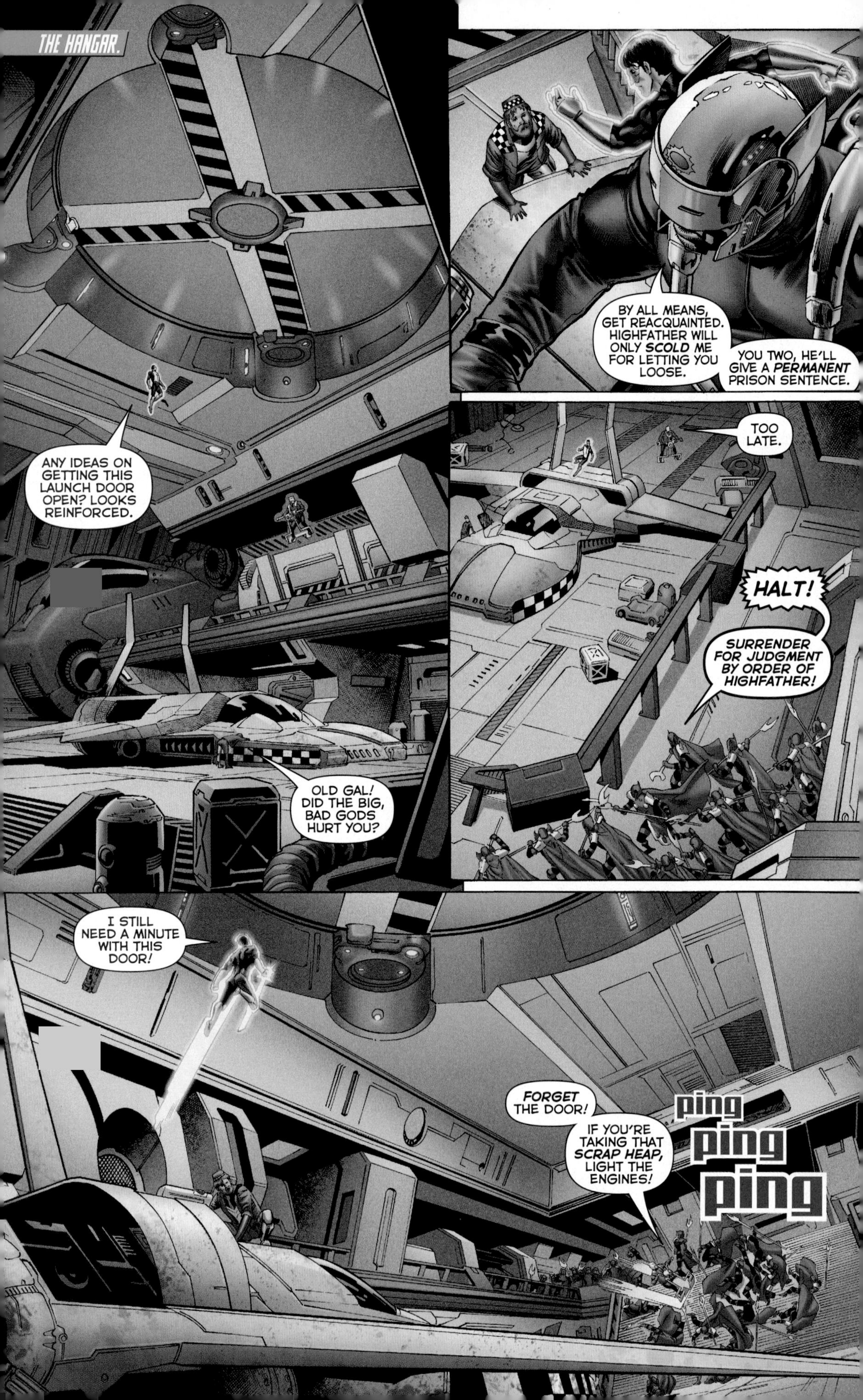
THE HANGAR.
ANY IDEAS ON GETTING THIS LAUNCH DOOR OPEN? LOOKS REINFORCED.
OLD GAL! DID THE BIG, BAD GODS HURT YOU?
BY ALL MEANS, GET REACQUAINTED. HIGHFATHER WILL ONLY SCOLD ME FOR LETTING YOU LOOSE.
YOU TWO, HE'LL GIVE A PERMANENT PRISON SENTENCE.
TOO LATE.
HALT!
SURRENDER FOR JUDGMENT BY ORDER OF HIGHFATHER!
I STILL NEED A MINUTE WITH THIS DOOR!
FORGET THE DOOR!
IF YOU'RE TAKING THAT SCRAP HEAP, LIGHT THE ENGINES!
ping
ping
ping

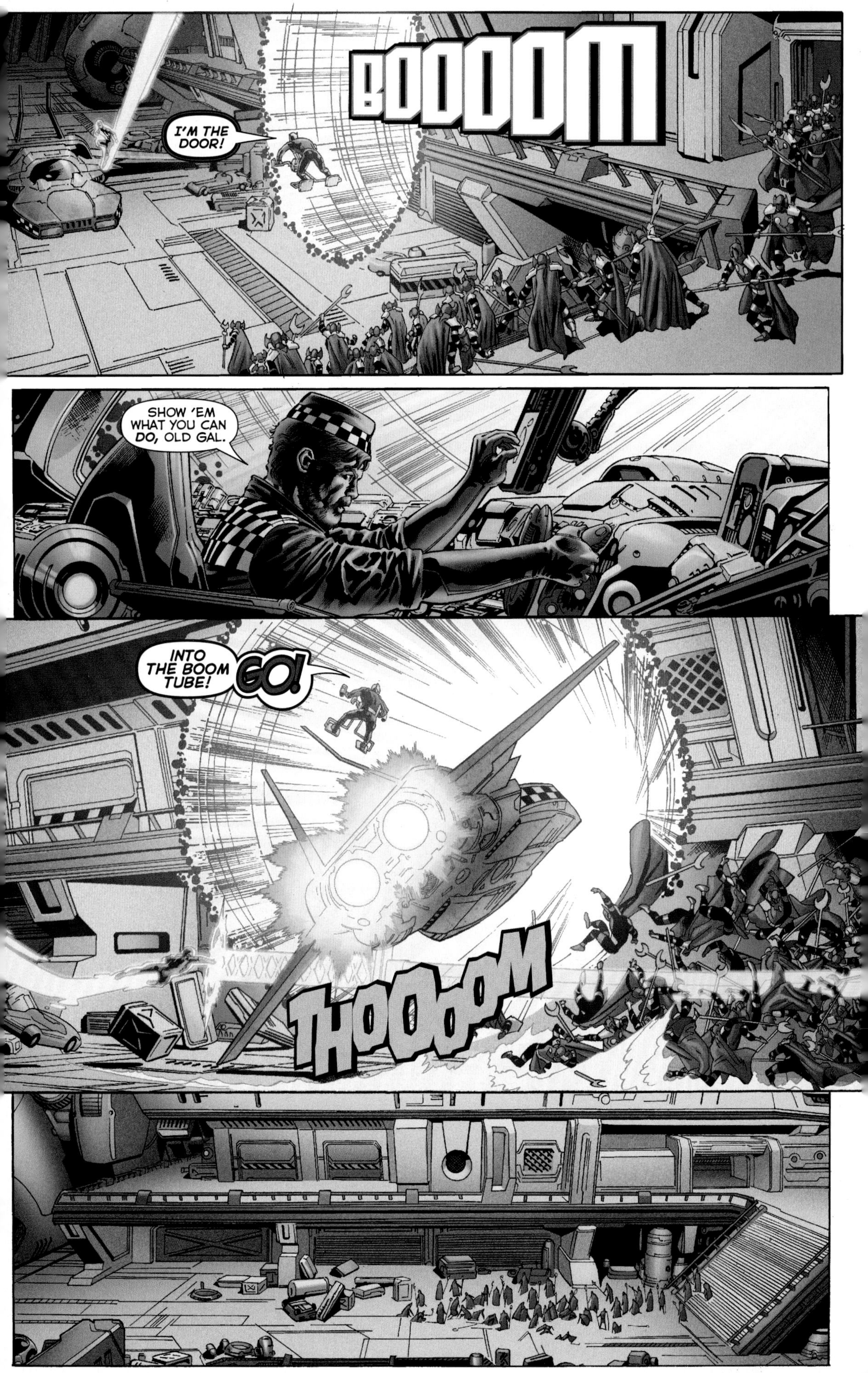
BOOOOM
I'M THE DOOR!
SHOW 'EM WHAT YOU CAN DO, OLD GAL.
INTO THE BOOM TUBE!
GO!
THOOooM

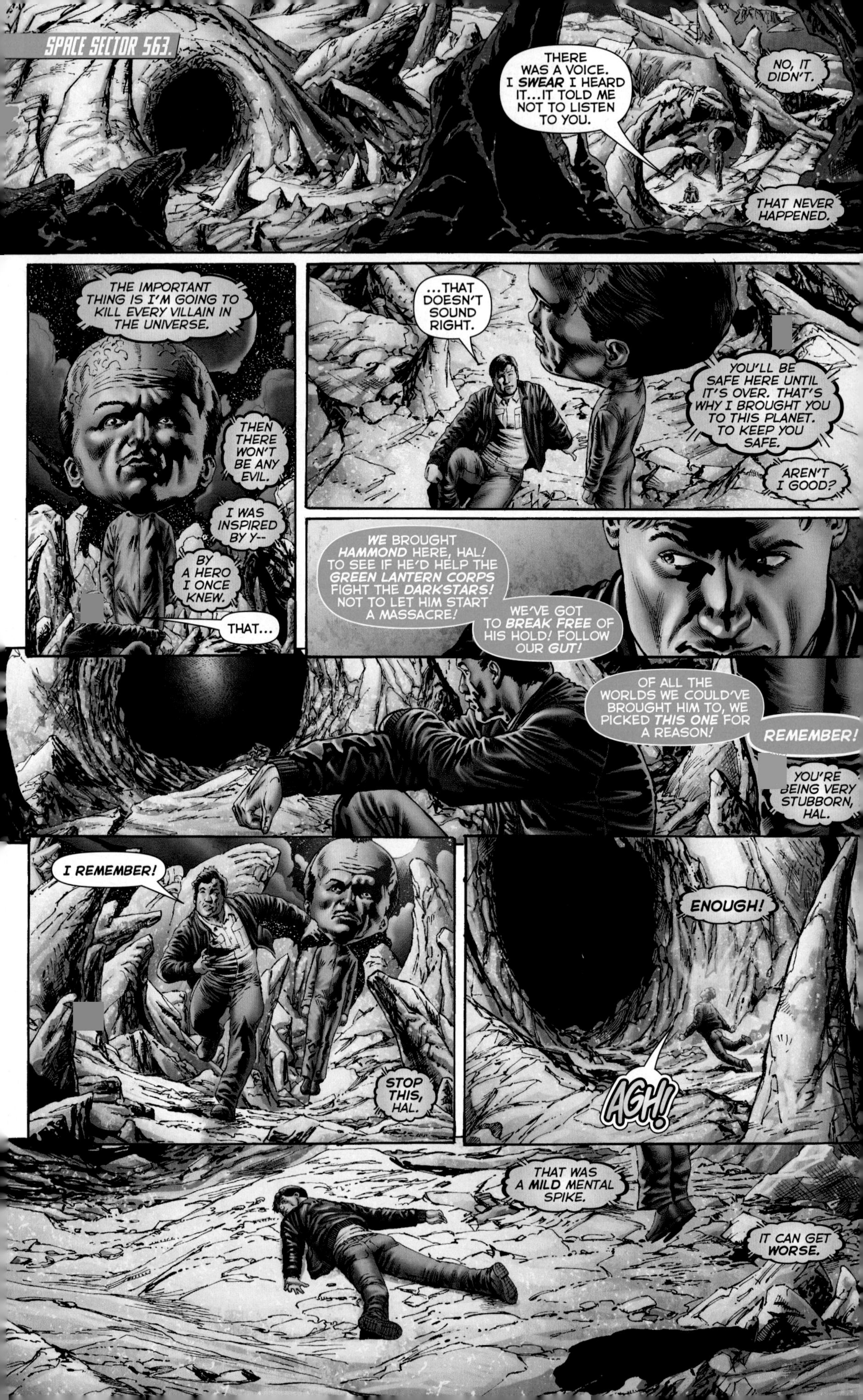
SPACE SECTOR 563.
THERE WAS A VOICE. I SWEAR I HEARD IT...IT TOLD ME NOT TO LISTEN TO YOU.
NO, IT DIDN'T.
THAT NEVER HAPPENED.
THE IMPORTANT THING IS I'M GOING TO KILL EVERY VILLAIN IN THE UNIVERSE.
THEN THERE WON'T BE ANY EVIL.
I WAS INSPIRED BY Y--
BY A HERO I ONCE KNEW.
THAT...
...THAT DOESN'T SOUND RIGHT.
YOU'LL BE SAFE HERE UNTIL IT'S OVER. THAT'S WHY I BROUGHT YOU TO THIS PLANET. TO KEEP YOU SAFE.
AREN'T I GOOD?
WE BROUGHT HAMMOND HERE, HAL! TO SEE IF HE'D HELP THE GREEN LANTERN CORPS FIGHT THE DARKSTARS! NOT TO LET HIM START A MASSACRE!
WE'VE GOT TO BREAK FREE OF HIS HOLD! FOLLOW OUR GUT!
OF ALL THE WORLDS WE COULD'VE BROUGHT HIM TO, WE PICKED THIS ONE FOR A REASON!
REMEMBER!
YOU'RE BEING VERY STUBBORN, HAL.
I REMEMBER!
STOP THIS, HAL.
ENOUGH!
AGH!
THAT WAS A MILD MENTAL SPIKE.
IT CAN GET WORSE.

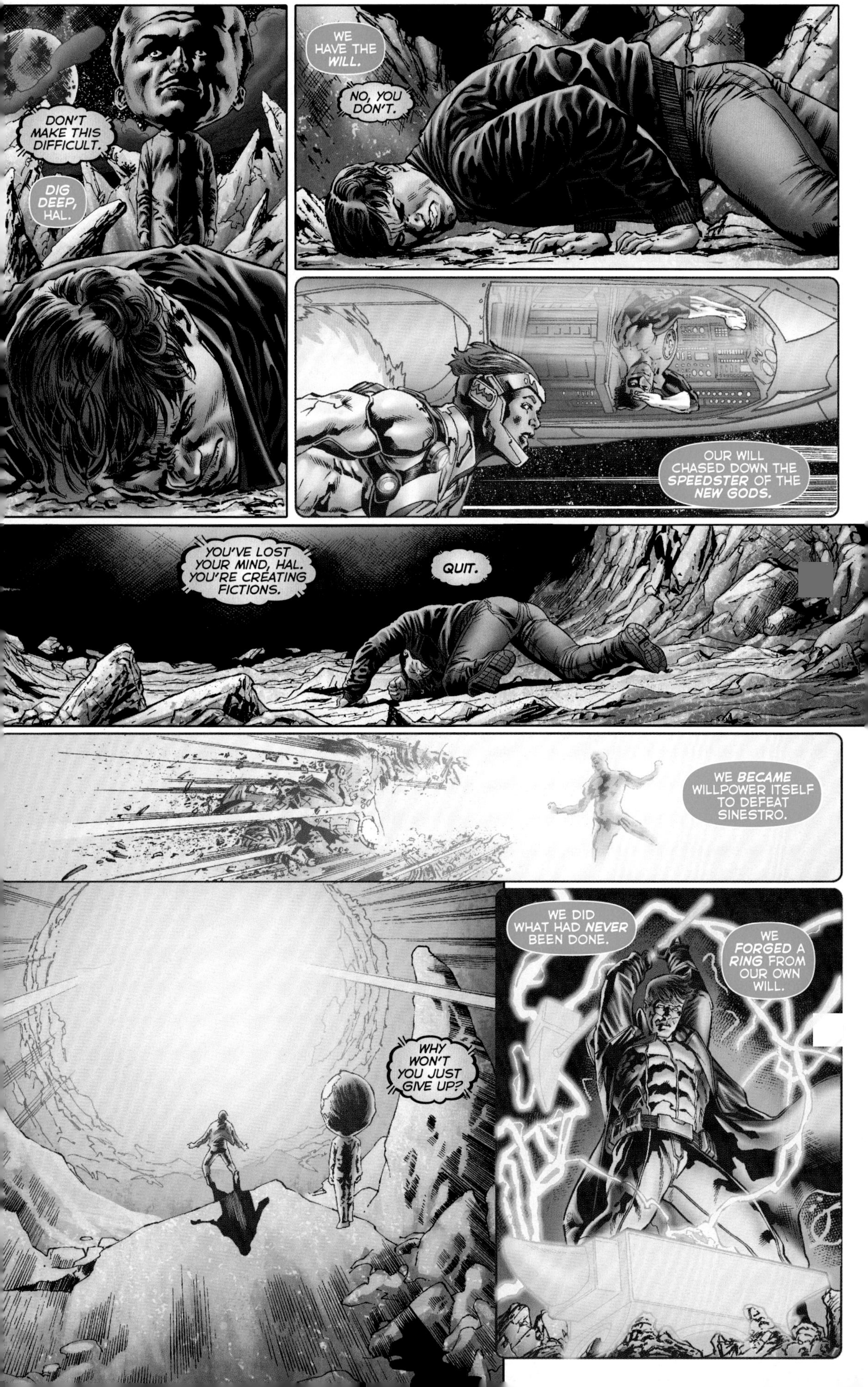
DON'T MAKE THIS DIFFICULT.
DIG DEEP, HAL.
WE HAVE THE WILL.
NO, YOU DON'T.
OUR WILL CHASED DOWN THE SPEEDSTER OF THE NEW GODS.
YOU'VE LOST YOUR MIND, HAL. YOU'RE CREATING FICTIONS.
QUIT.
WE BECAME WILLPOWER ITSELF TO DEFEAT SINESTRO.
WHY WON'T YOU JUST GIVE UP?
WE DID WHAT HAD NEVER BEEN DONE.
WE FORGED A RING FROM OUR OWN WILL.

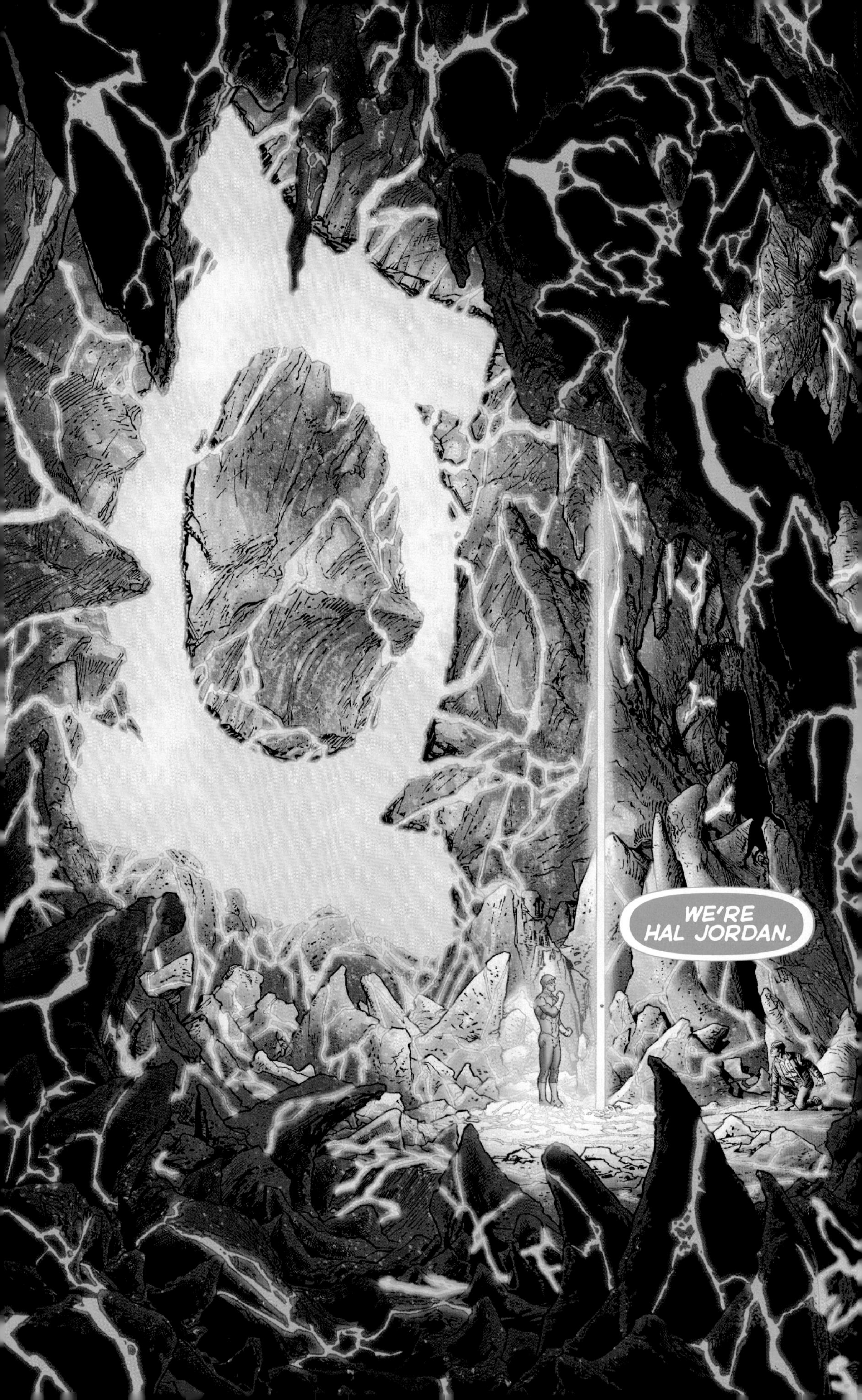
WE'RE HAL JORDAN.

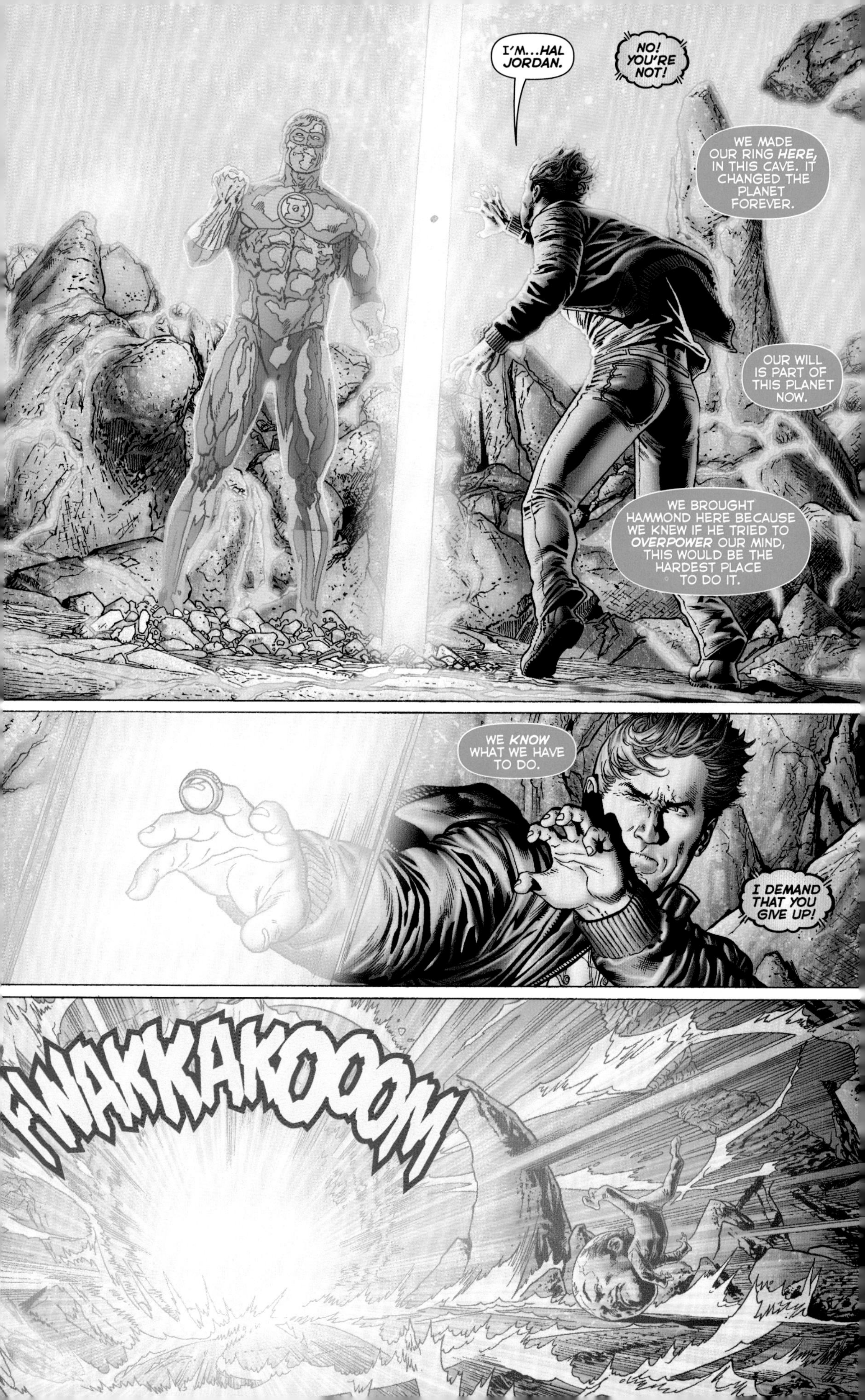
I'M...HAL JORDAN.
NO! YOU'RE NOT!
WE MADE OUR RING HERE, IN THIS CAVE. IT CHANGED THE PLANET FOREVER.
OUR WILL IS PART OF THIS PLANET NOW.
WE BROUGHT HAMMOND HERE BECAUSE WE KNEW IF HE TRIED TO OVERPOWER OUR MIND, THIS WOULD BE THE HARDEST PLACE TO DO IT.
WE KNOW WHAT WE HAVE TO DO.
I DEMAND THAT YOU GIVE UP!
WAKKAKOOOM

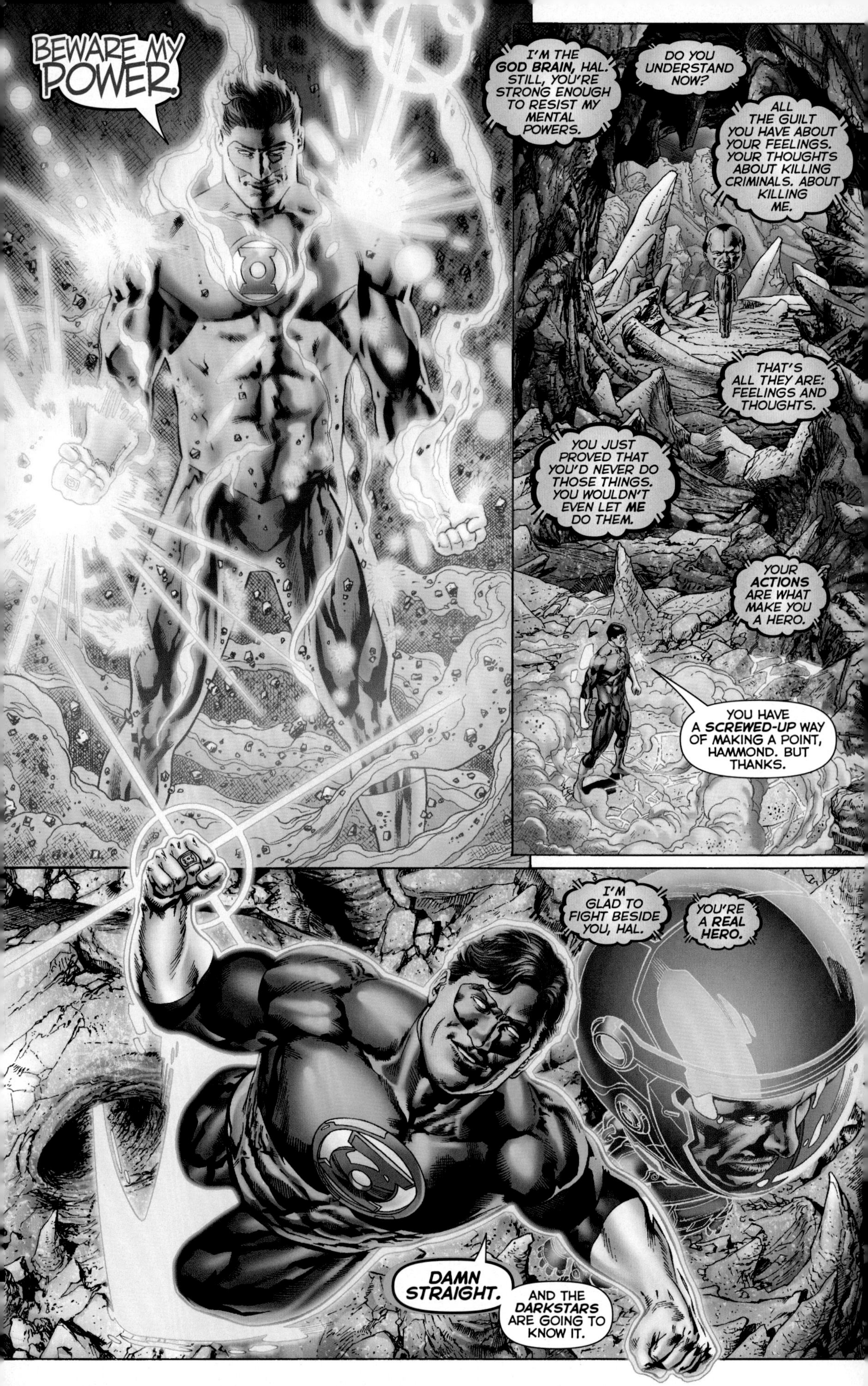
BEWARE MY POWER.
I'M THE GOD BRAIN, HAL. STILL, YOU'RE STRONG ENOUGH TO RESIST MY MENTAL POWERS.
DO YOU UNDERSTAND NOW?
ALL THE GUILT YOU HAVE ABOUT YOUR FEELINGS. YOUR THOUGHTS ABOUT KILLING CRIMINALS. ABOUT KILLING ME.
THAT'S ALL THEY ARE: FEELINGS AND THOUGHTS.
YOU JUST PROVED THAT YOU'D NEVER DO THOSE THINGS. YOU WOULDN'T EVEN LET ME DO THEM.
YOUR ACTIONS ARE WHAT MAKE YOU A HERO.
YOU HAVE A SCREWED-UP WAY OF MAKING A POINT, HAMMOND. BUT THANKS.
I'M GLAD TO FIGHT BESIDE YOU, HAL.
YOU'RE A REAL HERO.
DAMN STRAIGHT.
AND THE DARKSTARS ARE GOING TO KNOW IT.

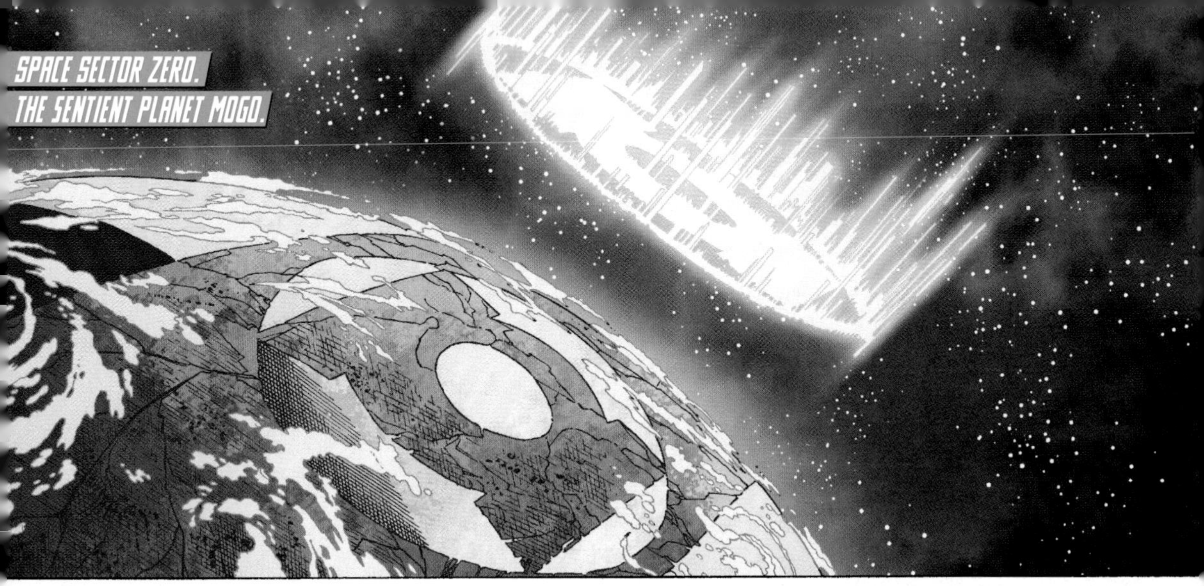
SPACE SECTOR ZERO.
THE SENTIENT PLANET MOGO.

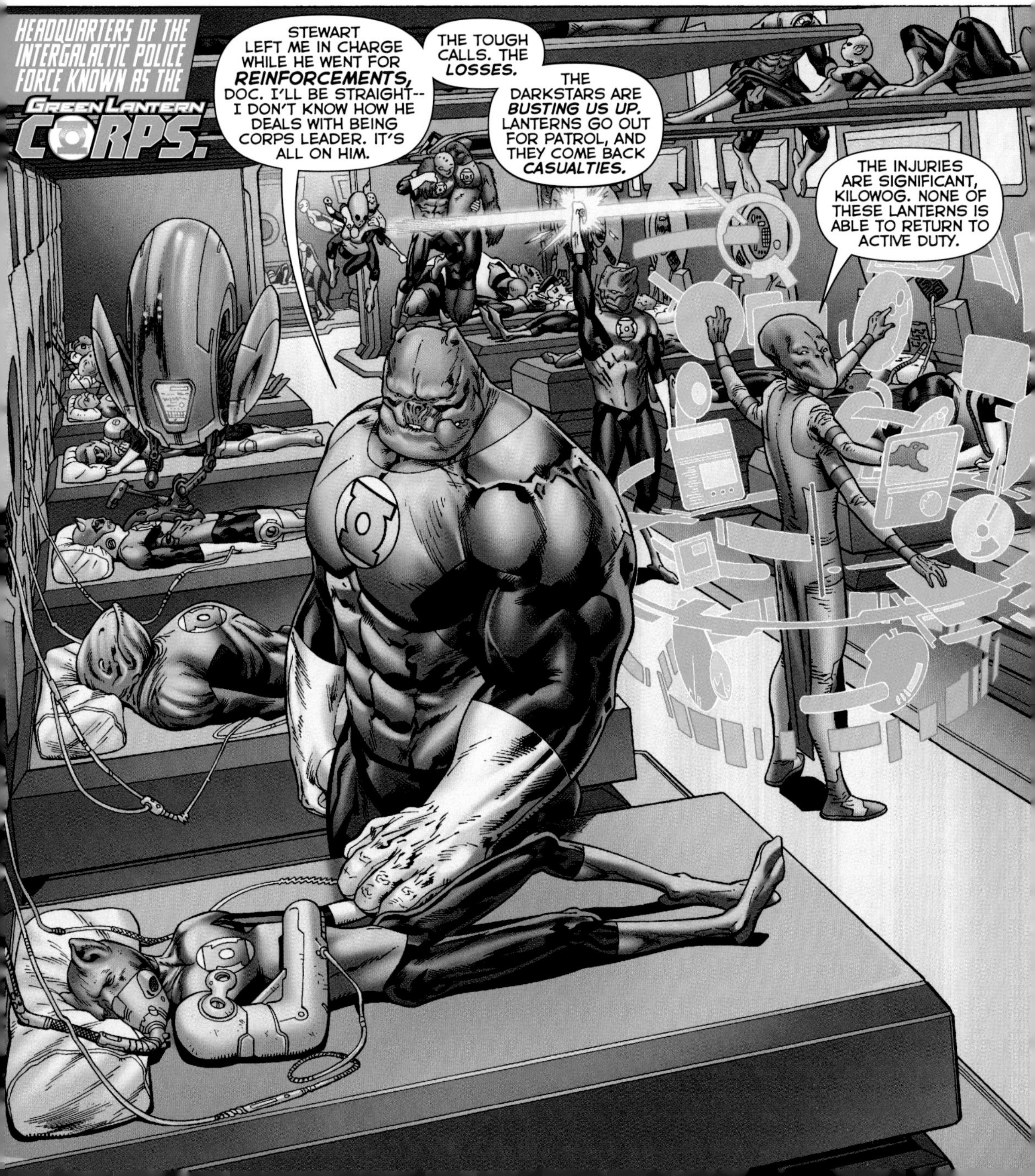
HEADQUARTERS OF THE INTERGALACTIC POLICE FORCE KNOWN AS THE GREEN LANTERN CORPS.
STEWART LEFT ME IN CHARGE WHILE HE WENT FOR REINFORCEMENTS, DOC. I'LL BE STRAIGHT-- I DON'T KNOW HOW HE DEALS WITH BEING CORPS LEADER. IT'S ALL ON HIM.
THE TOUGH CALLS. THE LOSSES.
THE DARKSTARS ARE BUSTING US UP. LANTERNS GO OUT FOR PATROL, AND THEY COME BACK CASUALTIES.
THE INJURIES ARE SIGNIFICANT, KILOWOG. NONE OF THESE LANTERNS IS ABLE TO RETURN TO ACTIVE DUTY.

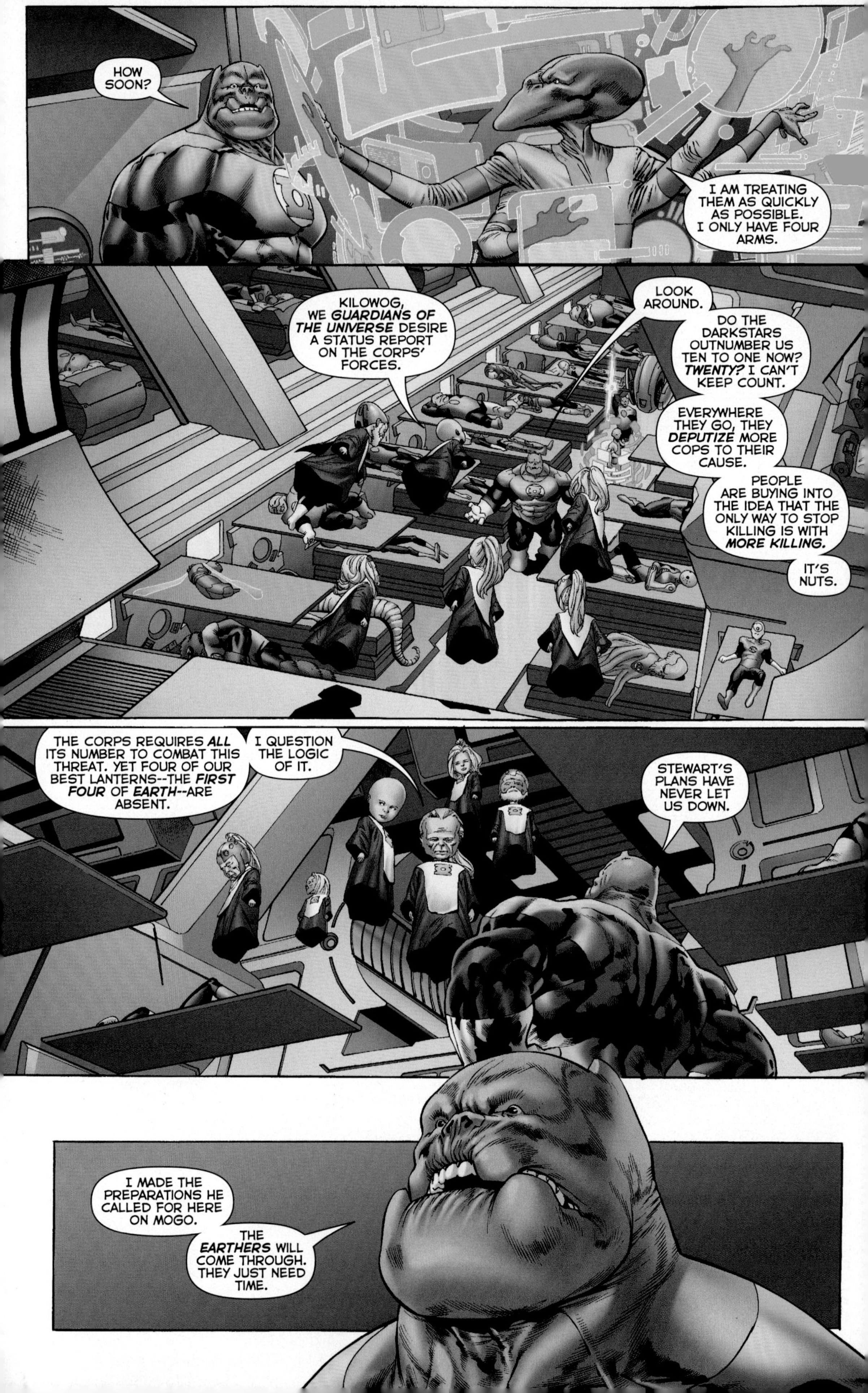
HOW SOON?
I AM TREATING THEM AS QUICKLY AS POSSIBLE. I ONLY HAVE FOUR ARMS.
KILOWOG, WE GUARDIANS OF THE UNIVERSE DESIRE A STATUS REPORT ON THE CORPS' FORCES.
LOOK AROUND.
DO THE DARKSTARS OUTNUMBER US TEN TO ONE NOW? TWENTY? I CAN'T KEEP COUNT.
EVERYWHERE THEY GO, THEY DEPUTIZE MORE COPS TO THEIR CAUSE.
PEOPLE ARE BUYING INTO THE IDEA THAT THE ONLY WAY TO STOP KILLING IS WITH MORE KILLING.
IT'S NUTS.
THE CORPS REQUIRES ALL ITS NUMBER TO COMBAT THIS THREAT. YET FOUR OF OUR BEST LANTERNS--THE FIRST FOUR OF EARTH--ARE ABSENT.
I QUESTION THE LOGIC OF IT.
STEWART'S PLANS HAVE NEVER LET US DOWN.
I MADE THE PREPARATIONS HE CALLED FOR HERE ON MOGO.
THE EARTHERS WILL COME THROUGH. THEY JUST NEED TIME.

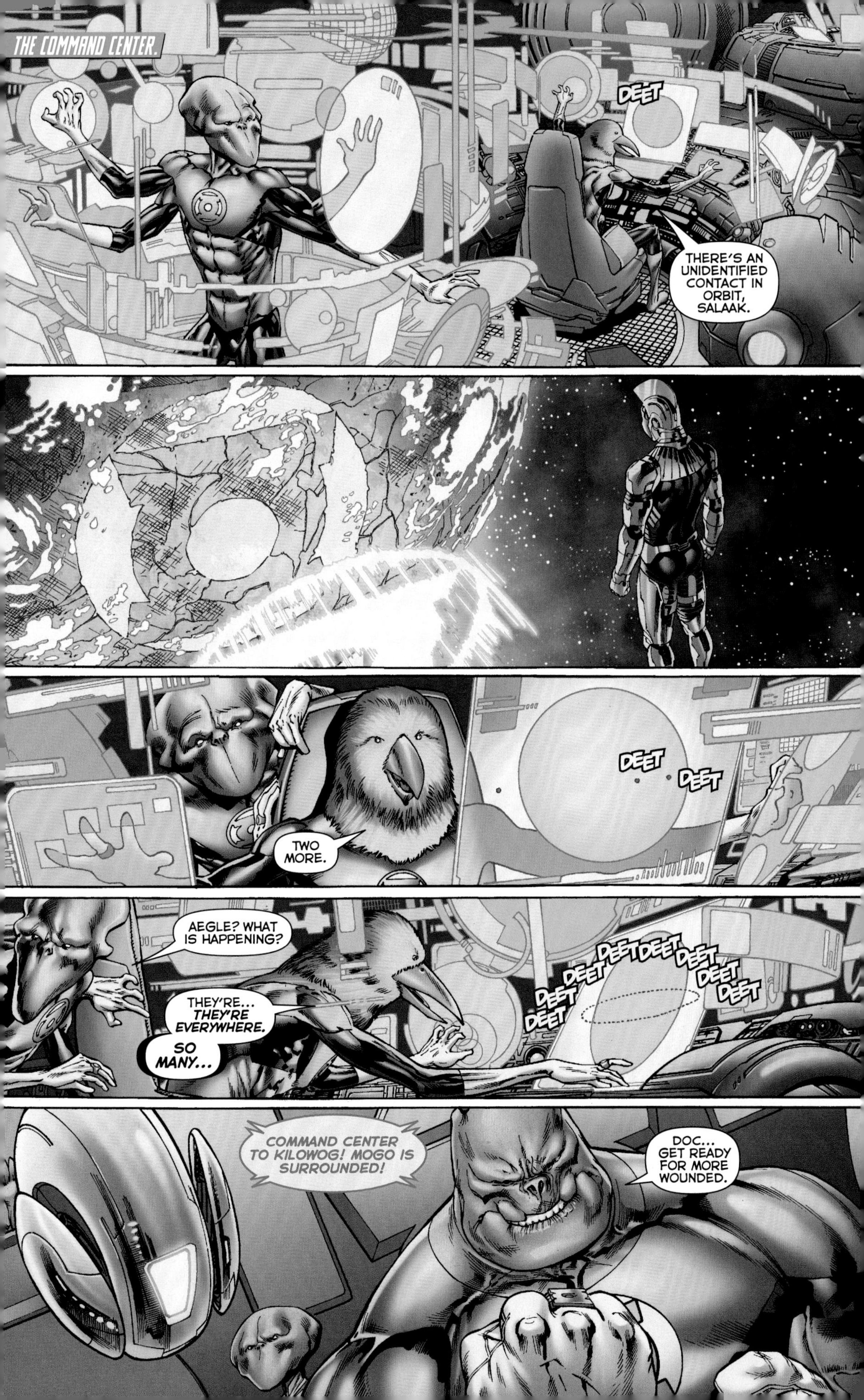
THE COMMAND CENTER.
DEET
THERE'S AN UNIDENTIFIED CONTACT IN ORBIT, SALAAK.
DEET
DEET
TWO MORE.
AEGLE? WHAT IS HAPPENING?
DEET DEET DEET DEET DEET DEET DEET DEET
THEY'RE... THEY'RE EVERYWHERE.
SO MANY...
COMMAND CENTER TO KILOWOG! MOGO IS SURROUNDED!
DOC... GET READY FOR MORE WOUNDED.

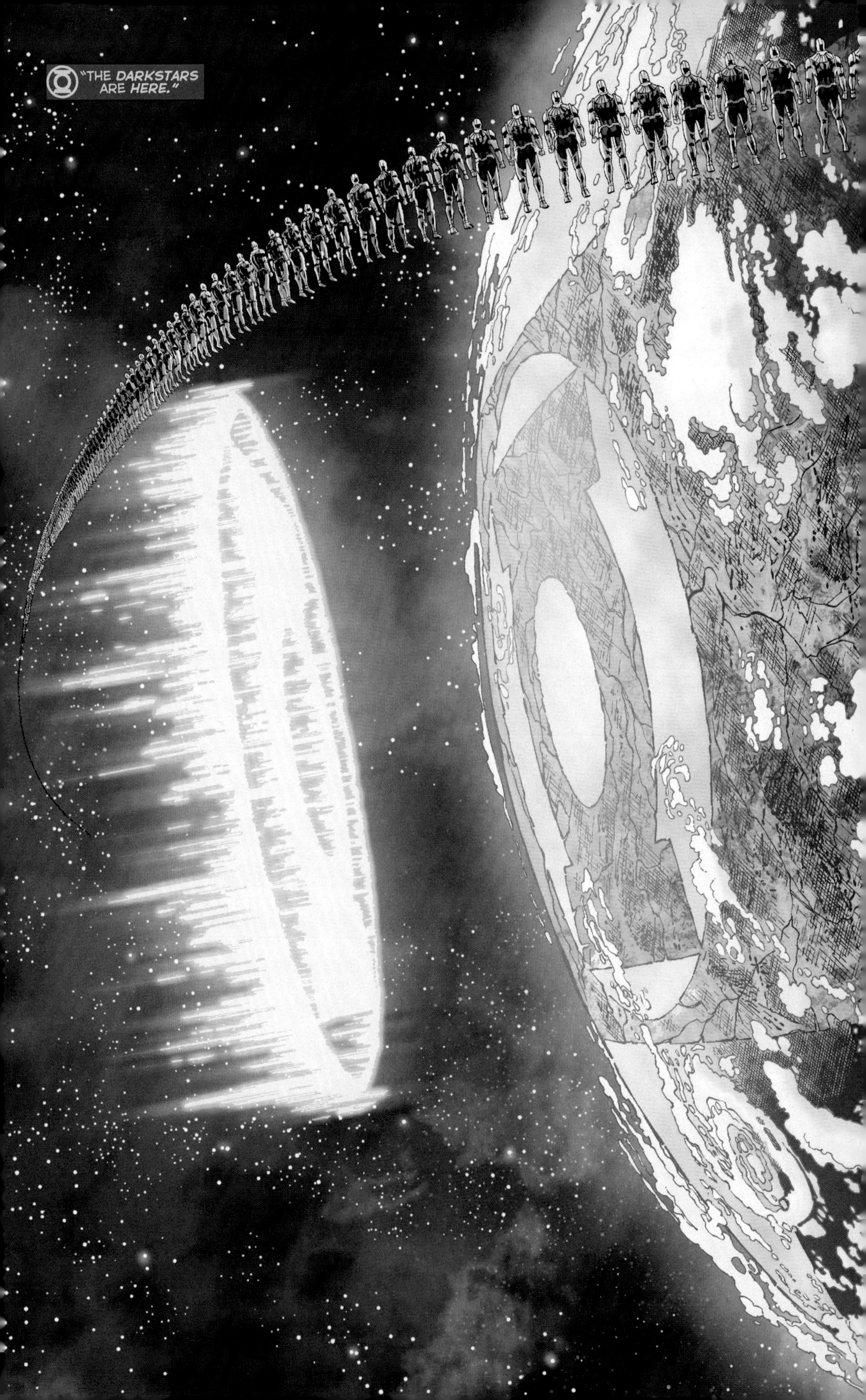
"THE DARKSTARS ARE HERE."

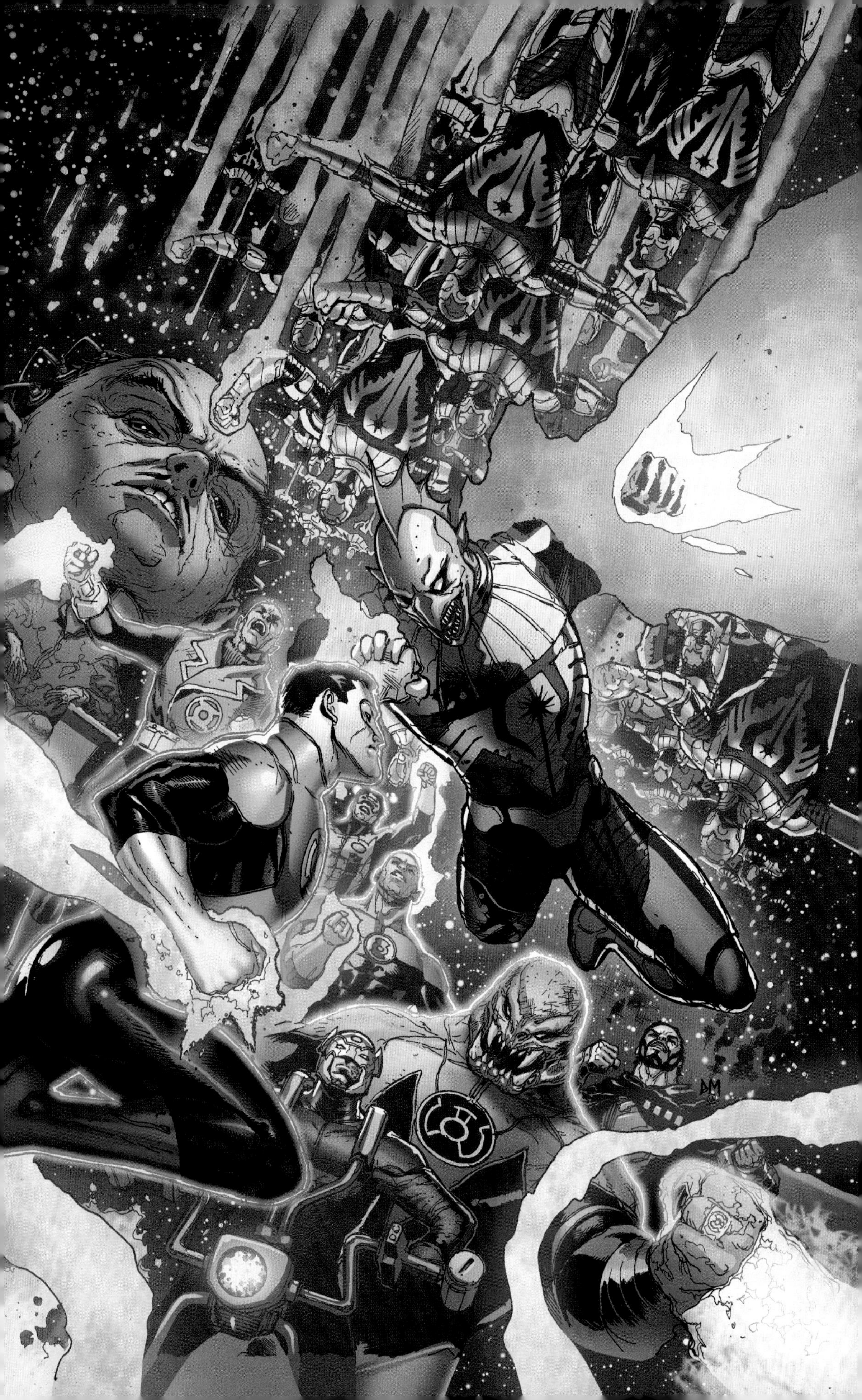

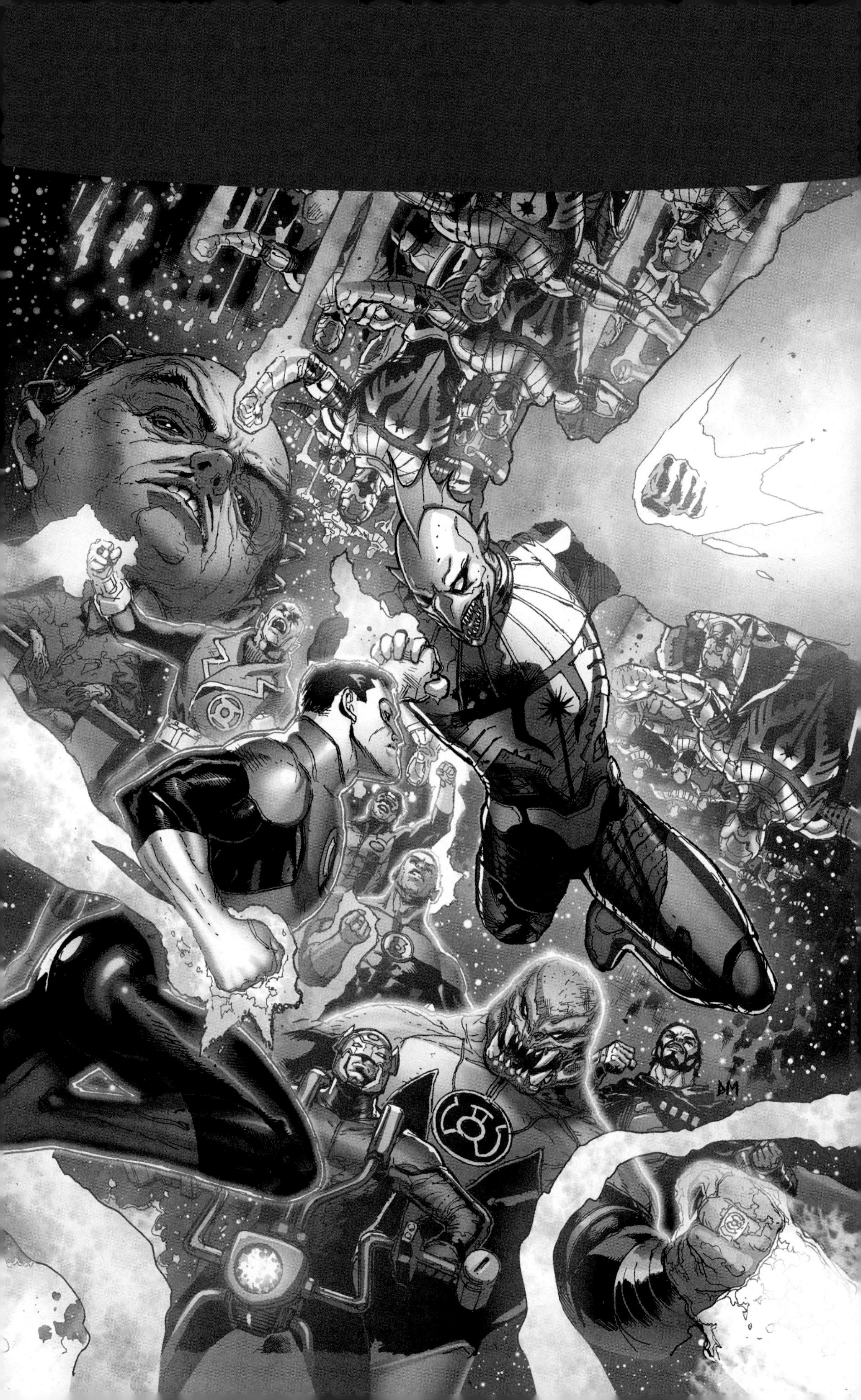

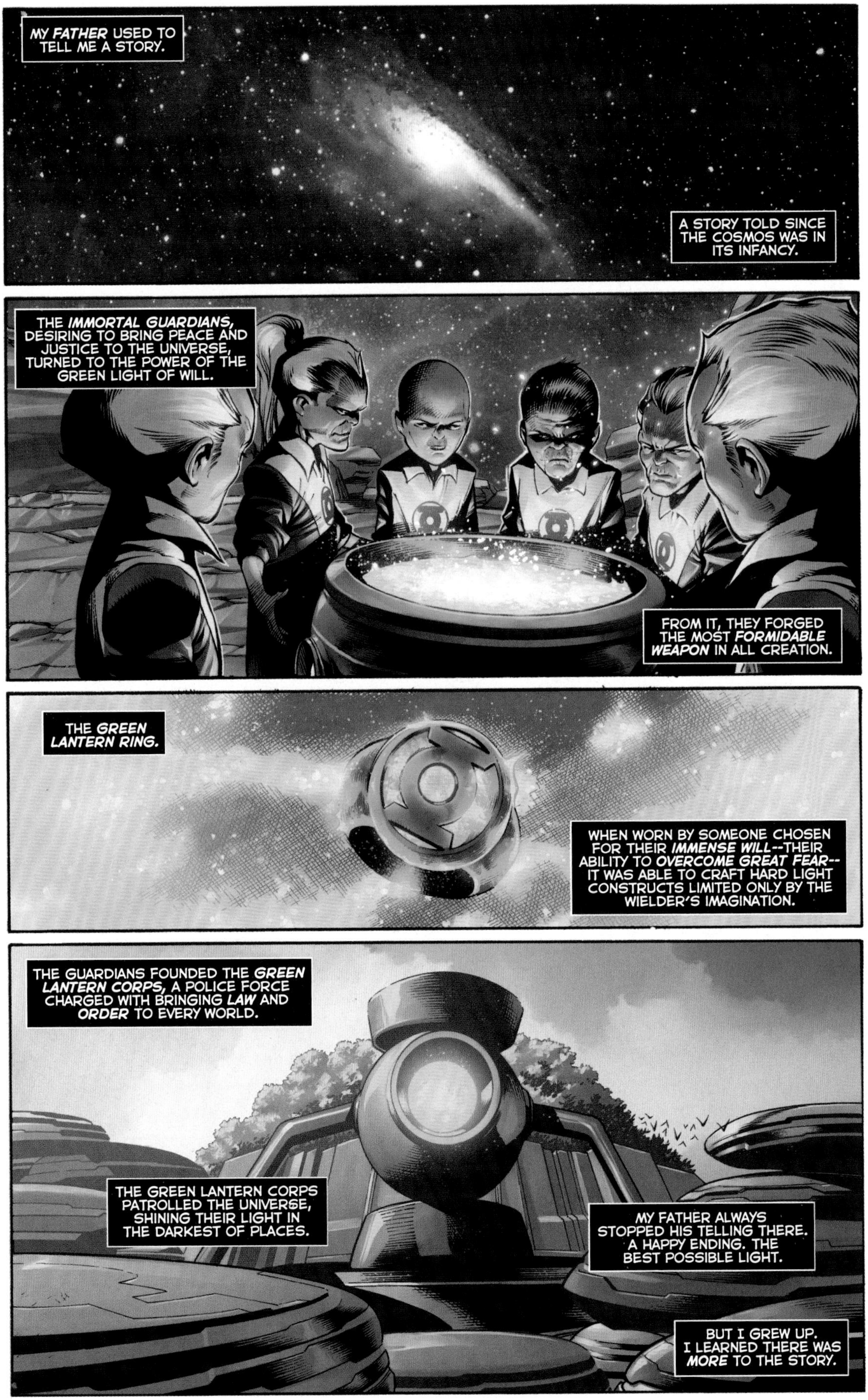
MY FATHER USED TO TELL ME A STORY.
A STORY TOLD SINCE THE COSMOS WAS IN ITS INFANCY.
THE IMMORTAL GUARDIANS, DESIRING TO BRING PEACE AND JUSTICE TO THE UNIVERSE, TURNED TO THE POWER OF THE GREEN LIGHT OF WILL.
FROM IT, THEY FORGED THE MOST FORMIDABLE WEAPON IN ALL CREATION.
THE GREEN LANTERN RING.
WHEN WORN BY SOMEONE CHOSEN FOR THEIR IMMENSE WILL--THEIR ABILITY TO OVERCOME GREAT FEAR--IT WAS ABLE TO CRAFT HARD LIGHT CONSTRUCTS LIMITED ONLY BY THE WIELDER'S IMAGINATION.
THE GUARDIANS FOUNDED THE GREEN LANTERN CORPS, A POLICE FORCE CHARGED WITH BRINGING LAW AND ORDER TO EVERY WORLD.
THE GREEN LANTERN CORPS PATROLLED THE UNIVERSE, SHINING THEIR LIGHT IN THE DARKEST OF PLACES.
MY FATHER ALWAYS STOPPED HIS TELLING THERE. A HAPPY ENDING. THE BEST POSSIBLE LIGHT.
BUT I GREW UP. I LEARNED THERE WAS MORE TO THE STORY.

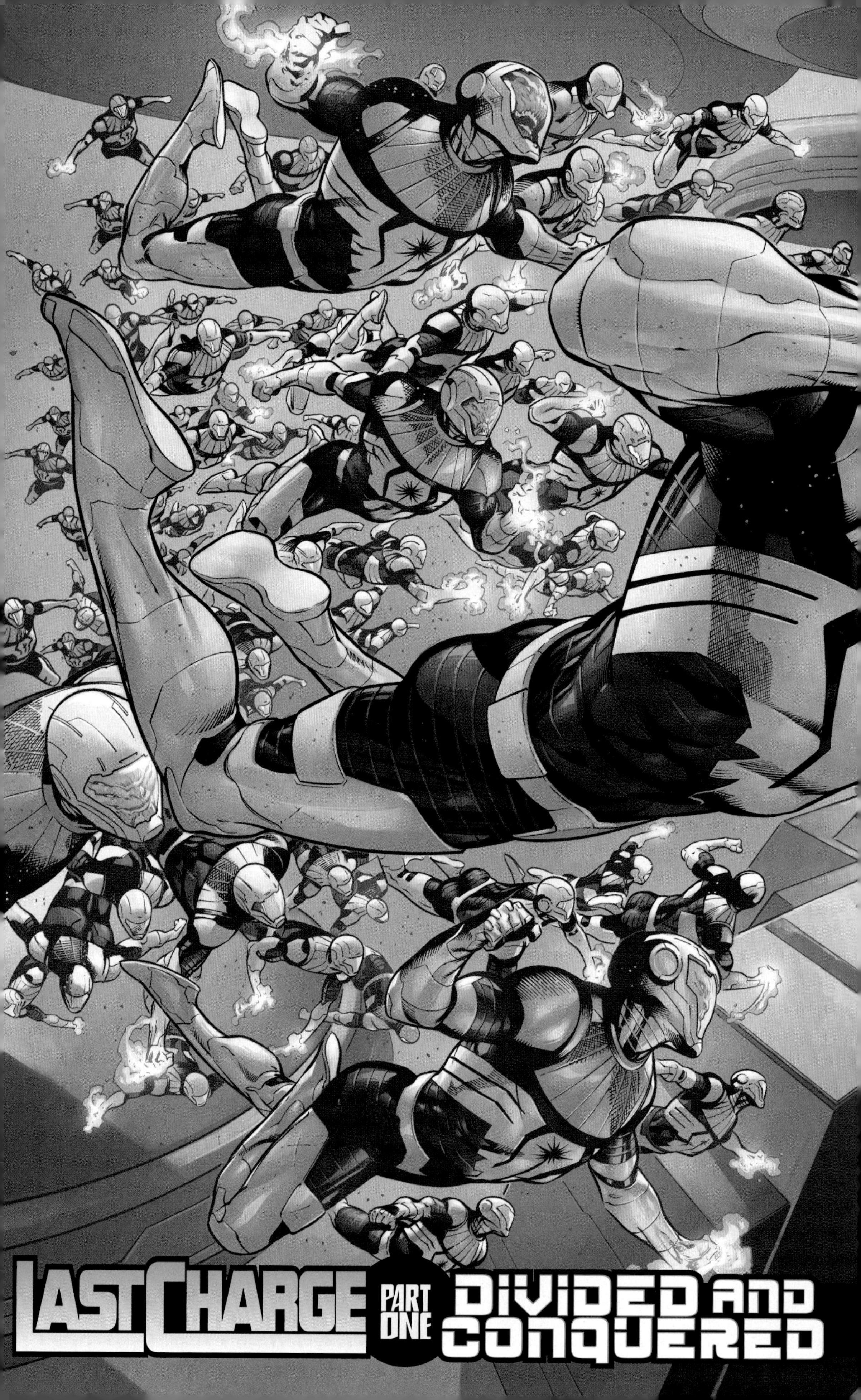
LAST CHARGE
PART ONE
DIVIDED AND CONQUERED

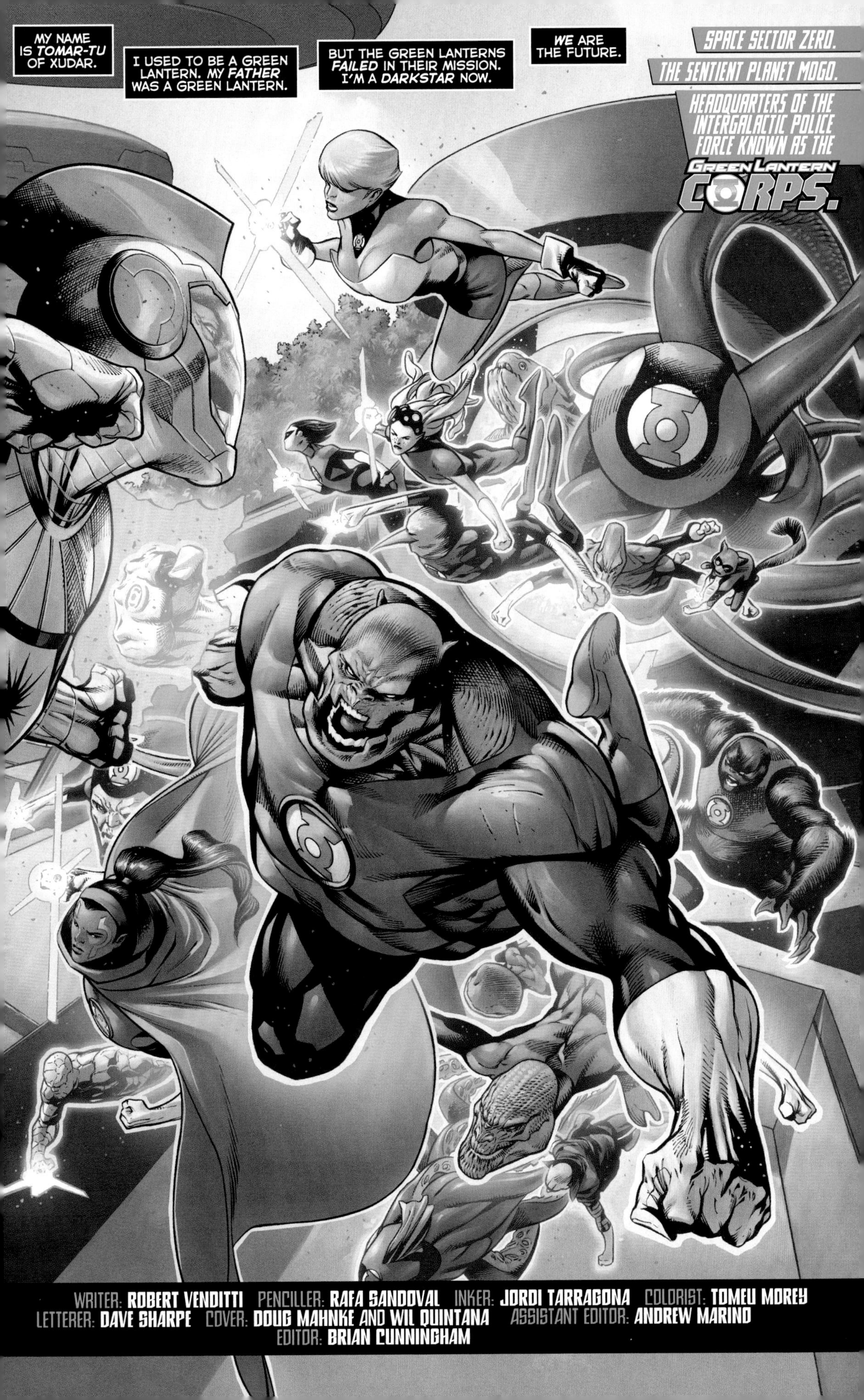

MY NAME IS TOMAR-TU OF XUDAR.
I USED TO BE A GREEN LANTERN. MY FATHER WAS A GREEN LANTERN.
BUT THE GREEN LANTERNS FAILED IN THEIR MISSION. I'M A DARKSTAR NOW.
WE ARE THE FUTURE.
SPACE SECTOR ZERO.
THE SENTIENT PLANET MOGO.
HEADQUARTERS OF THE INTERGALACTIC POLICE FORCE KNOWN AS THE
GREEN LANTERN CORPS.
WRITER: ROBERT VENDITTI PENCILLER: RAFA SANDOVAL INKER: JORDI TARRAGONA COLORIST: TOMEU MOREY
LETTERER: DAVE SHARPE COVER: DOUG MAHNKE AND WIL QUINTANA ASSISTANT EDITOR: ANDREW MARINO
EDITOR: BRIAN CUNNINGHAM

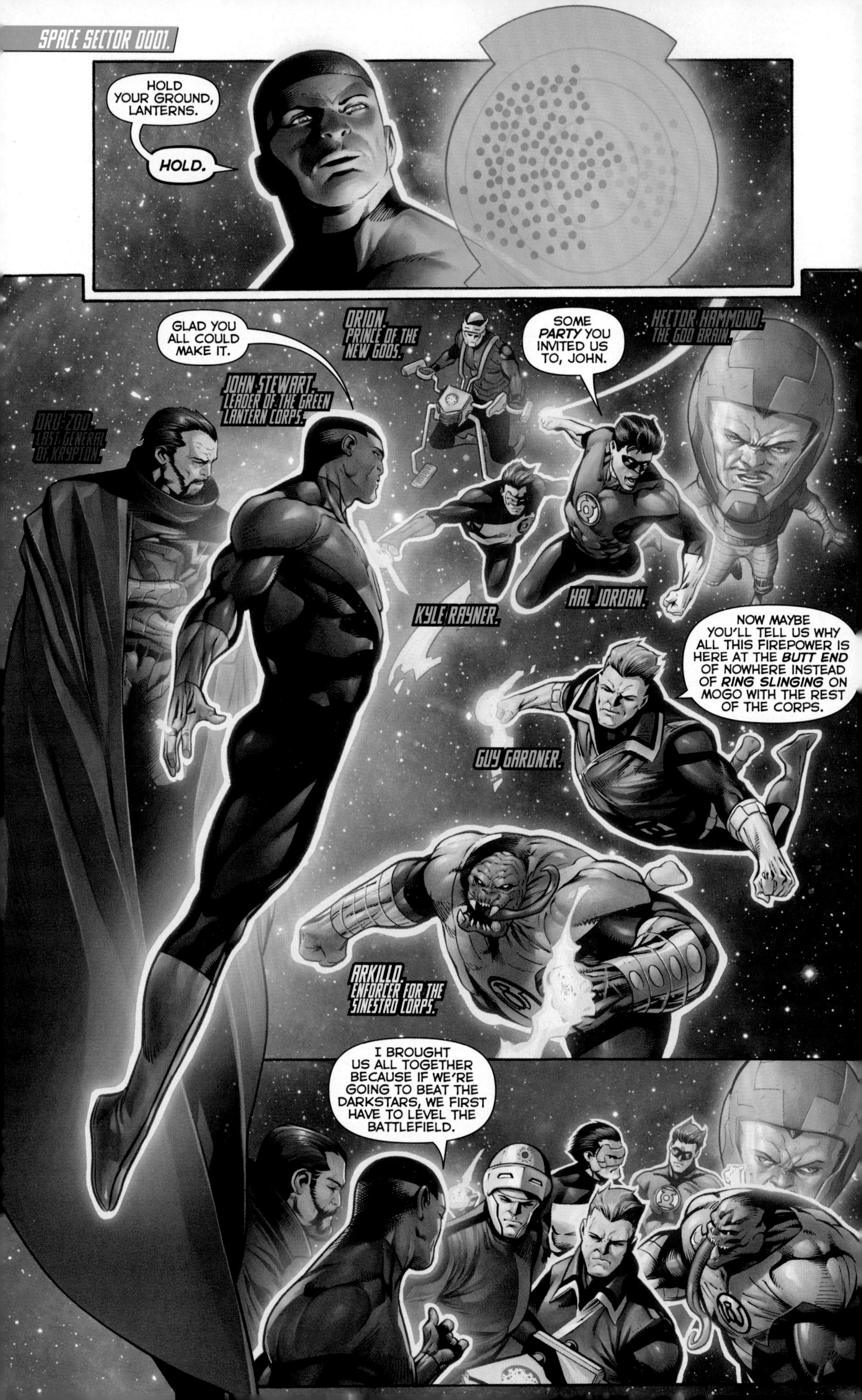
SPACE SECTOR 0001.
HOLD YOUR GROUND, LANTERNS.
HOLD.
GLAD YOU ALL COULD MAKE IT.
ORION. PRINCE OF THE NEW GODS.
SOME PARTY YOU INVITED US TO, JOHN.
HECTOR HAMMOND. THE GOD BRAIN.
JOHN STEWART. LEADER OF THE GREEN LANTERN CORPS.
DRU-ZOD. LAST GENERAL OF KRYPTON.
KYLE RAYNER.
HAL JORDAN.
NOW MAYBE YOU'LL TELL US WHY ALL THIS FIREPOWER IS HERE AT THE BUTT END OF NOWHERE INSTEAD OF RING SLINGING ON MOGO WITH THE REST OF THE CORPS.
GUY GARDNER.
ARKILLO. ENFORCER FOR THE SINESTRO CORPS.
I BROUGHT US ALL TOGETHER BECAUSE IF WE'RE GOING TO BEAT THE DARKSTARS, WE FIRST HAVE TO LEVEL THE BATTLEFIELD.

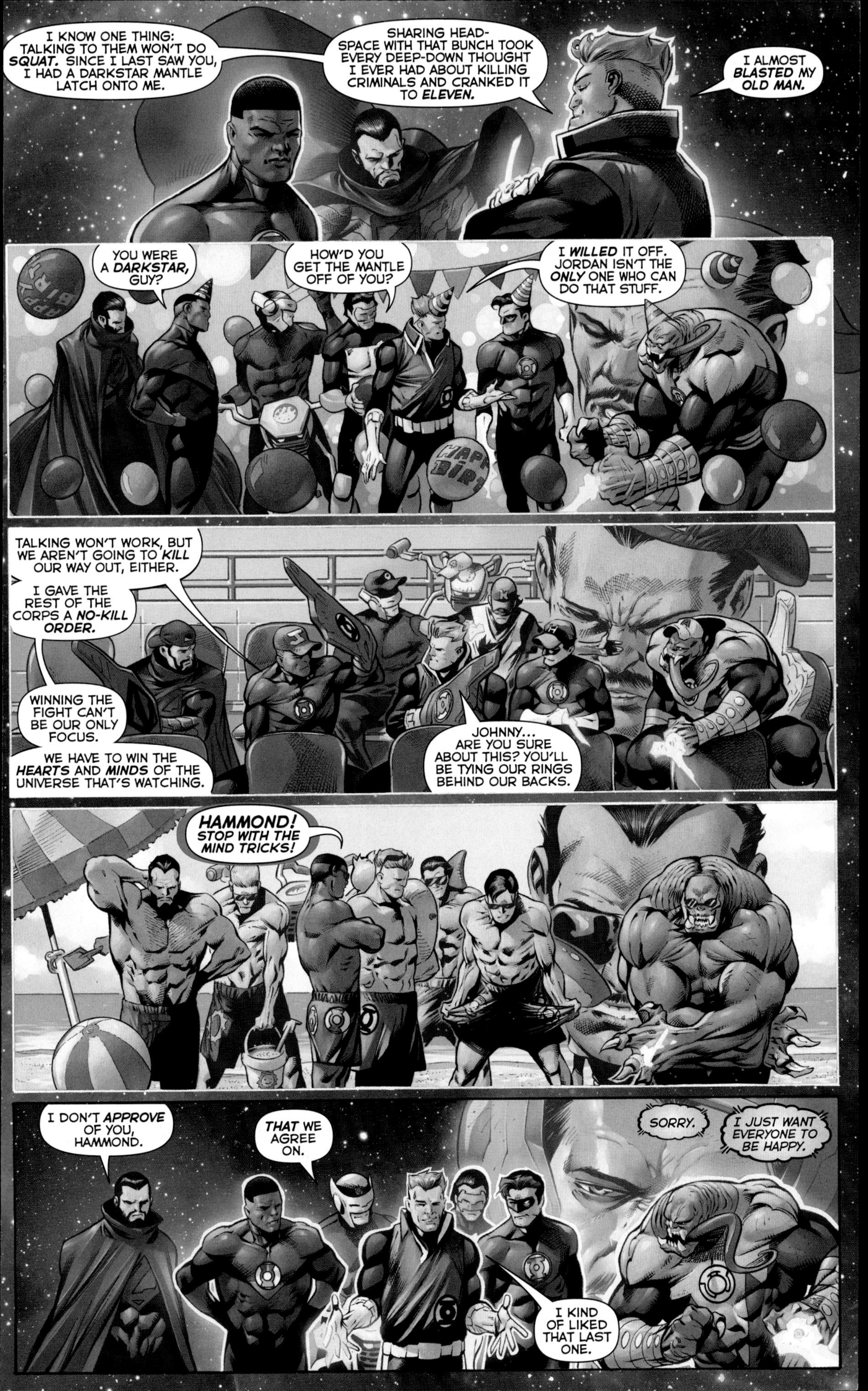
I KNOW ONE THING: TALKING TO THEM WON'T DO SQUAT. SINCE I LAST SAW YOU, I HAD A DARKSTAR MANTLE LATCH ONTO ME.
SHARING HEAD-SPACE WITH THAT BUNCH TOOK EVERY DEEP-DOWN THOUGHT I EVER HAD ABOUT KILLING CRIMINALS AND CRANKED IT TO ELEVEN.
I ALMOST BLASTED MY OLD MAN.
YOU WERE A DARKSTAR, GUY?
HOW'D YOU GET THE MANTLE OFF OF YOU?
I WILLED IT OFF. JORDAN ISN'T THE ONLY ONE WHO CAN DO THAT STUFF.
TALKING WON'T WORK, BUT WE AREN'T GOING TO KILL OUR WAY OUT, EITHER.
I GAVE THE REST OF THE CORPS A NO-KILL ORDER.
WINNING THE FIGHT CAN'T BE OUR ONLY FOCUS.
WE HAVE TO WIN THE HEARTS AND MINDS OF THE UNIVERSE THAT'S WATCHING.
JOHNNY... ARE YOU SURE ABOUT THIS? YOU'LL BE TYING OUR RINGS BEHIND OUR BACKS.
HAMMOND! STOP WITH THE MIND TRICKS!
I DON'T APPROVE OF YOU, HAMMOND.
THAT WE AGREE ON.
SORRY.
I JUST WANT EVERYONE TO BE HAPPY.
I KIND OF LIKED THAT LAST ONE.

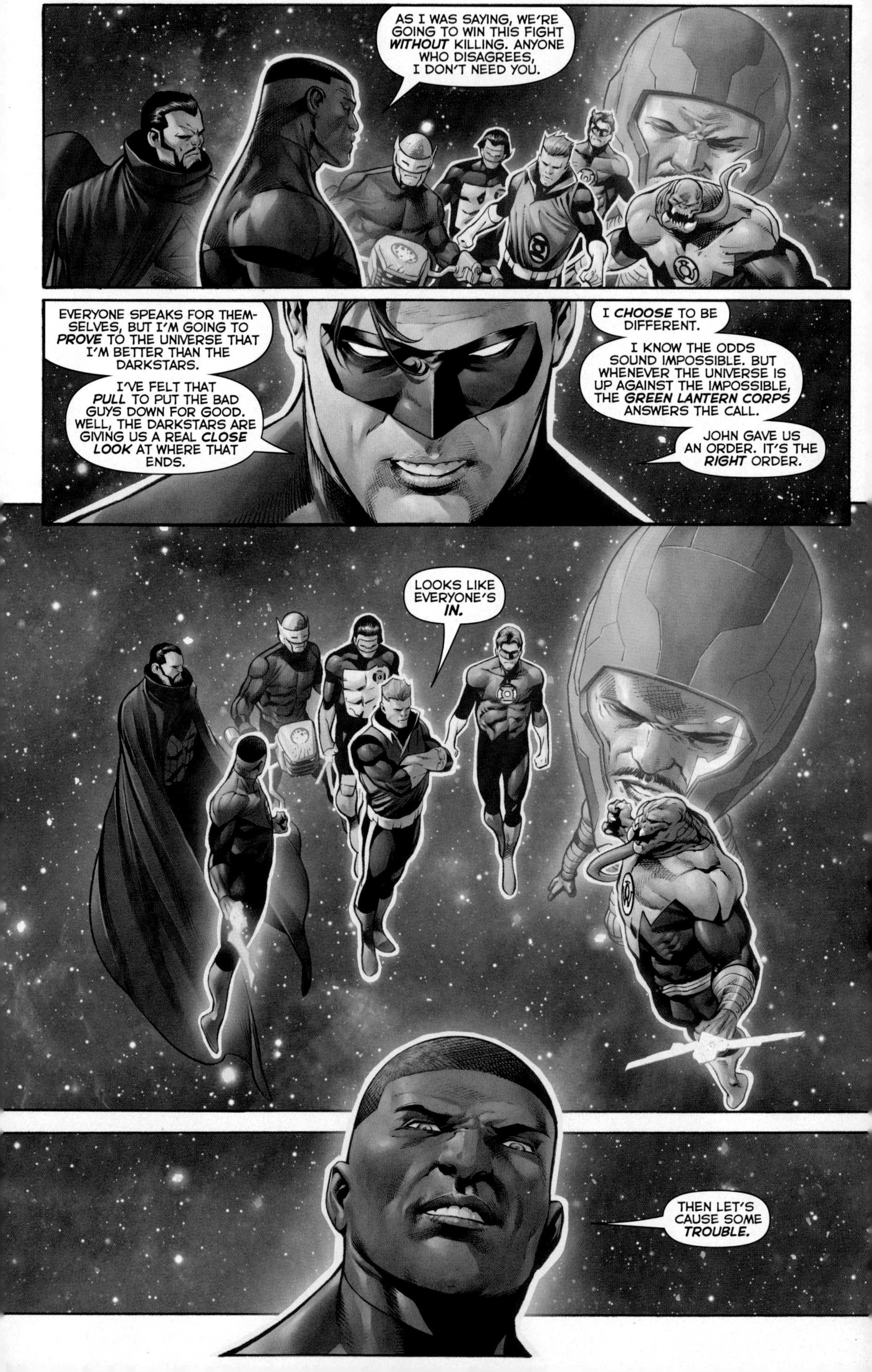
AS I WAS SAYING, WE'RE GOING TO WIN THIS FIGHT WITHOUT KILLING. ANYONE WHO DISAGREES, I DON'T NEED YOU.
EVERYONE SPEAKS FOR THEM-SELVES, BUT I'M GOING TO PROVE TO THE UNIVERSE THAT I'M BETTER THAN THE DARKSTARS.
I'VE FELT THAT PULL TO PUT THE BAD GUYS DOWN FOR GOOD. WELL, THE DARKSTARS ARE GIVING US A REAL CLOSE LOOK AT WHERE THAT ENDS.
I CHOOSE TO BE DIFFERENT.
I KNOW THE ODDS SOUND IMPOSSIBLE. BUT WHENEVER THE UNIVERSE IS UP AGAINST THE IMPOSSIBLE, THE GREEN LANTERN CORPS ANSWERS THE CALL.
JOHN GAVE US AN ORDER. IT'S THE RIGHT ORDER.
LOOKS LIKE EVERYONE'S IN.
THEN LET'S CAUSE SOME TROUBLE.

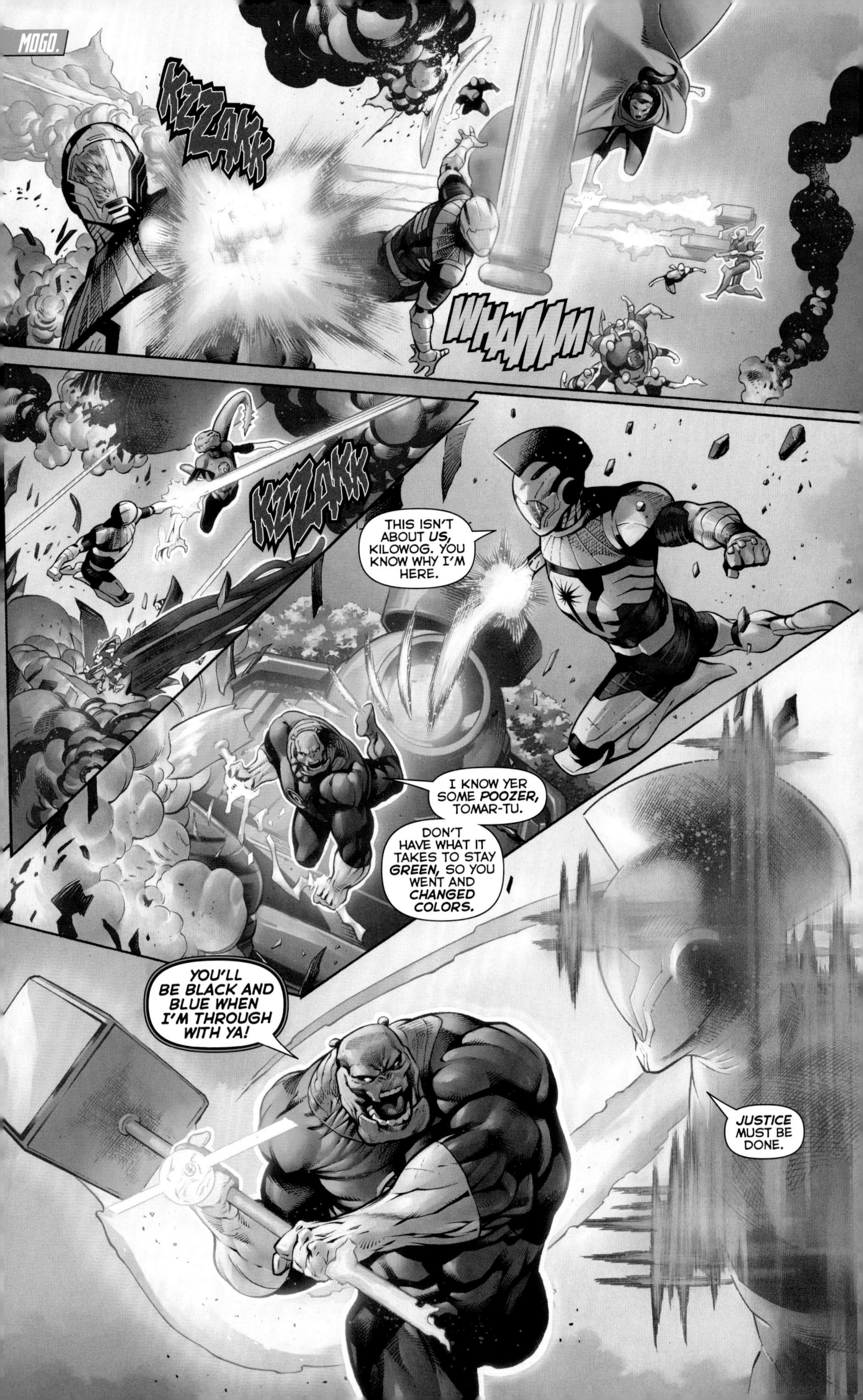
MOGO.
KZZAKK
WHAMMM
KZZAKK
THIS ISN'T ABOUT US, KILOWOG. YOU KNOW WHY I'M HERE.
I KNOW YER SOME POOZER, TOMAR-TU.
DON'T HAVE WHAT IT TAKES TO STAY GREEN, SO YOU WENT AND CHANGED COLORS.
YOU'LL BE BLACK AND BLUE WHEN I'M THROUGH WITH YA!
JUSTICE MUST BE DONE.

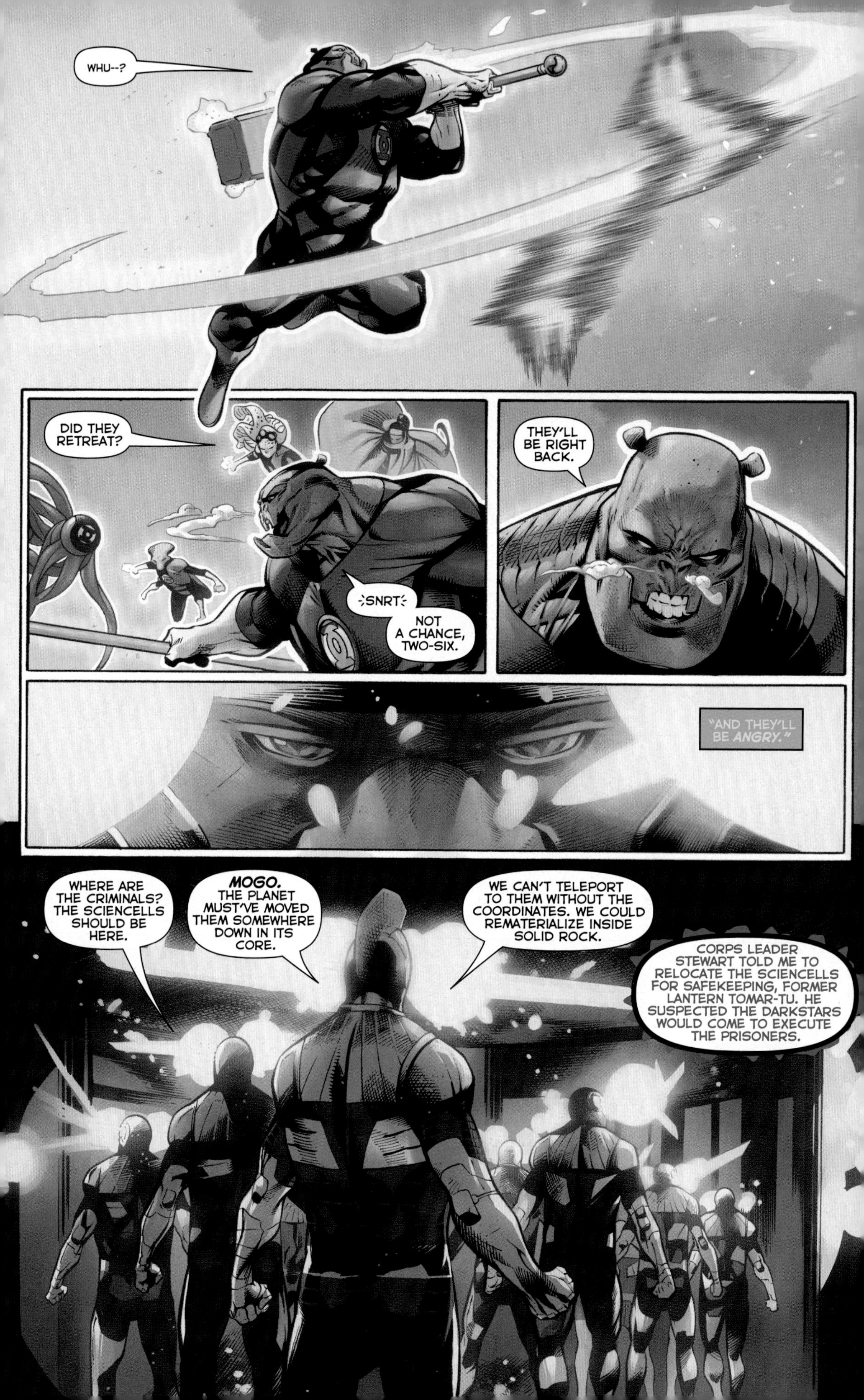
WHU--?
DID THEY RETREAT?
THEY'LL BE RIGHT BACK.
SNRT
NOT A CHANCE, TWO-SIX.
"AND THEY'LL BE ANGRY."
WHERE ARE THE CRIMINALS? THE SCIENCELLS SHOULD BE HERE.
MOGO. THE PLANET MUST'VE MOVED THEM SOMEWHERE DOWN IN ITS CORE.
WE CAN'T TELEPORT TO THEM WITHOUT THE COORDINATES. WE COULD REMATERIALIZE INSIDE SOLID ROCK.
CORPS LEADER STEWART TOLD ME TO RELOCATE THE SCIENCELLS FOR SAFEKEEPING, FORMER LANTERN TOMAR-TU. HE SUSPECTED THE DARKSTARS WOULD COME TO EXECUTE THE PRISONERS.

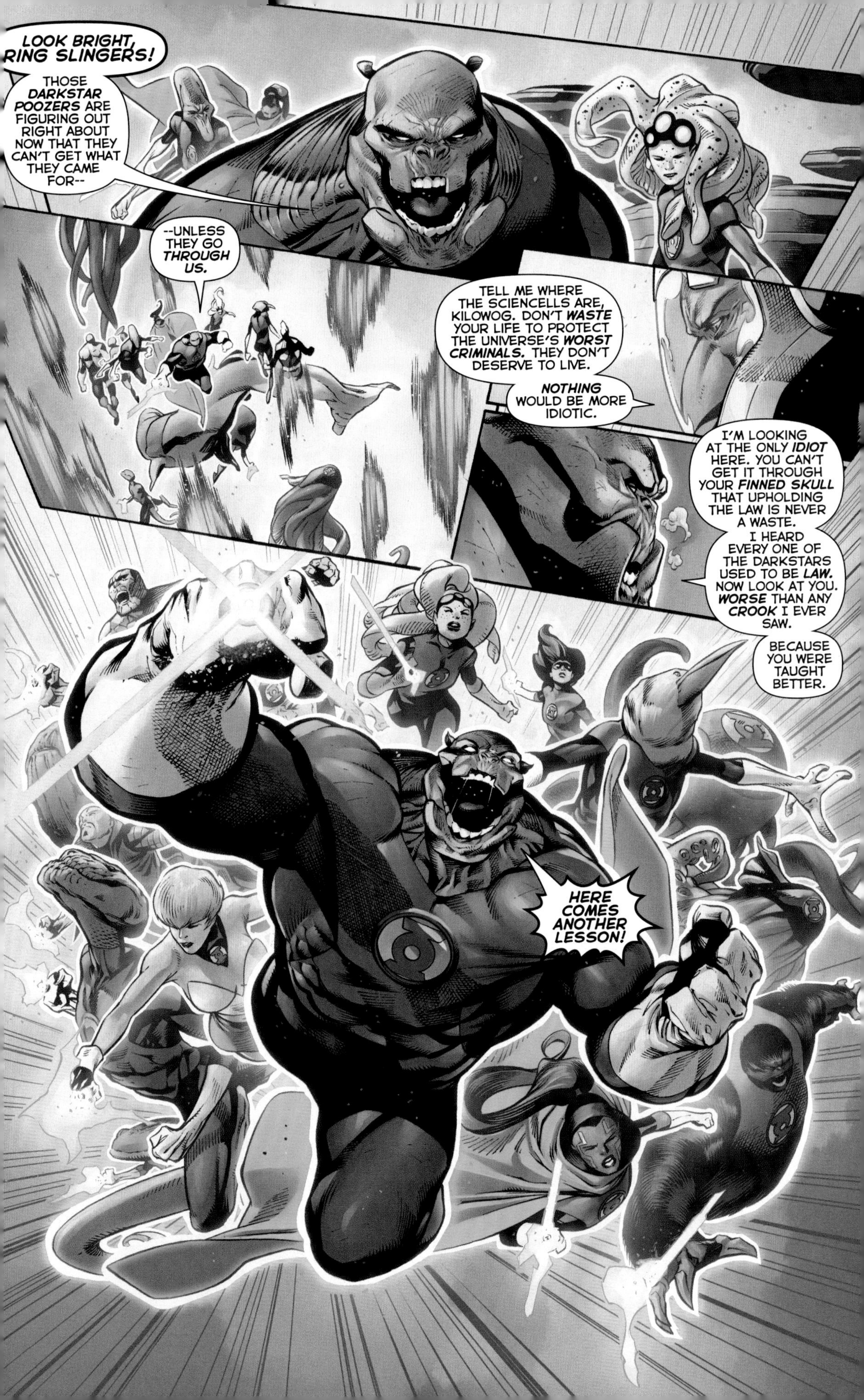
LOOK BRIGHT, RING SLINGERS!
THOSE DARKSTAR POOZERS ARE FIGURING OUT RIGHT ABOUT NOW THAT THEY CAN'T GET WHAT THEY CAME FOR--
--UNLESS THEY GO THROUGH US.
TELL ME WHERE THE SCIENCELLS ARE, KILOWOG. DON'T WASTE YOUR LIFE TO PROTECT THE UNIVERSE'S WORST CRIMINALS. THEY DON'T DESERVE TO LIVE.
NOTHING WOULD BE MORE IDIOTIC.
I'M LOOKING AT THE ONLY IDIOT HERE. YOU CAN'T GET IT THROUGH YOUR FINNED SKULL THAT UPHOLDING THE LAW IS NEVER A WASTE.
I HEARD EVERY ONE OF THE DARKSTARS USED TO BE LAW. NOW LOOK AT YOU. WORSE THAN ANY CROOK I EVER SAW.
BECAUSE YOU WERE TAUGHT BETTER.
HERE COMES ANOTHER LESSON!

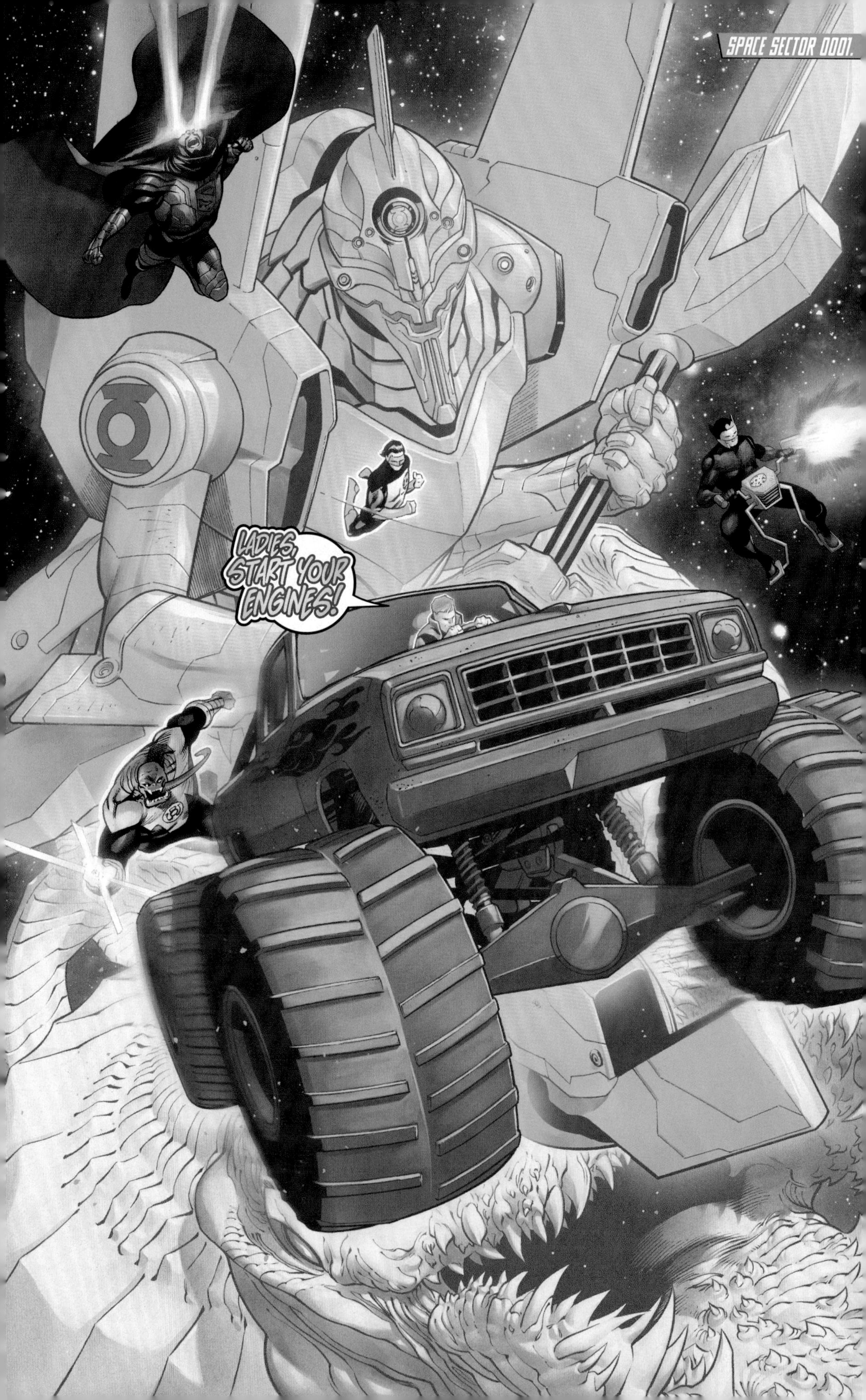
SPACE SECTOR 0001.
LADIES, START YOUR ENGINES!

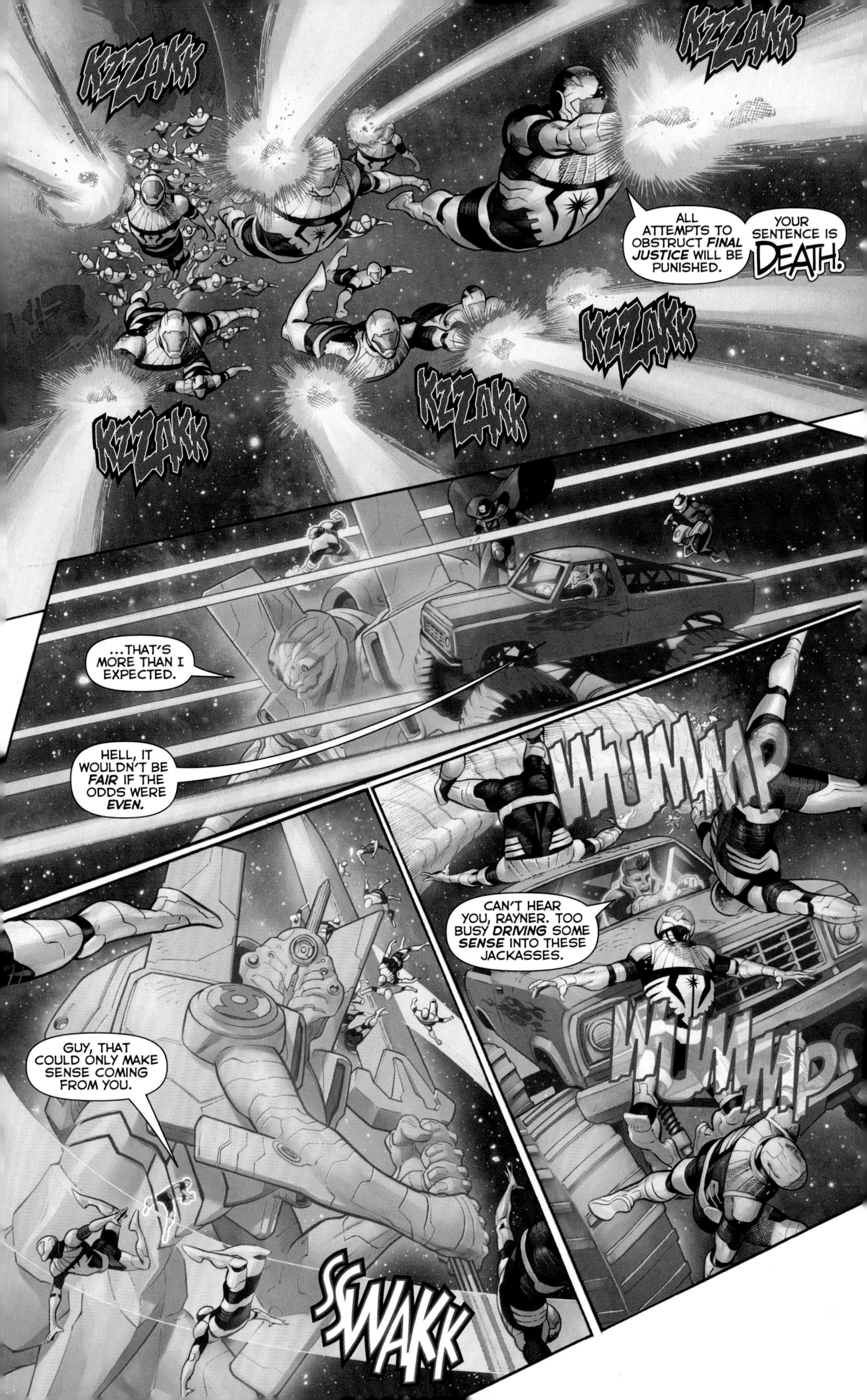
KZZAKK
KZZAKK
ALL ATTEMPTS TO OBSTRUCT FINAL JUSTICE WILL BE PUNISHED.
YOUR SENTENCE IS DEATH.
KZZAKK
KZZAKK
KZZAKK
...THAT'S MORE THAN I EXPECTED.
HELL, IT WOULDN'T BE FAIR IF THE ODDS WERE EVEN.
WHUMMP
CAN'T HEAR YOU, RAYNER. TOO BUSY DRIVING SOME SENSE INTO THESE JACKASSES.
WHUMMP
GUY, THAT COULD ONLY MAKE SENSE COMING FROM YOU.
SSWAKK

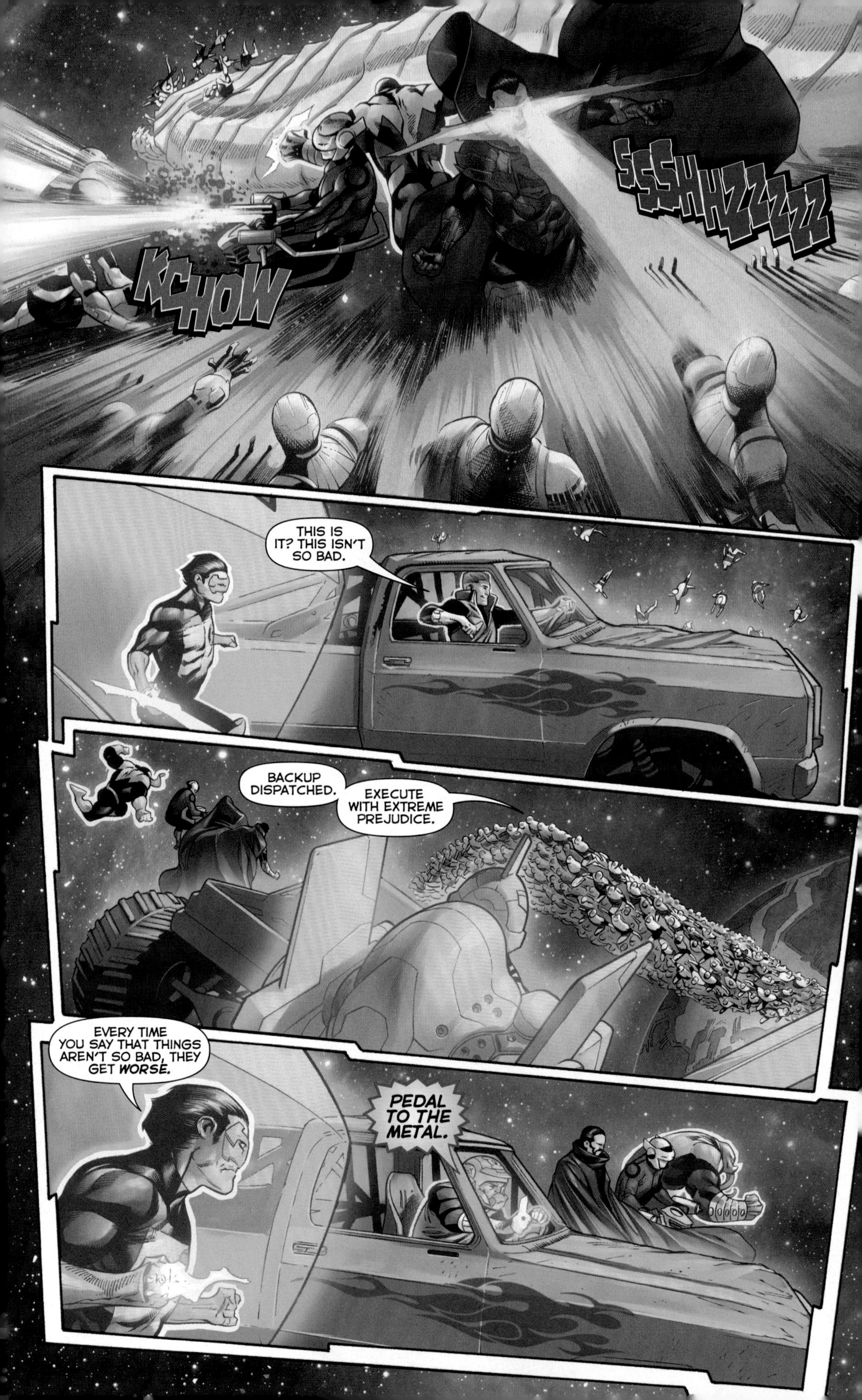
SSSHHZZZZZZ
KCHOW
THIS IS IT? THIS ISN'T SO BAD.
BACKUP DISPATCHED.
EXECUTE WITH EXTREME PREJUDICE.
EVERY TIME YOU SAY THAT THINGS AREN'T SO BAD, THEY GET *WORSE*.
PEDAL TO THE METAL.

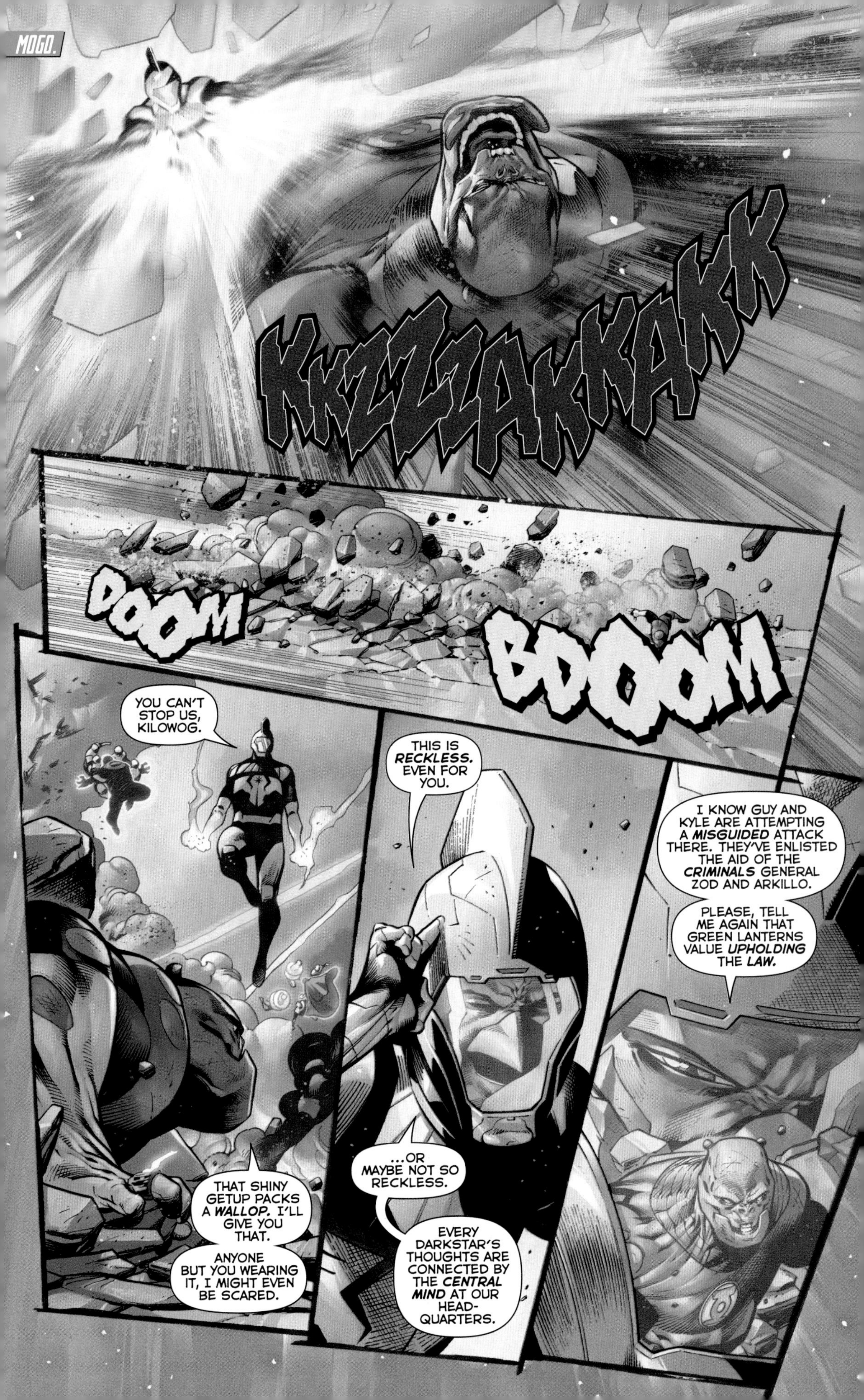
MOGO.
KKZZZAKKAKK
DOOOM
BOOOM
YOU CAN'T STOP US, KILOWOG.
THAT SHINY GETUP PACKS A WALLOP. I'LL GIVE YOU THAT.
ANYONE BUT YOU WEARING IT, I MIGHT EVEN BE SCARED.
THIS IS RECKLESS. EVEN FOR YOU.
...OR MAYBE NOT SO RECKLESS.
EVERY DARKSTAR'S THOUGHTS ARE CONNECTED BY THE CENTRAL MIND AT OUR HEAD-QUARTERS.
I KNOW GUY AND KYLE ARE ATTEMPTING A MISGUIDED ATTACK THERE. THEY'VE ENLISTED THE AID OF THE CRIMINALS GENERAL ZOD AND ARKILLO.
PLEASE, TELL ME AGAIN THAT GREEN LANTERNS VALUE UPHOLDING THE LAW.

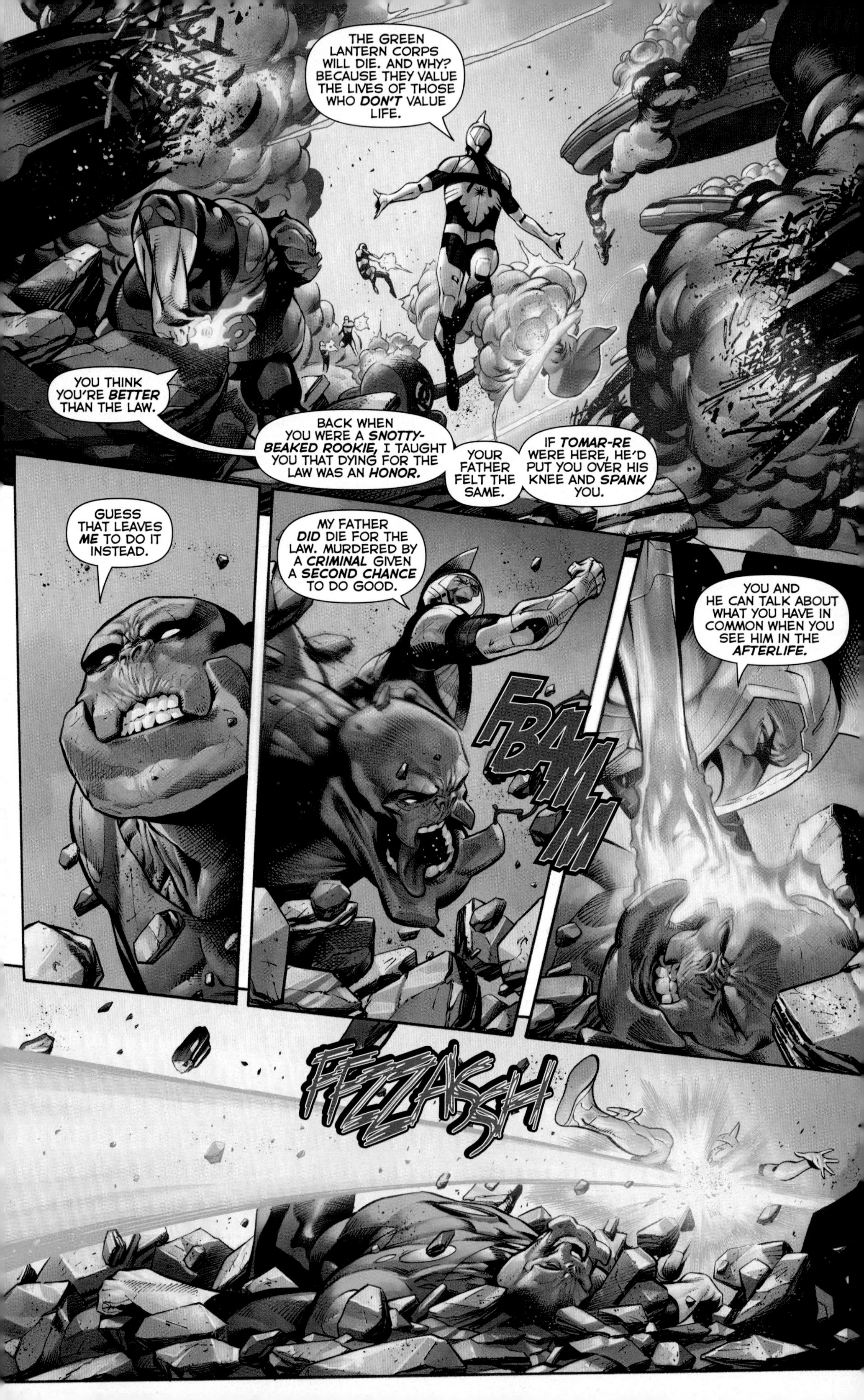
THE GREEN LANTERN CORPS WILL DIE. AND WHY? BECAUSE THEY VALUE THE LIVES OF THOSE WHO DON'T VALUE LIFE.
YOU THINK YOU'RE BETTER THAN THE LAW.
BACK WHEN YOU WERE A SNOTTY-BEAKED ROOKIE, I TAUGHT YOU THAT DYING FOR THE LAW WAS AN HONOR.
YOUR FATHER FELT THE SAME.
IF TOMAR-RE WERE HERE, HE'D PUT YOU OVER HIS KNEE AND SPANK YOU.
GUESS THAT LEAVES ME TO DO IT INSTEAD.
MY FATHER DID DIE FOR THE LAW. MURDERED BY A CRIMINAL GIVEN A SECOND CHANCE TO DO GOOD.
FBAMM
YOU AND HE CAN TALK ABOUT WHAT YOU HAVE IN COMMON WHEN YOU SEE HIM IN THE AFTERLIFE.
FFZZASSH

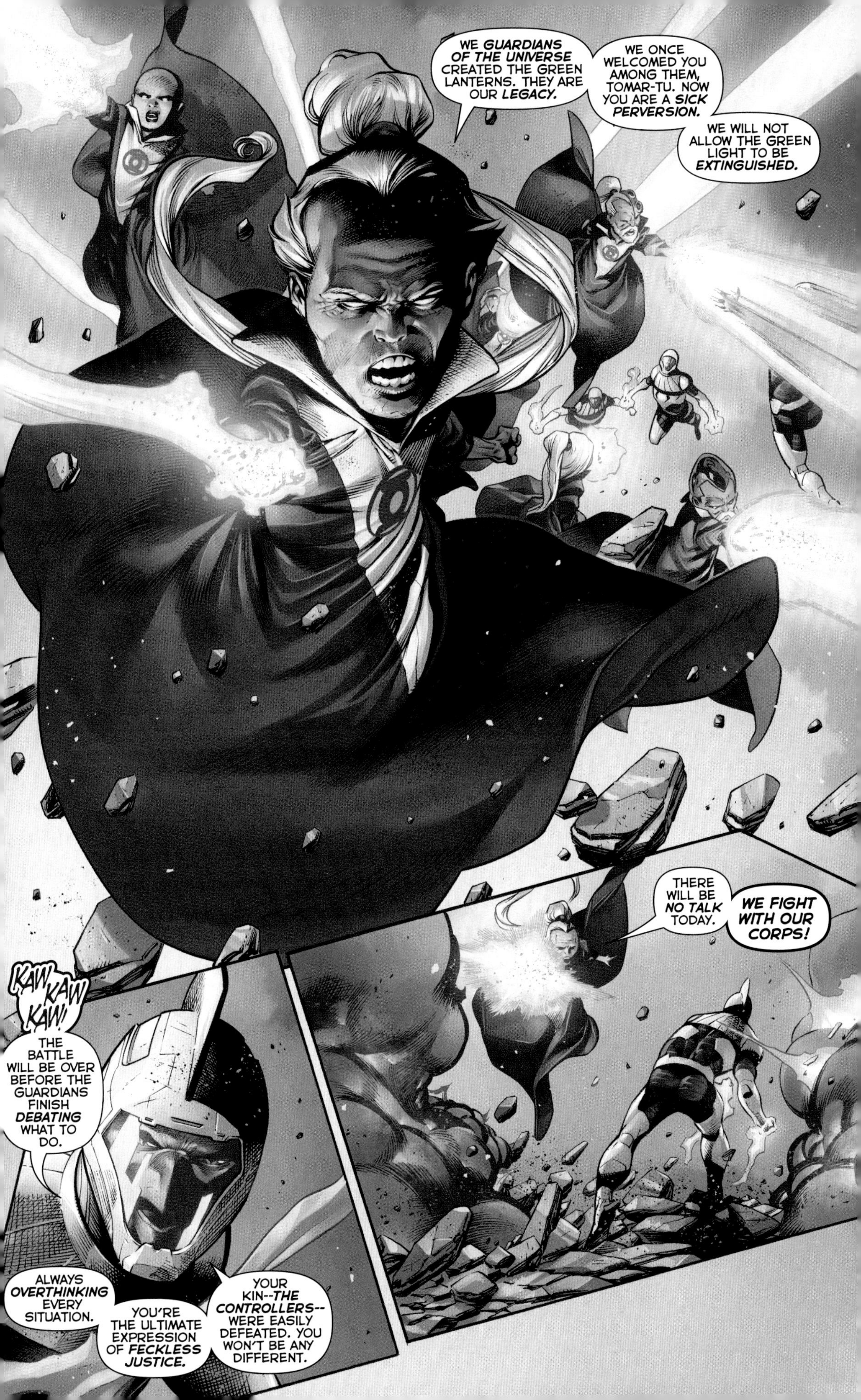
WE GUARDIANS OF THE UNIVERSE CREATED THE GREEN LANTERNS. THEY ARE OUR LEGACY.
WE ONCE WELCOMED YOU AMONG THEM, TOMAR-TU. NOW YOU ARE A SICK PERVERSION.
WE WILL NOT ALLOW THE GREEN LIGHT TO BE EXTINGUISHED.
THERE WILL BE NO TALK TODAY.
WE FIGHT WITH OUR CORPS!
KAW KAW KAW!
THE BATTLE WILL BE OVER BEFORE THE GUARDIANS FINISH DEBATING WHAT TO DO.
ALWAYS OVERTHINKING EVERY SITUATION.
YOU'RE THE ULTIMATE EXPRESSION OF FECKLESS JUSTICE.
YOUR KIN--THE CONTROLLERS--WERE EASILY DEFEATED. YOU WON'T BE ANY DIFFERENT.

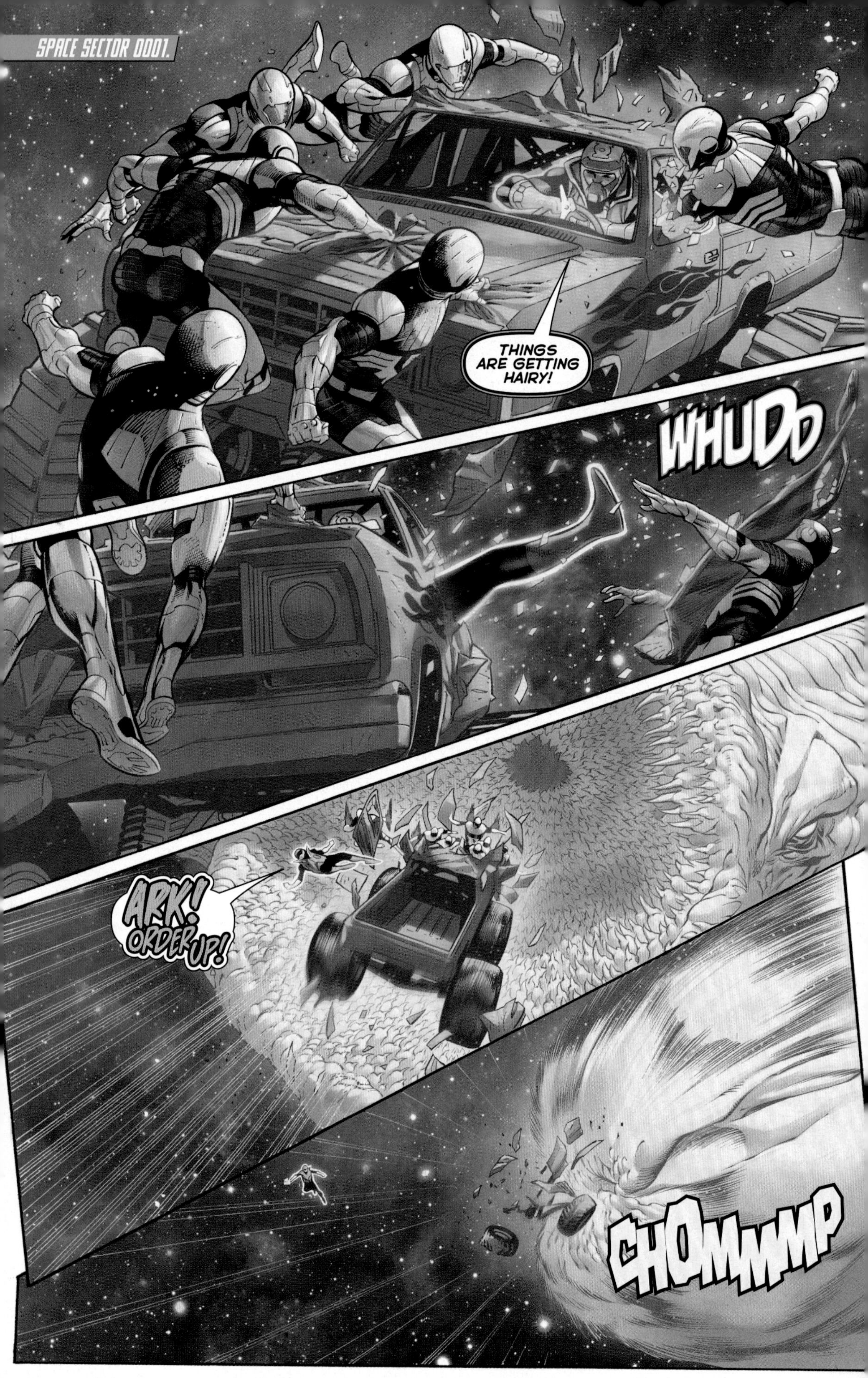
SPACE SECTOR 0001.
THINGS ARE GETTING HAIRY!
WHUDD
ARK! ORDER UP!
CHOMMMMP

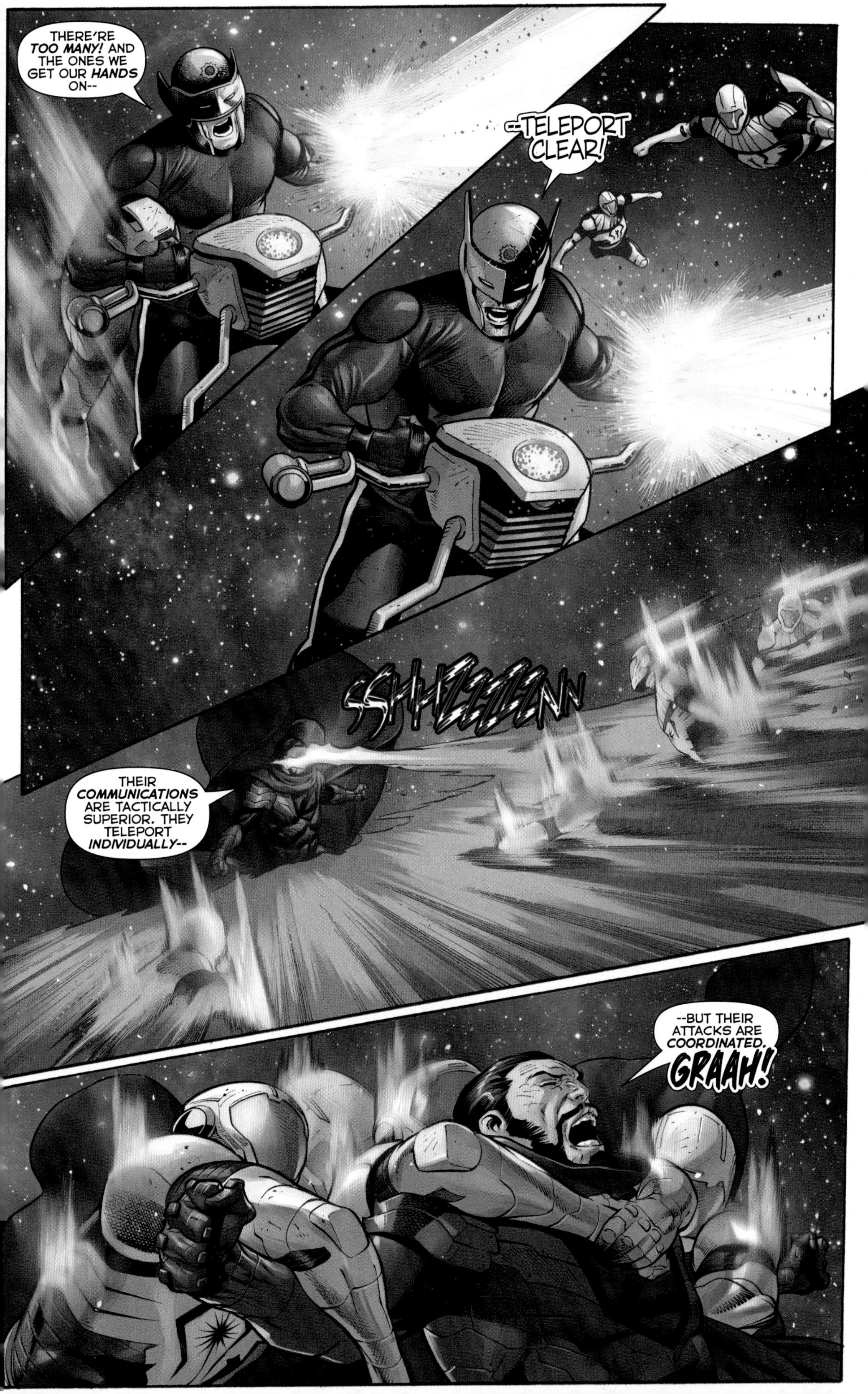
THERE'RE TOO MANY! AND THE ONES WE GET OUR HANDS ON--
--TELEPORT CLEAR!
SSHHZZZZZNN
THEIR COMMUNICATIONS ARE TACTICALLY SUPERIOR. THEY TELEPORT INDIVIDUALLY--
--BUT THEIR ATTACKS ARE COORDINATED.
GRAAH!

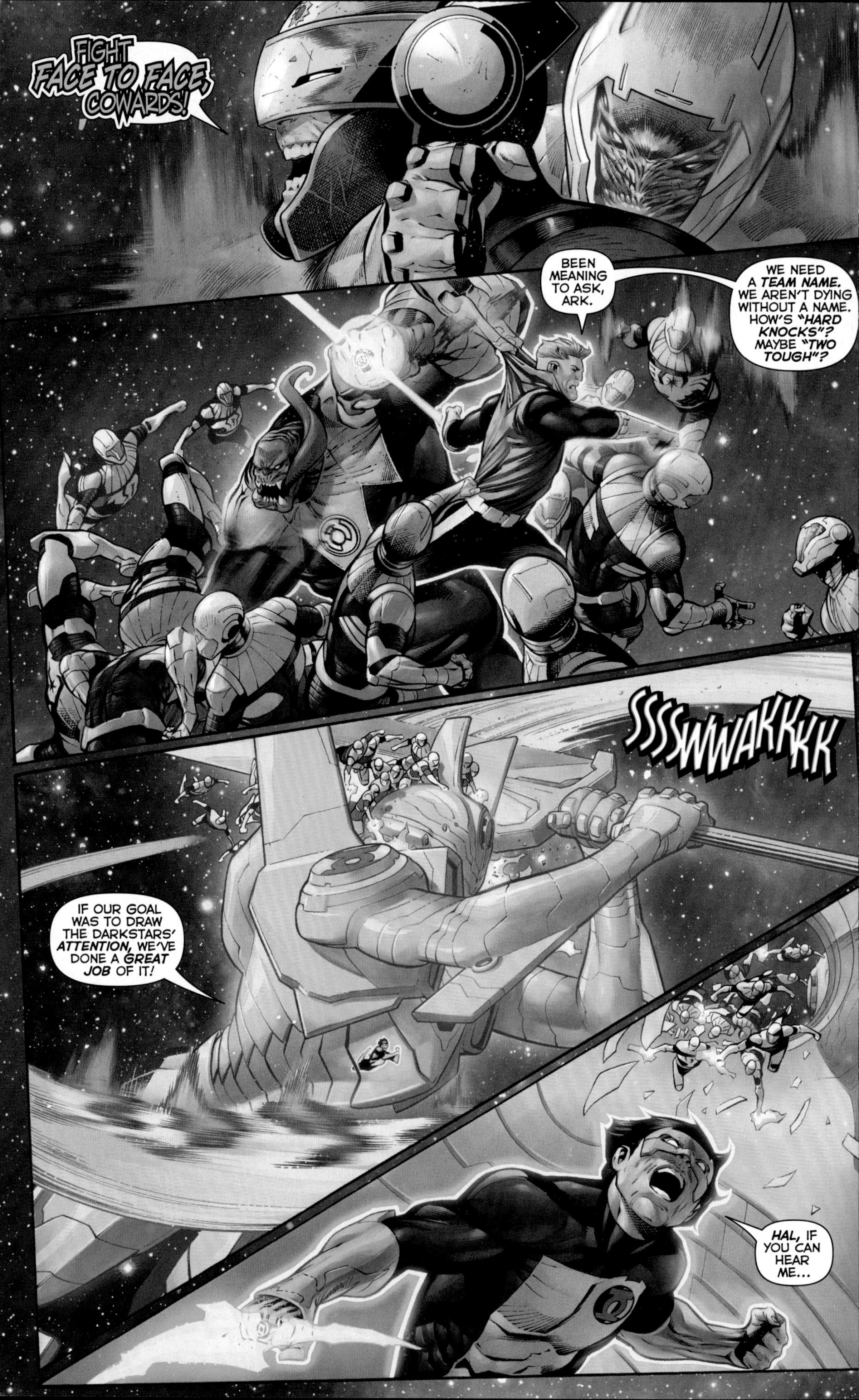
FIGHT FACE TO FACE, COWARDS!
BEEN MEANING TO ASK, ARK.
WE NEED A TEAM NAME. WE AREN'T DYING WITHOUT A NAME. HOW'S "HARD KNOCKS"? MAYBE "TWO TOUGH"?
SSSWWAKKKKK
IF OUR GOAL WAS TO DRAW THE DARKSTARS' ATTENTION, WE'VE DONE A GREAT JOB OF IT!
HAL, IF YOU CAN HEAR ME...

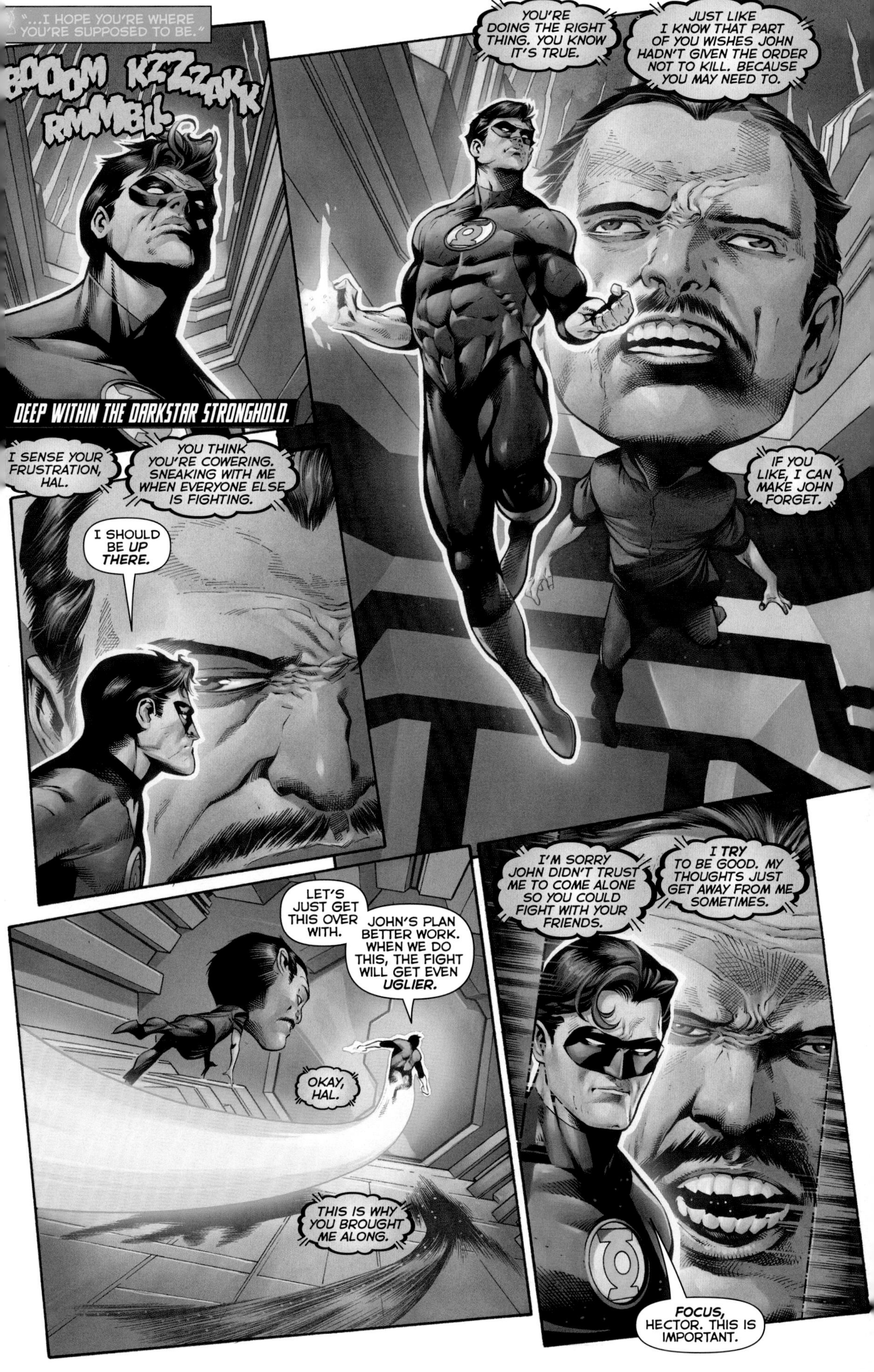
"...I HOPE YOU'RE WHERE YOU'RE SUPPOSED TO BE."
BOOOM KZZZAKK RMMBLL
DEEP WITHIN THE DARKSTAR STRONGHOLD.
I SENSE YOUR FRUSTRATION, HAL.
YOU THINK YOU'RE COWERING. SNEAKING WITH ME WHEN EVERYONE ELSE IS FIGHTING.
I SHOULD BE UP THERE.
YOU'RE DOING THE RIGHT THING. YOU KNOW IT'S TRUE.
JUST LIKE I KNOW THAT PART OF YOU WISHES JOHN HADN'T GIVEN THE ORDER NOT TO KILL. BECAUSE YOU MAY NEED TO.
IF YOU LIKE, I CAN MAKE JOHN FORGET.
LET'S JUST GET THIS OVER WITH.
JOHN'S PLAN BETTER WORK. WHEN WE DO THIS, THE FIGHT WILL GET EVEN UGLIER.
OKAY, HAL.
THIS IS WHY YOU BROUGHT ME ALONG.
I'M SORRY JOHN DIDN'T TRUST ME TO COME ALONE SO YOU COULD FIGHT WITH YOUR FRIENDS.
I TRY TO BE GOOD. MY THOUGHTS JUST GET AWAY FROM ME SOMETIMES.
FOCUS, HECTOR. THIS IS IMPORTANT.

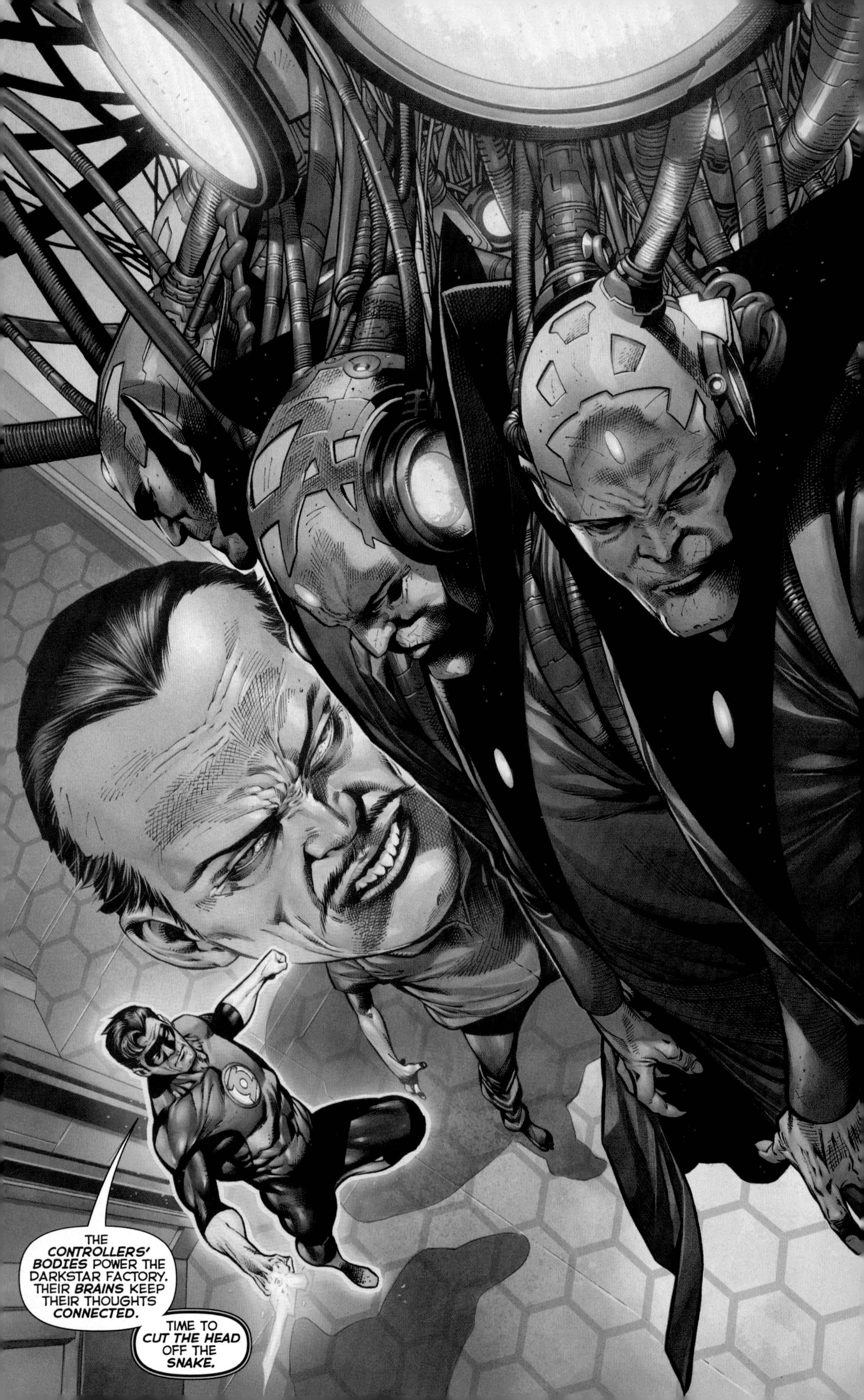
THE *CONTROLLERS' BODIES* POWER THE DARKSTAR FACTORY. THEIR *BRAINS* KEEP THEIR THOUGHTS *CONNECTED.*
TIME TO *CUT THE HEAD* OFF THE *SNAKE.*

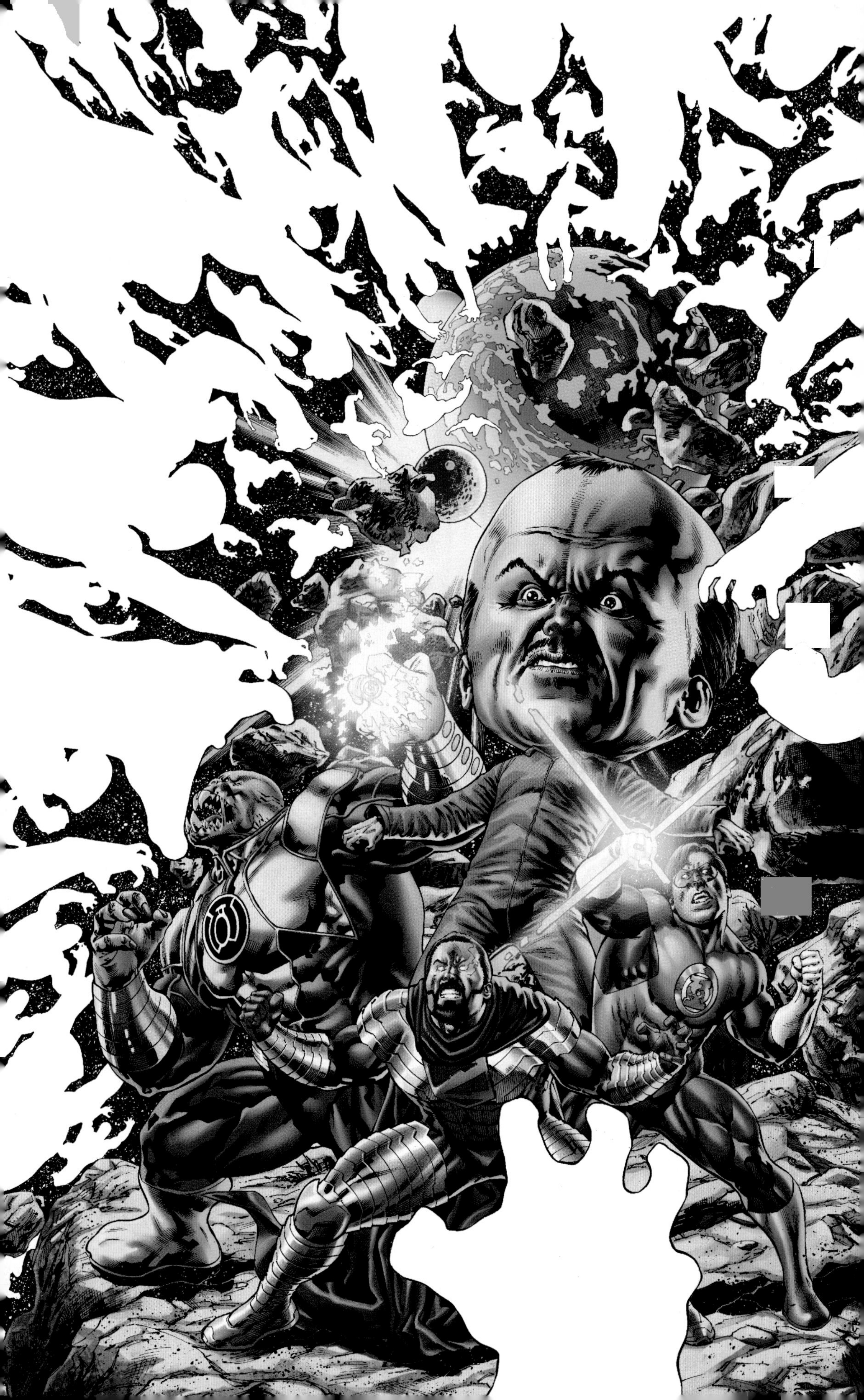

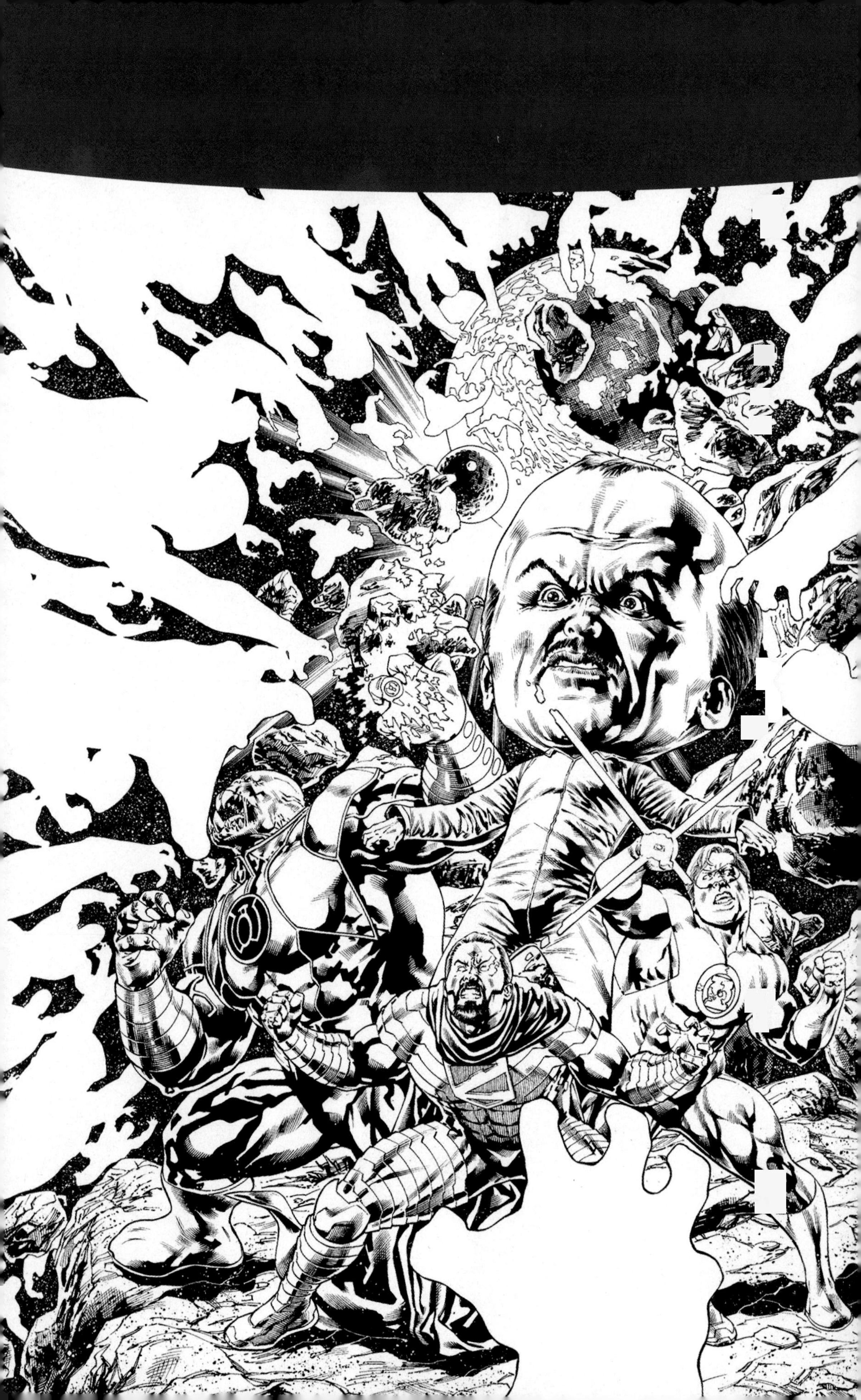

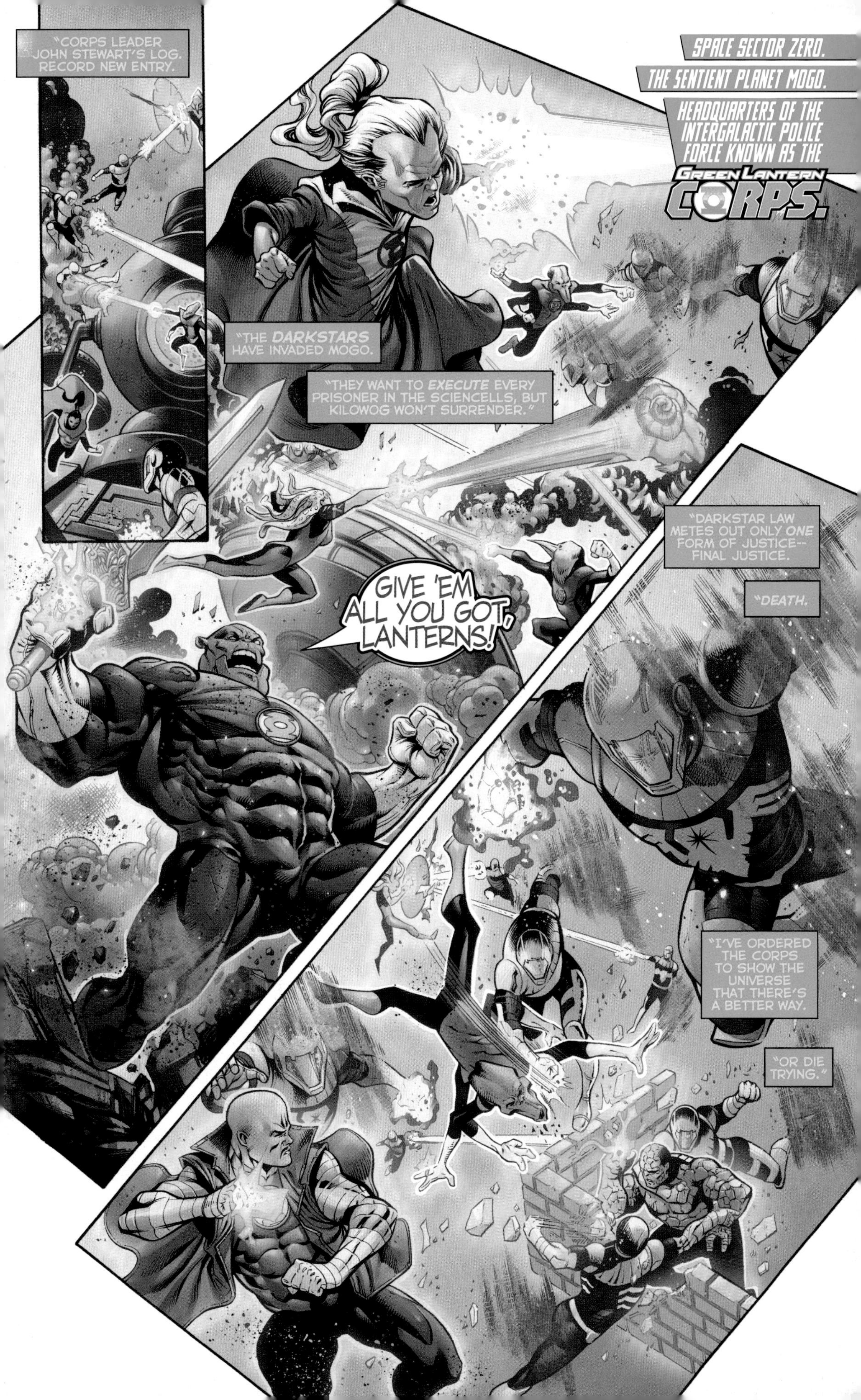
"CORPS LEADER JOHN STEWART'S LOG. RECORD NEW ENTRY.
SPACE SECTOR ZERO.
THE SENTIENT PLANET MOGO.
HEADQUARTERS OF THE INTERGALACTIC POLICE FORCE KNOWN AS THE
GREEN LANTERN CORPS.
"THE DARKSTARS HAVE INVADED MOGO.
"THEY WANT TO EXECUTE EVERY PRISONER IN THE SCIENCELLS, BUT KILOWOG WON'T SURRENDER."
GIVE 'EM ALL YOU GOT, LANTERNS!
"DARKSTAR LAW METES OUT ONLY ONE FORM OF JUSTICE-- FINAL JUSTICE.
"DEATH.
"I'VE ORDERED THE CORPS TO SHOW THE UNIVERSE THAT THERE'S A BETTER WAY.
"OR DIE TRYING."

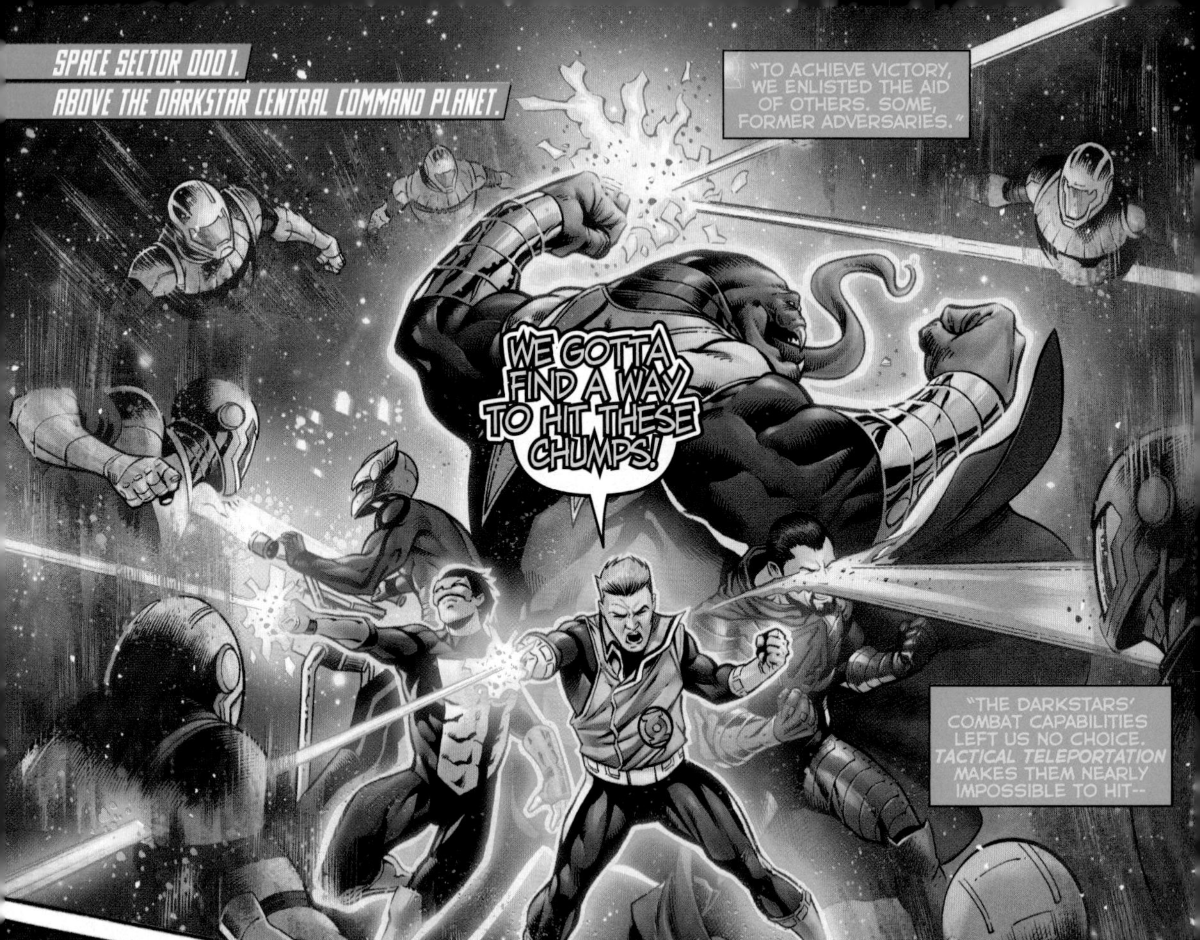
SPACE SECTOR 0001.
ABOVE THE DARKSTAR CENTRAL COMMAND PLANET.
"TO ACHIEVE VICTORY, WE ENLISTED THE AID OF OTHERS. SOME, FORMER ADVERSARIES."
WE GOTTA FIND A WAY TO HIT THESE CHUMPS!
"THE DARKSTARS' COMBAT CAPABILITIES LEFT US NO CHOICE. *TACTICAL TELEPORTATION* MAKES THEM NEARLY IMPOSSIBLE TO HIT--

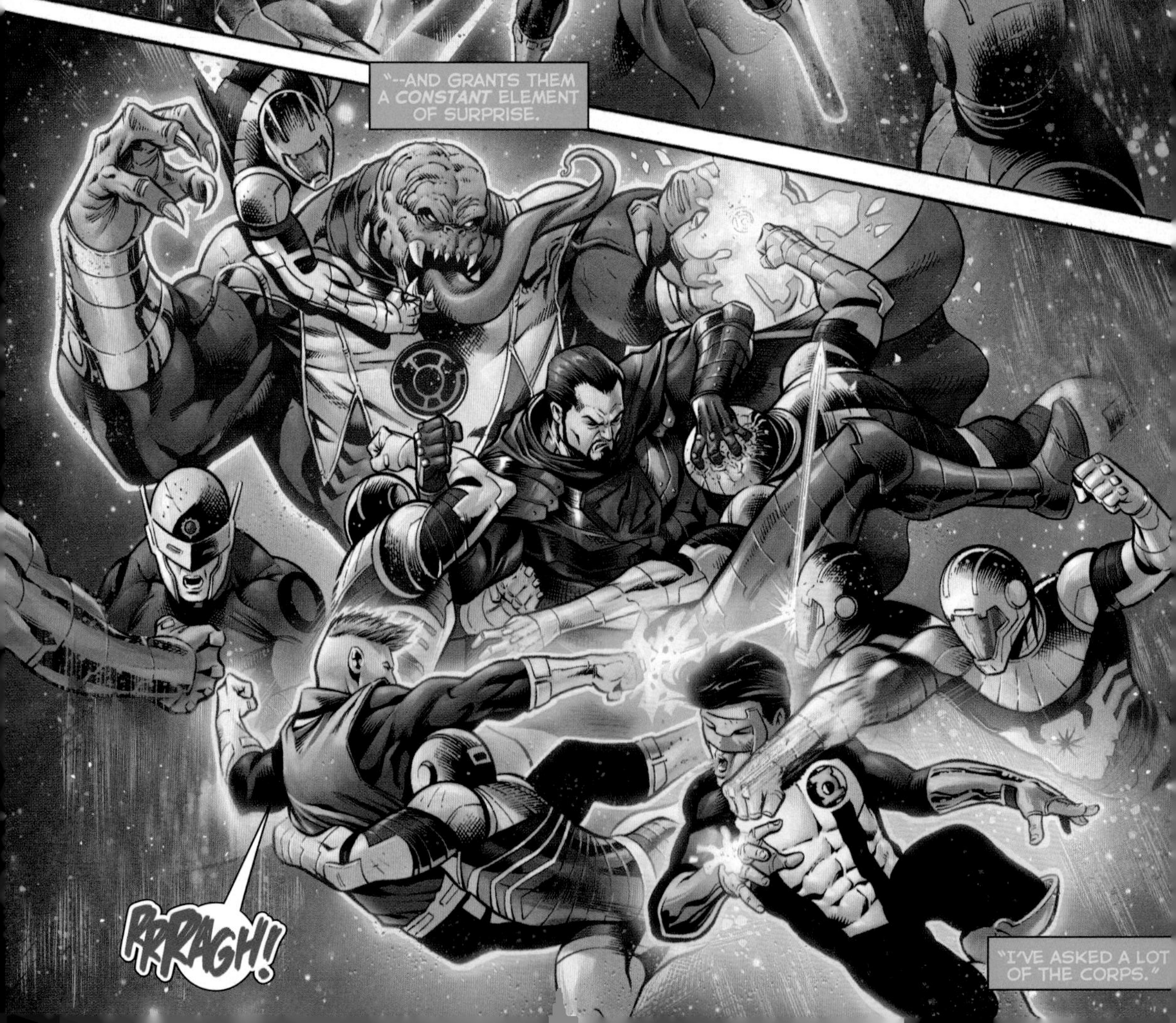
"--AND GRANTS THEM A *CONSTANT* ELEMENT OF SURPRISE.
RRRAGH!
"I'VE ASKED A LOT OF THE CORPS."

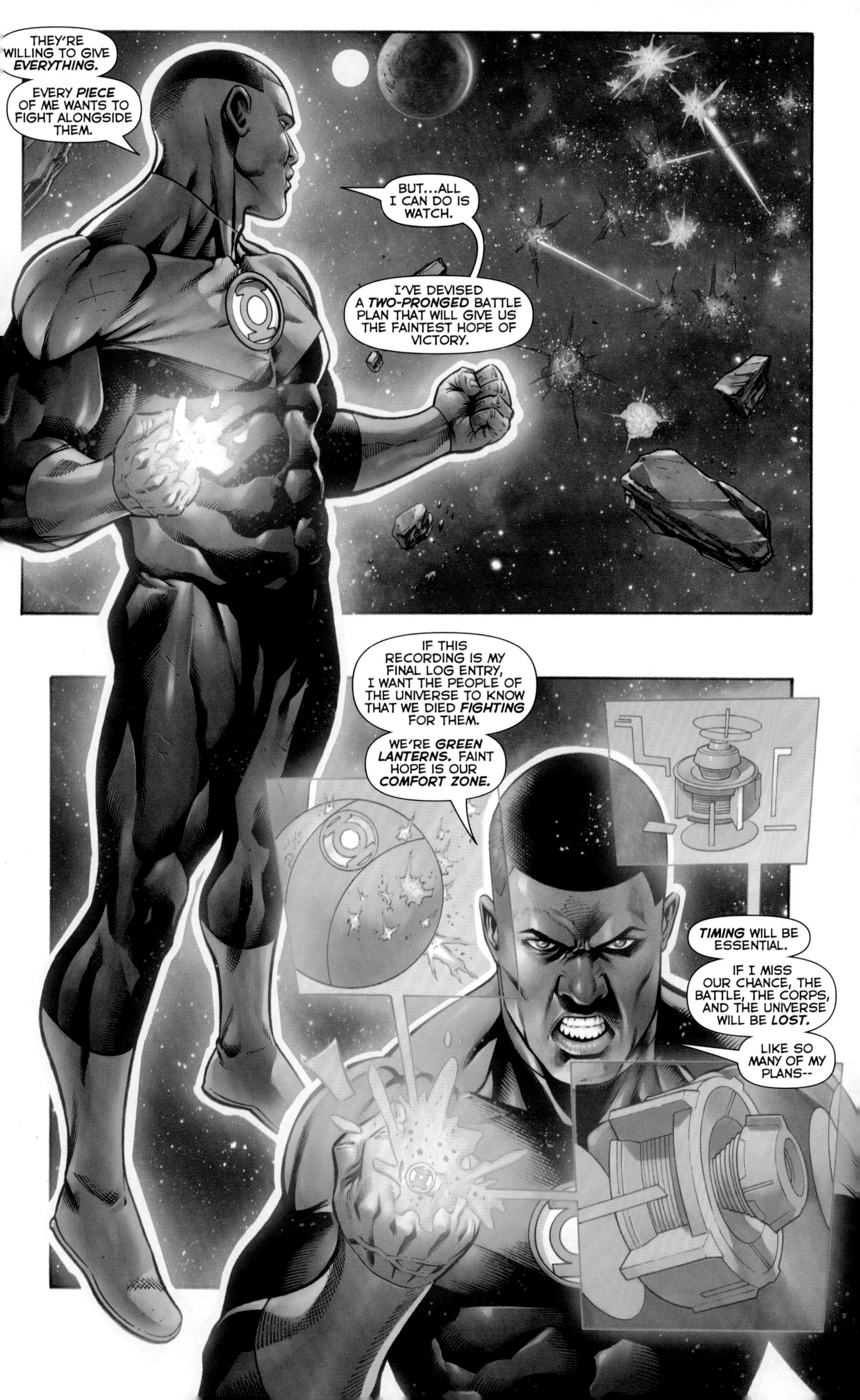
THEY'RE WILLING TO GIVE *EVERYTHING.*
EVERY *PIECE* OF ME WANTS TO FIGHT ALONGSIDE THEM.
BUT...ALL I CAN DO IS WATCH.
I'VE DEVISED A *TWO-PRONGED* BATTLE PLAN THAT WILL GIVE US THE FAINTEST HOPE OF VICTORY.
IF THIS RECORDING IS MY FINAL LOG ENTRY, I WANT THE PEOPLE OF THE UNIVERSE TO KNOW THAT WE DIED *FIGHTING* FOR THEM.
WE'RE *GREEN LANTERNS.* FAINT HOPE IS OUR *COMFORT ZONE.*
TIMING WILL BE ESSENTIAL.
IF I MISS OUR CHANCE, THE BATTLE, THE CORPS, AND THE UNIVERSE WILL BE *LOST.*
LIKE SO MANY OF MY PLANS--

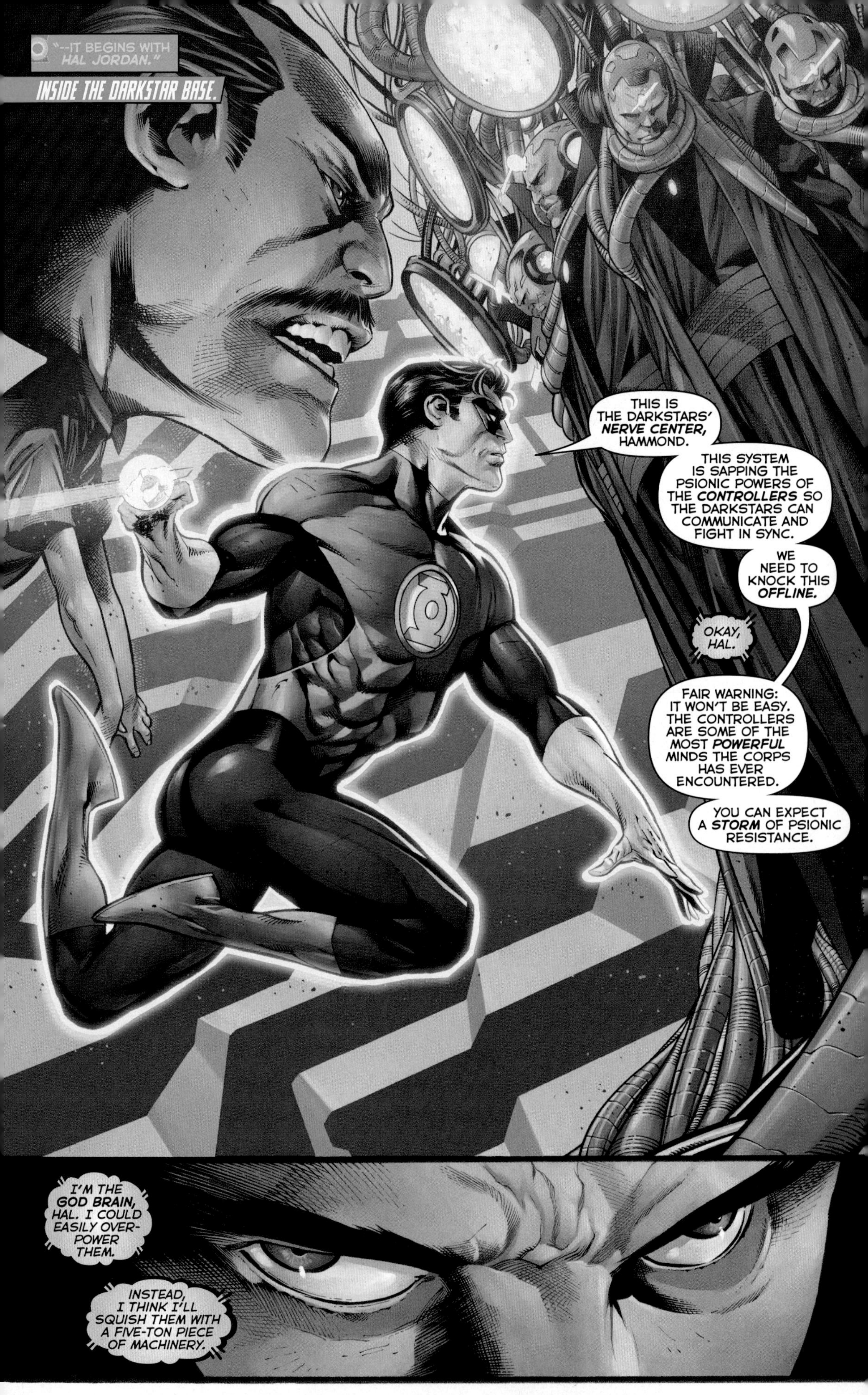
"--IT BEGINS WITH HAL JORDAN."
INSIDE THE DARKSTAR BASE.
THIS IS THE DARKSTARS' NERVE CENTER, HAMMOND.
THIS SYSTEM IS SAPPING THE PSIONIC POWERS OF THE CONTROLLERS SO THE DARKSTARS CAN COMMUNICATE AND FIGHT IN SYNC.
WE NEED TO KNOCK THIS OFFLINE.
OKAY, HAL.
FAIR WARNING: IT WON'T BE EASY. THE CONTROLLERS ARE SOME OF THE MOST POWERFUL MINDS THE CORPS HAS EVER ENCOUNTERED.
YOU CAN EXPECT A STORM OF PSIONIC RESISTANCE.
I'M THE GOD BRAIN, HAL. I COULD EASILY OVER-POWER THEM.
INSTEAD, I THINK I'LL SQUISH THEM WITH A FIVE-TON PIECE OF MACHINERY.

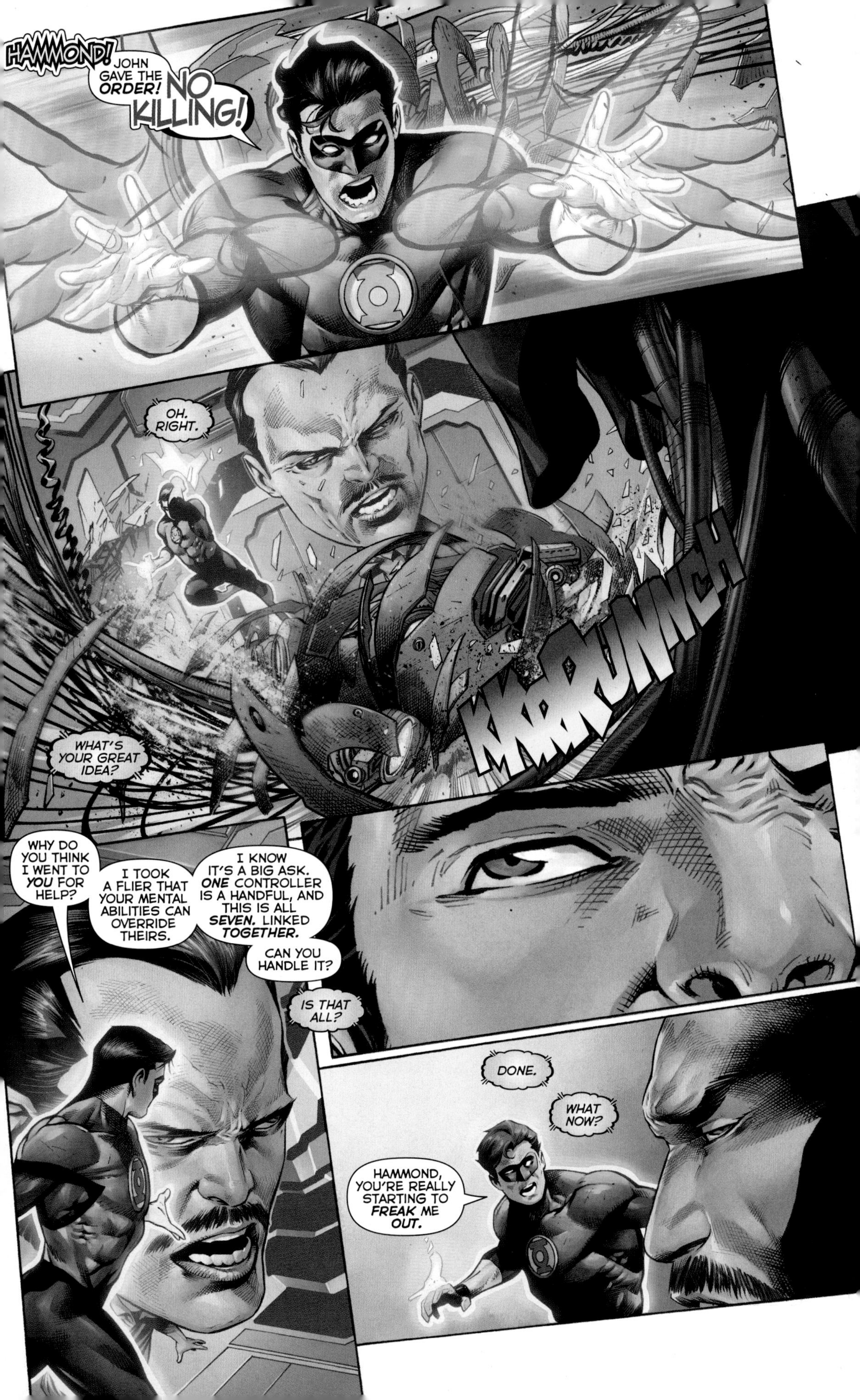
HAMMOND!
JOHN GAVE THE ORDER! NO KILLING!
OH. RIGHT.
KKRRUNNCH
WHAT'S YOUR GREAT IDEA?
WHY DO YOU THINK I WENT TO YOU FOR HELP?
I TOOK A FLIER THAT YOUR MENTAL ABILITIES CAN OVERRIDE THEIRS.
I KNOW IT'S A BIG ASK. ONE CONTROLLER IS A HANDFUL, AND THIS IS ALL SEVEN. LINKED TOGETHER.
CAN YOU HANDLE IT?
IS THAT ALL?
DONE.
WHAT NOW?
HAMMOND, YOU'RE REALLY STARTING TO FREAK ME OUT.

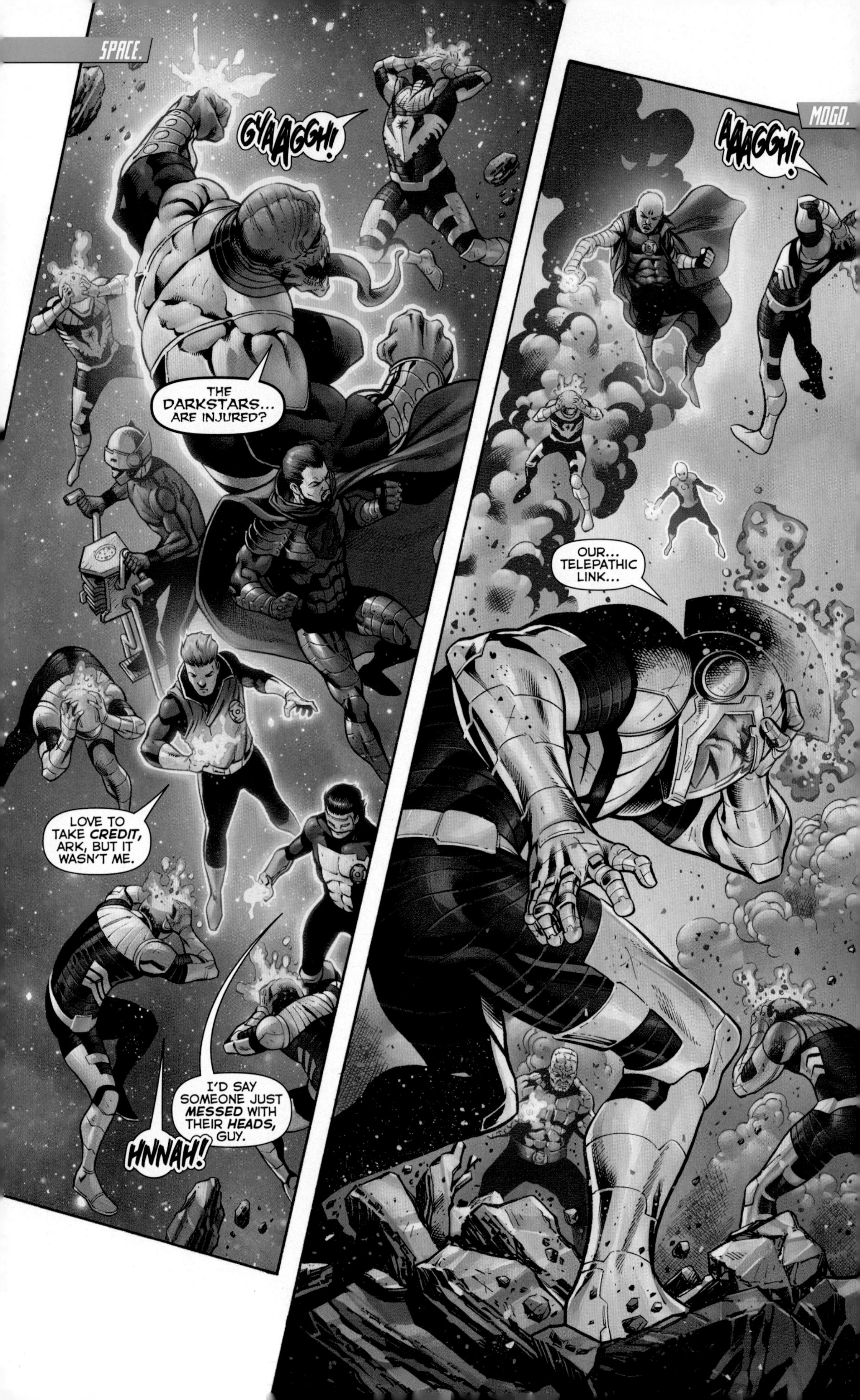
SPACE.
GYAAGGH!
THE DARKSTARS... ARE INJURED?
LOVE TO TAKE CREDIT, ARK, BUT IT WASN'T ME.
HNNAH!
I'D SAY SOMEONE JUST MESSED WITH THEIR HEADS, GUY.
MOGO.
AAAGGH!
OUR... TELEPATHIC LINK...

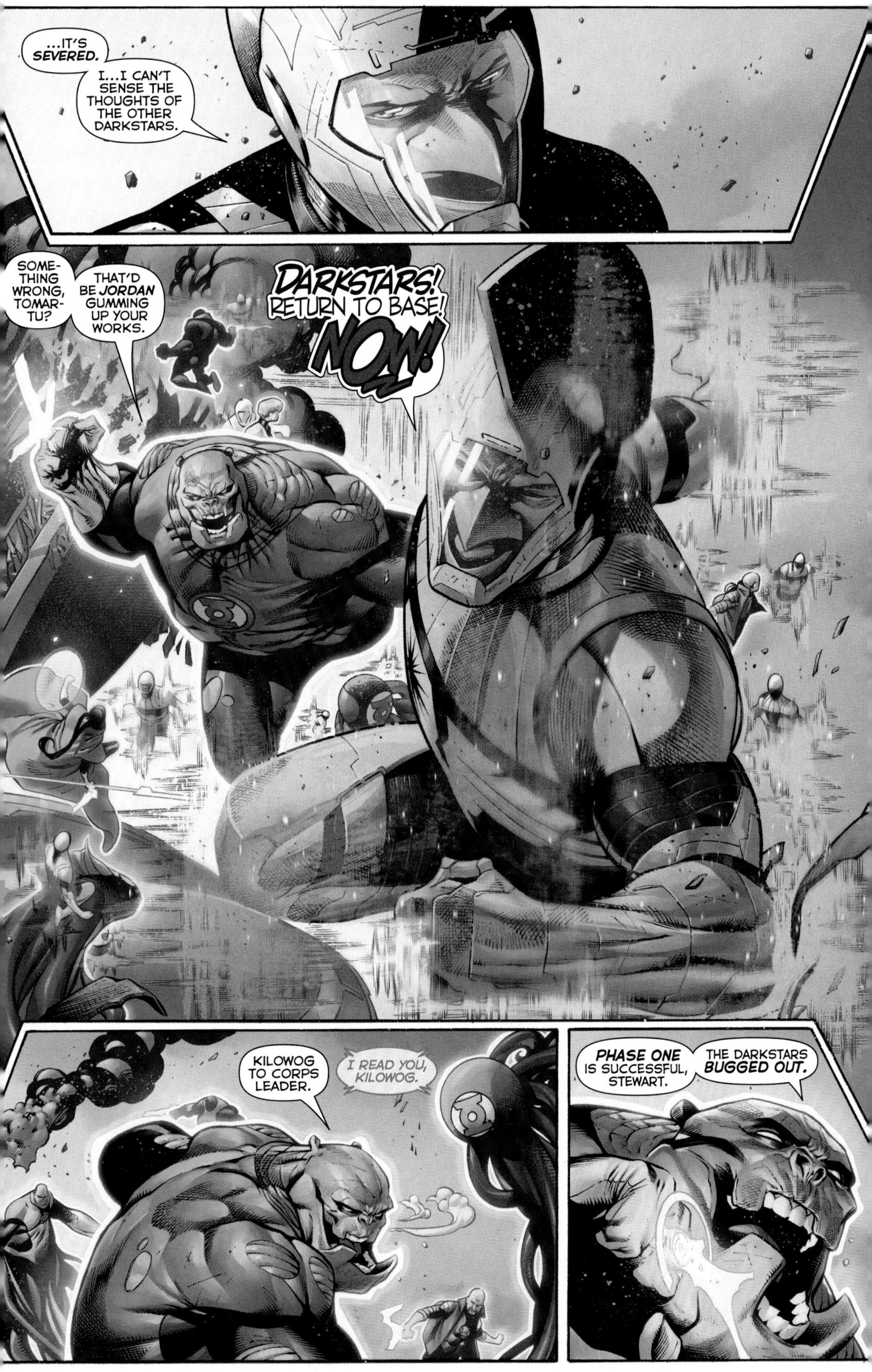
...IT'S SEVERED.
I...I CAN'T SENSE THE THOUGHTS OF THE OTHER DARKSTARS.
SOME-THING WRONG, TOMAR-TU?
THAT'D BE JORDAN GUMMING UP YOUR WORKS.
DARKSTARS! RETURN TO BASE! NOW!
KILOWOG TO CORPS LEADER.
I READ YOU, KILOWOG.
PHASE ONE IS SUCCESSFUL, STEWART.
THE DARKSTARS BUGGED OUT.

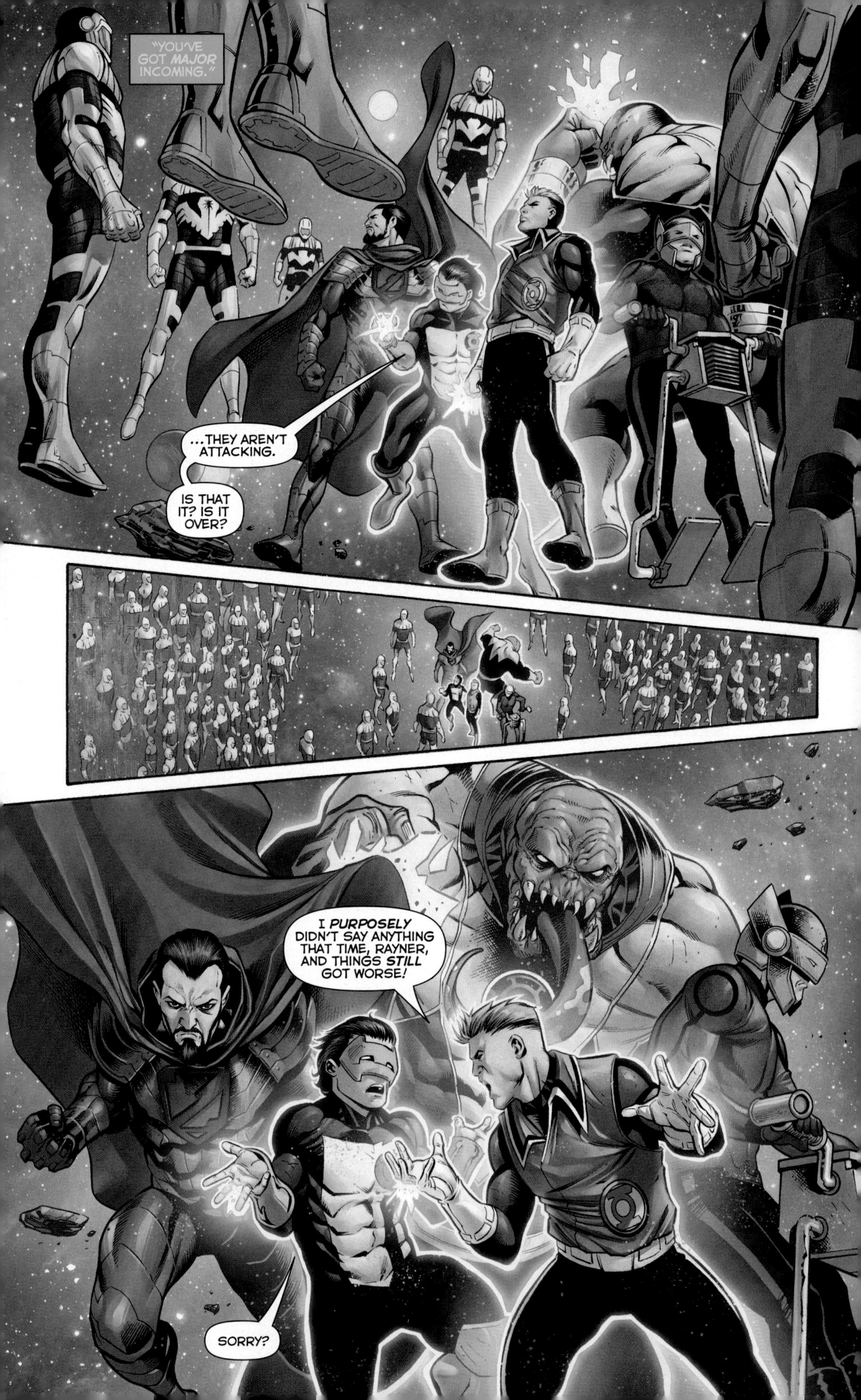
"YOU'VE GOT *MAJOR* INCOMING."
...THEY AREN'T ATTACKING.
IS THAT IT? IS IT OVER?
I *PURPOSELY* DIDN'T SAY ANYTHING THAT TIME, RAYNER, AND THINGS *STILL* GOT WORSE!
SORRY?

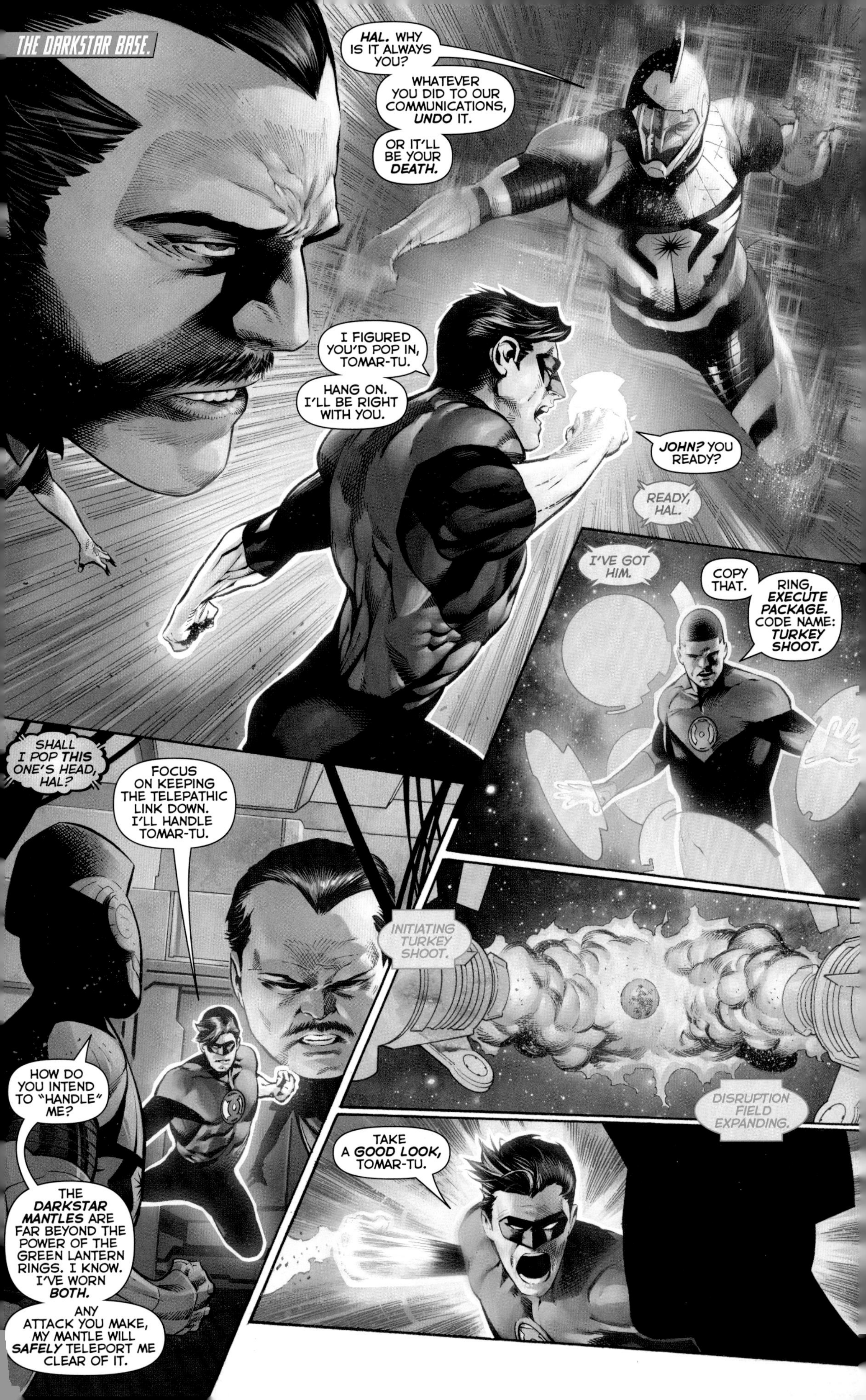
THE DARKSTAR BASE.
HAL. WHY IS IT ALWAYS YOU?
WHATEVER YOU DID TO OUR COMMUNICATIONS, UNDO IT.
OR IT'LL BE YOUR DEATH.
I FIGURED YOU'D POP IN, TOMAR-TU.
HANG ON. I'LL BE RIGHT WITH YOU.
JOHN? YOU READY?
READY, HAL.
I'VE GOT HIM.
COPY THAT.
RING, EXECUTE PACKAGE. CODE NAME: TURKEY SHOOT.
SHALL I POP THIS ONE'S HEAD, HAL?
FOCUS ON KEEPING THE TELEPATHIC LINK DOWN. I'LL HANDLE TOMAR-TU.
INITIATING TURKEY SHOOT.
DISRUPTION FIELD EXPANDING.
HOW DO YOU INTEND TO "HANDLE" ME?
THE DARKSTAR MANTLES ARE FAR BEYOND THE POWER OF THE GREEN LANTERN RINGS. I KNOW. I'VE WORN BOTH.
ANY ATTACK YOU MAKE, MY MANTLE WILL SAFELY TELEPORT ME CLEAR OF IT.
TAKE A GOOD LOOK, TOMAR-TU.

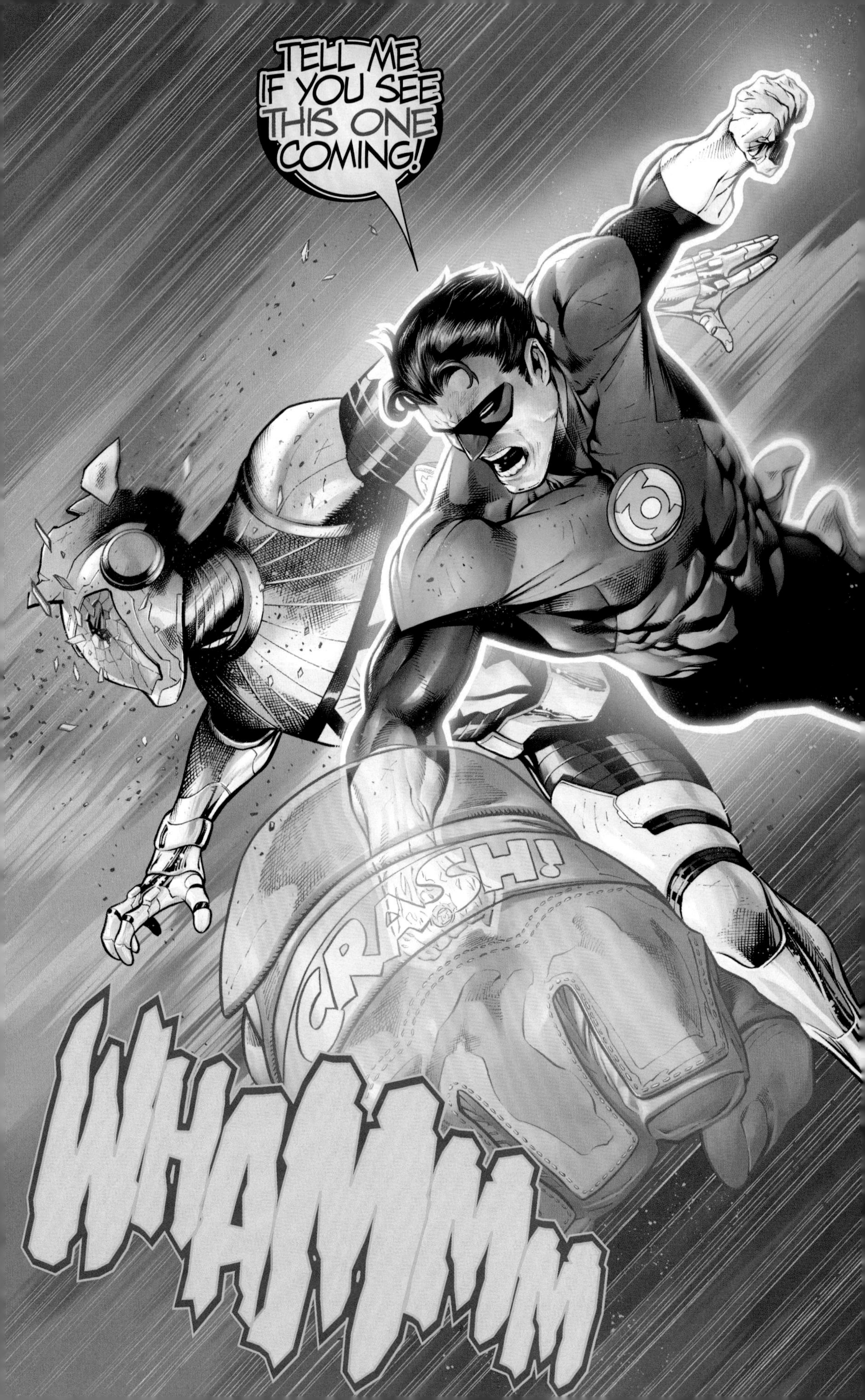
TELL ME IF YOU SEE THIS ONE COMING!
CRASSH!
WHAMMM

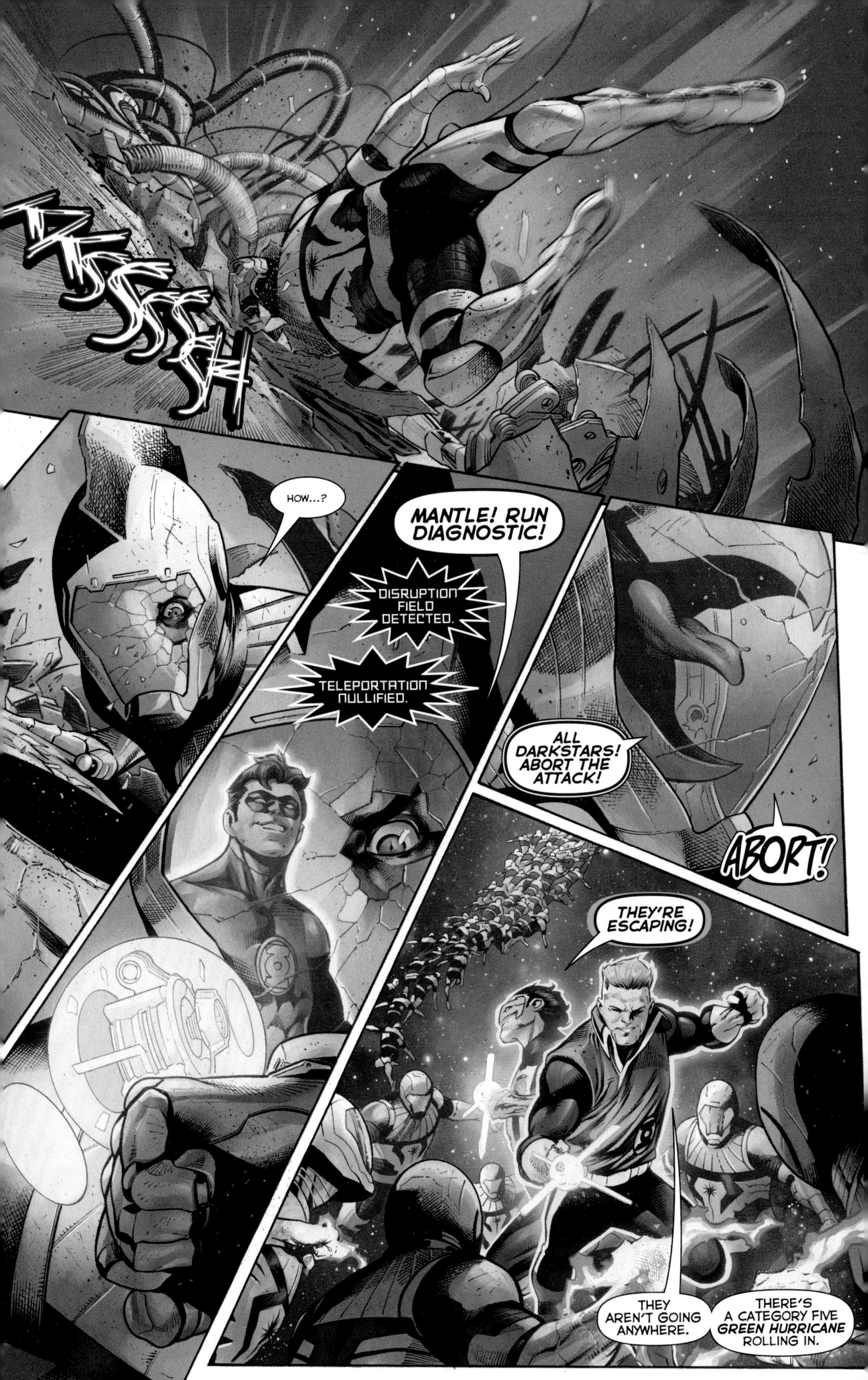

KRASSSH
HOW...?
MANTLE! RUN DIAGNOSTIC!
DISRUPTION FIELD DETECTED.
TELEPORTATION NULLIFIED.
ALL DARKSTARS! ABORT THE ATTACK!
ABORT!
THEY'RE ESCAPING!
THEY AREN'T GOING ANYWHERE.
THERE'S A CATEGORY FIVE GREEN HURRICANE ROLLING IN.

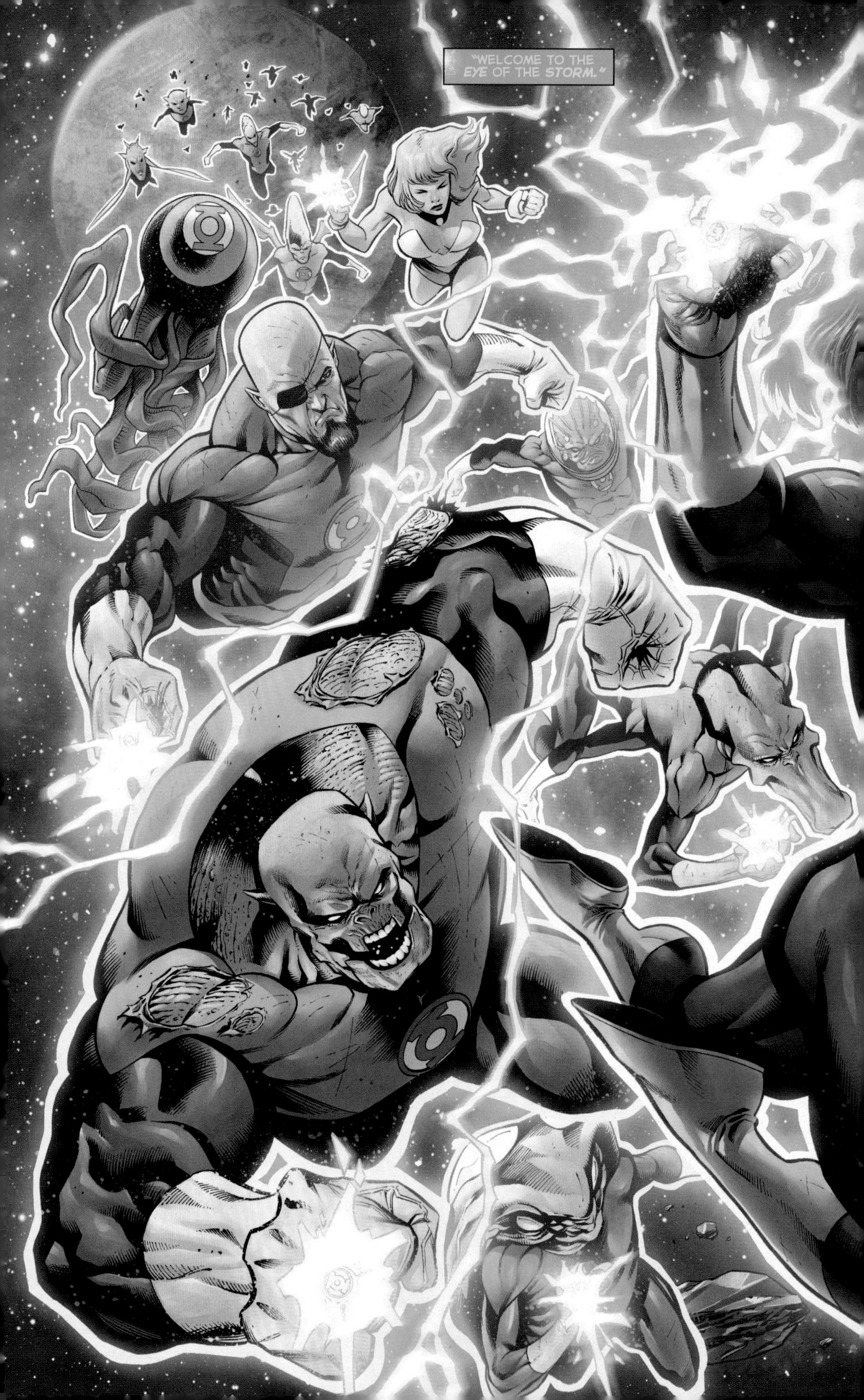
"WELCOME TO THE EYE OF THE STORM."

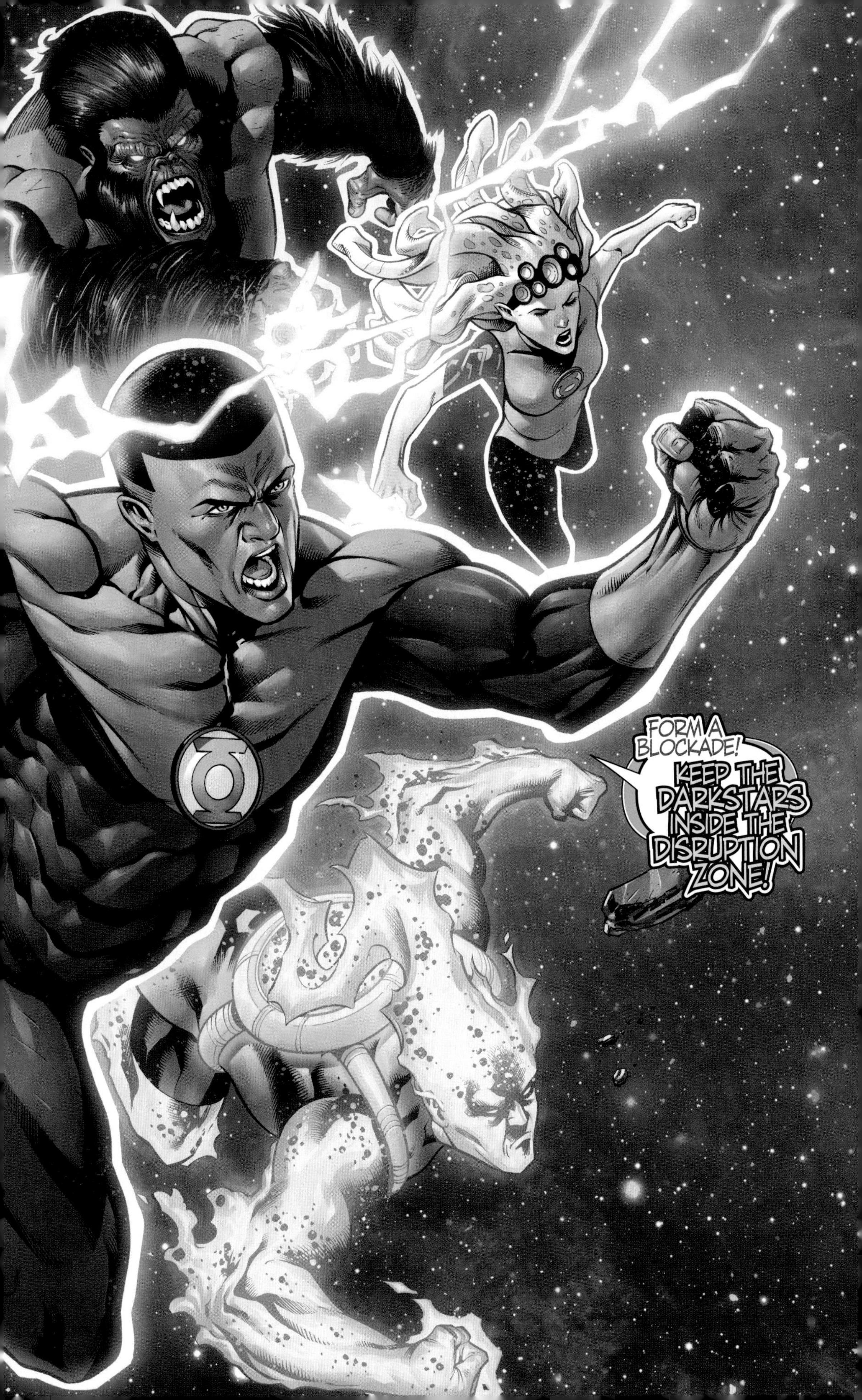
FORM A BLOCKADE!
KEEP THE DARKSTARS INSIDE THE DISRUPTION ZONE!

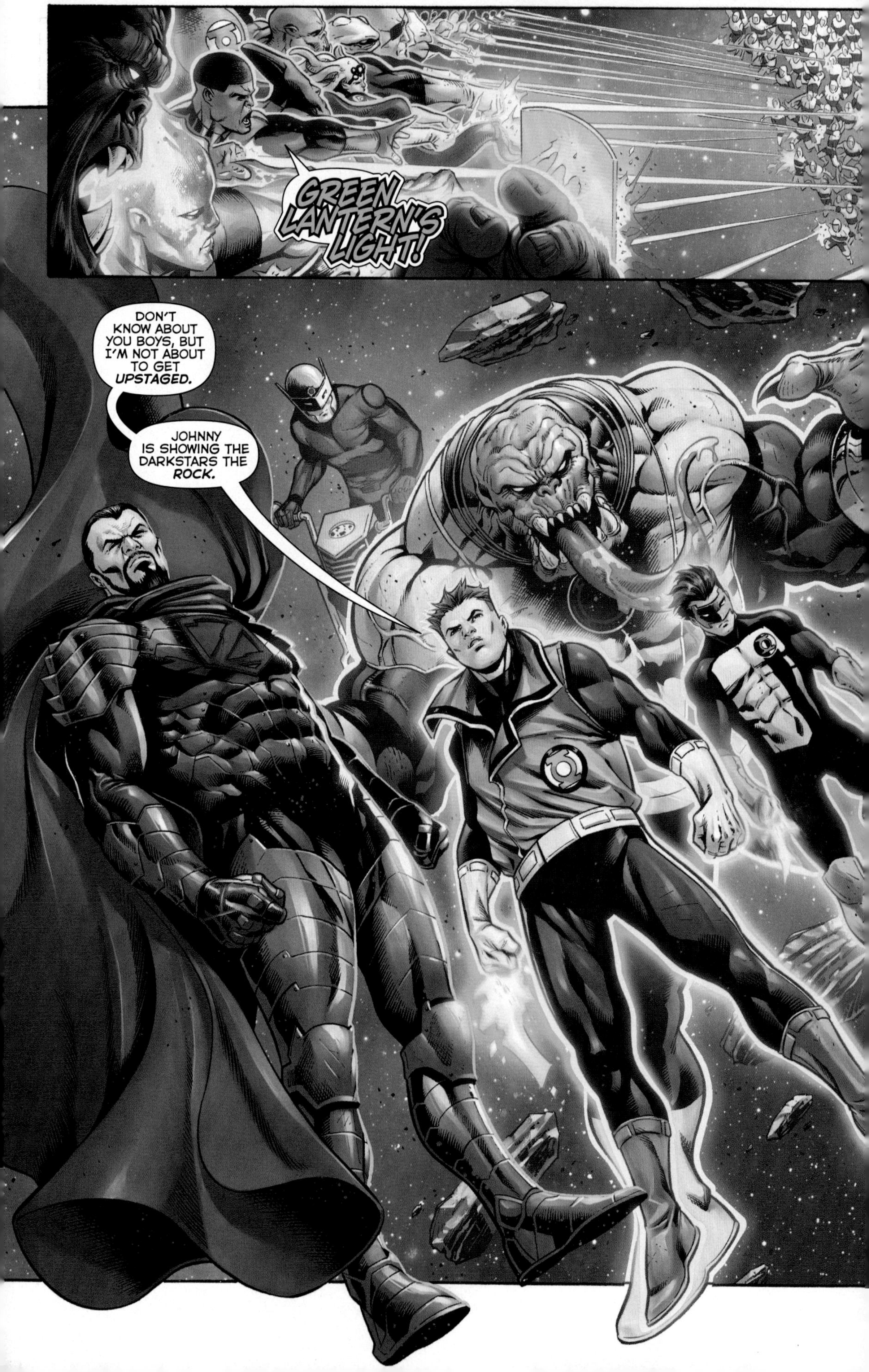
GREEN LANTERN'S LIGHT!
DON'T KNOW ABOUT YOU BOYS, BUT I'M NOT ABOUT TO GET UPSTAGED.
JOHNNY IS SHOWING THE DARKSTARS THE ROCK.

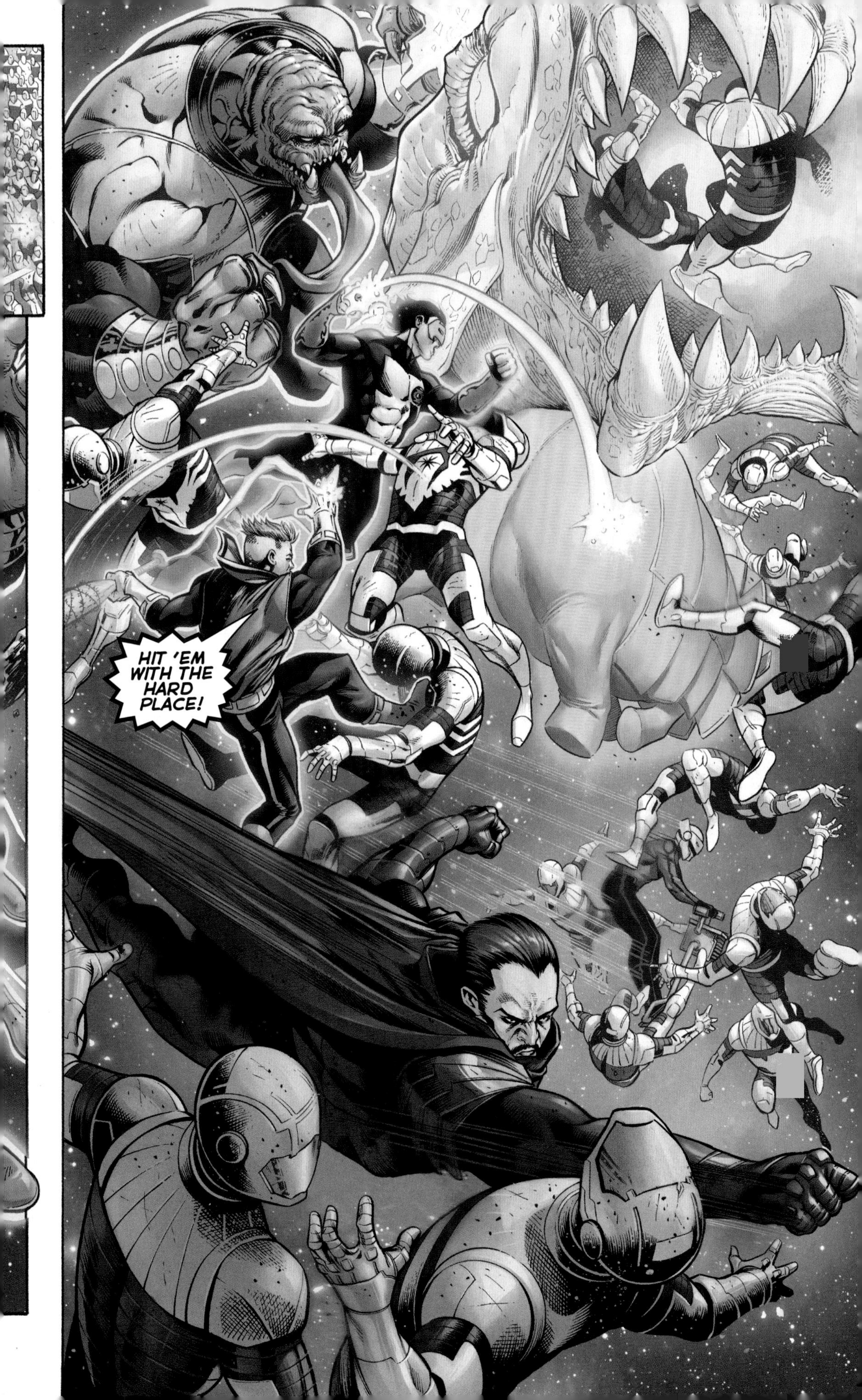
HIT 'EM WITH THE HARD PLACE!

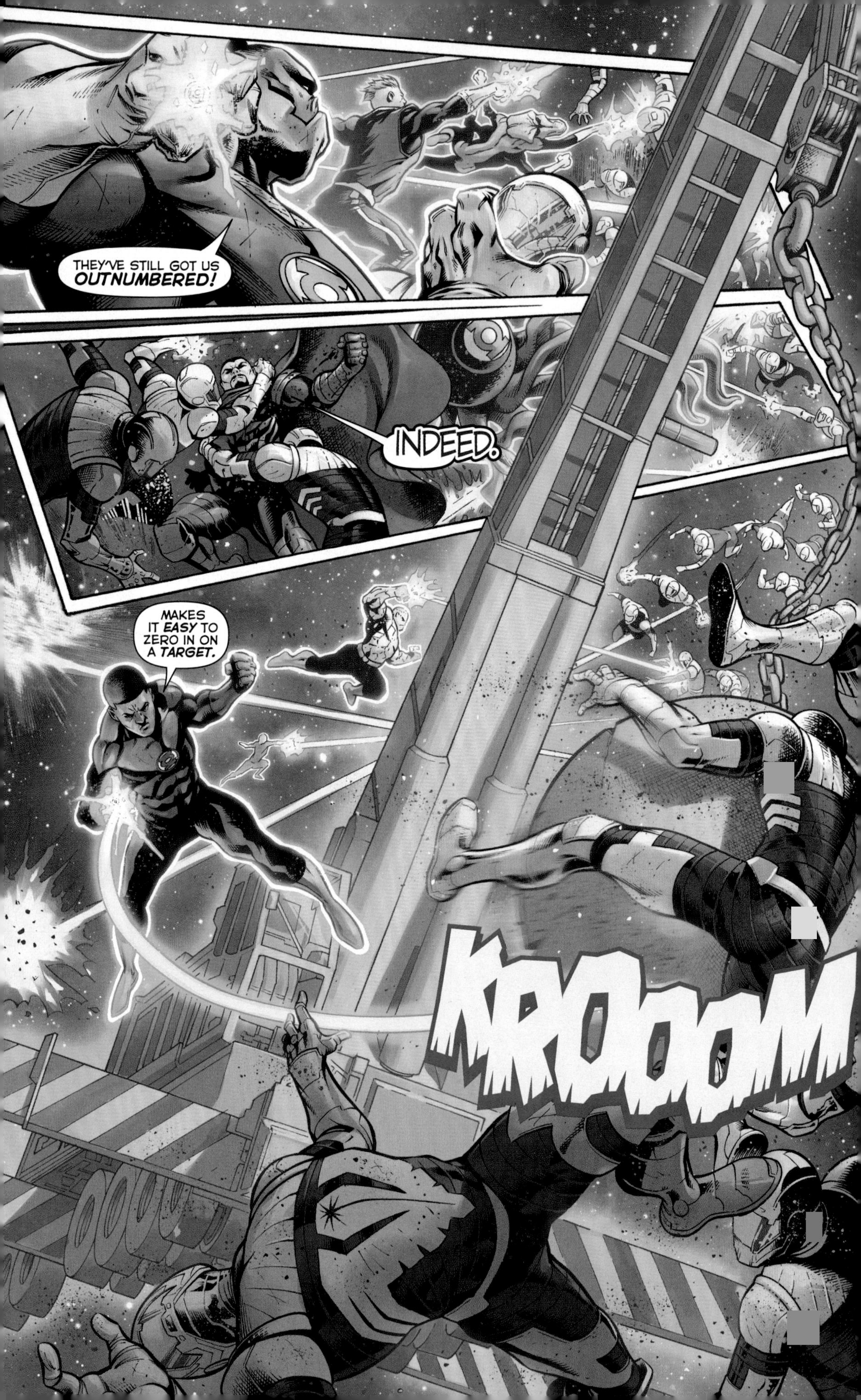
THEY'VE STILL GOT US OUTNUMBERED!
INDEED.
MAKES IT EASY TO ZERO IN ON A TARGET.
KROOOM

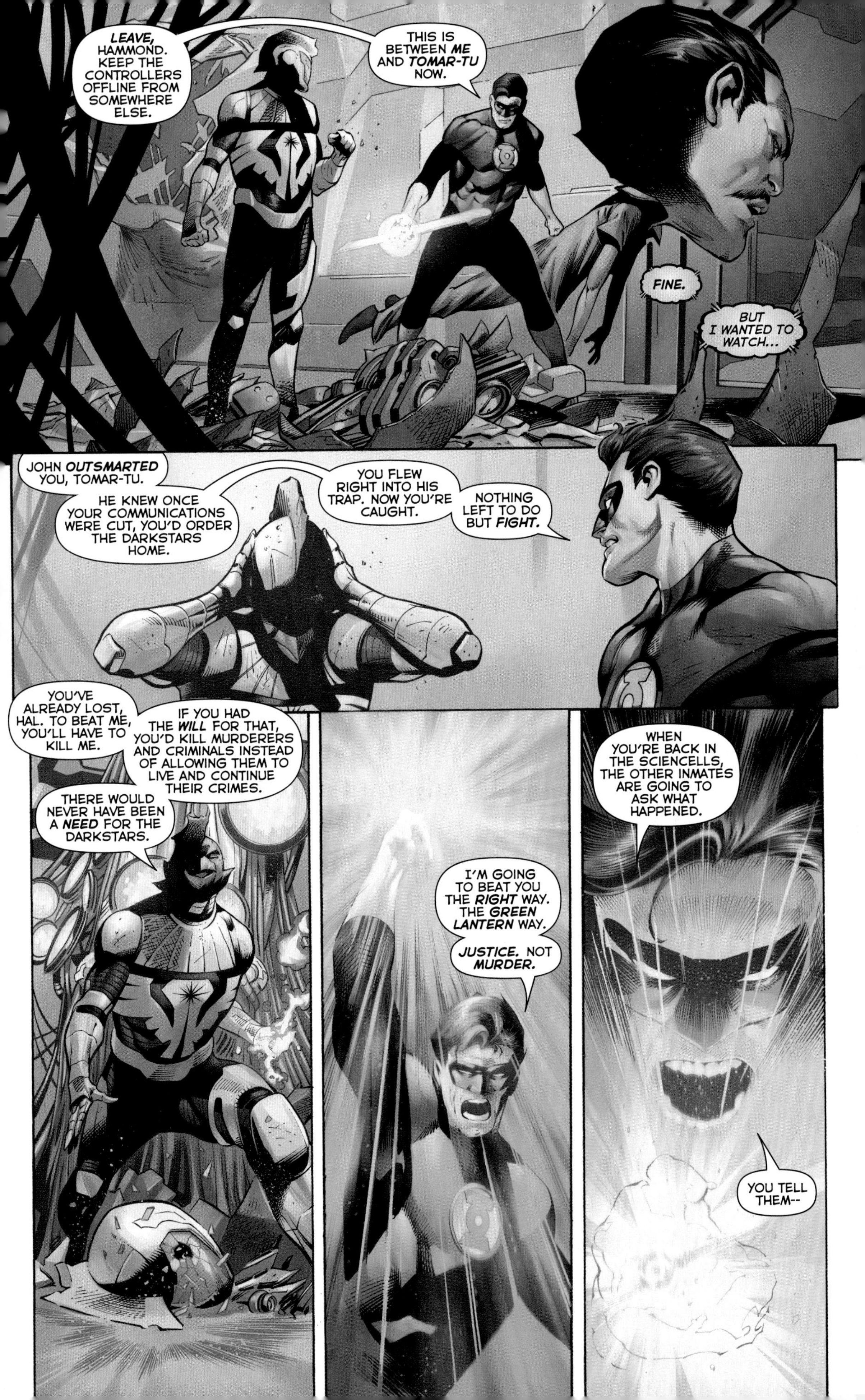
LEAVE, HAMMOND. KEEP THE CONTROLLERS OFFLINE FROM SOMEWHERE ELSE.
THIS IS BETWEEN ME AND TOMAR-TU NOW.
FINE.
BUT I WANTED TO WATCH...
JOHN OUTSMARTED YOU, TOMAR-TU.
HE KNEW ONCE YOUR COMMUNICATIONS WERE CUT, YOU'D ORDER THE DARKSTARS HOME.
YOU FLEW RIGHT INTO HIS TRAP. NOW YOU'RE CAUGHT.
NOTHING LEFT TO DO BUT FIGHT.
YOU'VE ALREADY LOST, HAL. TO BEAT ME, YOU'LL HAVE TO KILL ME.
IF YOU HAD THE WILL FOR THAT, YOU'D KILL MURDERERS AND CRIMINALS INSTEAD OF ALLOWING THEM TO LIVE AND CONTINUE THEIR CRIMES.
THERE WOULD NEVER HAVE BEEN A NEED FOR THE DARKSTARS.
I'M GOING TO BEAT YOU THE RIGHT WAY. THE GREEN LANTERN WAY.
JUSTICE. NOT MURDER.
WHEN YOU'RE BACK IN THE SCIENCELLS, THE OTHER INMATES ARE GOING TO ASK WHAT HAPPENED.
YOU TELL THEM--

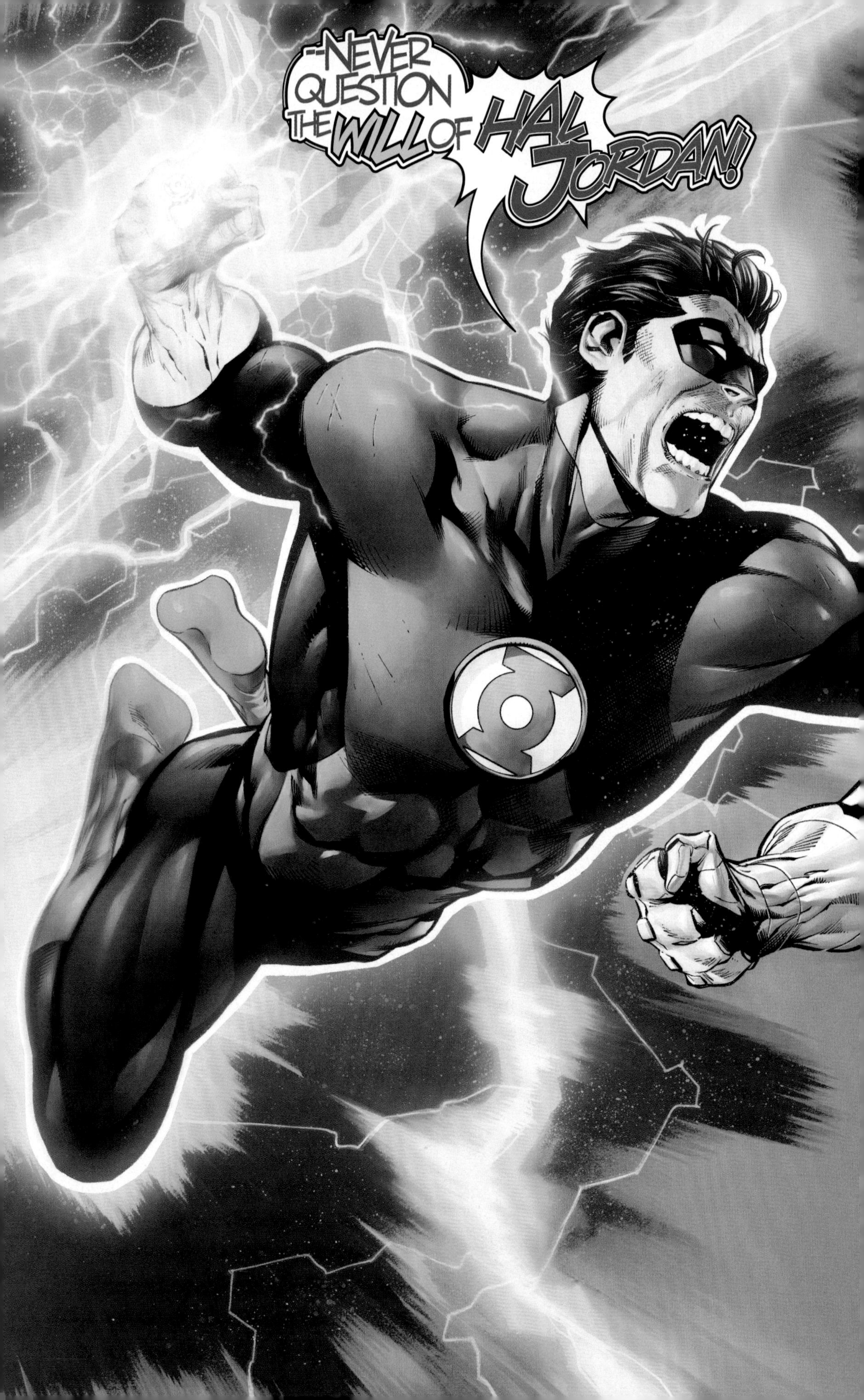
--NEVER QUESTION THE WILL OF HAL JORDAN!

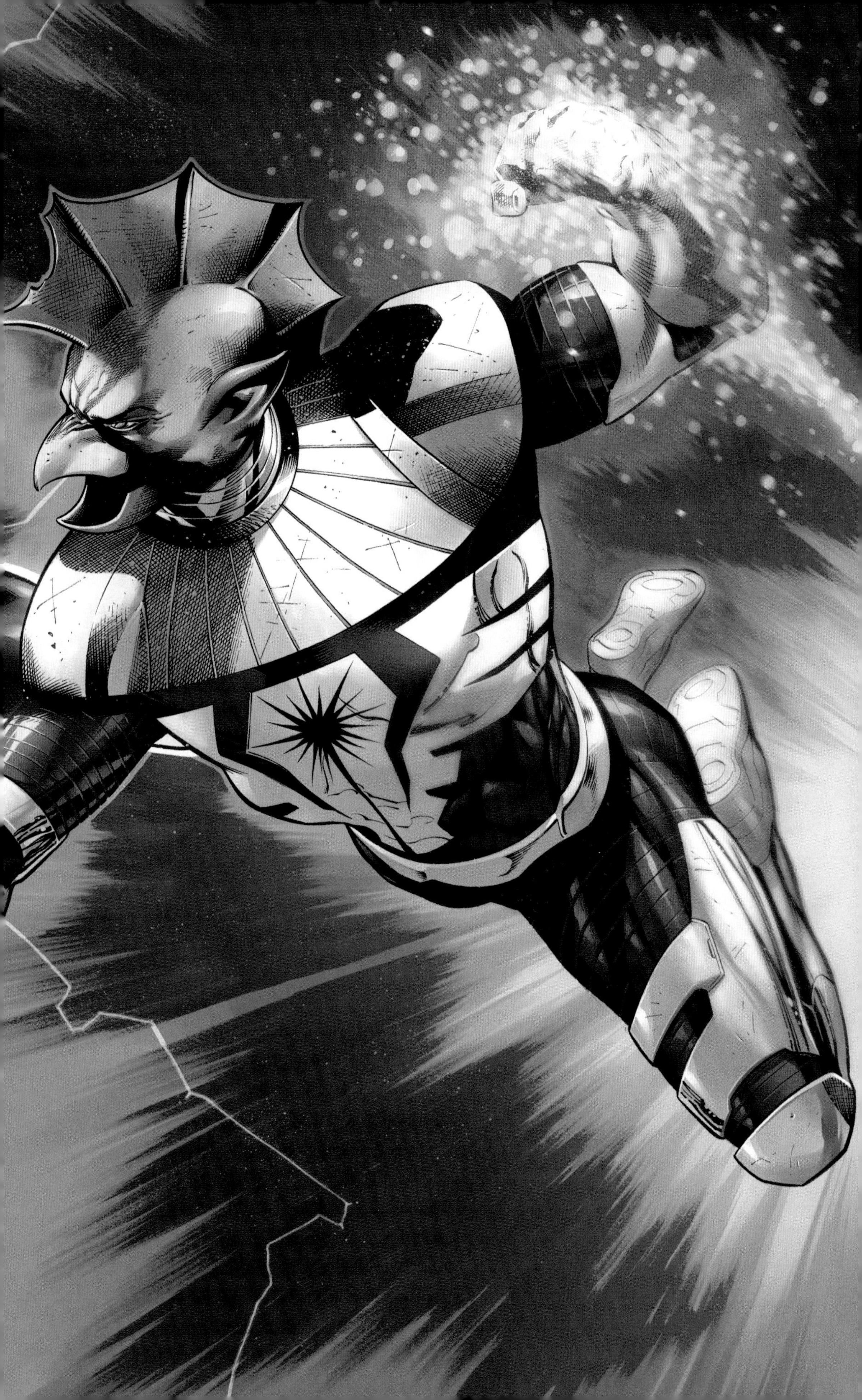

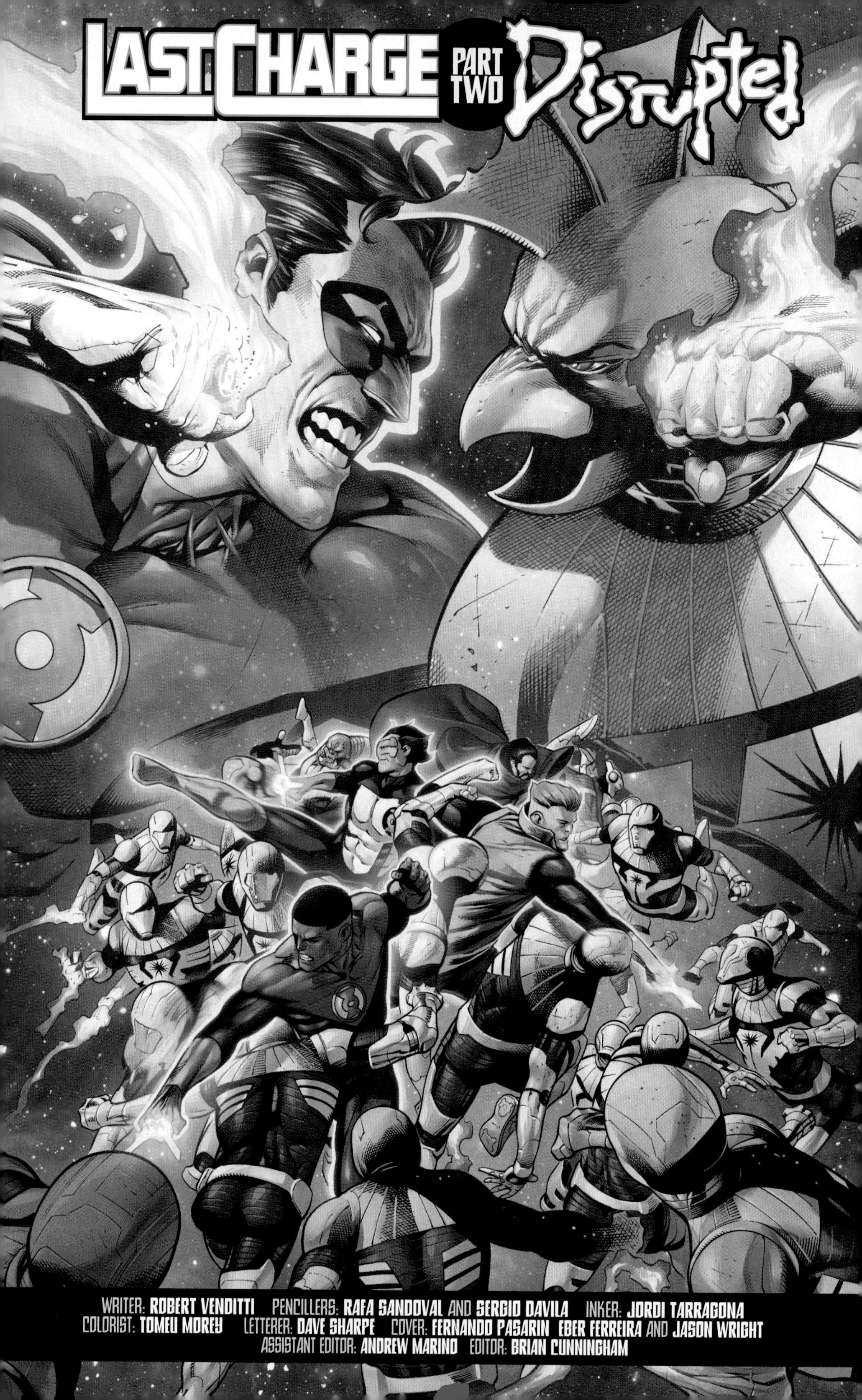
LAST CHARGE PART TWO Disrupted
WRITER: ROBERT VENDITTI PENCILLERS: RAFA SANDOVAL AND SERGIO DAVILA INKER: JORDI TARRAGONA
COLORIST: TOMEU MOREY LETTERER: DAVE SHARPE COVER: FERNANDO PASARIN EBER FERREIRA AND JASON WRIGHT
ASSISTANT EDITOR: ANDREW MARINO EDITOR: BRIAN CUNNINGHAM

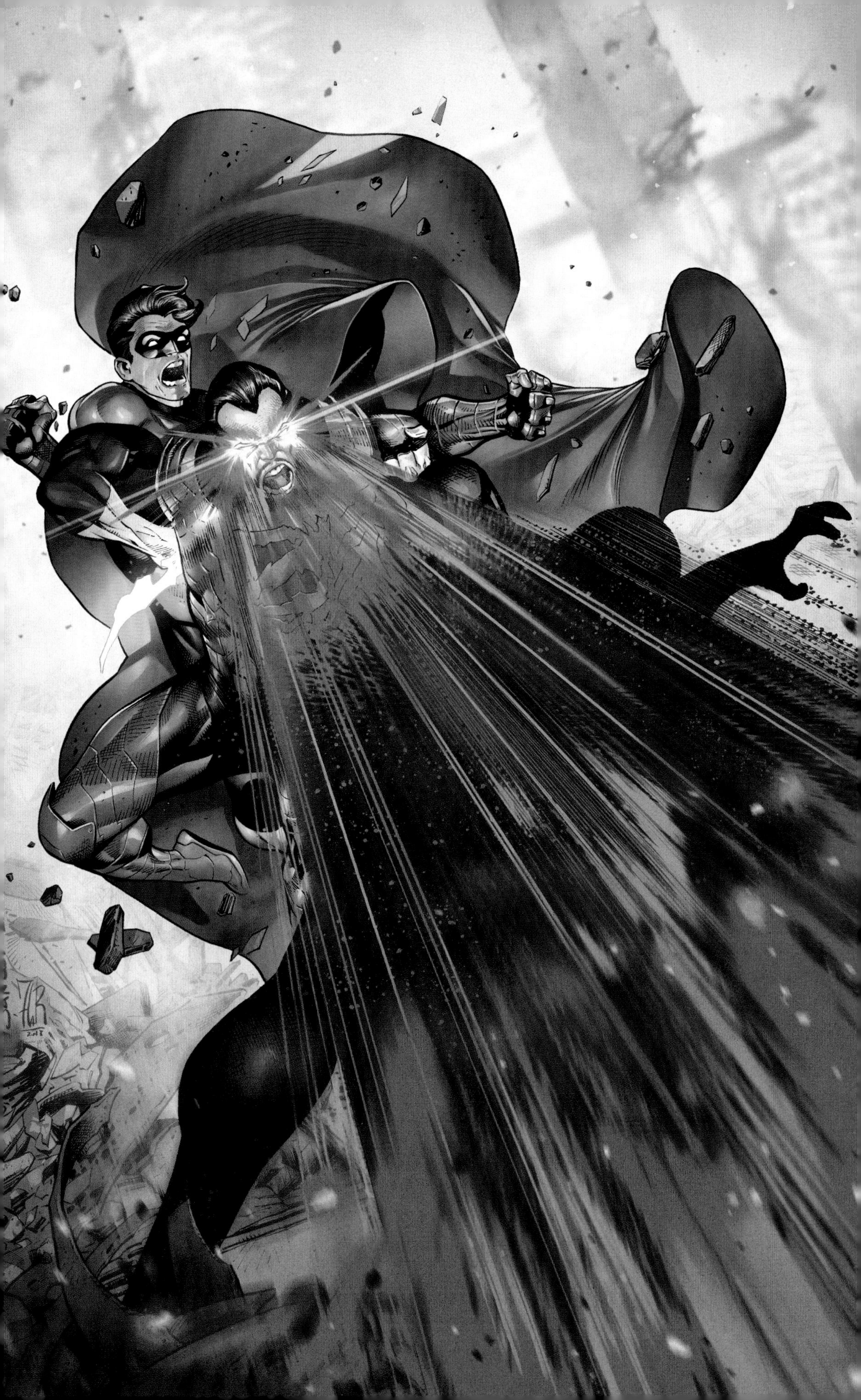

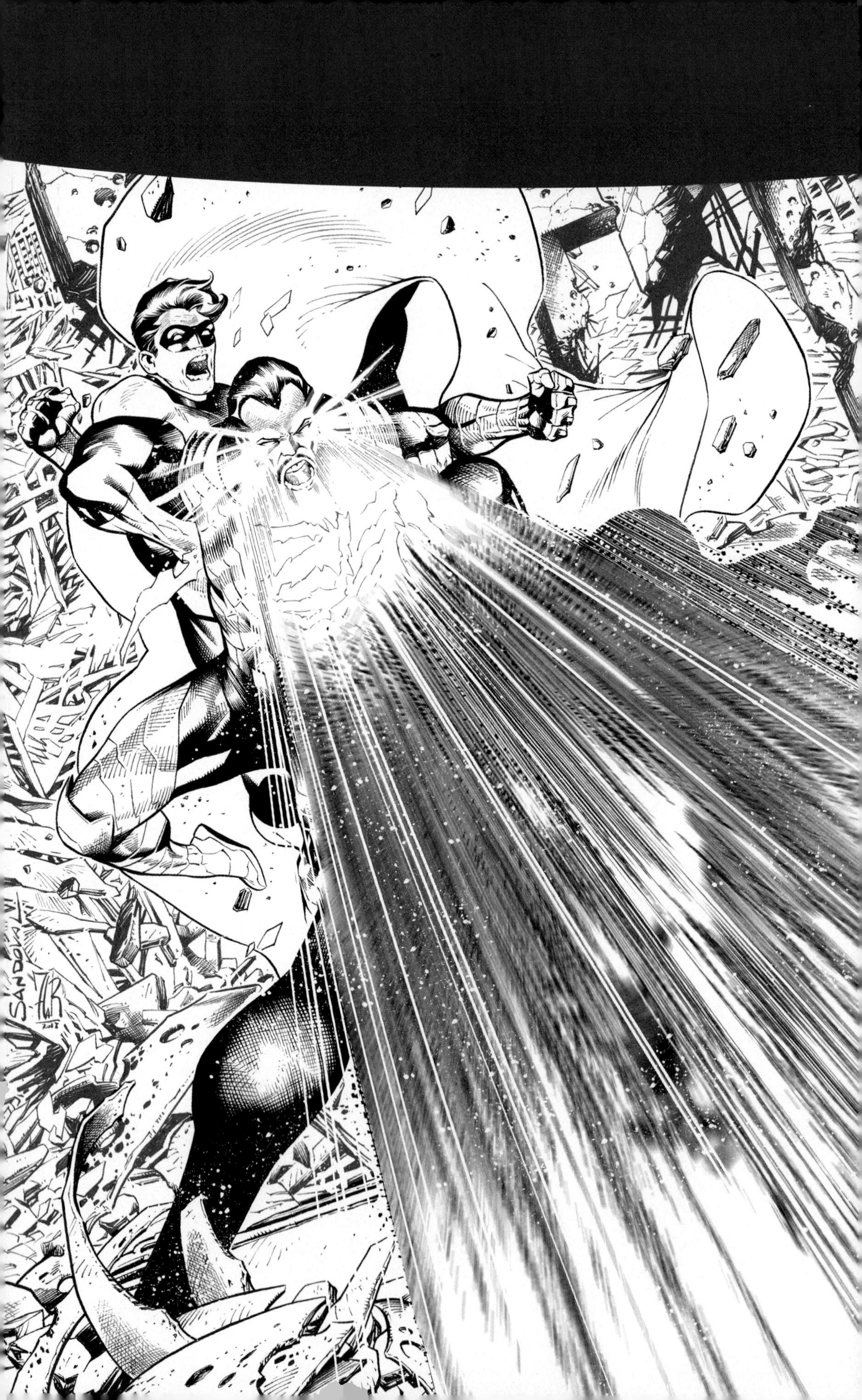

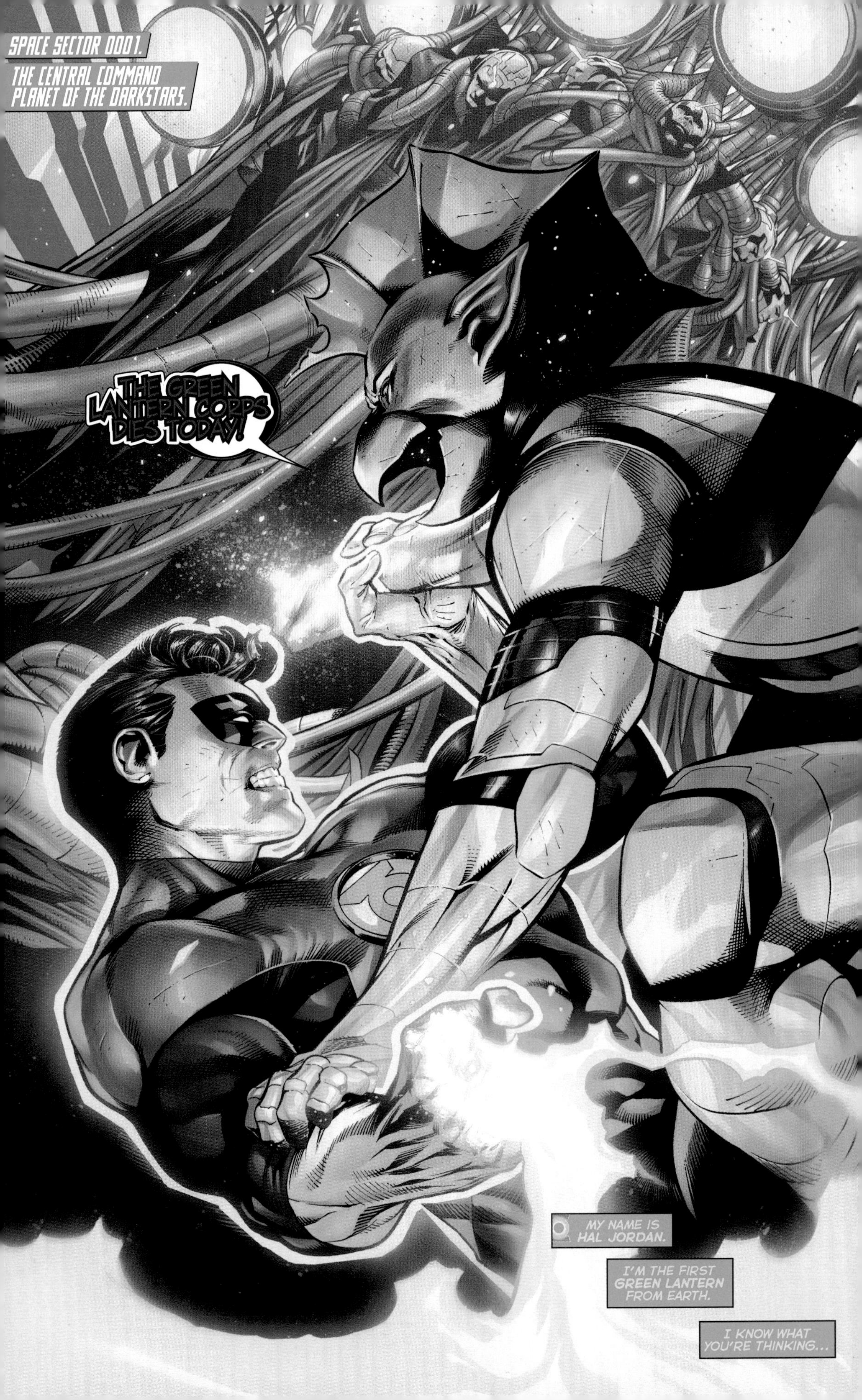
SPACE SECTOR 0001.
THE CENTRAL COMMAND PLANET OF THE DARKSTARS.
THE GREEN LANTERN CORPS DIES TODAY!
MY NAME IS HAL JORDAN.
I'M THE FIRST GREEN LANTERN FROM EARTH.
I KNOW WHAT YOU'RE THINKING...

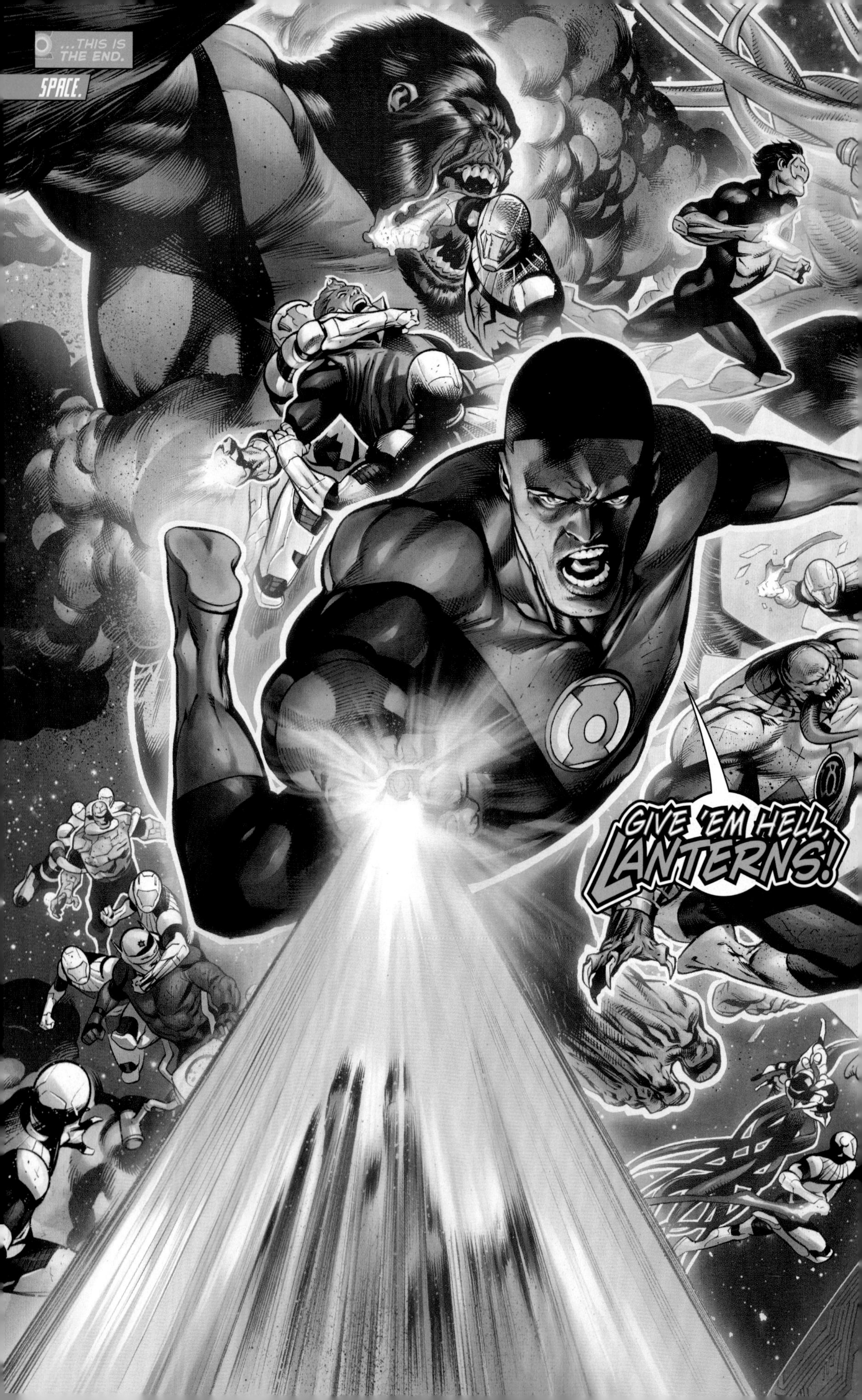
...THIS IS THE END.
SPACE.
GIVE 'EM HELL, LANTERNS!

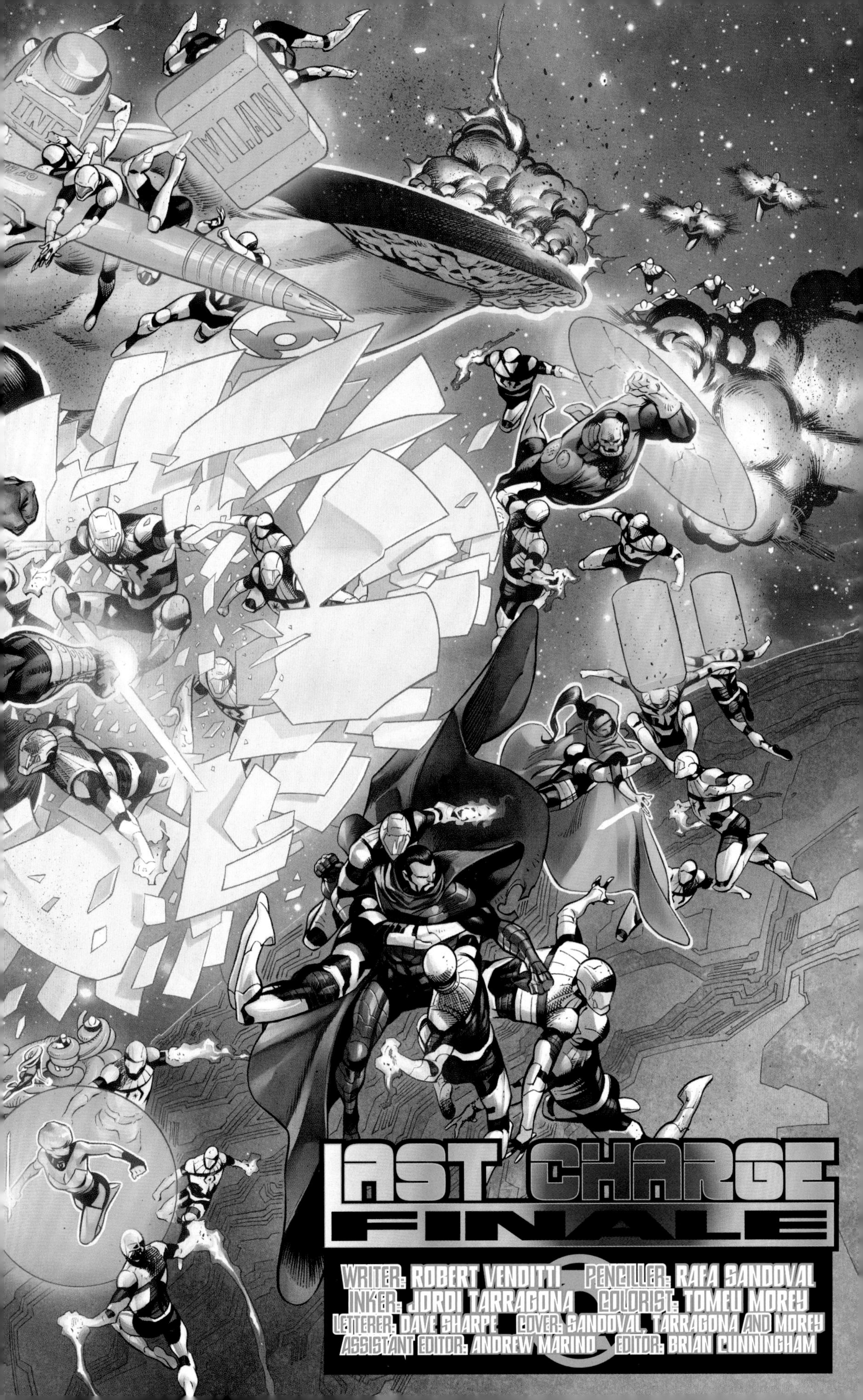
LAST CHARGE
FINALE
WRITER: ROBERT VENDITTI PENCILLER: RAFA SANDOVAL
INKER: JORDI TARRAGONA COLORIST: TOMEU MOREY
LETTERER: DAVE SHARPE COVER: SANDOVAL, TARRAGONA AND MOREY
ASSISTANT EDITOR: ANDREW MARINO EDITOR: BRIAN CUNNINGHAM

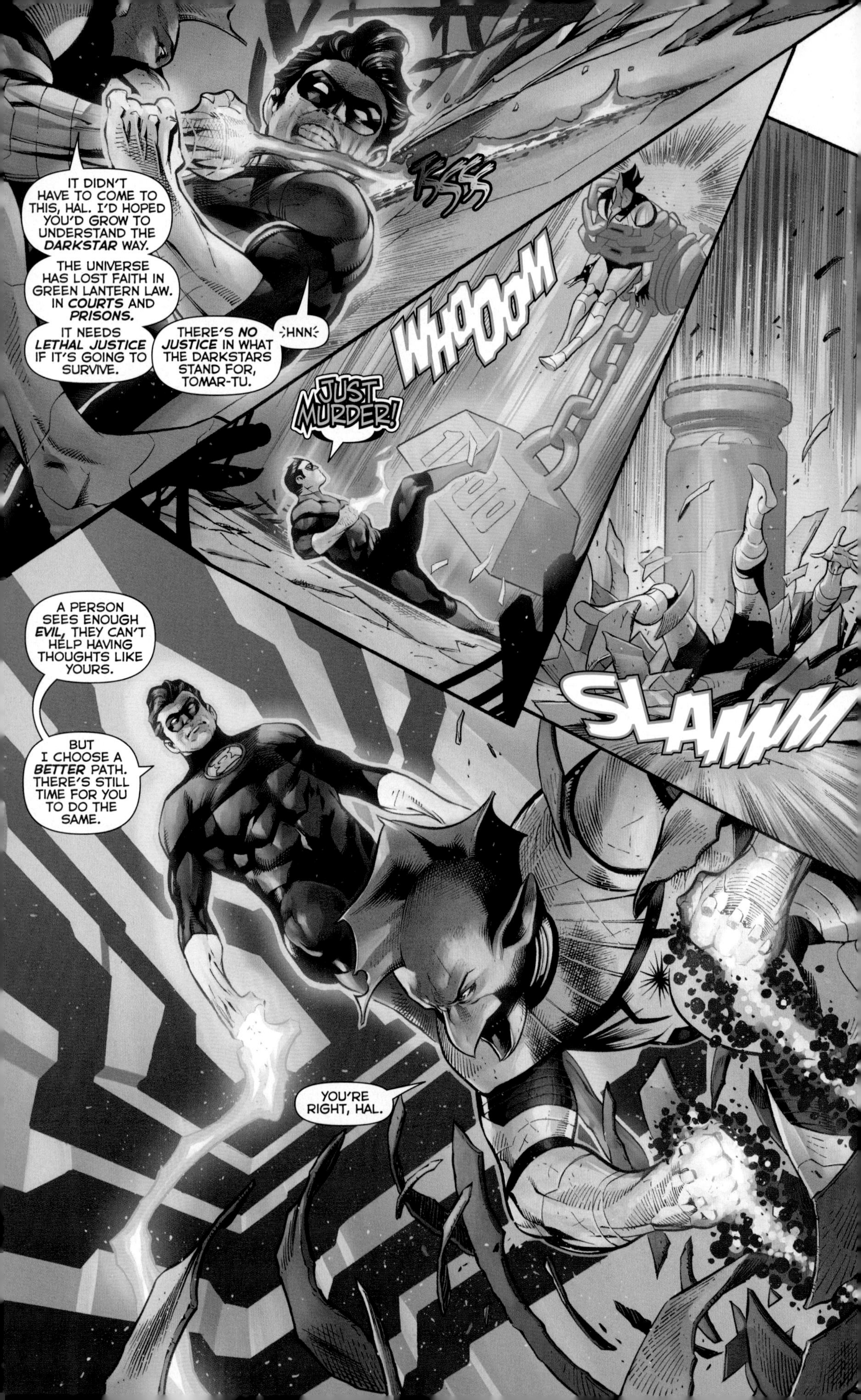

IT DIDN'T HAVE TO COME TO THIS, HAL. I'D HOPED YOU'D GROW TO UNDERSTAND THE DARKSTAR WAY.
THE UNIVERSE HAS LOST FAITH IN GREEN LANTERN LAW. IN COURTS AND PRISONS.
IT NEEDS LETHAL JUSTICE IF IT'S GOING TO SURVIVE.
HNN
THERE'S NO JUSTICE IN WHAT THE DARKSTARS STAND FOR, TOMAR-TU.
WHOOOOM
JUST MURDER!
SLAMM
A PERSON SEES ENOUGH EVIL, THEY CAN'T HELP HAVING THOUGHTS LIKE YOURS.
BUT I CHOOSE A BETTER PATH. THERE'S STILL TIME FOR YOU TO DO THE SAME.
YOU'RE RIGHT, HAL.

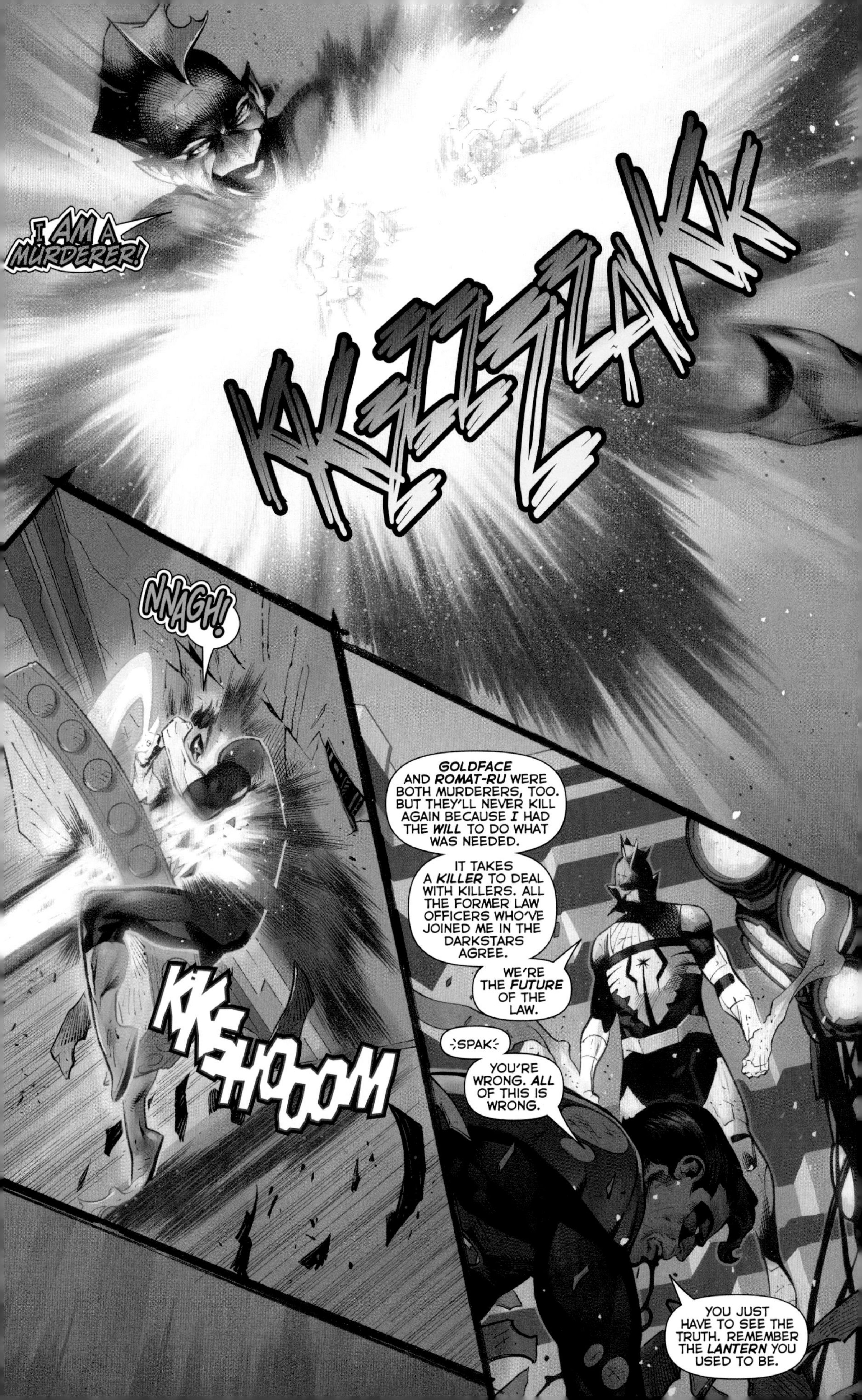
I AM A MURDERER!
KKZZZZAKK
NNAGH!
KKSHOOOM
GOLDFACE AND ROMAT-RU WERE BOTH MURDERERS, TOO. BUT THEY'LL NEVER KILL AGAIN BECAUSE I HAD THE WILL TO DO WHAT WAS NEEDED.
IT TAKES A KILLER TO DEAL WITH KILLERS. ALL THE FORMER LAW OFFICERS WHO'VE JOINED ME IN THE DARKSTARS AGREE.
WE'RE THE FUTURE OF THE LAW.
SPAK
YOU'RE WRONG. ALL OF THIS IS WRONG.
YOU JUST HAVE TO SEE THE TRUTH. REMEMBER THE LANTERN YOU USED TO BE.

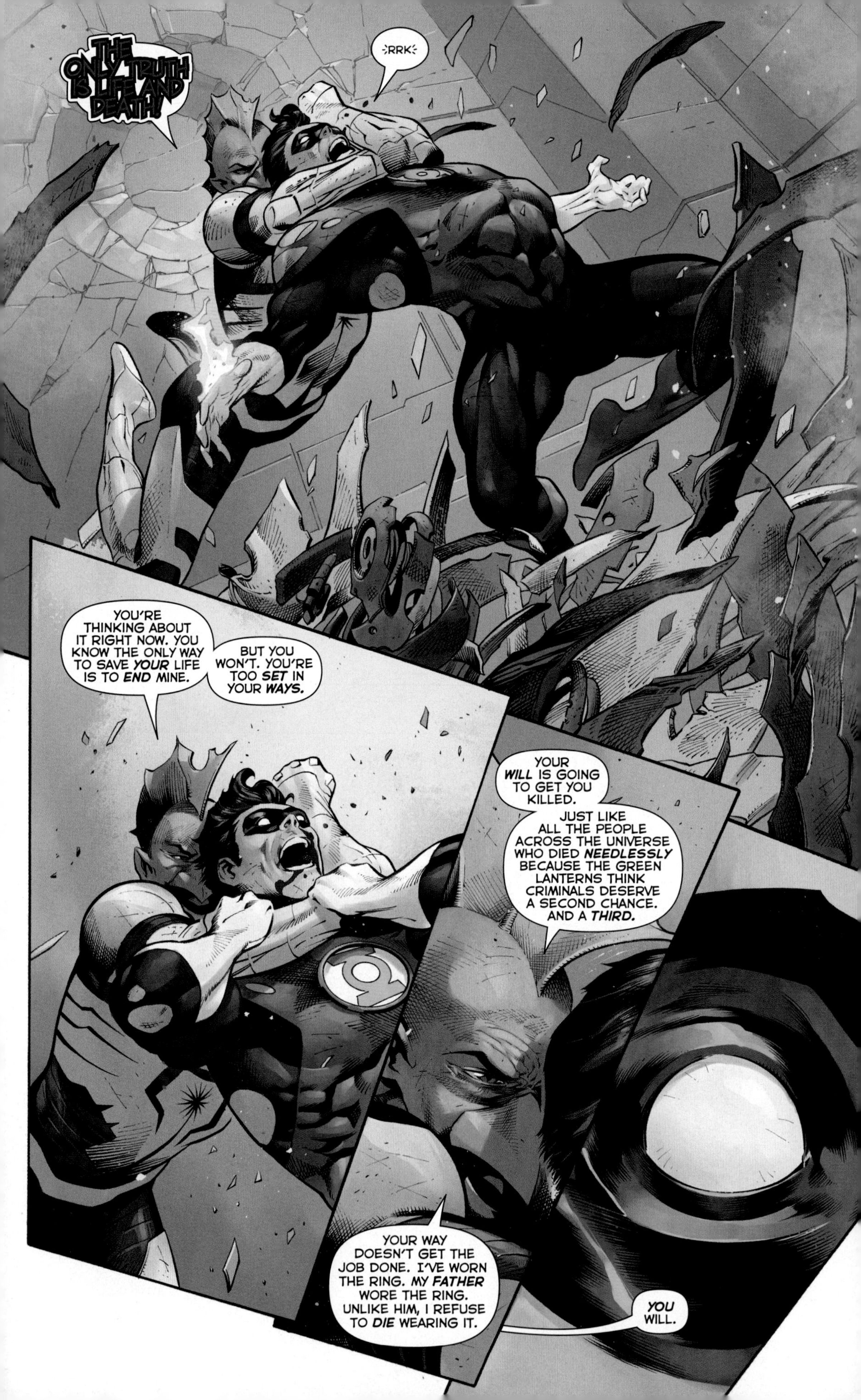
THE ONLY TRUTH IS LIFE AND DEATH!
RRK
YOU'RE THINKING ABOUT IT RIGHT NOW. YOU KNOW THE ONLY WAY TO SAVE YOUR LIFE IS TO END MINE.
BUT YOU WON'T. YOU'RE TOO SET IN YOUR WAYS.
YOUR WILL IS GOING TO GET YOU KILLED.
JUST LIKE ALL THE PEOPLE ACROSS THE UNIVERSE WHO DIED NEEDLESSLY BECAUSE THE GREEN LANTERNS THINK CRIMINALS DESERVE A SECOND CHANCE. AND A THIRD.
YOUR WAY DOESN'T GET THE JOB DONE. I'VE WORN THE RING. MY FATHER WORE THE RING. UNLIKE HIM, I REFUSE TO DIE WEARING IT.
YOU WILL.

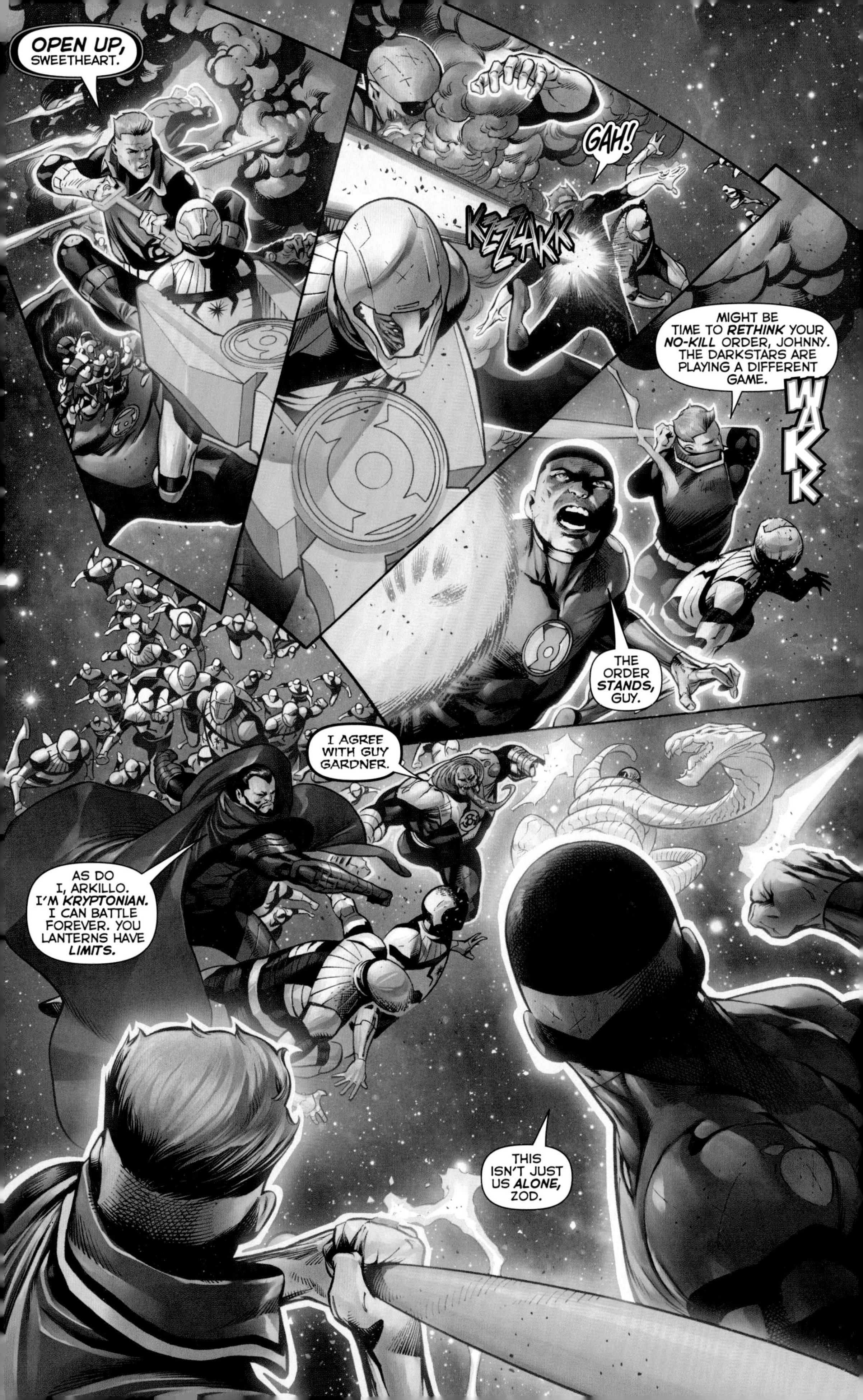
OPEN UP, SWEETHEART.
GAH!
KEZZAKK
MIGHT BE TIME TO RETHINK YOUR NO-KILL ORDER, JOHNNY. THE DARKSTARS ARE PLAYING A DIFFERENT GAME.
WAKK
THE ORDER STANDS, GUY.
I AGREE WITH GUY GARDNER.
AS DO I, ARKILLO. I'M KRYPTONIAN. I CAN BATTLE FOREVER. YOU LANTERNS HAVE LIMITS.
THIS ISN'T JUST US ALONE, ZOD.

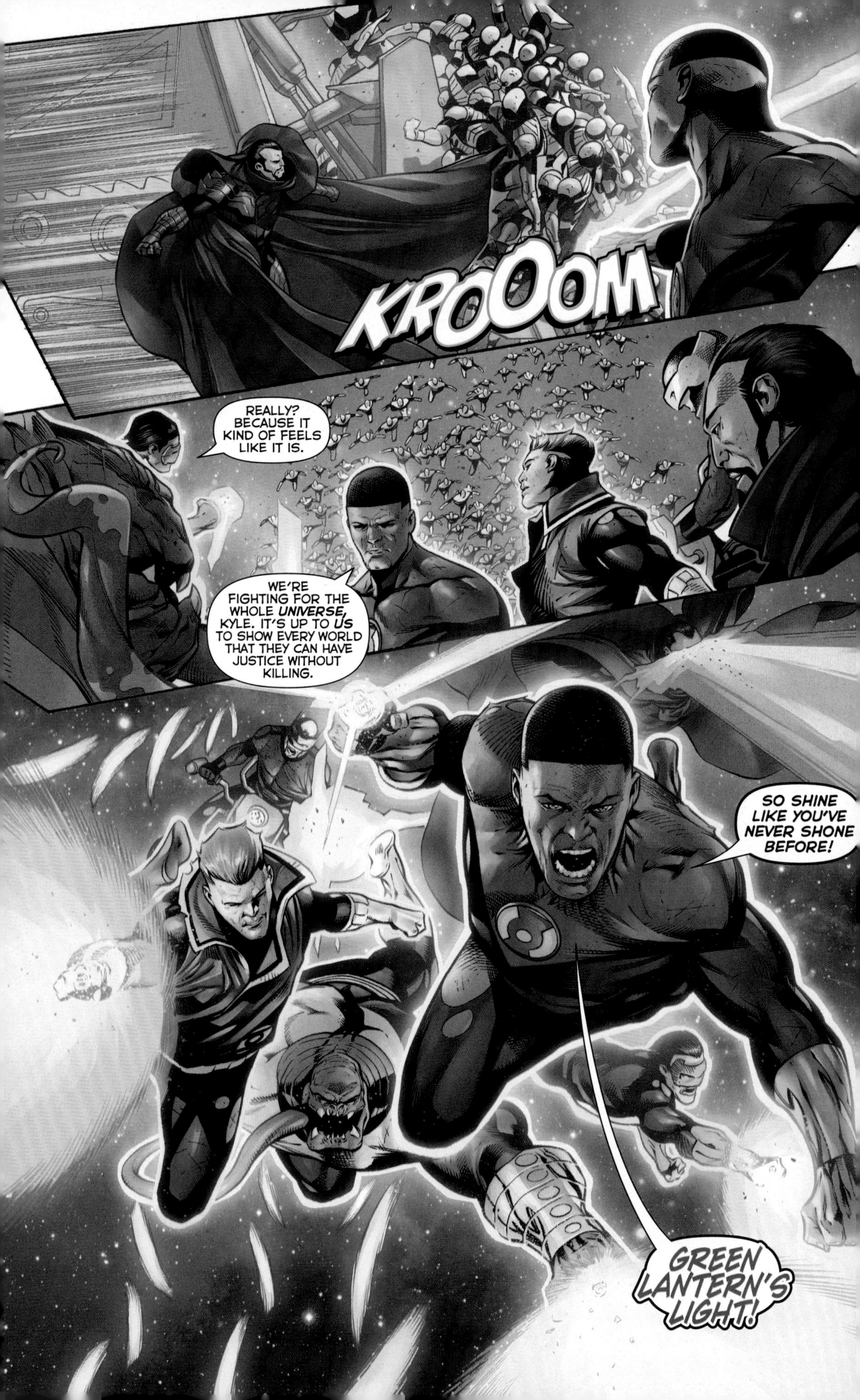
KROOOM
REALLY? BECAUSE IT KIND OF FEELS LIKE IT IS.
WE'RE FIGHTING FOR THE WHOLE UNIVERSE, KYLE. IT'S UP TO US TO SHOW EVERY WORLD THAT THEY CAN HAVE JUSTICE WITHOUT KILLING.
SO SHINE LIKE YOU'VE NEVER SHONE BEFORE!
GREEN LANTERN'S LIGHT!

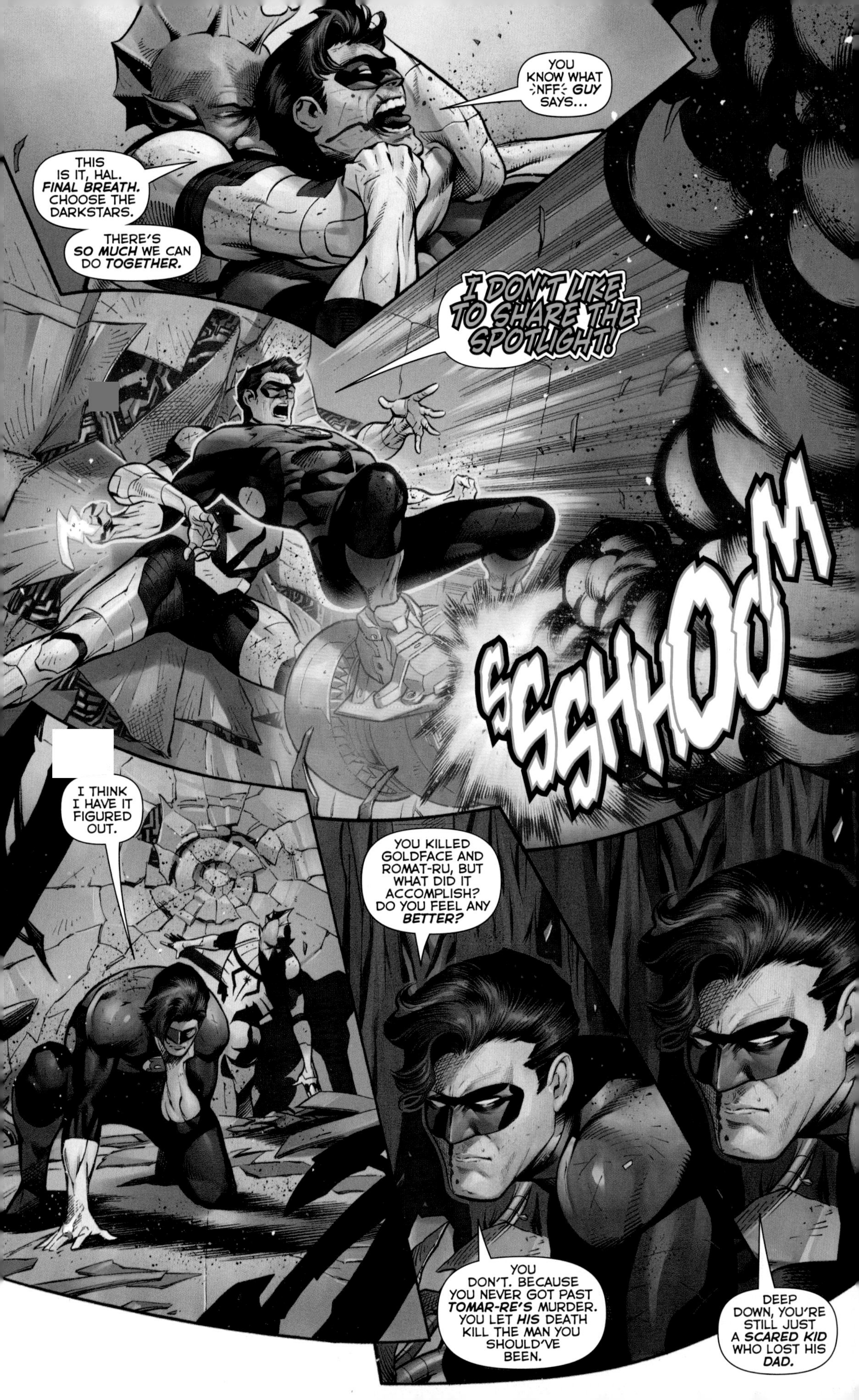

YOU KNOW WHAT -NFF- GUY SAYS...
THIS IS IT, HAL. FINAL BREATH. CHOOSE THE DARKSTARS.
THERE'S SO MUCH WE CAN DO TOGETHER.
I DON'T LIKE TO SHARE THE SPOTLIGHT!
SSHHOOM
I THINK I HAVE IT FIGURED OUT.
YOU KILLED GOLDFACE AND ROMAT-RU, BUT WHAT DID IT ACCOMPLISH? DO YOU FEEL ANY BETTER?
YOU DON'T. BECAUSE YOU NEVER GOT PAST TOMAR-RE'S MURDER. YOU LET HIS DEATH KILL THE MAN YOU SHOULD'VE BEEN.
DEEP DOWN, YOU'RE STILL JUST A SCARED KID WHO LOST HIS DAD.

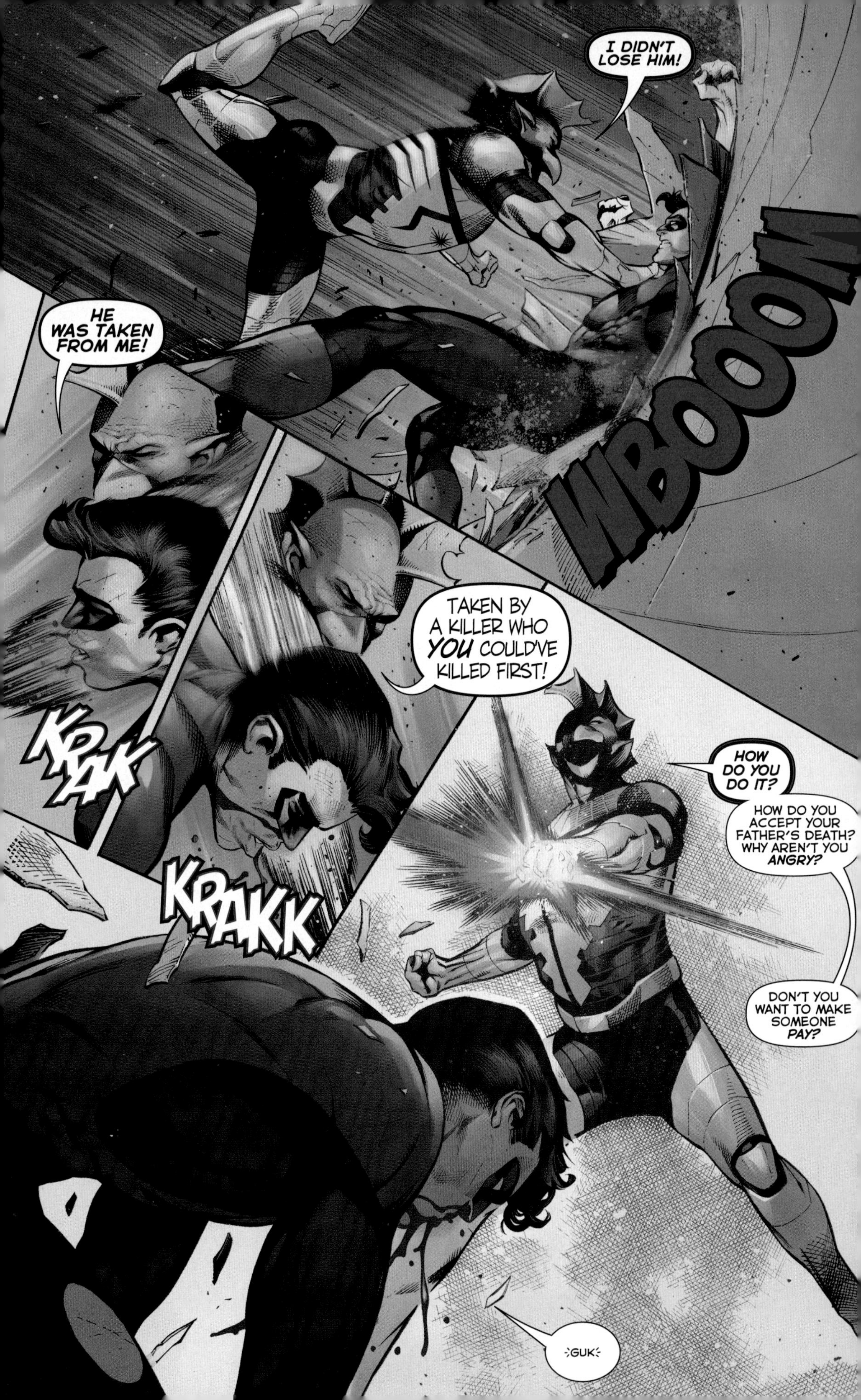
I DIDN'T LOSE HIM!
HE WAS TAKEN FROM ME!
WBOOOOM
TAKEN BY A KILLER WHO YOU COULD'VE KILLED FIRST!
KRAK
KRAKK
HOW DO YOU DO IT?
HOW DO YOU ACCEPT YOUR FATHER'S DEATH? WHY AREN'T YOU ANGRY?
DON'T YOU WANT TO MAKE SOMEONE PAY?
GUK

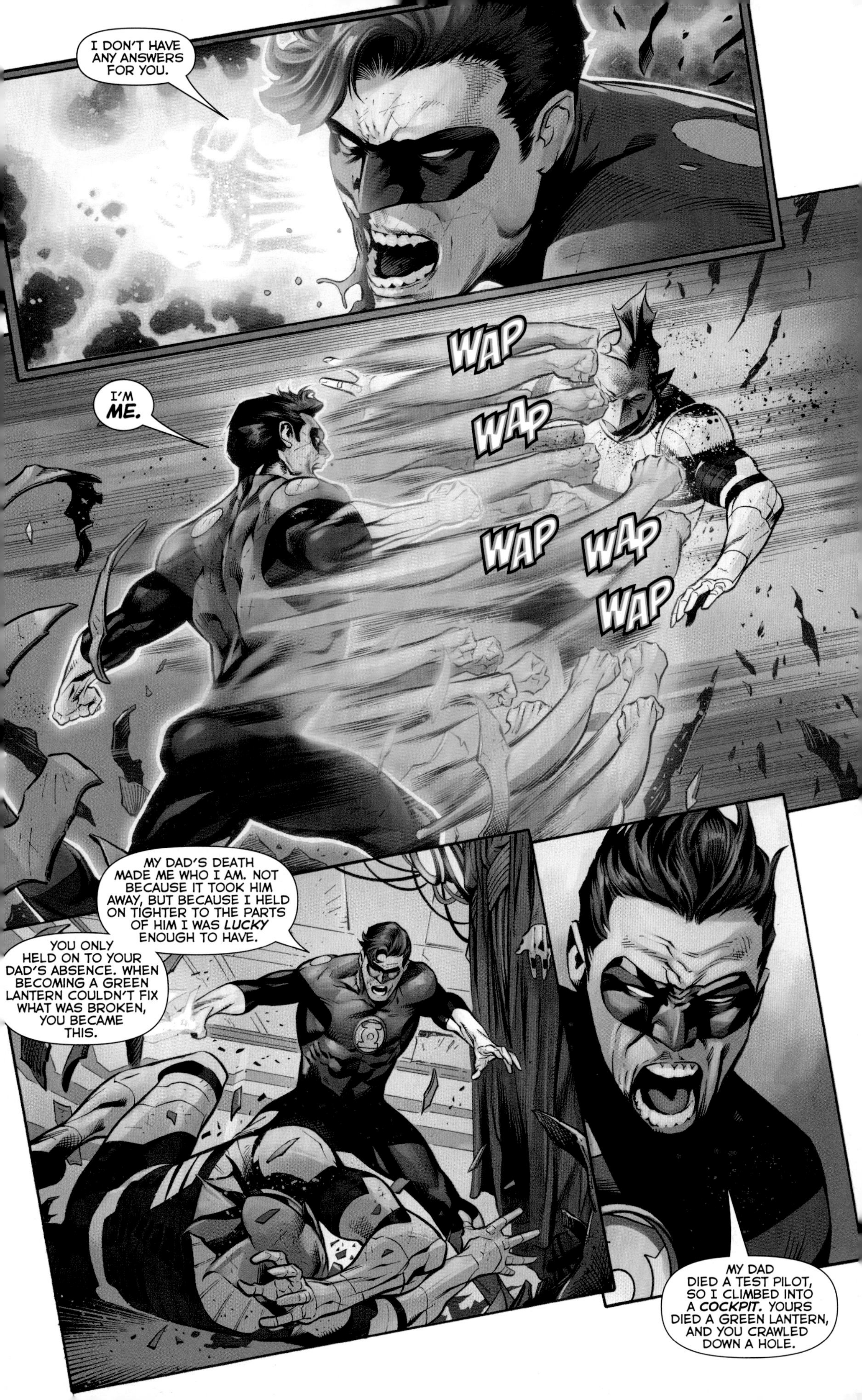
I DON'T HAVE ANY ANSWERS FOR YOU.
I'M ***ME.***
WAP
WAP
WAP
WAP
WAP
MY DAD'S DEATH MADE ME WHO I AM. NOT BECAUSE IT TOOK HIM AWAY, BUT BECAUSE I HELD ON TIGHTER TO THE PARTS OF HIM I WAS *LUCKY* ENOUGH TO HAVE.
YOU ONLY HELD ON TO YOUR DAD'S ABSENCE. WHEN BECOMING A GREEN LANTERN COULDN'T FIX WHAT WAS BROKEN, YOU BECAME THIS.
MY DAD DIED A TEST PILOT, SO I CLIMBED INTO A ***COCKPIT.*** YOURS DIED A GREEN LANTERN, AND YOU CRAWLED DOWN A HOLE.

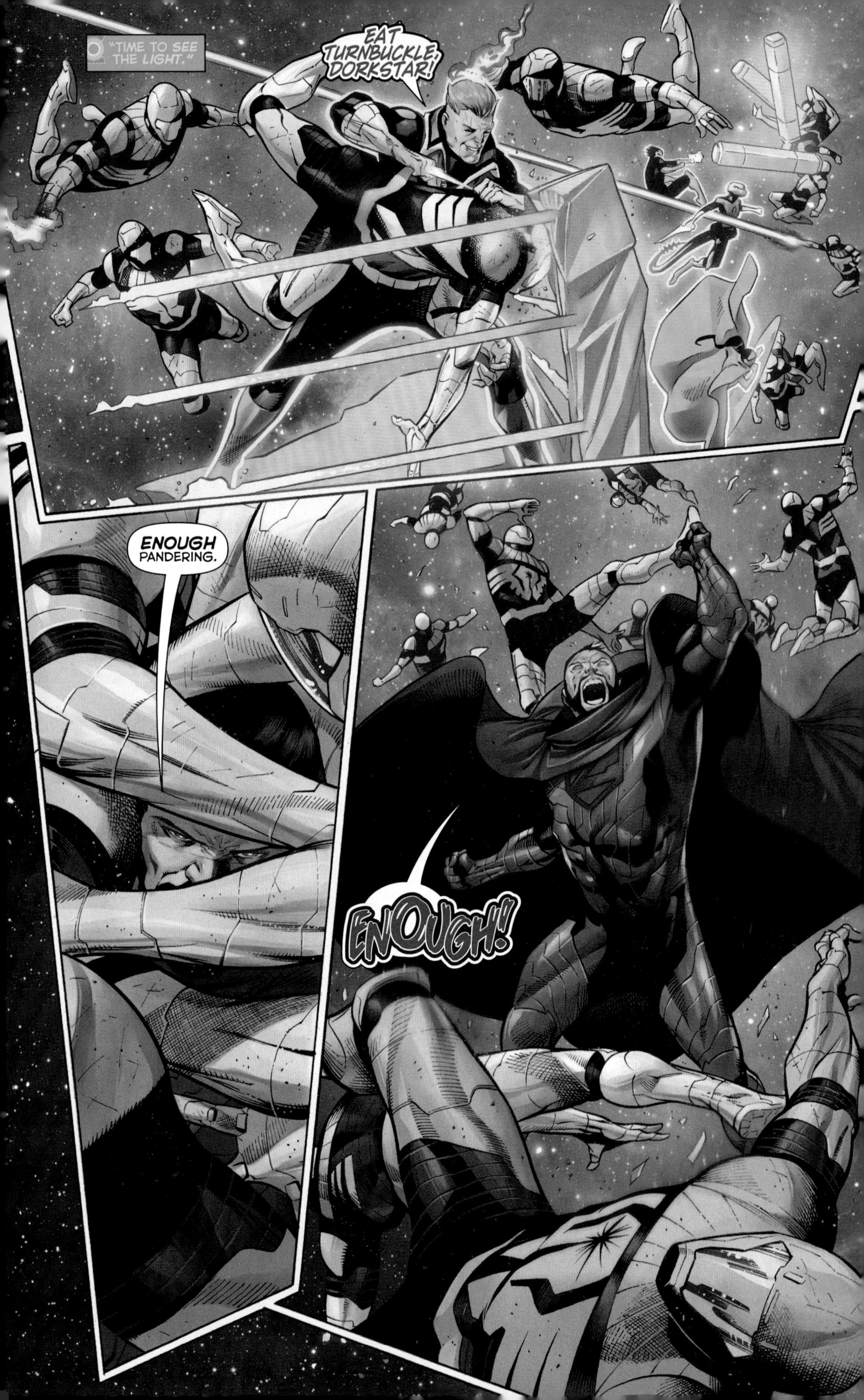
"TIME TO SEE THE LIGHT."
EAT TURNBUCKLE, DORKSTAR!
ENOUGH PANDERING.
ENOUGH!!

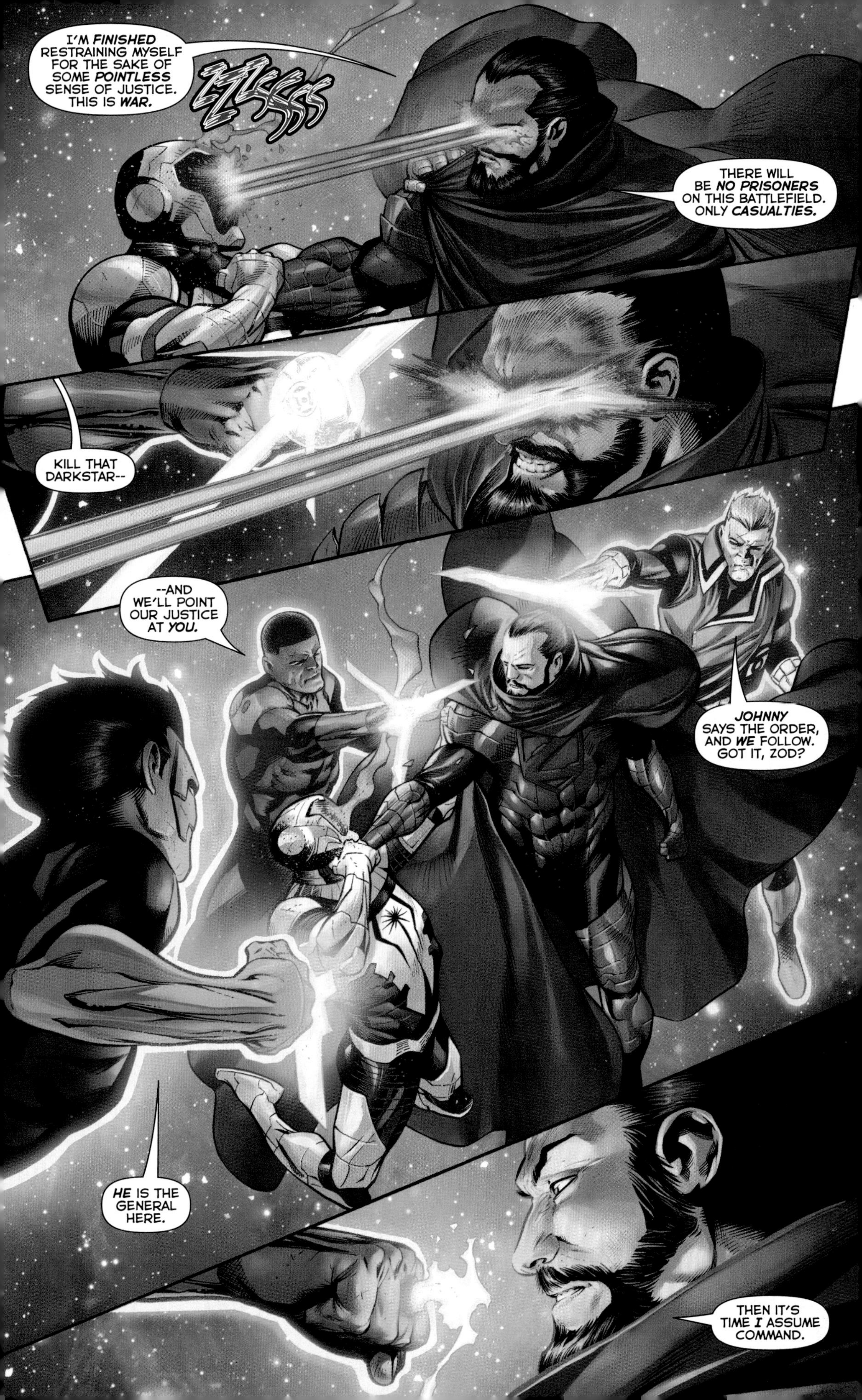
I'M FINISHED RESTRAINING MYSELF FOR THE SAKE OF SOME POINTLESS SENSE OF JUSTICE. THIS IS WAR.
ZZZKKKSSS
THERE WILL BE NO PRISONERS ON THIS BATTLEFIELD. ONLY CASUALTIES.
KILL THAT DARKSTAR--
--AND WE'LL POINT OUR JUSTICE AT YOU.
JOHNNY SAYS THE ORDER, AND WE FOLLOW. GOT IT, ZOD?
HE IS THE GENERAL HERE.
THEN IT'S TIME I ASSUME COMMAND.

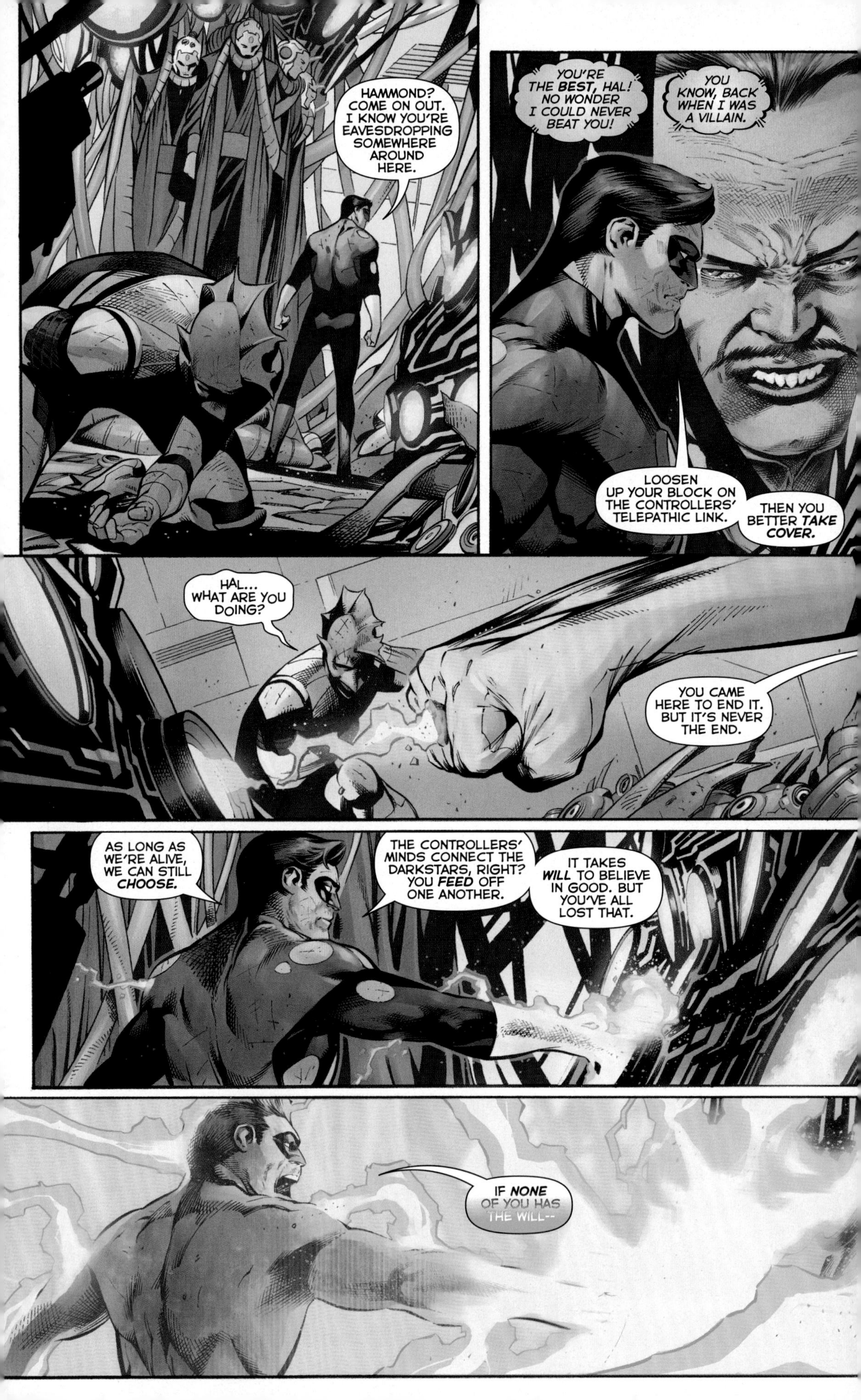
HAMMOND? COME ON OUT. I KNOW YOU'RE EAVESDROPPING SOMEWHERE AROUND HERE.
YOU'RE THE BEST, HAL! NO WONDER I COULD NEVER BEAT YOU!
YOU KNOW, BACK WHEN I WAS A VILLAIN.
LOOSEN UP YOUR BLOCK ON THE CONTROLLERS' TELEPATHIC LINK.
THEN YOU BETTER TAKE COVER.
HAL... WHAT ARE YOU DOING?
YOU CAME HERE TO END IT. BUT IT'S NEVER THE END.
AS LONG AS WE'RE ALIVE, WE CAN STILL CHOOSE.
THE CONTROLLERS' MINDS CONNECT THE DARKSTARS, RIGHT? YOU FEED OFF ONE ANOTHER.
IT TAKES WILL TO BELIEVE IN GOOD. BUT YOU'VE ALL LOST THAT.
IF NONE OF YOU HAS THE WILL--

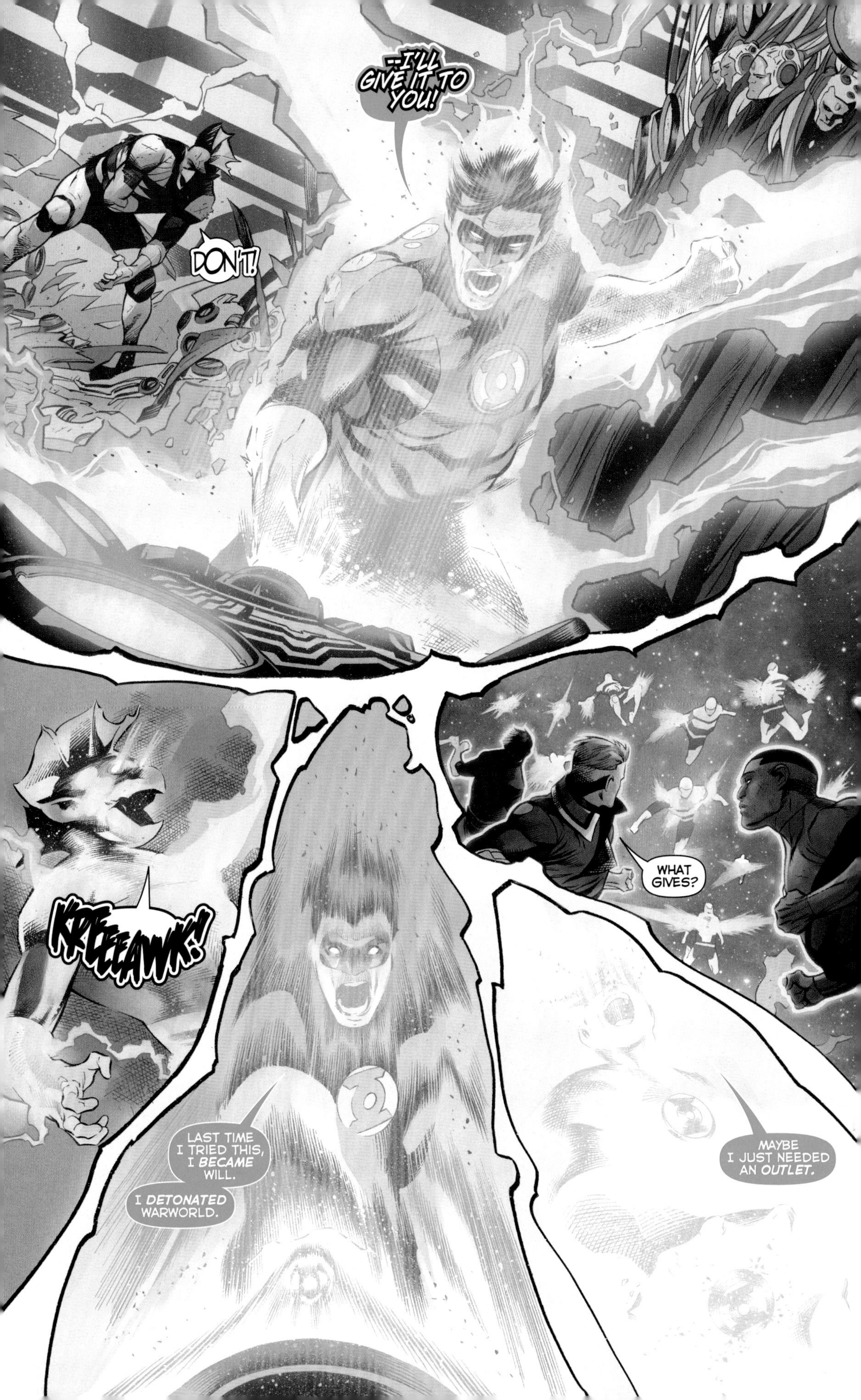
--I'LL GIVE IT TO YOU!
DON'T!
KREEEAWK!
WHAT GIVES?
LAST TIME I TRIED THIS, I *BECAME* WILL.
I *DETONATED* WARWORLD.
MAYBE I JUST NEEDED AN *OUTLET*.

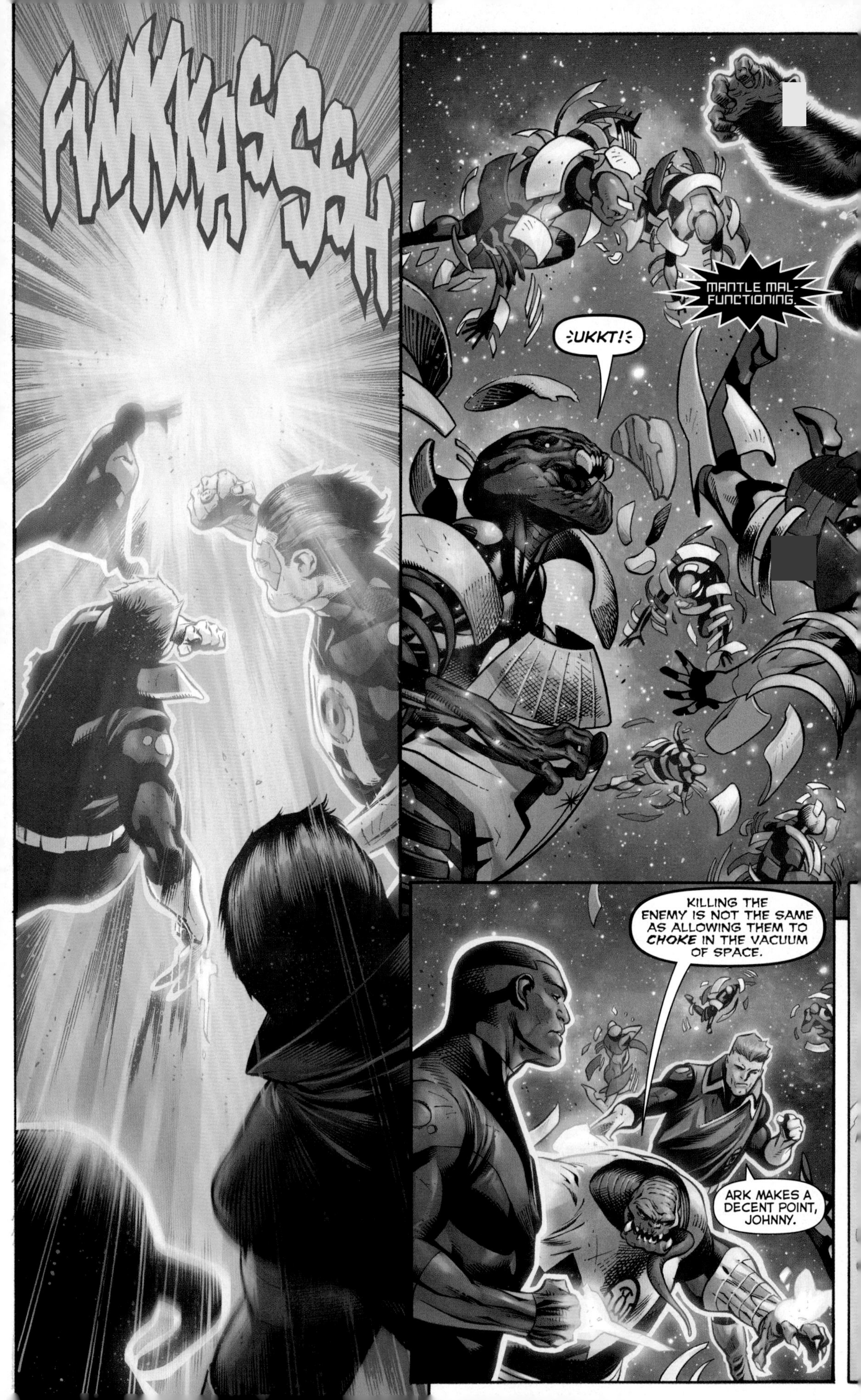
FWKKASSSH
MANTLE MAL-FUNCTIONING.
UKKT!
KILLING THE ENEMY IS NOT THE SAME AS ALLOWING THEM TO CHOKE IN THE VACUUM OF SPACE.
ARK MAKES A DECENT POINT, JOHNNY.

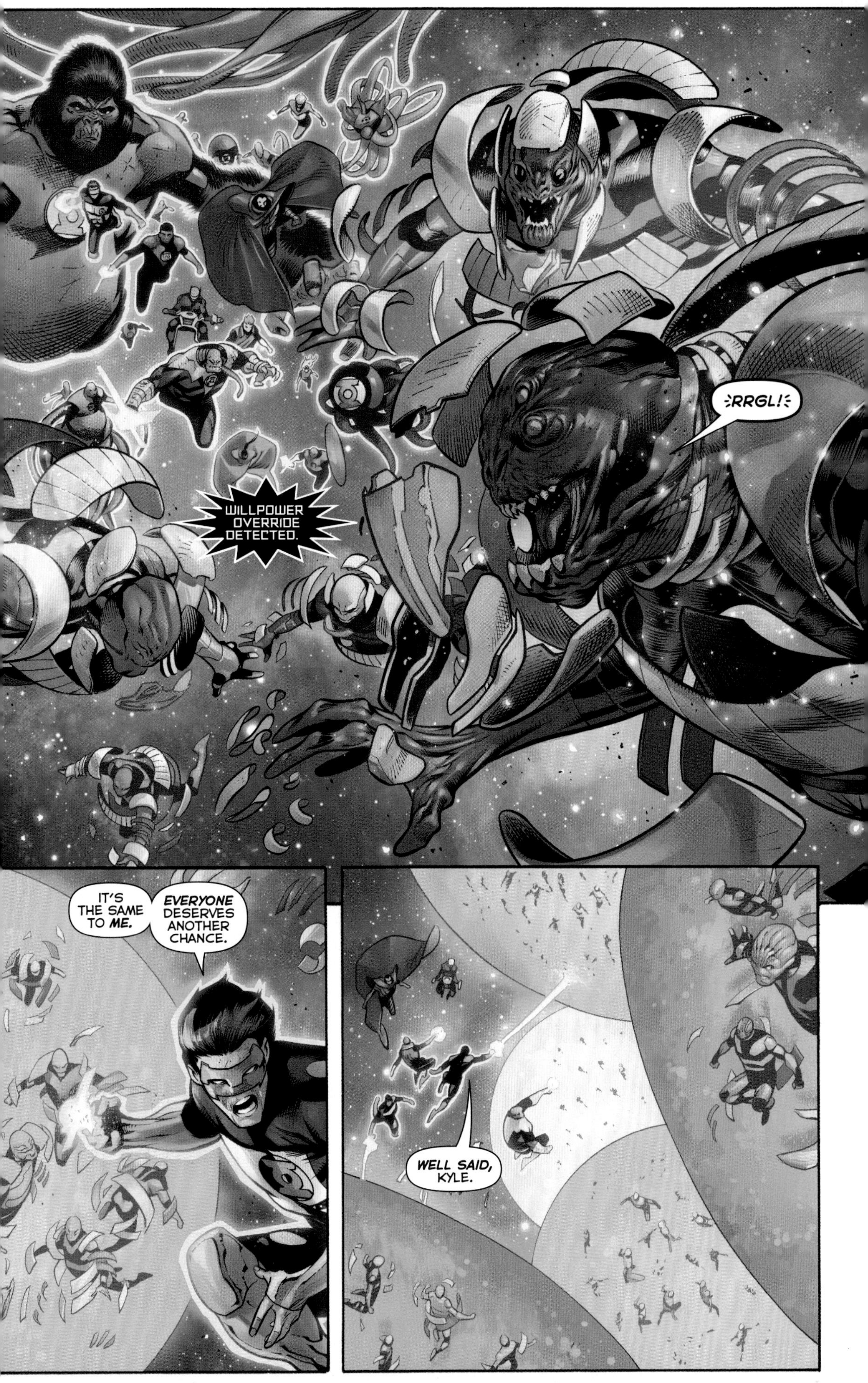
WILLPOWER OVERRIDE DETECTED.
RRGL!
IT'S THE SAME TO ME.
EVERYONE DESERVES ANOTHER CHANCE.
WELL SAID, KYLE.

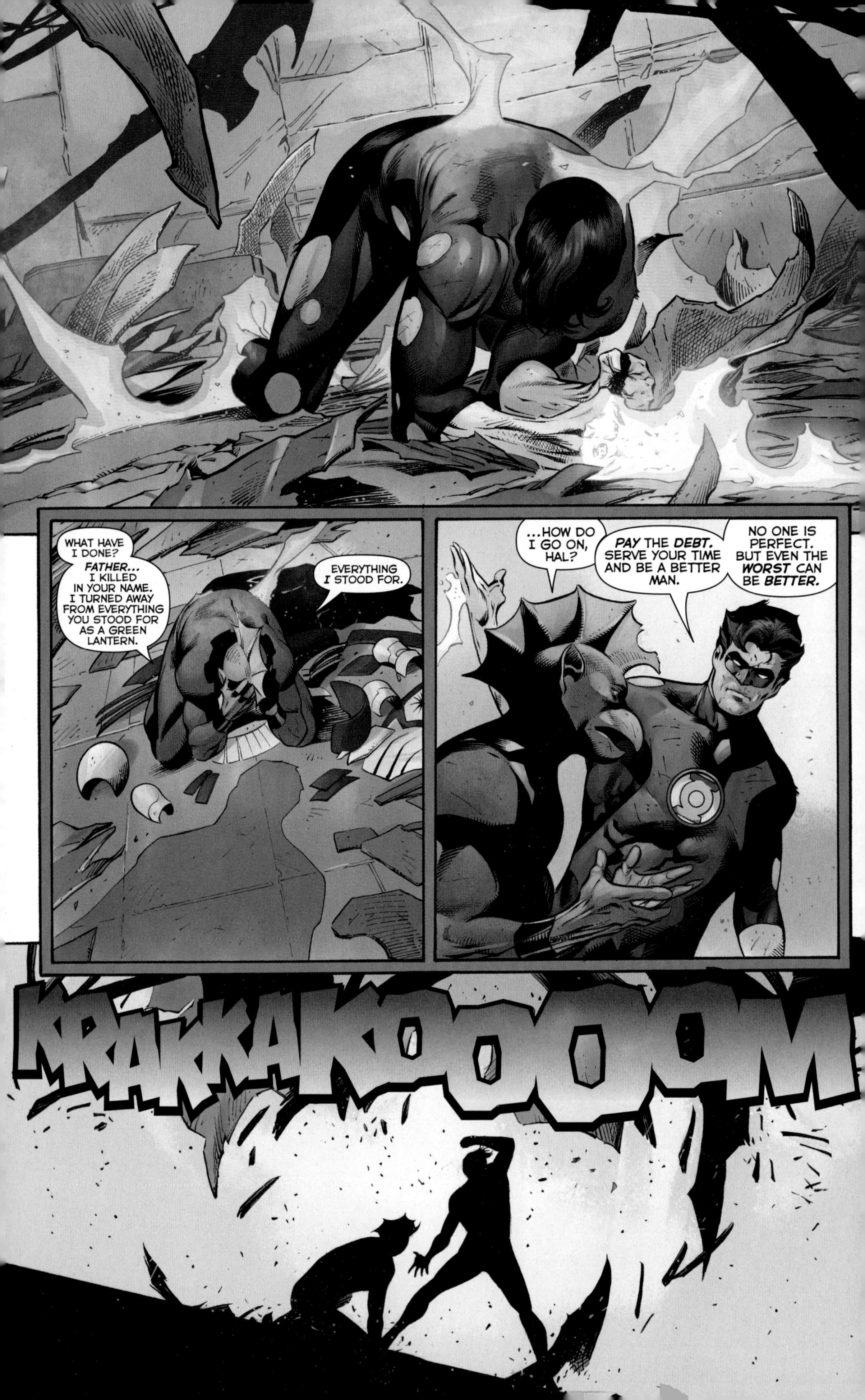
WHAT HAVE I DONE? FATHER... I KILLED IN YOUR NAME. I TURNED AWAY FROM EVERYTHING YOU STOOD FOR AS A GREEN LANTERN.
EVERYTHING I STOOD FOR.
...HOW DO I GO ON, HAL?
PAY THE DEBT. SERVE YOUR TIME AND BE A BETTER MAN.
NO ONE IS PERFECT. BUT EVEN THE WORST CAN BE BETTER.
KRAKKAKOOOOOM

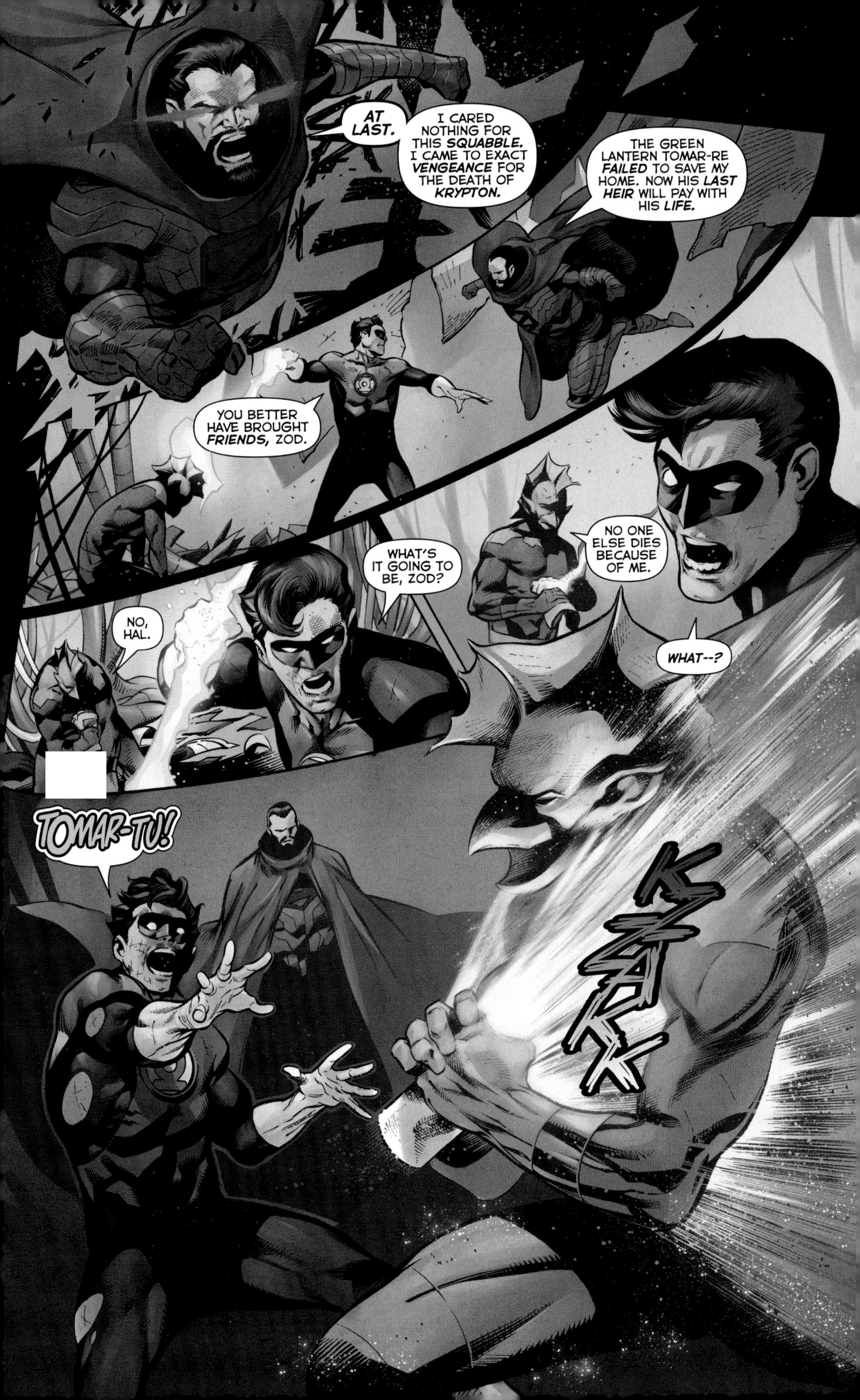
AT LAST.
I CARED NOTHING FOR THIS SQUABBLE. I CAME TO EXACT VENGEANCE FOR THE DEATH OF KRYPTON.
THE GREEN LANTERN TOMAR-RE FAILED TO SAVE MY HOME. NOW HIS LAST HEIR WILL PAY WITH HIS LIFE.
YOU BETTER HAVE BROUGHT FRIENDS, ZOD.
NO ONE ELSE DIES BECAUSE OF ME.
WHAT'S IT GOING TO BE, ZOD?
NO, HAL.
WHAT--?
TOMAR-TU!
KZZAKK

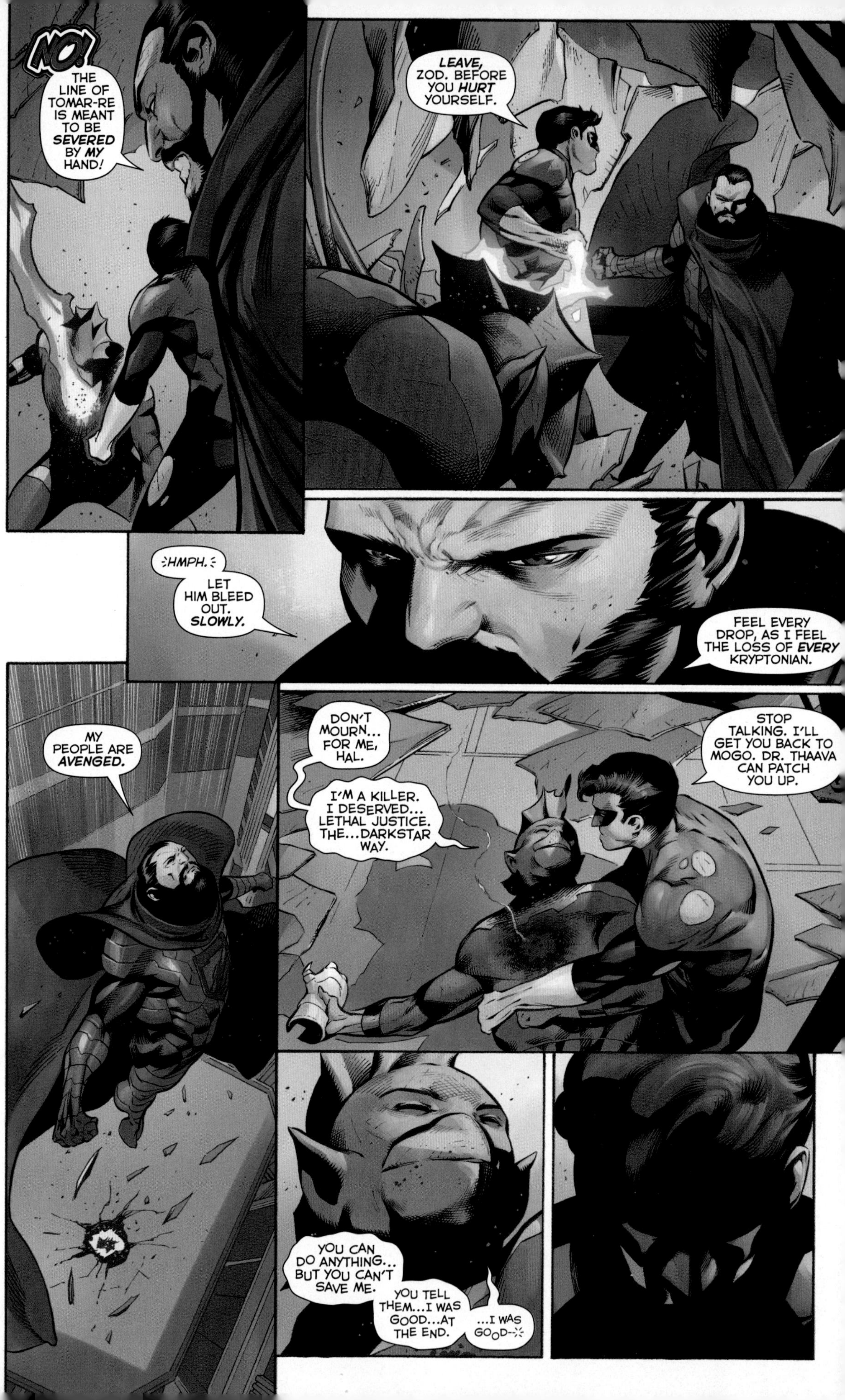
NO!
THE LINE OF TOMAR-RE IS MEANT TO BE SEVERED BY MY HAND!
LEAVE, ZOD. BEFORE YOU HURT YOURSELF.
HMPH.
LET HIM BLEED OUT. SLOWLY.
FEEL EVERY DROP, AS I FEEL THE LOSS OF EVERY KRYPTONIAN.
MY PEOPLE ARE AVENGED.
DON'T MOURN... FOR ME, HAL.
I'M A KILLER. I DESERVED... LETHAL JUSTICE. THE...DARKSTAR WAY.
STOP TALKING. I'LL GET YOU BACK TO MOGO. DR. THAAVA CAN PATCH YOU UP.
YOU CAN DO ANYTHING... BUT YOU CAN'T SAVE ME.
YOU TELL THEM...I WAS GOOD...AT THE END.
...I WAS GOOD--

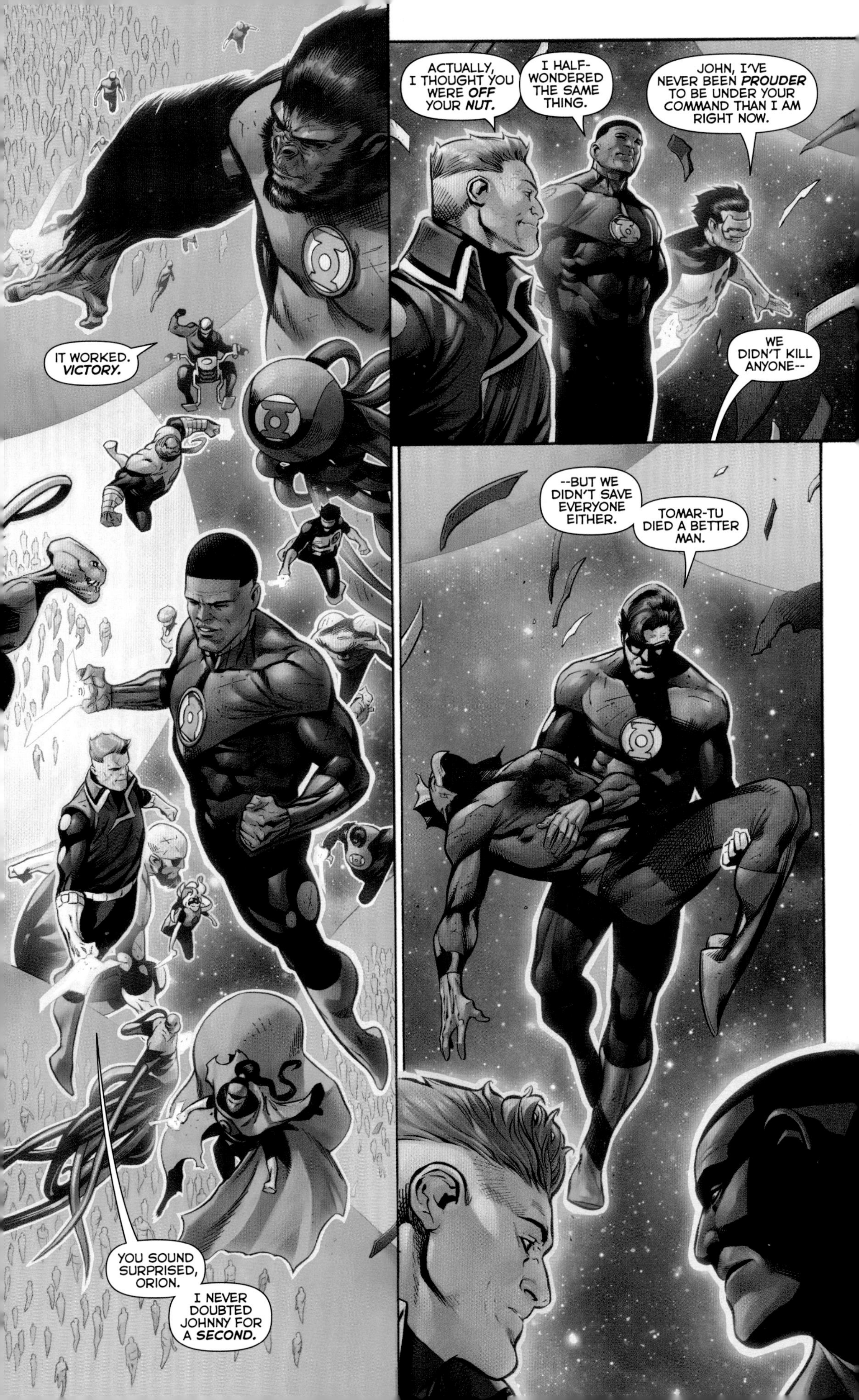

IT WORKED. *VICTORY.*
YOU SOUND SURPRISED, ORION.
I NEVER DOUBTED JOHNNY FOR A *SECOND.*
ACTUALLY, I THOUGHT YOU WERE *OFF* YOUR *NUT.*
I HALF-WONDERED THE SAME THING.
JOHN, I'VE NEVER BEEN *PROUDER* TO BE UNDER YOUR COMMAND THAN I AM RIGHT NOW.
WE DIDN'T KILL ANYONE--
--BUT WE DIDN'T SAVE EVERYONE EITHER.
TOMAR-TU DIED A BETTER MAN.

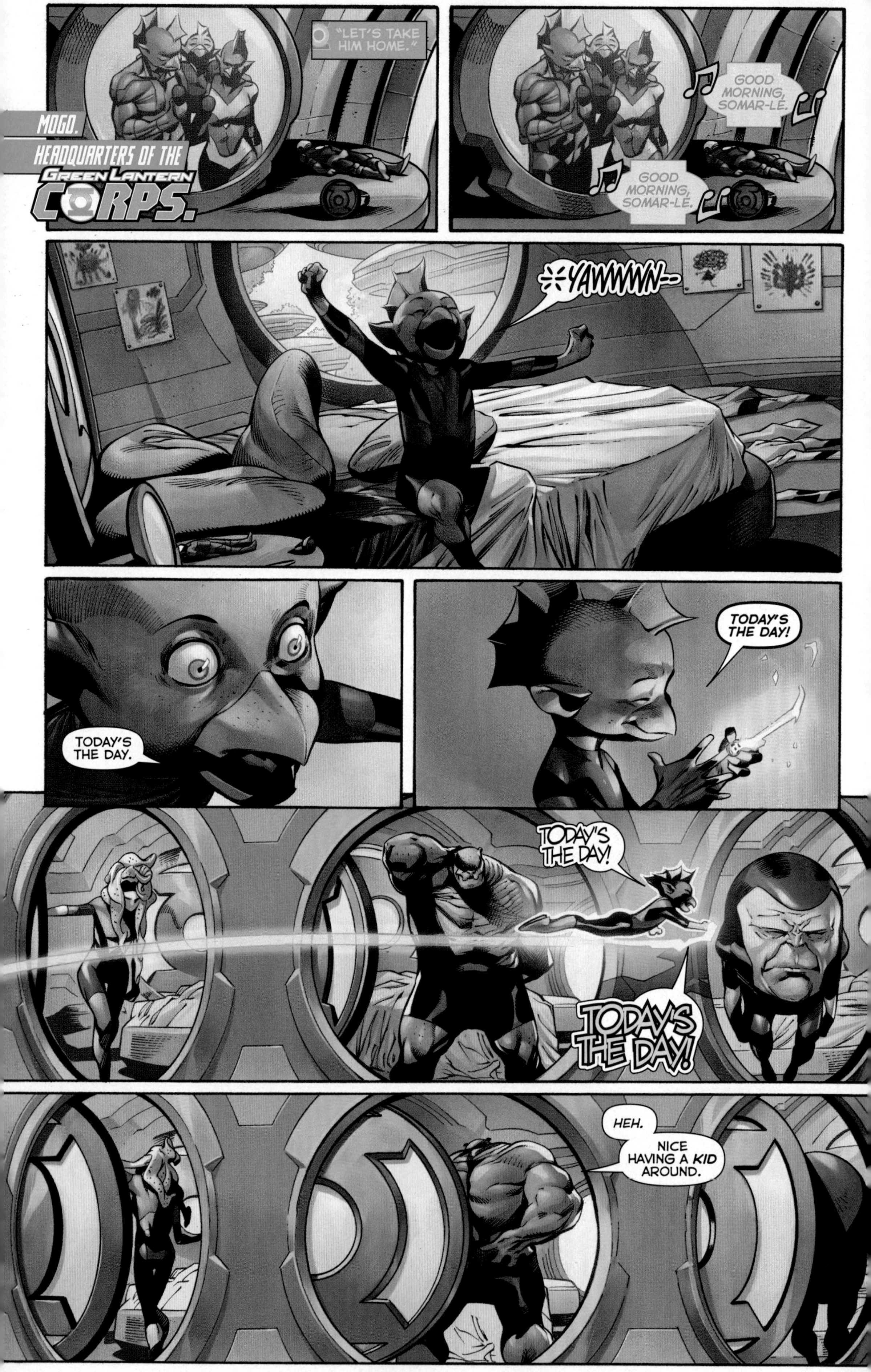
MOGO.
HEADQUARTERS OF THE
GREEN LANTERN
CORPS.
"LET'S TAKE HIM HOME."
GOOD MORNING, SOMAR-LÉ.
GOOD MORNING, SOMAR-LÉ.
YAWWWN-
TODAY'S THE DAY.
TODAY'S THE DAY!
TODAY'S THE DAY!
TODAY'S THE DAY!
HEH.
NICE HAVING A KID AROUND.

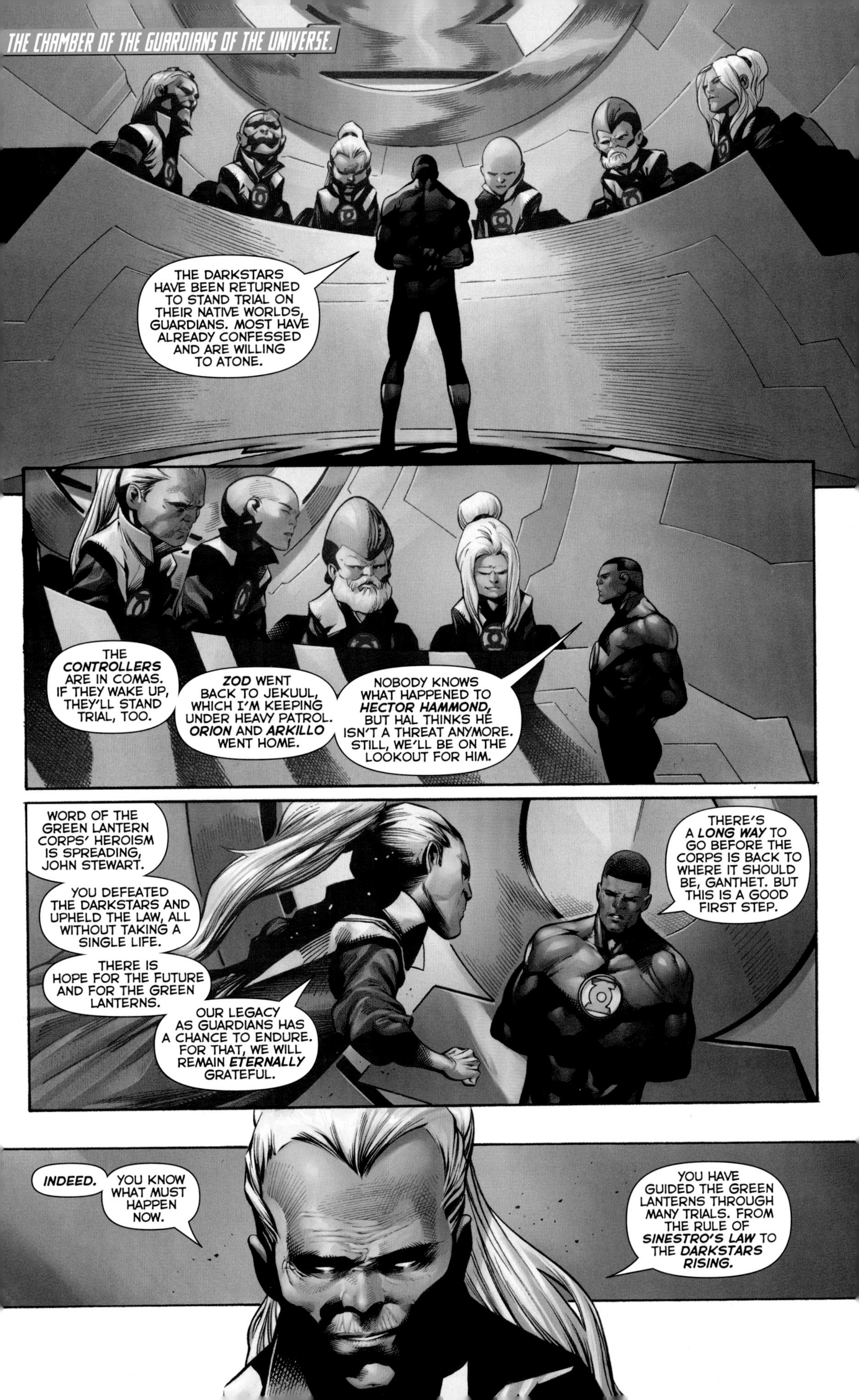
THE CHAMBER OF THE GUARDIANS OF THE UNIVERSE.
THE DARKSTARS HAVE BEEN RETURNED TO STAND TRIAL ON THEIR NATIVE WORLDS, GUARDIANS. MOST HAVE ALREADY CONFESSED AND ARE WILLING TO ATONE.
THE *CONTROLLERS* ARE IN COMAS. IF THEY WAKE UP, THEY'LL STAND TRIAL, TOO.
ZOD WENT BACK TO JEKUUL, WHICH I'M KEEPING UNDER HEAVY PATROL. *ORION* AND *ARKILLO* WENT HOME.
NOBODY KNOWS WHAT HAPPENED TO *HECTOR HAMMOND,* BUT HAL THINKS HE ISN'T A THREAT ANYMORE. STILL, WE'LL BE ON THE LOOKOUT FOR HIM.
WORD OF THE GREEN LANTERN CORPS' HEROISM IS SPREADING, JOHN STEWART.
YOU DEFEATED THE DARKSTARS AND UPHELD THE LAW, ALL WITHOUT TAKING A SINGLE LIFE.
THERE IS HOPE FOR THE FUTURE AND FOR THE GREEN LANTERNS.
OUR LEGACY AS GUARDIANS HAS A CHANCE TO ENDURE. FOR THAT, WE WILL REMAIN *ETERNALLY* GRATEFUL.
THERE'S A *LONG WAY* TO GO BEFORE THE CORPS IS BACK TO WHERE IT SHOULD BE, GANTHET. BUT THIS IS A GOOD FIRST STEP.
INDEED.
YOU KNOW WHAT MUST HAPPEN NOW.
YOU HAVE GUIDED THE GREEN LANTERNS THROUGH MANY TRIALS. FROM THE RULE OF *SINESTRO'S LAW* TO THE *DARKSTARS RISING.*

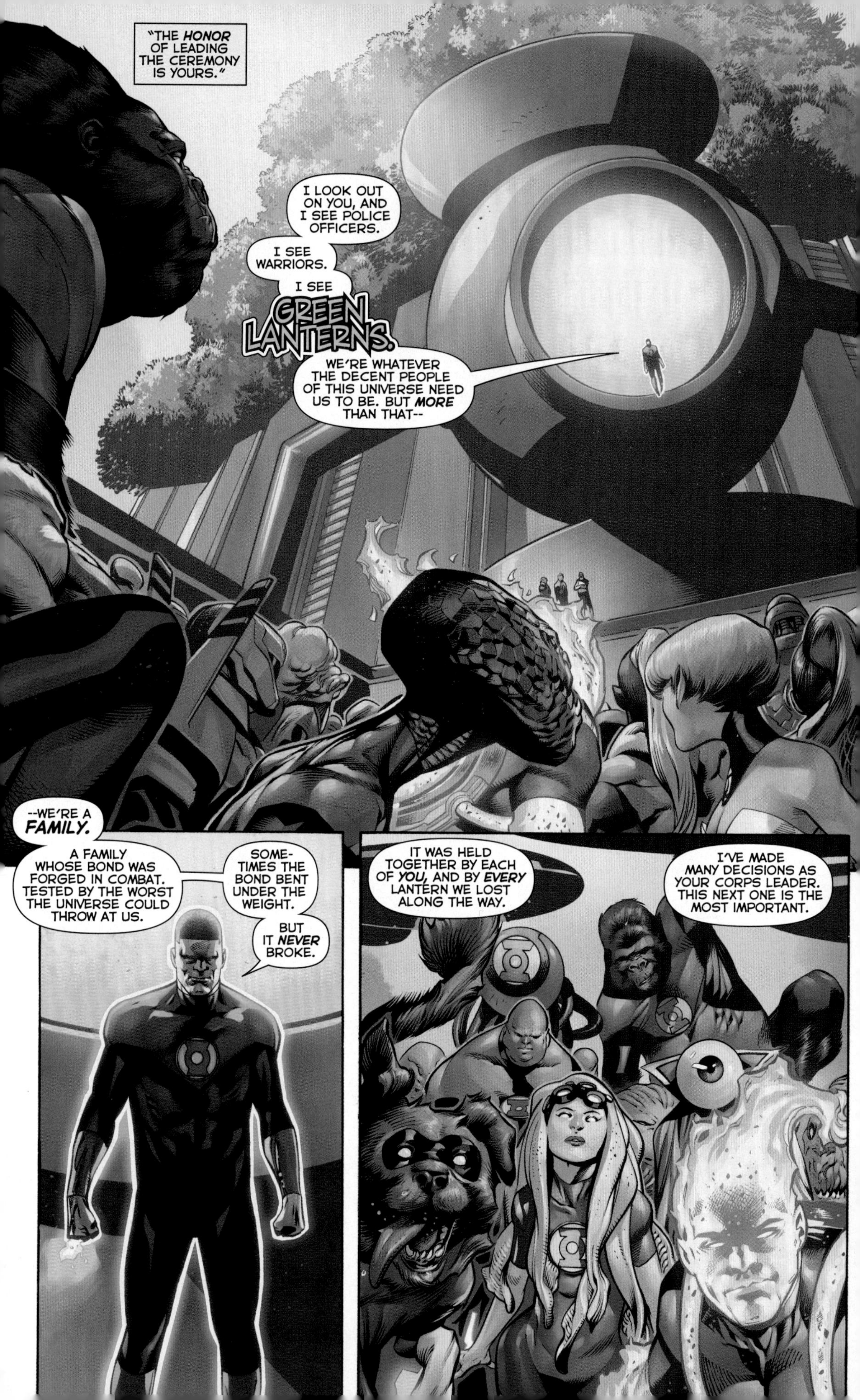
"THE HONOR OF LEADING THE CEREMONY IS YOURS."
I LOOK OUT ON YOU, AND I SEE POLICE OFFICERS.
I SEE WARRIORS.
I SEE GREEN LANTERNS.
WE'RE WHATEVER THE DECENT PEOPLE OF THIS UNIVERSE NEED US TO BE. BUT MORE THAN THAT--
--WE'RE A FAMILY.
A FAMILY WHOSE BOND WAS FORGED IN COMBAT. TESTED BY THE WORST THE UNIVERSE COULD THROW AT US.
SOME-TIMES THE BOND BENT UNDER THE WEIGHT.
BUT IT NEVER BROKE.
IT WAS HELD TOGETHER BY EACH OF YOU, AND BY EVERY LANTERN WE LOST ALONG THE WAY.
I'VE MADE MANY DECISIONS AS YOUR CORPS LEADER. THIS NEXT ONE IS THE MOST IMPORTANT.

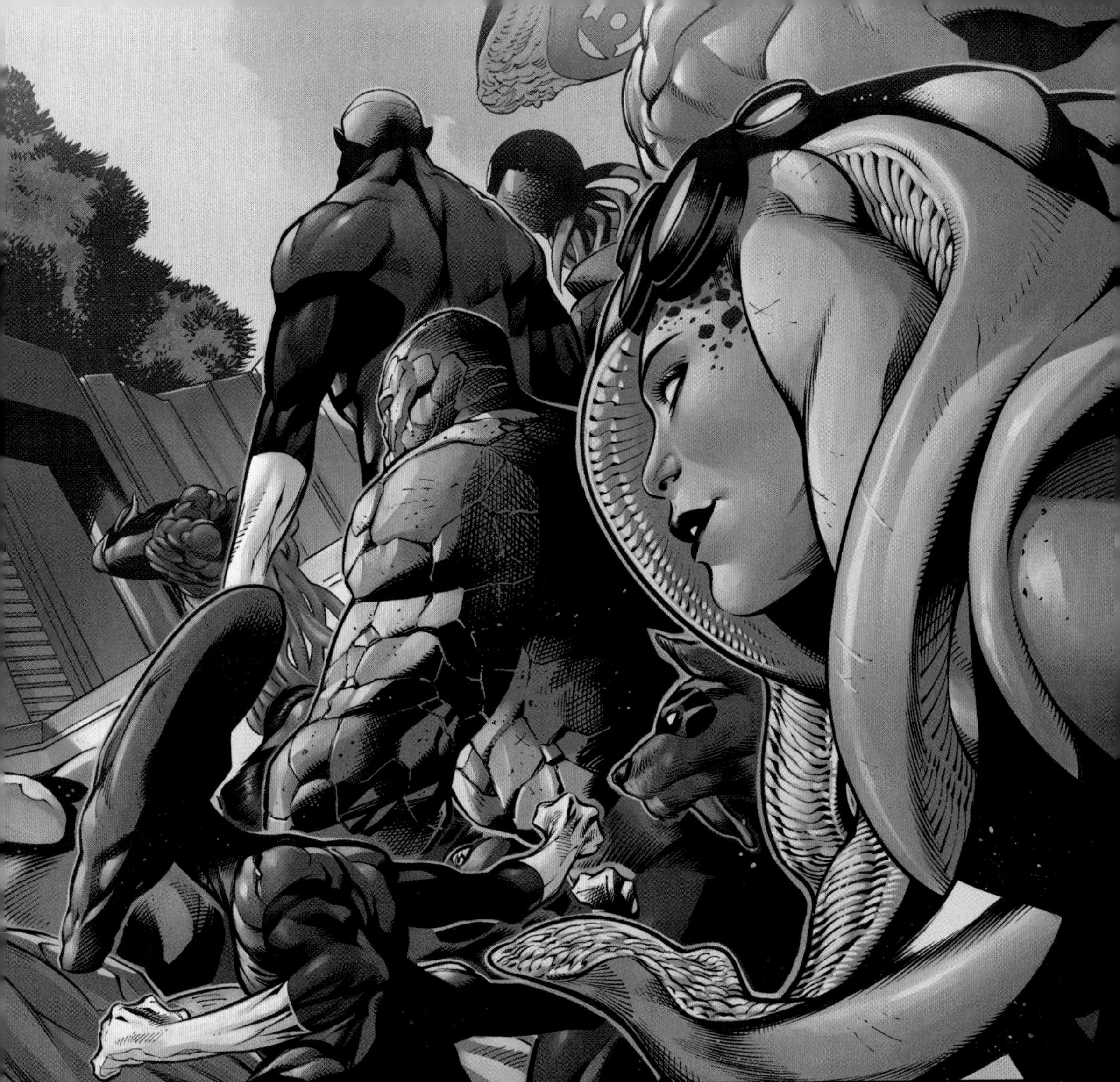

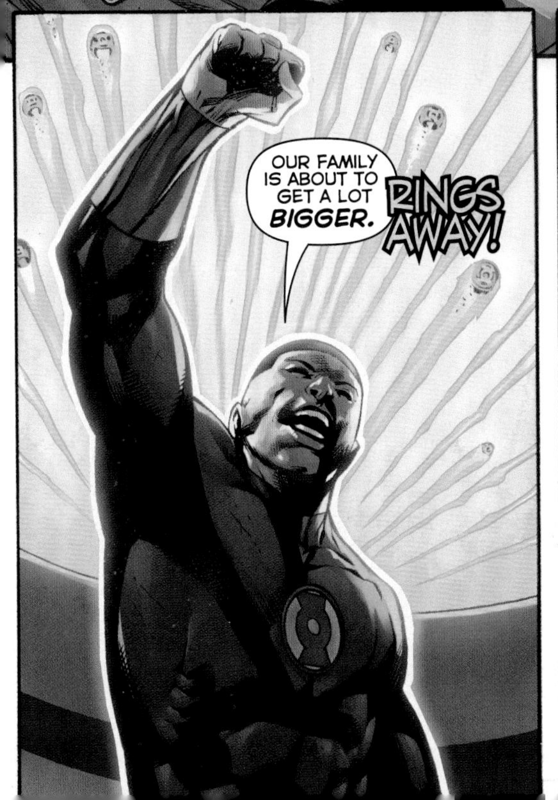
OUR FAMILY IS ABOUT TO GET A LOT BIGGER.
RINGS AWAY!

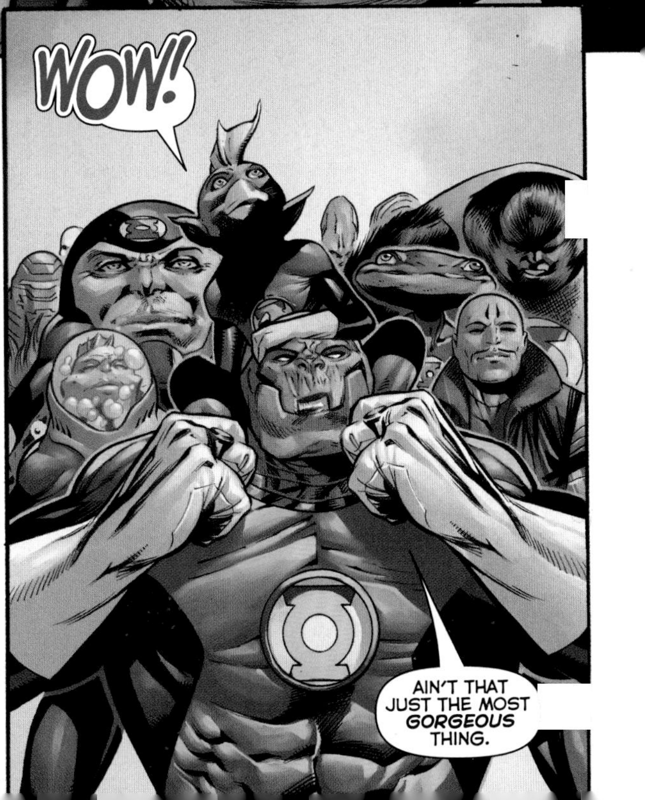
WOW!
AIN'T THAT JUST THE MOST GORGEOUS THING.

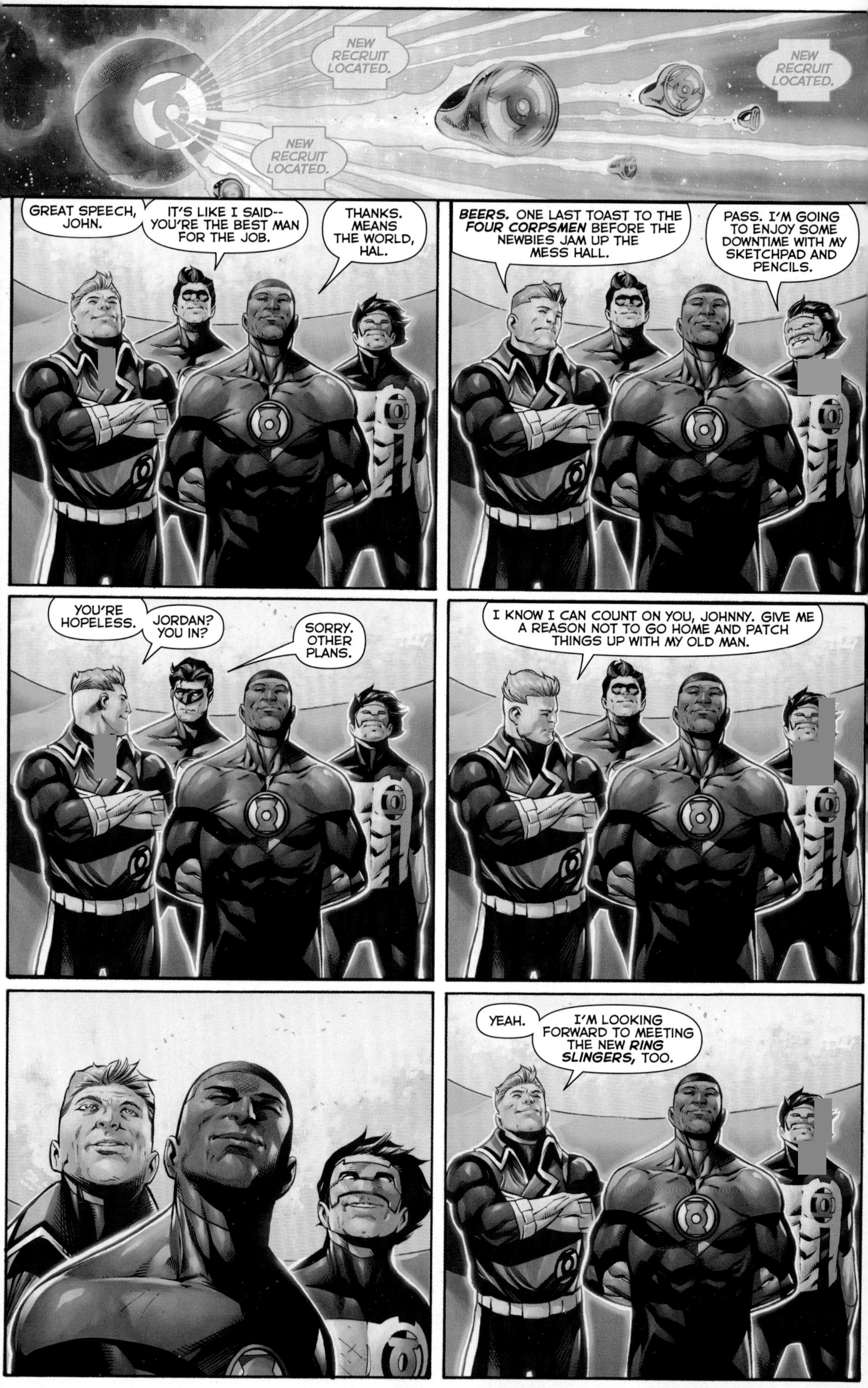
NEW RECRUIT LOCATED.
NEW RECRUIT LOCATED.
NEW RECRUIT LOCATED.
GREAT SPEECH, JOHN.
IT'S LIKE I SAID-- YOU'RE THE BEST MAN FOR THE JOB.
THANKS. MEANS THE WORLD, HAL.
BEERS. ONE LAST TOAST TO THE *FOUR CORPSMEN* BEFORE THE NEWBIES JAM UP THE MESS HALL.
PASS. I'M GOING TO ENJOY SOME DOWNTIME WITH MY SKETCHPAD AND PENCILS.
YOU'RE HOPELESS.
JORDAN? YOU IN?
SORRY. OTHER PLANS.
I KNOW I CAN COUNT ON YOU, JOHNNY. GIVE ME A REASON NOT TO GO HOME AND PATCH THINGS UP WITH MY OLD MAN.
YEAH.
I'M LOOKING FORWARD TO MEETING THE NEW *RING SLINGERS,* TOO.

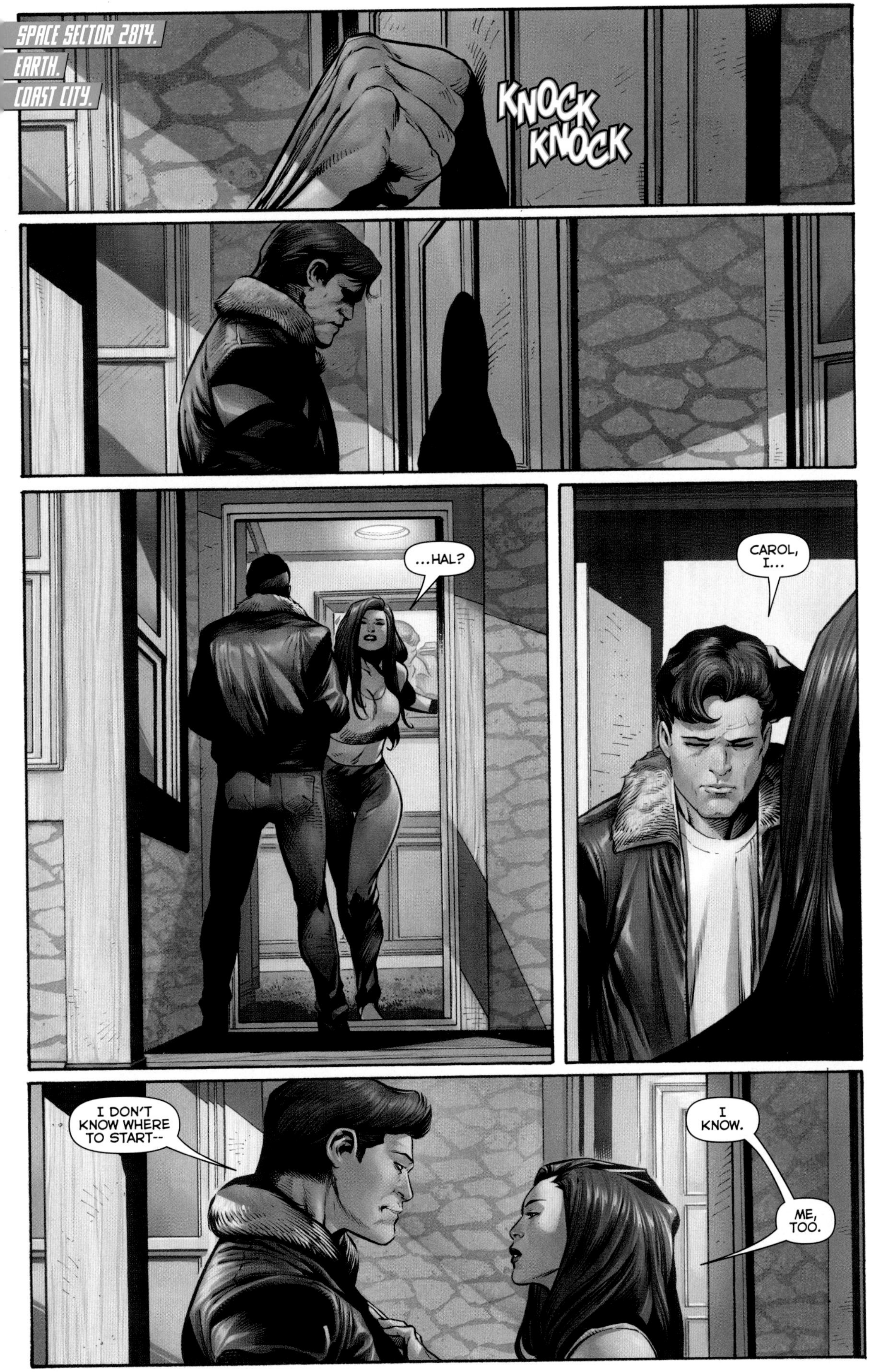
SPACE SECTOR 2814.
EARTH.
COAST CITY.
KNOCK KNOCK
...HAL?
CAROL, I...
I DON'T KNOW WHERE TO START--
I KNOW.
ME, TOO.

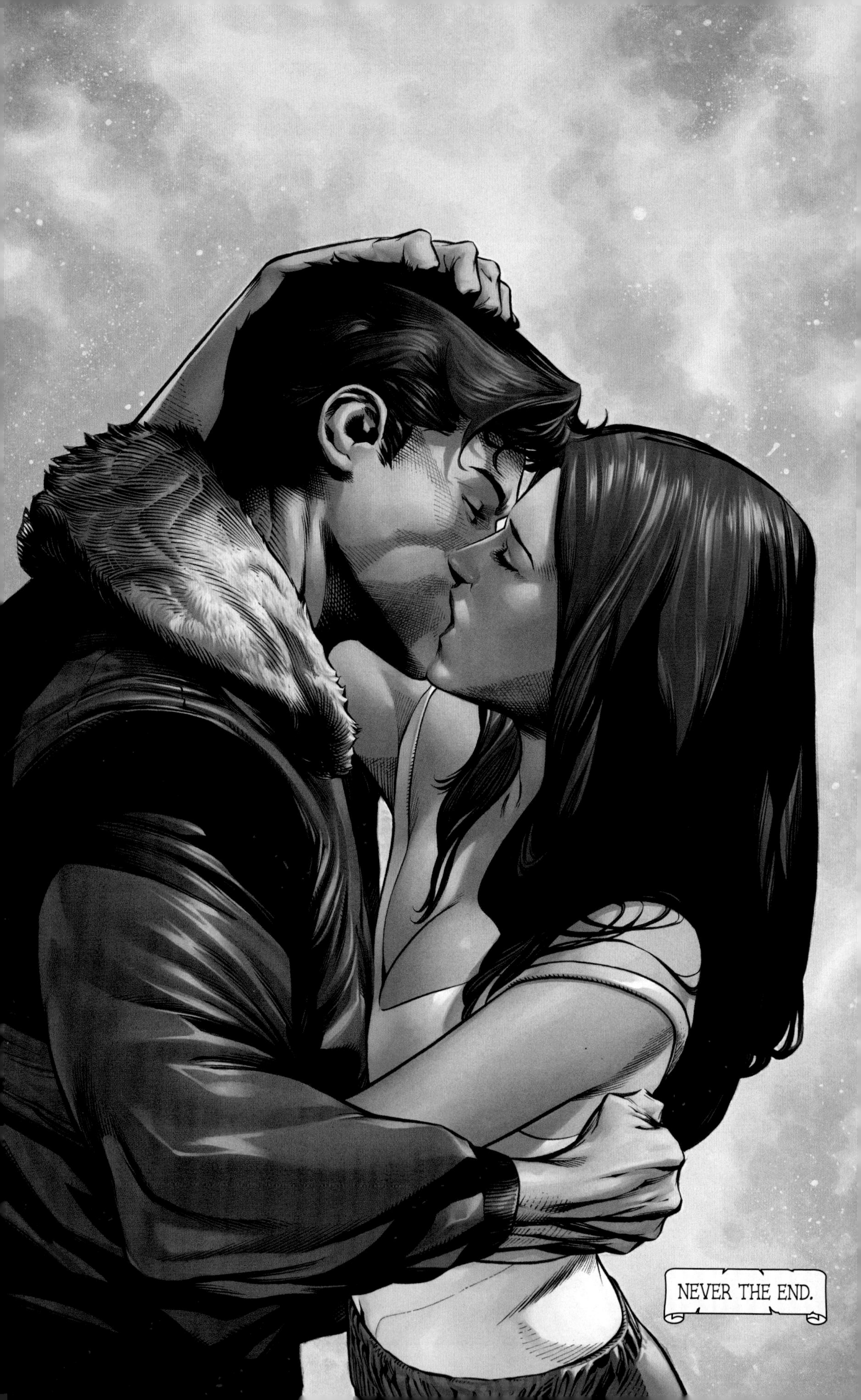
NEVER THE END.

HAL JORDAN AND THE GREEN LANTERN CORPS

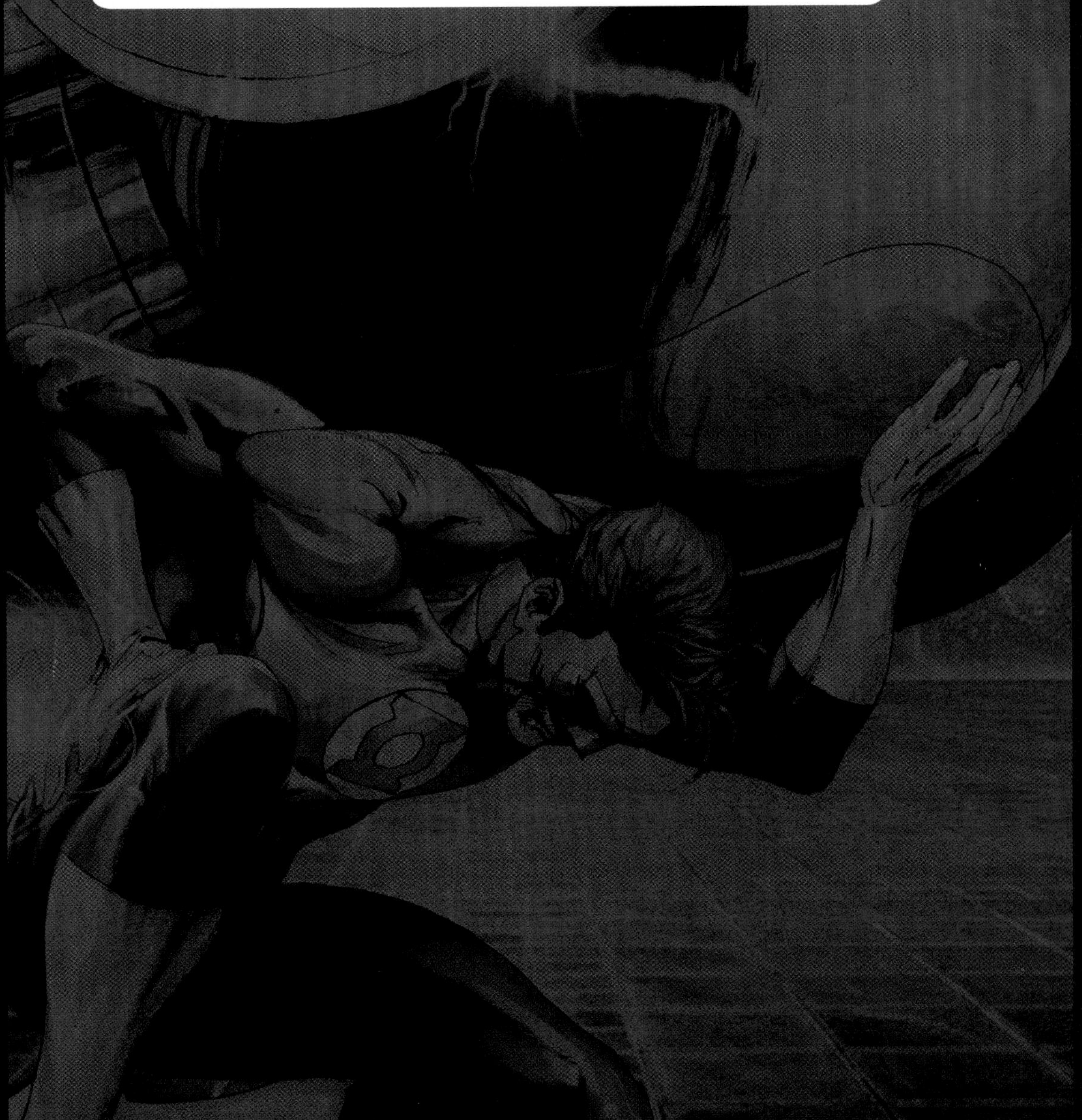

VARIANT COVER GALLERY

HAL JORDAN AND THE GREEN LANTERN CORPS #42 variant cover
by TYLER KIRKHAM and ARIF PRIANTO

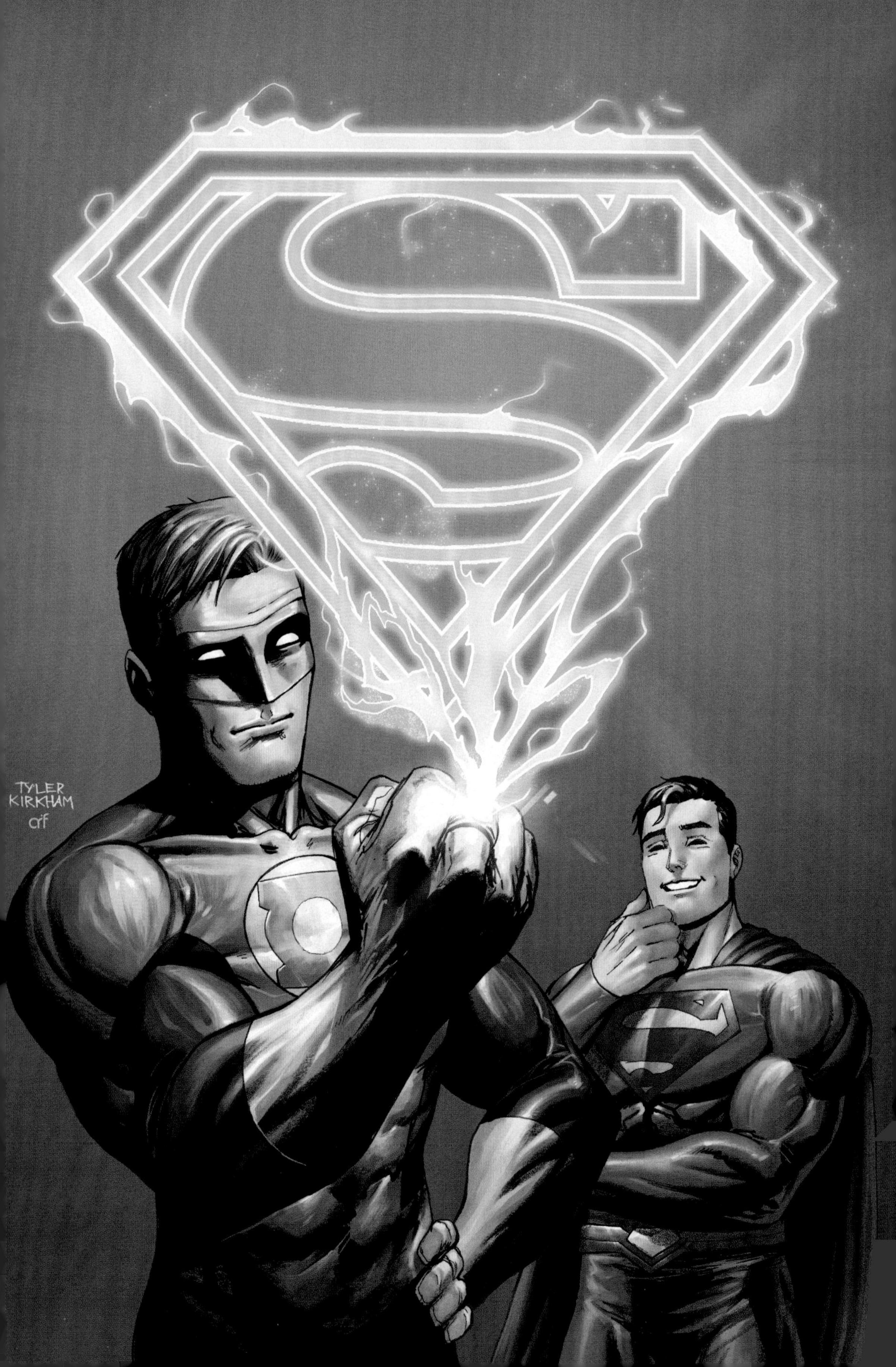

HAL JORDAN AND THE GREEN LANTERN CORPS #43 variant cover
by TYLER KIRKHAM and ARIF PRIANTO

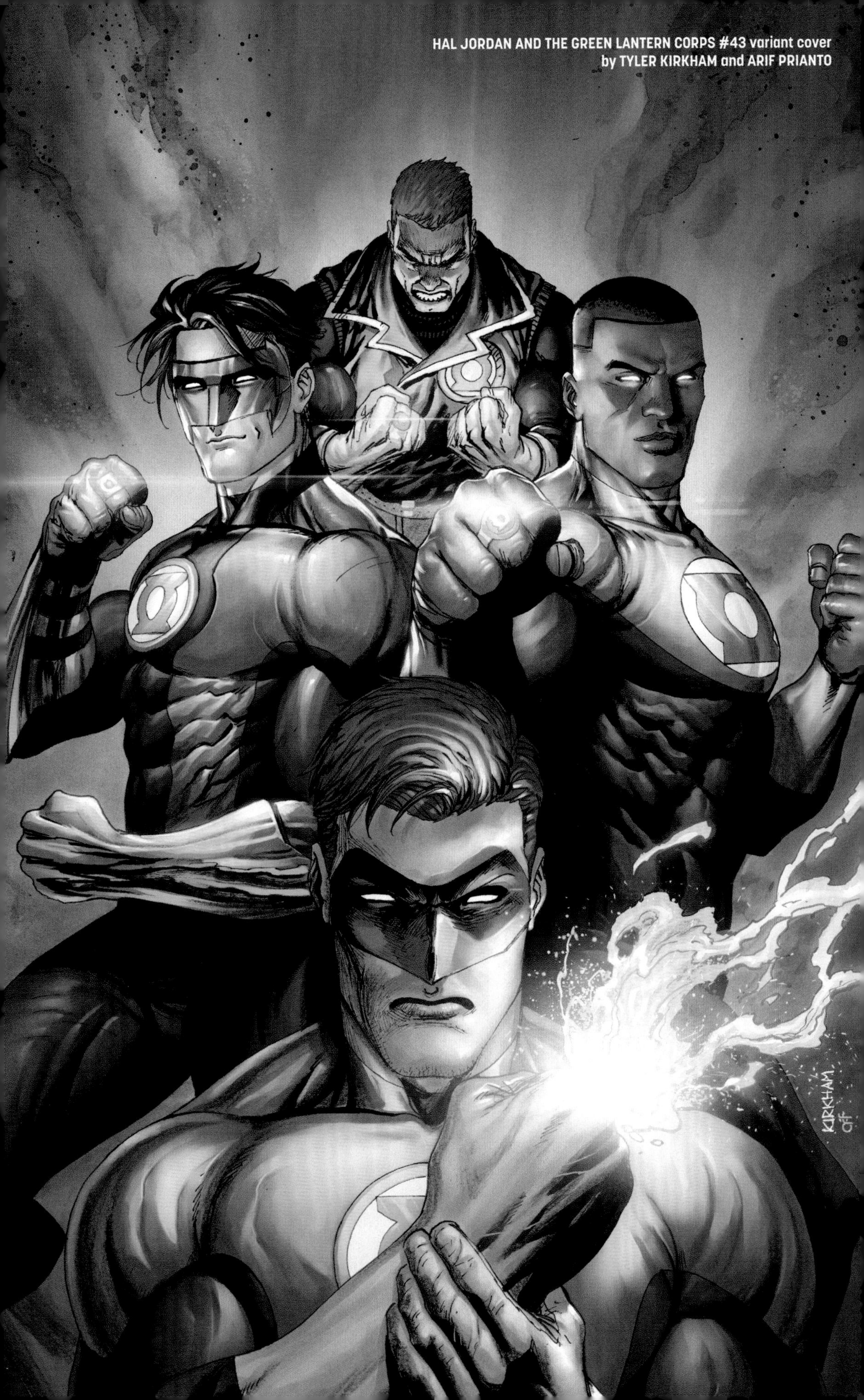
KIRKHAM

HAL JORDAN AND THE GREEN LANTERN CORPS #44 variant cover
by TYLER KIRKHAM and ARIF PRIANTO

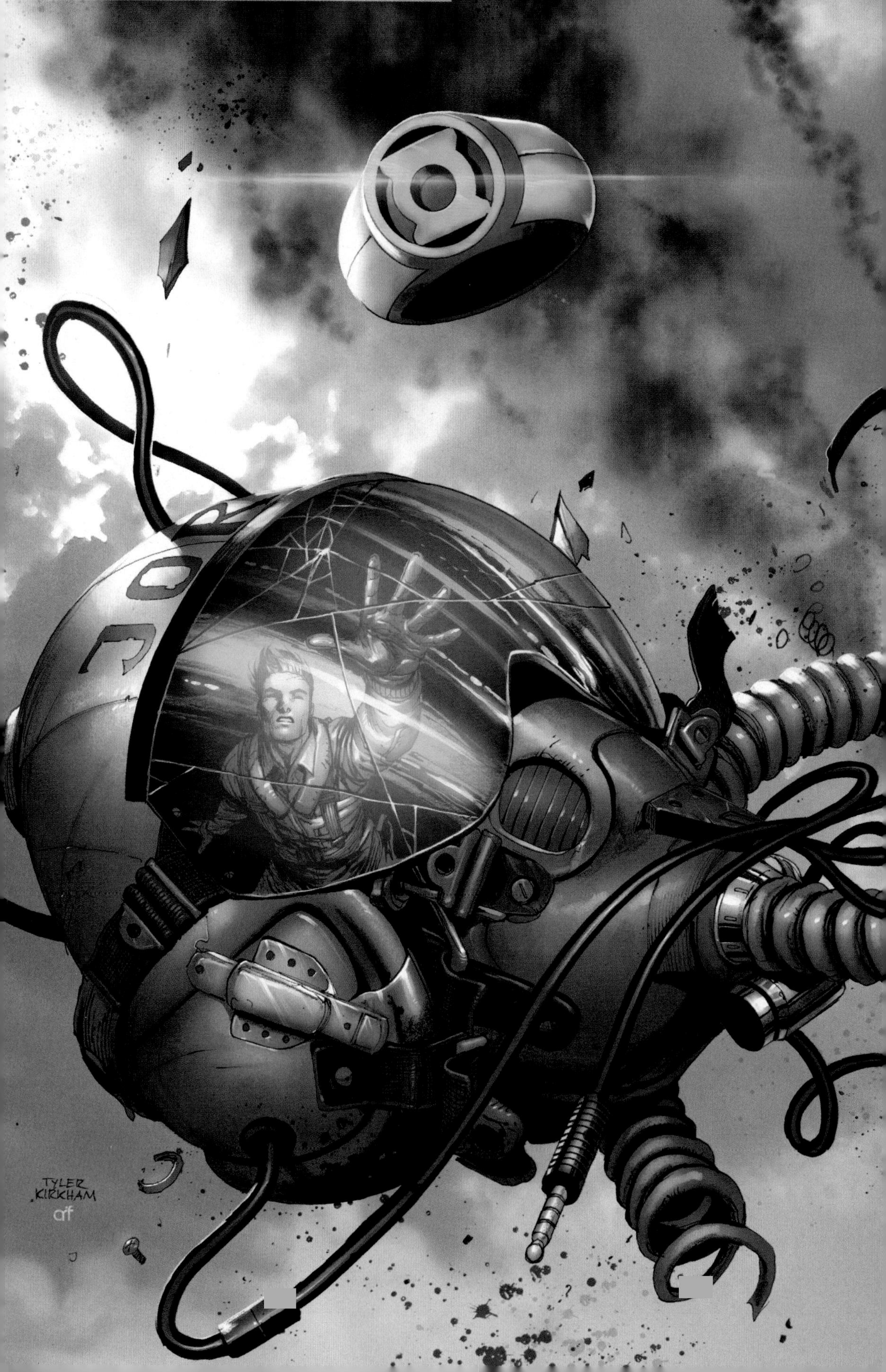
TYLER
KIRKHAM
af

HAL JORDAN AND THE GREEN LANTERN CORPS #45 variant cover
by TYLER KIRKHAM and ARIF PRIANTO

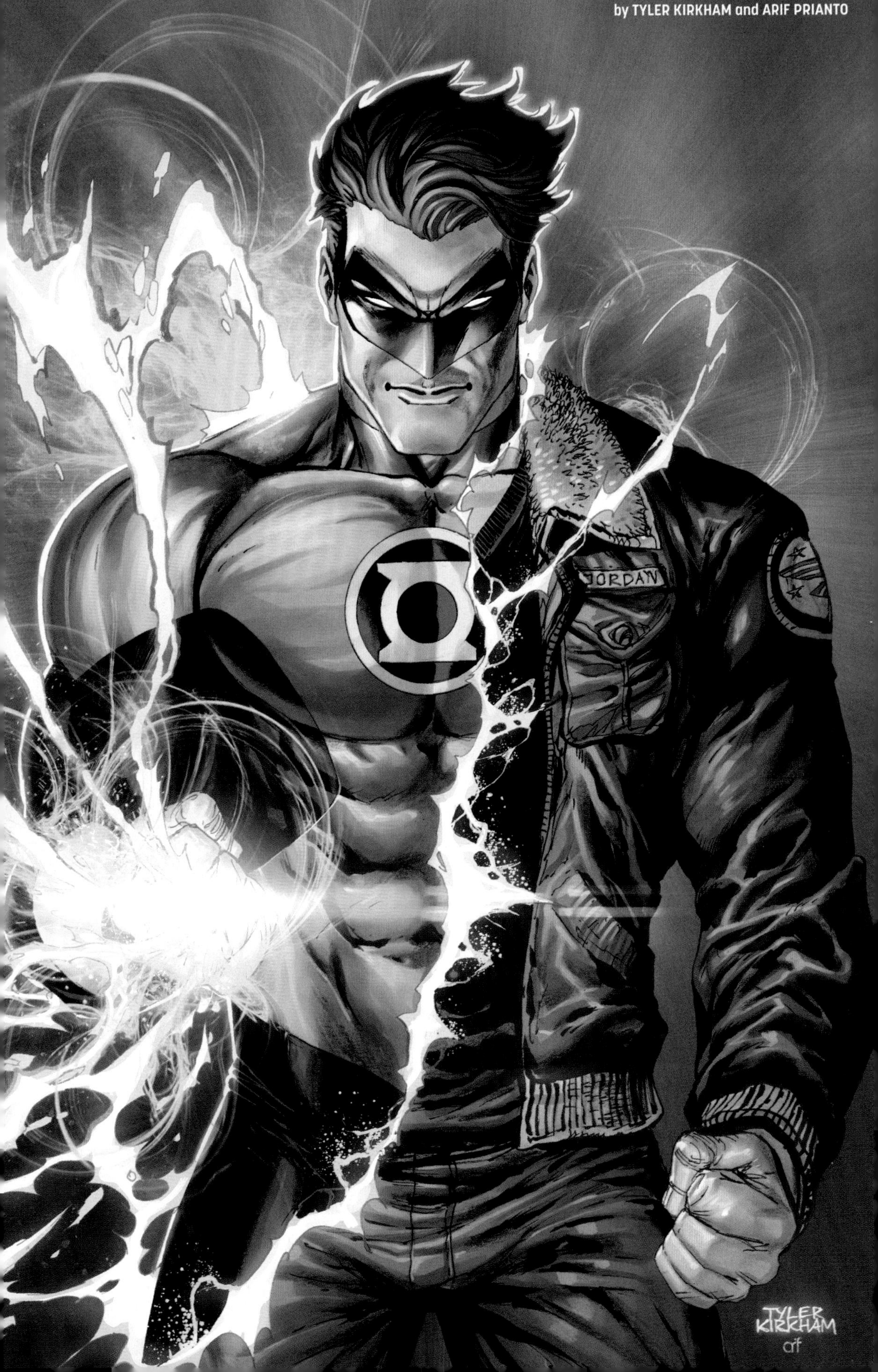
JORDAN
TYLER KIRKHAM
af

HAL JORDAN AND THE GREEN LANTERN CORPS #46 variant cover
by TYLER KIRKHAM and ARIF PRIANTO

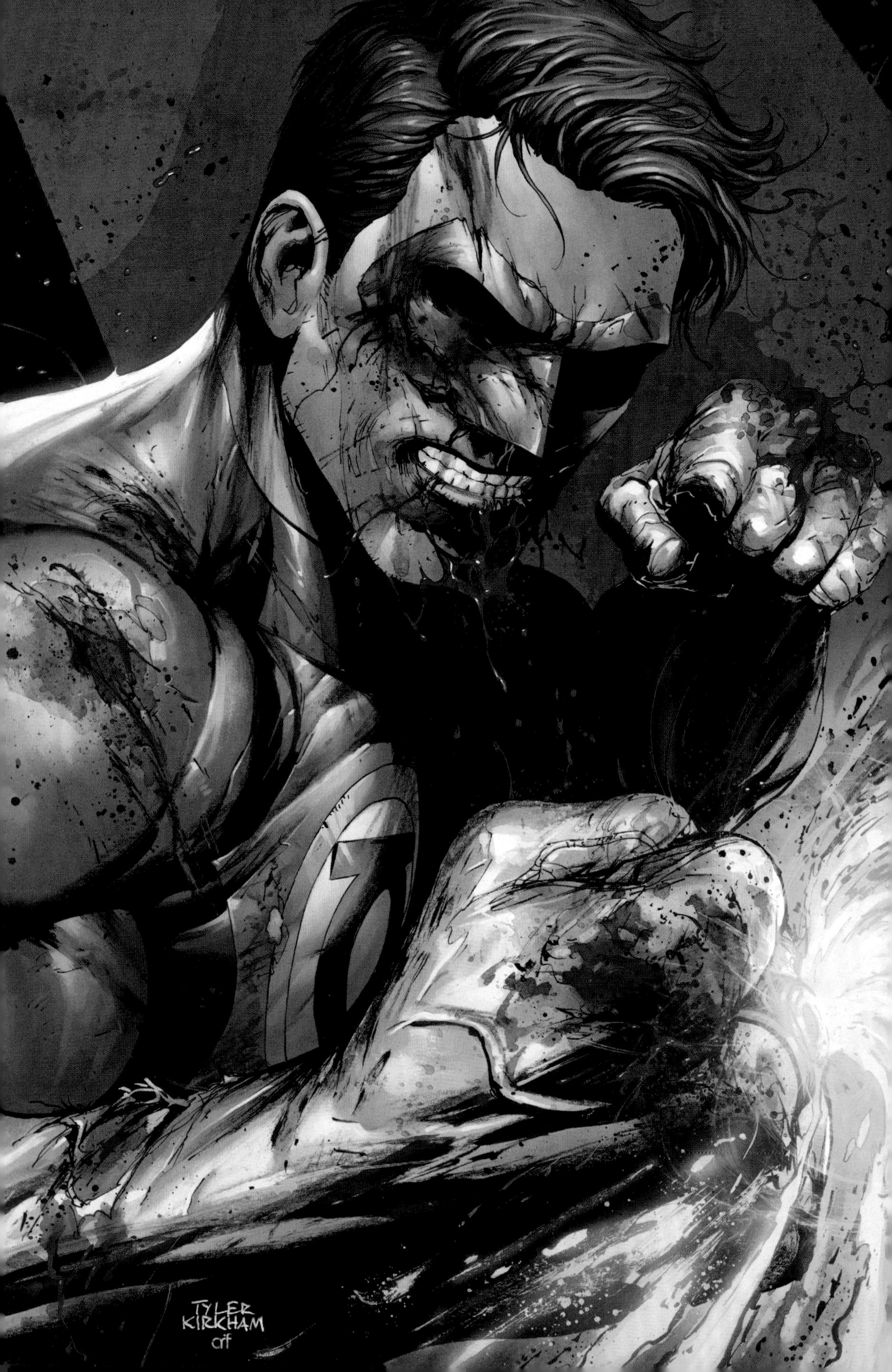
TYLER
KIRKHAM
arf

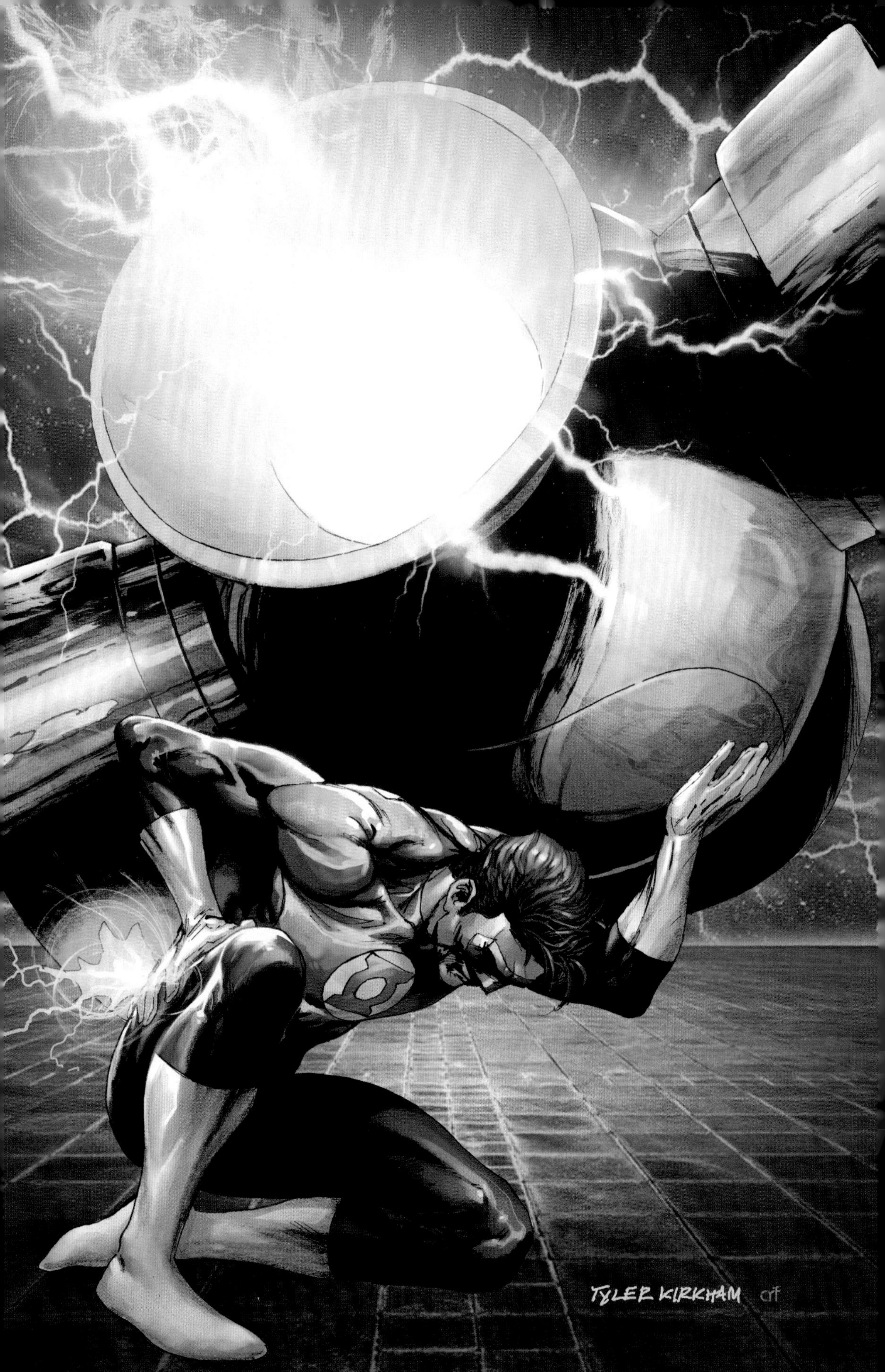
TYLER KIRKHAM
arf

HAL JORDAN AND THE GREEN LANTERN CORPS #47 variant cover
by TYLER KIRKHAM and ARIF PRIANTO

HAL JORDAN AND THE GREEN LANTERN CORPS #48 and #49 variant covers
by TYLER KIRKHAM and ARIF PRIANTO

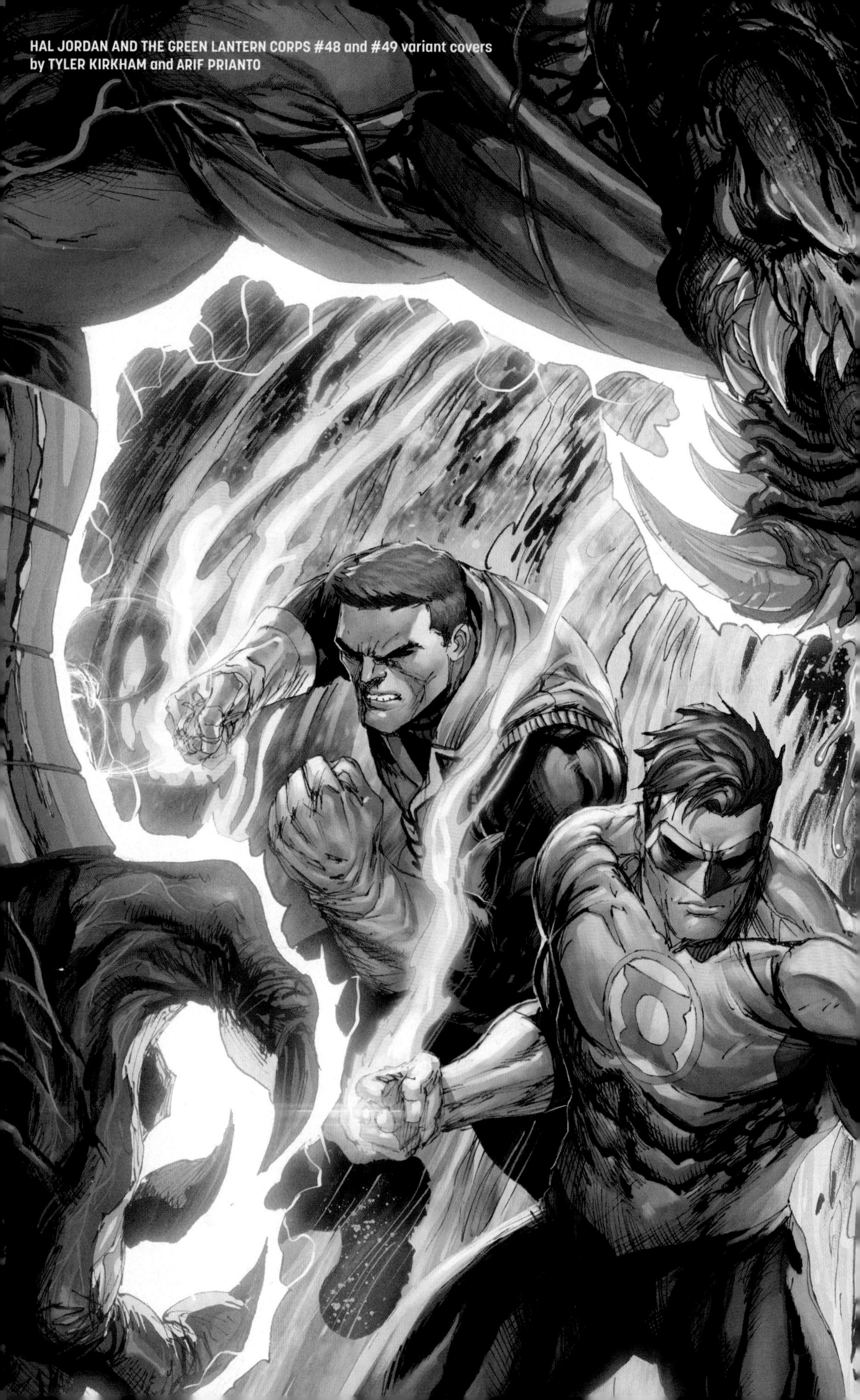

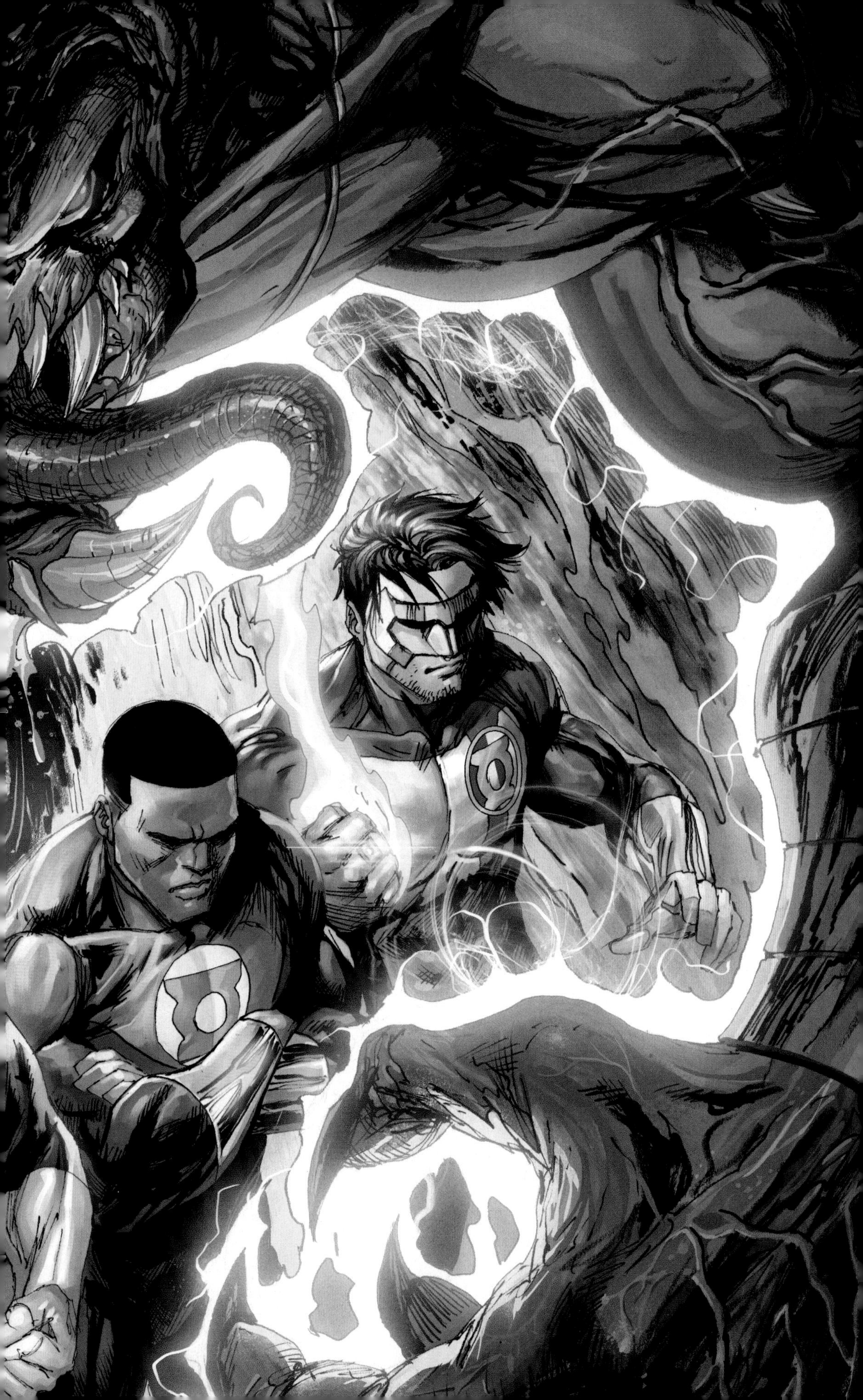

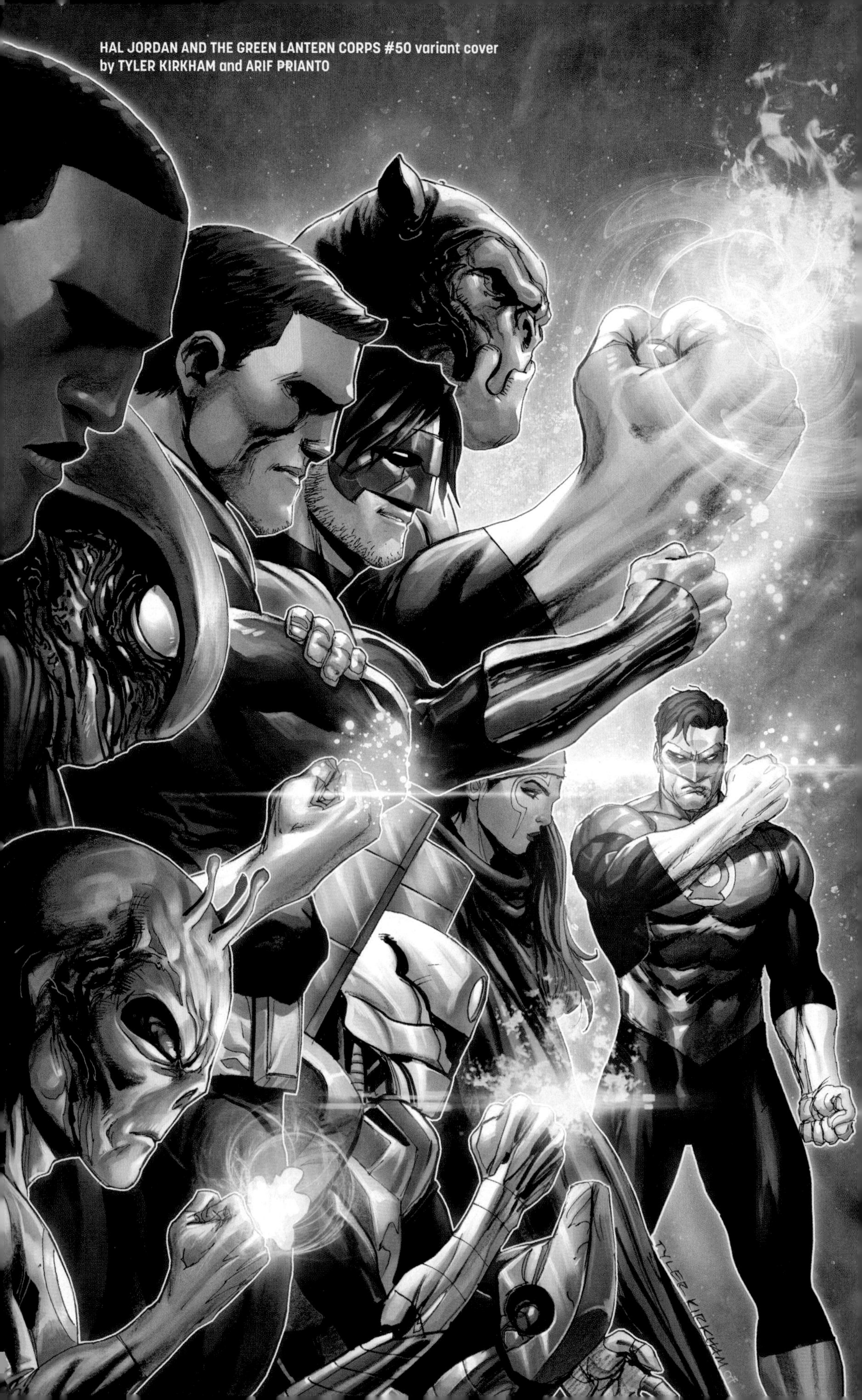
TYLER KIRKHAM

HAL JORDAN AND THE GREEN LANTERN CORPS #50 variant cover
by TYLER KIRKHAM and ARIF PRIANTO

HAL JORDAN AND THE GREEN LANTERN CORPS #49
Cover concept sketch by ANDY KUBERT
Cover sketches and pencils by FERNANDO PASARIN

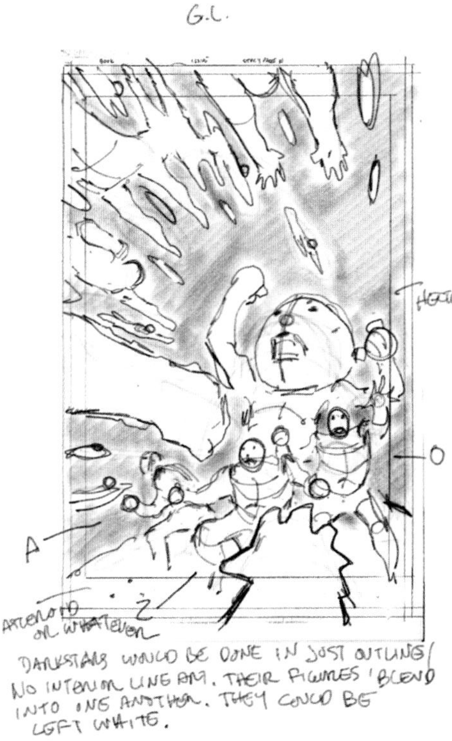

G.L.
HECTOR
O
A
Z
ASTEROID OR WHATEVER
DARKSTARS WOULD BE DONE IN JUST OUTLINE/ NO INTERIOR LINE ART. THEIR FIGURES 'BLEND INTO ONE ANOTHER. THEY COULD BE LEFT WHITE.

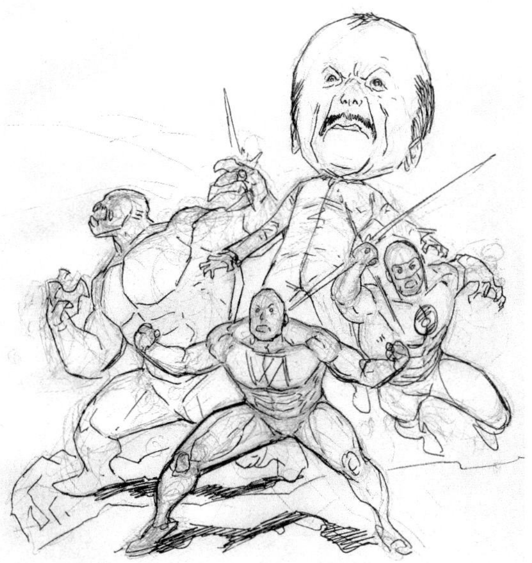

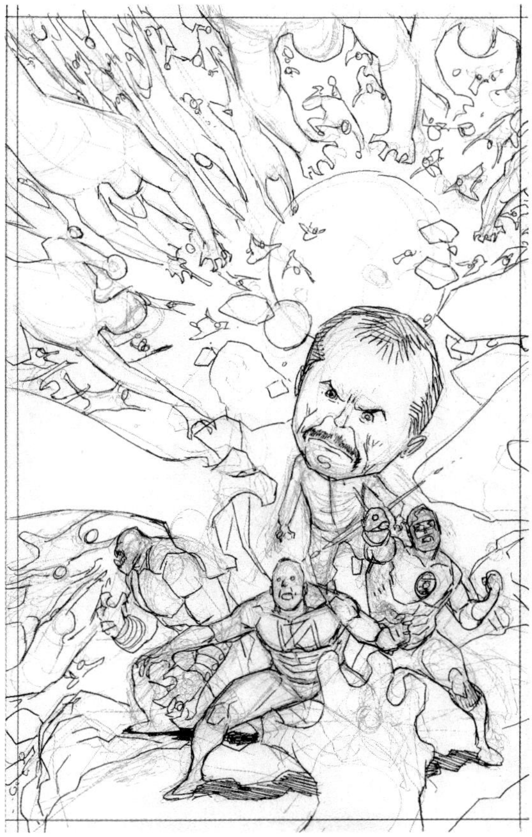

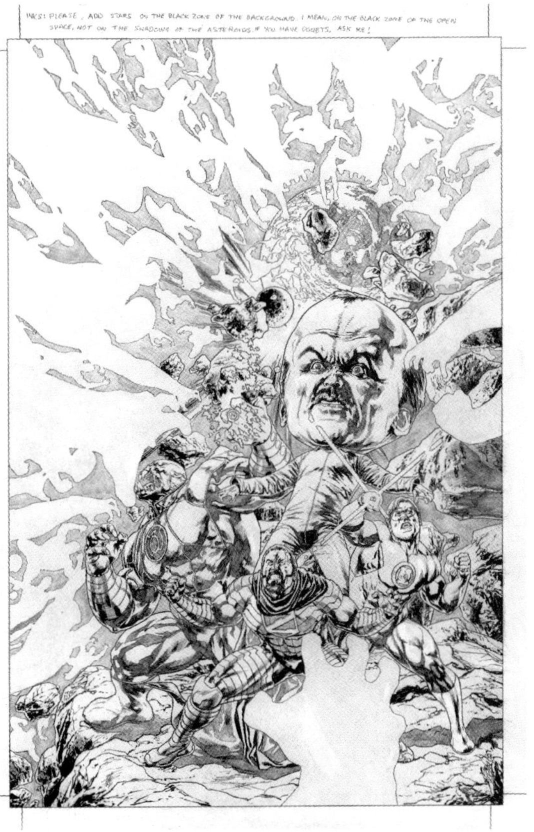

INKS: PLEASE, ADD STARS ON THE BLACK ZONE OF THE BACKGROUND. I MEAN, ON THE BLACK ZONE OF THE OPEN SPACE, NOT ON THE SHADOWS OF THE ASTEROIDS. IF YOU HAVE DOUBTS, ASK ME!

HAL JORDAN AND THE GREEN LANTERN CORPS #43, pages 10-11
Pencils by RAFA SANDOVAL

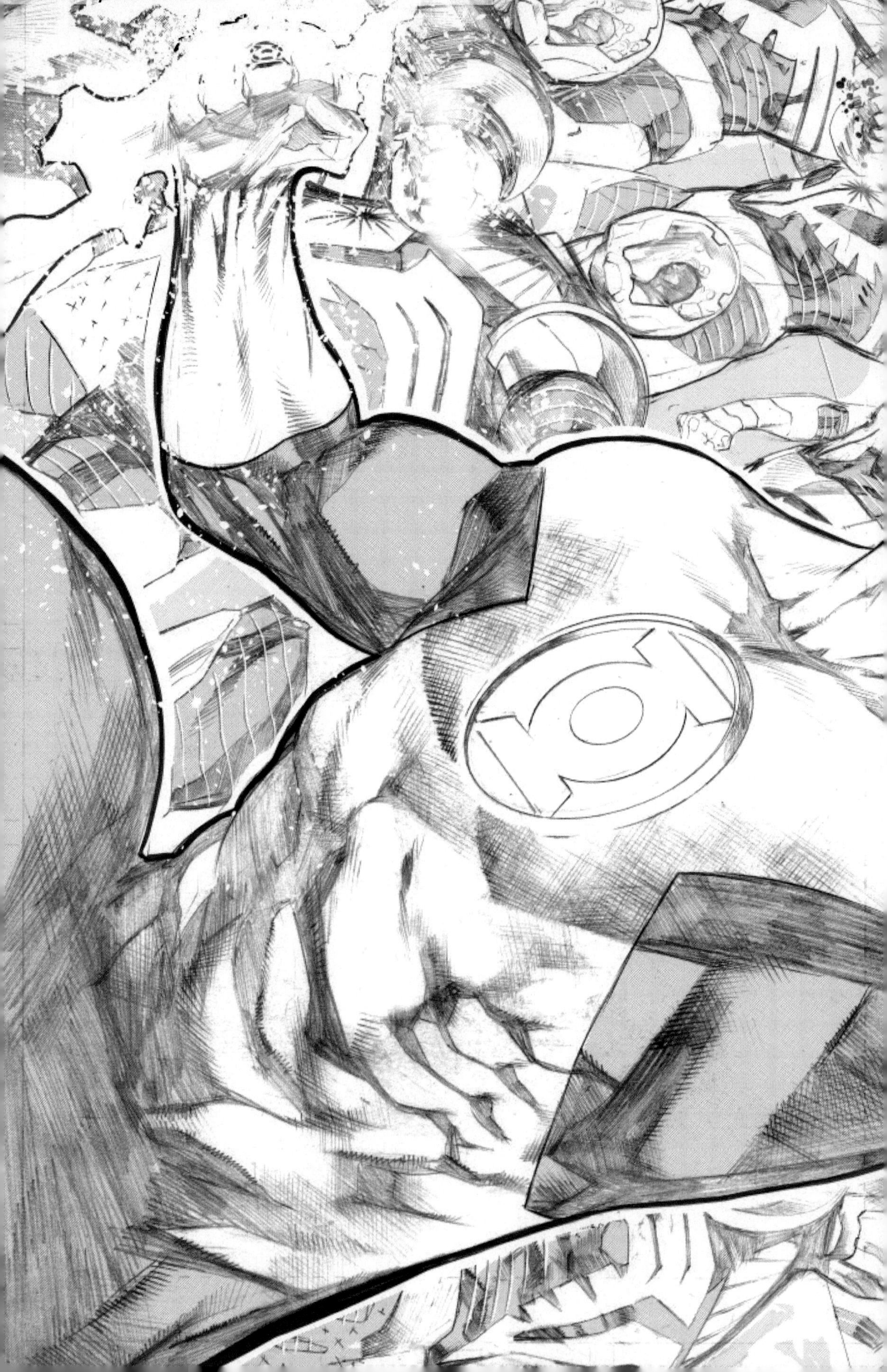

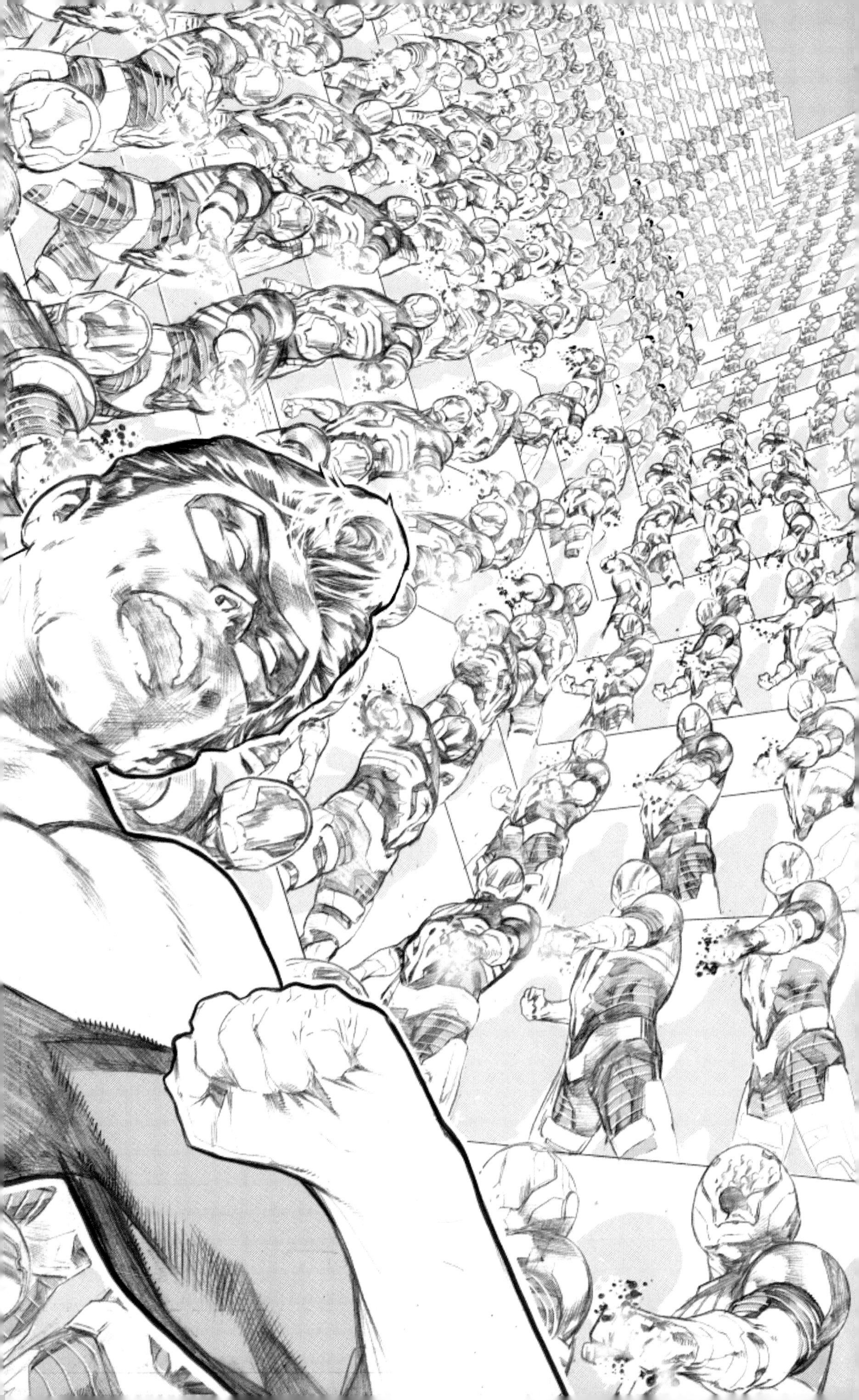

HAL JORDAN AND THE GREEN LANTERN CORPS #50, page 28
Pencils by RAFA SANDOVAL

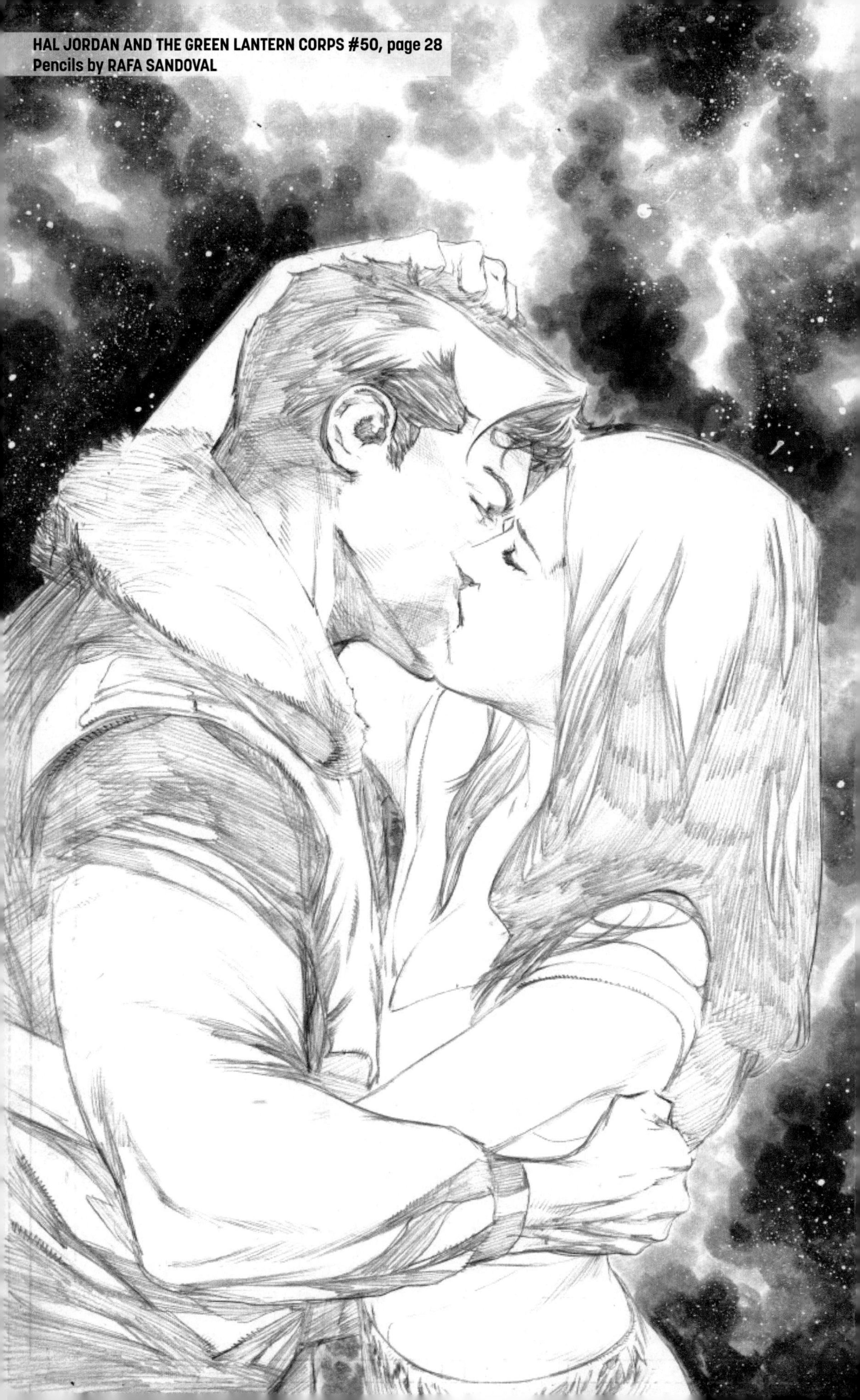